BEETON'S ALL ABOUT GARDENING

A POPULAR ENCYCLOPÆDIA OF THE THEORY AND PRACTICE OF HORTICULTURE

BEETON'S ALL ABOUT GARDENING

A POPULAR ENCYCLOPÆDIA OF THE THEORY AND PRACTICE OF HORTICULTURE

BRACKEN BOOKS
LONDON

RL5119/Bestseller Pubs/All About Gardening (8)

First setting 16.6.87

Job Disk 373/092 CFD4

Previously published by Ward Lock & Co.

This edition published 1987 by Bracken Books
a division of Bestseller Publications Ltd
Princess House, 50 Eastcastle Street
London W1, England

ISBN 1 85170 137 0

Printed and bound in Great Britain
by
Adlard & Son Ltd, The Garden City Press, Letchworth, Herts

TABLE OF CONTENTS.

PREFACE.

THE object of the present volume is to afford to that very large class of persons who in the present day take an interest in Gardening, accurate information upon the theory and practice of it. The Dictionary form has been adopted as being that best suited to easy reference, and the greatest care has been taken in the selection of the terms under which the information has been given. It is sincerely hoped that the explanations may be found plain and practical, and calculated to convey sound instruction to the most uninitiated. Illustrations have been added wherever necessary to assist verbal explanations, and to show clearly how any difficult Gardening operation may be performed.

No department of the science has been omitted; full cultural directions are provided for fruit aad vegetables, as well as flowers, also monthly calendars of work.

It must be admitted that a knowledge of garden management

is as essential to every possessor of a garden as a knowledge of domestic management is to every mistress of a house. The present volume is offered to the public as a companion to "Mrs. Beeton's Dictionary of Everyday Cookery," with a firm conviction of the truth of this statement, and in the hope that the contents may prove equally useful.

THE

PHILOSOPHY OF GARDENING.

CHAPTER I.

HISTORICAL SKETCH.

IT would be difficult to assign a greater antiquity to any industrial art than that which may be claimed for gardening, for, of necessity, it must have formed the earliest occupation of created man. This, of course, can be said of gardening only in its rudest aspect, as indicating the amount of cultivation given to the soil for the mere support of existence. Scientific gardening results from a high degree of civilization. "When ages do grow to civility and elegancy," says the great Lord Bacon, "men come to build stately sooner than to garden finely, as if gardening were the greater perfection." The traditions and historical notices of this art refer to periods of very remote antiquity. Ancient legends celebrate the gardens of the Hesperides and of Alcineus, and authentic history tells of the hanging gardens, by means of which the mighty king of Babylon sought to reconcile his median queen to the flat and naked country of her adoption. The Persians appear to have cultivated gardens from the earliest period. Xenophon, the historian, says of Cyrus: "Wherever he resides, or whatever place he visits in his dominions, he is careful that his gardens shall be filled with all that is beautiful and useful that the soil can be made to produce." The ancient Grecians followed in the same steps: they formed gardens not merely for fruit and vegetables, but for the cultivation of flowers with them. The narcissus, the violet and the rose were in high repute; myrtles and box trees were clipped into fantastic forms; and things out of season were produced in their forcing pits, for violets in profusion could be bought in the markets of Athens while the snow was thick upon the ground. Of the doings of ancient Rome in this respect we have plenty of information. When Tarquin the Proud was planning with the "false" Sextus the betrayal of the city of the Sabines, he took the messenger who was sent to him into his garden, and, without a word spoken, cut off the heads of all the tallest poppies growing there, to show that their end could be gained only by removing, one after another, the chief men in the city to be betrayed. The wealthy Lucullus had gardens of an immense extent, and imported from Persia the apricot, the cherry and the peach. The gardens of Sallust are also much praised, as well as those of the Emperors Nero and Hadrian. Flowers and fruits, we learn, were placed by the Romans under the guardian care of special Deities, and floralia or flower festivals instituted; indeed, to such a pitch of extravagance was the passion for flowers carried that at one period it became necessary that sumptuary laws should be enacted to restrain it. At one single supper, given by the luxurious Cleopatra, the roses alone are said to have cost an Egyptian talent, about two hundred pounds of our money, and the prodigality of Heliogabalus reached even a higher pitch. Still there is not much ground for believing that any great variety of flowers, fruits, and vegetables was to be found in ancient Rome. Pliny, the naturalist, enumerates in his history about one thousand plants of all descriptions; but of these, according to his testimony, only a very few were in general cultivation.

Mr. Loudon, after much laborious research, expresses the opinion that the following lists include all the culinary plants and fruits in use at the time of the fall of the Roman Empire.

CULINARY PLANTS.—Peas, beans, vetches, lentils, kidney beans, gourds, cucumbers, melons, cabbages of several sorts, turnips, carrots, parsnips, beet, skirret, radishes, sorrel, asparagus, onions, garlic, and some few other alliaceous plants; also endive, lettuces, succory, mustard and other salads, parsley, celery, orach, alexanders, elecampane, fennel, and chervil.

FRUITS.—Figs, almonds, citron, peach, pomegranate, apricots, plums, and cherries, 22 sorts of apples, 36 sorts of pears, services, quinces, and medlars, many kinds of grapes, mulberries, nuts, walnuts, chesnuts, stone pines or pignons, olives, and caroks.

There can be little doubt that flowers were forced under lights with sashes of talc; and in all probability cucumbers and fruits also were so grown.

During the unsettled times which were consequent upon the breaking up of the great Roman Empire, the art of gardening would seem to have been lost, or at any rate to have fallen into disuse. Its revival, there can be no doubt, was due to the monks. In the great religious institutions which rose and increased so rapidly during that period of European history which is usually called the Dark Ages, the arts of peace and civilization were maintained and cherished, while war and rapine engrossed the thoughts and energies of the outside world. The enclosure of every monastery embraced a piece of ground which, for exercise as well as utility, was cultivated by the inmates; and even the hermit's cell had its little plot for the growth of a few herbs, and perhaps a few choice flowers for the chaplets and garlands of some favourite saints.

The chief step, however, taken in the way of general gardening was in the time of Charlemagne. That wise monarch, in his *Capitularies*, commanded the formation of gardens throughout his dominions, and gave special directions for the cultivation of certain plants most useful for diet and for medicinal purposes. At a later period the Italians became noted for their exertion in this respect. Alfonso D'Este, Duke of Ferrara, established botanical gardens in several places—the chief of these being known as Belvedere, on the banks of the Po. The fashion once introduced, Naples, Florence, Pisa, Padua, and other large Italian cities soon followed, and the subject was taken up in such a manner, and so extensively, as to give rise to what we shall shortly have to describe as the Italian style.

In our own country, gardening as an art, and especially so as a science, is of comparatively very modern date. It is, however, only common justice to remark, that in no country have the advances made been equal to those of our own. Our gardening literature is also more copious than that of any other country.

Our ancestors in all probability derived their first notions of gardening from the Romans. Strabo, writing in the first century, tells us that the people of Britain were ignorant of the art of cultivating gardens. The continual wars in which Britain was engaged from the fifth century, when the Romans vacated the island, probably rooted out all traces of an art so civilizing as that of gardening, although there are indications that vineyards planted in the third century, under the Emperor Proteus, existed in the eighth century, where they are mentioned by the Venerable Bede. William of Malmsbury also, writing in the twelfth century, commends the vineyards of the county of Gloucester; and Pliny tells us that cherries, which Lucullus had introduced into Italy about a century before, were grown in Britain in the first century. Throughout the transition period which succeeded the Roman conquest, the warlike barons and discontented people were probably too much occupied in looking to their personal safety to think much of gardening. The opulent Earl of Northumberland, whose household consisted, in 1512, of a hundred and sixty persons, had but one gardener, who, according to the "Household Book," attended "hourly in the garden for setting of erbes, and clipping of knottis, and sweeping the said garden clene." In Scotland—if we may trust to the authority of the royal poet, James I.—that poor country had already established some claims to the reputation which has since carried so many of her sons over the world as gardeners. In his poem of the "Quair," written early in the fifteenth century, he speaks of—

> "A garden fair, and in the corneris set,
> Ane herbere green with wandes long and small.
> Railit about, and so with treeis set
> Was all the place, and hawthorn hedges knet,
> That lyfe was non, walkying there forbye
> That might within scarce any wight espye,
> So thicke the bewis and the leves grene."

Towards the end of the fifteenth and in the early part of the sixteenth century the wise and politic Henry VII. had nearly succeeded in rooting out the feuds of the Roses, red and white, and a long period of interruption no doubt prepared the people for the revival of gardening with the other arts of civilization, which took place in the succeeding reign of Henry VIII. The royal gardens of Nonsuch were laid out by this monarch with the greatest magnificence. "Nonsuch," says its historian Hentzner, "is so encompassed with parks, delicious gardens, groves ornamented with trellis-work, cabinets of verdure, and walks so embowered by trees, that it seems to be a place pitched upon by Pleasure herself to dwell in along with Health. In the pleasure and artificial gardens are many columns and pyramids of marble; two fountains spout water one round the other like a pyramid, upon which are perched small birds that stream water out of their bills. In the grove of Diana is a very agreeable fountain, with Actæon turned into a stag as he was sprinkled by the goddess and her nymphs. There is besides another pyramid of marble with concealed pipes, which spirt upon all who come within their reach." Such a garden might well claim pre-eminence, and justify the poet, who tells us—

> "This, which no equal hath in art or fame,
> Britons deservedly do Nonsuch name."

In Elizabeth's reign, Holland and Hatfield House were both laid out. Of the former, part of the original plan still remains. Of Hatfield, Hentzner says, "The gardens are surrounded by a piece of water with boats rowing through the alleys of well-cut trees and labyrinths made with great labour." Mazes and labyrinths and concealed pipes, by means of which visitors might find themselves lost one minute and deluged with water at the next, seems, indeed, to have been the taste of that day—a jocular sort of hospitality, "more honoured in the breach than the observance."

During the reign of James I., Theobalds was planned and erected. "A large square, having all its walls covered with phillyrea, and a beautiful *jet d'eau* in the centre, the parterre having many pleasant walks, part of which are planted on the sides with espaliers, and others arched all over. At the end is a small mount, called the Mount of Venus, placed in the midst of a labyrinth, and which is, upon the whole, the most beautiful spot in the world." It was now that this subject engaged the comprehensive mind of Bacon, with little immediate result. However, the contempt he expresses for "images cut out of juniper and other garden stuff" was not without its weight a few generations later, when a purer taste came to prevail. Hampton Court, Chatsworth, Wooton, and many other of the finest gardens in England, were laid out in Charles II.'s reign. Garden structures also began to be erected. Le Notre planted Greenwich and St. James's Parks, under the immediate directions of Charles, Versailles being the model, although only at a humble distance. Clipped yew trees and other Dutch tendencies, scarcely redeemed by the magnificent gates and iron railings now introduced, became the rage in the reign of William and Mary,—"terraced walks, hedges of evergreens, shorn shrubs in boxes, orange and myrtle trees in tubs, being the chief excellences." In 1696 an orangery with a glass roof was erected at Wollaton Hall, Nottinghamshire, said to have been the first structure of the kind in England. These gardens were laid out in the Italian style, with terraces, statues, fountains, and urns, and, next to Chatsworth, they seem to have been the finest in England. Like Powis Castle, and some other fine old terraced gardens, they were sacrificed to the rage for improvement ushered in a century later by Kent and Brown and their followers.

The addition of gardens, on an extensive scale, to the houses and castles of the nobility, as well as the establishment of parks and gardens in large cities, both at home and abroad, have done much to increase and improve the public taste.

The Dutch at an early period became noted for their love of flowers, and their skill in the cultivation of them. Their wealth, and their commerce with the Cape of Good Hope, the East Indies, and other remote parts, gave them extraordinary facilities over other nations in the acquisition of plants, and to them we ourselves are indebted for the introduction, not only of many beautiful flowers, but of vegetables now in common use. For a long time their gardens at Leyden were considered the richest in the world. Through the zeal of the wealthy Dutch merchants, in less than a century—that is, between the years 1633 and 1720—the number of the different species of plants in these gardens was raised from 1104 to upwards of 6000, as shown by the catalogue of Boerhaave, who was at the time Professor of Botany there.

Great encouragement of late years has been given to gardening in Germany and France, and most continental nations. The gardens of Berlin, Munich, Vienna, Paris, &c., have all exercised considerable influence upon popular taste; but nothing has been done elsewhere to equal, or even to approach, the improvement which has taken place in Great Britain; and this improvement has by no means resulted from any direct encouragement given by the Government, but is altogether due to individual enterprise. The subject of gardening about the early part of the present century was taken up by men of taste and education and a better style introduced than that which we had borrowed from our continental neighbours—something more natural, and therefore more suitable for general adoption. The effect of this is manifest. No continental nation possesses such multitudes of good private gardens as we do. That which in most other countries is a luxury to be enjoyed only at the public expense, is with us regarded as a necessity, which every householder, from the cottager to the nobleman, is unwilling to forego. No Englishman now, except his lot be cast within the confines of some dense city, where bricks and mortar cover everything, is contented to live without a few square yards of ground which he can call his garden; and even under the most untoward circumstances of want of space, and smoky atmosphere, auricolas, carnations, and other fancy flowers, may be seen growing and cared for in windows, even in the poorest streets and alleys of our most crowded cities.

There is with us a growing popular taste for gardening, which has both created a great commercial enterprise, and is itself fed from the same source. The demand for flowers has made it worth while for men of intelligence and capital to turn their attention to them—to establish correspondents in every part of the world, and to keep alive the popular appetite by the continual introduction of something new. The rich can now luxuriate in winter gardens, filled with the products of tropical climes. Glass houses can be constructed of any size and shape, and by artificial heating they can be raised to any temperature required. Whatever is found growing elsewhere can be made to grow with us. And even more than this can be effected; for the skill of our florists can increase, by hybridizing and other processes, the specific varieties of such plants as are placed under their care, until their number becomes almost endless.

Our historical sketch must of necessity be brief; but we must not fail to mention among the chief operating causes which have made gardening an art so popular in this country, the great encouragement given by garden allotments, and village flower shows. Some useful practical information upon these points will be found in the Dictionary, under the articles "Allotment Gardens," "Cottagers' Horticultural Society," and "Gardening for Smoky Cities and Large Towns."

CHAPTER II.

DIFFERENT STYLES OF GARDENING.

NATIONAL styles and peculiarities in most things, especially throughout the European Continent, are now rapidly passing away. Such are the facilities and the extent of intercourse, that anything worthy of imitation is speedily introduced everywhere. Every year we live there is less difference apparent in the dress, the manners, the modes of living, the houses, and the gardens of neighbouring nations. Still, for all this, peculiarities in style are remarked; and their stamps are fixed perhaps as indelibly as they ever were as historical facts.

With regard to gardening, there are generally said to be four characteristic styles, viz., the Italian, the French, the Dutch, and the English, or, as it is frequently called, the "natural style."

The Italian style is probably a continuation only of that of the Romans, with whom it was an amplification of the house itself—

> "A pillar'd shade,
> With echoing walks beneath,"

broad paved and sunny terraces and shady colonnades connected in their style with the house. Marble fountains, statuary, and vases, and other vestiges of ancient art found in the ruins, out of which they have been raised, are the chief characteristics of the magnificent gardens of modern Italy, and nothing can be nobler than this style when the accessories are all in keeping. "In spite of Walpole's sneer," says Mr. Bellenden Kerr, "about walking up and down stairs in the open air, there are few things so beautiful in art as stately terraces, tier above tier, and bold flights of stone steps, now stretching forward in a broad, unbroken course, now winding round the angle of the terrace in short, steep descents—each landing affording some new scene, some change of sun or shade: a genial basking-place or cool retreat—here the rich perfume of an ancestral orange-tree, which may have been in the family three hundred years—there the bright blossoms of some sunny creeper; while at another time a balcony juts out to catch some distant view, or a recess is formed, with seats for the loitering party to 'rest and be thankful.' Let all this be connected, by means of colonnades, with the architecture of the mansion, and you have a far more rational appendage to its incessantly artificial character than the petty wildernesses and picturesque *abandon,* which have not been without advocates, even on an insignificant scale."

The objections, in our opinion, to this style are, first, its non-natural appearance, and secondly, its want of adaptation to general purposes. It is only a few gardens of the wealthy that can be so fitted up. The appendages are too elaborate and expensive to be suited to the generality of villa residences, or even to the more extensive grounds belonging to country houses. If well carried out, and attached to a palace in keeping with it, a garden in the Italian style may be agreeable to some persons; but to our notion there are always too many architectural embellishments to produce a pleasing effect, or to make it consistent with the quiet and unpretending houses in which we are contented to live.

Though the French are said to have introduced a distinct style of gardening, they have most certainly not exhibited in it much originality. As far as we are able to judge, they have worked up the worst feature of the old Italian style with more modern inventions. In their larger gardens there is nothing natural—everything is strained and theatrical. Even at Versailles in its best days, though representing two hundred acres in extent, and we believe something like eight millions sterling in value, the geometric style in Le Notre has little to recommend it except what is due to its extent and magnificence. In the elaborate productions of this school there is far too much formality—

"Grove nods at grove, each alley has its brother,
And half the garden just reflects the other."

A grand effect and display may be produced, but certainly not the scenery or landscape of nature, by a labyrinth, in which thirty-nine of Æsop's fables are represented by means of copper figures of birds and beasts, each group being connected with a separate fountain, and all spouting water.

The French have done much for this art; but their skill has not shown itself in design. We are greatly indebted to them for new methods of propagating plants and increasing the varieties of them; also for novelties in such operations as pruning and training; but their garden arrangements are by no means equal to our own.

The Dutch style is more consistent, and exhibits a far greater amount of originality. Having no picturesque scenery in their own country to imitate, these practical and industrious cultivators of the soil make no attempt at producing an effect which the eye of every beholder would at once detect as being unnatural to them. Their skill has shown itself in the arrangement of beds, terraces, and grassy slopes. They are fond of large broad spaces, filled with beds in geometrical figures, separated by lines of well-clipped box edgings. Different portions of their gardens are also shut off from view by hedges of evergreens, frequently cut into fantastical forms. The Dutch style exhibits a profusion of ornament of this sort, mostly on a small scale.

"Trees cut to statues, statues thick as trees."

They have, moreover, canals and watercourses made to accommodate the bridges thrown across them, caves, fountains, and the never-failing "lust-haus," or summer-house, with a profusion of trellis-work and green paint. In the more extensive pleasure-grounds, a banqueting-hall is not unfrequently to be found. Notwithstanding all that may be said against the Dutch style, there is one remark to be made upon it, which is very greatly in its favour. There is neatness everywhere. Whatever is seen in a Dutch garden, we may rest assured—be it fruit, flowers, or vegetables—is worth growing, and is taken care of accordingly. The Dutch style has this great superiority over the Italian and the French, that it is not suitable to the palace merely, but it can enlist the sympathies of the most humble cottager.

All these different styles have at times been introduced into our own country, and found advocates. Happily, however, we have escaped being victimized by any of them, and upon their ruins we have raised a style for ourselves, which, according to Gray, "is the only taste we can call our own, the only proof we can give of original talent in matters of pleasure."

Loudon and Wise were among the earliest innovators, and they are highly praised in the *Spectator* for the manner in which they laid out Kensington Gardens. Bridgman followed, hewing down many a verdurous peacock and juniper lion. Kent, the inventor of the ha-ha, came next, and broke up the distinction of garden and park; and Brown (Capability Brown, as he was called) succeeded him with round clumps and boundary belts, artificially winding rivers and lakes, with broad drives terminating in summer-houses.

There were, it must be admitted, many noble gardens in England prior to this period, well and artistically designed.

It is not surprising, perhaps, that when taste revived the opponents of the old style rushed, at a very early period, to the opposite extreme; many fine old gardens were recklessly pulled to pieces; in the words of Sir Walter Scott, "Down went many a trophy of old magnificence—

court-yard, ornamented enclosure, fosse, avenue, barbican, and every extensive monument of battled wall and flanking tower."

Brown is admitted by everyone to have been a man of genius, and he astonished the gardening world by the skilful manner in which he arrested the river and formed the beautiful lake at Blenheim; but he could not be everywhere, and he found many ignorant imitators. Sir Walter Scott tells an amusing story of one of these conceited pretenders, who was employed by Lord Abercorn in laying out the grounds at Duddingston. The house embraces noble views of Craigmillar Castle on the one side, backed by the Pentlands; on the other, by Arthur's Seat and the Salisbury Crags; and, on a third, the eye is carried past the precipitous rocks on which stands the Castle of Edinburgh, across the rich plains of Midlothian: the improver conceived it to be his duty to block out every glimpse of this noble landscape. Duddingston Loch is a beautiful piece of water, lying at the foot of Arthur's Seat: he did the same for this, and would have done as much for the surrounding hills, but they were too grand objects to be so treated. Lord Abercorn laughed at his absurdities, but he was too indolent to interrupt his vagaries.

Sir Uvedale Price, who went a certain length with the prevailing mania, which he afterwards was still more active in arresting, expresses bitter regret for the destruction of an ancestral garden on the old system which he condemned before he found out his error. He was afterwards led to write strongly in favour of the preservation of the remains of ancient magnificence still untouched, with modifications calculated to redeem them from the charge of barbarism.

During the present century, this question of gardening style, which at its commencement was one of chaos, has acquired form and consistency. The distinction which Sir U. Price, Whately, and a host of writers sought to establish and simplify, was insisted upon by Sir Walter Scott, Sir Henry Stewart, Sir Thomas Dick Lauder, Gilpin, and many others, ably seconded by Repton, and another Gilpin—a professional landscape gardener—Sir Joseph Paxton, and other well-known practical gardeners; and it is now universally admitted that the garden surrounding the house, whether an architectural terrace or bedded lawn, must of necessity possess uniformity; that the shrubbery immediately adjoining must partake of the same character, somewhat modified; while the more distant portions of the grounds are given over to the skill of the landscape gardener.

The true English style, then, aims at being natural, and in various degrees of modification it is adapted to every garden, however extensive or however limited.

All modern writers agree that the pleasure-garden should be contiguous to the house, and its contiguity will, of course, have much influence upon the character of it. Certain styles of architecture require corresponding styles of gardening as their proper accompaniments. An imposing and highly-finished façade seems to demand formal terraces and geometric gardens. We can have here, then, something of the Italian, French, and Dutch styles, which are all branches of the formal or geometric style, and may be described as presenting regular forms, or groups of beds arranged in mathematical figures. This is much the most useful and effective style of flower-garden. The groups may be sunk beneath the surface, when they are called Dutch gardens; or the figures can be edged with stones or tiles, and thus be constituted architectural gardens. The character and design of the edging should also correspond with the architecture of the house, and it may require to be supported by retaining walls, with massive piers for vases, and embellished with fountains. As a transition from the house to the garden, nothing can be more pleasing than a geometric pleasure-garden, laid out in turf or gravel, connected with the house by an upper and lower terrace, and descending by broad stone steps, notwithstanding what Horace Walpole satirically remarks about "walking up and down stairs out of doors."

This should be succeeded by a portion of ground laid out in what is often called the Gardenesque style, which may be described as a skilful disposition of trees and shrubs, in regular or irregular figures, or singly and at equal or unequal distances, preserving, amid apparent irregularity, a certain degree of uniformity. The chief feature of this style is, that no two plants shall be planted so close together as to touch each other, and that flowers of the same species are kept distinct. This style is generally employed in arboretums and pinetums, and is the only one capable of exhibiting individual plants, shrubs, and trees in perfection. It forms a tasteful gradation between the geometric and the picturesque style. The latter Mr. Loudon defines as imitating nature in a wild state, according to art. He also gives an example of this:—"A gravel pit would be improved, according to art, if foreign trees, shrubs, and plants, even to the grasses, were introduced instead of indigenous ones; or a Swiss cottage instead of a hovel. Rock scenery, aquatic scenery, dale or dingle scenery, forest scenery, copse scenery, and open glade scenery, may all be imitated on the same principle, viz., that of substituting foreign for indigenous vegetation, and laying out regular walks. This is sufficient to constitute a picturesque imitation of natural scenery." Thus the picturesque style may be said to consist of irregular groups of figures, masses, or clumps, disposed at regular intervals; for in this style the grouping is everything—individual effect nothing. It is the connecting link, as it were, between the garden and the natural scenery outside.

This is essentially the English style of gardening, and under it our villas and country houses have been enabled to reach their present state of comfort and adornment. No country in the world can show such good general gardening as our own. But the end is not yet attained. We have still much to do before it can be said that we have reached perfection.

CHAPTER III.

SOILS AND THEIR CHARACTERISTICS.

No one can turn up a spadeful of earth in different parts of the country, much less travel any distance by railways through their different cuttings, without being struck with the variety of soils and subsoils that are to be met with. Perhaps he may ask himself whence this great variety, and what are the constituent particles of these different soils.

The chemist will answer readily enough that they are compounded of a great many chemical substances, and repeat the names of some fourteen, which are present in varying proportions in all fertile soils. The practical cultivator, with equal readiness, reduces them to some five or six well-ascertained varieties of soil, characterised according to the preponderating proportions of silica, lime, clay, vegetable mould, marl, or loam, which they contain. According to his rough estimate—

I. SANDY soil contains 80 per cent., or thereabouts, of silica; that is, of the crumbling *débris* of granite or sandstone rock.

II. CALCAREOUS soils contain 20 per cent. and upwards of lime in their composition.

III. CLAY soils contain 50 per cent. of stiff unctuous clay.

IV. VEGETABLE mould, the richest of all garden soils, contains from 5 to 12 per cent. of *humus*—that is, decomposed vegetable and animal matter.

V. MARLY soil is the *débris* of limestone rock decomposed and reduced to a paste.

VI. LOAMY soil, in which the proportion of clay varies from 20 to 25 per cent. sand, and various kinds of alluvium making up the remainder.

But both chemist and cultivator still confine themselves to generalities. If, therefore, we want to know something more of the origin of soils than this, we must consult the geologist. From him we learn a strange and wonderful chapter in the history of creation.

The framework of the globe we inhabit, he tells us, is a dense mass of primitive rock, of igneous origin, which has been proved by fire and tempered by water—vast masses of rugged granite and porphyry towering to the skies in our own and other countries; overlying which are the rocks of secondary formation, in which it is sometimes embedded; but more frequently the shaly slate and old red sandstone are thrown around it in their order of stratification—a mantle, as it were, thrown over the shoulders of these giants of creation.

These rocks of secondary formation are distinguished by their colour and by their structure, but above all by their fossiliferous remains, by means of which the naturalist has been able to trace the history of creation through a vast lapse of ages. These rocks of secondary formation are—

1. The Silurian group or Clay system.
2. The Old Red Sandstone.
3. The Carboniferous system.
4. The Permean system.
5. The New Red Sandstone.
6. The Oolite formation.
7. The Cretaceous or Chalk formation.

The tertiary formation, however, which forms another great chapter in the history of creation, is that which more directly belongs to our subject—the formation of soils—for it is concerned about the upper portion of the earth's crust.

When this period began there is every reason to believe that the British Islands were merely a long, straggling archipelago of rocky pinnacles rising out of the great deep, and a geological map of the period may readily be constructed by laying under water every part of the country which does not rise 800 feet above the level of the sea. Taking the whole range of the country, it will be found that it is rugged and mountainous on the west, north-west, and south-west; extensive elevations, intermingling with valleys, dales, and intersected by rivers and plains, much more extensive at the central, eastern, and south-eastern parts.

Such is the sketch which geologists give us of our country before those agencies came into operation, whereby the valleys have been left dry and the rocks themselves crumbled into soil. The agencies acting in the formation of soil and rock are both chemical and mechanical. Atmospheric oxygen and carbonic acid, which is so largely contained in rain-water, as well as vegetable and animal life, combine in the work of disintegration. It would be beyond our purpose and also exceed our space to go deeply into this subject: our observations must be confined to soils seen from a gardener's point of view.

That portion of the earth's crust which falls under the operation of gardening admits of a fourfold division. These soils are:—1. Silica, sandstone, or gravel; 2. Clay; 3. Loam; 4. Humus, or mould, formed from decayed vegetable or animal matter. These, combined in varying proportions with certain chemical substances, form the hazel loam, brown loam, clayey loam, sandy soil, garden mould, fat or rich soil—terms which are so continually on the tongue of every gardener.

Sandy soils are loose, friable, open, and dry, and for that reason easily cultivated. They rest chiefly on the old red sandstone, and granite and coal formations. When alumina and calcareous matter are absent, however, they are nearly barren: they absorb manures without benefit to the land. Where alumina and lime exist, they are more compact and adhesive, and grow good crops of beans, peas, spring wheat, and turnips. They are capable of improvement by admixture with clay, marl, chalk, and other adhesive soils, which communicate their constituent properties to them.

Calcareous soils resting on the upper chalk formation are usually deep, dry, loose, friable, and fertile in their nature; but others, resting on the shaly oolite, are stony, poor, thin soils. Leguminous plants, as peas, beans, vetches, sainfoin, and clover, do well on such soils, lime being essential to their growth. Where pure clay is present in such soils, they are called loams or calcareous clays; where silica is in excess, they are termed calcareous sandy soils.

Clay soils are characterised by stiffness, impenetrability, great power of absorbing and retaining moisture, and great specific gravity; they are, consequently, cold, stiff, heavy, and impervious, costly to cultivate, and often unproductive. Perfect drainage, burning the soil with wood fagots, branches of trees, grass sods, and vegetable refuse, and mixing chalk and sand, are the only remedies. Burning is the most efficient remedy; the burnt clay acting chemically as a manure, its constituents being rendered more soluble. Provided a moderate heat has been applied to the process, the potash is rendered soluble, and liberated from the clay in which it occurs in an insoluble combination. Thus treated, clay soils become the most fertile for all heavy crops.

In the absence of that amount of geological and chemical knowledge, so necessary for a correct analysis of the nature of soils, many practical gardeners attach great importance to the vegetable products they throw up spontaneously, in the form of weeds. The late Mr. Loudon has recorded, in his laborious work, a sort of vegetable index to soils based on this idea.

The leading soils for the cultivator are the clayey, calcareous, sandy, ferruginous, peaty, saline, moist or aquatic, and dry.

ARGILLACEOUS. — Tussilago farfara; Potentilla anserina, argentea, and reptans; Thalictrum flavum; Carex, many species; Juncus, various species; Orobus tuberosus; Lotus major and corniculatus; Saponaria officinalis. But the coltsfoot, Tussilago-farfara, is a certain and universal sign of an argillaceous soil, and is the chief plant found on the alum-grounds of Britain, France, and Italy.

CALCAREOUS.—Veronica spicata; Galium pusillum; Lithospermum officinale, and purpuro-cæruleum; Campanula glomerata and hybrida; Phyteuma orbiculare; Verbascum lychnitis; Viburnum lantana; Berberis vulgars; Cistus helianthemum; Anemone pulsatilla; Clematis vitalba; Hedysarum onobrychis.

SILICIOUS.—Veronica triphyllos and verna; Echium italicum; Herniaria glabra and hirsuta; Silene anglica, and other species; Arenaria rubra; Spergula arvensis; Papaver hybridum; Argemone, &c.

FERRUGINOUS.—Rumex acetosa and acetosella; Sheep's sorrel.

PEATY.—Vaccinium myrtillus, uliginosum, and Oxycoccus palustris; Ericas, Spergula subulata; Tormentilla officinalis.

SALINE.—Salicornia, 4 species; Zostera marina; Ruppia maritima; Pulmonaria maritima; Calystagia; Soldanella; Illecebrum verticillatum; Chenopodium maritimum; Salsola kali and fruticosa; Sisum verticillatum; Arenaria maritima, &c.; Atriplex laciniata.

AQUATIC.—Caltha palustris; Hippuris vulgaris; Pinguicula vulgaris; Lycopus europæus: Valeriana dioica; Hottonia palustris; Samolus valerandi; Thysselinum palustre; Epilobium tetragonum; Lythrum salicaria; Ranunculus lingua and flammula.

VERY DRY. — Arenaria rubra; Rumex acetosella; Thymus serpyllum; Acynos vulgaris; Trifolium arvense.

Though we cannot say that these plants are in all cases to be depended upon, it may safely be affirmed that the Sainfoin is always an indication of a calcareous soil, the common Coltsfoot of blue clay, the Arenaria rubra of poor sand, the small Wood-sorrel of the presence of iron. It would be wise, of course, to get the opinion of both scientific and practical men before finally deciding such an important matter. However, a successful cultivator, quite unable to give a correct definition of the character of the soil, is generally the safest of all judges as to its quality.

CHAPTER IV.

SELECTION OF A GARDEN SITE.

IT must be conceded at once that in a general way the house regulates the situation of the garden—that is to say, that the latter is dependent upon the former, and not the former upon the latter. Such is, undoubtedly, the case with the thousands of comfortable-looking villas which surround not only the Metropolis, but every city and country town in England. There may be some few instances in the country where a particularly good site for a garden has induced the building of a suitable house, but this can hardly even be said of gardens near large towns. These, for the most part, have to take their chance as to situation. They are entirely dependent upon what is considered the most suitable situation for the house, and must be set out and arranged in the best manner possible when the land for building purposes has been marked out. It must not, however, be supposed, because the garden is of necessity subsidiary to the dwelling-house, that the difference between a good and a bad site is small, and unimportant. both the enjoyment and productiveness of a garden are dependent upon its situation.

Seclusion is one great point to be kept in view; and in villa residences, even though detached from each other, this is often a hard matter to be gained. Still it is most essential to enjoyment, for everybody knows how unpleasant it is not to be able to work in and to walk about our gardens without being overlooked. A shrubbery of evergreens should in all cases, if possible, be made to skirt the public way, and both flower and kitchen garden be so managed as to be screened from the broad view of passers by. The judicious arrangement of ornamental shrubs will frequently effect all that is required; and if not, arches for roses, clematis, and other climbers, also trellis-work for the same purpose, may be introduced.

The next important requisites are a dry soil and subsoil, and, happily, these are equally important for the comfort and healthiness of the house. No house can be well situated that is built upon a heavy, close, and tenacious soil. It is quite true that drainage may do a good deal towards improvement; but if the subsoil be impervious to water, the site can never be desirable either for a house or for a garden. Under the article "Drainage," in the Dictionary, the reader will find the *rationale* of this most important operation explained and illustrated, as well as much practical information for carrying it out. There are very few soils which do not need to be improved by drainage.

The best subsoil, both for house and garden, is either chalk, rock, or gravel. And if we can find any of these, with a rich loam overlaying it to the thickness of three or four feet, we have secured an excellent site for the growth of both flowers and vegetables.

Aspect is another important consideration. A slope to the north, or north-east, embracing at any rate the entire garden, is highly objectionable, and a free exposure to all or any of the following points, viz., south-east, south, south-west, and west, will be found most suitable. An occasional border, with a north aspect, may prove useful however, and as much shelter as possible should be sought for on the north and north-east. Also, in the case of gardens situated on the western side of an island, shelter is desirable towards the west from the fierce winds that at times blow across the great Atlantic Ocean. For a flower garden, a sloping situation has many advantages. It admits of more effect being produced in laying it out than when the surface is a perfect flat. For a kitchen garden, on the other hand a level is to be recommended, or at most a very gentle inclination towards the south. If any portion of the ground is to be laid out in shrubberies, nothing is more agreeable than to have as many "ups" and "downs" in it as possible; these, with a good disposal of ornamental trees, and a judicious arrangement of walks, may be the means of causing a very small piece of ground to appear much larger than it really is. Salubrity or healthiness of situation is of course a matter of primary importance in the selection of a new home. Without health nothing can be enjoyed; with it, the humblest home and smallest garden may become a perennial source of happiness. Men rarely build a house or form a garden more than once in a lifetime; and an unfavourable choice will not only cause disappointment, but perhaps engender misery throughout an entire existence Too much caution, therefore, cannot be exercised on this point. No advantageous offer of a cheap plot of land; no contiguity to a town or railway; no desire even to be near your business, beyond what necessity requires; or to be near old friends; no theoretical fancies about the ameliorating influence upon climate of thorough drainage, or the effect of scientific cultivation, should induce anyone to build in an unhealthy locality. Four sufficiently striking characteristics will generally distinguish a healthy site: it will be dry, warm, liberally supplied with pure water, and elevated more or less above the surrounding country.

The advantages of a good supply of water for garden purposes cannot be too strongly insisted upon. If a brook or river passes through the garden, so much the better; for beyond an easy water supply, the banks can in general be turned to a very good account, and made both profitable and ornamental. The charm of a running stream, however, cannot in all places be secured; but almost everywhere a good pond may be brought in and rendered useful.

With regard to the enclosure of a piece of ground, there are many things to be considered. In a general way, there are three modes of enclosure—fences, hedges, and walls; and which of these is the most suitable must be determined by circumstances. Fences and hedges are undoubtedly the most ornamental, but walls are the most permanent and useful, and on these accounts are more generally adopted. Dr. Patterson, in his admirable little book on the Manse Garden, is loud in his condemnation of garden walls. "An equally high and four-cornered garden wall," he says, "staring in the open fields, is the most unseemly thing that can be set down on the surface of the earth." He then adds, "If your house stand within such a garden, it looks like a prison, and all the flowers within such a boundary of stone, appear not otherwise than as a parterre for the amusement of Bedlam." This is strong condemnation, and we are very far from yielding an unqualified assent to it. There are hundreds and thousands of houses and gardens in England, enclosed within walls, where a little good taste and good management in laying out the grounds have entirely kept from view not only all that is "unseemly," but all other disadvantages resulting from a brick-wall enclosure. Clumps of trees, ornamental evergreen shrubs, arches for roses, &c., trellis-work and rock-work, may be so disposed as to screen, or at any rate break the view of walls from any part of the flower-garden and pleasure-ground; and in the kitchen-garden, no one can possibly consider a brick wall to be out of place. Without it, what is to become of our wall fruits? and what, too, of such vegetables as tomatoes and others that require such support and protection? The different varieties of ivy may also be made use of in any place where the sight of a brick wall is offensive; and so also may the Virginia creeper, the bignonia, and a variety of those lovely clematis which have been introduced of late, and which of course require to be grown against a wall, and cannot well be had without one.

In laying out a garden, even of the smallest dimensions, there is always ample scope for the exercise of good taste, and it matters not, in our opinion, how the land selected is enclosed, for a little ingenuity will soon make a pretty garden out of it. Evergreens, both trees and shrubs, can be made to do wonders, and in a short time to convert the most unpromising spot into a paradise.

We have ourselves the greatest possible objection to a garden of one idea. By this expression, we mean a garden wherein as soon as we have entered, the eye takes in everything at a glance: and if this be bounded by four brick walls uncovered and staring red, we agree with Dr. Patterson that the sight is "unseemly." However well kept the lawn, however gay with flowers the beds upon it, there is always a deficiency in walking about such a piece of ground as this. The eye longs for variety in scene, and here it has none, for everything is seen at one glance. Let the walls, however, be covered, as we have pointed out, and let only two or three clumps of evergreens and a few ornamental conifers be well placed on such a lawn as this and a landscape can be made at once. Beds and shrubs, in reference to each other, now change their position and aspect as we walk about, and an agreeable variety is produced. A very small lawn will, in this way, appear much larger than it really is, and the beds, from the simple fact that they cannot all be seen at once, will seem to be more numerous than they are.

When the space is very limited there may at first sight appear to be an objection to the planting of shrubs upon a lawn, but we must remember, as will be remarked in our next chapter upon ornamental planting, that there are shrubs suited in growth to gardens of the smallest dimensions. The upright Irish yews, several sorts of cedars, and the beautiful thujas take up very little space. A clump of three of them may stand within a circle whose diameter is only three or four yards and yet ample space be left to walk among them. Thuja aurea erecta is beautiful as a single specimen, and takes no room. There are also light foliaged and silver varieties of conifers which may be introduced to form contrasts, but of these full information will be found in succeeding pages.

If the lawn be a dead flat, a large mound of earth may be thrown up to break the uniformity, often with a very good effect, for it can be planted with laurestinus, the sumach, &c., and, if space admits, a crab or a double-blossomed peach on a tall stem may be introduced; rock-work also comes in with its assistance, and trellis-work does the same. Under these two terms, in the Dictionary, will be found sufficient information for all practical purposes.

CHAPTER V.

ORNAMENTAL PLANTING.

EVERY possessor of a garden is more or less interested in the subject of our present chapter; for, whatever be its extent, some portion of it is certain to be occupied by plantation or shrubbery. The space of ground before the house generally requires to be screened from the road; and in almost every case there are some unsightly objects,—some sheds or blank walls which must be shut out from view by the judicious arrangement of a few trees and evergreens. Of course, the greater the extent that can be devoted to pleasure-ground the more care and attention must be bestowed upon ornamental planting.

At the present time, and in our own country especially, there are the greatest possible facilities afforded for beautifying our parks, pleasure-grounds, lawns, and shrubberies by the careful disposal of many of those choice evergreens, deciduous trees, conifers, and American plants which of late years have been introduced. The intercourse of nations, the steamboat and the rail, coupled with the rapid strides which have been made in botanical knowledge and research, have done and are doing much to assimilate all parts of the world as to their vegetable products. In a general way, the organization of plants, as of animals, is adjusted to the course and action of the elements; but nature to a great extent accommodates itself to the requirements of art, and in this way the plants of foreign countries become acclimatized.

Those who have visited the countries between the Tropics speak with admiration of the luxuriant profusion and rich variety of the vegetable productions of those regions. The system under which it goes on is far more favourable than in our own latitudes. Every zone, however, has its peculiar vegetable productions, though some may be more luxuriant and beautiful than others. If we look at the indigenous plants of Asia and Europe, northward from the Equator, we find a very varied succession. At the Equator there are the natives of the Spice Islands, the clove and nutmeg trees, the pepper plant and cinnamon bushes, which are common in Ceylon. In the East Indies there are the odoriferous sandal wood, the ebony tree, the banyan and the teak tree. In the same latitude, in Arabia, we have balm, frankincense and myrrh, the coffee tree and the tamarind. While in these countries—at any rate in the plains — the trees and shrubs which decorate our more northerly climes are wanting. At every step we take, the vegetable group changes both by addition and subtraction. In the thickets, west of the Caspian Sea, we read of apricots, citrons, peaches, and walnuts. In the same latitude, in Spain, Sicily, and Italy, we find the palm, the cypress, the chestnut, and the cork tree; oranges and lemons perfume the air with their blossoms; the myrtle and pomegranate grow among the rocks.

Crossing the Alps we have the vegetation which belongs to Northern Europe, of which England affords an evidence. The oak, the beech, and the elm, are natives of Great Britain. The wych elm is peculiar to the North of England and Scotland. Still further north the forests change their character. In Northern Russia are found forests of the various species of firs—the Scotch, the spruce fir, and the larch. In the Orkney Islands no tree is found but the hazel, which is also the case along the northern shores of the Baltic. As we proceed into colder regions we meet with other species, which appear to have been made for their situation. North of Stockholm there is the hoary alder (alnus incana); the sycamore and the mountain ash grow at the head of the Gulf of Bothnia; and as we pass the boundary line of the spruce and Scotch fir, we come upon those minute shrubs known as the dwarf birch and dwarf willow. Near to, and even within the Arctic region, if no trees are to be met with, there are still wild flowers of great beauty, and when these fail us there is reindeer moss. As we have just observed, Nature kindly accommodates itself to the wants and wishes, and especially to the industry, of man. Our woods and shrubberies and gardens may now be adorned with the vegetable production of all climates and countries. The Eastern and the Western world, especially Brazil, California, Japan, New Zealand, and Australia, have added many beauties to our scenery which were unknown to our forefathers. The oak, the ash, the elm, the lime, the beech, and the maple, in all parts of the country, testify by their size either to indigenous growth or to the length of time during which they have been known among us. But then, even these, until comparatively recent periods, were in no great varieties; or, if there were varieties, there was so little specific difference that they were generally regarded as being the same sorts.

Anyone who feels sufficient interest in the subject to take up the catalogues of our large growers of ornamental trees and shrubs will see that he has a great variety to select from, and perhaps it may surprise him to find that, though many of these are eminently beautiful, they are but specific varieties of plants well known, and that the generic names are old, common, and familiar.

Let us take the following as examples :—

Of the oak, *Quercus*, in addition to the common English oak, Quercus pedunculata, he will find Q. variegata, a beautiful variegated variety, calculated to produce a fine effect in distant scenery; Q. coccinea and Q. rubra, both scarlet oaks; Q. nigra, a black oak, with leaves as black as the purple beech; Q. alba, a white, American variety; Q. macrocarpa, with its long acorns; and Q. macrophylla, with its long leaves. These are only a few among many.

Of the ash, *Fraxinus*, besides F. excelsior, the common ash, there is F. pendula, a weeping ash, and F. aurea pendula, a golden weeping ash; also F. aucubefolia, the aucuba-leaved ash, and F. crispa, curled.

Of the elm, *Ulmus*, in addition to U. campestris, which is the old English elm, we find U. foliis variegatis, a variegated elm; U. glabra pendula, a smooth weeping elm; and U. rugosa pendula, a rough weeping elm; also U. latifolia, the broad-leaved, and many others, all valuable as large trees, for, though they require a rich, deep soil, they will live and flourish in the smoky atmosphere of our crowded towns.

Of the lime, *Tilia*, the common variety of which is T. Europea, there are T. alba, the white-leaved lime, and T. pendula, the weeping lime, both of which may be planted separately, or interspersed with other trees with very good effect.

Of the beech, *Fagus*, F. sylvatica, the common beech, is a fine tree and exceedingly useful, as it will grow well in both sandy and chalky soils. It is surpassed, however, by several of its varieties: F. asplenii-folia, the fern-leaved beech, and F. purpurea-major, the large purple beech, are noble trees.

Of the maple, *Acer*, A. campestre is the common maple, which is a showy tree, beautiful in growth and foliage; but there are several others which are even more beautiful: A. macrophyllum, the long-leaved maple, is very striking; and so, also, are A. lanciniatum, the cut-leaved maple, A. albo variegatum, the white variegated, and A. rubrum, the scarlet maple; also A. striatum, the snake-barked variety, which almost rivals the cork tree.

These which we have mentioned are a few only of the ornamental varieties of our most common forest and park trees. Others there are almost as common which admit of several varieties. Under the generic name, *Æsculus*, the horse chesnuts, are contained not only Æ. hippocastanea, the common horse chesnut, but Æ. flore pleno, a double-blossomed variety, Æ. rubicunda, with its scarlet blossoms, and one or two others.

The Spanish chesnut also, *Castanea vesca*, itself so beautiful in shrubberies, offers an agreeable variety in C. aspleniifolia, the fern-leaved, C. Knightii, and C. variegata.

Take, again, the *Populus*, or poplar, which is a handsome, quick-growing tree under almost any circumstances of soil and climate. Here we have that most beautiful variety, of which there are several splendid specimens standing singly to be met with: viz., P. alba, the Abèle poplar; also P. fastigiata, the Lombardy variety, and P. grandidentata, the large American aspen, and P. tremula pendula, the weeping aspen.

Then, there is that large genus *Cratægus*, the thorn or hawthorn—old as the hills, but for which care and cultivation have done much. Flowering and fruit-bearing, various in colour and in growth, the whole family is worthy of a place wherever there is room for planting. So hardy are they, that the most severe frost will never injure them, and so easy of culture, that they do not refuse to grow in almost any soil and under a smoky atmosphere. As no doubt we shall have to speak of the thorns again, we shall only here mention that the best recommended are C. apiifolia minor, the small parsley-leaved thorn; C. Maroccana, the Morocco thorn; C. pendula, the weeping hawthorn; C. rubra, the red hawthorn; and C. Leeana, Lee's variety.

Next let us invite attention to the genus *Pyrus*, which includes under it, apples, crabs, pears, aronias, the service tree, and the mountain-ash: some of the most ornamental of our smaller trees, whether we consider flowers, fruit, or foliage. There are Pyrus aria, the white beam tree; P. prunifolia, the Siberian crab; P. spectabilis, the Chinese crab; and many variegated and weeping varieties, which, as standards upon lawns, form very pretty objects. Anyone who intends to plant, cannot do better than select such of these as may suit his garden site, and assist the landscape which he is preparing.

In addition to these, which may be called the principal deciduous trees under cultivation, there are a large number of deciduous shrubs which should not be neglected by anyone who wishes to beautify and improve his plantations. Most of these shrubs blossom freely; many are very handsome, and produce an excellent effect when blended with evergreens, of which we shall have to speak presently. There are the different sorts of *Berberis:* Amygdalus communis amara, the bitter almond; A. dulcis, the sweet almond; Buddlea globosa, the globe-flowered buddlea, which is very ornamental; the Daphne mazereum, the common mazereon; also D. albo flore, the white-flowered variety;

also three or four varieties of the elegant and free-flowering Deutzia. Nor must we omit the different sorts of *Genista*, or Broom, the Robinia, and the many kinds of Spiræa, than which it is hardly possible to find any genus more richly varied and more profuse in flowering. Many other small deciduous shrubs, useful for filling up gaps in plantations and borders, are brought into notice in this work.

We must now pass to the description of those many shrubs of an evergreen character, which are not only highly ornamental in themselves, but so extremely valuable as preserving a fresh appearance in nature, even during the dreary months of winter; also in affording a continual shade and shelter to other things. It is here somewhat difficult to determine whether to begin with the Ilex aquifolium, the common holly, or Quercus Ilex, the evergreen oak. Both are handsome evergreens, and rich in varieties, but we must give the preference to the former. Not only is the holly the brightest green of all evergreens, but its magnificent scarlet berries give to it an additional charm. There are many varieties of the Ilex, and few things are more interesting than a good collection of these within an arboretum, or space so limited as to afford an opportunity for observing their differences of growth and foliage. I. albo marginatum, the silver-edged holly, and I. aureo marginatum, the golden-edged, are very beautiful; so also are I. ciliatum, the hairy holly, and I. ferox, the hedgehog holly; I. ovatum, the oval-leaved, I. pendulum, the weeping, and I. latifolium, the broad-leaved, are all striking. Second only to the Ilex, is the genus *Quercus*, Q. Ilex being the common evergreen oak. When standing singly on a lawn or in a park, Q. Fulhamensis, the Fulham oak, is very imposing; and so, also, is Q. Luccombiana, the Luccombe oak, which is of the same character. The acorns of each of these are very handsome. In some situations these choice varieties do not fruit freely. The past summer has been most favourable to the development of all kinds of seed, and no doubt a large quantity of these acorns have been secured for the seed bed.

The different sorts of box, *Buxus*, are very ornamental. They do not attain much height; but they grow well in shade, and always look fresh and nice. B. sempervirens is the common box; B. aurea and B. argentea, the gold and silver varieties, form an agreeable change; B. Balearica is a good sort, and so is B. latifolia; B. Hardwickii is a very quick-growing variety.

Of *Phillyreas* there are several sorts, all of which, from their dark, shiny leaves, form excellent masses, and grow freely in almost any soil. The Cerasus tribe must not be omitted, for to it belong the common laurel, Laurocerasus, and Cerasus lusitanica, the Portugal laurel, both of which are too valuable to be passed by; Laurus nobilis, the common bay, is useful as well as ornamental. Every seaside garden can grow the tamarisk; and, however smoky the atmosphere, Rhamnus alaternus, the common alaternus, and others of the same genus, which are all of quick growth, will live and do well, provided only they have shelter from the wind.

There yet remains to be noticed a class of trees, without which it can hardly be said that much has been don in ornamental planting.

This class contains the conifers and taxads, which have been so extensively improved and so freely cultivated of late years. The conifers and taxads are considered the grandest of ornamental trees. They are evergreen, thriving, for the most part, in common soil, disliking manure, except in a thoroughly decomposed state. They are best raised from seed, but some kinds are not yet obtainable in that way, and are found to do perfectly well grafted, when united to a proper stock. Where there is sufficient space, the pines and firs should enter largely into the composition of scenery; in more limited grounds the junipers, cypresses, arbor vitæs, and yews are equally valuable. A few only thrive well in the vicinity of large towns, but as such are very desirable from their distinct and handsome forms, they should not be overlooked when planting. In extensive pleasure-grounds, a " pinetum," that is, a space allotted to this division exclusively, is by no means uncommon. One of the most complete, although of comparatively recent formation, is that of W. R. Baker, Esq., of Bayfordbury, Hertfordshire. It consists of several acres, formed on rising ground, with slopes of different aspects to suit the requirements of the different trees.

First among the conifers, let us take the genus *Pinus*. It is hardly possible to do justice to the rich variety which is here included. There are pines adapted to every soil and every situation; also for every purpose of ornament and profit. What more commanding than a fine specimen of P. excelsa? Then there are P. Devoniana, the Duke of Devonshire's pine, P. insignis, and P. Jeffreyii, and very many others. The last-mentioned is certainly the best of the long-leaved varieties. Nor must we omit the magnificent Wellingtonia gigantea, which is certainly a pine, and the noblest and hardiest of pines; nor Araucaria imbricata, the Chillian pine, a very distinct variety. Then, the genus *Abies*, the fir; A. excelsa, A. grandis, A. Hookerii, A. nobilis, A. Nordmanniana, A. Pinsapo, are all eminently noble: this latter variety is a particularly handsome tree, having its numerous branches arranged in whirls in the most perfect order; as a single tree upon a lawn nothing can surpass it. In its own country, Spain, it attains a height of 70 or 80 feet. Again, there is A. Douglasii, the most distinct and beautiful ever introduced. It was discovered and named after the persevering explorer whose name it bears, and upon whose authority it is stated to attain the great height of 250 feet, and 12 feet diameter at base. It is thoroughly hardy, of sound constitution, and very rapid in growth. The flag-staff, 159 feet high, erected in Kew Gardens, is a specimen imported from Vancouver's Island. Independent of its great attractions as an highly ornamental tree, its value as timber can scarcely be estimated; it is fine-grained, elastic, strong, heavy and free from knots, easily wrought, and capable of receiving a high polish, very durable, and not subject to split.

Next in order from which to make a selection is the genus *Cedrus*, the cedar. Here C. deodora is conspicuous. It should have a place on every lawn which is large enough to admit it, and where it can have shelter from the wind. In its original habitat it attains 200 feet in height, and is frequently 40 feet in circumference; it is distinguished from all others by its handsome pyramidal form and beautiful glaucous green foliage. In speaking of its excellence as a timber tree, Mr. Loudon says, "The wood is very compact and resinous, and has a fragrant smell, remarkably fine, and of close grain, capable of receiving a very high polish, so much so, indeed, that a table formed of a section of a trunk four feet in diameter, sent by Dr. Wallich to Mr. Lambert, has been compared to a slab of brown agate." Dr. Royle informs us that the wood is particularly durable, and is much used in the construction of Himalayan houses. In Cashmir it is used for both public and private buildings, and likewise for bridges and boats. Strips of it are also burnt as candles.

Of the cypresses, *Cupressus*, there are many varieties. Conspicuous among them are C. Lawsonia argentea and C. Lawsonia aurea, the silver and gold cypresses, both of which, we understand, owe their origin to Mr. John Waterer, of Bagshot. All the cypresses require a dry soil and situation; if these conditions cannot be obtained, their places would be better occupied by junipers.

The junipers, *Juniperus*, are very similar to the above class, but much hardier. All the taller varieties are striking in shrubberies and plantations, and the smaller very ornamental on grass-plots and lawns; almost all junipers have a close habit, which renders them valuable in small gardens. J. excelsa, J. Virginiana, J. fragrans, J. thurifera, are some of the best and tallest; J. Chinensis is a handsome shrub, and so is J. Hibernica, the Irish juniper.

Of the *Thuia*, or arbor vitæ genus, the varieties are mostly of middle size. They vary in colour from a bright yellowish green to golden. They are most valuable in small gardens from their contrast with shrubs of both lighter and a darker tint. They are also not particular as to soil or situation.

There yet remains the yew, *Taxus*. Trees of this genus are generally of the darkest shades of green; they can, therefore, be planted either singly for contrast, or in masses, to give an effect of shade. They are all hardy, and, with the exception of T. baccata, they do not attain any great size, so that they are very suitable for small gardens. T. canadensis is, we believe, the lightest coloured variety. T. elegantissima, T. variegata, and T. foliis aureis have a fine golden tinge.

Our lawns and gardens already show that there is throughout the country a growing taste for plants of this character, and no doubt a time will come when the appearance of our English scenery will be improved by the introduction of ornamental trees and shrubs on a larger scale.

On referring to the catalogues of Messrs. Paul, of Cheshunt, Messrs. Waterer, of Bagshot, and other large growers, we are surprised to find at what prices plants can be supplied. Many of those we have enumerated are now quoted by the hundred at prices which but a few years ago were asked for a single specimen; and no doubt, when the selection is left to the grower, they may be purchased on even more favourable terms, Under good cultivation there is no limit to the increase of these things. Time alone is required to raise seedlings and strike cuttings.

CHAPTER VI.

THE MODERN FLOWER-GARDEN.

WITHOUT fear of contradiction, it may be asserted that no country in the world can show such a floral display during the summer and autumn months as is to be seen in England. Go where you will, throughout the length and breadth of the land, to the cottage or to the palace, and the love of flowers will be found predominant. Still it must be confessed that the system which of late years has been so fashionable is open to very serious objection, and that from the signs of the times an important alteration is at hand. Our flower-gardens during the long months of spring have been left without flowers, and this has been done to accommodate the cultivation of a limited class of plants. Bedding plants, properly so called, under which name are included verbenas, calceolarias, geraniums, petunias, and some few others, have almost driven out of notice a very long list of herbaceous plants and choice spring flowering bulbs. It is most certainly true that during the months of spring the great majority of our gardens have of late years been as bare of flowers as fallow fields. We can call to mind hundreds of villa gardens, and gardens attached to larger houses, that are literally a blaze of blossom during summer and autumn while these bedding plants are in perfection, from which it would be quite impossible to gather half-a-dozen different flowers at any other season. Now, this is not as it should be, and before a few years are over we shall see a very great improvement. There are flowers in abundance suited to all seasons; and it is only in the depth of winter that, comparatively speaking, flowers out of doors need be scarce. Some persons may say that the soil requires a period of rest, and that if we exhaust it with spring flowers we shall have to pay the penalty when summer comes. Every good gardener, however, can provide for this. There is no degree of exhaustion which cannot be repaired, and there should always be at hand a sufficient amount of compost to meet this difficulty. An entire change of soil in beds and borders is often not only beneficial, but absolutely necessary. This may be effected by deep trenching, if the subsoil be good enough, or by replacing the top soil by fresh mould taken from a field or some part of the kitchen garden. No one who takes any interest in the subject would urge this as an excuse for being without flowers in spring. The fact is, the fashion has been to garden for the summer only, and to sacrifice everything else to a good display of bedding plants. We have not one word to say in disparagement of any of the popular flowers, so called. They are all beautiful in their way, and well worthy of the care and attention which they have received. The advance which has been made by careful cultivation with verbenas, geraniums, petunias, and some few others, is marvellous : it rivals the degree of perfection which has been achieved in the case of florist's flowers, properly so called. The prize pansy and noble dahlia of our shows hardly excel their rude originals more strikingly than do the geraniums of the present day the plants which represented them some twenty-five years ago. Cultivation has effected for them that degree of improvement which is its natural result. Few sights are more attractive than fine plants of L'Orient, the Black Prince, and others, with flowers, large and rich in colour, springing from three, and even four, eyes in the new wood. The foliage varieties are also worthy of the highest praise. But we do not consider that any or all of these popular bedding plants should be cultivated to the exclusion of all plants of a different character. The public taste has of late been so absorbed by them that it can take interest in nothing else. The sweetness of the old-fashioned cabbage rose, unsurpassed, and perhaps unsurpassable, the delicate beauty of the old-fashioned London Pride, the simple modesty of the Fair Maid of Perth, and the general excellence of many of these favourites of bygone years, have failed to preserve them from neglect. In the march of fashion these and innumerable other perennials of great beauty have almost entirely disappeared. However small the garden, room must be made for summer bedding plants, and all perennials—herbaceous or ligneous—must be rooted out. We maintain that such a system is wrong—not an unqualified wrong, for we gladly give it credit for the good it has done in the improvement of some most useful and ornamental plants, but wrong inasmuch as it has well-nigh sent out of cultivation innumerable others. In the interest of floriculture generally we desire to see some modification of it. We do not advocate the giving up of bedding plants altogether : but what we would ask is that the space allotted to them should be circumscribed, and that the beds on lawns and borders should be planted on what may be called the mixed system. Almost every lawn has a centre bed. Instead, then, of the usual practice of filling this with one sort of plants of the same colour, or of different colours in ribbons, let bedding plants of all sorts be mixed in it, and some few herbaceous perennials of suitable growth be added. If the bed be a circle, it should, of course, slope uniformly from the centre to the edge, and much care and judgment will be requisite in planting to effect this. In very large gardens there may be plenty of space for the maintenance of both systems: but our work is intended not for the few, but for the many, and we are persuaded that the mixed system is the best for general adoption. By means of it flowers can be had in spring, as well as in summer and autumn.

Flowers for spring cultivation consist of flowering shrubs, herbaceous plants, and bulbs—the last-mentioned are perhaps the most numerous. Under the title of "Spring Flower-Gardens," in the Dictionary, will be found a list of the most useful varieties of bulbs, and full cultural instructions concerning them. We need not therefore enlarge upon this point here. Our remarks at present had better be directed to the two other classes of plants which serve to make a garden gay in spring: these are spring flowering shrubs and herbaceous plants. Of spring flowering shrubs, the Laurestinus and the Daphne mezereum are perhaps the best known. Of the latter there are two varieties, one with white and the other with dark red flowers, both equally hardy, and common enough throughout Southern Europe. They should find a place in every English garden. As is the case with several other winter and spring flowering shrubs, the flowers of the mezereum appear before their leaves; but they are, as the poet says—

> "Though leafless, well attired, and thick beset
> With blushing wreaths, investing every spray."

In addition to these, there are several American plants, rhododendrons, azaleas, &c., quite hardy, and which put forth their beautiful blossoms almost before winter leaves us. The earliest spring flowering sorts are some of the English hybrids, R. dauricum, a good purple, which, weather permitting, will be in bloom in January, and R. nobleanum, a dark pink, flowering from February to April. There are many other varieties equally good, single plants of which can be had at about 3s. 6d. each, and at a much less price when large quantities are taken. A few dozen azaleas also will add much to the beauty of a garden during spring. They are not in flower so early as the rhododendrons we have mentioned, but in favourable situations they are not very far behind them. The yellow azalea pontica, and light rose-coloured A. canescens are among the earliest sorts. These, as all other American plants, prefer a peaty soil; and to promote early flowering another year, the old flowers should be picked off as soon as they can be spared, and the plants kept well watered during the summer months. While speaking of the American plants, we must not forget certain varieties of hardy heaths and the beautiful andromeda. Though the lovely white blossoms of the latter are seldom fully open before May, still the buds themselves are highly ornamental, and they are several weeks in formation. Of heaths, Erica arborea, white, will blossom in March, and so will E. Australia, which is of a reddish purple colour. The weigela are also handsome, shrubby plants, adapted for ornamental planting and spring decoration. W. rosea has pink flowers, and W. lutea, yellow; both prefer the shelter of a wall, but in a warm situation they will thrive and flower profusely as standards.

We have now to speak of herbaceous plants—those, of course, which blossom in spring have the first claim. And here we must single out for especial notice the alyssum, the arabis, and the pretty little hepatica. The alyssum, with its bright yellow flowers, so thickly set as to form a golden ball, is extremely showy. Patches on beds and borders, in contrast with the purple arabis and the pink and blue hepatica, have a most charming effect. It is, as most other perennials, of very easy cultivation. Young plants may be obtained from cuttings and division of roots. In favourable situations, near sandy gravel, seedlings will be found in great abundance. Every year hundreds of young plants are hoed up by us in the gravel walks which skirt a piece of rock-work near the house, for upon this several old plants of alyssum are growing. There is a variegated sort, very dwarf and well suited to rock-work; also another variety with white flowers, A. calysinum. This is generally used as an edging to beds. The arabis flowers about the same time as the alyssum. Of this there are two sorts, the purple and the white, and their flowers make a pleasing contrast with the yellow alyssum. They are very dwarf, and when planted in patches on beds, or borders, contribute an important share to the floral beauty of the spring season. In any ordinary garden soil they will grow without trouble; all the attention they require being that the patches should be well pulled in as soon as they have ceased flowering. The hepaticas are great favourites, and the colours being various, they make an agreeable contrast when planted in patches. We have seen woods full of the single blue sort in Switzerland, and a very pretty sight it is, for the foliage, in shape and colour, is almost as ornamental as the flowers. The plumbago, or lead-wort, is another useful perennial, to be grown mixed with bedding plants. The foliage is good, and its rich blue flowers are valuable, for blue flowers are at all seasons somewhat scarce. It flowers later in the season than those we have already mentioned. In a similar manner the different varieties of Dianthus may be introduced. Under this generic name are included some of the most beautiful of our florists' flowers, as well as some choice species from China and Japan, and elsewhere. The former include, of course, pinks, picotees, carnations, and sweet Williams, and the latter, Dianthus hedwigii, imperialis, &c., all of which are easily raised from seed. The hybrid Dianthus, commonly known as the mule pinks, are very showy when growing among other things in a mixed bed. Of border plants, suited also to beds of very large dimensions, we must not forget the Dietytra, delphinium, penstemon, and chelone. A few years ago Dietytra spectabilis was regarded as a greenhouse plant, and, indeed, many persons now cultivate it only under glass; but experience has proved that it does far better in the open ground. It is most easily cultivated; any small piece of the root, with an eye in it, will grow. Of the delphinium, or larkspur, there are many varieties, the choicest of which are the star, meteor, and gigantea. Hendersonii, also, which was one of the earliest of the improved sorts, still holds its place. The penstemon and chelone are very much alike: indeed, though divided in gardeners' catalogues, they are plants of the same class and require in every respect the same treatment. The penstemon generally requires protection during the winter months, and it is, perhaps, the neglect of this which causes many persons to be dissatisfied with them as border flowers. The hybrid varieties are the hardiest and best.

We come now to phloxes of the dwarf sorts, P. Nelsonii and P sectacea are good bedders, and make a beautiful show in the spring; the taller sorts should be planted in borders. Plants of the lychnis tribe are also very ornamental. L. Chalcedonia, commonly known as the scarlet lychnis, of which the sorts are single and double, is very showy; L. coronata and L. fulgens are more dwarf and better suited for beds; the roots of both of these, however, require some little protection during winter; Linum flavum, also, with its profusion of bright yellow blossoms, is very attractive. Among the potentillas, which are so numerous, there are several admirably adapted to mixed summer beds. Intertwining with the stiff-growing bedding plants, they serve to mass the whole, and in this way produce a very grand effect. Neither the vinca nor the veronica should be neglected. Of spirœas, also, some of the dwarf sorts may be well introduced, especially S. trifoliata and S. venusta; the latter is of a beautiful rose colour. There are sedums and saxifrages innumerable to add to the plants we have mentioned, and many of these we have seen, with most admirable effect, introduced into beds upon lawns in southern Germany and Austria.

Herbaceous perennials form a class of plants most valuable for botanical study, as well as for ornamental purposes, and we feel persuaded that the more generally they are cultivated the better they will be liked. The bedding system, which was introduced with the verbena, about a quarter of a century ago, has well-nigh driven these most interesting plants out of cultivation; but there are signs of better things for the future. Mixed beds are taking the place of those hitherto devoted to one sort of flowers, and into these mixed beds suitable perennials are finding their way. Judiciously planted upon this mixed system, beds and borders during summer will not be less gay than hitherto, while in spring they will be enlivened with flowers, and even in winter present an appearance of something better than merely bare ground.

CHAPTER VII.

PROFITABLE GARDENING.

NOTWITHSTANDING almost every one who has a house desires to have a garden also, it is a very general complaint that a garden does not pay—that vegetables cost those who grow them for their own use twice, and even three times, as much as they can be bought for. This complaint is, in our opinion, neither reasonable nor just; and if in any case it is true, we unhesitatingly affirm that it must be the result of gross ignorance and gross mismanagement. There are very few persons who attempt to keep any separate account of garden expenses and returns, and in most cases it would be a very troublesome matter to do so; still it is quite possible to form a tolerably correct estimate, and to compare this with a greengrocer's bill, based upon the experience of a few weeks. Where the complaint we have mentioned is seriously entertained, we shrewdly suspect that a great error has been made in keeping the account, and that the kitchen garden has been made to bear the whole of the wages of the gardener. The majority of English gardens are managed by one man, who has generally several other things to occupy his time besides the growing of vegetables and fruits. Not unfrequently the gardener has some housework to perform, in the way of cleaning boots and knives and forks; sometimes he has a horse and carriage to look after, and most certainly the flower garden and shrubbery must fall under his charge. His entire time is in no case taken up in the cultivation of vegetables, and consequently the kitchen garden ought not to be charged with the whole of his wages. When full allowance is made for all other sorts of work which a gardener is called upon to do, there must be gross mismanagement somewhere if his garden crops do not pay. Few cultural occupations are more profitable than kitchen gardening, when carried on to supply the markets of any large town. It has been stated by Mr. Middleton that an acre of land has been made to return the enormous sum of £220 for its gross produce. Mr. Middleton tells us that he had the account from the market-gardener who occupied the land, and the items sold were as follows:—Radishes, £10; cauliflowers, £60; cabbages, £30; celery, first crop, £50; second crop of celery, £40; endive, £30. Total, £220. The land was most favourably situated for the sale of vegetables, and no expense was spared in the cultivation of it. It is quite ridiculous after this to affirm that a vegetable garden in private occupation, when properly managed, does not pay. A visit to any of the good market-garden grounds in the neighbourhood of London, and of Paris also, will serve to show how a vegetable garden may be profitably cultivated. An abundance of manure, constant tillage, and a rapid succession of crops would seem to be the three great essentials. In the grounds about London the whole surface of the soil seems at times converted into a hot-bed. Every crop is forced to perfection with marvellous rapidity, and removed and sold as soon as its proper growth has been attained. Double cropping is frequently practised: for no one fears that the soil will be exhausted so long as a supply of manure can be had. In some cases, if the soil and situation are suitable, fruit trees are permitted, and vegetables, which do not require much sun, are grown under them. Raspberries and other bush fruit are planted in rows, several feet apart, so as to leave ample space for vegetables between.

The market-garden grounds in the neighbourhood of Paris are even closer cropped than our own. Mr. Robinson's account will be read with interest:—"In addition to an abundant watering and rich manuring, the Parisian market gardeners owe a great deal of their success to a close system of rotation, eight crops per year being frequently gathered from the ground. Were it not so, the cultivators could not exist, so limited is the ground that each possesses. A considerable portion of the surface of one garden I visited," he continues, "was devoted to cos lettuce, and very fine specimens of it; but beneath them there was a dark green carpet of leaves, very close to the ground — the leaves of the scarolle, which forms such an excellent salad, and is, indeed, one of the very best of all salads, and not yet sufficiently grown in England. The young plants have plenty of room to grow now among the closely tied up cos lettuce; but the moment the cos is cut for market the scarolle has full liberty, and, with abundance of water, soon makes wide heads. Then, perhaps, some young plants of another vegetable are slipped in at regular intervals in the angles between four plants of scarolle, which crop will be vigorous and half way towards perfection when the great, smooth endive is ready for the market. As an illustration of the cropping, the cultivator described to me that of a portion of his ground for the past year. In the earliest spring the ground was occupied by cos lettuces, and from between them a crop of radishes was gathered. Cauliflowers were planted early among the cos, and as they approached maturity the ground was, of course, wholly occupied by them, as one could not well put anything beneath a crop of perfectly-grown cauliflowers. When they were cut in May and June, an opportunity occurred of giving the ground that thorough culture and preparation which such a course of heavy cropping demands. Then a crop of spinach was sown, and, in the spinach, cos lettuce. As soon as the spinach was cleared off, a crop of endive was placed alternately with the cos. Then small cauliflower plants were put in, yielding a fine crop in the autumn, and after them a small quick crop, like corn salad, and afterwards the ground was covered with frame."

It would not, perhaps, be practicable, neither would it be necessary, to adopt such a system as this in the kitchen gardens attached to private houses. We have drawn attention to the mode of cultivation adopted by the market gardeners of London and Paris, not for the sake of pointing out what crops should be grown and the rotation of those crops, but to show what by good management land may be made to produce, and to prove the error of the complaint too generally adopted that a kitchen garden does not pay! If it does not pay, and a debtor and creditor account, correctly taken, can show this, all we can say is that the fault rests with the cultivator who has not made the most of his ground. It is high cultivation only, both in gardening and in farming, that can be said to pay. The soil is always most liberal to those who treat it best. The market gardeners, we are free to admit, have very many advantages over the private growers. They can, of course, crop more often, because they can remove an entire crop for sale at once, or at any rate in a few days after it has arrived at maturity. This the private grower cannot do, for his object is to make his crop last out as long as possible for the daily supply of his table. Still, by careful management, he can keep this principle in view, and provide a successive crop for every rod of land as it becomes vacant. The rotation of crops is a most important subject. Plants, like animals, do not appropriate all the food which comes within their reach—they seize upon that which suits them, and reject that which does not: this is thrown off from their roots in a sort of slime, which is injurious to all plants of the same kind, but is capable of forming nourishment for others.

Gardeners commonly say that the "ground gets tired" of growing the same crop; but this does not express the whole truth, for it is not merely that the soil becomes exhausted and loses its nutrimental properties by growing the same crop; but the crop itself has left behind it a deposit which acts as a slow poison upon a crop of the like sort which follows it. Some vegetables suffer more than others from inattention to this. The potato soon degenerates by successive cropping; but beet and onions may be grown upon the same land year after year with better success. However, it is not advisable, unless under absolute necessity, to make any exception even with these. For small gardens some useful hints upon cropping will be found in the Dictionary under the head of "Allotment Gardens." The ordinary wants of a family, of course, must, to a great extent, regulate not only what shall be grown, but the quantity of each crop. But matters can always be so managed that no two crops of the same family follow each other. After peas it is unadvisable to plant either peas or beans, notwithstanding the sorts selected be different. After cabbage neither broccoli nor any of the brassica family should be planted, and so again it is best to avoid planting any root crops in succession. For all general purposes it is a good plan to divide a kitchen garden into four portions. Now, if we give up one of these to such permanent crops as asparagus, seakale, herbs, rhubarb, &c., we have three-fourths to be devoted to successive crops, one of these each year will be occupied by potatoes, which is usually considered the most important produce; and in the intervening years other vegetables in succession may be grown, spindle, or tap-rooted crops, such as carrots and parsnips, being succeeded by those which have fibrous roots, such as peas and beans.

The selection of good seed is also of essential importance to ensure good growth and an abundant produce. Many gardeners prefer to save their own seed, and when this can be conveniently done, there is of course a saving attached to it; but there is little profit in reserving merely the refuse for seed. For instance, peas and beans intended for seed should be left ungathered, because the earliest pods contain the finest seed; again, with potatoes, much injury is done by indifferent seed. The best shaped and hardest tubers should always be reserved for this purpose. They should be thoroughly ripe before they are taken up, and kept stored with the greatest care. For small gardens, as a matter of economy, we do not think it answers to save seed.

GLASS HOUSES.—Both hot-houses and green-houses may be turned, under proper management, to a very profitable account. They are often regarded as pieces of extravagance, but it is by no means necessary that they should be so. We have frequently heard of a grapery which has paid the rent of the house. No one need hesitate to grow grapes on the score of expense, if willing to take money value for the whole, or even part of the crop. Any master or mistress of a house, who has a taste for such employment, and does not disdain to undertake with their own hands some of the lighter portions of the labour of cultivation, will find that the growing of grapes and other fruit, under glass, will yield a very profitable return. There is another portion of the gardener's art, admirably adapted to the amateur, which may frequently be entered upon with great success. We allude to the production of new varieties of plants, by hybridising and other means. If followed up with judgment, and with an accurate knowledge of the true principles of cultivation, the production of seedlings may be undertaken with very good results. All the florists' flowers admit of improvement, and improved varieties constitute, as it were, copyrights, and are valuable in proportion as they are superior in size, shape, and colour to other flowers of a like sort. Seedling pelargoniums, fuchias, azalias, roses, &c., &c., are continually being sold at what might seem to be extravagant prices. We have heard of the stock of a single dahlia selling for as much as £100. Roses are often sold at a higher price. New fruits, also the result of cultivation, have most handsomely rewarded the trouble bestowed upon them. The stock of the Muscat Hamburg grape is said to have realized for its cultivator upwards of £800, and the Golden Hamburg more than double that sum. It should be remarked, too, that in these days, owing to the care bestowed upon this subject by Sir Joseph Paxton and others, the construction of glass-houses is far better understood, and the cost of them far less expensive, than it used to be.

THE

DICTIONARY OF GARDENING.

ACA'CIA (nat. ord. Legumino'sæ).

Elegant-growing plants, natives of Australia, the East Indies, and Mexico: nearly all are evergreen. During winter and early spring they flower freely in greenhouses, but they are not hardy enough to endure our climate unprotected except in the summer, when they may be plunged with their pots in borders with good effect. Of Acacias there is a great variety; all may be grown readily from seed, which is best imported, and from cuttings in pots of very fine mould, set in a hot-bed. Among the most beautiful varieties are *A. albicans*, with fine silver foliage; *A. balsamea*, yellow, about 6 ft. high; *A. Drummondii*, yellow; *A. Ixiophylla*, golden yellow; *A. odoratissima pendula*, yellow, with fine long pendent blossoms, very fragrant; *A. spinosa*, rose-coloured and white. The roots of the Acacia have generally a very poisonous smell, which renders them unpleasant and unhealthy in confined houses.

Culture.—All kinds require a sandy loam, well drained.

ACAN'THUS (nat. ord. Acantha'ceæ).

Perennials attractive for the beauty of their foliage: natives of Southern Europe. The most common varieties are *A. mollis* and *A. spinosa.* From the former of these the original idea of the capital of the Corinthian order of architecture is said to have been derived.

Culture.—All the sorts grow readily from seed, or they may be increased by dividing the roots. They require a sandy soil and free space.

ACHIME'NES (nat. ord. Gesnera'ceæ).

A genus of truly splendid plants, suitable either for the sitting-room, greenhouse, or stove, and especially adapted for hanging-baskets; they combine great individual beauty with a variety of rich, and brilliant colours rarely to be met with. Some of them are remarkable for their peculiar markings, others for their large handsome flowers, while all are so exceedingly effective as amply to recompense the amateur for his care and attention, which are trifling compared with what some plants of far inferior beauty require.

Culture.—Use a compost of peat, loam, and leaf-soil; or leaf-mould, loam, and silver-sand, and secure good drainage. Plant five to seven tubers in a five- or six-inch pot, with their growing ends inclining towards the centre, and their root ends towards the circumference of the pot, and cover them with about an inch of the compost. While growing, they should be well supplied with liquid manure; start them when convenient in heat, and when an inch and a half high they may be removed to the green-house. To keep up a succession, commence starting them in heat in January; and as one lot is taken out another should be put in, till May: do not neglect tying up the stems, or they will fall down and get injured.

Planted in pans or baskets, and suspended, they will become objects of the greatest interest, falling gracefully over the sides, and literally covering the pot or basket with their truly magnificent flowers.

Messrs. Barr and Sugden are supplying—

		s.	d.
3 each of 12 splendid varieties, for	..	10	6
2 ,, ,, ,,	..	7	6
1 each of 12 splendid varieties	..	4	6

AGAPAN'THUS (nat. ord. Hemerocallida'ceæ).

An African lily blooming in August, combining graceful foliage with large handsome heads of blossom. In flower-beds or masses, the blue variety is lovely; planted in a strong rich soil, it produces a splendid effect, and when mixed with Gladioli, either of the Ramosus or Gandavensis sections, the effect is unique. Protect the bed or patch during winter with a thatched frame.

Culture.—A nine-inch pot will be ample for a strong plant, but a large pot or tub is required for several plants; and this is the most effective and more usual way of growing the Agapanthus. Use a strong rich loam, and during the summer months give abundance of water, and liquid manure twice a week. In winter protect from severe frost, and water sparingly.

Seed, 4*d.* per packet; roots, 5*s.* per dozen.

AGERA'TUM (nat. ord. Compos'itæ).

Useful half-hardy annuals. The shades are blue, white, and red. The seed should be sown in a warm border in a light soil in April or May. Price 3*d.* per packet.

AH-AH.

A park or garden-fence, so called, it is said, from the time of the regency of George IV., who exclaimed "Ah! ah!" when stopped by one of these sunken fences in a day's hunting.

The object of the ah-ah is to make a fence entirely invisible, or to make

what is a very dwarf fence from the inside, a tall one from the park. Invisible ah-ah's are thus formed, with the aid of a brick wall from 4 to 6 feet high, which should batter slightly; or the wall may be dispensed with, and a small iron fence substituted, as in the cut. Sometimes an upright fence is

placed in the bottom of the ditch; but this is the worst of all forms of the ah-ah,—if, indeed, it deserves the name at all. Another form of ah-ah is to have a dwarf iron fence, with a brick or stone wall, of a plain or ornamental character, rising to the height of 1, 2, or 3 feet, as seen below. These walls may have a solid base, and the greater part be composed of open balustrades, finished with a massive coping, furnished with vases, thus:

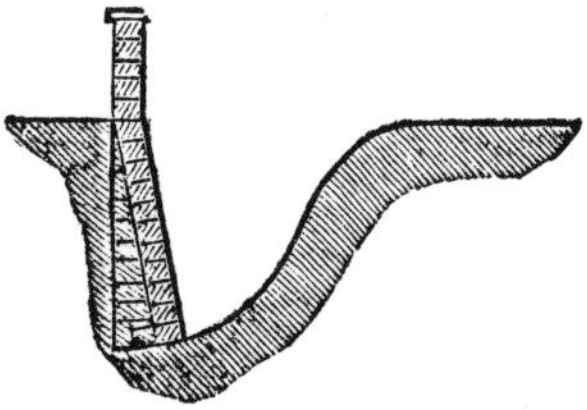

AILAN'THUS, or TREE OF HEAVEN (nat. ord. Xanthoxyla'ceæ).

A noble tree, resembling a gigantic stag's horn sumach, invaluable for avenues, groves, shrubberies, or wherever trees of stately growth and large ornamental foliage are required. Succeeds in any poor shallow soil. The leaves are largely used in France as food for the new species of silkworm, Phalæna Cynthia. *Hardy.*

ALLOTMENT GARDENS.

It would be beyond our purpose to point out the many and great benefits which result from the allotment of a small portion of land for a garden to every cottage. These are so obvious that we may take them for granted here, and proceed at once to show how such allotments may be managed to the best advantage. Many cottages, especially in our small agricultural parishes, have land enough attached to them for the purpose of forming a garden which shall supply the wants of the family. The case, however, is different with cottages situated in populous villages and on the outskirts of large towns. Here, for the most part, a rod or two of land in front, and the same quantity for a yard at the back, the cottages being generally built in rows, is all that can be attached to each: now, under such circumstances, the want of a garden is well supplied by the allotment system. The field selected for garden allotments should, of course, be situated as near as possible to the cottages for which they are required, and it should have the convenience of a supply of soft water either from a pond or running stream. The rent at which allotments are let must be determined by the value of land in the neighbourhood. It should include all rates, taxes, and other outgoings of a like nature, and may be fixed somewhat higher than the rent of ordinary farm-land, but not so high as market-garden ground. The extent of each allotment should be not less than a quarter of an acre, nor more than half an acre. Little benefit can be derived from less than the former quantity, and if half an acre be exceeded, there is great danger that the cottager will become unsettled as a day-labourer or mechanic, while his occupation will not be large enough to make him either a farmer or market-gardener. Spade husbandry must be insisted upon, and each allotment, to all intents and purposes, be treated as a cottage-garden. In an allotment of half an acre it is quite allowable that one-fourth may be cultivated in wheat or some other cereal, and one-fourth in potatoes each year, or half in wheat and half in potatoes in alternate years; but certainly, in all cases, one quarter of an acre should be stocked with what are properly called garden vegetables. The same portion of land should not be cropped with wheat and potatoes in continual succession, but after two years a change should be made with the other portion which has been cropped with garden produce. Indeed, the soil must naturally be very good, and also be well done by, to admit of such a close succession of wheat and potatoes. Barley or rye may, with advantage, be made now and then a substitute for wheat, and mangold wurzel will at times profitably take the place of potatoes; some provision, of course, having been made for a sufficient quantity of these for the use of the family. In agricultural parishes, the growing of seeds—turnip, mangold wurzel, carrots, and parsnip seeds—either on a portion of the allotment ground, or, what is better, on the land attached to a cottage, is found profitable; especially where there are children who can assist in keeping off the birds while the seed is ripening. Seed-growing will make a good change with wheat and potatoes; but it should not be encouraged, except in cases where the allotment exceeds the quarter of an acre.

The laying-out and division of a field into its proper allotments is a matter of taste, and must be regulated by the shape of the enclosure. A square field of ten or more acres may be divided by two walks cutting each other in the centre at right angles; and another walk may be made along each side, and at such a distance from the hedge or enclosure as the size of the field may suggest. These walks, if thought desirable, can be made broad enough for a small cart to pass along. Beyond these, all that is required would be alleys, or small walks between the different allotments; these last may be measured into the allotments, half to each occupier; but the larger and more important walks should not be measured in. If the field be enclosed with a bank and hedge, these should be kept in order at the joint expense or labour of the different occupiers of the land; and so also should the garden pump, if, from the absence of any supply of soft water, it should be necessary to sink a well. Dwarf apples and pears, &c., and all bush fruit should be considered admissible; but no high trees should be allowed, as they may do harm to a neighbouring allotment. Nor should any occupier be allowed to erect a greenhouse or shed, except under especial permission. Ordinary garden-frames can, of course, be used, wherever they are desired. The land taken for allotment gardens, previous to being let to the different tenants, should be drained, and proper water-courses provided. Many persons recommend the building of a large shed for garden-tools, &c., for the joint occupation of the tenants; but, as far as our experience goes, this is better avoided. Much ill-feeling is often engendered among the tenants by the taking of each other's implements; and where property is left upon the ground in this unprotected state, an opening is given to petty thieving. It can be no great difficulty for a man, whenever he has an hour or two to spend in his garden, to take with him on his barrow, his spade, rake, and hoe, or whatever he may require; and if the allotment be too far off for him to carry these things to and fro, in our opinion he is better without it. Very strict attention should be given to the payment of rent. The land should be let from Michaelmas to Michaelmas, and the rent paid half-yearly—the first half-year's rent to be paid on account at Midsummer, and the remaining half at the year's end. No cottager, except of good moral character, should be accepted as a tenant. Proper cultivation, neatness, and order should be strictly enforced, and, where these are not attended to, the tenant should have notice to quit: a three months' notice, expiring at Michaelmas, is the fairest arrangement for all parties. Allotment gardens are best managed under direction of a small committee. A piece of glebe land, if such lie convenient, is perhaps the best that can be occupied for the purpose, and the clergyman of the parish should be chairman of the committee.

We make here these general observations, which are the result of many years' experience, rather than give copies of rules which are actually of no use; for all rules, though they embody the principles which we have laid down, must be adapted to their own particular case. With regard to the cropping of allotment ground, the remarks which have already been made, and which will be found elsewhere in this volume, upon cottage gardening, will supply ample information. The following rotation of crops is very simple, and has been strongly recommended. It applies to a rood or quarter of an acre, and supposes the breadth of the land to be 27½ yards, and the length 44 yards, which makes just one rood. Of this piece of land make three equal divisions, and crop as follows :—

First Division.—Plant, first week in March, 22 rows of potatoes, 2 feet between each row; sets to be 1 foot apart in planting. *Sorts:* York Regents, Flukes, and Fortyfold, or a portion of each. An alley of one foot between this and the next division.

Note.—Winter and spring brocoli, and winter cabbage and spinach; take this division directly the potatoes are off.

Second Division.—Plant, middle of March, 2 rows of Windsor beans.

Early in March, 4 rows of hollow-crowned parsnips.

End of February, 4 rows of Altringham carrots, and 6 rows of onions, globe or James's keeping.

End of March, 1 row of Windsor beans.

Early in May, 4 rows of turnips, and 2 rows of mangold wurzel.

First week in May, 1 row of scarlet runners, with a foot alley between each.

Note.—Root crop. This division is to be trenched for the main crop of potatoes next year directly the roots are off.

Third Division.—Plant, last week in February, 2 rows of ash-leaved kidney potatoes and 3 rows of matchless cabbage, or York cabbage.

Early in March, 1 row of marrowfat peas and 3 rows of ash-leaved kidneys (Cape brocoli after).

Last week in February, 6 rows of ash-leaved kidneys (celery after) ; 1 row of early long-pod beans, and 1 row of early peas (celery after).

End of March, 1 row of cauliflowers (stone turnips after).

Plant, as early as possible, 2 rows of lettuce (autumn cabbage after), with a foot alley between each.

Note.—Mixed or early crop. This division is to be occupied with flying crops, such as turnips and lettuces, &c., in the autumn, and to be sown with the usual root crops next spring.

ALYS'SUM (nat. ord. **Crucif'eræ**).

Free-flowering, useful, pretty little plants for beds, edgings, or rockwork. The annual species bloom nearly the whole summer; the perennials are amongst our earliest and most attractive spring flowers. The varieties are :—

Alyssum argenteum, — yellow, with silvery foliage, hardy perennial, 1 ft., from Switzerland.
Alyssum atlanticum,—fine light yellow, very ornamental, hardy perennial, ¾ ft.
Alyssum Benthamii,—white, very fine, hardy annual, 1 ft.
Alyssum sexatile,—yellow, extremely showy, hardy perennial, 1 ft., from Candia.
Alyssum sexatile compactum,—golden-yellow, very compact, free-flowering and beautiful, hardy perennial, ½ ft.
Alyssum, sweet (Kœnigia maritima),—white, very sweet, hardy annual, ½ ft., British.

Price of seed, 3*d.* to 6*d.* per packet.

AMARAN'THUS (nat. ord. **Amarantha'ceæ**).

Half-hardy annuals, very graceful, with highly ornamental foliage. *A. ruber*, with dark carmine foliage, is a most strikingly beautiful plant for bedding, ribboning, or massing. Other varieties are bicolor, leaves crimson and green, and tricolor, red, yellow, and green.

Culture.—Sow in heat in early spring; plant out in May and June in very rich soil. Price of seed, 3*d.* to 6*d.* per packet.

AMARYL'LIS (nat. ord. **Amaryllida'ceæ**).

Flowers of rare beauty, whose large, drooping, bell-shaped, lily-like blossoms range in colours from the richest crimson to pure white, and striped with crimson or scarlet. They are easily cultivated, and with a little management a succession of bloom may be secured throughout the year. Some varieties do not require heat. A moderate supply of bulbs will serve the purpose.

Varieties which do not require heat are,—

Bella-Donna purpurea (Bella-Donna Lily),—white flushed with rosy purple.

Bella-Donna blanda.
Formosissima (Sprekelia formosissima),—rich crimson.
Longifolia alba (Crinum capense alba),—white, sweet-scented.
Longifolia rosea (Crinum capense alba),—rose, sweet-scented.
Lutea (Sternbergia lutea),—yellow, flowers in autumn.

Others must always be started in a hotbed; as,—

Aulica,—reddish-brown with greenish stripes, flowers very large.
Cleopatra,—dark red, margined with white, of great substance and very showy.
Crocea grandiflora,—vermilion.
Crocea superba,—bright orange, large flowers.
Johnsonii,—scarlet, with pure white stripes, very showy.
Johnsonii, striata,—striped.
Prince of Orange,—bright orange, large and handsome.

Culture.—When heat is not required, place the bulbs in front of a wall facing south, at least six inches under the surface, giving them a little winter protection: should the growing season be dry, water freely till the plant blooms, but when at rest the bulbs should be kept as dry and warm as possible. When heat is required, use six- or seven-inch pots, placing at the bottom a handful of potsherds and covering them with turfy peat, filling up the pot with a compost of rich loam, leaf-soil, and silver-sand, leaving only the neck of the bulb uncovered; the pots should then be either placed in a stove-frame or any other root-temperature, such as the modified heat of a tank or flue, and a few weeks will develop the flowers: immediately the leaves appear, give abundance of water, and encourage a vigorous leaf-growth. When the plant has done blooming, gradually withdraw the water, and give the bulbs in entire cessation from growth for eight or ten weeks, when they may again be re-potted and forced as before.

AMERICAN PLANTS.

Under this general name are included rhododendrons, azaleas, kalmias, ledums, andromedas, and others, which are supposed to require what is called bog earth. This, however, is not absolutely necessary to their successful cultivation.

The following materials, all of them within the reach of most persons, may be made to form a compost adapted to their culture. Rotted leaves, spent tan, sawdust, old thatch or straw, weeds, grass-mowings, and vegetable refuse of all kinds—old manure, even the bottoms of old wood-stacks. Any or all of these in a decomposed state, blended with a certain proportion of garden soil, may be rendered fit to grow American plants; but as it is the character of all decomposed vegetable matter fit to enter rapidly into the composition of the vegetable fabric, to subside rapidly, this must be guarded against by employing also such organic matter as tree-leaves, lumps of peat, peaty turf, or other vegetable matter, which will take long before decay takes place. Where old tan or sawdust is liberally used, the leaves should be fresh; those which have been used as linings for hotbeds by preference, from their tendency to mass together. Old thatch, or litter, forms an excellent basis for the whole clump, and weeds and other vegetable refuse, when burnt or charred. This compost, with a subsoil sufficiently retentive of moisture, and situation not too much exposed to the direct influence of the sun, will grow these beautiful shrubs in great perfection.

Mr. Errington, a good authority in such matters, says:—"In consequence of some alterations at Oulton Park, an old rubbish-yard had to be turned into the ornamental portion of the grounds, and an elevated mound of American shrubs planted on the site. The first proceeding was to burn, or rather char, the decayed vegetable matter in the yard, and throw the ground into shape; and a coating of coarse clayey matter happening to be the nearest commodity, was spread over the surface a foot thick. Next we applied several loads of leaf-mould, and, finally, three inches of fine heath soil from Delamere Forest. All these materials were thoroughly blended together to a considerable depth, the raw and undecomposed rubbish, as it came up again, being buried in the bottom of the trench. On the mound thus raised the shrubs were planted, and nothing can exceed their robustness. The ericas, especially, exceed all I have ever seen, from the admixture of the clay with heath and leaf-mould."

These materials, with their proportions, stand nearly as follows:—Sand one part, clayey subsoil matter two parts, decomposed vegetable matter two parts, undecomposed vegetable matter five parts, and at the bottom of all a quantity of rubbish and raw vegetable matter, which the roots of the more vigorous plants will reach, and find food in abundance in due time.

ANDROM'EDA (nat. ord. Eri'ceæ).

Deciduous heath-like shrubs, natives of North America; many of them are also evergreen. They delight in bog, like all other so-called American plants, and their roots should never be suffered to become quite dry; for if this occurs, the plant has seldom vigour enough to send out a sufficient quantity of new roots, and in general dies. All the kinds may be propagated by layers.

ANEM'ONES, or WIND-FLOWERS (nat. ord. Ranuncula'ceæ).

Amongst the numerous forms of floral beauty which enrich the flower-garden, from the first opening blossoms of spring to the last rose of summer, the Anemone takes a foremost place, having many points of interest and special characteristics of colour. Its blossoms are of the most dazzling hues of scarlet, purple, and blue, self-coloured and striped. The foliage is elegantly cut, and the growth is neat and compact, so that in beds, groups, ribbons, or as an edging to tulip or hyacinth beds, arranged either in distinct colours or mixed, they produce a unique effect.

The flowers of the double anemone are extremely handsome; they have outer guard petals, resembling a semi-double hollyhock. If planted from October to December, they will bloom in succession during the early spring months, while those planted in February and March will bloom from April to June.

The single anemone, with its beautiful poppy-like blossoms, may be had in bloom at pleasure, from February to December, and, in sheltered nooks, even in January, by simply arranging the time of planting.

Culture.—The Anemone delights in a light, rich, loamy soil, but generally succeeds in any which is well drained. Sea-sand, or a little salt mixed with the soil, is a good preventive of mildew; in other respects, the culture and after-management should be precisely such as we shall recommend for the Ranunculus.

They are usually regarded as spring flowers, and most undoubtedly always flower best at that season. In certain soils and situations, however, the tendency to growth and flowering in anemones is such that they have no sooner died down after spring-flowering, than they throw out fresh leaves and flower again in autumn. This, however, is not desirable, for it weakens the tubers, and the flowers soon degenerate. Autumn-flowering may generally be prevented by excluding light and air from the beds, by means of heavy top-dressings of well-rotted manure during the summer months. Many persons take up anemone tubers as soon as the leaf has died down; but this is not necessary, nor is it a good plan, unless the soil of the bed requires renovation, for the tubers will not keep many days out of the ground. The finest flowers are generally produced the first spring after a new sowing; but soil and situation have always a great effect upon them.

Messrs. Barr and Sugden offer their Paxtonian section of the double anemones,—

		s.	d.
500 in 20 splendid varieties ..	..	63	0
300 " " ..	..	42	0
150 " " ..	..	21	0
100 " " ..	..	15	0
50 " " ..	..	8	0
25 " " ..	..	4	6
Splendid mixed, all colours	per 100	5	6

Single Anemones :—

	Per 100. s.	d.	Per doz. s.	d.
Choice Mixed, all colours ..	3	6	0	6
Brilliant Scarlet	5	6	1	0

ANNUALS.

Plants so termed, as their name implies, spring up and flower and die in one single year, and they naturally divide themselves under three heads,—hardy, half-hardy, and tender. Let us take them in order, merely affirming, on the outset, what every seed farm in the country proves, that a rich and varied floral display may be maintained by annuals from April to November. A judicious selection of varieties is, of course, necessary; but this may be left to any respectable seedsman. What the public require to know is, what to do with the seeds when they have got them. First, then, as to—

Hardy Annuals.— *Culture.— Preparation of the Ground.*—Dig or trench the land to a depth of 18 inches at least; for slender-growing kinds, in warm, dry localities, the soil can hardly be made too rich; a liberal allowance of rich well-decayed manure should, therefore, be well incorporated with it; in cold and wet situations, however, a dressing of leaf-soil will be more suitable, especially for strong-growing varieties, as much care being necessary to grow these to perfection as is required for "bedding plants." Annuals, like all quick-growing plants, require a deep soil and an open situation, being unable to bear checks in their growth; the ground should therefore be well prepared: the time and trouble will be amply repaid by the increased duration and beauty of the flowers.

Time and Manner of Sowing.—The proper time for sowing hardy annuals depends entirely upon the period at which it is desired that they should bloom. For a spring display, sow early in September (a fortnight earlier or later according to soil and locality), in beds 4 feet wide, with an alley 1 foot wide between the beds, in rows 9 inches apart, and if the weather be dry, well water the drills before sowing, and cover the seed very lightly with fine soil. Before winter, the plants, if too thick, must be slightly thinned out, and early in March carefully lifted in patches containing three or four plants, and planted where they are intended to bloom, regulating the distance between the patches by the known habit of the plants; but as this sowing is expected to produce an early and effective display, rather than a long continuance of beauty, they may be planted rather thickly. To furnish a succession, a piece of ground proportioned to the quantity of plants required should be set apart in an open situation, and laid out in beds 4 feet wide, with alleys of 18 inches between; the soil should be prepared with a dressing of decayed leaves, and if stiff, some sharp sand should be added; manure had better be avoided, except in light soil, where a moderate dressing of thoroughly decayed manure would be most suitable. On this ground successive sowings of the best kinds should be made at short intervals, keeping the ground always occupied, and a good stock of plants ready for transplanting when required; thus a supply will always be at hand for removal into the beds or borders, to fill up vacancies occasioned by the removal of bulbs or autumn-sown annuals. Many of the spring-sown annuals, if properly attended to, will continue in bloom throughout the season, or as long as almost any other plants. Those intended for the principal summer display should be sown from March to May, either where intended to bloom, or in the reserved ground. By adopting the system of raising the plants in the reserve beds and transplanting, the beds and borders of the flower-garden can be kept filled with plants in full beauty.

Half-hardy Annuals.—These are less liable to suffer from drought than the hardy varieties; they do not arrive at maturity so quickly; therefore, with these, successive sowings cannot be practised with any advantage. Sow early in May where intended to bloom, or early in April on a hotbed or on nicely-prepared soil in a frame, or under a hand-glass, and transplant them when sufficiently strong and the weather is favourable.

When sowing in a hotbed is necessary, place a layer of four inches of leaf-mould on the top, then a layer of the same depth of fine sifted soil, consisting of equal parts of loam, leaf-mould, peat, and sand. Sow the seeds in drills, formed about a quarter of an inch deep, with the point of a stick; for very small seeds, one-eighth of an inch will suffice. Carefully sow, label, and cover the seeds as you proceed. If the soil is in a proper medium state in reference to moisture, and it is shaded from the midday sun, no water will be necessary until the seeds appear. The frame must not be allowed to rise above 45° or 50°, and should never sink below 40°. The atmosphere should be changed daily by the admission of air, and the surface of the soil looked over frequently, to see if any mould or fungus is making its appearance on the surface; for if so, it must be at once removed, and the spots where it appeared dusted over with quick-lime. With proper treatment, most of the plants will appear in from a week to a fortnight of the time of sowing.

Transplanting and after-management of Annuals.—The plants should be carefully taken up, so as not to injure the roots, retaining as much soil about them as possible, and the roots should not be exposed to the air longer than necessary. If the ground is dry at the time of transplanting, the bed in which the plants are growing should have a good soaking of water at least twenty-four hours before taking them up; they must also be liberally watered as soon as planted, and in dry, hot weather this must be repeated as often as necessary to keep the ground moist; the plants, indeed, should be moistened overhead every evening until they get established. Those transplanted early in spring will seldom require water; but if it is necessary, it should be given in the morning. In transplanting for summer blooming, the plants must be allowed sufficient space to develop their natural size; if closely planted, they will not throw out the side branches, which furnish a succession of bloom. Some plants will require four or six inches, others three or four times that distance from plant to plant. This must be regulated by the habit of the plant, and to some extent by the nature of the soil and locality; but it is better in all cases to have the plants too far apart than too close. In dry weather, watering will be indispensable to keep the plants, whether of hardy or half-hardy annuals, in vigour, and secure a continuous bloom. When necessary to water in summer, the soil should be thoroughly saturated, and as soon as the surface is dry, it should be slightly stirred between the plants. Occasional waterings of *weak* guano-water will heighten the colour of the flowers and increase the growth.

Tender Annuals.—These are plants which must be kept the whole period of their growth under glass; they may be sown in pots of light, rich earth, and plunged in a hotbed early in February or March. To bring the plants to perfection, they must be pricked out when they are an inch up, then as soon as possible be transplanted simply into the smallest-sized pots, and continually shifted as their roots increase. During the whole process of shifting they should be kept in a temperature of from 70° to 80°, and so abundantly supplied with water that the air should be constantly charged with moisture. When, however, they begin to flower, they may be removed to a dry and airy situation, and the temperature gradually lowered. This will greatly improve both the size and colour of the flowers.

ANTIRRHI'NUM (nat. ord. Scrophularia'ceæ).

The Antirrhinum, popularly called Snapdragon, is a hardy perennial, and one of our most showy and useful border plants. Amongst the more recently improved varieties of this valuable genus are large finely-shaped flowers of the most brilliant colours, with beautifully-marked throats; they succeed in any good garden soil, and are very effective in beds. *A. nanum* and varieties are valuable for rockwork and old walls. Choice mixed seed, 3*d.* per packet.

ANTS, TO DESTROY.

Place an inverted garden-pot over the nest, and the ants will work into it. Remove the pot in a day or two by placing a spade underneath it; then plunge it, with its contents, into boiling water, and repeat the process if necessary. Ants may be expelled from any particular plant by sprinkling it well with sulphur; they may also be kept away from wall-fruit, and other fruit while ripening, by drawing a broad band with chalk along the wall near the ground, and round the stem of the trees.

APHIDES.

Aphides, or plant-lice, and their congeners, are indicated by an unhealthy appearance in plants; the leaves and young shoots curl up, and multitudes of ants, which seem to feed on their secretions, are seen about the stems. The remedy is repeatedly syringing the leaves and stems with tobacco or lime-water, or with gas-tar water when that can be obtained; but plants should be carefully examined in May, and the winged parent of the *Psilla Pyra*, and its congeners, destroyed before they have deposited their eggs. Lady-birds (*Coccinelidæ*) render great service in destroying myriads of aphides, which ought to insure them the protection of gardeners.

APPLE.

The apple is a somewhat capricious fruit, some sorts affecting clay soils, while others do better in sandy loam, and even in well-drained peat soils. Apple-planting, therefore, requires some discrimination as well as observation as to the sorts most successfully grown in the locality. The following are among the most useful varieties.

Dessert Apples.

Early Harvest,—ripens end of July.
Margaret,—early in August.
Calville rouge d'Eté,—middle of August.
Devonshire Quarrenden,—middle of August.
Barowski,—end of August.
Early Julian,—in August and September.
Summer Pippin,—beginning of September, but of short duration.
Monstrous Pippin,—September and October.
Oslin, a high-flavoured apple,—ripens in September.
King Pippin,—end of September.
Reinette blanche,—in October and November, in France.
Quatre Gouttes côtelées, in October and November, in France.
Scarlet Crofton,—ripens with us in October.
Early Nonpareil,—in October, and keeps till March.
Potmaston Nonpareil,—in October, and keeps till March.
Court of Wick,—in use from October, and keeps till March.
Calville de St. Saveur,—ripens in November, in France.
Belle Fleur de Brabant,—in November, in France.
Reinette d'Angleterre, — in November, in France, and keeps till March.
Downton Pippin,—ripens in November, and keeps till January.
Golden Pippin,—popularly supposed to be extinct, grows vigorously on a warm soil and in sheltered situations, ripening in November, and keeping till March.
R inette dorée (Golden Reinette),—ripens in November, and keeps till April.
Ribston Pippin,—in November; keeps till May.
Ross Nonpareil,—in December; keeps till February.
Cornish Gillyflower,—in December; keeps till February.
Queen of the Reinettes,—in December; keeps till February.
Reinette du Canada,—in January and February.
Royale d'Angleterre,—in January, and keeps till March.

Wyken Pippin,—in January; keeps till March.
Old Nonpareil,—in November; keeps till May: a fine high-flavoured dessert apple.
Lamb's Pearmain,—in December; keeps till June.
Reinette Franche,—in use from February to July and August.

Cooking Apples.

Keswick Codling,—fit for use in July and August.
Monk's Codling,—fit for use from July till February.
Golden Winter Pearmain,—in use from October till January, as a kitchen as well as dessert apple.
Beauty of Kent,—in use from October till February.
Bedfordshire Foundling,—in use from January till March.
Winter Pearmain,—in use from November till April.
Winter Majetin,—in use from January to June.
Norfolk Beefing,—keeps till June.
Gooseberry Apple,—ripe in January, and keeps till June or July.

The modern system of dwarfing fruit-trees, by which space is so much economized, is produced by a special course of pruning, commencing a year from grafting, when the apple-tree should be pruned back, leaving about eight buds on the shoots. In the second year the head will exhibit eight or ten shoots, and a selection must now be made of five or six, which shall give a cup-like form to the head, removing all shoots crossing each other, or which interfere with that form; thus leaving the head hollow in the centre, with a shapely head externally, shortening back the shoots retained to two-thirds or less, according as the buds are placed, and leaving all of nearly the same size. In the course of the summer's growth the tree will be assisted by pinching off the leading shoots where there is a tendency to overthrow the balancing of the head. At the third year's pruning the same process of thinning and cutting back will be required, after which the tree can hardly go wrong. The shoots retained should be short-jointed and well-ripened; and in shortening, cut back to a healthy, sound-looking, and well-placed bud. After the third year, little or no shortening back will be required, especially where root-pruning is practised; the tree should now develop itself in fruiting stems, which will subdue the tendency to throw out gross or barren shoots.

Large standard trees in their prime only require pruning once in two or three years. At these intervals cross-growing or exhausted shoots, especially those in the centre of the tree, require thinning out, bearing in mind that the best fruit grows at the extremities of the branches, and that these branches must be kept under control.

APRICOTS.

Apricots, as most other fruit-trees, flourish best in a good sound loam. For planting, prepare the soil about a yard deep, and manure with rotten leaves,—one part of leaves to four or five of soil. Place a substratum of brick or other imperishable material below each tree. The apricot, when in a healthy state, produces more natural spurs than most other trees, and although some kinds will blossom and bear fruit on the young wood, yet the chief dependence for a crop of fine fruit must be on the true spurs. In pruning, stop all leading shoots, and pinch off to a few buds all shoots not required to fill up vacant places on the wall. Thin partially all fruit where it is thickly set, but reserve the final thinning until the fruit has stoned. The apricot, and especially the finest of them (the Moor Park), is subject to a sudden paralysis: first a branch, then a side, dies away, until scarce a vestige of the tree is left; and this generally occurs on fine sunny days in spring and early summer, when the sap-vessels are young, and the sap is easily exuded by a few sunny days. In this state a frost occurs, the sap-vessels are burst by the thawing of the frozen fluid, and the whole economy of the plant deranged. Under these circumstances, which are so often occurring, the injured limb having consumed the sap, can draw no further supply; it yields to the solar influence, languishes and dies. Such is briefly Mr. Henry Bailey's diagnosis of the disease under which this delicate tree suffers. The remedy is to retard, or rather prevent, premature vegetation, and when that can no more be done, to provide protection ; for this he recommends netting made of sedge, of about four-inch mesh, to envelop the main branches.

APRIL (Monthly Calendar).

Aspect of the Month.—The Aprilis of the Latins, from *aperire*, to unveil oneself, fairly lands us amidst the glories of spring. The opening buds and blossoms respond to the returning warmth of the sun, although in our northern and sea-girt climate there is, perhaps, little of that genial temperature which suggested the name of the month.

The variations in the temperature are still very great, the thermometer ranging from 75° to a degree or two below the freezing-point in the meridian of London ; the mean maximum of an average of ten years being 57·82° in the atmosphere, and the mean minimum being 35·33° ; the temperature being lowest at sunrise, there being, on an average of ten years, six frosty nights in the month. An unusual fall of rain in April is supposed to indicate a dry season for the harvest.

Flower-Garden and Shrubberies.—All seeds intended to flower during the summer should be sown during this month. In places where hardy annuals are extensively grown, another sowing might be made. It would be best to sow now where they are intended to remain. The modern system of furnishing the flower-garden has limited the use of annuals. In gardens, however, where the family may not be always at home, or where the proprietor is indifferent to more permanent and durable flowers, a very brilliant display may be made for several months with annuals.

Swindon, in his "Beauties of Flora," gives some very ingenious ideas of planting. He gives a list of eighty-nine different sorts, arranged in six different classes. By affixing a number to each sort, he readily indicates on his plans the kinds employed, and their relative position. He also arranges a circular clump, including all the eighty-nine sorts, the six heights being placed in six concentric circles, placing a large persicaria, or oriental mallow, in the centre. The general appearance, he says, is the same on every side, rising gradually from the edge upwards, the highest plants meeting nearly in a point at the centre, and no two flowers of the same colour or shape being seen together. His principle is excellent, and might be of great service, although many of the varieties he specifies are now comparatively worthless.

Mr. John Caie, than whom no gardener living occupies a higher position for taste in such matters, has proposed several geometrical flower-gardens of great beauty ; he has also laid down plans for furnishing them, so as to have blossom the greater part of the year. Although his plan differs in many respects, especially in many of his beds being in pairs, the accompanying design will give a general notion of the manner in which he

carries out his idea, which is to show the possibility of avoiding acute-angled beds, while retaining ample variety of outline ; fig. 7 being represented by the five triangular beds within the outer circle.

Arrangement for—

February and March.

1. Helleborus niger,—white and pink.
2. Beds of Crocus reticulatus,—blue.

April.

3. Eranthis hiemalis,—yellow.
4. Galanthus plicatus,—white.
5. Narcissus minor,—yellow.
5. Erythronium Dens canis albiflorum,—white.
7. „ Dens canis,—purple.

April and May.

1. Anemone apennina,—blue.
2. Arabis præcox,—white.
3. Cheiranthus alpinus,—yellow.
4. Aubrietia purpurea,—lilac.
5. Alyssum saxatile,—yellow.
6. Iberis saxatilis,—white.
7. Tulipa oculus solis,—red and black.

Hardy Annuals for April and May.

1. Silene pendula,—pink.
2. Nemophila atomaria,—white.
3. „ insignis,—blue.
4. Escholtzia crocea,—orange-yellow.
5. Collinsia grandiflora,—blue-purple.
6. „ bicolor,—white and lilac.
7. Clarkia pulchella alba,—white.

May to November.

1. Geranium Lucia-rosea,—rose.
2. Verbena,—Princess Royal,—white.
3. „ Heloise,—dark lilac.
4. „ White Perfection,—white.
5. „ Duc d'Aumale,—bluish.
6. Calceolaria viscosissima,—yellow.
7. Verbena,—Robinson's Defiance,—scarlet.

Perhaps some more recent varieties of the verbenas, Clarkias, geraniums, and calceolarias, might be substituted with advantage; but the kinds named are very beautiful in masses.

Fancy ribbon borders could easily be formed with annuals. Cheapness, worth, and beauty may be happily combined here. For a ribbon of two strips of colour, sow *Clarkia pulchella alba* and *Clarkia pulchella* in two separate rows thirteen inches apart. For three bands of colour, sow *Nemophila insignis* in front; *Sanvitalia procumbens* or *Bartonia aurea*, second, and Purple Candytuft third; or White Alyssum first, Virginian Stocks second, and *Escholtzia californica* third. Three rows of Nemophila alone would form a pretty ribbon,—*insignis* in front; 2. *maculata*; 3. *discoidalis*. For four bands or strips of colour, sow *Nemophila insignis* in front, Sweet Alyssum next, *Clarkia pulchella* third, and *Erysimum perofskianum* fourth. If another row is wanted, add Prince's Feather,

April.

which will tower above the Erysimum. These are not given as the best possible combination, but merely as samples of what any one, for a few pence, and with a yard or two of ground, may accomplish.

Mignonette and ten-week Stocks may be sown in patches or beds, for transplanting on a warm border, and *Perennials and Biennials* may still be transplanted.

It is now late for planting in shrubberies, and anything that has been left till this month must have copious watering. The holes dug for the roots should be well soaked with water before the plants are put in. This expedient will prove the safety of many a late-planted shrub. Rhododendrons and kindred American plants may still be set out either singly or in masses.

Gravel Walks and Lawns.—Walks should be broken up and turned, if not done in March; if turned then, roll twice a week at least. Lawns should now be mown once a week, and carefully, for nothing looks worse than the marks of the scythe on an otherwise smooth lawn. All gaps in box-edging should be made good, well watered, and trimmed. Place stakes to all such plants as require support, bearing in mind that "as the twig is bent the plant inclines;" fix the sticks firmly in the ground, bring the stalks to the stake, and tie them neatly but firmly to it, without galling the plant; remove all straggling, broken, or decayed shoots, and keep all clear of weeds, raking smooth with a small rake.

Rose Garden.—All pruning and any planting not done last month must be finished early in this, and all recently-planted trees copiously watered, the ground stirred, but left rough,—at least unraked. Beds for tea-scented roses should be prepared for planting towards the end of this month or in May. Good ordinary garden soil will produce roses large enough for ordinary purposes; but to grow them in perfection, a hole in the ground should be opened two feet square and a foot deep. This station should be filled with a compost consisting of two good-sized spadefuls of thoroughly-rotted dung for each plant, mixing it well with the soil. Upon the soil thus prepared the standard rose is placed, the collar just above the level of the surface, and the fibres carefully spread out over the soil. Fill in the remaining soil and replace the turf, treading it gently until it forms a small mound, out of the centre of which the tree rises. A stake is now to be driven into the ground, near enough to support the stem, which is tied to it.

The season for planting may be any time from the fall of the leaf till the buds again begin to swell, in April or the beginning of May. After that there is danger of the tree dying off.

In pruning newly-planted roses, the object is to balance the head to the vital powers of the fibrous root, so as to give a graceful form to the bush. If there be only one shoot from the bud, cut it down to two eyes; if there be a regular head formed, cut away every shoot down to the lowest eye that points outwards or downwards, and cut all weak shoots that come in the way of a better, back to their base, leaving only such as are required to form the head of the tree. When the buds begin to break, rub off all that grow inwards,—all that would cross other branches,—all that are coming weakly, and all that would crowd the head and destroy its cup-like form.

As the growth proceeds, examine every bud, every curled leaf and shoot, for insect larvæ; for maggots, if not detected at once, soon destroy the vitality of the flower-bud. Do this daily, syringing, also, with a fine rose syringe, very forcibly applied, which may destroy the green-fly, the thrip, and other enemies. If these enemies get established, nothing but hand-picking, washing with tobacco-juice, or smoking with tobacco, will get rid of them.

Florists' Flowers.—Polyanthuses require protection from sudden storms and cold winds. Auriculas are now in bloom, and require attention,—the

trusses thinned, and deformed pips removed. Weak manure-water should be applied in the mornings, shading the plants afterwards from the sun. Seed should now be sown in shallow pans, and lightly covered with soil, and the pans placed in some gentle heat. Dahlia-roots may now be planted out in the beds, three or four inches deep, and five feet asunder; tulips protected from cold winds and frosty nights by netting thrown over hoops, and by mats, in severe weather, on the beds, leaving plenty of light and air. Ranunculuses require the soil to be loosened as they come up, and watering with weak manure-water: a watering with lime-water will destroy any worms in the beds.

Carnations in pots should have the surface stirred, and a little new compost added, and be watered with lime-water, to destroy worms. Sow seeds in pots or boxes during the month, place them in a west aspect, and cover them with a sheet of glass. Some fine hybrids have lately been raised, between the Anne Boleyn class and other varieties. *Pansies* will now be interesting: water the fresh-potted plants sparingly, until the roots reach the edge of the pots: top-dress the beds with rotten manure; look for and destroy black slugs; plant out seedlings, and put in cuttings. Hollyhocks kept in pots during the winter should be planted out, about six feet apart, in deep rich soil. Cuttings of choice sorts are more tender than seedlings, and would be safer with a little protection for six weeks after planting. Seed may also be sown now in the reserve garden for autumn flowering.

Tender Annuals sown last month should be pricked out three or four inches apart on a fresh hotbed, prepared as described in March; on this they will grow without interfering with each other for three or four weeks. At the end of this time they must either be transplanted to a fresh hotbed, or thinned by removing every second plant. A hotbed for this removal should have seven inches' depth

April.

of earth laid equally over it; the plants carefully removed with a ball of earth round the roots, and replanted six inches apart, or singly in pots, to be plunged into hotbeds; the whole being lightly watered to settle the earth about the roots. Shade from the sun till rooted, after which give air every day, and water whenever the plants seem to flag. As the plants approach the glass, let the frames be raised about six inches, repeating the operation from time to time, so as to keep the plants a few inches from the glass.

Half-hardy Annuals may now be sown in warm sunny borders. Give them the protection of hoops and mattings at night and in severe weather; sow hardier sorts in the beds and borders, in small patches, where they are to flower, observing that their position is to be regulated according to their height and colour. The mode of sowing is to form a shallow basin in the soil, such as might be made with the convex side of a breakfast saucer; in this hollow sow the seeds, and sift half an inch of fine earth over them. Thin out the patches as the plants begin to grow.

Kitchen Garden. — Supposing the accompanying diagram to represent an acre of ground, the length to run east and west, which gives the advantage of a good peach wall, *a—b* is the line beyond which it is not advisable to crop; *c* is a border twelve feet wide, which may be devoted to early crops, or espaliers, pillar, or bush fruits. The same may be said of the borders *f* and *g*. The east and west walls may be trained with plums, cherries, pears, mulberries, walnuts, medlars, or other trees: *i* is supposed to be a low wall, fence, or hedge; *h*, a border, where late fruits or salading may be grown during the summer time, when a little shade is an advantage to them; *d*, main walk, six feet wide, running round the quarters; *e*, cross-walks, four feet wide between them. The main body of the kitchen-garden is divided into eight squares, two of which are devoted to each group. Let six

April.

be planted with:— 1. asparagus; 2. globe artichokes; 3. seakale; and 4. rhubarb. Of course the space for each will be determined by the requirements of the family, but the proportions indicated may serve as a guide. Let 5 be planted with bush-fruits, as currants —including red, white, and black; gooseberries and raspberries; and root-pruned trees. Horseradish may be planted between these. To keep all

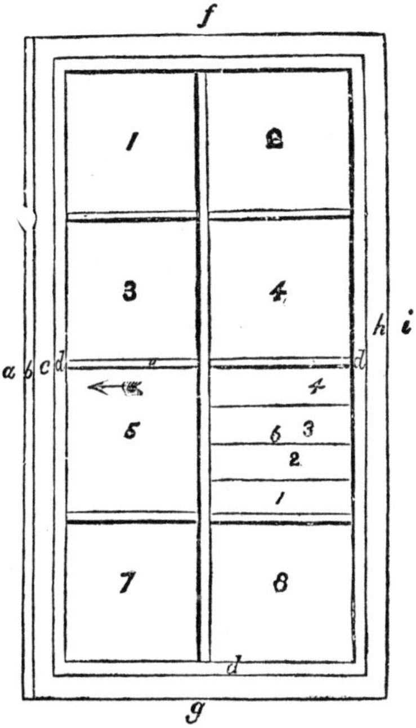

these in proper condition, a few of each should be removed every year; the asparagus, seakale, and rhubarb for forcing: the artichokes can be separated for propagation, and the raspberries divided and replanted. 7 and 8 are supposed to be planted with preparers, which comprise beet, celery, carrots, turnips, leeks, onions, peas, scorzoneras, salsafy, beans, cardoons, Jerusalem artichokes, potatoes, parsnips, scarlet-runners: these are some of the principal kitchen crops, and comprise about one-fourth. Then, again, let 1 and 2 be devoted to surface-crops, which, for the sake of equalizing them with the other groups, will comprise numerous light crops,—as salads, sweet herbs, and similar crops; the exhausters, comprising another fourth of the whole,—brocoli, cabbage, including Dutch, red Braganza, &c.; Savoys, Brussels sprouts, cauliflower, kale, or borecole. These will occupy 3 and 4. As these two squares become vacant, the deepeners may fill the space left by them, until, in course of time, 3 and 4 become filled with the latter. The exhausters will have taken the place of the surface-crops on 1 and 2; the latter will be transferred to 7 and 8, previously occupied with preparers, which have followed the deepeners on 5 and 6; and thus a perpetual rotation may be maintained, which will improve the ground instead of impoverishing it.

In the suburbs of large towns, where ground is valuable and space limited, it often happens that kitchen-gardens are severely overtasked, through a prevailing notion that high tillage and abundant manuring make up for extent of room. This is true; but it has its limits; for instances are not wanting to show that serious and vexatious results are traceable to this cause. The ground gets filled with insects,—undecomposed manure is worked into the soil after each crop,—it is trenched in, dug in, or laid on the surface as mulch sometimes; all manner of undecomposed rubbish and garden refuse is trenched three or four feet deep. The result is obvious; for where there is decomposition and putrid fermentation, many agencies are attracted thither to hasten the work; insects are bred in vast numbers; club and canker become prevalent; and good gardening becomes impossible. The remedy for this state of things is either a copious manuring with unslaked lime, burning the soil, or the substitution of new soil, if the surface-parings of a pasture are conveniently attainable. But prevention is always better than cure. The manure should be thoroughly decomposed or rotted, so that it is not likely to breed insects, and before it is applied to the ground, it should be well incorporated with an equal quantity of loamy soil. Where ground is heavily worked, as, for instance, where a spring crop of lettuces, an autumn crop of potatoes, and a winter crop of greens have been obtained from the same piece of ground, manure alone will not supply the whole of the loss, though the addition of new soil may do so. Another mode of prevention is to adopt a well-defined system of rotation: such a measure will keep the ground in good heart.

Jerusalem Artichokes may still be planted where not previously done. Give four feet one way, and three or four feet the other. This should not be delayed after the first week this month.

Globe Artichokes.—The best method of propagating these is to take offsets from them in this month, and plant them, three feet apart, in a row, and the rows five feet apart. They will bear little or nothing the same season, but will produce abundantly the following. To keep them in good bearing, it is advisable to plant a fresh row every year, and remove one of the old ones. If they are protected with straw, fern, or leaves in winter, they bear rather earlier in summer. When left unprotected, they are killed to the ground, but break up strong in the spring. Before planting, the soil should be trenched three feet deep.

Parsley, Chervil, &c. should be sown for the purpose of keeping a stock of young plants to gather from, as young leaves are best.

Spinach may still be sown, and is often useful for colouring green pea-soup in the summer. Sow in a shady spot, if possible; it will last the longer.

Potatoes for the main crop must be got in this month. As the ground is more likely to be dry at this time, they may be dibbed in whole, which yields food for the young shoot till it can find its own. When potatoes are cut, it is best to expose them for a day or two, to render the surface callous. In planting them, let it be in rows two feet apart; or, if space be limited, allow three feet, which admits of planting later crops between, before they are taken up. Although little is gained by allowing too much room, much is lost by too little; for root-crops are apt to run to haulm or top if too crowded. Two feet from row to row, and fifteen inches from plant to plant, is a good average. If the ground be light or dry, they may be dibbed in; that is, a line is stretched where the row is to be, on one side of which the holes are made with a potato-dibber—this is a pole or shaft three feet long, having a cross-piece of wood on the top for the handle, and a treadle for the foot eight inches from the lower end, and of sufficient thickness to make a hole that a potato may drop in easily. A potato or set is dropped in each hole, and the holes are filled up by drawing a wooden rake over them. It is objected to this, that the pressure of the dibber hardens the soil all round, and checks the spreading of the young tubers: making drills with a spade, and planting that way, is therefore preferable. Potatoes may be planted as the ground is dug, merely placing a line, cutting the drill, placing the potatoes fifteen inches apart, then digging backward two feet, placing the line, cutting another drill, and so on.

If the ground be wet, heavy, and, indeed, under any circumstances, a good plan is to cut a drill with the spade six or eight inches deep. In this place the sets fifteen inches apart, then move the line to the next row, cut another drill in the same manner, but fill up the preceding drill with the soil taken out, covering the sets in it. This is an expeditious mode, and will do on any soil. On stiff soils the dibber should never be used, because it forms a basin in which water is likely to stand and rot the potato. About the end of March or beginning of April the main crop may be planted, or it may be deferred till quite the end of the latter month, and smaller plantings may be made till midsummer. When the potatoes have grown about eight or ten inches high, a little earth should be drawn up to them—just sufficient to cover any tubers that may grow near the surface; too much produces luxuriance of growth in the haulm, and is contrary to nature. The ground should be thoroughly drained. It is generally admitted that disease is most prevalent in wet soils, or wet seasons. Some recommend cutting off the haulm as soon as the blight appears: this may save them in a great measure from the rot, but it stops the growth of the tubers, and whether any real advantage is derived from it is still undecided. It is advisable to pick off all the flowers, unless seed is wanted: this will throw the strength of the plant into the process of forming tubers. As to sorts, they are known to change character when transferred to different soils; but, for early crops, the Ash-leaved Kidney is deserving of culture, especially in its improved form. The Early Fulham and Early Manly are both good; the Forty-fold, a pink potato, is good for main crop; Regent and Flourball are good general croppers; and Fluke's or Kirk's kidney for late crops.

Turnip.—A sowing of early Dutch turnip may be made in this month. This crop is very apt to run to seed instead of swelling at the root, if sown too early; but a great deal depends on the kind of soil: it does best on a rather retentive soil; but should be in an open, unshaded piece of ground, for it never does much good if shaded or overhung by trees. A dressing of soot at the time of sowing seems to benefit turnips greatly. The seed should be sown evenly but rather thin,—a small quantity of it will cover a large piece of ground, if regularly scattered. Broadcast sowing is preferable for this crop; but if sown in drills, let them be fifteen inches distant from each other, and the plants left not less than a foot apart in the rows; even a greater distance is better, as turnips resent anything like crowding. If sown in drills, let them be very shallow—half an inch is deep enough. As soon as they are up, use the hoe unsparingly, and see that they are thinned to the proper distance before the roots begin to swell. If attacked with the fly, which happens in dry weather, dust with lime or soot while the dew is on them: on light soils turnips will repay copious watering.

Carrots may still be sown; and those who know the sweetness and delicacy of the short-horn kinds, in their young state, will take care to have a supply of them. They may be sown till the latter end of July.

Cabbages.—The first week in this month is a good time for sowing the various sorts of *Brassicæ* for main crop, selecting the beginning of the month for the meridian of London, and a fortnight later north of Cheshire and Lancaster. If sown earlier, except for early use, they are apt to make superfluous growth. The treatment for all sorts is nearly the same. Let the seed-beds be open, and away from trees or other shelter, tolerably dry, but not parched, at the time of sowing. Mark out for each sort its allotted space: give plenty of room,—at least a square rod; sow the seed broadcast regularly over the ground; tread it well in, unless the ground be wet and binding; in that case stand in the alleys, rake level, and pat the surface with a piece of flat board: this will press the seed in without hardening the ground. If dry enough to tread, rake the surface even. If the weather be dry, and continue so, it will be necessary to give the seed-bed a copious watering. When the seed is up, keep the beds moist, so as to promote vigorous growth; giving a liberal dusting of lime, salt, or soot now and then, which will benefit the young plants, and prevent the attacks of the fly. When large enough to handle, thin them, and prick out those drawn, in nursery-beds five or six inches apart from each other.

Peas for late crops may be sown any time this month. The tall-growing sorts are best to sow now, and if sticks be plentiful, these should have the preference. If on good soil, or well mulched, the yield is far above all other sorts; the *Ne plus ultra* yields an enormous crop: sow them six or seven feet apart from row to row, or ten or twelve feet, where crops of cabbages can be sown between the rows. Any of the wrinkled or marrow peas do well sown at this time: earth-up, mulch, and stake those sufficiently advanced. Good peas for sowing at this time are Hair's Dwarf Green Mammoth, Knight's Dwarf Green, British Queen, Tall White Mammoth, *Ne plus ultra*, Knight's Tall Green. The first two grow about three feet high, the others about six feet.

Salading.—Lettuces should be sown for succession; the large drum-head, or Maltese, does well sown at this time; but Cos lettuces are generally preferred, as being most crisp: any sort will do sown at this season. *Chicory* is used both as a salad in spring and also the roots as a vegetable: it should be sown late this month and the two following. Sow in shallow drills a foot apart, and thin to eight or ten inches in the row: they need not be disturbed again until taken up for use, or put in a frame to blanch the tops: in common with all crops, they must be kept clear of weeds. *Parsley* may be sown at any time; a principal sowing is usually made now. Some make sowings in shallow drills, eight or ten inches apart; but broadcast is preferable, at least if the ground is in condition to be trodden. Use the small hoe as soon as up, and thin out gradually, till the plants are ten inches or a foot apart. *Chervil* is sown and treated in a similar manner, and is much used in some families. See that a good curled sort is sown. *Marjoram*, of the sweet, or knotted kind, is usually sown this month, on a clear open spot: the seed is small, and should be sown on the surface, trodden, and raked evenly, and watered in dry weather. In common with most herbs, it requires a long time to germinate; so that care should be taken that it is not choked with weeds. They should be removed by the hand, until the plants are large enough to use the small hoe with safety. *Pot Marjoram*, winter and summer *Savory*, *Thyme*, and other herbs, may be sown and treated in the same way.

The Fruit Garden.—Planting of all kinds, except in cases of absolute necessity, should now be over for the season. Should it still be necessary to plant, precautions must be taken to protect the tender roots, while they are yet foreign to the soil, both from frost and heat, by mulching with long stable manure, or, as some recommend, by placing a layer of pebbles over them, on a bed of sand, and covering this, during the spring months, with ferns, haulm, or other rubbish. All winter pruning will now be completed. Peaches and nectarines are advancing towards blossom, and apricots, on a south wall, will be showing their bloom. These now require the greatest attention. If the autumn and winter months have been wet and cloudy, the fruit-bearing branches will be weak and watery. Every protection from spring frost should be given under these circumstances. In such seasons, especially in the months of August and September, the young shoots being unripened in the previous autumn, the trees are subject to the ravages of the green-fly, and if not observed at once, they commit very serious damage. Tobacco-water, in the proportion of 2 oz. of tobacco infused in a quart of boiling water, is a remedy as well as a protection, when applied cool to the tree with a brush. A weaker decoction may be applied with the syringe with advantage.

The question of protection is one on which authorities are by no means agreed; Mr. McIntosh and some of the best gardeners recommend temporary projecting copings to the walls, and canvas or calico curtains depending from them. Others find a worsted netting of small mesh and thickish thread a sufficient protection, while it

leaves a freer play to the natural atmosphere round the trees. Another object of protection in the early spring is to retard the blossoms by shading from the sun. For this purpose canvas, suspended during the heat of the day, is the most efficient.

The perfect-bearing shoots of the peach and nectarine are known by their buds towards the base of the shoots. Some of these are pointed, single buds, with a brownish envelope: these are leaf-buds. Next to these, and higher up the shoot, are triple buds,—a plump, silver-coated one on each side, and a thin one in the centre. This central one is a leaf-bud, the outer two are blossom-buds; and it should be the aim of the pruner to cultivate as many of these as possible.

Apples and Pears, which bear their fruit on spurs, when cultivated in gardens, are usually trained as espaliers, as pyramids, or dwarf. In the mature state they require care in selecting the shoots to be retained, preferring ripe, short-jointed, brownish shoots, shortening back these to a bud which will extend the growth of the tree, studying,—first, the production of spurs; second, to keep the heart of the tree open; third, as the finest fruit is borne on the extremities of the branches, to keep these as compact as possible.

Vines are now pushing forth their young shoots in great numbers. At this season only those which are obviously useless, and especially those issuing from old wood, unless wanted for future years' rods, should be rubbed off with the finger and thumb close to the stem. The useless ones being disposed of, those left should be trained close to the wall, at regular distances apart, so that all may enjoy the light, heat, and air.

Strawberries, which have been under mulch all the winter, should now be uncovered; the old foliage would be cut down in March, as directed; and after clearing away all weeds and useless runners, a spring dressing of half-decayed material from the cucumber-frame, mixed with soot and decayed leaves, will be useful, watering frequently towards the end of the month.

Gooseberries and Currants, pruned in January and top-dressed in March, by removing an inch or two of soil, and replacing this with a compost of loam and decayed dung, in equal proportions, will require little attention till the fruit begins to form.

Flowers under Glass.—Conservatory.—While any probability of spring frosts remains, ventilation must be cautiously given, especially with newly-potted plants and tender flowers from the stove or forcing-house. As they begin to grow, air should be given whenever it can be done with safety. Where artificial heat is used, ventilation may be rendered safe by using extra firing. Camellias and other plants with large coriaceous leaves, if not perfectly clean, should be washed with sponge, and, if necessary, with soft soap, to eradicate insects; and a moist, genial heat maintained by sprinkling the floor, stage, and pipes. Boronias, Lechenaultias, Chorozemas, and Tropæolums will now be fit to remove to the conservatory. Place them in as airy a situation as possible, maintaining a temperature of 45° to 50° at night, rising 10° or so from sun-heat.

It may be partly from contrast with the dormant state of plants out of doors, but chiefly on account of the intrinsic beauty of its occupants, that the conservatory is so much more beautiful for the next three months than it ever is afterwards throughout the year. There is a delicacy and fragrance about spring flowers that never seem equalled afterwards.

In addition to the plants named last month, this perfume will now be enlivened by the lily of the valley, roses, sweetbriar, and violets. Each is exquisite alone; but, all combined and added to the odour of lilacs, hyacinths, narcissus, and other spring flowers now filling with fragrance an artificial, partially confined atmosphere, constitute a delicious odour.

Greenhouse Plants divide themselves into hard- and soft-wooded plants. Among the former are Boronias,

Hoveas, Acacias, and Chorozemas, Epacridæ, Genistas, and Pultenæas, which will now be coming into bloom, if well managed.

Azaleas will be coming forward, where there is a good stock of such plants as *A. lateritia*, *Gladstonesii*, Prince Albert, *præstantissima*, and others of similar habit: their bloom should be retarded by placing them on the shaded side of the house. Plants that have been forced should have the seed-vessels picked off, and shifted, if the pots are tolerably full of roots.

Heaths in full growth require an astonishing quantity of water at this season of the year; mere driblets are certain death to them. When the pots are full of roots, they should be gone over two or three times a week, and filled to the brim with water. The longer the water is in passing through (provided the drainage is all right), there is the greater necessity for repeating the dose, as dry peat-earth is one of the worst conductors of water. When the water remains longer than ten minutes on the surface, a cold bath for twenty-four hours is the only remedy. Unless the soil is hopelessly dry, this will cure it, and it must not be watered again until the ball is turned out and examined. The evil of excessive dryness is often increased by excessive drainage. Heaths, while they cannot endure stagnant water, like a moist genial soil when making rapid growth. They resemble neither epiphytes nor orchids, and yet some of them naturally inhabit almost swampy districts. Give air more liberally as the sun strengthens and the days lengthen, but avoid the cutting draughts so characteristic of this month.

Pelargoniums, and other soft-wooded plants, now growing rapidly, require every attention. Water carefully, so as to avoid any check in their growth, using manure-water occasionally, composed of equal parts of sheep-, cow-, and horse-dung, and a little lime. Fill up the tub with soft water, mix it well, and draw it off clear, when settled, into another tub; to this mixture add two parts of soft water to one of the

April.

liquid, and water once a week with it during the growing season. Ventilate freely on warm sunny days, and syringe with water of the temperature of the house. *Scarlet Geraniums* require similar treatment to promote their growth. Cuttings struck now in 48- or 32-sized pots will fill the pots with roots by the autumn, and bloom through the winter months. *Calceolarias* should now have a final shift, using a light rich compost, and pegging them down to encourage roots up the stem, watering cautiously when dry, and fumigate for green-fly, ventilating freely every opportunity.

Fuchsias.—This is still a good time to buy in plants. The variety now is endless; but many of them are almost the same, with a new name. Favourite flowers are—

Souvenir de Chiswick, with rosy crimson sepals and tube, and violet corolla, and beautifully-recurved broad sepals. As a party-coloured variety of perfect habit, nothing can exceed Venus de' Medici, with white tube, blush-white sepals, corolla deep violet.
Rose of Castile,—blush-white sepals and tube; rosy purple corolla.
Sir Colin Campbell,—crimson tube, and sepals well reflexed; corolla dark purple.
Madame Cornelissen,—sepals very long; pure white corolla. The flowers of these are not only good, but the *habit*, a great point in double fuchsias, is also excellent.
Amazement is said to be the best double fuchsia,—sepals rich crimson, reflexed; corolla rich dark purple.
Bianca,—scarlet tube and sepals.
Black Prince,—broad sepals, carmine-scarlet; corolla very dark purple.
Catherine Hayes,—sepals scarlet; light-blue corolla; excellent habit.
Coronal,—sepals vermilion, nice-curved; corolla violet and rich purple.
Crown Jewel,—sepals crimson; corolla black; habit distinct; leaves long and peculiar.
Dr. Livingstone,—delicate white tube; petals well recurved; corolla blush; very distinct and delicate-looking.
Duchess of Lancaster,—white tube and sepals; violet corolla.
Fairest of the Fair,—white tube and sepals; corolla rich violet.
Forget-me-not,—sepals scarlet and carmine; corolla violet, red, and purple.
Goliath,—coral-red, with immense fruit, of a light green colour.
Guiding Star,—blush-tinted tube; sepals white, nicely recurved; corolla velvety purple.
La Crinoline,—sepals crimson; corolla bluish.
Leoline,—sepals crimson; violet-blue corolla.
Le Prophète,—sepals crimson; corolla violet.

April.

Leviathan,—sepals very broad, rich crimson, reflexed, and completely recurved; corolla deep purple, of an immense size; altogether, a fine bold flower.
Lord Elcho,—sepals carmine-scarlet; corolla violet-blue, beautifully cupped.
Marvellous (an immense double variety),—crimson sepals and dark corolla; bad habit.
Perseverance,—sepals carmine, salmon-tinted; corolla rosy lilac.
Prince of Orange,—sepals scarlet, wide-curved; habit excellent.
Prince Frederick William of Prussia,—sepals carmine and red; corolla plum-colour; good shape.
Queen of Hanover,—sepals white; corolla carmine.
Star of the Night,—sepals rich carmine; corolla violet-purple, a fine striking variety.
Tricolour and Tricolour flower, both striking and pretty varieties, *three*-coloured.
Victor Emmanuel,—sepals red; corolla slate-coloured.
White Lady,—one of the best white varieties,—an improvement on Princess of Prussia.

Begonias.—Most of the variegated varieties do best treated as half-deciduous. Retaining a few plants for winter decoration, compel the main stock to rest for the winter; that is, keep them warm and very dry, so that many of the leaves fade. Now is the time to shake over the dry soil, re-pot, and plunge into a bottom-heat of 75° or 80°; or they will start very nicely on a stone shelf. The rapidity of the change from semi-death to vigorous life is like a resurrection. Start a few pots of *Caladiums*. Their adder-tongued-looking leaves have a striking effect, and with foresight, some may be had throughout the year. Keep dormant plants quite dry. The beautiful Argyrites is often killed by attempting to keep the plant in leaf all winter, and by watering it to secure this object. Nature tells them all to rest for three or four months, and they will sooner perish than grow.

Orchids.—As soon as these begin to grow, a general potting should take place. The beautiful palm-like leaved cyrtopodiums should be shaken out and potted in a compost of equal parts loam, leaf-mould, turfy peat, sand, broken crocks, and charcoal. They are noble-looking plants. Bletias may be treated in the same manner, using more loam, however, for them and the beautiful dove-plant, *Peristeria elata.* Plunge Aerides, Vandas, &c., in water, when their flower-stems appear, until they are thoroughly soaked. Shift into fresh baskets Longaras, Brassias, Cropegias, &c. Keep Oncidiums rather dry at present. The beautiful old *Goodyera discolor* will now be in full blossom. Its striking dark purple-veined leaves, and noble heads of pure white blossom, make it still a charming object. Clean all plants when in a dormant state, and secure a moist growing atmosphere of 70° to 75°. Mechanics and cottagers who have no glass may make their houses very gay by taking up a few patches of crocuses, violets, hepaticas, pinks, &c., carefully potting them, and placing them in a sunny window.

Fruit-Culture under Glass.—The changeable temperature of the early spring months is a source of immense anxiety to the gardener. From cloud to sunshine, and from sunshine to storm; warm days succeeded by frosty nights, and cold winds by perfect calms, are constant occurrences, and keep the gardener and his assistants in a continued state of uncertainty. With every attention and skill, proper ventilation at this period is a work of great difficulty, from the fact that on the brightest days the air is often only a degree above the freezing-point. Unless provision is made for introducing the external air through a heated chamber, no *front* air should be admitted until the end of April or beginning of May. It is always dangerous to give direct air in front of vineries until the fruit is ripe. In the absence of some better means of partially heating the air admitted at the back or top of the house, before it reaches the plants, a close woollen net, or double or treble Nottingham netting, might be fixed over the ventilators or open spaces where the lights run down. The force of the current would be broken, and the air would be partially heated as it *sifted* through the fine meshes of the netting. If it were practicable to keep this netting wet, evaporation would tend largely to moderate the temperature of the air, and prevent its being so rapidly raised by the influence of the sun. But an equable temperature is scarcely more important than the amount of moisture contained in the air. Hydrometers, although not yet common, will soon be felt to be as necessary as thermometers. At present, every gardener worthy of the name is a living hydrometer, and it is astonishing how perfectly the *seasoned* ones can gauge the amount of water suspended in the air.

As soon as grapes begin to swell, a rise of 10° may take place, which may be continued until the first spot of colour appears. The minimum may then be from 60° to 65°, with a *little air constantly* in the house, never omitting to close it at night. Successional houses will now require great attention,—disbudding, thinning, and tying the shoots, &c. Raise the temperature through the different stages. Stop young shoots a joint beyond the bunches, excepting always the leading shoots on young vines. After a few stoppings, if the leaves become crowded, take the young wood off at the same point at every stopping, as two or three large leaves beyond the bunch are sufficient to supply its wants, and more useful than a number of small ones.

Pines.—Shift all the succession plants as soon as possible. It will facilitate this operation very much if one man places his arms carefully round the leaves and another slips a tie of soft matting round the plant, sufficiently tight to compress, without bruising, the leaves. This will render the plants manageable, and enable you to *pot* without *gloves.* If the plants have been properly kept during the winter, remove the crocks, gradually unwind the roots, take away as much of the old soil as possible, pull off from three to six inches of the bottom; place the plant two or three inches deeper in the new pot than it was in the old, as pines root up the stem, and have no permanent collar; press in the earth firmly, and the work is complete. Turfy loam, mixed with a little charcoal and broken bones, is the best compost; enrich this with manure-water during the rapid growing and fruiting stages. If ferns or leaves be used for bottom-heat, these will now require renewing. This work should proceed at the same time as the potting, so that the plants may at once be moved back to their proper quarters. Keep the plants level during the process of plunging the pots, and after two rows are plunged, cut the ties and arrange the leaves of the back row; plunge another row, then cut and arrange the second row; and so on throughout. A mild day must be chosen for these operations, as five or six hours' check from cold will often throw a whole pit of succession pines into premature fruit—one of the greatest calamities that can happen to the cultivator.

Figs.—A dry close atmosphere often causes the embryo fruit to drop. Dryness, or excessive moisture at the root, may produce the same results. When the fig is in full growth, the latter evil is almost impossible; but there appears to be but little demand upon the roots for moisture until the leaves are fully expanded. Maintain a temperature of 60°, and syringe the leaves daily.

Orchard-House. — Unless this is heated, keep it constantly open when the outside temperature is above 32°. Success here depends upon retarding the trees as much as possible. If they start now, and we have a sharp frost in April, the chances are you will lose the crops. If a pipe runs round part or the whole of a house, it may now be allowed to move at a temperature of 40° to 45°. Place plums, apricots, and cherries in the coolest part, nearest the ventilators. See that the trees in pots and borders are well watered previous to starting, and give all the air possible to keep down the temperature during frosty weather.

Strawberries.—Give plenty of air when in bloom, maintaining a drier atmosphere during that process. After they are fairly set, they will bear a temperature of 70° to swell off; but 60° to ripen, with abundance of air, is quite enough. On shelves, place each pot in a pan, or within a second pot half-filled with rotten manure. Water with manure-water, syringe twice a day, and keep the plants clear of insects.

Hotbed and Frame Cultivation.—*Cucumbers*, in growing condition, require more air in the day-time as the sun acquires more power; healthy plants will bear the full light without shading: if they droop under its influence while air is given freely, something is wrong at the roots or collar, and fresh plants should be raised to supersede them, provided they do not recover. Air should be admitted in proportion to the weather; and as this varies every day, more or less, watchfulness and care are necessary. Peg down the bines, and pinch off shoots that are not wanted, and all shoots above the fruit; add fresh soil and fresh linings outside as required.

Melons should be syringed occasionally with water of a temperature rather higher than that of the bed: all shoots not wanted pinch off, so that the strength of the plant can go into the fruit. Fresh cucumbers and melons should be started for successions. The heat of the dung now lasts longer, and is not counteracted by severe frosts, and the sun begins to yield more heat; the days also are longer, the plants receive more light, and consequently are likely to be more stocky and short-jointed; the dung, however, must be well prepared. Much time is saved by raising the plants in pots upon the fruiting-bed already going; if none are in operation, make a small bed with part of the dung, and cover it with a frame or hand-glass. Hotbeds at this time of the year are of the greatest importance in gardens where other appliances for raising plants are limited. The most tender plants may be raised from seed, and cuttings of almost all plants strike root most readily in them.

A melon-pit, divided into compartments of two or more lights each, will be useful at this time, and will answer most of the purposes to which frames are applicable. Vegetable marrows, ridge cucumbers, tomatoes, capsicums, chillies, tea-plants, egg-plants, may be sown and raised with the aid of manure, managed as for melons. This is a good time to raise all these, or to pot them and plunge them in the dung, if already raised.

Seakale should, when cut, be removed; the roots planted in the open ground, if required for increase.

Asparagus should be watered with weak liquid manure, but care should be taken not to overdo it: be rather sparing of stimulants than otherwise.

Potatoes may be tried by scraping away the earth near the collar. The largest tubers are generally near the surface, and may be removed without disturbing the plants, which should be left to perfect the smaller ones: water, if required; but liquid manure is not necessary.

French beans that are flowering should receive plenty of light and air, and be kept tolerably dry overhead, and tied up to sticks if they hang over: keep the roots moderately moist; but, if allowed to root through the pots, they will require no other stimulus.

Strawberries will require plenty of water and a liberal supply of liquid manure. While the fruit is swelling, give, if possible, more heat and more air; if kept close, the fruit is apt to fog or mould without swelling. In damp weather, tilt the lights; in dry sunny weather, push them down.

Tender Annuals should now be sown in heat, and half-hardy ones in cold-frames. Pot or prick off any that may be up. Balsams, cockscombs, and globe amaranths still require heat, and should be kept near the glass, to prevent being drawn up. Cuttings of all soft-wooded plants should be struck in great numbers for bedding out: these root and grow freely in hotbeds.

Salads may still be sown in cold-frames, and a good plan is to move the frames from place to place, merely using them to protect the seeds from birds: a frame placed over rhubarb will bring it on fast: lettuces, &c., may be urged on in the same way.

Mushroom-beds may be made out of doors this month. Prepare the dung by turning it over five or six times; mix a portion of loamy soil with it—some recommend a sprinkling of salt; build the bed up in a ridge of four feet high and five or six wide; dig a trench round it to drain it; beat it firmly, and when about 80°, spawn it by making shallow holes with one hand, thrusting pieces of spawn into them with the other. Some recommend waiting a day or two after making the bed, asserting that the weight of the casing, as it is called, causes a rise in the temperature, which might endanger the spawn. It is as well to be cautious: case the bed with two or three inches of loamy soil, rather stiff, and cover with six or eight inches of clean straw; and to keep this in its place, cover it with mats. This will protect it from winds and rain. Mushrooms are sometimes grown in large pots, boxes, or baskets. In any case the process is this:—Prepare some stable-dung as for making a mushroom-bed. When well worked and sweetened, fill the pot, &c., five-sixths, and press it firmly down; then lay in pieces of spawn and top with loamy soil, placing it in a warm place, as under the stage in a warm greenhouse or stove, forcing-house or pit, or even a hotbed frame. Mushrooms come into bearing rather quicker this way than on a bed: they are often grown on shelves, the house being quite dark and furnished with hot-water pipes. This is the most satisfactory mode of growing them, the other being a makeshift. In this case, a mixture of horse-, cow-, and sheep-dung, loam, and road-sand is well worked together, and placed on the shelves, mixed with pieces of spawn, and the whole pressed firmly down, and heat applied of an average of 70°. Vapour-troughs should be provided, for the mushroom will not bear a dry heat. Water should be applied when required, but very gently, and rather sparingly than otherwise, and of a temperature rather above that of the bed at the time.

AQUATIC PLANTS, for ornamenting Ponds, the Sides of Running Streams, and other Artificial Pieces of Water.

Vegetation of some sort, and generally of an interesting character, is sure to be found in the neighbourhood of water. There are, however, many plants which are to be preferred to others when we undertake to cultivate a piece of water on the margin of a stream. Flowers for water, as Mr. Loudon reminds us, are of two kinds: aquatics, plants for the water, and marsh plants, to place round the banks. Aquatic plants are propagated by seed, and frequently by division of the roots. The seeds when sown must be placed under water; in other respects they require the same general treatment as other herbaceous plants. We extract from Mr. Loudon's large work on the practice of gardening the following useful list of plants, with the colour of their different flowers and times of flowering.

Aquatic plants with showy flowers.

MAY. *Red.*—Equisetum fluviatile, Hydrocolite vulgaris. *White.*—Nasturtium officinale, Ranunculus aquatilis. *Yellow.*—Ranunculus aquatilis. *Blue.*—Veronica Beccabunga.

JUNE. *Red.*—Equisetum palustre, Butomus umbellatus. *White.* — Hydrocharis morsus-ranæ, Phellandrium aquaticum. *Blue.*—Myriophyllum spicatum, M. verticillatum, Pontederia cordata, Veronica anagallis. *Green.*—Potamogeton densum. *Brown.*—Potamogeton lucens, P. pectinatum.

JULY. *Red.*—Hippuris vulgaris, Polygonum amphibium. *White.*—Alisma damasonium, A. natans, A. plantago, Calla palustris, Nymphæa alba, N. odorata, Poa fluitans, Stratiotes aloides. *Yellow.*—Iris Pseud-Acorus, Villarsia nymphæoides, Nuphar advena, N. lutea, Utricularia minor. *Purple.*—Utricularia vulgaris, Trapa natans, Sagittaria sagittifolia. *Green.* — Ceratophyllum demersum, Cicuta virosa.

AUGUST. *Red.* — Hydropeltis purpurea, Polygonum hydropiper. *White.* — Cerastium aquaticum, Poa aquatica. *Yellow.* — Potamogeton natans. *Blue.*—Alisma ranunculoides, Lobelia Dortmanna. *Brown.* — Potamogeton perfoliatum, Scirpus fluitans, S. lacustris, S. triqueter.

Marsh plants with showy flowers, for the borders of ponds, the margins of streams, and ornamental pieces of water. Time for flowering, May and June.

HEIGHT, FROM 0 TO ¾ OF A FOOT. *White.*—Pinquicula lusitanica. *Blue.* — Pinquicula vulgaris. *Brown.*—Carex dioica.

FROM ¾ TO 1½ FOOT. *White.*—Œnanthe peucedanifolia. *Yellow.*—Carex flava, Ranunculus flamula, R. repens. *Green.*—Carex disticha, C. pulicaris, C. precox, C. stricta, C. muricata, C. elongata. *Brown.*—Carex cæspitosa, C. digitata, Schœnus nigricans.

HEIGHT FROM 1½ FOOT TO 2½ FEET. *White.* — Œnanthe fistulosa. *Purple.* — Comarum palustre. *Brown.* — Carex paludosa, C. riparia, Juncus conglomeratus.

HEIGHT FROM 2½ FEET to 3½ FEET. *Green.*—Carex pseudo-cyperus, C. vulpina, Cyperus longus, Juncus compressus.

HEIGHT FROM 3½ FEET UPWARDS.—*Red.* Scrophularia aquatica. *White.* — Œnanthe crocata. *Yellow.*—Senecio paludosus.

Marsh plants, &c., which flower in July and August.

HEIGHT FROM 0 TO ¾ OF A FOOT. *Red.*—Teucrium scordium. *White.*—Littorella lacustris, Samolus Valerandi, Schœnus albus. *Yellow.*—Hyperocum elodes. *Blue.*—Schœnus mariscus. *Variegated.*—Scutellaria minor. *Brown.*—Schœnus compressus, Scirpus acicularis, S. cæspitosus.

HEIGHT FROM ¾ TO 1½ FOOT. *Red.*—Menyanthes trifoliata. *White.*—Galium palustre, G. uliginosum, Pedicularis palustris. *Yellow.* Hottonca palustris, Rumex maritimus. *Purple.*—Pedicularis sylvatica, Triglochin maritimum, T. palustre. *Brown.* — Juncus squarrosus, Schœnus nigricans, Scirpus palustris, S. sylvaticus.

HEIGHT FROM 1½ FOOT TO 2½ FEET. *Yellow.*—Acorus calamus, Myosotis palustris, Rumex palustris. *Blue.*—Phormium tenax. *Purple.*—Aster tripolium. *Brown.*— Scirpus maritimus, Rumex crispus, Juncus sylvaticus.

HEIGHT FROM 2½ FEET TO 3½ FEET. *White.* Rumex obtusifolius. *Yellow.*—Cineraria palustris, Senecio aquaticus. *Green.*—Juncus effusus. *Brown.*—Scirpus holoschœnus.

HEIGHT FROM 3½ FEET UPWARDS. *Red.*—Malva sylvestris. *White.*—Dipsacus pilosus, Selinum palustre. *Yellow.*—Sonchus palustris. *Variegated.*—Angelica sylvestris. *Brown.*—Rumex aquaticus, Cyperus longus, Juncus acutus, J. maritimus.

To those who desire to ornament any piece of artificial water, the above lists are invaluable. The situation best adapted for hardy aquatics will be found to be in accordance with their height. Many that are not hardy may be introduced for summer decoration in pots sunk either wholly or half deep in water. These can be removed in winter to warm-water tanks under cover of glass. Every year something new in aquatics is being introduced, for the water-plants of the tropics are inexhaustible, and very many of them supremely beautiful. Most of the plants which have been mentioned in the above lists prefer a shady and sheltered situation, and will be found to flourish best when protected by overhanging trees. Rock-work and root-work form admirable receptacles for plants on the margins of streams, and afford all the protection they require, when properly arranged. We shall have more to say on this subject when we give lists of those plants which are suitable for rock- and root-work.

ARBORETUM.

A place set apart for a collection of trees and shrubs, containing only one or two plants of each kind, and arranged according to system. An arboretum may be of any extent; but to render it useful, each tree and shrub should be named. The following lists may be serviceable to those who are planning an arboretum.

Partial or entire Evergreens.

	FEET.	
Arbutus Unedo	10 to	20
,, ruber	10	20
,, hybrida	10	20
,, laurifolia	8	10
Quercus Fulhamensis	50	100
,, latifolia	30	100
,, Lucombeana crispa	30	100
,, Ilex (evergreen oak)	40	80
,, latifolia	20	—
,, variegata	20	—
,, Suber (cork-tree)	20	30

Deciduous Trees.

	FEET.	
Acacia Julibrissin	20 to	—
Acer platanoides (the Norway maple)	40	70
,, Pseudo-platanus (the sycamore)	30	60
,, albo variegatum	30	50
,, rubrum	30	50
Æsculus Hippocastanum (the horse-chestnut)	30	70
,, ,, flore pleno	30	40
,, rubicunda	20	30
,, rosea	20	30

Arboretum.

	FEET.	
Ailanthus glandulosa	60 to	—
Alnus glutinosa (common alder)	30	60
,, laciniata	30	60
,, cordifolia	30	60
Amygdalus (the almond)		
,, communis amara	20	—
,, dulcis	20	30
,, orientalis	8	10
Betula alba (common birch)	50	60
,, pendula	50	60
,, excelsa	60	70
Carpinus Betulus (common hornbeam)	30	60
,, americana	15	30
Castanea vesca (the Spanish chestnut)	30	70
,, asplenifolia	40	50
,, variegata	40	50
Cavya (the hickory)		
,, tomentosa	50	60
,, porcina	60	80
Catalpa syringifolia	20	30
Celtis occidentalis	40	50
Cerasus sylvestris flore pleno	20	30
,, semperflorens (the All Saints' cherry)	20	—
,, Padus (the bird-cherry)	12	40
Corylus Avellana (the common hazel, and varieties)	20	—
Cratægus coccinea	15	20
,, pyrifolia	15	30
,, Crus-galli	15	20
,, splendens	15	20
,, nigra	15	20
,, apiifolia	10	20
,, oxyacantha (the common hawthorn)	12	30
,, multiplex	10	20
,, rosea	10	20
,, ,, flore pleno		
,, præcox (the Glastonbury thorn)	10	20
Cytisus albus	7	—
,, Laburnum	20	—
,, alpinus (the Scotch laburnum)	20	30
,, odoratus	40	—
,, Waterer's hybrid	20	—
Euonymus europæus	10	20
Fagus sylvatica (the common beech)	60	100
,, purpurea	50	80
,, foliis variegatis	40	50
,, latifolia	40	50
Juglans nigra	50	60
,, regia (the common walnut)	30	60
Liquidambar Styraciflua	30	50
,, imberbe	10	20
Liriodendron tulipifera (the tulip-tree)	30	90
Magnolia glauca	10	20
,, acuminata	30	40
,, conspicua	20	30
,, Alexandrina	10	15
,, speciosa	10	15
Mespilus germanica	15	20
And other varieties of medlars, as the Nottingham, Dutch, and stoneless.		
Morus nigra (the common mulberry)	20	30
Negundo fraxinifolium (the ash-leaved maple)	30	[illegible]
,, crispum	20	[illegible]

Arboretum.

	FEET.	
Negundo variegatum	20 to	30
Ostrya vulgaris (the hop hornbeam)	30	40
Pavia rubra	10	20
,, erecta	15	—
Platanus orientalis (the plane-tree)	60	80
,, occidentalis	70	80
Populus alba (the Abele poplar) ..	80	90
,, tremula (the aspen poplar)	50	70
,, monilifera (the black Italian poplar)	100	120
,, fastigiata (the Lombardy poplar)	100	120
,, balsamifera	40	50
Punica Granatum (the pomegranate-tree)	10	20
Pyrus communis (the common pear)	20	30
,, foliis variegatis	20	—
,, Malus (the wild apple) ..	30	35
,, prunifolia rosea	10	20
,, spectabilis	20	30
,, aucuparia (the mountain ash)	20	30
,, pendula		
Quercus pedunculata (the common English oak)	50	100
,, sessiflora	50	100
,, Cerris (the Turkey oak)..	50	100
,, rubra (the champion oak)	80	90
,, coccinea	80	—
,, laurifolia	50	60
Robinia pseudo-acacia	40	80
,, microphylla	40	80
,, hispida (the rose acacia)	12	20
Salix americana pendula	10	—
,, babylonica (the weeping willow)	40	50
,, fragilis	40	50
,, Russelliana	50	60
Sambucus nigra (the common elder)	20	30
,, rotundifolia	10	20
Tilia europæa (the common lime)	60	90
,, rubra	50	80
,, pubescens	50	70
,, heterophylla	30	50
Ulmus campestris (the English elm)	60	80
,, latifolia	60	80
,, cornubiensis	60	80
,, montana (the Scotch or Wych elm)	30	60
,, vegeta (the Huntingdon elm)	50	80

Evergreen Shrubs.

	FEET.	
Acuba japonica	4 to	8
Berberis dulcis	2	5
,, Aquifolia	3	—
,, Darwinii	3	4
,, japonica	3	—
Buxus (box) latifolia, glauca, marginata, argentea, varying from ..	4	8
Ceanothus azureus	5	10
,, dentatus		
Cerasus lusitanica (the Portugal laurel)	10	25
,, Laurocerastus (the common laurel)	10	20
,, parviflora	5	10

Arboretum.

	FEET.	
Cistus purpureus	3 to	4
,, latifolius	3	4
,, cyprius (the common gum cistus)	5	6
,, lusitanicus	3	—
Cotoneaster rotundifolia	3	4
,, thymifolia	3	4
,, buxifolia	35	—
Cratægus pyrocantha	4	10
Daphne pontica..	4	5
,, latifolia		
,, Cneorum	1	—
,, indica rubra	3	—
Helitanthemum candidum	3	—
,, New Double Yellow ..	1	—
,, New Double Orange ..	1	—
Hypericum calycenum	1½	—
Ilex Aquifolium (the common holly)	10	30

As many varieties of the plain and variegated as you can find room for. There are about fifty varieties grown in most large nurseries, all beautiful and worthy of cultivation. Find out, if possible, the sorts that thrive best in your neighbourhood, and purchase them only.

	FEET.	
Laurus nobilis (the sweet bay) ..	20 to	30
,, salicifolia	10	20
,, crispa	5	20
Ligusticum vulgare buxifolium lucidum (the Chinese privet)	10	20
Mahonia fascicularis	3	6
,, trifoliata	3	4
,, Fortunii	3	4
Phillyrea latifolia	10	12
,, media	10	15
Ruscus aculeatus (the butcher's broom)	1	2
,, racemosus (the Alexandrian laurel)	4	—
Spartium junceum (the Spanish broom)	8	10
Tamarix gallica	5	10
Ulex europæa (the furze)	4	5
,, ,, flore pleno	4	6
Viburnum Tinus (Laurestinus) ..	8	10
,, lucidum	4	—
,, variegatum	3	—
Yucca gloriosa	3	5
,, ,, foliis variegatis ..	4	—
,, superba	3	6
,, filamentosa	1	—
,, ,, foliis variegatis	1	—

Deciduous Shrubs.

	FEET.	
Aralia japonica	10 to	12
Buddlea globosa	10	—
,, Lindleyana	4	6
Calycanthus floridus	6	8
,, ovatus	4	6
,, rubracaulis	4	6
Ceanothus americanus	2	3

	FEET.	
Chinonanthus fragrans	6 to	10
,, grandiflorus	6	10
Cornus sanguinea (the common dog-wood)	10	—
,, alba	6	10
,, siberica	6	10
Coronilla Emerus	4	10
Daphne Mezereum	4	—
,, ,, flore pleno ..	4	—
,, autumnalis	4	—
Deutzia scabra	4	6
,, corymbosa	4	6
,, gracilis	2	—
This variety requires a sheltered warm place.		
Euonymus europæus	20	—
,, ,, fructu albo ..	13	—
,, nanus	2	—
Forsythia viridissima	3	4
Genista radiata	2	3
,, hispanica	1	—
,, tinctoria	1	3
,, ,, flore pleno.. ..	1	—
,, prostrata	6 in.	
Hibiscus syriacus foliis variegatis ..	5 ft.	
Also the double purple, white and red	3 to	—
Hydrangea arborescens	4	5
,, hortensis	3	—
,, japonica	3	—
Hypericum, all the varieties	3	5
Kerria japonica	3	5
,, ,, flore pleno	3	5
Leycesteria formosa	6	8
Ligustrum (the privet) all the varieties	6	10
Lonicera (the honeysuckle)	4	—
,, Xylosteum (the fly Honey-suckle).		
,, fragrantissima	4	—
,, albiflora	4	6
,, cærulea	3	5
Pæonia Moutan, all the varieties ..	4	5
Philadalphus coronarius (Syringa) ..	10	12
,, ,, flore pleno	1	10
,, variegatus	6	—
,, latifolius	8	—
,, grandiflorus	8	10
Potentilla fruticosa	2	4
,, glabra	2	—
Ribes speciosum	4	6
,, sanguineum flore pleno ..	4	8
,, atro-rubens	5	—
,, the whole species, from ..	2	6
Rubus laciniatus	4	10
,, fruticosus flore pleno ..	4	—
,, ,, flore pleno roseo	6	12
Spiræa corymbosa	4	5
,, salicifolia	4	—
,, arifolia	6	8
,, grandiflora	6	—
And the whole are beautiful, varying in height from	3	8
Syringa vulgaris (the common lilac)	10	20
,, ,, flore pleno		
,, alba	10	20
,, Charles X.	10	—
,, persica (Persian lilac) ..	4	6
,, rothomagensis	6	8
,, Siberian lilac	6	8

All are beautiful.

	FEET.	
Viburnum sterile (Guelder rose) ..	10 to	—
,, prunifolium	6	10
,, dentatum	4	6
Wiegelia rosea	5	6
,, amabilis	5	6

ARDI'SIA (nat. ord. Myrsin'eæ).

Stove shrubs, several of which will flourish and fruit in a moderately warm greenhouse. All require loam and peat; and they may be increased by cuttings, which root very freely in sand. *A. crenulata* is a very favourite variety. Its bright red berries, which last so long, render it invaluable in a conservatory.

ARRANGEMENT OF COLOUR.

The following observations are generally allowed to be correct by those who have made the harmony of colours their special study. They may be acted upon in gardening.

I. The complementary arrangement is superior to any other for harmony of contrast. To produce the best effect, the colours should be as nearly as possible of the same tone: white comes in best in the complementary arrangement of blue and orange, and worst in a combination of yellow and violet.

II. The simple colours,—red, yellow, and blue,—combined in pairs, go together better than one simple colour and one binary colour containing that simple one. For example :—Red and yellow harmonize better than red and orange; red and blue better than red and violet; yellow and red better than yellow and orange; yellow and blue better than yellow and green; blue and red better than blue and violet; and blue and yellow better than blue and green.

III. In an arrangement of one simple colour with a binary colour containing the simple one, the brighter the latter is, when compared with the former, the better the contrast; or, in other words, in arrangements of this sort, the tone or intensity of the simple colour ought to be lower than that of the binary colour. For example :—Red and violet contrast better than blue and violet; yellow and orange better than red and orange; and yellow and green better than blue and green.

IV. When two colours harmonize badly, they had better be separated by something white.

V. Black never produces a bad effect when combined with two bright colours. In such cases, indeed, it is often better than white, especially when separating the one colour from the other. For example,—Black produces a harmony of contrast with the following binary arrangements—viz., red and orange, red and yellow, orange and yellow, orange and green, yellow and green.

VI. Black associated with dark colours, such as blue and violet, or with bright colours with a deep tone, produces harmonies that often have a good effect. For example, an arrangement of black, blue, and violet is better than one of white, blue, violet, white, &c.; the latter being too violent.

VII. Black with two colours, one bright and the other dark, is not so good as when the two colours are both light; and in the first case, the brighter one of the colours, the more the effect produced. Thus, in the following arrangement, black is inferior to white:—Red and blue; red and violet; orange and blue; orange and violet; yellow and blue; green and blue; green and violet.

Lastly, with yellow and violet, if not inferior to white, black, at all events, produces but a middling effect.

VIII. Grey, with two luminous colours, though perhaps it does not produce a decidedly bad effect, makes the arrangement look flat, and is inferior to black or white. With red and orange, perhaps grey may be better than white; but it is inferior to it, as well as to black, when placed with red and green, red and yellow, orange and yellow, orange and green, or yellow and green; it is also inferior to white, with yellow and blue.

IX. Grey associated with dark colours, such as blue and violet, and with bright colours of a deep tone, does not produce so good an effect as black in the same cases. If the colours do not look well together, it is better to separate them.

X. Grey and two colours, one bright and the other dark, is better than white, if the latter produces a contrast of too deep a tone, and better than black, if the latter increases the proportion of dark colours too much. For example, grey is better than black with green and violet, green and blue, orange and violet.

XI. When two colours harmonize badly, they had better be separated by white, black, or grey; but, in so doing, attention must be paid to the tone of the colours, and to the proportion of light and dark colours. For example, as to the tone of the colours, the effect of white with red and orange is lessened in proportion as their tones are deepened. Black, on the contrary, does very well with the same colours at their normal tone; that is, when, without containing any black, they are as intense as possible. Lastly, grey is not so good as black with red and orange, nor does it produce so violent a contrast as white.

ARTICHOKES (GLOBE).

These are best propagated by offsets taken in March. The plants bear best the second or third year after planting; so that it is advisable to plant one or more rows every year, and remove the same quantity of old roots. The ground should be deeply worked and well manured: let the manure be incorporated with the soil, not laid in a mass at the bottom of each trench. It is better to trench the ground first, and fork the manure well into the surface-spit, which gives the plants a better chance of immediately profiting by it. The offsets may be dissevered with a knife, or slipped off and cut smooth afterwards, and planted with a dibber. Some plant in threes, a yard apart, and four feet from row to row; or they may be planted singly, two feet apart in the row, and four feet from row to row. They should be well watered, and the ground kept loose between.

ARUM.

This splendid plant, with its snow-white flower, its yellow tongue and arrow-shaped leaves, is not hardy with us; but it admits of an easy cultivation even where there is no greenhouse, and it is so ornamental in a room or hall, that it is well worth the little trouble which it requires. The Arum grows freely from offsets, which are very freely produced. The plants should be repotted every October, in rich, light mould, with a few drainers, the offsets having been carefully removed, and all the old soil well shaken from their roots. From this time till June, or earlier, if the plants have flowered and are off blooming, they should have abundance of water; but after this they must be kept quite dry, and may be put away in an outhouse till the following October, when the same treatment should be renewed. The Arum, in a growing state, requires so much moisture that it is best to keep the pot always standing in a deep saucer full of water. Under this culture, offsets may be brought into flower in their third year.

ASPAR'AGUS.

Preparation of the Land.—A deep, mellow, light loam, or sandy soil, is most suitable, but ordinary garden soil, if properly prepared, will yield fair crops. The ground should be well drained to a depth of four feet, and heavily manured, the surface being covered to a depth of at least three inches, with rich, well-decayed farm or stable-yard manure. If the soil is of a clayey or strong, tenacious nature, sharp sand, or finely-sifted ashes, may be added with advantage. Trench to a depth of two feet six inches, well intermixing the manure as the work proceeds. The bottom of the trench should be loosened a spade's depth still lower, if the subsoil is such as will retain moisture, or otherwise benefit the plants; but if it is gravel, it had better be left undisturbed. If the ground can be trenched in the autumn before planting, and ridged up roughly for the winter, levelling the ridges as early in spring as the ground may be fit to work, and then forking over the surface two or three times when in a dry state, the exposure to the weather which will thus be effected will be of great service to strong soils, and beneficial to any.

Time and Manner of Sowing.—As early in April as the ground can be found in fair working condition, sow in drills about an inch deep, scattering the seed very thinly and covering it evenly with the finest of the soil. The seed may be sown in drills fifteen inches apart, thinning out the plants so that they may stand four inches apart in the rows, to furnish plants for transplanting after one or two seasons' growth; or it may be sown at once where the crop is intended to stand. In the latter case the drills should be two feet six inches or three feet apart, or they may be made in beds five feet wide, with two-feet alleys between the beds, putting three drills in a bed; in either case the plants should be thinned out, so that they may stand about a foot asunder in the rows. Except on strong tenacious soils, which are easily injured by treading when gathering the crop in wet weather, we recommend sowing in consecutive lines. Where the land is clayey, the ground should be set out in beds, the soil dug out of the alleys to the depth of twelve or fifteen inches, and placed on the top of the beds; there will then be little danger from lack of surface-drainage. The Asparagus is very impatient of stagnant moisture about its crowns during the winter, and, on strong soils, trenches should be made of moderate size, say three inches deep and wide, and filled with sharp sand previous to sowing. The plants will probably not make as much progress in the first season as if they had been sown in the soil, but the roots will soon extend beyond the sand, and in after-years this will prevent water lodging about the crowns and rotting them.

Transplanting and after-Manage-

ment.—The plants, if sown with the intention of transplanting, after one or two seasons in the seed-lines, should be encouraged by an occasional soaking of manure-water during the growing season; and a liberal dressing of rich manure should be spread between the rows in winter. Transplant in April, when the ground is in good working order. If the ground has been properly prepared, set a line and take out a trench sufficiently wide and deep to allow of spreading the roots, and cover the crowns about two inches. On strong, heavy, imperfectly-drained soils, place sand about the roots and over the crowns, as recommended under the head of Sowing. The roots should be carefully taken up, avoiding all cutting or injury; and any that are decaying should be rejected. During the growing season keep the ground free from weeds, and the surface free and open by frequent hoeings; a soaking of manure-water may be given with advantage when the weather is droughty. Clear off the haum in autumn, when it will part from the crowns by a slight pull, and apply a dressing of well-decayed manure, which may be lightly forked in between the lines, at once or in spring. During the second and following growing seasons too much manure-water can hardly be given, and on light, sandy soils a sprinkling of salt applied two or three times in the course of the summer will be of great service, particularly where manure-water cannot be used freely. The plants should not be cut for use until they become strong and throw up fine grass, and cutting should not be continued very late in the season. The ground between the lines must be liberally manured every autumn.

Grayson's Covent Garden Giant Asparagus, per oz. 3*d.*; per lb. 2*s.*

ASPARAGUS (French Method).

The French practice with asparagus is to dig a trench five feet wide and the length of the bed, laying aside the best of the soil for surface-use. On the bottom of the trench is laid, first, six inches of rich stable manure; above it, eight inches of turf; again, six inches of well-rotted dung, and then eight inches of the reserved soil sifted; over this six inches of thoroughly decomposed manure, and six inches more of the soil thrown aside in making the trench, well mixed together by digging. The beds thus formed are five feet wide, with alleys between, two feet wide. The roots are planted in the beds in rows 18 inches apart, and 18 inches apart in the rows; a handful of fine mould is placed under each plant, over which the roots are carefully spread, the crown being an inch and a half below the surface; a spadeful of fine sand is now thrown over the crown, and the operation is completed. In order to procure an early supply of this delicious vegetable, they prepare a moderately warm hotbed, on which six inches of rich mould is laid, and a sufficient number of asparagus from an old bed planted. Over this they lay a few inches of the same soil, covering the whole with sufficient litter to keep out the frost, or by mats over the frame. The plants will soon start into growth. A little liquid manure applied occasionally will keep up a vigorous growth, and the plants, if properly managed, will be ready to cut by Christmas.

ASPARAGUS IN FRAMES.

Early Asparagus is forced in the following manner with the most satisfactory results. In an ordinary melon-pit, about the beginning of February, a quantity of stable dung is set to work, by turning and shaking, to sweeten and regulate the heat. By the middle of the month, as much of this is thrown into the pit as will fill it to within a foot of the glass. Two days afterwards, this is covered with a layer of three inches of mellow soil. On a mild day previous to this, a quantity of asparagus-roots should have been grubbed up from an old bed (these make the best plants for forcing), and placed ready. As soon as the fermenting material has arrived at a safe temperature—about 80°, these roots should be packed thickly together on the three inches of soil, and more soil thrown on them, just sufficient to cover them, without increasing the weight too suddenly or too much. This precaution is necessary, because the addition of ten inches of earth would cause a rapid sinking and proportionate rise in the temperature of the dung, to the injury of the roots. Four days after planting, sufficient earth should be put on to cover the crowns about six inches. In ten days the crowns will begin to appear.

ASPARAGUS-CUTTING.

Cutting Asparagus is an operation of some delicacy. It should be cut with a saw-edged knife, having a straight, narrow, tapering blade, about six or eight inches long, and an inch broad at the haft, rounding off at the point. When the shoots are fit to cut, the knife is to be slipped perpendicularly close to the shoot, cutting, or rather sawing, it off slantingly three or four inches below the surface, taking care not to touch any young shoot coming out of the same crown.

AS'TERS (nat. ord. Compos'itæ). Half-hardy Annuals.

This splendid class of plants is not only one of the most popular, but also one of the most effective of our garden favourites, producing in profusion flowers in which richness and variety of colour are combined with the most perfect and beautiful form. The Aster is indispensable in every garden or pleasure-ground where an autumnal display is desired. In our flower-beds and mixed borders it occupies a deservedly prominent position, whilst for grouping or ribboning it stands unrivalled.

The Aster may be divided into two sections—French and German. The French, as improved by Truffaut, has flat petals either reflexed or incurved; the former resembling the Chrysanthemum, whilst the latter, turning its petals towards the centre of the flower, forms, when well grown, a perfect ball, and is best described by its resemblance to the Pæony. The German varieties are quilled, and the most perfect flowers are surrounded by a circle of flat or guard petals, as in the Hollyhock. The flowers of these are particularly admired for the exquisite symmetry of their form. The dwarf bouquet varieties of this beautiful plant grow from six to nine inches high, and are particularly adapted for small beds, edgings, or for pot-culture; they often flower so profusely as entirely to hide their foliage. All the varieties delight in a deep, rich, light soil, and in hot, dry weather should be mulched with well-rotted manure, and frequently supplied with manure-water: this labour will be amply repaid by the increased size, beauty, and duration of the flowers. Seed from 4*d.* to 1*s.* per packet.

AUBER'GINE—EGG-PLANT (nat. ord. Solana'ceæ). Half-hardy Annuals.

Several varieties are eatable, and extensively cultivated in the South of Europe. As pot plants they are curious and interesting, being covered in autumn with beautiful egg-shaped fruit: the scarlet variety is a great novelty. In warm localities they succeed out of doors on a south border. Seed from 3*d.* to 6*d.* per packet.

AUGUST.

Aspect of the Month.—The eighth month of the Julian year received its name from Augustus Cæsar, as July commemorated that of the greater Julius. Less rain falls this month than in July, and the mean temperature is a little higher; the nights are certainly hotter. Mean temperature of August—61·28° at the surface, 61·80° at a foot, and 61·26° two feet below.

Flower-garden and Shrubberies.—The flower-garden will now be in its greatest beauty, and every means must be taken to keep turf, gravel, and edgings of all kinds in neat order; dead flowers should be picked off daily, and stray growth reduced within proper limits. Trailing and climbing plants should frequently be gone over to keep them neat and secure after high winds: for the same purpose examine hollyhocks, dahlias, and other tall-growing plants. After removing the dead flowers from roses, encourage the production of autumn blooms in perpetuals, by watering with liquid manure and mulching the surface of the ground. Continue the propagation of plants for next season: no time must be lost with the more delicate pelargoniums, in order to get them established before winter.

Many of our most beautiful flowering-plants may be propagated this month; among them may be classed crassulas, lantanas, hydrangeas, mesembryanthemums, &c., all of which should be struck early, to flower freely the following season. Petunias, verbenas, heliotropes, salvias, and lobelias may be taken in hand next, reserving calceolarias till the last, as they strike better during the cold weather of autumn than earlier in the season. Verbenas and calceolarias may be struck under hand-glasses, or in a cold frame. Geraniums, including the scarlet varieties, will strike freely on a south border inserted in sandy soil. Anagallis, maurandyas, and lophospermums, may be rooted in sandy soil, if placed in a cold frame, and shaded in bright sunny weather. Ten-weeks stocks, of various colours, should be sown before the middle of the month, and intermediate stocks to be kept in pots throughout the winter for spring-flowering; pot a quantity of Bromptons for the same purpose, planting others in a sheltered spot to take their chance through the winter.

Roll lawns well, and meet the rapid growth by frequent mowing. Gravel-walks will likewise require frequent rolling and surface-weeding, especially in shady places, or the application of salt-and-water, to eradicate the smaller weeds, mosses, &c., after which they should be well rolled to make the surface firm and even.

Plant out all recently-struck pinks, double wallflowers, and pansies, keeping a few of the latter in pots for protection during the winter. Now that the planting-out season may be considered over, attention should at once be directed towards furnishing a supply for another year. Be careful to provide a good stock of cinerarias.

Seeds sown in the beginning of August, and potted off into store pots when large enough, make good plants for spring purposes. Potting into store pots prepares them for separate potting. The process of stopping retards their bloom, and strengthens the flowers: where earlier bloom is required, a modified treatment is to be adopted. When the flowering season is over, remove the plants to a shaded place, preserving all the leaves, and watering slightly, guarding them from insects until August, when cuttings may be taken from the old roots. When these are separated from the plant, the roots may also be separated and potted out; every particle of the root being capable, under proper treatment, of propagating a plant: these old ones are the best for early flowering; they may be divided even up to October.

Geraniums may be propagated by thinning out the beds here and there, and inserting the cuttings in small beds on a border, putting a little silver sand in the holes made to receive them. Intermediate stocks should be sown early in the month, and ten-weeks stocks before the middle. All double-flowering perennials that have done flowering may be propagated by slips, and parting the roots towards the end of the month, taking up the whole plant, and dividing it into as many separate plants as there are roots with buds, eyes, or stems. Let every root be trimmed by cutting off the straggling parts; pick off all dead leaves, then re-plant them in some shady border, and give some water. *Pyramidal Saxifrage* should be propagated: the offsets rise from the sides of the plant, and may now be taken off and planted either in borders or pots.

Flower-borders, shrubberies, as well as grass and gravel walks, now require the most vigilant attention; the borders should be gone over with the hoe and rake; all weeds being raked off, and straggling shoots either removed, shortened, or tied down, and dead footstalks and flowers removed. In shrubberies prune off all exuberant branches, keeping up a dwarf and full foliage, and watering where required. Grass walks and lawns must be mown once a week or fortnight, according to growth. Keep the turf short, thick, and even, and choose dewy mornings for mowing.

Autumnal Bulbs, such as colchicums, narcissuses, Guernsey lilies, and amaryllis, may still be planted in borders, beds, or pots, in light sandy loam.

Florists' Flowers.—Carnations and *Picotees* should now be layered, but without shortening the grass. Where seed is required, pick off all decaying petals, to prevent damp injuring the pods. If not wanted for seed, cut the old plant down.

Dahlias require constant watering and attention in tying out lateral shoots, removing superfluous ones, and relaxing the ties. Stir the soil, but not deeply, and give special attention to seedlings, selecting those worth preserving, and throwing away worthless varieties. Attend to the training and thinning of the shoots of dahlias; place small inverted pots, with a little dry moss in them, on the top of stakes, for a trap for earwigs.

Hollyhocks require the same attention as to staking and selecting.

Pinks.—First-struck pipings may now be planted out, potting a quantity in order to fill up vacancies which may be caused from the ravages of the wireworm, &c. Make pansy-beds.

Clean and prepare tulip-beds, and arrange the plants in their drawers, discarding stained varieties, and adding new ones in their place.

Rose-Garden.— Perpetual - flowering roses in dry weather require copious supplies of water. If mildew appear, syringe the plants with soft water in the evening, and dust the affected parts with flour of sulphur. Towards the end of the month any roses budded last month may have their bandages removed, the place examined to see that nothing has interfered with the bud, and the bandage restored. Cuttings of Tea-scented, Noisette, China, Bourbon, and Hybrid perpetuals, may be struck in light sandy soil over a gentle hotbed. When rooted, pot off and replace the cuttings in the frames for a few days till the roots begin to move, when they may be removed and hardened off.

The Ayrshire, Boursault, Sempervirens, and other climbing roses, frequently send out very luxuriant shoots near the bottom of the stem. These, if not wanted to cover some weak part of the plant, should be removed. Roses standing in pots should never be crowded, but constantly watered and kept in a growing state.

Kitchen-Garden.—The kitchen-gardener who would have everything thrive and prosper, must exercise the greatest vigilance during this month. Apart from the necessity of cropping and removing such crops as have ceased to become profitable, his attention will be drawn towards the multitudes of garden pests, which exhibit their effects at this time of the year more than any other. Caterpillars should be looked for and destroyed. The ravages of these insects produce an effect at once unsightly and discreditable. Savoys and cabbages, riddled by caterpillars, are both unpleasant to the eye and suggestive of neglect. A free use of lime, scattered over the plants on dewy mornings, will, in a great measure, save them. The wireworm and other insects may be trapped by means of potatoes cut in half, and the cut sides laid downwards. It is a good plan to trench all the vacant ground at this time of the year; grubs and wireworm are then buried deep enough to destroy them. The effects of the club become apparent in hot, sunny days: cabbages, &c., hang down and turn blue, and are infested with aphis. This disease is one of the most vexatious with which the gardener has to deal. How far it may be prevented by the use of wood ashes, &c., is a matter of doubt. The causes of it may be traced, first, to an injudicious application of manure in small gardens that are already too manured; and secondly, an exhausted state of the soil, arising from the too unvaried use to which it is put. Plants that are subject to this disease are strong feeders, and exhaust the soil very much; it is, however, reasonable to suppose they leave food suitable for other plants. Instances are not rare of ground being left to weeds for several years, where, although cabbages clubbed badly before, they did not after the vacation.

Artichokes.—Cut these down as the heads are gathered, and fork the ground between,—they will come up again before winter.

Asparagus.—Keep the beds clear from weeds, especially where there are young plants. Unless seed is wanted, it is advisable to cut off most of the bearing heads, which would, if left, exhaust and weaken the roots in ripening seed: it is, however, as well to sow every year, and some seed may be left for this purpose.

Beans.—Pull up the haum of any that have done bearing: lay the stalks together, and they will soon rot, or dry them, and they will burn. Some may be cut in lengths, and dried for earwig-traps, to place among flowering plants.

Beans, Running, should be stopped after reaching the top of the sticks: they will set quicker than if left to grow as they please. Give plenty of water at the roots if necessary, but none over-head.

Beans, French.—A row or two should be left for seed. It is not advisable to leave any to ripen on bearing plants, as they cease to yield for the table while ripening seed.

Cabbages.—Sow early this month for a full crop of summer cabbage. Sow thinly on an open spot, that the plants may come up strong, and scatter lime on the ground to protect from birds and insects; dust also the young plants when up; get out a supply of early coleworts; they will most likely make small head in November.

Carrots.—Early sowings may be taken up and stowed away for use; but if the ground is not particularly wanted for other crops, it is quite as well to let them remain till required for use. A little seed may be sown early this month to stand the winter: plants will be useful in the spring, when the winter store is exhausted.

Cauliflowers should be sown two or three times this month: seed sown at the beginning, about the middle, and at the end of the month, will give a succession. Sow in the same way as cabbages. It will be necessary to give them the protection of frames or hand-lights during the winter; but the sowing may be in the open ground.

Celery.—This may be got out in any quantity. If young plants are used, and kept growing, they will stand the winter well, but must not be earthed-up till November: those put out in June may now be earthed-up for blanching. It is not advisable to earth-up too quickly, or too much at a time; but there is less danger of doing harm by it now than in cold or wet weather. As celery grows quickly at this time, three weeks will blanch it; but it should be quite moist at the roots before being banked up.

Endive.—Sow early this month for the last time this season; prick out the plants as soon as large enough: a good watering now and then, after planting, is all the attention they require. When endive is ready for blanching, use inverted flowerpots with the hole stopped; but by no means tuck the leaves into them: merely clap a 24-pot over the centre. This is the best way of blanching.

Leeks may still be transplanted; but the sooner the better, or they will not get any size before winter. Plant in deep drills two feet or so apart, and water freely; draw earth up to those in full growth. Liquid manure given occasionally will benefit them.

Lettuce.—The first week in this month sow cabbage-lettuce for winter use, and from that time onwards, both Cos and cabbage-lettuce may be sown to stand the winter for spring use; sow rather thin on an open spot, as it is desirable to have these plants as stout and strong as possible; they will stand the weather much better.

Onions will most likely be arriving at maturity, and had better be pulled up as soon as this is the case, and laid on their sides. Green thick-necked ones should be turned down at the collar, and used first. It is necessary to ripen onions thoroughly before storing them away. Potato-onions should be taken up as soon as the stalks have decayed. Garlic, shalots, &c., will most likely be fit to take up this month, and may be treated in the same way as onions; that is, ripened in the open air, and stored away in a dry airy shed, or left beyond the reach of frost. Sow Tripoli, globe, or Welsh hardy, to stand the winter, for planting out in spring, or for salading: a warm sunny border is the most suitable place for sowing them.

Parsnips.—Stir the ground well between, so that the rain may penetrate quickly. Destroy weeds, and keep the crops clean.

Peas.—Pull up as soon as all are gathered: it is not advisable to leave them a moment longer. The haum may be dried in the sun, and will be useful in winter for covering and protecting many things from frost. The sticks should be tied in bundles, and stowed away.

Potatoes.—Early crops will be ready for taking up; but they will take no harm if left in the ground till wanted. If the disease appears, remove the haum instantly from late crops; the tubers will not be so large, but small

and good are better than large and bad.

Radish may be sown any time this month. The Black Spanish should be sown early for winter use. This takes rather longer than other sorts to arrive at maturity, but it may be treated in a similar manner to the others, except giving them more room.

Spinach.—About the second week in this month, sow the main crop of winter spinach: where a good supply is wanted, it would be best to sow every week this month. The earliest sown will grow quickly, but the later will stand the winter best, and prove valuable in the spring: sow in drills a foot apart, or sow, thinly, broadcast, treading it in either case.

Tomatoes.—Attend to these as directed last month. To have them bear well in our short seasons, it is necessary to aid them as much as possible, by pinching out all superfluous growth, exposing the flowers well, and training as close to the wall as possible.

Turnips may be sown any time this month: they will not, probably, grow large, but will be useful in February and March for the early greens which they yield; they may be left thicker than the early sowings. Continue to use the hoe unsparingly among advancing crops: this is most important in the culture of the turnip.

The gathering and drying of herbs should not be left later than this month. The propagation of herbs, if not done before, should now be finished; they will do little good if disturbed after this.

Fruit-Garden.—Look well over wall-trees; for snails, wasps, and flies are as fond of choice fruit as man himself. Snails will attack peaches, nectarines, &c., before they are ripe, and spoil the appearance of every fruit they approach. Find out their haunts, and pick them out with the hand,—this is the best mode of dealing with them; they are, then, easily destroyed by throwing them into salt-and-water. Wasps and flies must be dealt with another way. An old-fashioned plan is to hang bottles, containing sugar and beer-dregs, about the trees, in order to entrap them : this, however, is objectionable on account of its unsightly appearance. Syringing with any solution or compound is also objectionable, for it might deteriorate the flavour of the fruit ; the best thing to be done is to cover the fruit with suitable netting.

Tack in all useful wood. This should not be omitted this month, and the trees will scarcely require it after : remove every shoot that is not really wanted ; every scrap of wood that is not useful may as well be removed now as at any other time. As it is not proper to drench the trees when the fruit is ripe, or ripening, any shoots infested with aphis should be cleaned with a brush.

Standard trees, where a regular thinning is not adopted, should be shaken occasionally, to bring down any fruit that may be blighted. These can be no good on the trees, and the sooner got rid of the better.

Towards the latter end of this month raspberries have generally ceased bearing, and the old canes may be cut down : as they will be of no further service, they should be got rid of. This will give the new canes a chance to strengthen. It will be advisable to fork the ground over, for this will destroy weeds, give a fresh appearance, and, besides, admit rain. All borders about fruit-trees should receive a forking about this time. If currant-trees are netted over so as to be impervious to birds, &c., the fruit will keep good till late in the year. Black currants will not keep on the trees, and had better be gathered as soon as ripe.

Strawberry-beds may be planted ; but it is advisable to get the planting done as soon as possible, if a crop of fruit is expected the following year. It is a good plan to lay the runners in pots, if it can be done ; but, generally, it will be found that strong runners have already rooted by this time, and may be removed with a trowel. Plenty of water is necessary at this time to newly-planted things.

July and August is generally the time for budding fruit-trees : if any stocks are to be budded with different or better sorts, it should be done without delay. Peaches, nectarines, and other wall-trees that are scanty, or unfurnished with wood in any part, may be improved considerably by the insertion of a few buds.

Plant-Culture under Glass.—Conservatory.—Flowers are now so abundant in the open ground that an equal profusion in the house is hardly required. Those plants that remain should now have plenty of room and a free circulation of air. Camellias and acacias now require copious watering, care being taken that they are not started into second growth. Sprinkle borders daily, and keep up a moist atmosphere. Train and prune all climbing plants in graceful festoons, avoiding stiff, formal tying-in, which prevents free flowering in plants of a climbing habit. All plants intended for early forcing should now be placed so that the wood may be thoroughly ripened : on this chiefly depends their future bloom. Strong-growing plants, such as diosmas, the epacridæ, chorozemas, which have been in shade to prolong their flowering, should now be placed in a bright sunny place. Late-flowering *Azaleas* require shifting and training, so that the foliage draws out properly before winter. On the slightest indication of thrips, fumigate. *Camellias* require shifting, if not done last month. When they have rooted in the new soil, give them plenty of air day and night, and syringe freely three or four times a week in fine weather. *Daphne indica*, both red and white, as well as *Magnolia fuscata*, are very suitable companions to the Camellia, requiring exactly similar treatment and temperature. *Pelargoniums* which have gone out of flower should be exposed in the open air to ripen their wood, preparatory to being cut down in September.

The principal plants that decorate

the conservatory at this season will be some of the more common,—fuchsias, scarlet geraniums, with achimenes; but where there is room, a considerable number of stove-plants and orchids may be safely introduced; and if a few palms, &c., be added, they will give the charm of tropical scenery to the house, and render it more attractive. Brugmansias, and other gross-feeding plants, may be liberally supplied with liquid manure to maintain them in vigorous health, and at the same time to prolong the period of their blooming.

The climbing plants will require going over at short intervals to keep the strong growers within limits: any shoots which have done blooming may be cut in: this will often induce a second flowering. Examine plants out of doors, and any appearing to suffer from rain, &c., should be at once removed under glass.

Some of the earlier-started orchids will have ripened their growth, and may now be removed to a cooler and drier house. As the plants approach maturity, more light may be allowed them, which will help to ripen the pseudo bulbs. Continue to plants yet growing the requisite amount of heat and moisture to carry on the present year's growth, but avoid unnecessary stimulants at this season, which might induce a fresh growth, and to many be injurious to the bloom of next season. Fires will be necessary during cold nights; but lessen the shade, except in bright weather. Plants suspended on blocks and baskets must be daily examined to see that the growing material is kept sufficiently moist, while, at the same time, stagnant damp must be avoided.

As stove-plants in the conservatory go out of bloom, remove them to a house of medium temperature to ripen, unless they are likely to bloom again, when they should be removed to the stove and be heated, so as to bring on successional flowers. Some of the free-growing stove-plants, as justicias, eranthemums, &c., may require a small shift, or the foliage is apt to become

sickly. Let all have air liberally to induce a stocky growth.

Towards the end of the month the conservatory and show-house will be gay with the different varieties of *Lilium lancifolium*, fuchsias, neriums, balsams, achimenes, &c., in addition to a selection from the stove and orchid-house. As light will now be decreasing, the conservatory climbers may be pruned back, selecting those shoots for the purpose that have nearly done flowering. This will allow more light to fall on the plants below, and will prove advantageous to the ripening of their wood. Vigorous-growing plants, whether out in the open border or in pots, must be liberally supplied with water. Amaryllids which have perfected their growth may be placed in a dry place to winter. There is one section of this tribe, however, with elongated bulbs, which will not bear to be kept entirely without water, even when in a state of rest. These latter, with *Pancratium speciosum* and *fragrans*, &c., should be placed on the back shelves of a vinery, or in any house of medium temperature, and supplied only with water sufficient to keep their foliage from dying off. Complete the potting of chrysanthemums, and plunge them in ashes or sawdust to save watering. Stake neatly, and stop mildew wherever it appears, by dusting a little flour of sulphur over the infected leaves. Water with liquid manure freely.

Achimenes, as they go out of bloom, may be placed in a frame to ripen their tubers, exposing them fully to the sun, but keeping them rather dry. If the different varieties of epiphyllum have made their growth under glass, they may be removed to a sunny spot out of doors. Pot off seedling cinerarias, Chinese primroses, and calceolarias from the seed-pans when the plants are large enough for the purpose.

Fruit under Glass. — *Vinery.* — Whenever the leaves in the early-house show indications of ripening, the sashes should be removed and the vines fully exposed: beyond stopping any late laterals, vines should not be touched until the leaves fall. While they are thus exposed, the sashes, rafters, &c., may be put into a state of repair, and painted, that everything may be in good order when the time for forcing again arrives. If the sashes are not wanted for repairing, they may be used for a variety of purposes, such as ripening grapes, peaches, &c., against walls, forwarding tomatoes, or to assist in the propagation of bedding-stuff. Young vines, planted during the past or present season, should be stopped when once they reach the top of the house. Where the rods are intended to carry fruit next season, and the vines are growing freely, six or eight joints beyond where it is intended to cut them back should be left, as a too close stopping might cause the principal eyes to break, and thus endanger next season's show of fruit. Lateral shoots may be kept stopped back pretty close, as the object will now be more to ripen the existing wood than to encourage fresh growth; besides looking over ripe grapes to remove decayed berries.

Fires, especially to houses containing Muscat grapes, should be made each evening, and during wet, dull days, that abundant ventilation may be kept on. Vines in pots, intended to fruit next season, must be closely watched to get the wood perfectly ripened. As they have now completed their growth, liquid manure may be given pretty freely to swell out the buds to carry next season's crop. The plants must be kept close to the glass, and thus exposed to the full influence of light: great care should be taken of the principal leaves as the wood assumes a brown hue. Lessen water by degrees, and allow (if practicable) a lower night temperature.

Pinery.—As soon as the house for next season's fruiting is ready, the plants should be transferred there at once: the most forward plants should be selected, and have their final shift before removal. When it is desirable to have fruit early, say in April or May, the fruiting-pot must not be too large, as it will be necessary to get the plants into rest early. As a rule, early fruiting pines should have their pots well filled with roots by the middle of September; and while growing, allow them all the light you can command, and a proportionate quantity of air. The best pines for very early forcing are the black Antigua common Queen, and the Providence: to assist them, a few Jamaicas may be started in October, as they take a couple of months longer to ripen. The plants for the summer crop may remain for a week or two, unless there are reasons for potting them immediately. They may have a larger shift than recommended for the above, and should be kept longer growing in the autumn.

As the plants are to ripen their fruit in the pots they are now placed in, the size will be regulated by the kind of pine grown, and in some measure by the size of the plant. For queens and pines of similar habit, pots of from twelve to fifteen inches diameter will be sufficiently large; while pots from fifteen to eighteen inches will be quite large enough for the largest Providences and Cayennes. We have recommended the largest-sized pots, supposing the plants are well grown and in vigorous health; but nothing but disappointment will follow placing pines in large pots, when the pots in which they are growing are not filled with roots sufficient to justify shifting. By far the easiest and cheapest way to grow pines, is to have them planted on a bed of soil furnished with bottom-heat, either by hot-water pipes, or by applying hot dung underneath; the soil being supported by brickwork and slates, or rough boards. The bottom-heat required will be from 85° to 95°, and the soil may be turfy loam and peat, with sand and leaf-mould, varying the latter as the loam is heavy or light. If the plants are growing in pots, they may be turned out into the beds whenever the bottom-heat is right for them, a few of the outside roots being liberated, and the soil carefully packed round the balls. The bed should be brought pretty close up to the glass: for as the plants will grow vigorously during the autumn, they will require an abundance of light, assisted by a liberal supply of air, to check vegetation and mature the fruit. In planting out, and growing in pots, always allow plenty of room between the plants, that the leaves may spread themselves in an horizontal direction, and thus expose their surface better to the light; it should likewise be a point that the light and air should reach the lower leaves, which can never be the case when they are crowded together. Directly the succession-plants are removed to the fruiting-house, the younger plants intended to succeed later next season, and suckers, should be re-shifted and plunged to occupy their places. After the suckers, &c. are potted and plunged, keep them rather close for a few days till they begin to grow, after which expose them to light and air.

Pines in fruit will require water often, as the pots at this time will be more full of roots than earlier in the season. Syringe well; warm, and close the house afterwards. The pines for winter fruiting will now be in bloom, and while this is the case be careful to keep the syringe from the flowers.

Peaches.—As the houses are cleared of fruit, the trees should be gone over, and the wood not required for fruit next season should be cut away: tie the remaining shoots neatly in, without injuring the leaves, removing the laterals as you proceed: this will allow more light and air to reach the shoots intended to carry next season's fruit, and assist towards maturing well-developed fruit-buds. To ripen the wood, close up the house early in the afternoon with a temperature of 85°. In the evening again open the house as much as the sashes will allow: fires should be made in wet weather, accompanied by air. The aim should be a dry and rather high temperature by day, and as cold a one by night as circumstances permit. Keep down red spider by well syringing every morning, with air on the house. When the leaves begin to change colour, and the wood becomes brown up to the point, the sashes may be removed. Fruit-trees in pots, intended for forcing, if the wood is well ripened, supposing they have been growing under glass, may be removed to the foot of a south wall, and in a few weeks to a shady cool place to rest.

Melons.—The late crop will be advancing; and as light is decreasing, keep the vines further apart, that the leaves, as they are formed, may not crowd each other. Attend carefully to bottom-heat, which must not be allowed to decline. Red spider must be kept in check, by now and then washing the interior walls with lime and sulphur. Water cautiously, but do not allow the growing plants to get dry, which would check them and induce the attacks of spider. To grow melons in perfection, they should progress regularly: hence the necessity for steady bottom-heat, and close watching as regards watering during the entire period of their growth.

Cucumbers, as the nights get colder, may have a slight covering, and the bottom-heat, if declining, should be renewed. Keep down mildew with sulphur: the covering by night, and the increased bottom-heat, will, however, help to keep this in check.

Hotbed and Frame-Cultivation.—In a large establishment there are many purposes to which frames can be applied at this time of the year, both for kitchen-garden, floral, and other departments. This is a good time to strike the winter stock of bedding-plants, for raising cinerarias, &c. Frames without hotbeds are very useful. Mignonette, Nemophila, and other annuals sown now in pots, and kept in cold frames, will flower in the winter. Horn carrots sown now in the manner described in January will be useful in the winter; that is, without making a new hotbed for them, but renewing the soil on an old one. Heat is unnecessary to raise them, but may be applied with advantage in the winter by means of fresh lining. Cauliflowers are often sown in a frame, to save them from birds, &c.; but it is necessary to uncover them as soon as the seed is up, to prevent a spindling growth. It is advisable to look forward to the winter, and sow everything in time to allow of making sufficient growth before it comes.

Cucumbers that have been carefully stopped, trained, and pegged down, will continue in bearing. If mildew appears, sprinkle the leaves, and dust with sulphur; but if very bad, it is better to start new plants. If started on new beds now, they will continue bearing until Christmas, and with care all the winter; but they should be on good 4-foot beds, so that linings may be applied; for, as the season wanes, and the weather becomes colder, heat must be provided accordingly. Give fruiting plants the benefit of gentle showers.

Melons.—The same directions apply to these now as formerly. Where the fruit is swelling, keep up a brisk heat and plenty of moisture; but where it is approaching ripeness, let the beds gradually dry off: also, where fruit is setting, maintain a moderately dry atmosphere, as it does not set well if kept damp at the time.

Sow corn salad in a cold frame for winter use. Also plant out parsley under glass for use in severe weather.

Mushroom-beds may now be made and spawned for a winter supply.

AURIC'ULAS (nat. ord. Primula'ceæ).

Florists' flowers of great beauty, well deserving of cultivation. They may be propagated by offsets at any time during autumn, but the earlier the better. New auricula borders may be made in October, and old ones should then be carefully gone over and renovated. Let it be remembered that the Auricula delights in shade, and will not bear excessive moisture. In planting offsets, be careful that the soil is well pressed round the roots. In this respect the young plants will require attention for some time. The more delicate sorts of auriculas will not flourish so well as border plants; but the harder varieties — the common purple, yellow, and green—form very effective edgings to beds, and even when out of bloom they have a pleasing appearance from the richness of their foliage. Of course offsets will only perpetuate the same varieties. New sorts are to be obtained from seed, which must be raised in a gentle heat.

Fine seed, which may be relied upon, may be had from Messrs. Barr and Sudgen, as under :—

Auricula, from finest stage flowers, various colours, half-hardy perennial, ½ ft., 1*s.* per packet.

Auricula, from finest mixed border varieties, hardy perennial, ½ ft., 6*d.* per packet.

AUSTRIAN BRIARS.

Austrian Briars, and other yellow roses, are difficult to flower, and require careful management. The old double yellow is remarkably capricious, and the Cloth of Gold, or Chromatella rose, in which rose-growers expected to find an unrivalled yellow, blooms in perfection only in very few places. "The general direction given," says Mr. Saul, of the Durdham Downs Nursery, Bristol, "is to grow it in a poor soil, as it is a strong grower. Now, this I consider very questionable advice. It belongs to the group of roses called Noisettes, many varieties of which have been crossed and raised from very dissimilar groups. The large section of tea-scented Noisettes will be found to differ most materially from the original Noisettes, from their affinity to the tea-scented, from which they have been raised. To this section belong the Cloth of Gold, Solfaterre, Clara Wendel, Lamarque, Triomphe de la Duchère, and many other fine roses; Solfaterre being very little inferior to the Cloth of Gold, both being raised from the same parent. The whole section requires peculiar treatment, approaching in some degree to what we give to the strong-growing tea-scented kinds.

"Under the starving system," he continues to add, "I have seen the Cloth of Gold so semi-double, small, and worthless, that, without positively knowing it, I should have doubted its identity. It is a shy bloomer under this system, covering a considerable space of wall, and standing year after year without producing a solitary bloom. I have seen it producing magnificent blooms from buds of the previous season if budded on strong stocks, as the Celine and Manetti rose. These buds, after having been headed back the first season, when fifteen to eighteen inches long, should have the leading points pinched out, when the laterals will generally bloom abundantly in the autumn. On the dogrose stem, growing standard and half-standard high, I have bloomed it freely in the same way; not that I recommend it for a standard, for it is unsuited for the purpose; but should any one wish to try it in that way, he should protect the head from extreme cold in winter, pruning hard in spring, and applying liquid manure liberally in spring and summer, stopping all shoots at fifteen or eighteen inches, to induce the lateral shoots to bloom."

AUTUMN FLOWERS.

In addition to the ordinary bedding plants—geraniums, verbenas, &c.—a good display of flowers in autumn requires a free use of autumnal roses, hollyhocks, dahlias, *Lilium lancifolum*, delphiniums, phloxes, foxgloves, the hardy bamboo, the holy thistle, pampas grass, *Arundo Donax*, tritoma, yucca; and for foliage, sundry kinds of ferns.

AYRSHIRE ROSE.

The rapidity with which this rose covers a wall or pillar, added to its intrinsic beauty, renders it invaluable to the gardener. Where its growth is encouraged, it climbs to the summit of the tallest trees, from which its long graceful shoots hang in festoons. The Ayrshire seems to have been first grown in the garden of the Earl of Loudon, at Loudon Castle, Ayrshire. It soon found its way into the nurseries in Scotland, whence, in 1811, it was transplanted to London by Mr. Ronalds, of Brentford. It was at first considered a variety of *R. arvensis*, afterwards of the evergreen rose, *R. sempervirens*. It differs in many respects from both; its long slender branches grow so rapidly as to throw out shoots thirty feet long in one season. *R. arvensis* never grows with this rapidity, and its branches are stronger and thicker. The evergreen rose far less resembles the Ayrshire in these properties.

There is more than one tradition connected with the introduction of this rose: that which is most likely to be authentic is supported by Mr. Reilly, who states, in his monograph in the *Edinburgh Philosophical Magazine*, that the seeds from whence it was obtained were part of a packet received from Canada, from which several plants were produced. Another account traces it to a Mr. Power, from Yorkshire, who brought the plant from some gentleman's garden in that county. Whatever truth there may be in these statements, it is pretty certain that no rose having the slightest resemblance to the Ayrshire has since been discovered on the American continent. It also appears that at different periods, two very distinct varieties have been grown in nurseries under the same name; one being descended from *R. arvensis*, and the other from the real Ayrshire, with very long slender branches.

The Ayrshire is the hardiest of climbing roses, and its cultivation and management is very simple. Layers of its long pendulous shoots root readily, and it strikes easily from cuttings; it will grow rapidly where other roses will scarcely exist, and when placed in good rich soil, its growth is so rapid that a large space is covered by it in

Azalea.

the second season of planting. It forms an admirable weeping rose when trained on wires. It is useful for trellis, verandah, or alcove, as well as in rough places of the park or shrubbery. Its luxuriant growth soon turns a rough and dreary waste into a flowery bank.

Like the other roses, the Ayrshire has yielded many hybrid varieties :—

Ayrshire Queen,—dark purple-crimson.
Bennett's Seedling. —pure white; forms a beautiful pendulous tree as a half-standard.
Dundee Rambler,—white, edged with pink; well adapted for a half-standard for the lawn.
Ruga,—pale flesh colour; very fragrant; a hybrid between Ayrshire and a tea-scented rose.
Splendens,—creamy white, approaching flesh-colour when full; crimson in the bud; large, double, and globular; one of the finest pendulous roses.
Queen of the Belgians,—creamy white: cupped, large and double; very sweet-scented.
Alice Grey,—creamy salmon-blush.
Countess Lieven,—creamy white; cupped and double; of medium size.

AZA'LEA (nat. ord. Rhodora'ceæ).

Beautiful flowering plants, natives of North America, Turkey, and China. The azaleas common in our gardens are deciduous shrubs, varying in height from 2 ft. to 6 ft. The loftiest of them is the *arborescens*, which will grow from 10 ft. to 15 ft. in height. With azaleas, as with rhododendrons, the best garden varieties are hybrids. The following are among the choicest named sorts :—

Ambrosia,—red, orange blotch.
Aurantia major,—orange-scarlet.
Beauty of Flanders,—fawn and pink, orange blotch.
Buckii,—fine scarlet.
Coccinea major,—fine scarlet.
Emperor of Russia,—pink, fawn blotch.
Honneur de la Belgique,—bright orange.
Julius Cæsar,—dark crimson.
Louis Bonaparte,—fawn and yellow.
Minerva,—salmon.
Nudiflora colorata,—bright pink.
Pontica,—large, yellow, very showy.
Prince of Orange,—fine orange.
Rosea rotundifolia,—rosy buff, yellow blotch.

For conservatory decoration the Chinese and Indian azaleas are most important. These plants require a similar growing season, after flowering, to the Camellia; and until the shoots are sufficiently numerous, or the plants as large as desired, they can be grown on throughout the entire year, and stopped four or five times during that period. This *pushing* treatment will, however, sacrifice the blossom; but if the plants are started early, they can be stopped twice, and yet the terminal buds be sufficiently matured in the autumn to develop flower-buds. After the growth is made, the plants should be gradually hardened off, and be placed during September full in the sun's rays out of doors, to thoroughly ripen their wood. Two parts of peat, two of loam, a sprinkling of sand, and one-sixth part of charcoal that has been steeped in manure-water suits them well. While growing, they will also bear watering with clear weak manure-water every time that they become dry. Before housing them for the winter, examine the plants, and dip them into a tubful of equal parts soot-water, made by throwing half a bushel of soot in soap-suds, and tobacco-water. Repeat this dose three times, and every thrip will either take itself off or die. Indian azaleas bear forcing well, and by inducing an early habit by the aid of the forcing-pit, the luxury of their beauty may be enjoyed in conservatory or sitting-room for six or eight months of the year.

There is an immense variety. The following azaleas, nice plants of which can be bought from 18*s*. to 42*s*. a dozen, according to size, are perhaps as good as any :—

Admiration, Alba, Alba magna, Alba striata, Albertii, Amœna lateritii, Ardens, Beauty of Europe, Beauty of Reigate, Blondin, Broughtonii, Chelsonii, Coronata, Criterion, Danielsiana, Distinction, Duc de Nassau, Duke of Devonshire, Empress Eugénie, Exquisita, Exquisita pallida, Fulgens, Gem, Gladstonesii, Gladstonesii excelsa, Gladstonesii formosa, Glory of Sunning Hill, Grande Duchesse Hélène, Formosa variegata, ditto alba cincta, ditto alba suprema, ditto elegans, Magnet, Mars, Optima, Petuniæflora, Prince Albert,

Queen of Whites, Queen Victoria, Leopold, Rosea punctata, Rosy Circle, Smithii coccinea, Striata formosa, the Bride, and Triumphans.

BABIA'NA (nat. ord. Irida'ceæ). Half-hardy Bulbs.

Dwarf, free-flowering Cape bulbs of great beauty, succeeding best in a sandy, peaty soil, and sheltered sunny situation.

Babiana villosa,—delicate violet, 1 ft.
" " fine mixed, various colours, 1 ft.

BALM (nat. ord. Labia'tæ). Hardy Annuals.

Sweet-scented plants, with ornamental foliage, very effective in mixed borders, and succeeding in any common garden soil.

Balm, Moldavian (Dracocephalum Moldavicum),—blue, 2 ft., from Moldavia.
Ditto,—white, 2 ft.

BALSAM (nat. ord. Balsamina'ceæ). Half-hardy Annuals.

Magnificent plants either for conservatory or out-door decoration, producing gorgeous masses of brilliant flowers. When grown in pots, and large specimens are desired, they should be shifted into 10 or 12-inch pots, using the richest compost at command, and the pots plunged in spent hops or tan, and liberally supplied with manure-water; when used for out-door decoration, the soil should be rich, the plants supported with neat stakes, and liberally supplied with manure-water.

Balsam, mixed, saved from all the most choice double varieties, including Webb's, Smith's, and Glenny's.
Balsam,—aurora-coloured, striking and very beautiful, 2 ft.
Balsam,—camellia-flowered, ten magnificent double varieties:—pink spotted, lilac spotted, purple spotted, scarlet spotted, rose spotted, rose spotted white, fine bronze spotted, crimson spotted, bright pink spotted white, beautiful crimson spotted white. Each colour separate, or the collection from Messrs. Barr and Sugden.

BANK'SIA ROSE.

The flowers of this elegant rose are produced in small umbels, each of three, four, and up to twelve flowers, at the extremities of small lateral shoots, branches of the preceding year's growth. The peduncles or stalks are slender and smooth, and about an inch and a half long, so that the flowers have a drooping habit when fully expanded. The scent of the flower is agreeably fragrant, not unlike to that of the sweet violet. This delicate rose was imported from China in 1807, and was named in compliment to Lady Banks. It was long treated as a greenhouse plant; but in 1813 two plants were turned out into the open ground at Spring Grove. In two years, although one of them died, and was replaced, they had covered both walls against which they were planted. In 1818 and 1819 these plants had covered forty feet of wall, each shoot producing at its extremity an umbel of flowers, which began to open in April, and the whole wall was covered with blossoms until the middle of June. This vigorous growth and bloom was produced by planting the rose in a rich sandy loam, and against a wall with a south or west aspect, nailing its shoots close to the wall; and when the wall was completely covered to the extent proposed, cutting away all the strong shoots as they appeared, leaving only those intended to produce flowers in the following spring. From August to February the only care required is to nail in all young shoots, only removing those that are superabundant.

BASKETS FOR WINDOWS.

A very important feature in window-gardening is the introduction of suspended baskets, usually made of wire, for the purpose of displaying to advantage the beautiful habit of trailing plants. These should be potted in ordinary flowerpots, and surrounded with moss in the basket, the latter being made to hook on to a staple in the ceiling, so that it may be taken away when the plant requires water. One of the most suitable plants for the purpose is *Saxifraga sarmentosa*, which does well under ordinary treatment; it is of variegated foliage and highly ornamental. Another is *Disandra prostrata*, with bright yellow flowers, and pretty foliage like ground ivy. Both these will trail eighteen inches or more from the basket in very graceful festoons.

Wire baskets, of ornamental patterns, to fit the window-sills, are planted, some with ferns and lycopods, and others with trailing plants. These baskets require lining with moss to make them hold the soil; the moss ought to be partially dried, but damped again before using. Some are made of wood, ornamented outside; and some with pieces of fir cones tacked over them, which gives to them a neat and rustic appearance. Others, again, are ornamented with bark, or different-coloured pieces of wood. Terra-cotta vases, surrounded with wires for suspension, are also in use for the same purpose. When the baskets are of wood, they shonld be lined with zinc: which makes them more durable; for wood, as it decays, is sure to breed fungus, which is injurious to plants.

In planting a basket, if it is to be filled with ordinary soft-wooded flowering plants, that is geraniums, verbenas, petunias, &c., the soil ought to be two-thirds loam to one of very rotten dung or leaf-mould, and a little sand; if planted with ferns or hard-wooded plants, as *Myoporum parviflorum*, *Monochæton ensiferum*, *Pultenæas*, and the like, the soil should be one half turfy loam and one half peat, using rather more sand than for the freer-growing plants.

If the baskets are made of wire and lined with moss, they are sufficiently drained; if of wood, there should be one or more holes in each to let out surplus moisture. In filling the baskets, put some rough lumpy soil at the bottom. This should lie hollow, so that surplus water may readily find an exit. The soil should be laid in roughly, with some broken pieces of potsherd mixed with it, in which way it will keep sweet for years.

The best plants for suspending in baskets are fuchsias of a pendulous habit, as Nil desperandum, the Duchess of Lancaster, a splendid white variety, and the Princess of Prussia, a neat-growing plant, very showy, the corolla of the flower being white, and the calyx and tube red.

Next to fuchsias, are ivy-leaved geraniums, petunias, and verbenas, which are of rich and varied colours. *Saxifraga sarmentosa*, of variegated foliage and pretty trailing habit; *Disandra prostrata*, with pretty yellow musk-like flowers. The common musk is also a very suitable plant: if a bit is planted in the centre, or some small pieces pricked about the surface, it will soon spread out and hang down the sides. The common moneywort (*Lysimachia nummularia*) does well and is effective; also the trailing snapdragon (*Linaria cymbalaria*), which will soon cover a basket and look very pretty.

Among hard-wooded plants, suitable for suspended baskets may be reckoned *Myoporum parviflorum*, bearing small white flowers in autumn, winter, and spring; *Pultenæa subumbellata*, a neat spreading plant, flowering in spring. There are also one or two acacias, as *A. rotundifolia* and *A. ovata*, which are of a pendulous habit. *Monochæton ensiferum* is a beautiful winter-flowering plant, but will require tying down at first, and training neatly over the basket. In planting the hard-wooded plants, it should be remembered that though it may be that the softer plants are more easy to cultivate, and thus safer to begin with, these are more permanent, and do not so soon outgrow their room. Of a like permanency are ferns, which require much the same soil as the last, that is, equal parts of peat, loam, and sand, having some broken crockery mixed with it. One of the best ferns for baskets is the common polypody, or *Polypodium vulgare:* this may be planted in nearly all moss, with a small portion of soil. Another excellent fern, and, indeed, one of the handsomest, is *Asplenium flaccidum.* Let this fern be placed in the centre of the basket: it will require nothing more, but will show over the sides and look exceedingly beautiful, being of a bright lively green, and one of the best and handsomest ferns in cultivation. *Pteris serrulata* and *P. rotundifolia* are also good ferns for baskets, and easily grown.

There are also several sorts of British ferns which may be grown in this way, particularly the true British Maidenhair (*Adiantum Capillus Veneris*), which, spreading at the roots, will soon cover the surface of the basket. Next to this we should place *Asplenium lanceolatum*, then *A. marinum.* Other kinds might do in the same way, but we would not recommend those who are not well skilled in fern-culture to grow more than three or four at first.

BASKET-BEDS IN FLOWER-GARDENS.

Basket-beds, especially upon lawns, form a very effective garden ornament. They are constructed with a raised base of wood, iron, brick, stone, or wicker-work, covered with ivy or other creeping plant, and generally having one or two rims bent over at a certain elevation above the bed, to convey the idea of a basket. Of course, the rims or handles are also enwreathed with climbing plants, and the whole have often a most fascinating and graceful appearance. Where they have two handles, the basket might be furnished with four distinct colours,—thus: orange, blue, scarlet, white, dividing the basket transversely.

BEANS.

Beans, like peas, can be sown in October, where the soil is light, well drained, and well sheltered; where the ground is heavy, they may be raised in a pit or frame by sowing three in a 4-inch pot, and planted out in March; but if the soil is cold, and no conveniences are at hand for starting in pots, they may be sown in the following manner:—Let the ground be laid in ridges 3 feet wide, and 15 or 16 inches high, ranging east and west; on the south side of each ridge draw a drill halfway between the top and bottom, in which sow the beans about 3 inches apart: by this means they will be above the wet, catch every ray of sunshine, and will be stronger than if raised under glass and planted out. Peas may be managed in the same way. When about 10 inches high, level the top of each ridge to the row of beans behind it: they will not require earthing up again. If sown in October, a succession may be sown in January, in the same manner; and so on once a month till June: they do not bear well if sown after that. Those sown on level ground should have some earth drawn up to the roots when three or four inches high: this induces them to emit fresh roots. They are sown in rows about 4 feet apart, which leaves room for a row of brocoli, spinach, or lettuce between; but those who are not limited as to space had better allow 5 or 6 feet from row to row. On light soils the usual method is to stretch a line along where they have to be sown, and dib holes 4 inches deep, planting a row each side of the line, 4 inches apart, zigzag fashion; but in wet soils it is better to drill them in, laying boards along the row to stand on, so as to avoid clodding the ground by treading on it. The sort usually grown for first crop is the early mazagan; but the early long-pod is equally early and prolific, and larger; so is the prolific long-pod, for main crop. The monarch long-pod is also very good. The green, and the hang-down long-pods are excellent beans. The royal dwarf is a good bearer. Whatever sort is grown, the culture is the same; but as beans are not a favourite vegetable with many persons, the young gardener should consider well how much ground can be devoted to them without encroaching upon the space required for more important crops. A crop which is not required involves a loss of time, space, and nourishment withdrawn from the soil.

BEDDING PLANTS.

Plants commonly known under the name of bedding plants consist of the common scarlet and other geraniums, verbenas, petunias, calceolarias, lobelias, and others; indeed all sorts of trailers and creepers used for covering beds in summer and autumn are so named. Most of these latter require pegging down; and in wet seasons, when the plants are apt to run too much to leaf, the lower extremities of the shoots may be slightly bruised, which will check their growth and promote flowering. Beds for all the ordinary bedding plants should be well drained, and the soil light and rich.

To grow bedding plants in perfection, the beds should have a dressing of manure annually, or a heavier application every second year. It would be almost as reasonable to attempt to grow two crops of cabbages in succession, without enriching the soil, as two crops of bedding plants. Many of them exhaust the soil more than any crop whatever; and to grow them rapidly, and in perfection, the beds must be liberally manured.

BEDS.

Divisions of a flower-garden formed in different-shaped figures. The following are some of the most pleasing varieties:—

Basket-beds of Ivy on grass-plots: these have a pretty appearance, and may be made round or oval, according to fancy. A frame of wicker-work should be made, the shape of the bed, about one foot or $1\frac{1}{2}$ foot high, around which, on the outside, should be planted, quite thick, either the large Russian, or the small-leaved and variegated ivy. In a year or two, with little care and attention, the wicker-work will be quite covered, when the ivy must be kept well cut in, and the earth in the basket may be raised or not at pleasure. With a little trouble, the ivy may be made to trail over wands, and form a handle to the basket.

Cross-shaped Beds.—The various sorts of crosses also form very ornamental beds, and have this advantage over fanciful figures, that they may easily be designated by their particular names. Nothing is more brilliant than a Maltese-cross bed, filled in each separate compartment with different shades of verbenas, or in the opposite compartments with the small dark blue lobelia and *Gazania splendens.* The St. Andrew's cross also forms a nice bed, and so do the different forms of upright crosses, when the stem and the transverse are filled with flowers of such shades and colour as contrast well with each other.

Leaf-shaped Beds.— Some of the prettiest beds for lawns may be made by cutting them out into the natural form of the leaves of trees, shrubs, and plants. The form of the common ivy-leaf makes a very pretty bed, so does the heart-shaped ivy; also the oak, the maple-leaf, the horse-shoe geranium, and an endless variety of others. Beds so formed have this advantage, that they can be called by the name of the different trees, shrubs, and plants from which they have been taken.

Oak and Holly Beds.—Acorns sown very thick round a bed in a drill about two or three inches wide, in the course of a year or two form a very pretty edging; and, owing to the thickness with which they stand, with an occasional clipping, the small oaks may be kept four or five inches high, and in this manner have a very good effect. Hollies also may be used in the same way; but in this case it is better to raise the plants on a seed-bed, and transplant them to the bed for which they are required as an edging, when about two or three inches high. They may be kept dwarf by cutting, and will not become too large for their position for some years.

Tile-beds for Grass-plots form very pretty and very ornamental objects made on grass borders, or on lawns of kitchen or mixed gardens. The tiles, or pipes, as they are called in some parts of the country, should be of bright red clay, twelve inches long and about three inches in diameter, and all carefully formed in the same mould. These should be placed upright in a circle, or any other figure, buried, according to taste, about four to six inches in the ground ; the earth and the beds being raised to the level of the outstanding part of the tiles. A very effective centre bed can be made with these tiles in three tiers, the edges of each tier being built in scallops, and a border left about one and a half or two feet in diameter. These three borders have a beautiful effect when filled with different plants. Take, for instance, *Calceolaria aurea floribunda* for the top department ; Tom Thumb's, or Frogmore's, for the middle border ; and Mangle's variegated geranium for the lower. These beds have an agreeable appearance even in winter when cleared, on account of the contrast between the bright red tiles and the grass ; and in spring they may be made very gay with hyacinths, crocuses, and other bulbs.

Pincushion Beds.—So named from having plants of different coloured flowers and different habits dotted on all over them. The old *Verbena venosa* dotted among Mangle's geranium forms a pretty pincushion bed. Other pincushion beds may be formed by mixing plant for plant, of Dandy geranium and *Lobelia speciosa*, and Lady Plymouth with Purple King verbena, or the old scarlet *Verbena Melindres*. The Variegated Alyssum or Cerastium, mixed with Lobelia, also makes a soft and chaste pincushion bed. Golden Chain geranium, dotted among white verbenas and edged with *Lobelia speciosa*, is also beautiful. Mrs. Pollock and Bijou, alternate on a ground of Lobelia or Purple King verbena, have a rich effect.

Tent Beds.—These are formed by the aid of chains, flexible wires, or ropes. Drive a tall stake of the desired height, say 10 feet high, in the centre; describe a circle with a radius of, say 8 feet. Insert six or eight stakes at equal distances on this line, say 6 feet high ; join the centre stake to each side one with a chain or wire, and the frame of a tent bed is formed.

BEET.

There are two or three sorts of beet for garden cultivation—one known as the Perpetual Spinach beet, the leaves of which may be gathered throughout the summer and used as spinach : another, called Seakale beet, the midrib of the leaf of which is from two to three inches broad, very white and delicate in flavour, and used as a substitute for seakale. The edible-rooted beet is, however, the most useful variety. It may be cultivated in the following manner :—

Preparation of the Soil.—Select for this crop deep and rich, yet rather light and loamy soil, which has been well manured during the previous season. If this cannot be done, the ground should be trenched two feet deep, and ridged up in autumn. If it is deemed necessary to apply manure, a sprinkling of guano after the plants are up would be preferable to farm-yard manure, which often causes the roots to grow rough and forked.

Time and Manner of Sowing.—For the first supply sow a small quantity early in April, and the main crop the first week in May; but where small roots are desired, sow as late as the middle of June. Sow in drills about one inch deep, and from 15 to 18 inches apart, covering with friable soil. If possible, select a dry day when the ground is in good working order for putting in the seed.

Cultivation and after-Management.—Thin out the plants so that they may be from six to nine inches apart in the rows. Keep the ground free from weeds, and open by frequently stirring the surface. By the end of October the roots will have attained their full size, and they should then be taken up and stored in soil not over dry. In an airy cellar or shed they will keep perfectly well until spring; but when drying winds occur, they should be transferred from the latter into a damp, cool cellar. In pulling and cleaning, be careful not to wound the roots, or cut off any large fibres, as this would cause bleeding, which greatly injures the quality and tends to induce decay; neither should the leaves be cut off too close to the crown. In stacking, place the crowns outwards.

Covent Garden,—extra fine, medium-sized, beautifully-shaped roots, of a rich deep blood-red colour; boils tender, and is of superior flavour.
Carter's St. Osyth's,—medium size, good shape, short top, rich deep blood-red colour; fine flavour.
Cattell's,—a useful sort.
Henderson's Pineapple,—compact short-topped variety, roots medium-sized, and of a fine deep crimson; boils tender, and is of very superior flavour.
White's Black,—large root, almost black.

BEGO'NIA (nat. ord. Begonia'ceæ).

There are no plants more worthy of admission into a conservatory than begonias, and the facility with which they may be cultivated is equal to their beauty. All they require is a good rich loamy soil, mixed with a little sand, and a little heat to start them. Either hotbed or stove answers every purpose, provided there is a conservatory or greenhouse in which they can be flowered; the chief requirements being heat, moisture, and shade.

There is a delicious fragrance about some of the species, which particularly recommends them for cultivation; others are recommended by their richly-variegated foliage and graceful habit, and they all hybridize with great facility. The following are a few choice sorts selected from more than 350 species known to botanists:—

B. fuchsioides,—remarkable for its graceful habit.
B. odorata,—remarkable for the fragrant odour, from which it derives its name.
B. nitida,—an almost perpetual bloomer, one plant having had three or four cymes of flowers always open for three years.
B. manicata,—produces a large mass of flowers at one time in the early spring.
B. octopetala,—a tuberous-rooted winter-flowering species, with large pure white blossoms.
B. splendida,—grown for its crimson velvety young leaves, which lose their beauty, however, as the plant approaches maturity.
B. splendida argentea,—equally beautiful; a pink tinge shining through the silvery hue of the leaves.
B. Griffithii, or picta,—richly variegated, with colours shading beautifully into each other.
B. xanthia Reichenheimii,—in which green bands follow the principal veins, the spaces between being pure white.
B. xanthia lazula,—having copper-coloured leaves, shining with a fine metallic lustre.
B. xanthia pectafolia,—the copper-coloured leaves relieved with large distinct white blotches.
B. Queen Victoria,—a hybrid raised in Belgium; the leaf milky-white, except the margin of green dots, and a few central dots.
B. argentea, the upper surface of the leaf of a pure delicate white.
B. amabilis,—the bright banded leaves very glossy and shining.

Many other begonias, both distinct species and hybrid varieties, are in cultivation, nearly approaching these in beauty; but none will be found to exceed them.

BELLADON'NA LILY.

An amaryllis, the flower white, flushed with rose-purple, very handsome. The bulbs may be purchased at 5*s*. per dozen.

BENTHA'MIA (nat. ord. Corna'ceæ).

An ornamental profuse-flowering half-hardy shrub; the flowers succeeded by reddish-yellow, strawberry-like fruit, which is eatable: succeeds against a south wall in any good soil.

Benthamia fragifera,—large cream-coloured flowers, 10 ft., from the East Indies.

BER'BERIS (nat. ord. Berberida'-ceæ). Hardy Shrubs.

Highly ornamental free-flowering shrubs; covered in spring with a profusion of rich yellow flowers, and in autumn with fruit of a very attractive character. The common Berberis is a most elegant plant when trained to a single stem and then allowed to expand its head freely on all sides. So treated, the branches become drooping, and have a fine effect every spring, when they are covered with their rich yellow blossoms, and in autumn from their long red bunches of fruit, which rival the fuchsias. The following varieties are all hardy, and may be grown from seed—to be had from Messrs. Barr and Sudgen, from 6*d.* to 1*s.* 6*d.* per packet.

Berberis Bealii,—yellow, very handsome, 4 ft.
,, crassifolia,—yellow, 3 ft.
,, dealbata,—yellow, evergreen with whitish foliage. 5 ft., from Mexico.
Berberis diversifolia,—yellow, foliage distinct, 3 ft., from Monte Video.
Berberis Fortunii,—yellow, evergreen, very handsome, 5 ft., from China.
Berberis heterophylla,—yellow, 4 ft., from the Straits of Magellan.
Berberis intermedia,—yellow, with beautiful foliage.
Berberis Japonica,—yellow, handsome foliage.
,, Knightii,—yellow, a superb species.
,, Leschenaultii, — yellow, handsome, 5 ft., from China.
Berberis Nepalensis,—yellow, beautiful foliage, 3 ft., from Nepal.
Berberis, species from Buenos Ayres,—yellow, 4 ft.

BILL-HOOK.

This useful tool for garden purposes, with single and double edges, may be purchased of Messrs. Barnard, Bishop, & Barnard, of Norwich, from 2*s.* 3*d.* to 4*s.* each.

BLANCHING.

Several vegetables in very general use require blanching—celery, seakale, endives, lettuces, &c. The first of these is blanched by earthing-up, full instructions for which will be given under the culture of the vegetable. Seakale is blanched under pots prepared for this purpose, and covered over with litter, sand, ashes, or leaves.

With regard to endive, the best plan is to place over each plant, when full-grown, a large tile or slate, which will effectually exclude all light, and blanch the endive in a few days. Some gardeners tie the plants up with bass or twine; but the plan is objectionable, as in wet weather the rain will run down the endive-leaves and rot the hearts of the plants. With lettuces there is no better plan than tying.

BLINDS FOR WALLS.

A most complete and effectual system of blinds to protect fruit-trees on walls from frost, &c., may be made as follows:—

About an inch below the coping, let a splint of wood, 2½ inches wide and 1½ inch thick, be firmly secured to the wall. This splint must be furnished with hooks about an inch long and a foot apart. Pairs of pulleys, 1½ inch in diameter and ½ inch deep, are to be fixed on this splint, at intervals of 8 feet apart, all round the wall. They must be let into the splint in a bevilled direction, by cutting off part of the top and front surface; and each firmly kept in its place by four screws, as in the figure. Small eyes are to be placed below

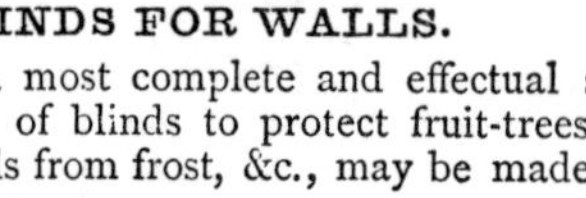

every other pair of pulleys, at distances of 16 feet apart. In the ground, about 4 feet 6 inches from the wall, and 16 feet apart, two posts, 4 inches square, must be firmly inserted, leaving about 3 inches above the surface. These posts are to be 2 feet 6 inches apart, and connected together with a strong piece of wood, 1½ inch wide and 3 deep, nailed on the inner or wall side of the posts. Another single post is to be placed in the centre of the space between the pairs, leaving a clear space of 8 feet between. The tops of the posts must be cut out in the middle, as here shown, and the single one furnished with a double hook for attaching a cord round. Splints of wood, ½ inch square and 10 feet 6 inches long, are then attached to the

hooks already referred to, by an iron eye attached to the upper end, the bottom end resting in the opening of the centre of the post. A canvas screen, 2 feet wide, attached to two similar splints of wood, is then hooked on to the top of the wall, resting on the pair of posts already adverted to. Wooden rollers, 16 feet long and 3¼ inches in diameter, furnished with a cast-iron wheel at both ends, 4½ inches in diameter, 1½ deep, and 1½ wide across the mouth, for the reception of cord. The other end of the canvas has pieces of zinc an inch square, with a hole in the centre, firmly sewn to it, a foot apart. These are for attaching to the hooks on the splint at the top of the wall, and the cord is then run through the hook *b*, over the end of the roller *c*, round the pulley at *d*, along the top to *e*, through the pulley at *e*, and drawn down on the outside of the canvas at *f*. It will be seen that

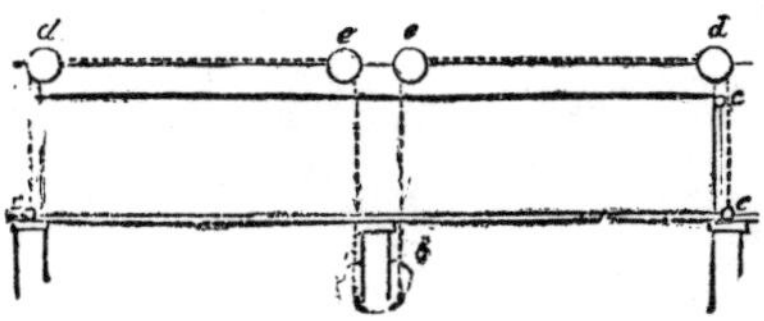

each roller is furnished with four pulleys and two cords, and can be moved up and down with the greatest despatch. The canvas screens fixed on the pairs of posts, while they support the end of the rollers, also allow plenty of space to work in. Angular screens can also be provided for filling the spaces at the end, so as to form a complete canvas house when the blinds are down. Such blinds carefully used will last a dozen years, and often save a crop in a single night; they are quite as useful in autumn in maturing the wood, as in spring for protecting the blossoms. In cold districts they would be equally useful for pears, plums, &c.

BORDERS.

Borders in flower-gardens differ from beds, in having a walk only on one side of them. They require much care, and the exercise of good taste in planting. Height, colour, and time of flowering are the main qualities to be regarded. The object ought to be to have an equal number of plants in flower in each of the floral months, and colours in agreeable contrast. Hardy herbaceous plants alone may keep a border perpetually gay, but they must be arranged with regard to height and colour,—pansies, daisies, primroses, silenes, &c., being dwarf; pinks, cloves, carnations, veronicas, &c., taller; phloxes, various sorts of campanulas, chrysanthemums, &c., and starworts, Rudbeckias, &c., being tallest of all. Plants of this class flower at various times of the year, from early spring to late in the autumn. Where spring-flowering bulbs are mixed up with them, it is not advisable to plant them near the edge, as is often practised. Plant them far back; as they flower when the borders are comparatively bare, they are sure to be seen to advantage; and the long grassy leaves do not disfigure the borders after they have flowered, as they do in the old method. Late bulbs, as gladiolus and lilies, being tall, should be placed far enough back to correspond with the other plants. A very pretty effect may be produced by planting a ribbon border or clump with plants of ornamental foliage. This may be done with the very commonest and cheapest of plants; for instance, a front row of variegated arabis; second row,

Henderson's beet, treated as an annual.—This is dwarf, very bright crimson-coloured, and grows about 8 or 10 inches high; third row, variegated mint—hardy; fourth row, *Perilla nankinensis*—annual; fifth row, ribbon-grass—hardy; sixth row, purple arack, *Atriplex rubra*—annual. These graduate in height and colour, have a very pretty effect, and will last the whole summer and autumn.

In planting a border, the ribbon style is very effective,—that is, supposing there be room for five or six rows, each row a foot or 18 inches wide,—a double row of *Lobelia speciosa* next the edging, followed by a row of verbenas,—Mrs. Holford's Snowflake, or any other white sort; these, again, followed by *Calceolaria aurea;* this by Tom Thumb geranium. If there is room for one or more rows, they may be followed by *Salvia patens* (blue), *Coreopsis lanceolata* (yellow), a row of white phlox, and a back row of dahlias. These should graduate in height and colour. This is merely given as a sample. There are many things that would do, in the same way; as *Kœnigia variegata.* Isotomas, *Phlox Drummondii*, all dwarf, and suitable for a front row; petunias, heliotropes, lantanas, &c., might form a second; ageratums, galardias, salvias, a third. Again, antirrhinums, still taller; then dahlias, and hollyhocks, tallest of all. Ribbons are very effective planted with annuals, as *Phlox Drummondii*, stocks, asters, zinnias, xeranthemums, and sweet peas, all which graduate in height, and vary in colour. These may be raised in frames in March and planted out in May, or sown in the open ground in May. Hardy annuals may be sown early in spring, allowed to flower, and then be followed by bedding-plants or by biennials, which are best sown in May and planted out.

BORECOLE.

Borecole and Curlies are a numerous tribe of Brassicæ, cultivated for their leaves in winter, and for their sprouts in spring. The first week in April or May, and again about the second week in August, is the time to sow. The borecoles are less exhausting to the soil than cabbages, and will follow peas without fresh manuring, if the ground is in tolerably good heart; or they may be planted between rows of peas or potatoes, to occupy the ground when these crops are removed.

The Horticultural Society have experimented on this tribe of Brassicæ, and issued a report; but the varieties are so numerous and so mixed, that the distinction between them is very indefinite. *Dwarf Curled Greens*, under half a dozen names, are the old Scotch curly, very dwarf in habit, and closely curled,—an excellent variety. The *Tall Green Curled*, also under a host of names, grow two or three feet high, stand severe frost, and afford the most delicate greens when frosted. *Purple Borecole* differs little from the preceding except in colour. Variegated borecole is a mere variety, very useful, and even ornamental, in the mixed gardens.

BORO'NIA (nat. ord. Ruta'ceæ).

A handsome free-flowering greenhouse evergreen shrub: succeeds best in rich fibrous sandy peat.

Boronia alata,—rose, very elegant, 3 ft., from New Holland.

BOSSIÆ'A (nat. ord. Legumino'sæ). Greenhouse Evergreen Shrubs.

A neat, elegant, free-flowering genus of plants, succeeding best in a compost of rich fibrous peat and silver sand.

Bossiæa biloba stenophylla, 3 ft., from New Holland.
Bossiæa linophylla,—orange, 3 ft., from New Holland.

BOURBON ROSE.

The *Bourbon Rose*, a variety of *Rosa indica*, was discovered in the Isle of Bourbon in 1817, by M. Breon, who flowered it and sent the seeds to M.

Bourbon Rose.

Jacques, at Château de Neuilly, near Paris. It was growing among a lot of seedlings raised to form a hedge. This parent of a numerous and lovely progeny, graduating from pure white to the darkest tints, has been hybridized with the Chinese, with the Noisette group, and with other Bourbon roses; and in the latest edition of Mr. Paul's "Rose-garden" they number 251 varieties.

The distinguishing characteristics of Bourbon roses are brilliancy and clearness of colour, large and smooth petals, falling in numerous and graceful folds. They are perfectly hardy, and thrive under the ordinary culture, delighting in a rich soil, like most of the roses, and requiring close pruning, except the more vigorous kinds. They are of slow growth, however, in spring, and thus they are best adapted for autumn-flowering roses.

"The kinds of vigorous growth," Mr. Paul tells us, "form handsome umbrageous trees, with heads as large as summer roses; they also look chaste and elegant trained on pillars. The moderate growers are pretty as dwarf standards. The dwarfs form striking and beautiful objects when grown on their own roots. A great many are excellent for pot-culture, and are beautiful objects in the forcing-house."

The following list embraces the best varieties of the Bourbon; those marked * partaking of the Bengal rose, *R. indica*:—

Sir Joseph Paxton, — flowers bright - rose, shaded with crimson; large, full, and cupped, with fine foliage.

Comice de Seine-et-Marne, — flowers open, crimson-scarlet, changing to rosy purple; produced in clusters, very double and cupped. One of the most beautiful of the group for standards, but surpassed by another raised from it at Lyons in 1852.

Mrs. Bosanquet,—creamy white; a profuse bloomer from June to November; moderate grower. This rose appears to be intermediate between the Chinese and what are called Bourbons. Will form a small clump, if possible more unique and beautiful than any other variety. A truly splendid rose.

Bouquet de Flore,—brilliant carmine; opens freely, and blooms profusely from June to November; a strong, vigorous grower, and admirably adapted for massing. A China striking rose, and suitable for pot-culture.

*Comte d'Eu,—brilliant carmine, very strong, and continues to bloom well through the summer and autumn; a moderately strong grower; forms a lovely bed, being distinct and very good.

Cérès,—a pale glossy rose, of compact form and thick petals; very large and double, of remarkably fine habit, and well adapted for pot-culture.

Paul Joseph,—a rich crimson-purple, shaded sometimes with fiery red; of large, full, and compact form, suitable for a dwarf or dwarf standard.

Proserpine,—a bright velvety crimson flower, of medium size and compact form; of dwarf habit.

Madame Souchet,—a rosy blush, margined with red or lake; large and very double, and compact in form.

Armosa,—deep pink, of full form and medium size, partaking of the Chinese; suitable for a standard or for pot-culture.

Amenaide,—flowers lilac rose-colour, produced in clusters; large, full, and cupped, partaking of the Noisettes.

Charlemagne,—flowers a clear blush, changing to pink; large and very double, and cupped.

Julie Deloynes,—flowers flesh-colour, cupped, very double; small, white, and sweet-scented, changing to white; partaking of the Noisette.

Apolline,—flowers silvery rose-colour, shaded; large, full, and cupped. A fine autumnal climbing rose.

Prince Albert,—fine scarlet-crimson; large, full, and cupped.

*Enfant d'Ajaccio, — scarlet - crimson, very bright; a moderately strong grower. Its only bad quality is that it will not open well in hot summer weather; but in autumn it is truly brilliant. The rains of October appear not to affect it in the least. Very beautiful and good.

Georges Cuvier,—rosy-crimson, tinted with light purple; fine shape, expands its blooms freely; a moderate grower. Distinct autumnal rose, with large, full, and compact flowers, with beautiful foliage.

*Grand Capitaine,—velvety fiery scarlet, very brilliant; opens its flowers both in summer and autumn. Not very double; dwarf habit; well adapted for a small bed, where the intense brilliancy of its flowers will show to advantage. One of the most distinct of roses.

Pierre de St. Cyr,—glossy rose; fine, large, double-cupped flower; expands well, and blooms profusely; a most robust grower. Will form a splendid clump to contrast with any of the strong-growing hybrid perpetuals. As a weeping rose it forms a splendid umbrageous tree, blooming through the summer and autumn.

Queen,—fawn-colour, shaded with salmon; very sweet-scented flowers; large, double, and cupped. One of the first and last in bloom, invariably expanding its flowers well, which appear in profusion. Rather dwarf habit, but will form a lovely small clump. Distinct and beautiful.

Souchet,—purplish carmine, sometimes a brilliant crimson; a large glossy flower, of full and compact form, and a good dark variety. A moderate grower, expanding its flowers with freedom. Superb.

Souvenir de la Malmaison,—white at the margin, approaching to flesh-colour, or fawn in the centre. Very large and magnificent flower, with very thick petals, blooming freely through the summer and autumn; a strong grower. This will make a gorgeous clump in contrast with such roses as Baronne Prevost, La Reine, &c.

BOURSAULT ROSE.

Boursault Rose owes its name to M. Boursault, an eminent French grower; it is a cultivated variety of the Alpine rose; the shoots are very long, flexible, and smooth, in many instances entirely without spines, and the eyes are further apart than in most other kinds. The flowers are produced in clusters suitable for pillars, and from their naturally pendulous habit they may be trained to form weeping roses. They should be well thinned out in pruning, but flowering-shoots should only have the points cut off. Mr. Paul describes the following as blooming from May to July:—

Amadis,—deep crimson-purple, shaded with lighter crimson; large, semi-double, and cupped; the young wood whitish-green.

Black Boursault,—flowers whitish-blush, with deep flesh centre; very double and globular; of pendulous habit; excellent as a climbing rose in a good aspect.

Drummond's Thornless,—opens a rosy carmine, changing to pink; flowers large, double, and cupped; habit pendulous.

Elegans,—flowers in clusters of semi-double rosy crimson; sometimes purplish, often streaked with white; erect in habit, and suitable for a pillar.

Gracilis,—flowers early; cherry, shaded with lilac-blush; full-formed and cupped; of branching habit; spines long and large; foliage a rich dark green.

Inermis,—rosy-pink, becomiug pale when expanded; large and double, and of branching habit; shoots spineless.

Old Red Boursault,—opens a bright cherry, becoming paler gradually; large and semi-double; of pendulous habit; a showy pillar or weeping rose.

Banksia,—flowers pink; a very early bloomer.

Weeping Boursault,—flesh-colour, like the blush: of a pendulous habit, and suitable for a weeping rose.

BOUSSINGAUL'TIA.

A handsome half-hardy greenhouse plant, bearing in July copious and graceful racemes of delicious fragrant white flowers. It grows freely in any common garden soil, and will blossom out of doors, if planted under a south wall, and protected during severe weather.

Boussingaultia baselloides,—white, sweet-scented.

BOX EDGING.

The box used for the purpose of edging is *Buxus sempervirens.* It is readily propagated by dividing the old plants, and it will grow in any soil not saturated with moisture. The best time for clipping box is about the end of June. To form edgings of box properly is an operation in gardening that requires considerable care. Mrs. Loudon gives the following excellent directions:—"First, the ground should be rendered firm and even: secondly, a narrow trench should be accurately cut out with the spade in the direction in which the edging is to be planted: thirdly, the box should be thinly and equally laid in along the trench, the tops being all about an inch above the surface of the soil: and fourthly, the soil should be supplied to the plants and firmly trodden in against them, so as to keep the edging exactly in the position required: the trench should always be made on the side next the walk, and after the soil is pressed down and the walk gravelled, the gravel is brought up over the soil, close to the stem of the box, so as to cover the soil at least an inch in thickness, and to prevent any soil being seen on the gravel-walk side of the box. This also prevents the box from growing too luxuriantly, as it would be apt to do if the trench were on the border side, when the plants would lean against the gravel, and the roots being entirely covered with soil, would grow with so much luxuriance that the plants would be with difficulty kept within bounds by clipping. A box edging once properly made and clipped every year, so as to form a miniature hedge, about three inches wide at bottom, three inches high and two inches wide at top, will last ten or twelve years before it requires to be taken up and re-planted; but if the edging be allowed to attain a larger size—say, six inches wide at bottom, six inches high and three inches wide at top, it will last fifteen or twenty years, and probably a much longer period."

BRACHY'COME (nat. ord. Compos'itæ). Half-hardy Annuals.

Beautiful free-flowering dwarf-growing plants, covered during the greater portion of the summer with a profusion of pretty cineraria-like flowers, very effective for edgings, small beds, rustic baskets, or for pot-culture; succeeding in any light rich soil.

Brachycome iberidifolia,—blue, ½ ft., from Swan River.
Brachycome iberidifolia albiflora,—white, ½ ft., from Swan River.

BRACHYSE'MA (nat. ord. Legumino'sæ).

A beautiful greenhouse climber, of a very ornamental character, exceedingly effective on low pillars or trellis-work; succeeds in any light rich soil.

Brachysema speciosum,—deep red, very handsome, from New Holland.

BRAVO'A.

A handsome greenhouse or conservatory plant, producing in July its beautiful crimson pentstemon-like flowers; succeeds also in a warm south border, with winter protection; thrives best in a sandy loamy soil.

Bravoa geminiflora,—crimson, blooming in pairs.

BROCOLI.

Preparation of the Soil.—All the

varieties of brocoli require a deep, rich soil, and the ground should be trenched to a depth of at least two feet, incorporating, as the work proceeds, abundance of rich manure. Indeed to obtain fine large heads too much manure can hardly be used.

Time and Manner of Sowing.—The early varieties, such as Purple Cape, Grange's White Cape, Walcheren, &c., should be sown from the middle of April to the middle of May, according to locality, and a second sowing of similar kinds shonld be made about a fortnight afterwards. These will succeed the cauliflowers, and will carry the supply on to Christmas. Two or three sowings of Snow's Winter White, put in from the beginning of April to the middle of May, will keep up the supply until the sprouting varieties are ready, and these again till the spring kinds come in. Sow the Purple Sprouting, and Lee's new White Sprouting early in March; and those intended to furnish the spring supply or main crop at the latter end of April or early in May. All the varieties should be sown in beds of well-pulverized rich soil. The surface must be made fine, and the seed then beaten gently into the ground and covered lightly with fine earth. When the plants are sufficienty strong, and before they are drawn by growing too closely together, transplant them into nursery-beds or lines, allowing about four inches intermediate space. This will insure strong stocky plants, and will also induce the formation of an extra quantity of roots. In transplanting the early varieties, great care must be used not to injure the roots; and the plants should be freely supplied with water until fairly established. In warm localities, where the soil is of a light sandy nature, it is considered, necessary by many growers to sow the seed in the situation permanently intended for the crop; but we think if moderate care is taken to keep the plants well supplied with water, they may not only be safely transplanted, but that thus treated they will be much less liable to form heads prematurely.

After-Management.—Plant in permanent situations as soon as the plants are sufficiently strong, in rows from 2 feet to 2 feet 6 inches apart, leaving about the same distance between the plants. Keep them well supplied with water until fairly established, especially the autumn flowering varieties, and these must also be liberally watered in all stages of their growth, during dry, hot weather. Keep the ground well stirred between the rows and free from weeds; and before severe weather sets in, the spring kinds should be laid over, with their heads facing the north. This operation checks the action of the roots, and the plants consequently become less succulent and better able to resist frost. They are thus also put in the best possible position for covering with stable or any other litter when such protection may be necessary.

Division I.—For cutting during the autumn and early winter months.

Grange's White Cape,—the best White Cape variety for succeeding the cauliflower.
Early Purple Cape,—very useful, may be cut from August to December.
Early Purple Cape,—new large-headed.
Walcheren,—a very valuable variety for cutting in September and October.
Dancer's Late Pink Cape,—a valuable succession to the Purple Cape.

Division II.—For cutting during the winter months.

Snow's Winter White, —fine heads may be cut from this variety in November, December, and January.
Covent Garden,—the variety supplied to the Covent Garden market in winter.
Early Purple Sprouting,—a very fine sprouting variety, sometimes called Asparagus Brocoli.
Lee's Early White Sprouting,—a wonderfully fine sprouting variety, extremely hardy.

Division III.—For cutting in March and April.

Adam's Earliest White,—the earliest spring brocoli, sometimes ready for use in February.
Imperial Early White,—a very superior variety, a fine succession to Adam's.
Dildock's Bride,—produces fine large heads, and forms a good succession to Imperial.
Beck's New Dwarf,—a first-rate early variety, very dwarf.
Knight's Protecting,—a very useful variety.
Sulphur or Brimstone,—very useful, extremely hardy and produces fine heads.

Division IV.—For cutting in April and May.

Chappel's Cream,—a fine variety, with large compact heads.
Dickson's Emperor (new),—said to be the latest of all brocoli; comes into use the end of May or beginning of June.
Frogmore Protecting (true from Turner),—very highly recommended.
Howden's Large Late Purple, —a valuable hardy variety.
Mammoth, or Giant White,—the largest and best of this division.
Wilcove,—a fine, large, late variety.

Messrs. Barr & Sugden's price of seed varies from 1*s.* to 2*s.* 6*d.* per oz.

BROMPTON STOCKS (Mathiola incana).

These are biennials. The seed should be sown early in May in a light sandy border with an eastern aspect. It succeeds best sown thinly in drills about six inches apart. As soon as the plants show their second leaves they should be watered every evening with a fine rose pot. When about three inches high they should be thinned out to at least six inches apart and the other plants removed to another bed. In about a month's time they should be thinned again and the alternate rows taken up, so as to leave the remaining plants about a foot apart every way. These may be suffered to flower where they stand, or they may be transplanted to the flower-borders in March or April. Great care is necessary in transplanting not to expose the roots, and the new soil should be of the richest description possible. The plants will require shading till they are established, and watering with liquid manure till they begin to flower. Thus treated the flowers will be splendid.

BROWAL'LIA (nat. ord. Scrophularia'ceæ). Half-hardy Annuals.

Very handsome profuse-blooming plants, covered with beautiful flowers during the summer and autumn months; growing freely in any rich soil.

Browallia Cerviakowskii,—blue with white centre, beautiful, 1½ ft.
Browallia demissa,—light blue, yellow and orange centre, 1½ ft., from South America.
Browallia elata alba,—white, 1½ ft., from Peru.
" " cærulea,—sky-blue, 1½ ft., from Peru.
Browallia elata grandiflora,—sky-blue, large and handsome, 1½ ft.
Browallia pendula,—bright blue, very pretty, 1½ ft.

BRUGMAN'SIA (nat. ord. Solona'ceæ).

Magnificent conservatory plants, with a profusion of large trumpet-shaped highly odoriferous flowers; growing freely out of doors during summer; in the centres of beds, mixed borders, or against south walls, they are very ornamental. They require rich soil and plenty of space for their roots.

Brugmansia Knightii,—white, splendid for winter decoration, 3 ft.
Brugmansia suaveolens,—white; flowers 1 ft. or more in length.

BRUSSELS SPROUTS.

Brussels Sprouts have the same treatment in the seed-beds as other Brassicæ, early in April being the best time for sowing in the open ground. Mr. Cuthill thinks March sowing would be better. "When thus sown," he adds, "I have had them three feet high, each stem producing a peck of large close sprouts." The after-treatment Mr. Cuthill recommends, is to "select a rich stiff loam, and plant them in rows 2 feet or 18 inches apart, keeping the ground loosened by hoeing; and as soon as the stems reach their full height, which is known by the top beginning to cabbage, it is cut. This throws all the strength of the plant into the sprouts on the stem, and makes the bottom ones as good as the top." Mr. McIntosh dissents from this practice of cutting the top: "From their form and position," he says, "they protect the sprouts during winter, and in wet weather, from frost, snow, and rain."

BUDDING.

Grafts of this description present the following characters: they consist in raising an eye or bud with a piece of the bark and wood, and transferring it to another part of the same plant, or any other plant of the same species. Budding is chiefly employed on young shoots or trees from one to five years old, which bear a thin, tender, and smooth bark.

The necessary conditions are, that the operation takes place when trees are in full growth, when the bark of the subject can be easily detached from the *liber*, and it may be performed

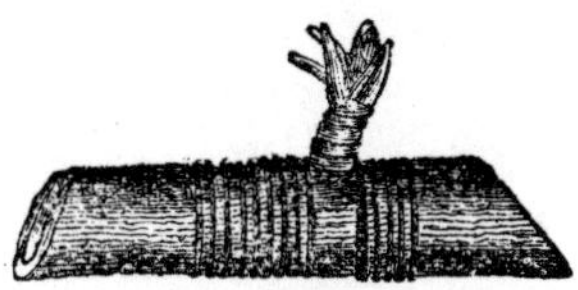

generally from May to August. The buds adapted for the operation should present well-constituted eyes or gemmæ at the axil of the leaf; if they are not sufficiently so, it is possible to prepare them by pinching the herbaceous extremity of the bud; thus producing a reflux of the sap towards the base; and in about twelve days' time the eyes will have become sufficiently developed: then detach the bud from the parent tree. Suppress all leaves, only reserving a very small portion of the petiole, or leaf-stalk, *c* (next page).

Budding.

Having fixed upon the intended stock and bud, take a sharp budding-knife, and with a clean cut remove the bud from its branch, with about a quarter of an inch of the bark above and below: remove all the wood without disturbing the inner bark of the eye; for it is in this liber, or inner bark, that the vitality lies. Now make a cross-cut in the bark of the intended stock, and also a vertical one, T, and shape the upper part of the shield, or bud, *a*, so as to fit it exactly.

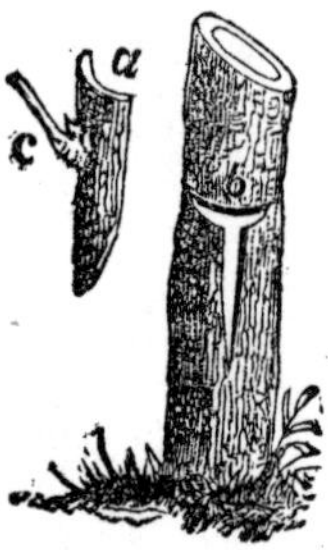

Having fitted the parts correctly, raise the bark of the stock gently with the budding-knife, and insert the bud; afterwards bandage lightly above and below the eye, bringing the lips of the bark of the stock together again over the bud by means of the ligature, in such manner that no opening remains between them, and, above all, taking care that the base of the eye is in free contact with the bark of the stock.

Some weeks after, if the ligatures seem to be too tight, they may be untied and replaced with smaller pressure. When the operation takes place in May, the scion will develop itself as soon as the suture is completed. In order to provide for this, cut the head of the stock down to within an inch of the point of junction immediately after the operation.

When the operation takes place in August, the head is never cut till the following spring, when the scion begins to grow. If the same practice as in earlier budding were followed, the consequence would be, that the bud would develop itself before winter; and, having no time to ripen its new wood, it would perish, or at least suffer greatly. When the buds begin to grow, they require to be protected from strong winds; otherwise they would be detached from the stem. This is done by driving a stake, *a*, firmly into the ground, attaching it by a strong cord to the stem of the stock above and below the junction, as in the engraving, and tying the shoot of the young scion firmly to the stake above, protecting it by a bandage of hay or other substance, to prevent the bark being injured.

The weather most suitable for budding is a subject of dispute among practical men. Cloudy weather has generally been preferred; but Mr. Saul, of Bristol,—no mean authority,—protests strongly in favour of warm sunny weather, provided the stock and buds are in proper condition. "In warm weather," he says, "the sap is more gelatinous, and the bud, on being extracted and inserted in the stock, quickly and properly tied, soon takes. On the contrary, in wet, cloudy weather, the sap is more thin and watery, and the bud will not unite so freely; besides this, a fall of rain, after the buds are inserted, likely enough, in such weather, will fill up the interstices, and rot the buds before they have time to unite with the stock."

Another question Mr. Saul agitates: —Is it necessary to extract the wood from the eye of the bud? "American writers say, no; but I answer, yes," he says. "It may suit their hot, dry climate, but I must give the preference to our old system of extracting the wood from the bud, not only for roses, but for fruit, ornamental, and forest trees. In rose-budding," he adds, "the bud in the shoot should be commenced with, cutting out from it about the eighth of an inch below the bud or eye, to about half an inch above it. Take out the wood without touching the liber or inner bark; next make an incision in the branch on which the bud is to be placed, quite close to the main stem, half an inch long, with a cross-cut at the upper extremity, thus: T. Raise the bark with the end of the budding-knife, without bruising it, and insert the bud, tying it well with worsted thread, giving one turn below, and two, or at most three, above the eye of the bud. Worked in this way, they grow out from the axil of the branch, and look neat and workmanlike; and after a season or two, when headed back and healed over, it presents a fine bushy head, growing apparently out of the main stem, without scars, wounds, or knots."

The shoots selected for budding or grafting, whether for fruit- or rose-trees, should be firm and well-ripened: watery shoots, or watery buds, are valueless. For grafting, the branches should be of the preceding year, well ripened under an August sun,—*aoûté*, as French fruitists say.

The stock should be in a state of vegetation slightly in advance of the graft; otherwise the flow of the sap is insufficient to supply the wants of the scion. In order to provide for this, the graft may be removed from the parent branch a little before the operation, and buried under a north wall: there it remains stationary, while the stock is advancing to maturity.

BUDDING ROSES.

To the foregoing remarks on budding generally, it may be well to add some special directions respecting roses.

In selecting buds of roses, take those of moderate size; clean off the thorn, cut the leaves off, leaving only about half an inch of the stalk or petiole to hold by; then with a sharp knife take out the bud, beginning half an inch above the eye, and bring the knife about the eighth of an inch below; with the point of the knife separate the wood from the bark, without interfering with the wood which remains in the eye, leaving it so that, when inserted on the stock, the wood left may be in immediate contact with its wood.

Having removed the thorns on the intended stock, open the bark at the most convenient spot for the insertion, by drawing the point of the knife down the centre of the shoot, and by a cross-cut, where the other begins, raise the corners of the bark sufficiently to introduce the lower end of the bud: press it down till it is opposite to the corresponding bud on the stock, and bind it up with a piece of fine bass or worsted thread, leaving the eye so that it is just visible. After three or four weeks it should be examined, and the band loosened a little. In cases where the bud does not separate freely from the bark, the wood may be tied in also; but the operation is both neater and more efficient when all the wood except that in the eye is removed. Cloudy weather is generally recommended for the operation; but Mr. Saul, of the Durdham Downs Nursery, Bristol, says he prefers bright, warm, sunny weather, provided the stocks are in proper condition. Rose-budding may be performed any time from June to September, and even as late as October, August being suitable for the greatest number of roses, the test being of course the maturity of the shoots.

BUD'DLEA (nat. ord. Scrophularia'ceæ).

Deciduous shrubs, natives of India and South America. They are not quite hardy enough to endure very severe winters with us out of doors; but in greenhouses they flower profusely. A loamy soil, mixed with peat, suits them best.

BUGLOSS.

The Bugloss (*Anchusa*) is a fine showy plant, mostly with large blue flowers. They may be propagated by slips, and by dividing the roots into as many plants as there are heads, when they have done flowering, as well as by seed saved in the autumn, and sown on a warm border in the spring.

BULBS.

The grand feature in the culture of bulbous-rooted plants is, that most of them, from peculiarity of constitution, or from their mode of increase, require to be taken up and replanted every year, or every second or third year at the furthest. Where this is not done, the flourishing bulbs are smothered with the quantity of small offsets that form around them. These offsets not only rob the larger bulbs of their food, in species in which the same bulb flowers for several seasons, but by shading them from light and air, prevent the elaboration of the little that is left into organizable matter for the formation of flowers the succeeding season. In species, again, that flower only once from the same bulb, as the numerous varieties of Gladiolus and similar plants, two or more bulbs are generally formed; and if they are left where formed, a number of weak, puny, flowerless bulbs will be the consequence. Other species, like the Crocus and similar bulbs, form their young bulbs on the top of the old ones; and by this process, repeated yearly, would speedily throw the original bulb entirely out of the ground; while the Narcissus, Tulip, Colchicum, and similar plants, form their new bulbs under the old ones, and would ultimately burrow so deep that the young bulbs would never reach the surface at all. To remedy all these evils, and insure for the bulb a period of perfect rest, all the most valuable varieties should be taken up annually. No special time can be named as the best adapted for this purpose. Bulbs vary so much in the period and habit of their growth, that any general instructions would only mislead. One rule, however, which must never be infringed, is, that no bulb is to be disturbed while the leaves are in a growing state. The bulb is never matured until the leaves die of their own accord. As soon as they thus die, the bulb may be taken up and stored away in a cool room, say in a temperature of 40°.

The period of rest allotted for different families must also vary. To save trouble, common border bulbs are generally replanted at once: all of them, however, would be benefitted by a period of perfect rest. If kept cool, the bulbs themselves will give unerring instructions concerning the right time of planting. If the store-room is too warm, their excitability will afford no criterion for safe practice. From one to three months will be a suitable resting period for most of the families. Bulbs so obviously increase themselves, either by the formation of young bulbs, above, below, or beside the old ones, that any instructions concerning their propagation would be well nigh superfluous.

Treatment of Bulbs in Borders.—Be careful to give a good dressing of well-rotted manure, and as much mulching from the liquid-manure tank as can be spared to all choice bulbs while their leaves are in a growing state; for it is at this time that Nature is making her greatest efforts, and will require, of course, the greatest support. Those who wish to increase the size of any single bulb, and so insure an extra fine flower for another year, will do well to cut off the flower-stalk as soon as it appears this season; but by no means to pluck or injure the leaves. In the case of all bulbs, the leaves should be suffered to die away naturally, notwithstanding the beds where they grow are not improved in appearance while the process is going on. In crocuses and narcissus for edgings the dying leaves may be curled round and made neat; but they must on no account be shortened or cut off. Nothing in the spring of the year makes a more effective display in a garden than different sorts of bulbs round the edges of the different beds, now of necessity empty of everything else. Yellow, purple, white, and variegated crocuses, may each have their own edging of a bed allotted to them; the little single daffodil, the winter snowflake, and hoop-petticoat narcissus, may be placed around others; but if these are to flourish and do well, they must not be disturbed; they must be well manured when in a growing state, and their leaves not removed until they have died down.

BULBOCO'DIUM.

A very pretty early-flowering plant, best known as *Red Crocus;* blooms about a fortnight before the ordinary Crocus, and, like it, may be cultivated in-doors.

Bulbocodium vernum,—purple-red; per 100 10*s.* 6*d.*, per doz. 1*s.* 6*d.*

BUSH FRUIT.

Under this title are included gooseberries, the different kinds of currants —red, white, and black,—and raspberries; fruits so extremely useful that they are to be found in every garden, and are grown extensively for markets in the neighbourhood of every large town. It too frequently happens that bush fruit, from the readiness with which it yields a crop, is left to take care of itself; but the quantity and quality of the fruit produced will be found to depend very materially upon the good management of the bushes. We shall give general directions for the different sorts, but further information will be found under the different heads.

Though the *Gooseberry* will grow on the poorest soil, it will not produce fine fruit unless planted in a deep, rich soil, and treated generously. Though hardy, it requires moderate shelter, and though rejoicing in moisture, it will not flourish in undrained land. Cuttings should be planted any time from October to March. Select for the purpose shoots of a medium size, not root-suckers, about a foot or more in length. Cut the base of the shoot square; no fruit canes should ever be planted with slanting heels; after this, remove with a knife every bud from the base to within two inches of the top. If the cuttings are fifteen inches long, and four heads are left at the top, the future stem will be a foot high, which will be ample for a useful tree. The lower buds are removed in order to secure a clean stem and prevent the formation of suckers. Plant the cuttings in the shade four inches deep, and fix the earth firmly about them. During summer, young growing shoots strike readily under a hand-glass on a shady border, and a season may frequently be saved in this way. The first season's growth of cuttings put in in autumn should be very little interfered with. If any pruning is requisite, it is best done by rubbing off buds and by pinching in shoots which would interfere with the proper shape of the bush. At the end of the season, cut back all leading shoots to two-thirds of their length, so as to cause them to break next spring and form well-shaped bushes. At first, it is frequently desirable to plant cuttings only a few inches apart, and after the second year's growth to plant them out finally about six feet apart. Each bush would then have about eight leading shoots to form a head, and must be kept in shape and order by yearly prunings. If large fruit is required, it is not desirable to shorten the shoots, except they grow too vigorously and incline too much downwards. Weak and superfluous shoots should be removed, and this is best done by taking them off as close as possible to the old ones, and removing all bottom buds, so as to prevent the formation of too many young shoots. The trees may be trained in many ways: sometimes the form of a fan or an espalier hedge is adopted, which has the advantage of being easily netted if birds are troublesome. The cup and funnel shapes are especially suited for the production of fine fruit, as air may be admitted to the centre of the trees. The best plan of protecting these from birds is by encircling the bush with wire netting, and covering the top with a piece of string netting, which can be removed when the fruit is to be gathered. The ordinary bush form can be protected in the same way.

With regard to the selection of sorts, we cannot do better than give the experience of so good a judge as Mr. Shirley Hibberd. The best of the old varieties, he tells us, still hold their ground. There are none equal to the Champagne for flavour. The Red Champagne is of the same quality, differing only in colour. The old Rough is the best for preserving, and Warrington is unequalled as a profitable late gooseberry. For early work, take Golden Drop, Ostrich, and Early Green Hairy. For the latest crop and for retarding, the best are Warrington, white; Viper, yellow; Pitmaston, green; and Coe's Late Red. The most profitable sorts are Keen's Seedling and Warrington, red; Globe and Husbandman, yellow; Profit and Glenton, green; Eagle and Wellington Glory, white. For large exhibition berries, the following are a few of the best established sorts:—Red: Companion, Slaughterman, Conquering Hero, and Dan's Mistake. Yellow: Leader, Leveller, Goldfinder, Peru, Catherina. Green: Thumper, Gretna Green, Rough Green, General, and Turnout. White: Snowdrop, Antagonist, and Lady Leicester. The Lancashire gooseberries, which are generally distinguished by long, drooping branches, bear the largest fruit. Seedlings have been shown at Manchester varying in weight from 20 dwt. to 26 dwt., and, we believe, even beyond this. Such fruit, however, is generally produced at the expense of the crop. When fruit is to be gathered green, it is most profitable to keep the bush as thick in shoots as possible: for ripening fine fruit, the more open the bush the better.

Currants, red and white, may be pruned and treated in the same manner; black currants require a different treatment. In managing the cuttings, proceed as directed for gooseberries. Plant out the second year, when the cuttings have about eight inches of stem and about five leading shoots. The pruning of both red and white currants is very different from that of gooseberries. When the requisite number of branches has been produced, so as to form a uniform bush, the greater part of the young shoots should be taken off annually, leaving only those that may be required for new branches, and shortening these to four or six inches with a clean cut just close to a bud. In pruning off the superfluous lateral shoots, take hold of each branch at its extremity with the left hand, and, with the knife in the right hand, remove every fresh lateral up the stem, leaving to each a short spur of a quarter or half an inch in length: from these spurs the bunches of fruit are produced. As the bush increases in age, it will be necessary to remove all old mossy wood, and also to thin out the spurs when they have become too crowded. Of late years, great improvement has been made in both red and white currants. Visitors to Covent Garden market frequently express surprise as to the size of the bunches and the berries. These currants are not only peculiar sorts, but very great pains are taken in the cultivation of them. To grow fine currants, make the plantation in an open sunny position, on a stiff, well-manured loam; plant the bushes five feet apart each way, and every autumn trench in a good dressing of half-rotten manure in such a way as not to injure the roots of the trees. At autumn-pruning all the young shoots must be cut in to two inches. The sorts which produce the largest fruit are White Blanche, with amber-coloured berries, and White Dutch. Of red currants, Cherry is the largest; La Fertile and Knight's Large Red are also excellent varieties.

Black Currants.—The cultivation of the black currant is almost the same as the gooseberry, and the pruning is the same, only not so severe, as the black currant does not form so many young shoots. All dead and unproductive wood should be removed each year, and the shoots thinned so that light and air may freely enter the bush. The best varieties are the Naples Black and Ogden's Black; both of which, under good culture, are profuse bearers, and very large. Black currants are best left to grow as bushes; they do not thrive well trained to walls, or as espaliers.

Raspberries.—Raspberries flourish in any good rich loam, and will grow to perfection in a dark unctuous soil. As a general rule, raspberries do well where black currants flourish, and neither of these are very productive where cherry-trees thrive best. Before planting, the ground should be well trenched and manured; for though the roots lie near the surface, it is well to induce them to strike downwards in the event of a dry season. The second or third week in October is the best period for planting. Strong canes should be selected, and great advantage is gained if they be taken up with soil upon their roots. They may be put in singly, in rows, or in bunches of three canes each. In this latter case, it is desirable to cut the canes of different heights; the strongest may be four feet, the second three feet, and the third two feet. Staking will be necessary before the plants begin to grow in the spring, and great care should be taken that the ground is not trodden in wet weather. The pruning of raspberries is an easy matter. In June the bushes should be gone over, and all suckers removed, except about six of the strongest. These, at a later period, may be reduced to four, and if the parent plant be weak, two or three will be sufficient. There is great benefit in cutting the canes of different heights, for as the top buds grow strongest, the young fruit-bearing shoots are more equally divided, and enjoy more air and light. The ground in which raspberries are grown should not be broken up, but have a top dressing of good rotten manure yearly. The most useful varieties of the raspberry are the Red Antwerp, Fastolf, Prince of Wales, and Vice-President, the Yellow Antwerp, and Large-fruited Monthly. By a little management, raspberries may be made to bear a crop of fruit during autumn. There are sorts called Double-bearing Raspberries, but the result is greatly due to pruning. For late bearing, as soon as root suckers show themselves in June, the old canes should be cut away entirely, so as to prevent summer fruiting; and encouragement given during July and August to such suckers as show blossom-buds, for these will bear fruit in autumn. Autumn-bearing raspberries must be kept thin, or they will not prove successful. The canes for this purpose should be planted in single rows, and not in threes, as recommended for summer fruiting. They should stand about one foot apart.

CABBAGES.

Cabbages, or *Brassicæ*, are the most important product of the garden, whether we look at them as a necessary or a luxury of life. They are also, except under a well-considered system of rotation cropping, the most exhaustive class of vegetables under the gardener's care. With such properties, it is not surprising to find that they were well known to the ancients, and that, in all probability, we are indebted to the Romans for their first cultivation in British gardens.

Gerarde is the oldest English author who has written on this useful vegetable : he mentions the white-cabbage cole, red-cabbage cole, the curled garden cole. The Savoie cole is, he says, numbered among the headed coleworts or cabbages. He notices the curled Savoy, but says, "the swollen colewort of all others is the strangest, and which I received from a worshipful merchant of London, Master Nicholas Lete, who brought the seed out of France, who is greatly in love with rare and fair flowers, and plants, for which he doth carefully send into Syria, having a servant there, at Alepo, and in many other countries; for the which myself and likewise the whole lande are much bound unto him." The same author says, "Rape cole is another variety; they were called in Latin, *caulo-rapum* and *rapo-caulis*, participating of two plants—the coleworts and turnips ; from whence they derive their name. They grow in Italy, Spain, and some places in Germany. They must," he says, "be carefully set and sown, as musk-melons and cucumbers." This variety has now become one of our hardiest field plants.

This important family of vegetables is biennial, triennial, and nearly perennial in some of the varieties. It may be divided into—

1. The Cabbages proper, which have heads formed of the inner leaves growing close and compactly round the stem, which are thus blanched into a whitish yellow by the outer leaves.

2. Red, or Milan cabbage, which grows in the same form, but differs in colour.

3. Savoys, distinguished by their curly wrinkled leaves, but retaining the tendency to form a head.

4. Brussels sprouts, producing the sprouts, or edible part, from the stem in small heads, like very young cabbages.

5. Borecole, of which there are many varieties, having a large open head with large curling leaves.

6. Cauliflower and brocoli, in which the flower-buds form a close fleshy head of a delicate yellowish-white, for which both are cultivated.

Of the first of these there are many varieties, some of them valuable for their precocity, which adapts them for early spring cultivation; others for more enduring qualities. They are all propagated by seed sown for main crops twice a year—namely, in April, for planting out in June and July, for autumn and winter use; and in August and September, for spring use; but it is usual to make sowings of smaller quantities every month for succession.

The Romans propagated the Brassicæ by seeds and cuttings, by which choice varieties may be perpetuated with greater certainty than from seed. This is done by slipping off the sprouts, which all the tribes produce on the stem, when about four inches long, exposing them to the air for a day or two to cauterize the wound, then dipping them in caustic lime, and planting them where they are to grow. Pliny tells us they are fittest for planting or for eating when the sprout has six leaves.

The Cabbage.—The seed is sown on beds four feet wide, and long in proportion to the sowing. A bed 4 feet by 20 will take 2 oz. of seed. Cover the seed to an eighth or a quarter of an inch with rich light soil, and rake it in : the after-cultivation will be gathered from the monthly calendars. The cabbage requires a rich retentive soil, and is improved by early transplanting. When about two inches in height, the young plants should be removed into nursery-beds thoroughly prepared by digging and manuring, and, if dry, by watering, where they are planted four or five inches apart. Here they must remain till well rooted. Their next remove is usually to the place where they are permanently to grow; but they will be rather improved than otherwise by an intermediate shift to a second nursery-bed.

In final planting cut, the ground being trenched and well manured, a drill is drawn, three inches deep, at a distance proportioned to the size and habit of growth of the variety; the small or early dwarfs at 12 or 15 inches apart in the rows, the larger sorts, as Vanack, at 18 inches. The subsequent culture is confined to weeding and occasionally stirring the earth during summer, and drawing it up round the stem when about eight or nine inches high.

The best varieties of the white cabbage are the Early York, Early Battersea, Early Dwarf Sugar-loaf, the Late Sugar-loaf, Vanack, the Portugal, or *Couve Trunchuda*—of all of which there are many varieties; as Atkin's Matchless, Sutton's Dwarf Combe, Sutton's Imperial, Enfield Market, Shilling's Queen. The conical Pomeranian is singularly hardy and very compact. The Vanack was subjected to experiment by the Horticultural Society, and Mr. George Lindley reported it as "always in season by timely sowings, making excellent spring coleworts; becomes white-hearted cabbage very early, and furnishes fine sprouts after the cabbage is cut." The red cabbage is chiefly used for pickling, and the varieties are confined to the Dutch, Aberdeen, and Dwarf Red. Their cultivation is in all respects the same as the white cabbage, and the vegetable is only gathered when the head is thoroughly formed, and when so gathered the stem is thrown away as of no further value.

CABBAGES IN MARKET GARDENS.

Towards the end of October, a well-conducted market-garden is full of cabbages just planted out, which, in November, are strong healthy plants. Before planting, the land is heavily dunged, a two-horse load being used for every thirty yards, which is dug into the ground as it is trenched, the planters following the diggers. This work is carefully superintended; every man has his twelve feet measured out to him, and the foreman walks before the workmen to see they do their duty. The lines are run along the land as soon as it is ready, at distances two feet apart, trod on in one direction all over the field. The lines are then shifted, and placed at right angles to the other, at the same distance apart, the workmen now only treading on the angles. This done, planting commences; the plants, which are usually large well-grown plants, are inserted at the angles; consequently, the plants stand two feet apart each way. Immediately after planting, the hoe is sent through the field to loosen the soil: this is frequently repeated, but no earthing-up. It is one remarkable peculiarity of this mode of culture, that slugs are unknown in a well-managed market-garden; the continual stirring and deep trenching seems to root them out. The moment these cabbages are off the ground, the land is again trenched, and prepared for a fresh crop.

CACTUS (nat. ord. Cacta'ceæ). Greenhouse Perennials.

An extremely curious and interesting genus, many of the varieties producing magnificent flowers of the most brilliant and striking colours. They succeed best in sandy loam, mixed with brick and lime rubbish and a little peat or rotten dung.

CALANDRIN'IA (nat. ord. Portulaca'ceæ).

Very beautiful free-flowering plants. *C. discolor* and *grandiflora* have large handsome flowers, and are fine for edgings; *C. umbellata* is of a trailing habit, and produces profusely its glowing *rosy violet* flowers in bunches; is invaluable for rockwork and dry hot banks, or similar situations, where it will stand for many years. They succeed best in a light rich soil. They may be raised from seed.

Calandrinia discolor,—rose-lilac, hardy annual, 1 ft., from Chili.

Calandrinia grandiflora,—rose-pink, hardy annual, 1 ft., from Chili.
Calandrinia umbellata,—rich rosy violet, hardy perennial ½ ft.

Seed 3*d*. per packet.

CALCEOLA'RIA (nat. ord. Scrophularia'ceæ). Half-hardy Perennials.

Plants of a highly decorative character, indispensable for the ornamentation of the conservatory and flower-garden. The herbaceous varieties are remarkable for their large, finely-shaped and beautifully spotted flowers; these are cultivated exclusively for in-door decoration. The half-shrubby kinds grow more compact, have smaller flowers, bloom more profusely, and by many are more highly prized than the herbaceous sorts; they are alike useful for in and out-door decoration, and succeed in any light rich soil. The calceolarias mostly used for bedding are the different shades of yellow and brown. These admit of a very easy cultivation.

Take the cuttings early in October, and having prepared a piece of ground in a north border, the soil of which must be well drained, and made light with a large admixture of sand, place the cuttings in, and press the earth well round them, water them well, and cover with a hand-glass, or place the cuttings in pots, and having sunk them in a north border, under a wall, place a hand-glass over them. In this way they may be kept without further attention till the following spring, unless the weather should be very frosty, in which case it may be well to throw some covering over the hand-glass. In the spring the cuttings should be repotted, and will soon become fine plants. It is to be observed that the state of atmospheric influence most favourable to all cuttings is when a change to moist growing weather succeeds, within two or three days, the warm dry weather during which the cuttings have been taken.

CALLIOP'SIS (nat. ord. Compos'itæ).

The Calliopsis, or, as it is sometimes called, Coreopsis, is one of the most showy, free-flowering, and beautiful of hardy annuals. The tall varieties are very effective in mixed borders and fronts of shrubberies; the dwarf kinds, from their close compact habit of growth, make fine bedding-plants, and are valuable for edgings. The different varieties make very pretty ribbons. Amongst the tall varieties, *C. filifolia Burridgii* is the most graceful and beautiful, and *C. bicolor grandiflora* the most showy and effective in mixed borders. All are hardy annuals except *C. Ackermannii*, which has a yellow, crimson centre, and is a hardy perennial; 3 ft., from North America.

CAMEL'LIA (nat. ord. Ternstromia'ceæ). In house.

Favourite winter and spring-flowering shrubs of great beauty. Almost any soil will grow camellias. Some persons grow them entirely in peat, some in strong loam, approaching to clay. The best soil, however, appears to be two parts fibry peat, one fibry loam, one-sixth part sharp silver-sand, and one-sixth part *rotten wood*, or clean leaf-mould. Keep them in a temperature of 55° to 60° until their growth is made and flower-buds formed. During this period they should be frequently syringed, and a humid atmosphere maintained. Towards the end of April gradually remove them by easy transitions, to a cool house or cold pit, and the last week in May to a sheltered situation out of doors, or they may continue in the same house or pit throughout the season. The pots must be placed on a hard bottom to prevent the ingress of worms, watered alternately with clean water and weak liquid manure, and finally removed under glass in October. With such treatment their blossoms will expand in November or December. As soon as the last flower has fallen, shift the plants into larger pots if the state of their roots require it.

Fine plants, from 18 inches to 2 feet high, of the following or equally good varieties, can be purchased at from 30*s.* to 42*s.* a dozen; larger plants, from 60*s.* to 120*s.* a dozen:—

Alba plena, Albertus, Amabilis, Archduchesse Marie, Beata, Chandlerii, Elegans, Countess of Ellesmere, Countess of Derby, Cup of Beauty, De la Reine, Duchesse d'Orléans, Eximia, Fimbriata, Lady Hume's blush, Grand Frederick, Grandis, Imbricata, Imbricata alba, Jenny Lind, Mathotiana, M. alba, Marchioness of Exeter, Princess Royal, Prince Frederick William, Reticulata, R. fiore pleno (this is still expensive), the Bride, Tricolor, Tricolor imbricata pleno, and Victoria magnosa.

CAMELLIAS in the open Air.

Among the evergreen plants which are suitable for the shrubbery or border, none can excel the Camellia; and there are a few varieties of this beautiful shrub which do well in the open ground. It may be useful to enumerate some of the sorts which are known to flourish and blossom freely against a north wall, or upon a north border, and to make one or two observations upon their culture and the soil best adapted for them. The sorts best suited to open-air cultivation are Carolina (double white), Pæoniflora, Prince Leopold, Perfection, Eclipse, Dahlia-flora, *Imbricata alba*, Duchess of Orleans, and Bealii. The soil in which they are planted should be a mixture of peat, leaf-mould, and cow-dung, about two feet deep. Great care should be taken that the plants never suffer from drought. After flowering they should be freely watered with liquid manure, especially if the season be dry. The surface of the ground just round the stems of the plants may frequently, with very good effect, be paved with small stones, which assist in keeping the roots cool and moist. As a general rule, the borders on which camellias are planted should not be disturbed more than is necessary to remove the surface weeds. A top-dressing of fresh soil may, with advantage, be given to them every winter. So treated, the sorts of camellias mentioned above will be found as hardy as most of our common evergreens, and require no protection, except, perhaps, in an unusually severe winter, when a few fir boughs may be placed before or around them. The snow should never be allowed to rest upon their branches. Some growers of camellias in the open ground bind straw round the stems of their plants, about five or six inches from the ground, when winter sets in: this is found a very efficient protection against frost.

CAMPAN'ULA (nat. ord. Campanula'ceæ).

A genus of exceedingly beautiful plants, characterized by the variety of their colours, profusion and duration of their bloom. Some of them are remarkable for their stately growth, others for their close, compact habit; of the former, *C. pyramidalis* grown in pots, placed about terraces, gravel walks, or the margins of lawns, produces a most striking effect. Visitors to Paris may have been struck with the free use made of this plant in the public gardens. Of the dwarf varieties, *C. Carpatica* is a most valuable bedding-plant. The whole genus deserves a prominent place in every garden.

CANDYTUFT (nat. ord. Cruciferæ).

The Candytuft, or Iberis, as it is also called, derives its name from the island of Candia, whence it first came. It springs up readily from seed sown in any light rich soil. Autumn is the best time for sowing.

The improved varieties of this favourite flower are exceedingly beautiful, and it may be questioned if there be two more effective annuals than Dunnettii and the sweet-scented; the one a rich crimson purple, the other pure white: they succeed in any soil.

Candytuft, Dunnettii, new dark,—crimson, exceedingly beautiful hardy annual, 1 ft.
Candytuft, Normandy,—lilac, 1 ft., from Normandy.

Candytuft,—purple crimson, very fine.
„ rocket, pure white, 1 ft.
„ rose, 1 ft.
„ sweet-scented, pure white, very fine, 1 ft., from Crete.

CAN'NA (nat. ord. Maranta'ceæ).

For the adornment of the conservatory, drawing-room, or flower-garden, these magnificent plants are unrivalled; their stately growth, combined with their rich and various-coloured flowers, and picturesque and beautiful foliage, render them the most strikingly effective of ornamental plants. When intermixed with other plants, or dispersed in pots about terraces, gravel walks, or on the margins of lawns or lakes, they impart quite an oriental aspect: during the summer months in the gardens around Paris, these plants create quite a sensation. Being of easy culture and rapid growth, no one need be without them. They may be propagated by dividing the roots or by seed. Steep the seeds for a few hours in hot water before sowing, then place the pot in a cucumber-frame, or some other warm situation; the plants will be ready to plant out in June, or to shift into larger pots for the decoration of halls, terraces, &c., where they soon become objects of great interest.

CAPE BULBS.

Charming in their foliage, abundant in their flowering, and of easy culture, these plants have but one fault,—they are a very short time in flower. Mr. M. Saul, the gardener to Lord Stourton, says of them, "I have seen hundreds of flower-gardens perfectly dazzling with scarlets, yellows, and blues of every shade; but I declare I have never witnessed anything to equal the beauty and grandeur of some beds of these truly delightful genera which I once saw in full flower in the open garden. They were protected from the north by a wall, behind which grew a row of trees, and consisted of the Gladiolus, Ixia, Sparaxis, Tritonia, Watsonia, and Anomatheca; all remarkable for the delicacy, brilliancy, and distinctness of their flowers."

In the open ground, a south border, sheltered by a north wall, is most suitable for their growth. It should be well drained, nothing being more prejudicial to them than a wet bottom; the soil turfy loam, a little peat or leaf-mould, and a little sand. The bulbs should be planted about six inches deep any time in October, and during the winter months the bed should be covered a few inches thick with tan or dry litter, removing it as soon as pretty fair weather sets in in the spring.

When grown in pots, the same soil will suit them; potted in October, they should be protected in a cold frame or pit. They will require little or no water till they begin to grow in spring. When they have made a little growth, they may either be planted out in a warm border, or placed on the shelves of the greenhouse near the lights, and watered regularly to keep them in a growing state till the foliage shows signs of maturity; water must then be withheld. When at rest they should be kept quite dry.

CAP'SICUMS.

Pretty ornamental plants, especially in autumn, when covered with their light scarlet fruit. From the Capsicum cayenne pepper is made.

Preparation of the Soil.—These thrive best in a rich, yet light and free soil; and whether grown in pots or planted out, the soil should be of this description.

Time and Manner of Sowing.—The seed should be sown early in March, in well-drained pots filled with light sandy soil, and placed in a cucumber-frame, or wherever a temperature of about 65° is maintained. Cover the seed to the depth of about half an inch, and keep the surface constantly moist until the plants appear. When the plants are strong enough to handle, pot them off, placing two or three plants in a 5-inch pot, and replacing them in the warmth. Keep them rather close until they become established, then shift into 7-inch pots; and when they are fairly established in these, remove them, if intended for the open ground, to a cold frame, and gradually prepare them for planting out by a freer exposure to the air. Those intended to grow in pots under glass should be shifted into 10-inch pots as soon as they require more space for their roots, and be stopped, so as to cause them to form bushy plants; they must be liberally watered and syringed over head during droughty weather. Those intended for the open garden may be planted in properly prepared situations towards the end of May, protecting them by hand-glasses or any more convenient contrivance till they are fairly established. They must be liberally watered during hot, dry weather. In favoured localities most of the varieties do better planted out than when grown in pots under glass; but they will not succeed in the open air except in warm, dry situations.

CARDOON.

A perennial in its native country,—the shores of the Mediterranean,—it becomes an annual in this country, the first sowing taking place in the beginning of March, on a very slight hotbed; in April, on the natural ground; and again in June, for next spring's crop. The trenches are dug as for celery, and moderately manured with well-decomposed dung. In sowing, two or three seeds are sown together in a clump, 12 inches apart. Should each vegetate, remove all but one, when six inches high. When the plant is 18 inches high, put a stake to it, and tie the leaves lightly to it, earthing-up the stem at the same time, like celery. Throughout the summer, water copiously and frequently with soft water and a little guano, to prevent flowering. In September, the early crop will be fit for use; remove the earth carefully, take the plant up by the roots, which cut off; the points of the leaves also cut off to where they are solid and blanched.

CARNATION.

This flower is the cultivated *Dianthus Caryophyllus*, found wild in many parts of England, although it is supposed to have reached this country in its cultivated state from Italy or Germany. Gerarde, writing in 1597, makes mention of it as received from Poland; and it is a remarkable instance of the effects of cultivation, that the named varieties of flakes, bizarres, picotees,—pink, purple, scarlet, and crimson, bear scarcely any resemblance to the original. They are propagated by *seeds*, which, however, do not ripen well with us, and are obtained chiefly from South Germany; by *pipings*, by *cuttings*, and by *layers*. The seed should be sown in May in pots of light rich soil, placing the pots in an airy, sheltered part of the garden. When the plants are up, and show five or six leaves, plant them out in beds in the same rich soil, and 10 inches or so asunder; protecting them during winter in a cold frame, or by means of matting. Many of them will bloom the following summer.

For layers, the propagating season is July and August. Having selected the shoots to be layered, and prepared pegs for pegging them down, and soil for their reception, add a little grey sand where the layers are to be placed. Prepare the shoot by trimming off all the leaves with a sharp knife, except five or six at the top; then with a thin-bladed knife make an incision half through the shoot, with an upward cut, beginning below a joint, and passing through it for an inch or so; bend the layer down into the sandy soil prepared for it, pegging it down in that situation in such a manner as to keep the slit or tongue open, and cover it over with rich light compost. Two days afterwards, when the wound is healed, a gentle watering will be beneficial.

Cuttings are made by taking off shoots which cannot be conveniently layered, cutting them right through a joint with an oblique angular cut, and planting them in pots or beds prepared with mixed compost and sand.

Piping consists in drawing out the young shoots from the joints, and inserting them into a light sandy soil, where they take root,—a process more generally applicable to pinks than carnations.

In preparing compost for carnations, take two-thirds good staple loamy soil, the turfy top-spit in preference; add to this one-third of thoroughly rotted cow or stable dung, and one measure of drift sand or other sharp grit, to ten measures of the compost. The alluvial deposit from watercourses, like a mill-head, is an excellent substitute for the maiden loam. In preparing the bed for carnations, having filled the bottom with sufficient drainage material, and secured an outfall for the water, fill in the compost till nearly full. On this surface spread out the roots horizontally, and fill up with fresh compost, pressing the whole firmly, but gently down, in that position.

The layers of carnations and picotees should be taken off as they begin to form fibre, and either potted or planted in a nursery-bed till October, in either case keeping them in a close frame till they have rooted. If potted, re-pot in October, and prune to a clean stem, leaving the lower pair of leaves half an inch from the soil, and removing all laterals over an inch long: most of them will strike in the beginning of October, and bloom strongly the second year, if they do not bloom the first.

The chief distinction between the carnation and picotee is, that the colour of the former is disposed in unequal stripes, going from the centre to the outer edge; that of the picotee is disposed on the outer edges of the petals, radiating inwards, and uniformly disposed. Flakes are carnations of two colours only, with large stripes going quite through their petals. Bizarres have their colours in variegated irregular spots or stripes. A perfect carnation should be not less than two inches and a half across; the lower petals six in number,—broad, thick, and smooth, and lying over each other so as to form a circle; each row of petals smaller than that immediately under it, rising in the centre so as to form half a ball. The colour should be clear and perfectly defined; and where there are two colours, the contrast should be bold and decided.

CARNATIONS FOR EXHIBITION.

The preparation of carnations and picotees for exhibition is quite an art, and to some a mystery. The base of the petals, which are mere threads issuing from the calyx, supports broad, heavy blades, which form the expanded blossoms; the largest-sized, which should be outside, being frequently in the centre. If the flower were left to itself, the calyx would probably be split all the way down one side, the other side not opening at all. To counteract this tendency, it is necessary to tie the calyx round the middle when the bud is nearly full-grown, and before it splits; and when the bud begins to open at the top, to pull back the five pieces which form the outer leaves of the calyx down to the point where it is tied: this enables the petals to develop themselves properly.

It is necessary, moreover, that these petals should be "dressed," to make them presentable. This is done by bringing all the petals into their proper places, passing the threads of the broadest petals outside those of the smaller, and guiding the others to the centre according to their size. This is obviously a very delicate operation, and should be commenced as soon as the petals begin to develop themselves. The larger petals are to be placed outside, and should form a complete circle; the next largest follow, making an inner circle, each petal lapping over the centre of that on which it rests; the third row being placed on the joinings of the second, and a fourth row, should there be one, on the joints of the third; while the whole continues to grow and expand, giving a natural effect to this artificial operation of dressing the flower.

The mode of operation is to take hold of the broadest part of the petal with a pair of smooth flat tweezers of ivory or bone, and by a gentle twist to bring the base round into the position it is to assume; the whole being usually supported by a card, in which a hole is cut large enough to let the calyx about halfway through, while the petals fall back upon, and are supported by, the card, which is circular in shape, to correspond with the expanded flower.

CARROTS.

Sow broadcast on beds, and thin to three or four inches for the smaller sorts: larger sorts are better sown in drills. If it is preferred to drill the seed, let the drills be one foot or 15 inches apart, as shallow as possible, and sow the seed continuously along the drill, or three or four seeds at intervals of six or eight inches: this economizes the seed, and admits of going amongst the plants without treading on them. Light ground should be trodden before it is drilled: the seed hangs together, and should be separated by rubbing it up with soil, if sown broadcast; but this is unnecessary if sown in drills. The seed is very light, so that a calm day should be chosen for sowing: a little wind is apt to blow it anywhere but into the right place: it takes from one to three weeks to germinate. As soon as the plants are well above ground, use the small hoe unsparingly, and thin out to not less than six inches apart; as they advance, continue using the hoe both to destroy and prevent the growth of weeds, and also for the benefit derived from loosing the ground. Carrots may be drawn for table as soon as large enough; but the main crop for storing should not be taken up till quite the end of October, or even later, unless severe frosts set in. There are many different sorts; but the Dutch Horn is generally used for forcing and early crops; Intermediate for second or late crop; the improved Altringham is good for main crop; but much depends on soil and locality. To produce carrots and parsnips of an extraordinary size, make a very deep hole with a long dibble; ram the earth well round it while the dibble is in, and when it is removed, fill up the hole with fine rich earth. Sow a few seeds on the top, either parsnips or carrots, as may be required, and when up, draw out all except the one plant nearest to the centre of the hole. Prodigious carrots and parsnips may be produced by this means.

CAULIFLOWERS (Brassica oleracea Botrytis).

The origin of the cauliflower, like all the family, is ascribed to the common wild cabbage, *Brassica oleracea*. It is of eastern origin, having been brought from Cyprus into France, and introduced from that country into England early in the 17th century.

With us the plant is treated as an annual, although it may, like all the race, be propagated from cuttings. In order to keep up a succession, three or four sowings should be made in the season, the first sowing being made on a slight hotbed in February, or very early in March. This is done by digging away a few inches of the soil the size of the intended bed, filling it up to a few inches above the surrounding soil with fresh stable-dung which has been well turned, covering the bed with the soil removed, raking it, and patting it smooth with the back of the spade. On this bed sow the seed, raking it in, or sifting fine soil over it, and covering it with hand-glasses, and otherwise protecting it when necessary.

Early in April a second and larger sowing should be made in the open ground, and a third and last sowing about the middle of August to stand through the winter. These sowings are made on beds of rich light soil, thoroughly pulverized by digging, and neither too dry nor too moist, 4½ feet wide, and long in proportion to the requirements of the garden, half an ounce of seed being sufficient for a 10-foot bed. In very dry weather, the seed-beds should receive a copious watering the night before sowing. When the plants are large enough to be handled, transplant them to nursery-beds of rich soil, well manured, pricking them out four inches apart each way. Some authorities recommend a second removal when the roots have formed a compact mass, in order to check the growth of stem and promote balling. In June the April sowings will be fit to plant out where they are to grow; in September they will be heading, and will continue to improve up to the frosts of early winter.

Like all the Brassicas, the Cauliflower requires a rich, deep soil and an open spot, but sheltered from the north. An old celery- or asparagus-bed, from which the plants have been lifted for forcing, is excellent. If none such is at liberty, let the ground be well trenched three feet deep, and manured with good rotten dung, thorougly incorporated with the soil in digging, bearing in mind that the delicacy and freshness of the vegetable depend on its rapid and vigorous growth when once started. On the ground thus prepared plant the young seedlings 2½ feet apart each way.

The after-cultivation is very simple; careful weeding, stirring the soil from time to time with the hoe, and drawing the earth about their roots, and copious watering at the roots in dry weather, include the necessary routine.

The autumn-sown plants are usually pricked out under frames for protection during winter, keeping them clear of weeds and decaying leaves, stirring the soil occasionally, and giving plenty of air in fine weather, protecting them from frost and rain. As they advance, and begin to head under hand- or bell-glasses, every opportunity should be taken of giving air: in severe weather, protect the frames and hand-glasses by packing litter round them.

When the heads begin to appear, shade them from sun and rain by breaking down some of the larger leaves, so as to cover them. Water in dry weather, previously forming the earth into a basin round the stem, and pour the water into the roots, choosing the evening in mild weather for so doing, and the morning when the air is frosty.

Mr. Henry Baily, of Nuneham Park, a well-known authority, transplants his autumn seedlings, as soon as they have made a few roots, into 60-sized pots, which he places in an open airy frame, or other sheltered place having facilities for protecting them from frost. As they fill the smaller pots with their roots, they are transplanted into larger ones, taking care that the roots never get matted in their pots; and early in February the first crop is placed out on a south border, the holes prepared for them having received a barrowful of thoroughly rotted dung, over which the mould is replaced, forming a little hillock on which the cauliflowers are planted. They are covered with the hand-glass till thoroughly established. By pursuing this course, Mr. Baily tells us (*Hort. Trans.*, v. 103), all check on the vigorous growth of the plant is avoided, while the tendency to increased luxuriance, so necessary in plants whose leaves or flowers are eaten, is encouraged.

After planting out, copious waterings should be given in the mornings in dull, cloudy weather, or in the evenings after bright sunshine.

On the approach of winter, the plants in flower may be taken up with as much earth at their roots as possible, and planted, or rather laid in by the roots, on their sides, in a light sandy soil, in some warm, sheltered place, where the frost can be excluded. In such a shed or frame they may be kept fresh and in condition for many weeks. Mr. Drummond, of the Cork Botanic Gardens, dug pits in the common soil, planting the cauliflowers in them, and covering them with frames of long wheat straw, tied together in small bundles, giving them air in fine weather.

The increase of so-called varieties led the Horticultural Society to test their qualities a few years ago, with the following results:—Eight kinds were sown on April 9th, and subsequently treated alike in every respect. Of the eight kinds tried, the large Asiatic and the Walcheren proved to be the most deserving of cultivation. It must be here remarked, however, that April 9th is much too late to prove some cauliflowers in this country; for every gardener knows that a kind which comes good in spring may be almost worthless in a dry, hot summer. The early varieties were failures, but the late kinds were good. In experiments upon vegetables, it is important that they should be proved in the best season for their particular growth, as many are trained to early spring, others to summer, and others again to autumn growth; and there is little doubt that these properties, within certain limits, become hereditary.

CEANO'THUS (nat. ord. Rhamna'ceæ). **Half-hardy Shrubs.**

An extremely handsome, free-flowering genus of highly ornamental shrubs, suitable either for conservatory decoration, or for covering fronts of villas, walls, or trellis-work in warm situations: they succeed best in peat and loam.

Ceanothus Americanus,—white, 4 ft., from New Jersey.
Ceanothus azureus grandiflorus,—sky-blue, flowers in bunches, 4 ft., from Mexico.
Ceanothus Baumannii, 3 ft.
„ Californicus,—blue, tinged with lilac, 4 ft., from California.
Ceanothus cæruleus microphyllus,—blue, small leaves, very pretty, 5 ft., from North America.
Ceanothus Delilianus,—white, shaded pale blue, beautiful, 5 ft., from North America.
Ceanothus floribundus,—dark blue, remarkably pretty, 3 ft.
Ceanothus Fontanesianus,—blue, shaded red, 4 ft., from North America.
Ceanothus grandiflorus roseus,—reddish blue, handsome, 4 ft., from North America.
Ceanothus Hartwegii,—blue, 6 ft., from Mexico.
Ceanothus ovatus,—white, elegant, 6 ft., from North America.

CELERY.

The celery-plant, *Apium graveolens*, is a biennial in its wild state, although the mode of cultivation adopted makes it an annual, except when grown for seed: it grows naturally in our marshy grounds, but we are indebted to Italy for this vegetable as well as the name, *celeri; ache* being the popular English name given to it by Ray and the older writers. It is propagated by seed, which is best obtained from the seed-shops. It may be sown in any month from Christmas to April. To get plants for the table in September, seeds should be sown in February in pans, which should be placed on a moderate hotbed: in about three weeks they will germinate, and, when about two inches high, the plants should be pricked out under glass, either in a frame or in pots, in a compost of loam, and three parts well-rotted dung. If in pots, shift them in April, and at the end of May plant them in shallow trenches in a warm part of the garden. If the trenches are dug out to the depth of two feet, six inches of hot dung placed in the bottom to stimulate the plants, the soil replaced, and the plants put in and covered with hand-glasses, an early crop will be the result. A second sowing should be made in March, still on a hotbed or on pans, or protected by sashes and mats until the plants are up; when fit to handle, they should be pricked out on a slight hotbed, or on a warm border. After a few weeks they should be again transplanted into a similar bed, and placed four or five inches apart each way. In July the plants will be fit to plant out in trenches for autumn use; a third sowing in April, treated in a similar manner, will be ready for winter use, pricking them out in fresh loam and decomposed leaf-mould when large enough to handle. When ready to plant for good in the trenches, mark out the ground into 4 feet clear spaces between the trenches, allowing 15 inches for the trench, if single rows, and 20 inches if double rows, are to be planted. Have not less than four feet clear space between the rows ; dig out the trenches one spade deep, throwing the soil on the spaces between ; then dig in the trenches a good dressing of rotten dung. If the weather is hot and dry, it is as well to wait for a shower of rain, unless the trenches can be watered both before and after planting. If in single rows, it is merely necessary to plant along the centre of the trench, a foot apart ; if double, stretch a line along the centre, and plant a row on each side of it. Let the youug plants be taken up and planted with a trowel : they should be well settled in with water. Celery is sometimes planted in this manner :—The ground is marked into one or more beds 4 feet wide ; if more than one, 5 or 6 feet is left between the beds ; the soil is dug out to the depth of 10 inches or a foot, and thrown on the intervening spaces ; a good dressing of manure is then forked into each bed ; the plants are then planted in rows across the beds, five plants in each row, the rows 15 inches apart. The only advantage of this plan is, that a greater number of plants can be grown on a given space. In earthing them up, it is necessary to have two pieces of board as long as the bed is wide. Place these between two rows, letting the boards rest close to the plants : this forms a trough into which the earth is to be thrown. Before earthing-up, as it is called, it is always best to gather up each plant with the hand and press the soil about it, to keep the leaves together, which prevents the soil falling into the heart of the plant. Never earth-up till about three weeks or a month before it is wanted,—before the month of October, when a little more time must be allowed for blanching. Early in November the final earthing-up should be done, unless in wet soils, when the plants might be protected with litter and earthed-up for blanching at discretion, otherwise sharp frosts might injure them. Some place dried leaves about the plants before earthing-up, and others, at the final earthing, cover the plants completely over ; but whether any advantage is derived from these practices may be doubted. It is advisable to dust well with lime before earthing, or to water with lime-water to destroy slugs. It is always best to earth-up gradually, that is, about four inches at a time, lest a too sudden change from exposure might rot the stalks. While growing, plenty of water should be given, and sometimes liquid manure ; for celery is a gross-feeding crop, and must be kept growing, or it will neither be crisp nor of good flavour. A very good way to grow celery is to plant about 15 or 18 inches apart, on a well-manured and well-pulverized piece of ground : let it grow to its full size, keep the ground well stirred between, give liquid manure or lay rotted dung between, and water in dry weather. When it is desired to blanch it, get a number of 4-inch drain-pipes, about 18 inches long ; place one over each plant, hold the leaves and stalks together, and fill up with sand : it will blanch clean, and is easily taken up. A great many more plants may thus be grown on a given space, the waste of room between the trenches, in the ordinary method, being avoided. To protect from frost, place litter between ; but very sharp frosts alone will require this.

In lifting celery, "always begin at one end of a row," says Mr. McIntosh, "taking the plants up by the roots, and carefully avoid bruising the stems or breaking the leaves. Cut the roots off, and bury them in the trench, but remove the plant to the vegetable-house. Remove the outer leaves to be washed, and reserved for soups. The centre parts carefully examine, and remove discoloured parts ; and when washed clean, dip it in clear salt-and-water, to dislodge any small worms : this done, it passes out of the gardener's care."

As frost sets in, a quantity of the crop for immediate use should be taken up ; removing the roots and soil, and tying the leaves together, convey them to the root-cellar, and lay them in sand, not too dry. Look to them from time to time, to see that they do not get too dry.

There are many kinds of celery in cultivation.

Early dwarf, solid white, is recommended.

Cole's superb white only differs in colour from his superb red; both highly recommended.

Manchester giant has a high reputation, but chiefly for its vigorous growth.

Old solid red, much grown by London market-gardeners.

Sutton's solid white, highly recommended for its colour and crispness.

Seymour's white champion is recommended for its compact, blanched, and crisp heart.

CELO'SIA (nat. ord. Amarantha'ceæ). Half-hardy Annuals.

Elegant and free-flowering plants, producing in the greatest profusion spikes of the most beautiful flowers. Some of the varieties have long, beautiful, slender flower-spikes, which may be dried for winter bouquets; others, again, have feathery or mossy plumes. Plants of the Celosia flower freely if planted out in June in a warm, sheltered situation; grown in pots, they are the most graceful of greenhouse and conservatory plants, and with a little management may be had in flower the whole winter. They are exceedingly valuable for dinner-table decoration. At the autumn flower-show of the Royal Horticultural Society, the collection of standard plants for dinner-table decoration which was awarded the first prize partly consisted of Celosias. They grow freely in rich loamy soil; favourite varieties are:—

Celosia argentea,—silvery white, shaded with bright rose, very handsome, 3 ft.
Celosia pyramidalis atrosanguinea,—dark red, very handsome, 3 ft.
Celosia pyramidalis aurea,—orange, exceedingly beautiful, 3 ft.
Celosia pyramidalis Ada Beaufleur,—white, tipped rosy purple, a splendid hybrid between C. pyramidalis and C. argentea; spikes of bloom 8 inches long, 3 ft.
Celosia pyramidalis coccinea aurantiaca,—scarlet and orange, very handsome, 3 ft.

CHAMÆ'ROPS (nat. ord. Palmæ).

The Chamærops, or Fan Palm, is a splendid plant of oriental appearance, producing a striking effect if planted out in lawns or pleasure-grounds, and protected during winter; it is also valuable for conservatory decoration: succeeds best in rich loamy soil.

CHELO'NE (nat. ord. Scrophularia'ceæ).

A beautiful hardy herbaceous plant, with showy pentstemon-like flowers, very effective in centres of beds, or groups in mixed borders: thrives in any rich soil.

CHINA ROSES.

The first introduction of the Chinese roses dates from 1789, in which year both the monthly rose and the crimson Chinese were introduced. The varieties which have sprung from these are innumerable. They have also been hybridized extensively with the tea-scented. Unlike other roses, also, the Chinese roses get a deeper and more brilliant tint by exposure to the sun. "Archduke Charles, and some other Chinese roses," Mr. Paul tells us, "are distinct and beautiful as variegated roses; they expand rose and white, soon become mottled with, then change entirely to, crimson, from the action of the sun's rays."

The common and Crimson China are very beautiful, either grown in beds or on walls. Among groups of bedding-plants mixed with Cérise unique, or Lady Middleton geranium, the common China rose, edged with the crimson, and surrounded with a white band of Alyssum or *Cerastium tomentosum*, is very effective, distinct, and striking. Towards the end of May or beginning of June, they will be in full beauty, and the mass of blush pink, with the setting here described, is peculiarly soft and beautiful. By cutting off the flowering-stems as soon as they begin to fade, a succession of flowers will be secured throughout the summer. If, however, a short hiatus should intervene, the geraniums will fill up the gap; and the varieties here named have the merit of harmonizing nicely with the roses. Several other China roses form beautiful groups for the flower-garden. The best for this purpose are, perhaps, the following :—

Cramoisie supérieure,—bright crimson.
Clara Sylvain,—pure white, large.
Prince Charles,—bright carmine.
Mrs. Bosanquet,—pale flesh, similar in habit to Bourbon Queen.
Aimée Plantier,—bright fawn and rose.
Eugène Hardy,—creamy pale blush.
Marjolin,—rich dark crimson.
Madame Bréon,—bright rose, large and good.

All the China roses require some protection in winter. Nothing is better than some coal-ashes over the roots—say eight inches thick, and a quantity of boughs of spruce, &c., bent over the tops, from six to eight inches in thickness.

Of the monthly China rose the following are very beautiful varieties :—

Anteros,—flowers white, tinged with sulphur, creamy centre; cupped, large and full; partaking of the tea-scented.
Archduke Charles,—light rose, margins almost white, changing to brilliant crimson; a profuse bloomer; moderate grower. One of the best changeable roses. Unique.
Belle Ferronnière,—flowers blush, with flesh centre, often tinged with pink; cupped, large, and double; excellent for massing.
Bourbon Armosa,—a bright pink.
Bourbon Angelina,—pale cream-colour, fawn in the centre.
Caroline de Berri,—flowers flesh-colour, tinged with fawn, and cupped.
Clara,—flowers white, with creamy centre, but petals often rosy; large, full, and cupped; good forcing rose.
Clara Sylvain,—pure white, cupped, large, and full; a superb flower, flowering freely from June till the end of October; moderate grower, suited for a small bed, and the best white for the purpose. Beautiful.
Chénédole,—flower a brilliant crimson; large, superb flower; magnificent for a standard, making long and vigorous shoots.
Cramoisie supérieure,—a beautiful rose, of bright velvety crimson.
Eugène Hardy,—flowers white, centre blush-colour; of medium size, full, and cupped; of drooping habit, and does best as a standard.
General Soyez,—flowers cherry-crimson, very large and full, cupped; a beautiful autumn rose.
General Jaquemont,—flower purplish-red, of very perfect shape; has taken prizes at all recent flower-shows.
George IV.,—flowers deep violet-crimson; raised by Mr. Rivers; one of the oldest and finest of the class.
Grenadier,—flowers rosy crimson, changing to pale rose; large, full, and cupped.
Madame Bréon,—flowers rich rose-colour, sometimes tinged with salmon; very large, full, and compact.
Madame Bureau,—flowers white, the centre inclining to straw; large, double and cupped. One of the finest autumnal whites.
Magna rosea,—flower light blush; a fine large rose.
Miellez,—flowers pale lemon, changing to white; of medium size, double, and cupped.
Reine de Lombardie,—flowers blush, changing to rosy crimson; large, full, and expanded.
Rival de Pæstum,—flowers yellowish-white; large and full.
Rubens,—flowers blush, lilac, and crimson; changeable; very large, full, and cupped.
Tancredi,—flowers light purple, suffused with crimson; variable, large, and cupped, with rich foliage.
Virginale,—flowers flesh-colour, of medium size; full, globular; requires forcing to bring out.

CHOROZE'MAS (nat. ord. **Legumino'sæ**).

A most interesting genus of plants from Australia, which bloom almost the whole year, more especially in the winter and early spring, and are consequently most acceptable additions to our greenhouses and conservatories. They are not very difficult to manage, and are alike useful for decoration and as cut flowers for bouquets, at a time when such flowers are valuable. They delight in a rich turfy peat, mixed with fibrous loam and leaf-mould and gritty sand. When recently potted, they require a close pit or the warm part of a greenhouse, and cautious watering, until they get into free growth. When thoroughly established, water with clear liquid manure twice a week.

Chorozemas are propagated by cuttings of the half-ripened young wood, taken off in July or August, taking the short, stiff, and weak or medium growth, but avoiding twigs of a robust habit. These, after being trimmed, should be about one inch long, and must be inserted in sand, under protection of a bulb-glass. In preparing the pots for the cuttings, take care to drain thoroughly, by half filling them with potsherd; then place fibrous peat about an inch deep over the drainage, and fill up with clean sand. After the cuttings are in, place the pots in a close cold-frame, water when necessary, and wipe the condensed moisture from the inside of the glass twice or thrice a week. Here the cuttings must remain until they are cicatrized, when they may be removed to a warmer situation, and the pots plunged in a very slight bottom-heat, and in a few weeks they will be ready to pot off. If it is late in the season before the cuttings are ready to pot off, they should remain in the cutting-pots through the winter, and be potted off in February; but if they are ready for single pots in September, they will be much benefited by being potted off early.

Attention must be paid to stopping the rude shoots, so as to induce close, compact, and healthy growth. If the plants progress as they ought, they will require a second shift during the season. They should be kept growing until the winter fairly sets in, at which time they should be brought to a state of rest. In the second year some of the plants will have a nice head of bloom; but in order to produce rapid growth, remove the bloom-buds when quite young, and keep the plants vigorously growing through the second season. If they are in good health and the pot full of roots, a shift any time between Christmas and October will not hurt them: never shift a plant until the pot is full of vigorous roots, and also take especial care that the roots do not become matted before you shift.

Manure-water in a weak state may be used with advantage; but use it with caution, and not more than twice a week. That prepared from sheep's dung and soot is best, and it *must* be used in a perfectly clear state.

The following are some of the most distinct and beautiful of the series which are met with in cultivation:—

C. angustifolia,—a remarkably graceful shrub, with long, slender, and somewhat scrambling stems, having linear acute leaves with recurved margins, and racemes of pretty flowers, of which the standard is orange-yellow and the wings crimson-purple. Flowers in March and April. New Holland. Introduced 1830: formerly called *Dillwynia glycinefolia.*

C. cordata,—an elegant dwarf shrub, with many slender branches, clothed with sessili-cordate, obtuse, spiny-toothed leaves, and bearing the flowers in more or less drooping racemes. They are orange in the standard, with scarlet or crimson wings, sometimes scarlet with purple. Flowers in March and April. New Holland. Introduced 1836.

C. Dicksoni,—a handsome dwarf bushy-growing shrub, furnished with narrow leaves, and bearing a profusion of beautiful dull scarlet and yellow flowers. Flowers in March to May. New Holland. Introduced 1836.

C. flava,—a very pretty and distinct form for the cultivator. It is of erect, slender habit, with elongated ovate leaves, sinuate, toothed on the margin; the teeth spiny: the flowers are in racemes, the standard deep clear yellow, the wings much paler or lemon-colour. Flowers in March and April. New Holland. Introduced about 1848.

C. ilicifolia,—a diffuse-spreading shrub, with oblong, lanceolate, pinnatifidly spinous leaves, and bearing scarlet flowers; the standard marked with yellow at the base. Flowers from March to August. Introduced 1803.

C. Henchmanni,—a hairy shrub, with short twiggy branches, covered with needle-shaped leaves, and bearing numerous axillary racemes of flowers of a light scarlet, with a yellow mark at the base of the standard. Flowers from April to June, and sometimes till September. Introduced 1825.

C. ovata,—a handsome shrub, with weak ascending winged stems, furnished with ovate-acute leaves, and bearing short racemes of showy flowers, usually scarlet, with crimson wings. Flowers from March to May. Introduced 1830.

C. spectabilis,—a very beautiful small shrub, with slender, twining or scrambling stems, the leaves of which are elliptic, lanceolate, obovate, or cuneate, and the flowers pale orange in the standard, tinged with crimson; the wings being crimson: they grow in long drooping racemes. Flowers from April to July. Introduced 1839.

C. triangularis,—a beautiful dwarf spreading shrub, of branching habit, with subhastate leaves, pinnatifidly spinous on the margin, and the flowers in short racemes, the standard scarlet, the wings purple. Flowers in March and April. Introduced 1830.

C. varia,—a dwarf compact-growing species, with variable leaves; in some forms broadly ovate, toothed, and spiny on the margin; in others almost entire, and sometimes nearly round in outline. The flowers are very numerous, in short racemes, large and showy, usually orange with crimson wings. Flowers from April to July. Introduced 1837.

The variety called C. varia nana, of remarkably dwarf habit, is the best for a limited collection, though there are two or three other very distinct and beautiful forms.

CLOTH OF GOLD ROSE.

To grow Cloth of Gold and its congeners freely, procure strong, healthy plants, budded on Celine or Mannetti stocks in spring; plant out on a south wall, on a properly-prepared border. If the soil is naturally good, enrich it with rotted dung, having the border previously well drained. Should the soil be indifferent, dig it out to the depth of 18 inches or 2 feet, and replace it with rich turfy loam, mixed with well-decomposed cow-dung in equal proportions, and a little leaf-mould. Every ten days in summer give the plant a good soaking of liquid manure, and as the growth proceeds, nail the shoots closely to the wall, and stop all shoots at 15 or 18 inches, by pinching off the points. Many, both of the stopped and unstopped shoots, will bloom freely. In cold situations protection should be given in winter. Spring pruning should not take place till the end of March, when all danger from severe frost is past. At this time prune hard, cutting out and shortening back considerably all old wood, to induce vigorous growth. In the following season give the same attention to pruning and watering with liquid manure. The south wall will be found greatly to facilitate the ripening of the young wood in autumn.

CHRYSAN'THEMUM (nat. ord. Compos'itæ).

Unusual importance attaches to the cultivation of Chrysanthemums, from the facility with which they may be grown in the very heart of large towns, as has been proved by the efforts of Mr. Broome in the Temple Gardens, where he has grown all the best varieties in a manner which has astonished many who have examined his collection. The flower is of easy culture, and cuttings may be struck almost up to the time of flowering. Nothing is finer than the display of these flowers in October and November, ranging as they do from pure white to a deep orange, from a pale blue to deep red and crimson; but, like the dahlia, the first frost sadly spoils them. Where the collection is a choice one, chrysanthemums are best trained against a wall, or in beds, where protection against sudden frost can be easily applied. By means of pot-culture, which is now extensively used, a splendid show of flowers may be preserved even up to Christmas, with comparatively little trouble.

Cuttings of chrysanthemums should be potted pretty thickly together in sandy soil, and the pots plunged to the rim in a gentle hotbed. If the number is not large, put them separately in thumb-pots, so that there may be no derangement of the plants when they are repotted. Nothing roots more certainly than the Chrysanthemum; and if rooted pieces of the old plant are taken instead of cuttings, propagation will go on without any trouble at all. In order to give the plants every advantage, they must never be either root-bound or allowed to flag from drought: these evils are to be avoided by frequent repottings and constant attention to watering. The blooming-pots should generally be 10 inches deep and 8 in diameter at the top; and between the thumb-pots and these final ones there should be at least three shiftings. Fresh rich soil must be used to fill up the space in the larger pot. Plenty of fresh air and sunlight must be afforded all through the growth of the Chrysanthemum, and as the plant absorbs rapidly, it requires some care to prevent the leaves from flagging. In hot sunny weather, half a dozen waterings in a day would scarcely accomplish this, and prevention must be tried by burying the pots up to the rim in the moist soil of the garden: thus treated, one or two good waterings in a day will be sufficient. Care must be taken that worms do not get into the pot, by placing them on bricks, slates, or coal-ashes. They should be turned round twice a week to prevent their roots striking into the material beneath the pots. Liquid manure may be supplied rather plentifully as the flower-buds begin to expand: when judiciously applied, it produces finer growth and deeper colour. The best compost consists of two parts light loam to one part of well-decomposed dung, freely mixed with sand. The Chrysanthemum may also be raised from seed. Messrs. Barr and Sugden say, "Really valuable varieties have been raised from the seed saved by our Sardinian correspondent. The seed we offer has been saved from the very finest of the new varieties, and is warranted to produce 75 per cent. of double flowers."

The Chrysanthemum, like other plants producing terminal flowers, has a tendency to send up one leading stem, which, if not interfered with, would produce a bunch of flowers at the top. This tendency is counteracted by stopping the terminal shoot, which produces a compact shrubby growth, and a great many more flowers. As a rule for the large-flowering kinds, stopping should cease in July; while with pompones it may be extended to August. The general law is, that letting the plants run up is favourable to fine flowers, and stopping, to a more plentiful supply. It is the practice of some growers to stop the plants at every third eye until the middle of August, watering freely with manure-water three or four times a week, and sprinkling the plants overhead with water every morning. Early in September the best plants are selected, and repotted into 12-sized pots, using the compost as before, and giving ample drainage, and placing them under a south wall; the smaller plants being transplanted at the same time into 24-sized pots, and placed under an east wall. By the middle of October the earlier plants will be showing flower, and should be placed in a cold greenhouse, or cold-pit, where they can receive plenty of air, leaving those intended for late flowering under the east wall as long as the weather will permit. By the middle of November all should be housed, or at least provided with shelter, and a good supply of bloom for the next two months should be the result.

The number for selection is well-nigh endless, and they have latterly been divided into Large, Pompone, and Anemone-flowered varieties. The following are good sorts, that cannot fail to give satisfaction. Those marked thus * are the most expensive; but they can, with a few exceptions, be supplied by most nurserymen at 6*s.*, 9*s.*, 12*s.*, and 18*s.* per dozen. The time to purchase them is when they are in bloom; and then you can please yourself both in colour, substance, shape, and size of flower, as well as in the habit of the plant:—

Large-flowering Varieties.

Alfred Salter,—fine form; light pink; first-rate.
Annie Salter,—fine golden yellow.
Aimée Ferière,—white, tipped rose-pink; incurved; fine.
Adriane,—cream, buff-tinted.
Aurora,—very full; ochre-yellow.
*Bacchus,—rosy fawn; large; incurved.
Beauté du Nord,—violet-carmine.
Boadicea,—creamy rose.
Cassy,—orange and rose.
Chevalier Domage,—fine gold.
Cloth of Gold,—fine; large.
Defiance,—fine; incurved; white.
*Dido,—white sulphur; incurved; dwarf habit.
*Draco,—incurved; dark red; free bloomer.
Dragon,—puce; light centre.
Etoile Polaire,—deep yellow; incurved.
Excelsior,—bright crimson; very full.
*Finstriatum,—primrose; fringed.
Formosum,—finely incurved; pale sulphur.
Golden Christine,—golden buff; large.
Golden Queen of England,—canary; fine.
*Guelder Rose,—pure white; finely incurved.

*Imbricatum album,—incurved; white.
King,—light peach; incurved.
La Reine d'Or,—golden yellow; fine.
*Lady St. Clair,—pure white; finely incurved.
Le Prophète,—golden fawn; a splendid flower.
Lord of the Isles,—creamy yellow and orange.
Marceau,—rose; bordered white.
Novelty,—large; blush.
Picturatum roseum,—salmon; incurved.
Prince Albert,—bright crimson.
Queen of England,—fine blush; incurved.
Queen of Lilacs,—fine; incurved.
Queen of the Isles,—white; large.
*Snowball,—fine white.
*Snowflake,—very dwarf.
Versailles Defiance,—rose and lilac; fine form.
Vesta,—ivory-white; one of the oldest and best.
Vulcan,—bright red crimson.

Pompone Varieties.—These are beautiful for front shelves in conservatories, or beds or borders out of doors; generally of compact, close growth, and the flowers about the size of large daisies, and rivalling the large ones in colour; they are at once the neatest and most ornamental plants for furnishing:—

Adonis,—rose and white.
Aigle d'Or,—canary-yellow.
*Apollo,—fine; incurved; chestnut-yellow.
Bob,—fine dark brown.
Brilliant,—crimson-scarlet.
Christina,—canary-yellow; brown tips.
Diana,—white; fine form.
*Fairy,—light lemon.
Fennella,—bright orange.
Hendersonii,—yellow; early flowering.
Ida,—pale clear yellow.
*Indian Prince,—carmine-red and gold; incurved.
*Lucinda,—rosy lilac and blush; full.
Madame Fould,—cream; one of the best.
Madame Mielly,—violet-amaranth.
Marabout,—white-fringed; fine.
Mrs. Salford,—white; fine.
Mrs. Modell,—fine white.
Nemesis,—bronzed orange.
President Ducaisne,—rosy carmine; scarlet.
Queen of Lilliput,—rosy blush.
Sacramento,—golden yellow.
Scarlet Germ,—crimson-scarlet.
Stella,—light-shaded pink.
The Little Pet,—blush-white; incurved.

Large Anemone-flowered Varieties.—These are not equal to the others in beauty. They differ from them in having a centre of close petals like an anemone, and a fringe of loose petals for an edging. Almost every one knows the Golden Orange-coloured Gluck; it is a perfect representative of this class:—

George Sands,—red, with gold centre.
Fleur de Marie,—large white.
Juno,—white.
King of Anemones,—crimson.
*Lady Margaret,—pure white, with row of ground petals.
Margaret of Norway,—red and gold.
Margaret of Versailles,—blush.
Louis Bonamy,—lilac; high centre.

Pompone Anemone-flowered Varieties:—

Reine des Anémones,—fine white.
Perle,—rose; lilac centre.
President Morel,—cinnamon; gold centre.
M. Astre,—golden yellow.
Madame Peuter,—pure white.
Golden Cedo Nulli,—golden canary.
Cedo Nulli,—white, with brown spots.
Boule de Neige,—pure white,
Ariane Amaranth,—gold centre; fine.

CINERA'RIAS (nat. ord. Compos'itæ).

Few plants are so effective for decorative purposes as these. "To make a truly fine cineraria," says Mr. Glenny, "we must have a white ground, which renders any colours a good contrast, the most striking being crimsons and blues. The edging should be even, forming an even band of colour alike all round, and having a well-defined circle of white surrounding a disk of some determinate colour. This disk, then, should be white on the ground, distinctly banded with a dense colour of some kind, the greater the contrast the better; the disk being small, dark-coloured, or bright yellow; the petals smooth and velvety,—no ribs or pinkers; the bloom flat and round; or if they deviate, by cupping rather than reflexing; the foliage spreading, green, and even; above which the flowers should form an even surface of bloom, the flowers setting edge to edge, and perfectly circular; the ends of the petals free from notch, with a distinct edge of colour; thick at the edge, and the flowers opening flat." Unless for exhibition, it is best to grow them annually from seed. The first sowing should be made in March, in pans filled with equal parts of peat and loam and one-sixth part sand. They should be well drained, made firm, and the seed slightly covered, and placed on a slight bottom-heat. Keep the pans and young plants, when they appear, partially shaded from the bright sun; put them into 3-inch pots as soon as they will bear handling, return them to the same place, and renew the same treatment until they are thoroughly established in their pots. Then gradually harden them by giving plenty of air, and place them in a sheltered situation out of doors towards the end of May. As the roots reach the sides of the pots, shift them into larger, giving them their final shift in September. The first flower-stems should be cut out close to the bottom when large plants are desired. This will induce them to throw out from six to twelve side shoots;—these may be reduced, or all left, at the option of the grower. Towards the end of September, they should be returned to a cold-pit, and they will begin to flower in October. No soil is better for growing them than equal parts rich loam, leaf-mould, and thoroughly rotted sheep- or horse-dung, liberally mixed with sharp sand or charcoal-dust, and used in a roughish state. They also luxuriate under he stimulating regimen of *rich* manure-water. Another sowing may be made in April, and a third in May, for very late plants. The treatment of old plants may be similar to this. Cut them down as soon as they are done flowering; shake them out, and pot each sucker separately in March; then proceed as above in every respect.

List of the best Varieties.

Acme, Adam Bede, Beauty, Brilliant, Duke of Cambridge, Bridesmaid, the Colleen Bawn, Handel, Incomparable, Mademoiselle Parepa, Magenta, Maid of Honour, Miss Marnock, Mrs. Livingstone, Perfection, Queen Victoria, Queen of Lilies, Regalia, Royal Marine, Solferino, Slough's Rival, the Wizard, and Wonderful.

CLARK'IA (nat. ord. Onagra'ceæ). Hardy Annuals.

Cheerful-looking flowers, growing freely from seed and blooming profusely under almost all circumstances. When planted in rich soil and properly attended to, they rank amongst the most effective of bedding plants, more especially *C. integripetala*, *alba*, and *marginata*, *C. Tom Thumb*, and *C. T. T. integripetala:* the large handsome flowers of the former render them strikingly attractive, and the latter, with their fine bushy habit, make useful plants for bedding or conservatory decoration. The new double variety, *C. pulchella* fl. pl., is of a rich magenta colour and very handsome. These new varieties are decided acquisitions.

CLIAN'THUS (nat. ord. Legumino'sæ).

A genus of magnificent free-flowering shrubs, with elegant foliage and brilliantly coloured and singularly-shaped flowers, which are produced in splendid clusters. *C. magnificus* and *C. puniceus* blossom freely out of doors in summer, against a trellis or south wall; *C. Dampierii* succeeds best planted in the border of a greenhouse, and is one of the finest plants of recent introduction; seeds sown early in spring flower the first year; succeed best in sandy peat and loam. They may also be raised easily by cuttings.

Clianthus Dampierii,—brilliant scarlet, with intense black spot in the centre of the flower; exceedingly handsome and showy, from New Holland.
Clianthus magnificus,—scarlet; beautiful, 4 ft., from New Zealand.
Clianthus puniceus,—scarlet, 4 ft.

CLIPPING HEDGES, &c.

All evergreens and hedges, especially evergreen hedges, should be cut to a point pyramidically; for if the top be allowed to overhang the bottom, the lower shoots will invariably die off. With hollies and laurels use the knife in pruning, to avoid the rusty appearance of the withering of half-cut leaves. Privet and thorn may be clipped with the garden-shears.

CLUBBING IN BROCOLI.

This disease, so destructive to a crop of brocoli, especially on poor land and under indifferent culture, may be prevented, in some degree, by dipping the roots, before planting, in a thick mixture, composed of $\frac{1}{4}$ peck of soot and 1 lb. of saltpetre, with water added to make it the consistency of paste. A more certain remedy, however, is found in a proper system of cropping and manuring, by which this exhausting vegetable is made to follow, in rotation, crops which act as deepeners and restorers of the qualities withdrawn by previous crops of Brassicæ.

COLLIN'SIA (nat. ord. Scrophularia'ceæ). Hardy Annuals.

An exceedingly pretty, free-flowering popular genus, remarkably attractive in beds, or mixed borders. *C. bicolor*, *C. bicolor alba*, *C. bicolor atrorubens*, and *C. multicolor marmorata*, contrast finely in ribbons.

COMPOSTS.

The successful flower-grower should always have at hand :—

1. All the leaves which can be got together, except those in the shrubberies, which should be dug in.
2. A heap of clean road-grit.
3. A heap of sand, silver or river.
4. A good stack of turfs cut from some pasture, three inches or less in thickness.
5. A heap of cow-dung.
6. A heap of stable-dung, which is most suitable for the present purpose when taken from an old hotbed.
7. A stack of turfy peat from a common.
8. All the waste of the garden should also be placed where it may rot, for it is a capital dressing ; because, when once fairly rotted into mould, it is next in value to pure leaf-mould.

We hear and read of all manner of exciting composts, such as guano, night-soil, bullock's blood, offal of the slaughterhouse, sugar-bakers' scum, and various other not very nice material ; but all this resolves itself into the single fact that all animal matter, as well as animal dung, enriches the ground,—bone-dust, shavings of horn and hoofs, among the rest. There is an uncertainty about the strength of all these materials which renders them unsuited for delicate and valuable plants, although, for farming operations and coarse-vegetable growing, they are valuable. A collection of florists' flowers cannot be played with, and their existence would be often placed in jeopardy by exciting composts, of which the strength is not easily ascertained ; whereas all those materials which we have recommended are known. Beyond these we may mention rabbit-, sheep-, and even poultry-dung, which may be obtained for the purpose of using as liquid manure after being thoroughly decomposed ; such liquid manure being made by stirring a pound of rotted poultry-dung, or half a peck of rabbit-, sheep-, or cow-dung, in eighteen gallons of water for two or three days, and, when settled, it is fit for use.

CONSERVATORY.

This structure may well be termed a winter garden, for such is its most useful purpose : it is really an essentially necessary adjunct to a well-ordered country-house of any pretensions, affording means of exercise to the ladies and visitors in inclement weather. In houses of smaller dimensions it is the storehouse for displaying the flowers as they are forced into bloom in the greenhouse or frames, as well as for growing certain climbing and creeping plants festooned and trained under its roof and over its walls, and for other plants only requiring protection from frosts, which occupy its beds and borders. Even in the absence of any heating apparatus, the conservatory, if properly glazed and painted, will bring the temperature of the atmosphere to about the degree enjoyed by our neighbours on the banks of the Loire, seven degrees farther south, without the great extremes of summer heat and winter cold to which they are exposed. In these days, therefore, of cheap glass, there is no reason why every house, suburban or country, should not have its glass house proportioned to its size.

There are some few points which should influence the choice of a site for every kind of plant-structure, the first and most important being, that it is not overshadowed on the south, east, or west, or exposed to the drip of trees or houses in any direction. A lean-to house, which, however, is the very worst form, may have any aspect between south and south-south-east; south, inclining a point or two to east, being the best, as it receives the early sun as it gradually rises, without being exposed to its full meridian glare. The span-roofed house would probably be well placed which ranged from north-west to south-south-east also: it would thus receive all the morning sun on one side, while the other would receive the meridian sun slightly oblique, and all the afternoon sun, varying according to the angle of incidence of the roof. This would also be the most favourable aspect for a ridge-and-furrow roof, whether it were supported against a back wall or had a rectangular roof with vertical lights on each side.

Conservatories, however, which are appendages to the house, must depend for their aspect on the position it occupies, except where the principal rooms lie to the north. No plant-house can possibly prosper in this aspect, since the house shades it from the south sun; nevertheless, with these rooms it must be connected, or it fails in its object; and a passage or corridor connecting it, covered with glass, must lead to some locality, either to east, or west, or south, where a more genial aspect can be obtained for the conservatory. Where a glass corridor becomes necessary, it should be made subservient to the objects of the conservatory by the introduction of baskets, trailing plants, vases occupying niches, and other attractions.

As regards its architectural style, the conservatory should, at least, be in harmony with that of the house: if ornaments are permitted, they should be Gothic, Tudor, or Grecian, according as the house is of one character or the other: in this, as in all other matters, congruity is to be studied.

The conservatory, properly speaking, is a house in which the plants occupy beds and borders as in the garden, but on a smaller scale: sometimes the plants are permanent ones, more frequently they stand in pots plunged into the soil, or in tubs standing on its surface, or in vases occupying pedestals. Much has been written on the arrangements of conservatories, and Mr. Noel Humphreys has propounded some ideas for their picturesque arrangement which would have a very pleasing effect in a house of sufficient size. Want of space prevents us from doing more than directing the reader's attention to his observations, which are well worth the notice of any one who contemplates adding a conservatory to his house. The shape and size of a conservatory must, of course, always be determined upon by the situation. It must suffice here to observe that the panes of glass should be large, with as little sash-work as possible, and that the best mode of heating is with hot-water pipes. The heating apparatus of the conservatory may generally be so managed as to warm the hall and staircase.

COPINGS FOR WALLS.

Coping to garden-walls has been a "much-vexed" question; it seems very well settled, however, that a stone coping, projecting an inch or two over the wall on each side, is necessary for the protection of the wall from the effects of rain, and to that extent it is useful in retarding the radiation of heat. Mr. Walker re-

Copings for Walls.

commends a coping, as improving the appearance as well as necessary for protection from the weather, and recommends one of two inches thick, bevilled off to three-quarters of an inch at the edges on each side.

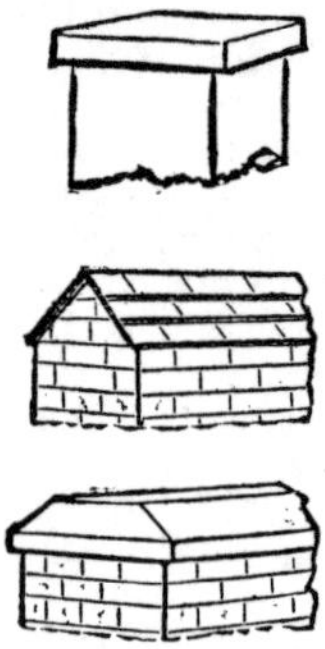

Admitting that the coping projecting two inches is necessary for the protection of the wall, and beneficial to the tree, the best horticulturists come to the conclusion that temporary copings, extending 18 inches beyond the wall, with protecting curtains depending from them, are very useful during the spring months; and Mr. Errington considers that by using them in autumn a fortnight is added

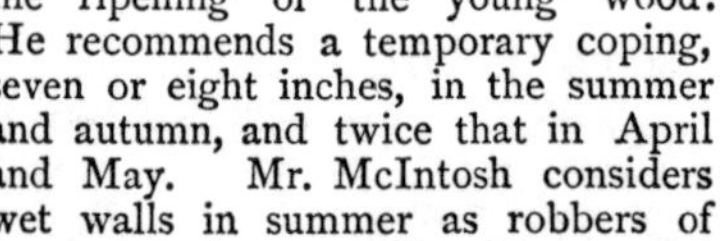

to the summer, and time given for the ripening of the young wood. He recommends a temporary coping, seven or eight inches, in the summer and autumn, and twice that in April and May. Mr. McIntosh considers wet walls in summer as robbers of heat, and that a wall with a good projecting coping, capable of being moved in the heat of the day, is invaluable after sunset. The portable coping at Dalkeith is a boarding nine inches wide, supported on iron brackets, to which the boards are attached by screws. In the Horticultural Society's Gardens the copings are more inclined, the stone coping projecting two inches; and six inches thick of York paving, Caithness flag, Ackworth paving-stone, and various heads of slate of the Pembrokeshire and other Welsh counties, make excellent coping stone. Roman cement has been tried; asphalt has also been tried successfully. Glass, six inches thick, and bevilled, has been thought the best material for coping, being perfectly indestructible by the weather; and cast iron has been found to answer. As to shape, the flat coping, with a groove to carry off the water, is supposed to be excellent. A very good coping is sometimes formed of brick and cement, as on the other side. Another form of coping strongly recommended is a stone, sloping on each side, laid on a flat one placed horizontally over the wall.

Copings projecting too far are said to deprive the leaves of the vigour they derive from summer rains and heavy dews, although they are useful in spring, when the trees are in blossom, and up to the time when the fruit is set. At this season, even in the far drier climate of France, it is found necessary to protect the tender blossoms from the late frosts, hail, snow, and cold rains of spring, which are very fatal to stone-fruit; the walls in France being generally trellised, in order to protect the trees from the intensity of the heat produced by radiation, as distinguished from our own more moist climate, where the practice is reversed: an angular framework of wood is attached to the trellis, projecting some 20 inches or so from the wall, at an inclination of 50°. When the tree begins to vegetate, towards the second week of February, hurdles of straw attached to rods of wood, 7 feet 4 in. in length by 2 feet broad (fig. A A), are placed on the triangular frame, so as to shelter the tree at the time when it is in blossom, and till it has begun

Copings for Walls.

to stone, resting on the trellis A D C. When the trellis is absent, projecting rods of wood are attached under the coping, upon which the hurdles are laid in lengths, at a similar angle.

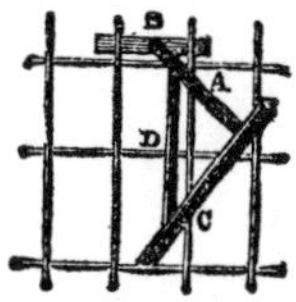

This shelter, M. Brieul assures us, is indispensable for stone-fruit. Apples and pears are also benefited by the shelter, especially when exposed to a north or west aspect, or in damp localities. This protection, however, according to the same authority, which suffices while the temperature stands at 1° or 1½° below zero, becomes useless whenever it descends to 3°, or even 2°, which too frequently sweeps away the hopes of the fruit-gardener. The walls should then be protected by means of a rough canvas, such as is used by paperhangers to cover walls before papering, which is attached to the projecting hurdles under the coping at B, and at foot to posts driven into the ground at an angle of 50°. This canvas covering permits the light and

air and warmth to pass; the vegetation is uninterrupted, and the protection is sufficient to exclude the strongest spring frosts.

Mr. Gorrie, a well-known and experienced horticulturist, found that the projecting coping added greatly to the warmth of the walls, the difference being from 4° to 11°; and it will be readily conceded that this advantage is a very important one. At the same time the cost of permanent coping adds greatly to the cost of the wall.

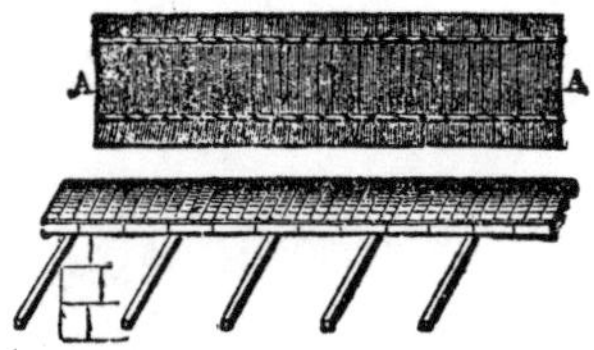

Mr. Gorrie proposed to train the Ayrshire rose on a projecting trellis under the coping, so as to give shelter to the fruit-trees while in blossom, the rapid spring growth of this rose being favourable for the purpose, while its deciduous habit admits of the full play of the wind in winter.

The Rev. John Lawrence, one of our oldest and best writers on fruit-trees, places among the causes of barrenness to which he directs attention cold seasons, and especially *frosts* and *blasts* in the spring. Having recourse to mats, although sometimes successful, has many objections, which put him to considering some more efficient remedy, and it occurred to him that horizontal shelters presented the one needful remedy. He experimented with thin bits of board or tile fastened to the wall, and found them to succeed to a marvel, securing fruit wherever they were placed. For this purpose he proposes to lay rows of tiles in the wall at distances regulated by the space between the lateral branches of the tree, and jutting forward from the plane of the wall about an inch and a half, not in continuous rows, but with gaps to receive the branches of the tree. By the help of these shelters, says Mr. Lawrence, "even in the most difficult year, a good quantity of fruit may *almost* be depended upon from such blossoms as are sheltered by the tiles. The fruit thus sheltered

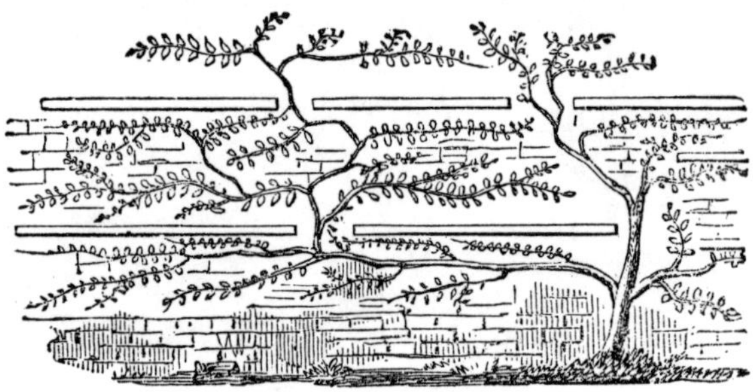

from perpendicular cold and blasts I have experienced to be much larger, better, and finer-tasted, than those of the same tree where exposed. They are also forwarder and earlier ripe than the others."

CORONIL'LA (nat. ord. Legumino'sæ).

Handsome free-flowering half-hardy shrubs, with silvery-looking foliage, and their pretty flowers dispersed in little tufts like coronets; easily cultivated from cuttings, growing freely in a mixture of peat and loam, and succeeding well against a south wall with a little winter protection.

Coronilla glauca,—yellow, 2 ft., from South of France.
Coronilla juncea,—yellow, 2 ft., from South of France.

COTTAGE GARDENS.

Cottage gardens and allotments vary in size and shape: some are square, some oblong, others angular; they also range in size from half a rod to a quarter of an acre. Taking a medium course, let us describe one of about thirty yards each way. Here, as in other cases, economy recommends simplicity of design. Supposing the frontage (3) to be laid out as a flower-garden; let the walks present a curve rather than sharp angles; let

the beds be circular or oval rather than pointed; and let the space for flowers be as open as possible. Nothing is more beautiful than a smooth green plat of grass, on which one or two of the smaller ornamental trees may be planted—such trees as

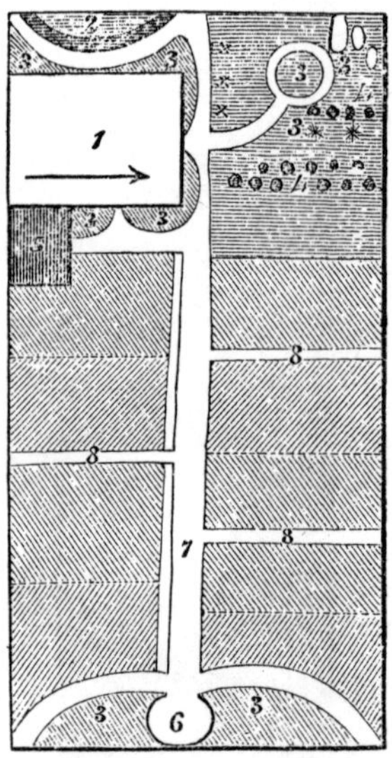

the silver birch, copper beech, or some sort of conifer, a pine, cypress—some of the araucarias, now easily procurable, or a deodara. Let the edgings be of box, if obtainable—nothing is so handsome; otherwise thrift, white alyssum, or some of the ornamental grasses. Ornamental tiles are both cheap and elegant. The path should be of gravel, if possible; if paved, let let it be with pebbles, or of coarse sand—road-sand is capital for kitchen-garden walks, so also is burnt clay. Let the main parts of the ground be devoted to kitchen crops. If drainage is necessary, ascertain where the water can be carried to. Open a trench along the whole breadth of the plat, either into the intended outlet or into a well sunk in the ground, and into this trench lead the several drains from the higher part of the ground from one end of the garden to the outlet, gradually sloping towards the lower trench. If this be left open and kept clear, it will carry off all superfluous water; but if some brushwood be laid along the bottom, it may be covered and cropped over. Brickbats or stones will do, but pipes or tiles are to be preferred. This done, let one main walk pass through the centre, of about five feet wide, or more if it is to be made a drying-ground. At the end of this main walk an arbour (6) may be formed of *Clematis Vitalba*, of the white jasmine, or yellow winter-flowering jasmine: all these are suitable for the purpose, being of dense growth and habit, and very cheap. On each side of the arbour flowers or herbs may be grown. On the sunny sides of the house let a vine, apricot, peach, or nectarine be planted in a proper station prepared for them. There is a wall having a southern aspect; let it be devoted to some of these also; if the fruit be not required for home use, it is saleable. The main part of the ground should be devoted to kitchen crops, following out a system of rotation-cropping, and using also a little caution in the application of manures: green, unprepared, or rank-smelling dung, breeds no end of insects, which become ruinous to crops. In preparing manures—which, however, are essential for maintaining the fertility of the soil—let it be remembered that all animal and vegetable refuse will be useful, when properly mixed. The droppings of cattle, sheep, pigs, and all house-sewage, should be collected and saved, and mixed with rather more than the same quantity of garden soil: the application of a little quick-lime will remove any offensive smell. Let the offal, dung, &c., be laid in layers, about nine inches thick, mixed with similar layers of garden soil and quicklime, remaining so till a good heap has accumulated, when it should be turned over and mixed thoroughly before dressing the ground with it. Applied in this way, it is not so likely to breed insects, and is more efficacious. The following is a list of fruit-trees and vegetables suitable for a cottage garden:—

APPLES.—*Early.* —White Juneating, Red Juneating, Red Quarrenden, Keswick Codlin, Manks Codlin. *Medium.* — Hawthornden, Kerry Pippin. *Late.* — Blenheim Orange, Fearn's Pippin, Lemon Pippin, Cockle Pippin, Ribston Pippin, King of Pippins, London Pippin, Scarlet Nonpareil, Old Nonpareil.

PEARS.—*Early.*—Ambrosia, or early Buerre, Buerre Gifford, Jargonel. *Medium.*—Buerre Diel, Duchess of Orleans, Marie Louise, Williams's Bon-Chrétien. *Late.*—Napoleon, Passe Colmar, Crassane d'Hiver and Catillac—baking.

PLUMS.—*Early.*—Goliath, Victoria, Greengage, Rivers's Prolific. *Late.*—Purple-gage, Magnum Bonum, Coe's Golden Drop, Damson.

VINES FOR OUT-DOORS.—Royal Muscadine, White Sweetwater, Black Cluster.

CHERRIES.—*Early.*—May Duke, Archduke. *Medium.*—Bigarreau, Kentish, Morello. *Late.*—Duke.

APRICOTS.—Moor Park.

PEACHES.— Mignonne, Noblesse, Malta, Royal George.

NECTARINES.— Pitmaston Orange, Roman (for well-drained soil), Scarlet.

GOOSEBERRIES.—*Green.*—Cocks's late Green, Greengage, Favourite. *Red.*— Champagne, Warrington, Lancashire Hero. *Yellow.*—Amber, Golden Drop, Early Yellow.

CURRANTS.—Large Grape,—red, Grape,—white, Black Naples.

RASPBERRIES.—Falstaff.

STRAWBERRIES. — Keen's Seedling, Sir Harry, Oscar.

Vegetables suitable for the Cottage Garden.

PEAS.—*Early.*—Emperor, Ringwood, Tom

Thumb and Bishop's Long-pod,—dwarf. *Medium.*—Auvergne, Blue Imperial, Scimitar. *Late.*—Knight's Dwarf Marrow, Knight's Tall Marrow.

BEANS.—Mazagan,—early, Sword Long-pod,—main crop.

CABBAGE.—Enfield Market,—main crop, Early York, East Ham, Colewort.

BROCOLI.—Early Cape, Purple Sprouting, Walcheren, or Cauliflower.

SAVOY.—Brussels Sprouts.

KALE.—Green Curled, Brown, or Ragged Jack.

LETTUCE.—Hammersmith,—for winter, Black-seeded Brown Cos,—all the year.

CARROT.—Early Horn, Intermediate.

TURNIP.—Early Dutch, Late Stone.

ONION.—Brown Spanish, Silver Globe.

SPINACH.—Round,—for summer, Flanders,—for winter.

POTATOES.—Improved Ash-leaved Kidney, Kirk's Kidney.

VEGETABLE MARROW.—Custard.

CUCUMBER.—Southgate,—for out-doors.

RADISHES.—Scarlet Short-top, Turnip, red and white.

CELERY.—Coles's Crystal,—white, Coles's Crystal,—red.

ENDIVE.—Green Curled.

PARSLEY.—Best Curled.

CORN SALAD,—for winter use.

COTTAGERS' HORTICULTURAL SOCIETY.

Few things are better designed to promote habits of industry and domestic tastes among the working classes than encouragement given to useful and ornamental gardening by means of Cottagers' Horticultural Societies, with village shows of vegetables, fruits, and flowers. A decided taste for gardening is soon called forth wherever these shows have been established. The influence of them tends upwards in society; we have frequently remarked what great improvement has taken place in the general appearance of the gardens of a neighbourhood where any encouragement is given to gardening among the lower classes. The upper classes do not like their gardens to be less gay or less productive than those of their poorer neighbours; an interest in garden operations is extended, a knowledge of gardening is sought for in books and practice, and great general good is the result. Following the plan adopted in our article upon garden allotments, we shall state, generally, how the management of such village societies ought to be conducted, rather than lay down precise rules, which can only apply to a particular place.

A Cottagers' Horticultural Society should be placed under the management of a committee, and must be supported by subscriptions from honorary members. In places where subscriptions are not readily forthcoming, a small payment—say 2*d.* or 3*d.* annually—may be taken from all who intend to exhibit for prizes, and also from visitors on the show days. If, however, sufficient can be collected for the prizes without them, both these payments are, in our opinion, better avoided. All cottagers, not being gardeners, should be invited to compete free of any charge. The shows should not exceed two in the course of the year. The first should be early in July, and the second about the middle of September. If only one show be deemed advisable, the autumn show is the best. Any useful garden produce may be offered for a prize; but no prize should be awarded unless there be two or three specimens, so as to make competition, and also unless, in the opinion of the judges, the specimens have reached a certain degree of merit. The following list will serve to show how vegetables, fruits, and flowers may be classed, so as to embrace a good general selection, and insure sufficient competition to promote good cultivation.

Potatoes.—Ash-leaved kidneys, 6 potatoes, Early kidneys, 6, Late kidneys, 6, Flukes, 6. Red variety, 6, Round potatoes, 6. *Onions.*—Spring sown, 6 roots, autumn sown, 6. *Parsnips,* 3 roots. *Carrots.*—Short horn, or early variety, 3 roots, Long carrots, 3, White carrots, 3. *Cabbages.*—Common cabbages, 3 heads, Savoys, 3, Brussels sprouts, 3 stalks, Cottagers' kale, 3, Red cabbage, 3 heads *Celery,* 3 roots, *Cucumbers,* 1. *Gourds,* 1. *Beans.*—Broad beans, 12 pods, French beans, 30, Runners, 30. *Peas,* 30 pods. *Lettuces.*—Cos, 3 heads, Cabbage, 3. *Turnips,* 3 roots. *Mangold Wurzel,* 3 roots. *Rhubarb,* 3 stalks. *Radishes.*—Turnip, 8, long, 8. *Apples.*—For dessert, of each sort, 6, for cooking, 6. *Pears.*—For dessert, 6 of a sort, for baking, 6.

Plums and other fruit may be arranged in the same way on plates. Specimens of plants in pots need not be all of the same sort, although, if there be three or four fuchsias and three or four geraniums, it will be well to class them together, and assign separate prizes. Cut flowers, wild flowers, and grasses, especially if exhibited by children, should not be neglected. Prizes also may, with great benefit, be given for the earliest swarm of bees and the heaviest hive of honey. All specimens shown for the purpose of gaining any prize must be the *bonâ fide* property of the persons showing them. They must have been raised by him, or, at any rate, have been in his possession for two months before the show. Everything intended for exhibition should be at the place appointed before ten o'clock a.m.; it should be ticketed with the owner's name, which should be folded up, or otherwise carefully concealed from view. Between ten and twelve o'clock the judges, who should be not more than three in number, and selected from the committee, should make their awards, and fix the prizes. At twelve o'clock the public might be admitted, and the prizes distributed at one. The judges' decision must, in all cases, be final; and any one who expresses dissatisfaction ought not to be allowed to compete for twelve months. We think it very desirable, especially where the subscriptions are small, that the prizes should be given in goods. Tools for the garden, hardware goods useful for the house, baskets and measures, crockery, and articles of clothing, are all good for prizes, and have a greater worth than their money value. It will be observed that we do not recommend set prizes for certain things: the selection of the prizes should be left to the discretion of the judges. Advantage may well be taken of such shows for the introduction of special prizes, which may be given by any one so disposed for any matter of cottage economy or cottage adornment; for rustic garden chairs and baskets, also for the best-kept cottage and neatest garden, and for the best-cultivated allotment: for these last purposes, if funds admit of it, a succession of prizes should be given; and even here, if the prize be given in money, the sum is better left uncertain, to be settled each year by the judges. The following rules, which have been adopted in our own village, are found to work admirably; all the cottages and gardens are visited twice in the year, and the money is distributed at the time of the show.

Prizes for Cottagers.—"£5 will be divided into as many prizes as the judges may think fit, for the neatest cottage and best-cultivated garden for fruit, corn, vegetables, and flowers; to be competed for by ordinary labouring cottagers. Also £1 (to be divided or not, as the judges may decide) for same as above; to be competed for by small tradesmen or cottagers whose average weekly income exceeds, in the judges' opinion, the labourers' earnings, and who are not allowed to compete for the £5 prizes. In all cases the number and age of family will be considered, and the judges' decision final."

Another special prize of 5*s.* for the best home-made 4-pound loaf of bread is also competed for.

COTTAGER'S KALE.

This is a variety of the tall cavalier cabbage which was raised at Sherburn Castle, Oxfordshire, from Brussels sprouts. Crossed with one of the varieties of kale, it was submitted to the Horticultural Society in the spring of 1858, and is said to be the most tender of all the greens, and of exquisite flavour. It stands four feet high when full-grown, and should be allowed an equal space to grow in, being clothed to the ground with immense rosette-like shoots of a bluish-green tint, which, when boiled, become a delicate green. The seed should be sown late in March or early in April, and the plants should have a rich deep soil assigned to them.

COW-DUNG.

Charred cow-dung is an excellent manure for almost all purposes, and by charring it, it is fit for immediate use. Take some old wood and build a cone two or three feet high; then procure some green cow-dung, and cover the cone nine inches thick; let it drain for a day or two; cover it with weeds or rubbish, and set fire to the wood, regulating the draught so as to prevent the fire burning too fiercely; and by the time the wood is consumed, you will have a fine crust of charred cow-dung. This mix, when broken up, with composts. A few pieces of it at the bottom of the pots in which calceolarias, pelargoniums, cinerarias, or pines or vines are grown, will be found a most excellent manure.

CROCUS.

For in-door decoration the Crocus properly managed is very useful; for the flower-garden, indispensable. When used as an edging to beds, borders, &c., the colours being nicely blended, they are remarkably attractive; while in the arrangement of any fancy designs, or grouped in distinct colours of from six to fifty, or even a hundred in a group, the effect is all that could be desired. We have seen large beds of Crocus planted in circles, each circle one colour: with the sun shining on them nothing could possibly be more brilliant, more especially when there chanced to be a good proportion of them yellow.

Culture in-doors, same as the Hyacinth, and, like it, they may be grown in any ornamental contrivance; but it is absolutely necessary, to insure success, that they be kept well supplied with water, close to the glass, and have abundance of *fresh air*, or they will produce leaves only.

Culture in the open ground.—They can be successfully grown in almost any soil and situation. Plant two to three inches deep, and not more than two inches apart.

Crocuses, however, are very accommodating in reference to the depth at which they are planted. When planted in beds devoted to bedding-plants, they will reach the surface and flower, if inserted four times that depth. As the young bulbs are formed on the top of the old ones, they thus possess a self-elevating power. Crocuses will flower freely for many years without being disturbed. The best growers, however, recommend dividing and replanting every third or fifth year. To secure perfect blooms, the foliage must be left to die down of its own accord. If planted in ribbon-beds, the following arrangement would look well:—Back row, David Rizzio, large purple; 2nd row, largest yellow; 3rd row, Flos niger, fine large blue; 4th row, Mont Blanc, or any other pure white: or the order may be reversed, or confined to three colours only,—yellow, blue, and white, or *vice versâ*. On wide borders, the same order may be repeated as often as necessary. The great point in this style of planting is to choose distinct colours only, and not varieties of colour.

CU'PHEA (nat. ord. Lythra'ceæ).

Profuse-blooming plants, equally valuable for the ornamentation of the conservatory, drawing-room, and flower-garden. *C. eminens* is of a graceful branching habit, covered with splendid long scarlet and yellow tubular flowers; *C. Zinampinii* is covered with red-violet, and *C. ocymoides* with rich purple-violet flowers. The perennial species, if sown early, can be used for bedding-plants the first year; the annual kinds may be treated like ordinary half-hardy annuals.

CURRANTS.

To grow these favourite fruits in perfection a deep and tolerably rich soil is required; and preparatory to planting, this should be deeply trenched and manured with thoroughly-rotted dung. Currants as well as gooseberries are propagated by cuttings, which should be well-ripened wood of last year's growth, slipped from the tree, and from 10 to 12 inches long. Having selected the slip and separated it from the parent stem, cut off the top, leaving four shoots : trim off all others. Make two or three incisions, penetrating half through the stem, to expedite the process of rooting, and plant the cuttings in a nursery-bed in rows a few inches apart each way. When they have made roots, transplant them into a bed of deeper and richer soil, pruning back the four shoots to five or six inches, and leaving two side shoots to each. Here they may remain a second year, the four shoots now multiplied to eight, and the head beginning to assume its permanent shape. This is produced by means of hooked sticks, by which straggling shoots are brought into cup-like form, and forked twigs, by means of which shoots inclining inwardly are pressed out to their proper position, which should be as nearly the horizontal as possible.

In the autumn of the second year the bushes may be planted out in their permanent stations, which may be from 3½ feet up to 7 or 8 feet apart, according to circumstances ; that is, if it is a plantation entirely devoted to well-selected bush-fruit, in which no other crop is to be cultivated, 3½ feet, or 4 feet, will do. Where they are planted with the intention of growing other crops between them, 6 feet to 8 feet will not be too much. If planted in rows to divide the quarters of the kitchen-garden, 6 feet will probably be a convenient distance. In planting, dig out the soil 18 inches deep, and of sufficient diameter to admit of the growth of the roots ; smooth and level the station with the back of the spade, and drive a stake firmly into the ground in the centre, leaving it six or seven inches above the surface of the soil. Having trimmed the roots of the bush, place it in the centre of the station with the roots radiating in all directions, regularly spread out, none of them spreading over others, and sprinkle two inches of the soil over them, pressing it gently all round into the roots ; over this spread a thin layer of well-rotted dung, and fill up the whole to the level of the surrounding soil. This done, water the roots well, and prune back all the shoots so as to form a cup-like bush, with branches radiating from the centre.

Currants produce their fruit both on the young wood and on the wood two, three, and four years old ; and generally along the branches. The general bearers, therefore, young and old, of proper growth and well-ripened, must be continued as long as they remain fruitful, cutting out from time to time such as are of irregular growth or too crowded,—all branches and decayed wood, together with the superfluous or over-abundant young wood of last summer ; but retaining a selection of young shoots where necessary, to fill up gaps in the tree ; the rule being, to keep the bushes trained to a single stem below, while the head, or general expansion of branches, is kept open and regular.

CUTTINGS.

Cuttings in general may be considered as of two kinds,—matured wood and young green shoots. The former, whatever they may be, strike readily, and with very little care. An American plan, which is very successful, is to lay them in slightly-damped moss, or to drop them lightly into a wide-mouthed bottle, having a piece of damp sponge at the bottom and a covering of muslin over the top. In either of these methods a callus is soon formed, and the cuttings readily throw out roots. Cuttings of young green shoots, however, require a very different treatment : they must be so managed as never to be allowed to flag, and the following appears to be the best method that can be pursued. Put silver-sand about an inch deep into shallow pans (common saucers answer every purpose), and in these plant the cuttings. Then pour carefully upon the sand enough water to make a thin sheet about it. The lower leaves of the cuttings are to be removed before planting, and the stalk fixed firmly into the sand before the water is poured on. These tender young green shoots, or cuttings, will be better for a little shade and heat. A piece of thin muslin or tissue-paper will provide the former, and heat may be had by placing the pan of cuttings over a basin of hot water, re-filled twice a day. These cuttings will be rooted and ready for potting off before the water in which they are grown has dried up.

Cuttings of all sorts of geraniums for bedding the following year should be struck early: from the last week in July to the end of the first week in August is very good time. They should be taken in dry weather, when the parent plant has had no water for some days, and they should be kept to dry twenty-four hours after they have been prepared for potting. The more succulent sorts, and any that appear difficult to strike, may with advantage be touched at the end with a small paint-brush dipped in collodion, which will serve to hasten the callus which the cutting must form before it will throw out roots. They may be potted four or six in a pot, according to sizes. It is essential that the pots be well fitted with drainers, that the soil be light and sandy, and that it be pressed tight round the joint of the cuttings, which should be buried in it as fleet as possible. When filled, the pots may be sunk in the ground on a south border, and well watered in the evening, when the sun is off. They will require no shading, except the sun be very scorching; and, in this case, they must not be kept from the light, but merely screened from the scorching rays of the sun. They may flag a little; but this is of no importance; in two or three days they will recover, and put forth roots. If they grow too freely before it is time to take them in for the winter, the top shoots should be broken off, and in this way they will make strong bushy plants.

To preserve cuttings from frost where there is no greenhouse, dig a pit about four feet deep, strew the bottom well with ashes, and sink the pots in the same. Over it place a common garden-frame, bank up the outsides with straw and a coating of earth. In such a pit, verbenas, calceolarias, fuchsias, &c. &c., may be preserved during the severest winters, provided the pots be kept in the dark by being well covered with matting during frost.

CY'CLAMEN (nat. ord. Primula'ceæ).

A genus of charming winter and spring blooming bulbous roots, with very pretty foliage, and flowers the most beautiful, graceful, and ladylike, so easily cultivated withal, that any one may enjoy these floral bijous either in the sitting-room window, conservatory, or greenhouse, from October to May, by a little management in the period of starting them into growth.

Culture.—Plant one bulb in a 5- or 6-inch pot, using a rich soil composed of loam and leaf-mould, rotted dung, and a little silver-sand, and, to secure good drainage, place at the bottom of the pot an oyster-shell or hollow potsherd, and over that some pieces of charcoal: the bulb should not be covered more than half its depth.

When the blooming season is over and the bulbs are at rest, plunge the pots in a shady well-drained border, and there let them remain till the leaves begin to grow, when they should be taken up, turned out of the pots, and as much soil removed as can be done without injury to the roots, and replaced with the compost already mentioned.

DAHL'IA (nat. ord. Compos'itæ).

The Dahlia, so named after Dahl, the Swedish botanist, belongs to the same family, and is a native of the same country, as the potato—namely, the mountains of Mexico. There it was found in the sandy plains 5,000 feet above the level of the sea, and was sent to Europe in 1789 by Cervantes, the Spanish director of the

Mexican Botanic Gardens, who named it *Dahlia coccinea*. Under the impression that sandy soil was its proper compost, it lingered in our gardens, a miserable scraggy plant, till 1815, when a fresh and improved stock was introduced from France, and it was taken up by the florists. Under the influence of cultivation, it has been so mucb improved in form as to become one of the finest flowers of the garden, while the shades of colour are so numerous, so diverse, and so opposite, that it would be difficult to find another plant at once so hardy and so showy. Probably its importer never dreamed that the naked stem and imperfect flower of *D. coccinea* would, by the efforts of cultivation, become so ornamental in European gardens; nevertheless, such it has become; and few gardens are now without their collection of dahlias, while the nursery lists of named varieties swell into hundreds, of every shade and colour, except the much-prized blue, which was for some years the object of the florist's pursuit.

Dahlias may be multiplied by seeds and by dividing the tuber, every eye, when separated with a portion of the tuber, making a plant. They will also grow from cuttings off the young shoots under the lower leaves, which may be struck in small pots filled with sandy soil. Experiments have even been made to ascertain how far grafting would succeed with the Dahlia.

Seedlings are procured by sowing the seeds in shallow pans and plunging them into a hotbed, or by sowing on hotbeds prepared for the purpose, in March. The soil should be light and sandy, with a mixture of peat-mould. The seed should be chosen from the best varieties only; it should be lightly covered with soil. A few days will bring them up, when they require all the air which can be given them safely. In April they will be ready for potting off either singly in the smallest-sized, or round the edge of 6-inch pots: this strengthens them for final planting out. Towards the middle or end of August, if successfully treated, they will begin to bloom: at this time they should be examined daily, all single and demi-single blooms thrown away, unless they present some new colour or show some peculiar habit of growth, in which case they may be improved by further cultivation and crossing. Caution in this respect is necessary, as it is a habit of the Dahlia to improve under a second year's cultivation, and some of our finest varieties have come up with indifferent flowers as seedlings. When done flowering, the young bulbs are taken up and treated as old tubers.

Cuttings are taken as follows:—In February or March, and even as late as the first week in April, the tuber, which has been carefully wintered in a dry place, is put into soil placed over a hotbed, and in a very short time as many shoots as there are eyes in the tuber make their appearance. As soon as these are two inches long, they are taken off just below the leaves, struck singly in small pots, and again placed in the hotbed. Some prefer cutting up the tuber as soon as the éyes are distinguishable, and replacing them either in the soil of the hotbed or in pots. Mr. T. Barnes, an undoubted authority, tells us that to obtain short-jointed, stout, and healthy plants, "they should be rooted from cuttings taken off in April, and struck in a gentle hotbed." As soon as rooted, they should be potted in 5-inch pots, and again placed in a gentle heat, but with plenty of air. "Cuttings struck at this time," he tells us, "are more healthy than those struck at an earlier period," and consequently form better flowering plants. A week after they are potted they should receive a watering of liquid manure made from guano and powdered charcoal, well mixed with rainwater, repeating this occasionally till the time of planting out; fumigating the frame with tobacco, should there be any appearance of the green-fly.

Early in May beds are prepared for the reception of dahlias, if they are to be grown in massed beds. The form of the beds will depend on the general design of the garden: if a portion of the garden is devoted to them, either for the plants or the flowers, they will be best displayed in beds three feet wide, with alleys between. The beds being marked by stakes placed at each corner, four inches of the surface-soil is removed, and four inches of thoroughly-rotted manure put in its place, and the whole deeply dug, and the manure thoroughly mixed with the soil in digging. In the beds thus prepared the plants are placed, the collars, as they have grown in the pots, being on the surface of the beds. The 3-foot beds will receive each a row; thé stakes are firmly fixed 4, 5, or 6 feet apart, according to the size of the plants; the plants themselves are set 4 inches deep, so that the crown of the plant is just above the surface. As the plant increases in growth, tying up commences; at the same time a diligent search should be made for slugs, earwigs, and other pests of the garden. These must be rooted out, or they will root out the dahlias, or at least destroy their flower. Where any of the plants show a weak and drooping growth, time will be saved by re-striking the top: although these will bloom later, the flowers will be stronger than they would be from a plant which has received a check.

During June and July dahlias require careful attention in watering and stirring the soil about the roots. As the lateral shoots attain sufficient length, tie them up so as to prevent their breaking, placing other stakes for the purpose, should that be necessary.. This prevents their clinging too near to the stem, and permits of a free circulation of air round the plants. When they are intended either for exhibition or for highly-developed flowers, only one bud should be left on a shoot, shading the flower both from the sun and rain by tin sconces, oil-skin caps, or inverted flowerpots, placed over the top of the stake to which it is tied, while all superfluous and useless shoots are removed, and the growth of the plant encouraged by every possible means. As autumn approaches, the swellng shoots render it necessary to examine those tied up, slacking the strings where necessary, to prevent them from galling.

Where dahlias are merely to fill a place in the general arrangement of the garden and shrubbery, care should be taken to supply them with suitable soil. Peat-mould, mixed with sand, is useful in developing stripes and spots on the flower. As the plants progress, the lateral shoots, as well as the central stem, require support by tying up, and the roots should be assisted by stirring the soil with a fork every two or three weeks, and by copious watering, removing all dead or straggling shoots, and keeping the plant trim and well-staked.

Dividing the Roots.—Another and more common practice in gardens is to place the whole tuber in some warm place in March, and, when the eyes show themselves, cut up the tubers, and in May plant them at once six inches below the surface, in the place where they are to bloom, staking them and leaving them to nature until they are sufficiently grown to compel attention; but even for common bedding-out purposes, and for filling up gaps, the plant is worthy of greater care than this amounts to. Light-coloured flowers are confirmed in their beauty by seclusion from sun and air while they are developing their bloom; darker flowers, on the contrary, lose much of their brilliancy if too much shaded: these should, therefore, only be shaded partially from the direct rays of the meridian sun.

In October the Dahlia begins to fail. This then is the time to revise the names, and see that they are all correct, and to take care that seed from such as it is desired to propagate from is secured before they are injured by the frost. Provide also against severe weather coming on suddenly, by drawing the earth round the stems in a conical form, which will protect the roots from frost while they are yet in a growing state, as well as diminish the moisture, which encourages growth. Even in November, in mild seasons, the Dahlia will remain fresh and gay if the weather is open and clear; but in general the earlier flowers will have passed away: their time of rest is come. When the frost turns their foliage brown or black, take them up, cut off the roots, leaving six inches or so of stem attached, and plunge them into a box of ashes, chaff, or sand, or any other method of preserving them from damp, frost, and heat, during the winter.

As to giving a list of dahlias, when it is considered that the eight or ten winners of prizes at the national dahlia-shows must exhibit upwards of 160 varieties, it will be obviously vain to attempt it. We may state, however, that Mr. Turner, of the Royal Nursery, Slough, has repeatedly carried off the great prizes for fifty dissimilar varieties, as well as for fancy varieties: it is pretty clear, therefore, that he can supply the very best selection possible.

DAISIES ON LAWN.

To clear a lawn of daisies, there is nothing equal to the continued use of the daisy-fork. With this ingenious little tool several square yards of apparently the most hopeless grass can be cleared in a few days. The fork should be used in moist weather, and the grass well rolled afterwards.

DAISY (nat. ord. Compos'itæ).

There are many varieties of this plant well worthy of cultivation. Among the most beautiful are the large double, the large quilled, and the hen-and-chickens. These, in a very rich soil, produce fine flowers, and are admirably adapted for edgings. Interesting specimens may be obtained from seed. Messrs. Barr and Sugden offer seed at 6*d*. per packet, saved from the finest Belgian varieties.

DAISY-FORK.

This is a useful little tool for removing daisy roots from lawns: it is fitted with two iron prongs, and acts as a lever by means of a long or short handle. Price, 1*s*. 6*d*. to 3*s*. 6*d*. each.

DAISY-RAKE.

The daisy-rake is for removing the flowers by drawing it over the grass. Price, 5*s*. to 7*s*. each.

DANDELIONS, TO KILL.

Cut the tops off in the spring, and place a pinch of salt, or a little gas-tar, on the fresh wound.

DAPH'NE (nat. ord. Thymela'ceæ).

Beautiful shrubs, remarkable for the elegance of their flowers and for their bright red poisonous berries. *D. Mezereum* is the most common variety. The dwarf daphnes are somewhat tender: they bear pink flowers very fragrant. There is a Chinese daphne, *D. odorata*, which is a great ornament in the greenhouse, but too tender for the open air.

DATU'RA (nat. ord. Solana'ceæ).

A tribe of highly-ornamental plants, hardy annuals, producing large sweet-scented trumpet-shaped flowers of the most attractive character, and succeeding in any light rich soil. *D. humilis* has magnificent golden-yellow double flowers; *D. Wrightii* has large white flowers bordered with lilac.

Datura ceratocaulon, — satin-white, striped purple, very handsome, 2 ft., from South America.

Datura Cuvilje, — white, stems and leaves mossy, handsome, 1¾ ft., from Africa.

Datura fastuosa alba,—pure white, double, 3 ft., from Egypt.

Datura fastuosa violacea,—fine violet, double, 3 ft., from Egypt.

Datura humilis flore pleno (chlorantha fl. pl.), —rich golden yellow, a magnificent, free-flowering, sweet-scented variety, 2 ft., from Texas.

Datura Knightii, — white, splendid double flowers with exquisite odour, 3 ft.

Datura quercifolia,—lilac, oak-leaved 3 ft., from Asia.
Datura Wrightii (meteloides), — satin-white, bordered with lilac; an exquisite, sweet-scented plant, 2 ft., from Asia.

DECEMBER (Monthly Calendar).

December, the last month of our year, was, as its name indicates, the tenth of the Roman calendar. Although the thermometer often sinks below freezing during this month, the frosts are seldom of long continuance. Rain and wind abound. The variations of temperature are smaller than in November. The mean temperature of the earth, one foot beneath the surface, is now 41·13°; at two feet, 42·83°; that of the atmosphere being 38·14°.

Though November is the best month for transplanting and for laying down turf for lawns, whatever in this respect has been left undone may still be accomplished if the weather remains open.

Flower-Garden and Shrubbery.—The pruning of deciduous trees and shrubs should also be proceeded with, unless during severe frost. Most evergreens are best pruned in April. Nevertheless, as that is a busy, and this a comparatively leisure season, the hardiest evergreens, such as laurels, &c., may be pruned now; any, however, that require cutting down, had better be left till that period. We prune mainly for three leading purposes: to improve the shape, curtail size, and to induce a profusion of bloom or fruitfulness. The first is entirely a matter of taste, the second of space, and the third the primary object for which all flowering shrubs and trees are cultivated: the two first are entirely effected by pruning the top; the last is more effectually secured by cutting in the roots. This latter does not necessarily, however, supersede the former; often both may proceed simultaneously with advantage. One of the chief points in the management of shrubberies is so to prune them and cut down the plants as always to preserve a dense thick bottom. The digging, pointing, top-dressing, and cleaning of old shrubberies, should also be proceeded with, the turf frequently swept and rolled, the gravel kept scrupulously clean, and every possible thing done to make this outside *winter garden* attractive during the bleak winter and spring months.

The beds in the flower-garden, now disrobed of their summer beauty, will either be furnished with shrubs, herbaceous plants, annuals, or bulbs, or simply roughed up for the winter. Previous to either being done, it is hoped that they received a liberal top-dressing of manure. It is as vain to expect to grow the majority of bedding-plants successively for years on the same soil without enriching it, as it would be to produce good vegetables on the same starving regimen; indeed, many of these plants (verbenas for instance) *draw* the soil as much as a crop of cabbages. If every bit of weed, short grass, and other refuse that comes off the garden annually, is conveyed to a heap, occasionally turned over and saturated with manure-water, a most valuable dressing for the beds will be provided at a cheap rate. Roses should have something richer: in fact, nothing is too good for them. Roses may still be planted, although the sooner this work is finished the better for next season's bloom. Plant as many on their own roots as possible: they are more durable, more beautiful in this form than any others. All newly-planted roses should be mulched over with 3 or 4 inches of light dungy litter on the surface. Examine and renew the labels on these and all other named shrubs and herbaceous plants; provide stakes and pegs, and make labels in bad weather. Take stock of, and finally decide on, the disposition of your bedding stuff; sweep and roll the turf, and mow, if need be, from the mildness of the season. Keep your gravel bright, clean, and as hard as adamant, and by such means make the flower-garden, *even in winter*, a cheerful, comfortable promenade.

Reserve Garden.—Annuals, to stand the winter here, will probably require

December.

some slight protection. Carefully watch against the inroads of mice, rats, snails, &c. Not only bulbs, but even young plants, are often devoured by the two former; and in mild winters a little black slug will clear off whole beds of annuals. Let every vacant space be roughly dug up, manured, &c.: choice beds of tulips, anemones, &c., sheltered in bad weather, and the whole examined daily to guard against accident and ward off disease.

Florists' Flowers. — Dahlia roots stowed away in cellars, &c., must be carefully and frequently examined to see how they are keeping, and any scarce sorts placed in heat towards the end of the month, to insure a large stock before May. Subjoined is a list of some first-rate fancy and show varieties:—

Fancy Class.

Blondin, — yellow-flaked; bright red, large, and good crimson, 4 ft.
Beauty of Etruria,—dark buff, spotted, and striped, 4 ft.
Confidence,—crimson-striped, 3 ft.
Eclat,—purple-tipped, white, 3 ft.
Gem,—rosy crimson; small tip, bright yellow, 3 ft.
Miss Jones,—maroon, tipped white, 3 ft.
Norah Creina,—orange, tipped white, 4 ft.
Pauline,—tipped white, 3 ft.
Striata,—superb lilac, striped deep purple, 4 ft.
Spotted Gem, — buff-striped, and spotted orange, 4 ft.
Summertide,—chocolate, tipped white, 4 ft.

Show Varieties.

Andrew Dodds,—darkest flower out, 3 ft.
Beauty of Hilperton,—purple, large, and fine, 4 ft.
Criterion,—rose-lilac; large and fine, 4 ft.
Etonia,—buff; fine shape, 4 ft.
Heroine,—soft peach, with bronze tip, 4 ft.
Joy,—blush-white, tipped with cherry, 3 ft.
Madge Wildfire,—bright light scarlet; fine, 4 ft.
Madame Perault,—bright pink-carmine, 3 ft.
Mrs. Barnes,—blush-white; constant, 3 ft.
Mrs. Crawford,—deep scarlet, 3 ft.
Mrs. H. Oakes,—primrose-yellow; fine shape, 5 ft.
Norfolk Hero,—chestnut-brown, 3 ft.

Carefully dry dahlia seed preparatory to sowing in pans next month, and see that all the labels are firmly attached to the roots. The above, and other equally good varieties, can be purchased at from 12*s.* to 18*s.* a dozen.

December.

Pinks and carnations in beds will require pressing firmly into the earth after severe frost. Examine the beds for slugs in mild weather, and see that the plants are not destroyed by rats and mice.

The same precautions are necessary with pansies in beds in the open ground. It is best to keep a stock of autumn-struck cuttings of these in pots, to fill up blanks and insure against accidental deaths. The following will be found good:—

Dr. Fleming,—shaded purple: large and fine.
General Havelock,—deep golden yellow.
Vesta,—primrose; self.
Lord Palmerston,—rich velvety purple.
Caroline,—white ground, heavy purple belting; fine.
Isa Craig,—medium belting; clear and fine.
Mrs. Hopkins,—white ground, purple belting; dense blotch.
British Sailor,—gold ground, heavy maroon belting.
Chancellor,—gold, with crimson maroon belting.
Richard Headley,—yellow ground, shaded bronze, belting fine.
President,—rich gold, dark maroon belting.
Wallace,—dark belting on a yellow ground; fine.

Fancy Class.

Anna,—yellow, shaded maroon; black blotch.
Belle Esquimoise,—white ground, immense dark blotch.
Butterfly,—white and blue upper petals, under bronze; striking and beautiful.
Duchesse de Brabant,—yellow and bronze; fine.
Etoile du Nord,—yellow-bordered, purple-lilac blotches; extra fine.
Iris,—light purple, lucid yellow; fine.
Miss E. Bining,—white; dark blotches; fine.
Noemi Demay,—gold, with immense blotches; fine.
Octave Demay, rich yellow, large blotch; fine.
Princess Alice,—creamy white, with dark blotch.
Talma,—yellow maroon top; immense blotches.
Zouave,—light yellow blush; purple belt.

Tulips.—If planted early last month, some of them may be peeping through the soil: if so, they must be protected by having a slight pyramid of sandy peat-earth or leaf-mould placed over them. During very frosty weather the beds or rows must be covered with mats, woollen nets, &c., as nothing injures these bulbs more than severe frosts on their crowns just as they are coming through the ground. The soil for these bulbs should be trenched from 2 feet to 30 inches deep, mixed with a liberal dressing of well-rotted manure. It is also a good plan to place a layer of manure about 6 inches from the surface, so that it may be readily and speedily available for the roots. The bulbs should be planted 6 inches square and 4 inches deep, and any period from the middle of October to the middle of December will do for planting them. For brilliancy of colour, diversity of height and time of blooming, and striking showiness, we have nothing to equal the tulip. Ribbon borders and masses of colour may be formed of this bulb alone, rivalling all our summer and autumn beauties. Of Dwarf Duc Van Thols alone, we have all the colours necessary to form effective ribbon borders with the exception of blue. And the splendid blue of the crocus is ever ready to supply the *blue* wants of the tulip. Thus, the

Back row, scarlet, next yellow, next red, next white. Front row, blue crocus, or yellow, scarlet, white, blue; or white, scarlet, yellow, red, white, blue, &c.

Other varieties of early, single, and double tulips afford even greater material for this kind of display. Among them there are several violet colours, such as Blue Flag, &c., which may take the place of blues. Nearly all the arrangements of colours which are recommended and illustrated in this work can be carried out by the aid of tulips alone, or, at least, slightly assisted with crocuses. Their neat habit renders them peculiarly adapted for describing patterns on beds or borders, and frames: circular, curved, or polychrome forms may be indicated by them to the greatest nicety. The following are good varieties :—

Single Tulips.

Bride of Haarlem,—white striped, crimson.
Canary-bird,—pure yellow.
Couronne Pourpre,—dark wall-flower.

Cramoise Royale,—white, with rosy-violet crimson.
Dorothea Blanche,—white, striped with cerise.
Duc de Brabant,—yellow, striped and feathered crimson.
Duchesse de Parme,—bronze-crimson, bordered yellow.
Globe de Regant,—white, striped with violet.
Grootmaester von Maltha,—white-striped rose.
La Belle Alliance,—brilliant scarlet.
Pax alba,—pure white; fine.
Pottebakker,—white.
,, red, striped yellow.
,, yellow.
Royal Standard,—white, striped bright red.
Silver Standard,—white, striped with scarlet.
Vermilion,—brilliant vermilion-scarlet.
Violet Hative,—purplish violet.
White and Red bordered,—white feathered.
White Swan,—pure white; very fine.

Double Tulips.

Blue Flag,—purplish violet.
Blanc Borde Pourpre,—violet, purple-bordered; white.
Conqueror,—pure white, feathered with violet-crimson.
Duke of York,—bronze-crimson; margined lines.
Gloria Solis,—crimson, striped golden yellow.
La Candeur,—pure white.
Mariage de ma Fille,—crimson, and white striped.
Over-winner,—violet and white striped.
Pæony Gold,—golden yellow; feathered crimson.
Purple Crown,—velvety crimson.
Tournesol,—scarlet and yellow.
Yellow Rose,—golden yellow.

Then there are the curious wonderfully showy Parrot Tulips, of which the following are as good as any.

Coffee-colour.
Constantinople red.
Margraff,—striped, red and yellow.
Monster Rouge,—crimson.
Perfecta,—scarlet and gold.
Fern,—brilliant scarlet.
And Monstrosa, which is monstrously beautiful.

Show, or late-flowering tulips, of which a single bulb used to be worth a fortune, are exquisite in shape and colour, and are divided into three classes,—bizarres, which have yellow grounds, feathered or striped with crimson, purple, or white; byblomens, white ground, flaked or striped with black, lilac, or purple; and roses that have white grounds, feathered or striped with crimson, pink, or scarlet. In each of these classes many exquisitely beautiful named flowers exist. Any one intending to grow these should visit some good collection, such as those at Battersea, St. John's Wood, or Slough, when they are in flower, and choose for himself.

Soon after tulips have finished flowering, their leaves will ripen and die off. They should be immediately taken up with all the soil that will adhere to the bulb, slightly dried, and put away in drawers or paper bags, each sort by itself. During the summer they should be frequently looked over to see that they are not decaying. On the 1st of October rub off all the offsets, plant these by themselves, and prepare for planting the entire stock as already directed.

Kitchen-Garden.—The experienced gardener knows the importance of winter operations. Respecting crops, individually, little can be done; but collectively, some attention should be given to the various stores of seeds and vegetables; the latter should be looked over occasionally, turned, sorted, and cleaned; kept moist without being damp, cool without frost, and where there is a free circulation of air. As to seeds, it is well to have them ready for sowing; that is, thoroughly dried and rubbed out, every particle of husk and light seed blown out, and carefully papered and labelled. Those that have to be purchased should be procured early. Go to respectable dealers, that you may be certain of the sorts being true to name. Note down and procure exactly what will be required for the season, so that no time is lost when they are wanted, and place each sort in its proper drawer or receptacle, that there may be no confusion. Also see to the tools or implements, and ascertain that they are in good condition; replace or repair any that are broken; never trust to just the right number if any are not in good condition; keep them dry, and clean well before hanging them up. Another thing to attend to, is proper composts and manures. These may be collected on a spare or vacant piece of ground in the kitchen-garden, where there will be plenty of room to turn them over and mix, and where all kinds of woody refuse can be collected and charred and mixed with them. In frosty weather, when the ground is hard, these should be wheeled on to vacant ground. Again, much time is saved in the spring and summer by making a general pruning and trimming of trees. Most trees will be improved by a little cutting-out: it prevents them making so much dead wood. Collect all these prunings; see what are useful for any garden purposes.

With regard to particular crops :—

Seakale.—Some may be covered for forcing. Place the kale-pot over a bunch of crowns; see that enough is covered: then, having previously prepared and shaken out the dung, and got it into a condition to maintain a moderate heat, cover the pots to a thickness of about three feet from the ground: too great a body of dung is apt to heat too violently and spoil the crowns. Give just enough to maintain a moderate heat, and no more: it will be ready to cut in about three weeks, according to the amount of heat. Some gardeners cover with leaves, which answer the purpose; but in collecting leaves, a great many slugs and other vermin are collected also. These do mischief to the kale; in other respects the effect is the same.

Rhubarb may be treated in a precisely similar manner, but requires larger pots; and none but the earliest sorts should be forced.

Peas and Beans of the early kinds may be sown on light ground; but it is not advisable to sow many. Those sown in February will be as early within a few days, and much more certain.

Celery.—Cover with litter in frosty weather. It will be so much better to take up, besides keeping it fresh and uninjured.

Parsnips and other crops that remain in the ground ought also to be covered with litter or leaves. The slightest covering will make a vast difference in case of sharp frost, which should always be bargained for at this time.

Endive.—Blanch with pots, and cover with litter; and a good supply may be kept up the whole winter without having recourse to frames, the litter helping to blanch it before the pots are put on; but a dusting of lime should be given occasionally to destroy slugs, which are very fond of endive.

Brocoli, &c.—It will now be seen what advantage there is in giving the various sorts of brassicas plenty of space. Those planted among other crops are shanky, and more exposed to the frost, while those planted open, are short, firm, and stocky, and far more likely to stand severe frost. Let this be considered in cropping next year.

This is the best time to make any general alterations. Where old bushes are to be grubbed up, and the ground prepared for cropping, or where young bushes are to be planted, also where drainage is necessary, now is a good time to do it before the winter rains make a swamp of the garden. Set the edgings and paths in order, and carefully remove any accumulation of rubbish which is likely to harbour vermin. *Herb beds* should be cleared, and made as neat as possible, both for the appearance and well-doing of the herbs.

Fruit-Garden. — December is the month of rest here as in other departments of the garden; but there is much to be done which is too often left undone. Planting may now be presumed to be over; at least, unless the weather is unusually mild, when it will be well to prepare the ground, and leave the planting until the early spring.

Peaches, nectarines, and other wall-trees now require pruning, and the shoots selected nailed in; but both operations should be avoided in frosty weather; pruning in such weather is apt to lacerate the sap-vessels and destroy the shoots, which die back under its influence.

Standard apples and pears should receive their final autumn pruning and thinning out, chiefly of the interior branches, so as to admit of a free current of air; badly-placed shoots should be removed. Espalier trees, and trees planted against a wall for horizontal training, do best when the shoots are tied down; in the absence of trellis on the wall, studs should be driven into it at convenient distances, in order to avoid the distortion the branches undergo in the old process of nailing with shreds.

Plants under Glass.—The re-labelling, cleaning, and arranging of all plants should be diligently forwarded, so that every plant should have its proper name and its best dress before Christmas. Climbers on roofs and pillars may also have their final pruning, cleaning, and tying; every dead leaf and every particle of dirt removed. This, so essential to health everywhere, is especially necessary in the conservatory, where nothing offensive to good taste should ever be seen. The interest of this house is often much increased at this season by introducing some pots of Christmas roses, hyacinths, narcissuses, &c., from the forcing-pit. The edges of the beds, shelves, and vases may also be decorated with variegated and plain holly, and pillars from which fuchsias or other climbers have been removed, be wreathed in the same manner. These, with occasional syringing, will keep fresh for six weeks, and very much increase the interest of the house. The chrysanthemums will continue flowering during the month, and camellias be coming on to supply their place. *Rhododendron arboreum,* grown for several years under glass, will also flower in the conservatory at this season without any forcing. With a very little forcing the following varieties might be brought into flower during the month. Except in very sheltered situations and mild seasons, they cannot be depended upon for out-of-door cultivation; but they are splendid for pot-culture:—

Album, superbum, campanulatum, pictum, Gloire de Gand, nobleanum, pulchellum, princeps, Smithii, Smithii coccineum, venustum, Chandlerii, and Victoria Regina. Beautiful plants of these can be bought for from 3*s*. 6*d*. to 10*s*. each.

Next to rhododendrons, and even superior to them in usefulness, are camellias. This is the month when these are especially useful. By inducing early growth and early maturity, they will flower from habit in December as well as, if not better than, in any other month. The same may be said of Indian azaleas, of winter heaths and epacrises.

The same principles will apply to giving air, &c., as in November; only, as we have generally more sun in December, more may be admitted. Care must, however, be taken to prevent a cold draught cutting off the beauty of any plant that may have recently come from a warmer house or forcing-pit. Frequently re-arrange the plants, and let the charm of change and freshness add grace to the glow of beauty, which should distinguish this house in winter.

Where a temperature of 45° is maintained, the various sorts of *Epiphyllum truncatum*, so often met with in stoves in winter, will bloom well in this house. There are now several varieties of this charming winter-flowering plant grown as dwarfs in suspended baskets, or as tall plants, umbrella-fashion, or as pyramids: worked on the Pereskia, it is exquisitely beautiful. Perhaps it flowers best in a cool stove, but it will flower for six weeks or two months in a warm conservatory. Potted in a rough mixture of peat, leaf-mould, loam, brickbats, old plaster, and charcoal, and kept in a temperature of 60°, its progress is rapid. During the summer and autumn months, the plants should be fully exposed to the sun in an airy house. Place them in a temperature of 55° towards the middle of October, and now every leaf will terminate in one, two, or three beautiful flowers.

In the stove the *Poinsettia* should now be in flower. No description can convey an exaggerated or sufficiently strong idea of the regal beauty of this plant. Half a dozen of them, from four to five feet high, with eight shoots each, terminated by bunches of enormous scarlet bracts, set off by the peculiar shape and colour of the true leaves, is a sight worth going twenty miles on any December morning to see. Any one with a plant-stove may have this treat at home, as few plants are more easily propagated or grown. They can be had in flower from October to March.

Euphorbia jacquiniflora should also be flowering. The brilliant effect of this plant among begonias, ferns, and other things, must be seen to be appreciated. Some late caladiums, grown for this purpose, will now be intermixing their beautiful leaves with the bright flower-stems of *Gesneria cinnabrina*, and others. The bright red berries of the *Ardisia crenulata* will also be exhibiting themselves in striking contrast with the shining green leaves.

Orchids.—Rest here also should be the order of the day; nevertheless that rest will be partially broken by the flowering of some or all of the following plants:—*Pholænopsis amabilis*, several Oncidiums, Cymbidiums, Epidendrums, Cattleyas, Zygopetalums, &c. Maintain a temperature of 60° to 70°, and avoid all stimulating treatment.

Greenhouses.—Preserve a minimum temperature of 40°; give as much air as possible; see that the stock is kept perfectly clean by occasional smoking, washings, dippings, &c.; put on a fire on dull mornings to expel damp; remove heaths, epacrises, &c., to the conservatory as they come in flower; shift young plants of kalosanthus into their blooming-pots as they require it, and keep everything in a quiet semi-dormant state until the new year awakens them.

Pelargoniums.—Early varieties for

cut flowers may be forced into bloom in a vinery or peach-house at work. The general stock will require careful treatment this month. The latest-flowering specimens may receive their final shift, and all will require careful training, a genial temperature of 45°, and great skill in watering and ventilating. Fancy varieties often show a disposition to bloom prematurely. These early flowers must be perseveringly removed, to throw the strength into the shoots, for a perfect inflorescence at the proper season. Keep the plants within a yard of the glass, if possible, to prevent their drawing, and fumigate as soon as one green-fly is visible.

Cinerarias.—The earliest of these will now be in flower, and few plants are more effective for decorative purposes.

Cold-Pits and Frames.—Water and cover with care; give all the air possible in mild weather. During severe weather these may remain hermetically sealed for a week with impunity at a temperature of 35° to 40°. After such a long nap, unwrap cautiously, and shade for a few days from the sun's rays. Examine the entire stock every favourable opportunity.

Forcing-pit.—Keep up a growing temperature of 55° to 60°. Introduce fresh batches of shrubs, roses, bulbs, and everything that will flower early, to supply the place of those draughted off for other service.

Fruit-culture under Glass.—*The Vines* are now showing branches. Bring artificial heat to your aid, and keep a night temperature of 60° and a day one of 70°; admit every possible ray of light: keep the leaves within nine inches of the glass, and create a midsummer climate in December. Examine frequently the state of the borders, and keep the roots as warm as the tops. Stop the shoots a joint beyond the branches; damp the floors, paths, and pipes, if these are used, during bright days; admit air whenever it is practicable, and try to secure strength rather than length. Where a succession of grapes is wanted, start another vinery; proceed as directed in November.

Continue to look over and preserve late grapes, and maintain for these a cool and equable temperature of 40° to 50°. If a gentle current of air can be kept up through the houses by night and by day, the fruit will keep all the better. Vine-borders may be formed, or old borders renewed during this month. Old vines may also be taken up where the borders are bad, the roots carefully preserved, a new border made and skilfully planted, and half a crop taken the first season. Young vines may be planted in a dormant state or first started in pots, and then put in the border in June or July. The great point in planting at any season is carefully to surround the roots, sprinkle leaf-mould over them, and keep them within six inches of the surface. A mulching of dung or some litter will be necessary to prevent them being dried up; and if the vine is in full growth when planted, the top must be shaded a few days until the roots have laid hold of the soil; then let the top run as far as it chooses. Leave laterals and all on. The more growth for the next four months the better, because the larger the top the greater the number of healthy roots. Upon the number, nearness to the surface, and strength of these, all future success may be said to depend.

Pines.—Keep fruiting pines almost entirely dry if you wish them to start in January. Maintain a day temperature of 70°; night, 60° to 63°. This drynesss is necessary to throw the plants into bloom. Nothing does this more effectually than a check, although the check must neither be too severe nor too long-continued. Beware of moisture settling upon any pines that may now be in flower, as it often prevents the proper fructification of the blossoms; and deformed fruit is the consequence. Embrace every opportunity of admitting air when the external atmosphere will permit, and keep the plants within one foot of the glass. Succession plants, if kept tolerably dry, may be wintered in pits, at a temperature of 60°, with perfect safety. Beware of an excess of heat, or any sudden change of temperature, lest you cause premature growth or start them into fruit.

Peach-house.—In many places the fruit-house is started this month. For instructions in the preliminary stages, see November. Beware of frost. The wood of trees under glass cannot bear cold so well as that nurtured out of doors.

Figs.—Lee's Perpetual fig is the best sort grown; the white Ischia and Marsella are perhaps a little better flavoured; but they are small. The first batch of strawberries should now be introduced. Cuthill's Black Prince the best for the early season, and if they can have a little bottom-heat, so much the better. Plants in 48-sized pots do best for early work, the cramping principle inducing fruitfulness.

Hotbed and Frame.—Little can be added to what has been already said. Let the weather be the principal guide as to giving air, &c.; be careful that the frames are ventilated without causing draught, which might injure the plants considerably. See that the heat is maintained, and cover with mats at night; but do not shorten the days more than they are. The mats should be taken off as soon as it is light in the morning, and not put on till it is getting dark at night, so that the plants may have all the daylight they can get.

DECIDUOUS FLOWERING SHRUBS.

Almost all these, which are very ornamental, are easy of cultivation; but they require an amount of care and observation, in order that they may be made to produce abundant and handsome flowers. Lilacs and also laburnums may, with advantage, occasionally be thinned out, but they ought never to have their shoots shortened; while Guelder roses, syringas, ribes, spiræas, and others, will be benefited by almost any degree of pruning, and can only be made to bear fine handsome flowers by having their spring shoots well cut in about the end of May and beginning of June. Appended is a list of—

Choice Deciduous Shrubs, &c.

Althæa frutex,—bears various-coloured flowers, like single hollyhock: blooms early.
Almond,—dwarf and tall; bears pink flowers; very early.
Azaleas.—These may be had of many colours,—scarlet, red, orange, yellow, pink, bronze-colour, and shaded; bloom early.
Buddlea globosa,—orange-coloured flowers.
Berberry,—flowers in bunches, yellow, and succeeded by scarlet berries.
Calycanthus floridus,—allspice-scented wood, with brown flowers.
Chimonanthus fragrans,—dull-coloured; flowers in the winter, highly scented, and before the leaves appear.
Cherry,—double-flowering.
Clematis (various). The common is very hardy and fragrant.
,, Siebaldii,—white, with blue centre.
,, Azurea grandiflora,—rich purple.
Cydonia (*Pyrus*) japonica,—scarlet flowers; blooming several months in the year.
Cytisus (Laburnum),—yellow, purple, and other varieties; flowering early in the spring.
Daphne Mazereum,—red and white.
Deutzia scabra,—flowers white.
Guelder rose,—bears white balls of bloom.
Thorne's Cratægus,—red, double and single; pink do.; white do.; and many varieties of fruit and foliage.
Jasminum nudiflorum,—yellow.
,, officinale,—white.
Lilac,—purple, pale, white, Persian, and other varieties.
Lonicera, an immense number of species and varieties, and nearly all good, ranging from 3 to 15 ft.
Magnolia conspicua.
,, purpurea; and many other excellent species and varieties.
Peach,—double-flowering.
Philadelphus Syringa,—highly-scented white flower; leaves small, like the cucumber.
Ribes sanguineum,—crimson flowers.
,, album,—white do.
,, aureum,—yellow do.
,, speciosum,—scarlet; a double variety,—and many others.
Robinia (Rose-acacia),—pink flowers; several varieties.
Roses.—There are upwards of 1,500 varieties and species; but a list of these will be found elsewhere.
Spiræa,—many varieties, and all pretty.
Virginian creeper,—will grow to the top of a house, and the foliage turns crimson in autumn.

DELPHIN'IUM (nat. ord. **Ranuncula'ceæ**).

A genus of profuse-flowering plants of a highly decorative character. Planted in large beds or groups, their gorgeous spikes of flowers, of almost endless shades, from pearl-white to the very richest and deepest blue, render them conspicuous objects in the flower-garden and pleasure-ground: they delight in deep, highly enriched soil. With the exception of *D. cardiopetalum* they are all hardy perennials.

DESMAN'THUS (nat. ord. **Legumino'sæ**).

A very pretty ornamental greenhouse shrub; succeeds best in peat and loam.

Desmanthus virgatus, — white, 1½ ft., from West Indies.

DESMO'DIUM (nat. ord. **Legumino'sæ**).

A pretty greenhouse plant, flowering in long spikes, and having curiously twisted seed-vessels; succeeds well in sandy loam and peat.

Desmodium Gangeticum,—lilac, 2 ft., from East Indies.

DEUT'ZIA (nat. ord. **Philadelpha'ceæ**).

A beautiful hardy shrub, when in bloom covered with pretty snowdrop-like flowers, exceedingly valuable for the spring decoration of the conservatory.

Deutzia gracilis,—pure white, very graceful, 3 ft., from Japan.

DIAN'THUS (nat. ord. **Caryophylla'ceæ**).

A beautiful genus, which embraces some of the most popular flowers in cultivation. The Carnation, Picotee, Pink, and Sweet William, all "household words," belong to this genus. *D. Sinensis* and its varieties may be considered the most beautiful and effective of our hardy annuals; the double and single varieties, with their rich and varied colours in beds or masses, are remarkably attractive; while the recently introduced species, *D. Heddewigii*, with its large rich-coloured flowers, three to four inches in diameter, close compact habit, and profusion of bloom, is unsurpassed for effectiveness in beds or mixed borders.

DIGITA'LIS (nat. ord. **Scrophularia'ceæ**). **Hardy Perennials.**

Remarkably handsome and highly ornamental plants, of stately growth and easy culture, especially adapted for shrubbery borders, woodland walks, and pleasure-grounds. They thrive in almost any soil and situation.

DISBUDDING.

The object of disbudding is to remove all useless sprays not required for next year's branches, which would not, from their position, ripen into desirable fruit-bearing wood; it is, in fact, to relieve the tree from nursing wood that must be cut away in the autumn-pruning; but it must be the care of the operator to avoid removing shoots well placed for future branches, or which would expose the tree to too severe a trial of its vital power.

DOCKS.

Docks, as dandelions, may be got rid of by cutting off the tops as soon as they appear, and placing a little salt on the wound.

DOG-TOOTHED VIOLETS.

Pretty little plants, with beautifully spotted leaves. When planted as an edging to beds or borders, they are remarkably effective, and do well in any light soil. To prevent decay, surround the tubers with about an inch of silver-sand.

Dog-toothed violets,—purple, per 100, 7*s.* 6*d.*; per doz. 1*s.*

Dog-toothed Violets,—rose or red, 1*s.* per doz.
,, white, 3*s.* 6*d.* per doz.
,, mixed, 1*s.* 6*d.* per doz.
,, yellow (*Erythronium Americanum*), 9*d.* each.

DRAINAGE.

However high and apparently dry a situation may appear, it is quite possible that it requires to be drained. The object of draining is not only to get rid of superfluous moisture, but also to prevent the little there may be from remaining stagnant. It is quite a common occurrence to find a piece of ground that is never too wet, but which is, nevertheless, sour and unfitted for the cultivation of delicate flowers. It should, therefore, be the first care of the florist to make drains from the highest part of the ground to the lowest, three feet from the surface, dug the shape of a V; and if there be no outlet at the lowest part, to dig a hole, or well, or pond, into which all these should lead, even when there is no apparent means of getting rid of the water. At the bottom of these drains a row of common 2-inch earthen pipes may be placed, end to end, and covered up again with the soil. These are too deep to cause any danger of disturbance in ordinary operations; and the effect is to let air into the soil, if there be no surplus moisture; and to prevent the lodgment of water anywhere: about a rod apart, in parallel lines, will be sufficiently close for the drains, and a larger drain along the bottom, or a ditch, may lead at once to the outlet or the receptacle for the water. Suppose, however, the soil is really surcharged with water, and there is no place but the pond made for the purpose into which this water can pass, and suppose, while we are imagining evils, that this pond or hole fills higher than the bottoms of the drains, it is obvious, in such cases, that the drains cannot empty themselves. Still, even such drains are of use; if they can only discharge all the water in the driest season, immense good is done by them. If the pond be not too large, a garden-engine may be set to work to lower the water by throwing it over the surface; and although it may fill as fast as the water is taken away, there is a circulation of water going on in the soil, instead of moisture being stagnant, and the ground made sour.

The rationale of drainage is very well explained by Mr. D. S. Fish. "Drainage," he says, "as popularly understood, means the art of laying land dry. This, however, is a very imperfect definition, both of its theoretical principles and practical results. Paradoxical as it may appear, drainage is almost as useful in keeping land moist as in laying it dry. Its proper function is to maintain the soil in the best possible hygrometrical condition for the development of vegetable life. Drainage has also a powerful influence in altering the texture of soils. It enriches their plant-feeding capabilities; elevates their temperature, and improves the general climate of a whole district, by increasing its temperature, and removing unhealthy exhalations. It lays land dry, by removing superfluous water; it keeps it moist, by increasing its power of resisting the force of evaporation; it alters the texture, by the conduction of water, and by filling the interstices previously occupied by that fluid with atmospheric air; it enriches the soil, by separating carbonic acid gas and ammonia from the atmosphere, and by facilitating the decomposition, absorption, and amalgamation of liquid and solid manures. It heightens the temperature of the earth, by husbanding its heat, and surrounding it with an envelope of comparatively dry air, and by substituting the air for water withdrawn through the interstices of the soil; for while the tendency of excessive moisture in the soil is to bind the whole mass into an almost solid substance, the tendency of air is to separate its particles into atoms, and render it porous: and the more porous a soil is, the greater is its power of resisting evaporation. For this reason, porous soils are more moist in hot weather than those of a more tenacious character.

"Drainage enriches soils in another way. All rain-water is more or less charged with carbonic acid gas and ammonia. Now, the larger the quantity of rain-water that passes through the soil, the greater will be the amount of these gases brought in contact with the roots of plants. Nor is this all: solid

1

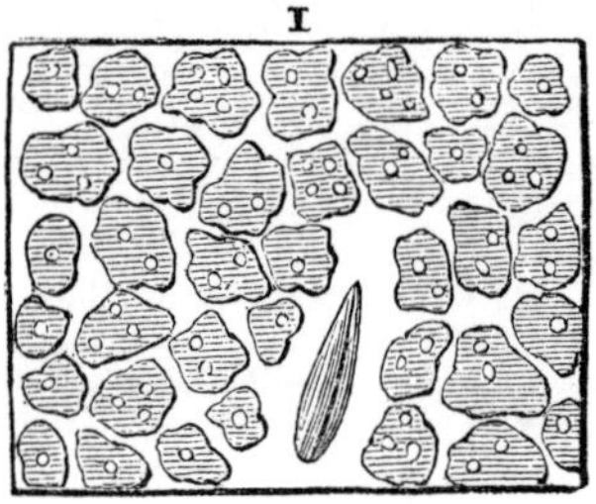

manures of the richest quality are comparatively useless on wet, heavy soils; for while a certain amount of moisture is essential to the decomposition of manures, an excess arrests the process, and all the most soluble portions are washed out long before it is sufficiently decomposed to enter into the composition of plants. Judicious drainage, therefore, places the soil in a proper hygrometrical condition for performing its importants functions."

2

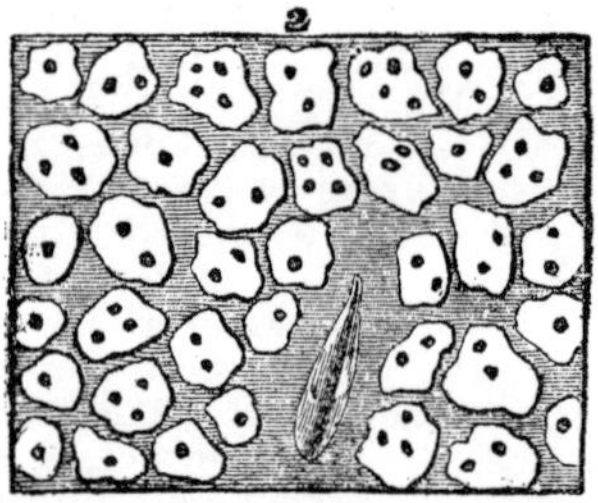

This will be rendered still more obvious by the accompanying diagrams, which prove the beneficial influence exercised by drainage upon the soil, and were exhibited before the Highland Agricultural Society by Dr. Madden, of Penicuik, in 1844. They are highly-magnified sections of soil in three different conditions. Under the microscope, soil is seen to be made up of numerous distinct porous particles. Fig. 1 represents it in a perfectly dry state; both the soil and the channels between being quite dry. Fig. 2, on the other hand, represents a soil perfectly wet; the particles themselves are full of water, and so are the channels between them. In fig. 3 the particles are moist, while the passages between them are filled with air. These diagrams show that soil in the condition exhibited in figs. 1 and 2 was totally unfit for the germination of seed. In fig. 1 there is no water; in fig. 2 there is no air; in fig. 3 both are pre-

3

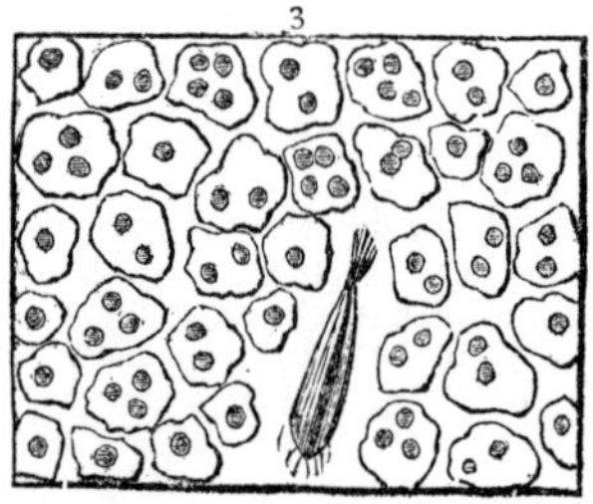

sent, in the proportions favourable to the growth of seeds, and these are requisite to insure the vigorous growth of the plant throughout all its stages; fig. 3, therefore, is the condition of soil desirable for all cultural purposes, and exhibits that congenial admixture of earth, water, and air, that plants delight in, and which efficient drainage only can provide.

DRAINAGE OF POTS.

The effectual drainage of pots does not consist so much in the quantity of drainage, as in the arrangement of it. A potsherd should be placed over the hole; some pieces of pot, broken rather small, over that; and these again covered with a layer of peat-fibre or rough earth. This gives efficient *drainage*, and need not occupy more than an inch and a half of the pot.

DRAINING IMPLEMENTS.

The implements used in draining are a spade, and in deep draining, and in a clay soil, a series of two or three spades, varying in size, and each sloping to the point, and slightly rounded, so as to make a circular cut; a spoon-like implement also is required for lifting

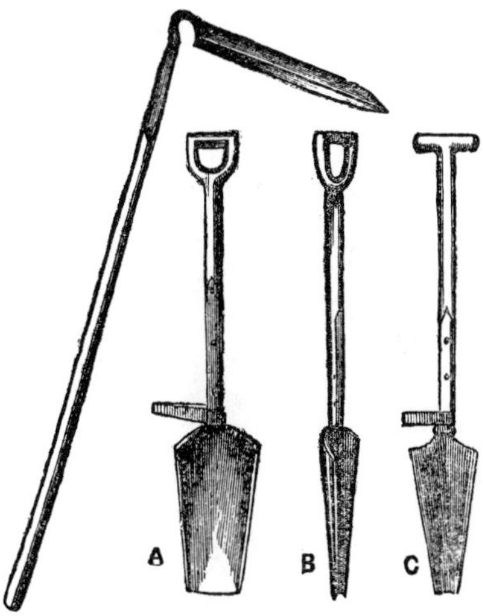

the loose soil clear out of the bottom of the trench; and a level, which may easily be formed by fixing three perfectly straight-edged boards in an upright position and in a triangular form, held together by a vertical board in the centre, with an opening at its base for a line and plummet.

DRAINING MATERIALS.

The materials employed for drains are very varied; brushwood, rubble, stones, bricks, and pipes being all in use. In clay countries it is no unusual thing to form pipes with the clay itself, by inserting an arched framework of wood, and withdrawing it when consolidated. The best and cheapest drains, however, are drain-pipes, which are now obtainable everywhere on moderate terms.

DRESSING TO DESTROY INSECTS' EGGS.

An excellent Dressing to destroy the Eggs, &c., of Insects that infest the bark of trees and old walls.—Take ½ lb. of tobacco, ½ lb. of sulphur, ¼ peck of lime; stir these ingredients well together in three or four gallons of water; leave them to settle, and syringe the trees and walls well with the clear liquid. More water may be added when the first is used up.

DUTCH HOE.

This is one of the most useful sort of hoes for the flower-garden. Its construction is too well known to need description. Messrs. Barnard & Bishop, of Norwich, advertise them from 3 inches to 10 inches at from 9*d.* to 2*s.* 6*d.* each.

DWARF FRUIT-TREES.

Modern fruit-gardens may be described as orchards in miniature. Certainly they are more manageable, doubly interesting, and equally productive with orchards. To make good dwarf trees, work apples on the Paradise stock, pears on the quince, and cherries and plums on the most dwarf stocks that can be procured. Careful summer stopping, root-pruning, and the pyramidal form will describe the main feature of their treatment and training; and abundance of good fruit will be the result. The trees may be planted in rows from 7 to 10 feet apart, and the same distance between each plant. On good soils they succeed well on the level of the ground; on heavy clays, or other unfavourable bottoms, the ground can be thrown into ridges or mounds. The bottom of these mounds may be occupied with a standard gooseberry or currant—these bear admirably trained a single stem in this manner; and the sides can be cropped with salading. A fruit-garden thus formed is quite a scene of beauty when the trees are in flower, and very enjoyable at all times.

EARWIG-TRAP.

The amateur's registered earwig-trap is to be obtained of Messrs. Barr & Sugden, price 7*s.* 6*d.* per dozen. Those who cultivate dahlias, roses, and such other plants as are subject to the depredations of earwigs, &c., will find this trap invaluable.

No. 1 engraving represents the trap as it appears fixed on a stake; No. 2

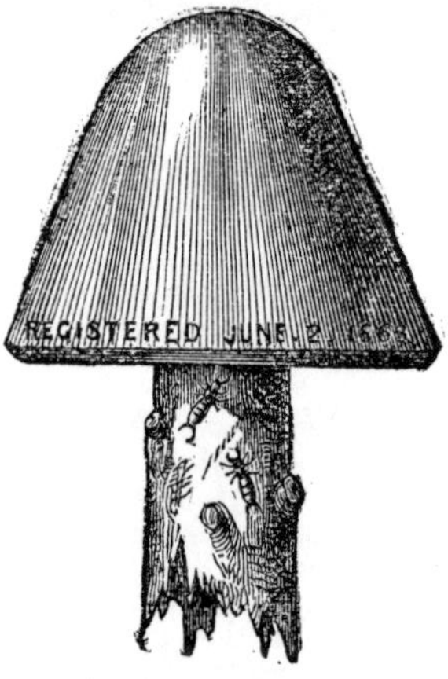

No. 1.

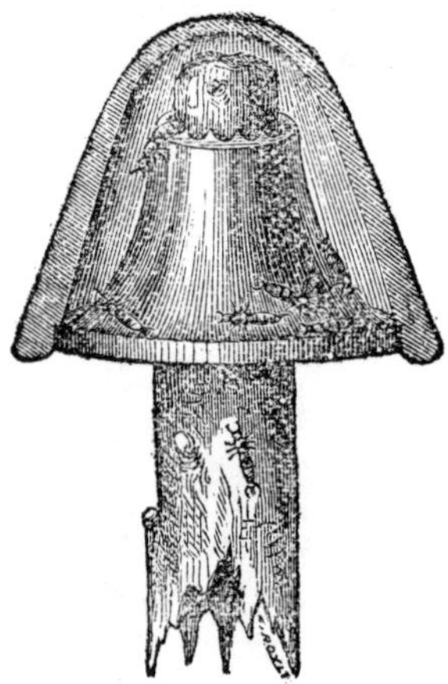

No. 2.

shows the section with the chamber (*from which there is no escape*), where the insects retire after their nocturnal depredations. The trap is then inverted, the inner cone removed, and the culprits dealt with as may seem good in the eyes of their captors.

EARWIGS.

To get rid of earwigs, place pieces, about four or six inches long, of the hollow stems of any plant, in an horizontal position, in different parts of the trees on which earwigs abound. The earwigs will congregate in these, and may be shaken out into boiling water and destroyed. Very small garden-pots containing a little dry moss may be inverted on the top of a stick, and in this way will form a good trap when placed among flowering plants.

ECCREMOCAR'PUS (nat. ord. Bignonia'ceæ).

A half-hardy climber of great beauty; bearing rich orange-coloured flowers in profusion. It will grow in any common soil, and may be easily raised from seed, which it ripens in abundance. Sow in autumn on a slight hotbed, and the plants, after two or three shiftings, will be ready for turning out in April or May. If cut down in autumn, and covered with dry leaves, the Eccremocarpus will live through any ordinary winter, and shoot up again vigorously in the spring.

ECHI'NOPS (nat. ord. Compos'itæ).

The Echinops, or Globe-thistle, is a strong-growing, free-flowering plant of considerable beauty, suitable for large shrubbery borders; it grows freely in any soil.

Echinops bannaticus,—blue ball, 3 ft., from Hungary.

EDGING.

Sometimes gardens are laid down on a mixed plan of grass and gravel. When each bed is edged with brick, stone, tile, or cement, these edgings are occasionally surrounded with from two to four feet of gravel, succeeded by the same or a greater width of turf. Flagstones are also used for this purpose instead of gravel, as well as to subdivide groups of figures close to the dwelling-house. Beds on grass, however, unless much elevated above the surface, are most effective without any edgings whatever; although, in certain situations, raised beds, with massive edgings of stone or rustic-work, look well. For beds on gravel, an edging of some kind becomes imperative. Of all living edgings box is the best; thrift, sedums, and saxifrages of various kinds, and that wonderful weed which was designed to banish grass from our lawns (*Spergula milifera*), follow each other in value and adaptability for this purpose. Ornamental stone, tile, brick, or cast-iron edgings, are probably better than any living edging whatever. These can neither harbour insects, exhaust the soil, nor look patchy through dying off; and although perhaps more expensive in the first instance, the first expense is the only one. They can be purchased on very reasonable terms, and of varied and elegant designs. Whatever edgings are used, they must vary in height and thickness with the size of the beds they define. Nothing can be in worse taste than a heavy massive edging surrounding a small delicate pattern, or *vice versâ*.

On sterile, uncongenial soils, it has een recommended by Mr. Loudon and others to inclose all the flower-beds with a brick wall to a depth of two or three feet, so that the soil could be entirely removed at pleasure. Where this is attempted, such walls would form an excellent base for the edging to rest on; and where such an operation is unnecessary, a layer of concrete six inches deep will afford the requisite solidity and stability. Ornamental wire-work often makes a very effective edging for different beds.

EDGING PLANTS.

There are many plants adapted for garden edgings. Among these we may enumerate *Buxus sempervirens*, thrift, cuttings of *Iberis saxatilis*, daisies, both white and red, the variegated alyssum, feather-grass, &c. &c.

EDGING TOOLS.

Lawns and beds cannot be kept in good order without the frequent use of edging-irons and edging-shears. The former is a spade-like tool for cutting the edges of beds; and the latter, as its name implies, is used for shearing off the long grass which grows on the edges. The price of the former is 3*s.* to 4*s.* 6*d.*, and of the latter, 6*s.* 6*d.* to 7*s.* 6*d.*, or 8*s.* 6*d.* if provided with a wheel.

EDWARD'SIA (nat. ord. Legumino'sæ).

Half-hardy shrubs and trees, beautiful for their foliage and curiously-shaped flowers. They are natives of New Zealand, and flourish best in our climate under protection of a wall. They seed freely, and in this way are easily propagated.

EGG-PLANT (Sola'num ovig'erum, nat. ord. Solona'ceæ).

A very singular and ornamental class of fruit-bearing plants (half-hardy annuals), especially adapted for conservatory or drawing-room decoration: they thrive best in very rich light soil.

Egg-plant,—white-fruited, 1½ ft., from Africa.
,, scarlet-fruited, beautiful, with handsome dark green foliage, 1½ ft., from Africa.
Egg-plant,—violet-fruited, 1½ ft., from Africa.

EGG-PLANT (Aubergine, nat. ord. Solona'ceæ).

This is the edible variety of the Egg-plant, so extensively cultivated in the south of Europe.

Time and Manner of Sowing.—The seed should be sown in March, or early in April, in well-drained pots of light rich soil, and covered lightly. Place the pots in a cucumber- or melon-frame, or where a moderate heat is maintained, and keep the soil moist. When the plants are fairly up, place them singly in small pots, using rich soil, and in the same temperature near to the glass. When they have started into growth, induce a bushy habit by frequently pinching out the points.

After-management.—As soon as the plants have well filled the first pots with roots, shift them into others two sizes larger, still using rich light soil. Keep them well supplied with water at the roots. If they are intended for decorative purposes, they should be shifted into 8- or 10-inch pots before the roots become matted. Stop the shoots at the first joint beyond the fruit as soon as this is set, and keep them in a moist, warm situation until the fruit attains a fair size, when they may be placed in a cool house. But if the plants are to be grown with the view of obtaining the largest possible crop of fruit, they should in favourable localities be planted out of doors, when the weather becomes warm, in prepared trenches, such as are recommended for ridge cucumbers. They should have the protection of hand-glasses until they are well established and the weather becomes settled and warm. If they can be planted out on a slight hotbed under the shelter of a frame, there will be more certainty of a good crop than by any other method of treatment. The plants when grown in pots are very subject to the attack of red spider, and will require frequent syringings to keep them clear of this pest. They must be liberally supplied with water at the roots, and weak manure-water after the fruit is set will be useful.

The varieties are—

Scarlet-fruited, very handsome; White-fruited, ditto; Violet-fruited, ditto; New striped, weighing from 1 lb. to 4 lb., ditto.

Seed from 3*d.* to 4*d.* per packet.

EMPEROR STOCK.

The Emperor or Imperial, sometimes called Perpetual Stocks, are hybrids of the Brompton, growing 18 inches high, and of a robust branching habit. Sown in March or April, they make splendid "autumn-flowering stocks," and form a valuable succession to the summer-blooming varieties. Should the winter prove mild, they will continue flowering to Christmas. Sown in June or July, they flower the following June, and continue blooming through the summer and autumn months.

	per pkt. *s.*	*d.*
8 splendid varieties, of the most beautiful colours	2	6
8 ditto, ditto, smaller packets	1	6
Splendid mixed, sufficient for a large bed	2	6

ENDIVE.

Preparation of the Soil.—Trench the ground to a depth of two feet, mixing a very liberal dressing of rich and thoroughly-decayed manure. For crops intended to stand the winter, a light, dry, and rather poor soil is best, and they should be planted in a sheltered situation.

Time and Manner of Sowing.—Make the first sowing about the middle of May on a bed of well-pulverized rich soil, scattering the seed thinly, and covering it lightly. For the main crop sow in the middle of June, and again about the middle of July. Plants to stand the winter should be sown early in August. When the plants are about two inches high, transplant into nursery beds upon rich well-prepared soil, taking special care not to injure the roots, as this, as well as want of water in hot, dry weather, very often causes them to run to seed. In dry weather supply them liberally with water.

Planting and After-management.—When the plants are about four inches high, transplant, lifting them carefully with as much soil as can be kept about their roots. Place them in drills about 3 inches deep and 12 to 14 inches apart, and leave about the same distance between the plants. Give a liberal supply of water immediately after planting, and as often as may be requisite to keep the soil moist. Beyond watering and keeping the surface of the soil open and free from weeds, the plants will require no further attention till they are nearly full-grown, when means should be used to blanch them. In the case of the earlier crops this may be done by tying them up when dry, after the same fashion as lettuce, and drawing the soil about them so as to fill the drills in which they are planted, then ridging up the soil two or three inches round each plant. But as late crops intended for winter use are liable to be injured by frost, these should be blanched by covering the plants with inverted pots. When severe weather is feared, a portion of the plants sown in July may be lifted with balls and planted closely together in pits or frames, where they can be protected from frost and wet, yet be fully exposed to the air when the weather permits. Tying or covering should be done at intervals, so as to have a continuous supply well blanched as they may be required for use. The August sowing should be planted out at the bottom of a south wall, or in some other sheltered situation. In many localities these plants require the protection of glass to winter them safely.

	per pkt. *s. d.*	per oz. *s. d.*
Green Curled, extra fine French —very superior variety ..	0 4	0 9
Batavian Green,—smooth broad leaves	—	0 9
Batavian White,—large and very superior	0 4	0 9
White curled,—very useful ..	—	0 9
New Moss curled	0 4	0 9

EP'ACRIS (nat. ord. Epacrida'ceæ).

These are heath-like shrubs, natives of New Holland. They all require a fine gritty peat soil, and flourish best in double pots, with moist moss between them. The pots should be well drained; but the roots of the plants must never suffer for want of moisture. They must have plenty of air and light, and just sufficient heat to keep them from frost. Cuttings of the young wood strike easily in sand with a little bottom heat.

These plants should be freely cut back as soon as they have done flowering; and after the shoots have grown afresh, two or three inches long, is the best time for potting them. Place them in a close pit, but by no means warm, for a few weeks; gradually inure them to the air, plunge in a sunny situation: see that the wood is brown and hard by the end of September. Remove to conservatory-shelf in October, and you will have a charming profusion and succession of tiny tubes of colour.

As no one ever saw, or ever will see, an ugly epacris, it seems almost a loss of time to specify varieties. However, all are not equally beautiful; therefore select the following, which can be bought from 9*s.* to 18*s.* per dozen:—

Epacris alba odorata, Albertus campanulata, Impressa, Alba carnea, Atleana delicata, Impressa alba, Impressa floribunda, Alba coccinea, Alba floribunda, Kinghornii magnifica miniata, Kinghornii splendens, Kinghornii compacta, Kinghornii major, Viscountess Hill. The following generally flower in the autumn: —Racemosa, Picturata, Mont Blanc, Exquisite, and Fireball.

EPIPHYL'LUM TRUNCA'TUM (nat. ord. Cacta'ceæ).

This is one of the numerous family of *Cacti*, an abundant flowerer, and requiring only greenhouse heat.

ERI'CAS (nat. ord. Erica'ceæ).

This important genus of greenhouse plants, which includes five or six hundred described species, and as many varieties produced by cultivation, is the great ornament of the greenhouse at a time when other flowering plants are scarce. Ericas or Heaths also have the advantag of furnishing flowers in summer and autumn, as well as in winter and spring.

Heaths are propagated by cuttings formed of the tender tops of the young shoots. The cuttings should be an inch or so in length, and should be tenderly used, so as to avoid bruising any part of the stem, and inserted in pots or pans filled with pure white sand, moistened and firmly pressed down. Having inserted the cuttings, water so as to settle the sand about the roots; give a little time for the moisture to subside, then cover them with bell-glasses, pressing the edges into the sand so as completely to exclude the air, only removing the glasses to wipe off accumulated moisture. They should be placed in the propagating-house, or in a spent hotbed. When they begin to root, which will be seen by the starting of the shoots, they should have air given daily to harden them preparatory to the removal of the bell-glasses.

The soil best adapted for heaths is that obtained from a locality where the wild heath grows luxuriantly, taking care it is not dug too deep: the turf must not exceed four inches; if deeper, it is more than probable that the good and nutritious upper soil will become deteriorated by an admixture of inert and mischievous subsoil. The summer is the proper season to procure and store up a heap which may safely be used after having a summer and winter's seasoning.

The next matter of importance is the selection of healthy dwarf-growing, robust plants, taking care to avoid anything like meagre, stunted plants, which might live for years, but cause nothing but disappointment to the cultivator.

To prepare the soil for potting or shifting, it should be cut down from the heap so as to disarrange it as little as possible, breaking the lumps well with the back of the spade, and afterwards rubbing the soil through the hands, which is far better than sifting, as it leaves more of the fibrous decomposing vegetable matter in it; add to this one-fifth good white sand, and well incorporate the two.

To convert plants into handsome well-grown specimens in a moderately short space of time, they must have a liberal shift. Young plants in a 60- or 64-sized pot may be shifted into a 24- or 9-inch pot, taking care that plenty of potsherds be used for drainage. Care must be taken, also, that the soil is thoroughly mixed, by pressing with the fingers in the fresh pots all round the ball of the plants, so as to make it quite firm and close. After being set away in a cool frame or pit, let them be well watered. The following is a list of the best kinds for spring, summer, and autumnal flowering:—

Spring-flowering Heaths.

Aristata, or Horned,—flowering from March to August; dark-purple and white; 18 inches high.
,, major.
Andromedæflora, — flowering from March to August; rose-colour; 2 ft. high.
Arbuscula,—a small heath of Sicily, bearing a red flower from February to August; 12 inches high.
Colorans,—whitish red; flowers in May; a greenhouse evergreen shrub.
,, superba.
,, blanda.
Denticulata, — purple; flowers in April; a greenhouse evergreen shrub.
Exsurgens,—dark orange; flowers in May; do.
,, coccinea
Ferruginea,—red; flowers in May; a greenhouse evergreen shrub.
Floribunda,—pale pink; flowers in May; ditto.
Florida campanulata,—red; flowers in May; ditto.
Gracilis,—purplish-red; flowers in March; do.
Grandinosa, or Hailstone, —a pretty heath, with white flower; in March and April; 6 inches high.
Hyemalis.
Humeana,—pink; flowers in March; a greenhouse evergreen shrub.
Incarnata,—pale red; flowers in March; ditto.
Lambertiana,—a delicate heath; flower rose and white; from May to August; 12 inches high.
Linnæana,—ornamental greenhouse shrub, of delicate habit, 18 inches high; purple and white; January to May.
Linnæoides,—linnæana-like heath; February to May; 18 inches high, and purple and red.
Metulæflora,—orange; flowers in April; a greenhouse evergreen shrub.
Mirabilis,—purple; flowers in May; ditto.
Mutabilis,—crimson; flowers in May; ditto.
Neilii.
Persoluta rubra,—red; flowers in March; a greenhouse evergreen shrub.
Pyramidalis,—pink; flowers in March; ditto.

Ericas.

Rubra-calyx.
Sanguinolenta,—a pretty heath, flowering May to July; flower crimson and red; height 9 inches.
Sebana lutea,—yellow; flowers in May; a greenhouse evergreen shrub.
Sindryana.
Smithiana (Smith's heath),—flowering in April and May; bears a purple flower; height 2 ft.
Sparsa (scattered),—flowering in April; flower purple; 18 inches high.
Tenella,—a delicate heath; flower purple; May to August; 2 inches high.
Transparens,—white; flowers in May; a greenhouse evergreen shrub.
Vernix.
,, coccinea.
Westcottii.

Summer-flowering Heaths (June to August).

Aitoniana,—whitish-purple; flowers in August; a greenhouse evergreen shrub.
,, turgida.
Ampullacea major,—whitish-red; flowers in June; a greenhouse evergreen shrub.
,, rubra.
,, elegans.
Bandoniana,—purple; flowers in July; a greenhouse evergreen shrub.
Banksiana purpurea,—purple; flowers in June; ditto.
Beaumontiana,—purple; flowers in June; do.
Bergiana,—purple; flowers in June; ditto.
Carniula,—purple; flowers in August; ditto.
Cavendishiana.
Clowesiana.
Depressa,—yellow; flowers in July; a greenhouse evergreen shrub.
,, floribunda.
Elegans,—green; flowers in August; a greenhouse evergreen shrub.
Eassoniana.
Eximia,—scarlet; flowers in June; a greenhouse evergreen shrub.
Fastigiata,—white; flowers in July; ditto.
Favoides elegans.
Florida,—red; flowers in July; a greenhouse evergreen shrub.
Hartnelli,—purple; flowers in July; ditto.
,, nana.
Inflata,—whitish-red; flowers in July; a greenhouse evergreen shrub.
,, rubra.
Irbyana,—whitish-green; flowers in August; a greenhouse evergreen shrub.
Jasminiflora alba,—white; ditto; ditto.
Jasminoides.
Jacksonii.
Laurenceana.
Longipedunculata,—pink; flowers in July; a greenhouse evergreen shrub.
Mammosa,—purple; flowers in August; ditto.
,, major.
M'Nabiana.
Massoni,—red-green; flowers in August; a greenhouse evergreen shrub.

Ericas.

Metulæflora bicolor.
Mundula,—purple; flowers in June; a greenhouse evergreen shrub.
Murrayana.
Nitida,—white; flowers in August; a greenhouse evergreen shrub.
Ollula,—pink; flowers in June; ditto.
Ovata,—purple; flowers in June; ditto.
Picta,—orange-yellow; flowers in July; ditto.
Princeps,—scarlet; flowers in June; ditto.
,, carnea,—flesh; ditto; ditto.
Propendens,—purple; flowers in July; ditto.
Regerminans,—red; flowers in June; ditto.
Retorta,—pinkish-white; flowers in June; ditto.
,, major.
Rubens,—dark red; flowers in July; a greenhouse evergreen shrub.
Sanguinea,—crimson; flowers in August; ditto.
Spannoniana,—whitish purple; flowers in June; ditto.
Splendens,—scarlet, flowers in July; ditto.
Sprengelii,—yellowish-purple; flowers in June; ditto.
Templeana,—2 ft. high; flowering in July and August; flower red and purple.
Tortulæflora.
Tricolor,—red-green; flowers in June; a greenhouse evergreen shrub.
,, Dunbariana.
,, elegans.
,, Wilsoni.
,, ,, superba,—pink; flowers in July; a greenhouse evergreen shrub.
,, ,, coronata.
Vasæflora.
Ventricosa,—flesh; flowers in June; a greenhouse evergreen shrub.
,, coccinea,—scarlet; ditto; ditto.
,, ,, minor.
,, Bothwelliana.
,, grandiflora.
,, splendens.
,, hirsuta,—flesh; flowers in June; a greenhouse evergreen shrub.
,, alba,—white; ditto; ditto.
Vernoni superba.
Vestita alba,—white; flowers in June and August; a greenhouse evergreen shrub.
,, ,, grandiflora.
,, coccinea,—scarlet; flowers in June; a greenhouse evergreen shrub.
,, rosea,—light red; flowers in August; ditto.
Webbiana.
Westphalingia.
Wilmorei,—pink; flowers in July; a green house evergreen shrub.

Autumn and Winter-flowering Heaths.

Archeriana,—dark scarlet; flowers in September; a greenhouse evergreen shrub.

Bowieana, — white; flowers in October; a greenhouse evergree shrub.
Cerinthoides; dark scarlet; flowers in September; ditto.
,, stricta.
Gracilis autumnalis.
Infundibuliformis,—pale red; flowers in September; a greenhouse evergreen shrub.
Sebana rubra.
Taxifolia,—purple; flowers in September; a greenhouse evergreen shrub.
Vernix ovata.
Verticillata major, — scarlet; flowers in September; a greenhouse evergreen shrub.

From this list varieties may be selected that will furnish plants for the whole year. Heaths like plenty of air: it must be given freely, but carefully. From exposure to dry, arid, cutting winds, plants that are growing freely are apt to get a rustiness that will so disfigure them that months will elapse before they are free from it. With respect to plants growing in the heathery, or other house, during the continuance of cold winds, the doors to the eastward should be closed, and air admitted from the front sashes, taking care to let down the top-lights, so as to insure a free circulation of air. When the plants are of free growth, and the weather is of a parching character, it will be necessary to look over them every day, and water them freely, taking care that none be allowed to suffer for want of it, which at this stage would prove destructive to the flowering of the plants, if not to their life.

ERIOSTE'MON (nat. ord. Ruta'ceæ). Greenhouse Evergreen Shrubs.

An interesting genus of New Holland plants, extremely elegant in growth, and producing in profusion beautiful star-shaped blossoms: they thrive best in sandy peat and loam.

Eriostemon amœnum,—blush, 3 ft.
,, cuspidatum,—red, 3 ft.
,, ,, rubrum, 3 ft.
,, densifolium,—pink, 3 ft.
,, intermedium,—white, 3 ft.
,, linifolium,—red, 3 ft.

ERO'DIUM (nat. ord. Gerani'ceæ).

Charming little plants for rockwork, edgings, and flower-borders; succeed in any soil.

Erodium pelargoniæflorum,—white and rose, upper petals very prettily striped, ½ ft., from Algiers. Hardy perennial.

ERYS'IMUM (nat. ord. Crucif'eræ).

Free-flowering, and exceedingly showy plants, producing in beds, mixed borders, and ribbons, a very fine effect; succeed in light rich soil.

Erysimum Arkansanum, — sulphur - yellow, handsome, 1½ ft., hardy annual, from North America.
Erysimum Barbarianum variegatum,—yellow, foliage prettily variegated, 1½ ft., hardy perennial.
Erysimum Peroffskianum, — orange, showy, 1½ ft., hardy annual, from Palestine.

ERYTHRI'NA (nat. ord. Legumino'sæ). Half-hardy.

A splendid genus of shrubs, with fine leaves and brilliant scarlet flowers. Planted in a warm, favourable situation out of doors they grow freely, but in most localities they succeed best in a greenhouse, with the advantages of a warm house early in the season; they succeed best in rich loam and peat.

Erythrina corallodendron (Coral-tree),—scarlet, 20 ft., from West Indies.
Erythrina Crista galli,—scarlet, 20 ft., from Brazil.
Erythrina Hendersonii,—scarlet, 4 ft.
,, laurifolia,—scarlet, 4 ft., from South America.

ESCALLO'NIA (nat. ord. Escallonia'ceæ). Half-hardy.

Handsome evergreen shrubs, with rich glaucous leaves and bunches of pretty tubular flowers; they succeed against a south wall, if protected in the winter, and thrive best in sandy peat and loam.

Escallonia floribunda, — white, 3 ft., from Granada.
Escallonia macrantha,—purple-scarlet, 3 ft., from Granada.

Escallonia macrantha carnea, — flesh-colour, very beautiful, 3 ft., from Granada.
Escallonia viscosa alba,—white, from Mendoza, 3 ft.

ESCHSCHOLT'ZIA (nat. ord. Papavera'ceæ).

An exceedingly showy profuse-flowering class of Californian annuals, quite hardy, remarkable for extremely rich and beautiful colours; valuable for bedding, massing, and ribboning. *E. tenuifolia* is exceedingly neat for small beds, edgings, or rockwork; delights in light rich soil.

Eschscholtzia Californica,—bright yellow, with rich orange centre, 1 ft.
Eschscholtzia compacta,—yellow and orange, 1 ft.
Eschscholtzia crocea,—rich orange, 1 ft.
,, ,, alba,—creamy white, 1 ft.
,, tenuifolia,—primrose, with orange centre, very compact, ½ ft.

ESPALIER TREES.

Fruit-trees of almost all kinds—apples, pears, gooseberries, currants, &c.—may be trained upon an espalier or trellis. In some situations this kind of training is not only extremely neat, but possesses peculiar advantages. The trees are more fully exposed to the influence of light and air, and in small gardens it is useful on account of the little space which the trees occupy, and because they will bear fruit earlier than when left as standards. The training of espalier is very simple. When the trees are young, one shoot must be trained perpendicularly and two others horizontally, one on each side; the two last must not be shortened, but the perpendicular shoot is to be shortened in the following year to three good buds; two of which are to form new side branches, and the other a leader as before, and so on every year, till the trees have attained the desired size: from six to nine inches is about the proper distance between the horizontal branches. Trellises are best made of wood (iron causes canker in the trees), and young larch—the thinnings of the plantation—is the best wood for the purpose.

ESPALIER ROSES.

Roses, as espaliers, may be made to assume a striking feature in the economy of an ornamental rose-garden. The espaliers should be formed of galvanized iron, five feet or so high, and of proportionate width. Hurdles of this material, if the bars be close enough, will answer very well; but the bars should not be more than six inches apart. This form of rose-training is especially suitable for varieties with weak footstalks, notably Maréchal Niel. The plants used should be of strong-growing habit, on their own roots or the Manetti, and planted upon the southern aspect, or as near to that as possible. Intertwine and mix the branches as thickly as may be, and tie them to the cross-bars with wire or tarred string. To construct a rose-terrace, let such espaliers as described above form the back rows of sloping beds; an ascent may thus be charmingly laid out in stages, with path and terrace alternately to the level ground.

The following climbing roses may be used in the espalier form:—

Laura Davant,—pink, double.
Russelliana,—dark crimson, double.
Madame D'Arblay,—white, blooming in clusters.
The Garland,—nankeen and pink, semi-double.
Frederick the Second,—rich crimson-purple.
Juno,—pale rose, very large.
Madame Pantier,—pure white.
Madeline,—pale flesh.

But it is useless to multiply names, the varieties of climbing roses are almost endless. The rose-grounds of Messrs. Paul & Sons, of Cheshunt, present an abundant choice for the most fastidious; the only difficulty is, amidst so many beauties, which to choose.

EUCO'MIS (nat. ord. Lilia'ceæ).

A very ornamental half-hardy bulb, with curious tuft-crowned spikes of flowers.

Eucomis punctata,—green and brown, 2 ft., from Cape of Good Hope.

EUGE'NIA (nat. ord. Myrta'ceæ).

The Rose-apple, a highly ornamental greenhouse evergreen tree, of considerable beauty; succeeds in loam and peat.

Eugenia Jambosa,—green and yellow, 15 ft., from East Indies.

EUPHOR'BIA (nat. ord. Euphorbia'ceæ).

Very ornamental, warm greenhouse evergreen shrubs; succeed in a mixture of peat loam.

For bouquets, vases, or head-dresses, this Euphorbia is one of the finest flowers in existence; a fine spike, 18 inches long, is a matchless wreath at once.

Euphorbia regis Jubæ,—red, 3 ft.
„ splendens,—bright scarlet, 2 ft., from Madagascar.
Euphorbia jacquiniflora.

EVERGREEN ROSES.

These are the progeny of *R. sempervirens*, which abounds throughout Europe in a wild state, and, like the Ayrshire, are employed as climbing and weeping roses. Their beautiful dark-green leaves grow on to the depth of winter, which has procured them the name, although, strictly speaking, they are deciduous. They are mostly trees of vigorous growth and abundant bloomers, adapted for pillar-roses; their small, but very double flowers, hanging in graceful cymes of fourteen to twenty on a branch. They require much thinning in the pruning season; the shoots left being merely cut at the points, the others cut close to the base.

Banksæflora,—creamy white, with yellow centre; cupped and double; produced in clusters.
Carnea grandiflora,—pale flesh-colour; large and double; cupped.
Donna Maria,—pure white, of medium size; full and cupped; a choice variety.
Félicité perpétuelle,—flesh-colour, changing to creamy white; produced in graceful trusses drooping from their own weight; a superb sort.
Fortune's five-coloured,—creamy white, striped with carmine.
Fortune's double yellow,—bronze and yellow; large and very distinct.
Myrianthes,—pale peach, the centre white; hanging in graceful trusses of full-cupped flowers; a fine pillar-rose.
Princess Louise,—creamy white, with black petals shaded with rose; large, double, and cupped; a fine climber.
Rosea major,—rosy flesh-colour, changing to white; large, double, and cupped, with fine glossy foliage.

EVERGREENS.

Few things afford stronger indications of the necessity of renovation and reform in a garden than the state of the evergreens and hedges. These are so easily and so insensibly suffered to grow wild, and are so seriously injured by want of care and the proper use of the knife, that neglect cannot go on very long without its ill consequences becoming manifest. Portugal laurels and many other evergreens may be cut in; but with the common laurel it is a saving of time to cut it down at once; so also with the arbutus and sweet bay. Privet, and holly hedges, which from years of neglect are found to be occupying too much space, must be cut in. The former may often be cut down with advantage to within a few inches of the ground, and the latter cut close on all sides to the single stems. In a few years new and fresh wood will fill up all vacant spaces, provided the soil is enriched and kept free from weeds.

EYED NAILS.

In stone walls—perhaps in brick walls also—copper or iron nails with eyes should be let into the interstices, to tie down the branches of the fruit-trees, taking care that they are let in with the eye close to the wall; for the radiation of heat from the wall is in proportion to its distance, and the heat which is one degree a foot off the wall, is a hundred and forty-four when in contact with it. The advantage of the eyed nails consists in preserving the wall. Thread dipped in pyroligneous acid, or flexible wire, may be used for the purpose of tying. This mode of fastening is much neater than shreds and nails.

FABIA'NA (nat. ord. Solana'ceæ).

A handsome erica-like greenhouse shrub of easy culture; succeeds best in sandy peat. It is almost hardy.

Fabiana imbricata,—white, 2 ft., from Chili.

FABRI'CIA (nat. ord. Myrta'ceæ).

An exceedingly ornamental conservatory shrub, with graceful delicate drooping foliage, and very beautiful star-like flowers; succeeds best in sandy peat and loam.

Fabricia glauca, — white, 6 ft., from New Holland.

FAN-TRAINING.

Numerous fanciful modes of training wall-fruit have been recommended; but trees to be healthy should be made to assume their natural position as near as possible. For peaches and nectarines the fan system is the best, because it is the most natural form that trees so artificially placed can be made to assume. Much injury is done to trained fruit-trees merely to give them an artistic appearance.

FANCY GERANIUMS.

The following list embraces some of the best varieties. Those marked * are the most expensive; but good selections may be had from 12*s.* to 60*s.* per dozen.

Annie, — deep purple-maroon; white throat and margin.
Advancer, — mulberry, light margin; lower petals blush.
*Amy Sedgewick,—rose; fine form and quality; clear white centre and edges.
Adèle,—light rose, white belt on each petal; good form.
Bridesmaid,—lavender-rose, edged with white; good form and substance.
Beauty of Slough,—rosy-crimson; white centre, fine.
Crimson King,—crimson, dwarf and showy; medium size.
Cassandra,—crimson and white.
Celestial,—bright light rose.
Claudiana,—crimson upper petals; light margin.
Cloth of Silver,—silvery white, with delicate rose blotch.
*Countess Waldegrave,—dense crimson; white throat; fine.
Decision,—mottled crimson; margined white.
Delight,—rosy crimson; upper petals bright cerise; delicate habit; light throat and edges.
Delicatum,—white, with delicate rose blotch.
Dictator,—mulberry, edged with white.
*Emperor of Morocco,—mulberry; lilac throat and edges.
Evening Star,—rich purple cirmson; white edge; fine.
Formosum,—rich carmine; lower petals mottled white.
Fairy,—pretty lilac; white upper petals.
Fleur de Marie, — clear white, with purple blotch and spots.
King of Roses,—carmine-rose; white centre.
*Mademoiselle Patti, — pink lower petals; violet-rose upper ditto.
Moonlight, — light rose; white margin and centre.
Negro,—very dark; white throat and margin.
*Painter, — violet-crimson; light margin on upper petals.
Princess Royal, — silvery white lilac; rose-blotch on upper petals.
Perfection,—violet-rose, margin white.
Rosabella, — carmine; white margin; lower petals white.
Sarah Turner,—crimson, suffused with purple· lower petals white; fine.
Sweet William, — various shades of colour; peculiar edge.
Undine, — very large, rosy lake, with light throat and edges.
Venus,—light; lower petals suffused with pale pink; upper petals rose; fine.
Vivid,—very bright rosy-crimson; white throat; fine.

FEBRUARY.

The mean temperature of February is nearly two degrees higher than January, and the average number of frosty nights is about eleven. Less rain falls this month than in any other, and hoar-frosts at this season generally precede it.

Flower-Garden and Shrubbery.—Where the beds are filled with shrubs in winter, they should be hoed deeply several times during the month, to expose a fresh surface to the air. Beds occupied with crocuses and snowdrops should have the surface broken with a rake occasionally, before the plants appear. Borders similarly furnished require the same treatment. This not only imparts additional neatness, but, by breaking the crust, enables the plants to appear more easily and speedily, and in dry weather it considerably modifies the power of the frost. Beds planted with herbaceous plants, as well as herbaceous borders, would be benefited by similar treatment, provided they were dug early in November. Finish digging among herbaceous plants, circumscribing, dividing, rearranging, and replanting all where necessary, during mild weather. The old-fashioned way of arranging these according to their height is still the most effective.

The great business of propagating tender plants for furnishing the flower-garden must now be vigorously prosecuted. Stock must be taken; calculations made, judgment and foresight exercised, and activity displayed, if the garden is to be liberally filled next May. For the last few months, the great object has been safely to keep what we have. During the next three, the plants we have must be used to furnish what is required to fill the garden in May. If the bedding system is to maintain its ground, the garden must be filled with *flowering plants* by the end of that month. To effect it, verbenas must be planted four inches apart, and geraniums from six to eight inches. Measure the superficies of your beds; calculate at these distances, and increase your stock accordingly. With the exception of calceolarias, and probably geraniums, nearly all other bedding plants grow and flower as well, if not better, when propagated in the spring than in the autumn. Geraniums grow equally well; but autumn-struck cuttings flower more freely, and certainly two, three, or four-year-old plants flower more freely than any cuttings whatever. Boxes of geranium-roots that have been stored in cellars through the winter may now be brought out into the light of day, and, if they have been carefully managed, the whole surface will be alive with buds and shoots. A hundred such roots will furnish a thousand well-rooted plants before bedding-out time, and leave the old roots still available—the best of all plants for the centres of beds. For this purpose, however, they must be placed in bottom-heat until the shoots are two or three inches long. Then thin the *stools* by heeling off the cuttings; that is, taking them off quite close to the old stems. Place the cuttings singly in small 60-sized pots, or three round a large 60; or in pots or boxes of any size: place them in a house or frame with a temperature of 60°, and in three weeks they will be well rooted. If a frame be used, it must have a little air night and day, as geraniums are very impatient of a close atmosphere. Verbenas also root well in the same way; but in bright weather they require shading. For verbenas, ageratums, and calceolarias, in the spring, no place is better than a pit or frame with top- and bottom-heat of from 60° to 70°. If any or all of these have been gradually hardened off in the winter, the store pots ought to be now plunged into a temperature of 50° or 60°, for a week or fortnight before the tops are removed for cuttings. Within certain limits, the more tender the shoots of such plants are, the more rapidly they will emit roots. Place dahlia-roots, also, in heat at this time, in order to excite healthy growth for cuttings.

Sweep and roll turf and gravel; finish laying turf; top-dress, turn, renew, and relay the edgings of walks; and let cleanliness and neatness compensate as far as possible for the absence of floral beauty.

Shrubberies.—Push forward the digging and clearing of shrubberies. The great point in the management of shrubberies, however, is so to plant, prune, and train the shrubs, as to render these operations unnecessary. The raw edges, and masses of bare soil, that render digging aud cleaning an injurious necessity, mar the beauty and grandeur of masses of shrubs. As a rule, their branches should sweep the edges of the turf; and the culture of

February.

herbaceous plants should never be attempted among them.

Where digging is necessary, it should assume the character of pointing. Among shrubs, this operation should be performed by running the spade along the whole length, about three inches beneath the surface, and inverting it. This process buries the leaves and rubbish, without injuring the roots. The growth of shrubs should also be regulated by pruning and training, as cleaning proceeds. Common laurels and lilacs will often be found overriding rhododendrons, or other shrubs: the most worthless should always be removed, or boldly cut in. Rhododendrons are often extremely effective as margins to masses of other shrubs, and they are also invaluable in groups by themselves.

Reserve Garden.—If the weather continues open, the following hardy annuals should be sown during the month:—

Alyssum calycinum (Sweet Alyssum).
Bartonia aurea.
Calandrinia speciosa.
Calliopsis Drummondii.
,, bicolor atrosanguinea.
Chrysanthemum coronarium.
Collinsia bicolor.
,, grandiflora.
Erysimum Peroffskianum.
Eschscholtzia californica.
,, crocea.
,, ,, alba.
Eutoca Manglesii.
,, viscida.
Gilia tricolor.
,, ,, alba.
,, ,, rosea.
Iberis coronaria (Candytuft).
,, mbellata.
,, ,, alba.
,, odorata.
Leptosiphon androsaceum.
,, flore albo.
,, densiflorum.
Limnanthes grandiflora.
Nemophila atomaria.
,, insignis.
,, discoidalis.
,, maculata.
Schizanthus porrigens.
,, pinnatus.
,, ,, Priestii.
Silene pendula.
Sphenogyne speciosa.
Viscaria oculata.

February.

There are many other beautiful hardy annuals, some of which, such as the Lupines, had better not be sown till March. Only half the packets of the above seeds should be sown in February, and the other half reserved for a second sowing, either in the reserve garden or on the borders and beds where they are to bloom. Those sown during March or the beginning of April are more to be depended on than the earlier sowings. The above, however, will prove quite hardy in ordinary seasons. If the weather continues mild, autumn-sown annuals may be transplanted during the month: from two to four inches square, according to the size and habits of the plants, will be a proper distance apart. With the exception of ten-week stocks, which should be sown in pots or a frame at once, the sowing of all other tender or half-hardy annuals may safely be deferred to next month; material, however, should be collected, and frames got in readiness for this purpose. A bottom- and surface-heat ranging from 50° to 55° will generally be amply sufficient for the germination of most flower-seeds; so that the quantity of material required will only be about one-half of what would be necessary to raise or grow cucumbers. Guard choice tulips, hyacinths, &c., against the attacks of mice and snails. An endless variety of traps have been invented for the former: no trap is more efficient for the latter than leaves of the cabbage tribe, laid flat on the ground, and carefully examined every night; if left till morning, possibly the leaves will be eaten, and the snail hid beyond our reach.

Florists' Flowers.—*Auriculas*, *Carnations*, and other florists' flowers in frames, must be carefully attended to. During dull weather, the lights should be tilted up, either at the sides or the top, in preference to pushing them down or drawing them up. This mode of ventilation will prevent the fog or moisture in the air from being deposited on the leaves, a point of the first importance during damp or frost. Never water unless absolutely necessary, and then do it thoroughly, taking care to keep the leaves dry, and not allow a drop to fall on the crowns of the plants. During mild weather, too much air can hardly be given; but avoid cutting draughts of cold air. On genial days, when the sun shines for a few hours, remove the lights entirely, and clean and gently stir the surface-soil, removing every decayed leaf, spots of fungus, and all impurities, both from plants and frame. A dirty frame will soon engender sickness and disease; and diseased plants will rapidly infect the frame: hence the necessity of perfect cleanliness. Whenever a fœtid, unhealthy atmosphere is discovered, the plants should be removed, the plunging material thrown out, the whole interior of the frame painted with hot lime-and-water, and fumigated with sulphur burnt over a hot coal. An hour's reign of the sulphur fumes will suffice to destroy every living thing, and drive out or neutralize the noxious malaria. The light or lights should then be removed, and be thoroughly washed with warm water and soap; fresh plunging matter (nothing equals clean coal-ashes) introduced, and the plants re-arranged. Such preventive measures often check incipient disease, and save valuable collections of plants.

Top-dress auriculas and pinks with rich soil, and re-pot all pansies that are intended to be bloomed in pots. Eight-inch pots are those most generally used for this purpose, but the size must depend upon the strength of the plants. To insure a good bloom, they should not be shifted into larger pots after this period.

Kitchen-Garden.—The operations in the kitchen-garden this month depend very much on the weather. In mild open weather, a sowing of radishes is made, and to protect them from birds and frost, cover lightly with straw or fern, uncovering the beds occasionally in mild weather. Netting stretched over the beds will admit light and air, and exclude the birds; white worsted will keep them off for a day or two; but they soon get used to it; and scarecrows are equally ineffective. A covering of tiffany, canvas, or calico stretched on laths, will be effective, and resist the March winds more than straw or fern: it need be but a few inches from the ground. If the ground is in condition for treading, it is best to do so, as, indeed, it is with nearly all seeds; but if the ground is apt to clod or bind, it should by no means be trodden, but covered with light soil, or pressed in with the rake. The ground, in such cases, should be marked into beds of convenient width, allowing a foot or fifteen inches between, for alleys, to stand in, never treading on the beds. Some gardeners, whose ground is limited, are in the habit of sowing parsley, carrots, onions, leeks, or some such crop, which takes longer to grow, along with radishes, sowing both together, the radishes coming off soon after the others are up. This may be a saving of time or room; but where there is plenty of space, it is not advisable to sow two crops together.

Seakale.—About this time begin forcing seakale: if forced earlier, it is not so good or abundant, and if left till March, artificial heat is almost unnecessary.

Continue to wheel manure on to vacant ground, and get all digging, trenching, and in fact all ground-work, as forward as possible, bearing in mind that much of the success of the season depends upon it; and how important it is to have the ground prepared a week or two before cropping, especially where it is heavy or retentive. None but a practised workman can appreciate the advantage of having the surface in that finely-pulverized condition that follows sharp-frost and drying winds.

Cauliflowers, under hand-glasses, should have all the air, sun, and light possible, and gentle showers in mild weather, where they are protected from frost, cold winds, or heavy rains. Dust them also occasionally with lime, to destroy slugs, and stir the earth about the roots.

Peas which are advancing should be earthed up, both to protect and to strengthen them. A dusting now and then with lime will protect from birds and mice; or white worsted stretched along the rows will do so, if rightly managed. One way is to have some half-circular pieces of board, a foot wide, with pegs nailed to them to thrust into the ground; then have five or six small nails on the upper edge at regular distances: these are fixed into the ground at each end of the row, and as many lines of worsted as there are nails passed over the peas. Some gardeners lay branchy sticks over them; others sow rather thickly and leave them fully exposed, affirming that, by allowing for loss, they are not too thick.

Dwarf peas may always be grown advantageously where sticks are an object, and these may be sown closer together. The Bishop dwarf, long-podded, is a good cropper, and may be grown without sticks; but where sticks or hurdles can be obtained, it is no saving to grow without them, for the taller sorts, which grow six or eight feet high, bear most enormously if in good soil and mulched. During this month it is advisable to get in some of the medium sorts, as Auvergne, Imperial, Scimitar, or Champion; the later sorts had better be left till next month.

Broad Beans of any sort may be got in for succession.

Cabbages.—Look over the rows of cabbages, and see if any are eaten by vermin. Dust with lime when the ground is wet, or early in the morning, to destroy slugs. It is a good plan at this time of the year to let a few ducks into the kitchen-garden for half an hour or so every morning; they will destroy immense quantities of slugs, snails, worms, and grubs. Replace all the plants that have been destroyed by frost or otherwise, and draw earth up to the stems. Sow under hand-glasses a little cabbage, of some quick-heading kind, as early York or Eastham: they will follow those which have stood the winter, and be very useful in July, August, and September. Some Brussels sprouts may be sown; also purple Cape and Walcheren brocoli for autumn use.

Parsley may be sown in drills, or broadcast, or as edgings or between dwarf or short-lived crops. The seed should be but slightly covered, trodden or pressed in, according to the state of the soil, and raked evenly. It takes several weeks to germinate at this season of the year.

Carrots of the Short-horn sort, if sown on a warm border now, will come into use in May. Sow rather thickly, and thin to two inches apart.

Onions for salading may be sown on a warm border. A small sowing of leeks may be made at the same time and in the same manner, but not quite so thick. A top-dressing of soot once a fortnight, or even oftener if the weather be rainy, will have a very great effect upon the onion crop, and will prove an effectual remedy against the maggot at the root, which so often destroys the entire crop, especially on highly-manured land.

Red Beet, if sown now, will be very useful late in the summer. Sow in drills nine or ten inches apart, or broadcast, and thin to the same distance. The white beet may be sown for the leaves, which are eaten like spinach in summer.

Early Potatoes may be planted on a south border, or under a wall having a sunny aspect. At this time it is well to plant middling-sized tubers whole. The early tops are apt to get cut off by spring frosts; but they bear none the less for it, and they may be recovered if not too severely frozen, by watering with cold water before the sun is up.

Salading and Potherbs.—Lettuces should be sown now for succession; mustard-and-cress also, under hand-glasses. American cress, which is much the same as watercress, may also be sown on a sunny border: it is very useful for salading, and easily cultivated. Chervil may be sown about the end of this month, and also other potherbs, as savory, marjoram, coriander, and hyssop: unless it is desired to have them very early, however, it is as well to defer sowing these till next month, though they are mostly very slow in germinating.

Scorzoneras, Salsafy, &c.—It is as well to defer sowing main crops of these things till next month: the advantage of having early crops is great, but they should be proportioned to the extent of room, the time they last, or the wants of the family. A square rod of ground will generally be sufficient for early sowings of most of the principal crops, but herbs and salads will do with less, and it is best to look forward to what is to be done during the whole season, and calculate to a nicety what can be grown on every part without wasting room, or crowding and over-cropping, and exhausting the soil beyond the power of manure to restore it. It may seem advisable to make early use of the ground, and get it three-parts cropped in February; but in May and June it will be seen that a fatal error has been committed.

Fruit-Garden—Strawberries.—If it is desirable to make new plantations of strawberries at this time, it may be done by taking up runners with a trowel, and planting them eighteen inches apart. It is easy to select plants that will flower and fruit the same year by the crowns, which, if plump and full, indicate flower-buds. After planting, mulch with dung. Old plants should be cleaned and mulched.

Raspberries should be pruned without delay, if not done before. Cut out all the old canes, and thin out the new to four or five; shorten them one-third, and if necessary support them with sticks, rails, or by arching them together. If this is done carefully, only tying two together, it will answer better than tying them to stakes.

Gooseberry- and Currant-bushes should be pruned where formerly omitted. In pruning gooseberries, the object is merely to thin out and regulate the shoots, which need not be shortened except to keep them off the ground. In pruning currants, the object is to produce short fruit-bearing spurs, so that all the shoots except the leaders should be cut in three-fourths, the leading shoots about one-half, or rather more.

February.

Black Currants should scarcely be cut at all; they do not bear well if much pruned; a little thinning or reducing into shape is all that ought to be done.

Apples and Pears.—Finish pruning all fruit-trees this month, whether standards, espaliers, dwarf-bushes, pyramids, pillars, or trained on walls. In pruning these, the main object is to produce short fruiting-spurs, so that all vigorous shoots should be shortened; but the stronger the shoots the less they should be cut; for too close cutting throws them into the production of wood and leaf, and not fruit. Figs on walls should scarcely be cut at all, and no trees should be cut in frosty weather.

Peaches, Apricots, and Nectarines, on walls, ought to be unnailed and pruned this month. Thin out the shoots till they lie about six inches from each other, and shorten or not according to the strength of the tree or shoot: if very strong, shorten but little; but if a weak shoot terminates still more weakly, cut back to a double bud—that is, one leaf-bud between two flower-buds: prune neatly in this way, and tack the branches up again with fresh nails and shreds. The trees should be gone over in this way every winter; it is important also that the shoots be thinned out and disbudded in summer.

Flowers under Glass.—In the conservatory camellias, arums, epacrises, *Salvia splendens*, Chinese primroses, a few heaths, lachenalias, and perhaps forced lilacs, azaleas, rhododendrons, with hyacinths, narcissuses, crocuses, and other bulbs, will now be in flower or coming into flower-bud. Keep a night temperature of from 40° to 45°, allowing a rise of 10° with sun-heat. Unless during very severe frost or cutting winds, give air daily, if only for an hour at noon, to change the atmosphere of the house-damp. Prune, and destroy scale and other insects on climbers and other permanent plants. All plants should be carefully examined before they are introduced into this house, in order to prevent an importation of insects. Smoking with tobacco, and other insect-destroying processes, are not only very disagreeable, but are most inimical to the beauty and longevity of the flowers. Examine, water, and top-dress if necessary, any of the borders. Remove all plants back to their respective quarters as soon as their flowers fade, and introduce fresh supplies from forcing-pits or stove; let no dead leaf or flower, or dirt of any description, be allowed to mar the sense of delight which the conservatory should ever inspire.

In the greenhouse more air may be given, and 5° less heat will suffice for this house than for the conservatory. Now is a good time to examine and clean the whole stock of plants. Many of the acacias and epacrises are apt to become infested with scale. So liable to this pest are many of them, that it seems to be a constitutional tendency; its eradication, too, is very difficult. Prevention is the only remedy, for a perfect cure is impossible. If any dust or soot has accumulated on the leaves of heaths and azaleas, they will be much benefited by a good washing. The best mode of proceeding is to hold the plant on one side over a tub of water, turning it round in all directions, while an assistant dashes the water violently upon it with a syringe. Very dirty plants may sometimes require sponging with soap-and-water in addition to this. Water with care, examining carefully the balls of the plants, which in heaths sometimes become so hard and dry that the water refuses to penetrate. If found in this condition, they should be plunged into a pail of water for twelve or twenty-four hours, until the ball is thoroughly soaked. Pick off the flowers of winter-blooming heaths as soon as their beauty has faded. Carefully watch weak downy-leaved varieties for the first symptoms of mildew, and refrain from syringing any of them overhead in dull weather.

Towards the end of the month several species of greenhouse-plants, such as kalosanthus, baronias, chorozemas, Dillwynias, pimeleas, and azaleas, might be shifted into larger pots. Most of these thrive well in good fibrous peat and a little loam, liberally intermixed with sharp silver-sand and charcoal. One of the chief things to be attended to before placing any plant, and especially any hard-wooded plant, into a larger pot, is to see that the old ball is in a nice healthy growing state. The extremities of the roots should also be carefully untwisted or unwound, to induce them to start at once in the fresh soil. The new soil must also be pressed firmly into the pots, or the water will pass through it, instead of penetrating through the old mass of roots. Many hard-wooded plants are destroyed through inattention to these points. At this season of the year green-fly often attacks pimeleas, leschenaultias, and other plants: let them be destroyed at once, by fumigating with tobacco-smoke.

Pelargoniums now delight in a temperature of from 45° to 50°, with 10° increase by sun-heat. Scarcely any rise of temperature should be permitted, however, before the house is slightly ventilated. The sun's rays striking upon plants with any drops of condensed moisture on the leaves, is certainly one cause of the *spot* on these plants. Cutting draughts of cold wind are doubtless another cause of the same disease. This must be specially guarded against on bright days, when the air is keen and harsh. Shifting the young successional stock should now be completed. The soil they delight in consists in two parts good turfy loam and one of leaf-mould, with a slight admixture of thoroughly-decomposed cowdung, and a liberal sprinkling of silver-sand. The chief work here at present will consist in stirring the surface of the large plants, staking, training, and watering. The water should be say 5° warmer than the temperature of the house, and the foliage must be kept dry.

Fancy Pelargoniums will bear a temperature of 5° or 10° more than the other varieties. They should be potted in lighter soil, and even more carefully watered, as altogether they are more tender. The shoots will now require thinning and training.

Calceolarias and Cinerarias enjoy a temperature of from 45° to 55°. Well-rooted plants of the former should be shifted into the compost recommended last month; and plants of the latter, for very late flowering, may also be shifted. The earliest cinerarias will now be opening their flowers in the conservatory, and a succession coming on. Green-flies are particularly fond of these plants: they must be destroyed on their first appearance.

Fuchsias, after re-potting, thrive best if plunged in a gentle bottom-heat. Water carefully until fresh roots are emitted; shade in bright sunshine to prevent flagging. Thin out plants that have been cut down to a single shoot, if the pyramidal shape is desired; if bushes are wanted, leave three or four, and maintain a genial temperature of from 50° to 60°. Never cut down and shift fuchsias at the same time, nor shake them out for re-potting before they have again begun to grow. After cutting down, allow the shoots to grow two or three inches: plants that have not been cut down must fairly *break* before they are re-potted. The young top-growths will then hasten the emission of roots, and, with a moist atmosphere provided for a few days, they will scarcely sustain any check.

Forcing-Pit or House.—This is an indispensable adjunct to a well-kept conservatory, and should now be occupied with bulbs for succession. Rhododendrons, azaleas, Ghent and Indian (most of which, especially the *Indica alba*, force admirably), roses, lilacs, Anne Boleyn white and other pinks, true carnations, cloves, &c., maintain at a genial growing temperature of 55° to 65°; on very cold nights, however, it may fall 5° or 10° with impunity.

Plant-Stove.—Maintain a temperature of from 60° to 65° fire-heat. Start the first batch of achimenes, gesnerias, gloxinias, &c. Prune plants of allamanda, dipladenia, clerodendron. &c. Pot *Glorissa superba* during the month: it thrives best plunged in a brisk bottom-heat. Many ferns, begonias, and other plants, should also be potted, and started into fresh growth. Some of the dendrobiums, Stanhopeas, and maxillarias should now be watered and pushed into flower. Prepare plenty of good peat and loam, broken potsherds, charcoal, &c. &c., for a general potting of all plants that require it.

Fruit under Glass.—In the present day this includes almost all known fruits. Proceed as follows:—

Vines.—Grapes are the most useful, if not the most delicious, of all fruits. Some think the pine preferable; but nothing can exceed in grace and beauty a noble vine, laden with its rich clusters. Where several houses are devoted to the culture of the vine, grapes may be had every day, from the 1st of January to the end of December. The successful cultivation of the grape-vine has been a leading object with all gardeners in this country from the time of its introduction by the monks to the present day. Every variety of soil and mode of treatment have been tried, and so marvellous is the power of the vine in adapting itself to varying circumstances, that most of them have been more or less successful. On the poorest and the richest soils; in borders eight feet and borders two feet deep; among masses of brick and stone and putrid carrion; in the wettest and driest situations,—good grapes have occasionally been produced. A few leading principles, however, seem to form the basis of the successful culture of the grape-vine. It should be planted on a dry bottom. The soil should be light, rich, and need not exceed three feet in depth. The roots should be kept at the same or a few degrees higher temperature than the branches. These three points will secure abundance of healthy roots. Upon this, and a liberal supply of food, will depend the health and strength of the top. The vine is, in certain stages of its growth, what is termed a *gross feeder*;—hence has originated the gross absurdity of men attempting to feed it with *carrion*. No sooner, however, does a vine-root reach carrion, than its course turns in another direction; or, if this is impossible, it plunges into the putrid mass and dies. It not only cannot absorb carrion, but carrion kills the spongioles, or feeding part of the root. The elements of the carrion might, indeed, afford nourishment to the vine, but man's stupidity has placed it exactly in the position to prevent it, for as long a period as possible, from being separated into its elements, and kept it in that state in which no root can absorb it. Exposed to the air or thrown into water, the carrion would soon have been decomposed, and become acceptable as plant-food. Buried in a vine-border, it is locked up for months, on wet soils for years, and becomes a poisonous instead of an enriching agent. The best mode of feeding vines during their growing and fruiting stages, is either by a liberal application of manure-water or a rich top-dressing of the very best manure. Both methods may be adopted, or only one, as seems best; but by either or both systems, the best food of the right quality, in such a state that the vine *can feed upon it*, would speedily be brought within reach of the roots.

Vines in houses, started in October, will now be swelling their fruit. Thin in time, and maintain a steady growing temperature of 65°.

Those started in January will show their bunches this month, and a temperature from 55° to 60° will be suitable. Some prefer leaving the disbudding until the bunches show, so as to leave the best. This is safe practice, and the buds up to this stage do not much exhaust the vine.

In many places the first or second house will be started this month. See that all loose bark is removed, that the vines are thoroughly cleaned with soap-and-water, and painted over with a thick coating of equal parts of sulphur, soot, lime, and cowdung, made into a paste with strong soap-suds, previous to starting them. Begin with a temperature of 45°, and slowly and gradually increase it during the month 10° or 16°. Maintain a genial atmosphere in all the houses, by sprinkling the paths, syringing, &c.; and give as much air as the weather will permit, allowing a rise of 10° or 15° during sunshine. Grapes grown in pots require the same general treatment as those planted out. It will very much hasten the ripening of the fruit, if the pots are maintained in a steady bottom-heat of from 70° to 80°.

Pines.—From 65° to 70° should be the minimum temperature during the month: the bottom-heat may range from 5° to 10° higher. During dull weather a dry atmosphere must be preserved. The plants should be carefully examined previous to watering, and this operation performed so as to prevent the water getting into the axils of the leaves. Plants swelling their fruit should be placed at the warmest end of the house, and those intended for autumn- or winter-fruiting kept steadily growing, carefully guarding against any sudden check. Succession-plants in pots must be kept rather dry, and the linings and coverings carefully attended to.

Peaches.—In their early stages these are very impatient of heat. Begin with a temperature of 40°, and gradually rise to 50°. This should not be much exceeded until the fruit is set; then, by gradual ascent, from 5° to 10° may be added; this is the maximum of fire-heat for peaches until the period of stoning is over. Syringe twice daily in bright weather, except when the trees are in flower. The borders should have a good soaking, if dry, before forcing commences. Give as much air as the weather will permit at all times. Unless bees make their appearance, the trees should often be gently shaken when in flower, and the pollen distributed by a camel-hair pencil, to insure the fructification of the blossoms.

Figs will bear a higher temperature

than peaches, and may be started at 50°. The terminal buds of the young shoot should be removed, to insure a good crop. Maintain a moist atmosphere, and water copiously when necessary.

Orchard-houses should stand open night and day, unless during severe frosts. Plants in pots must not, however, be allowed to become too dry. The trees would be benefited by being painted over with a similar composition to that recommended for vines. This would tend to prevent the attacks of insects, kill all moss and fungi, and render the buds safe from the ravages of birds, which often play sad havoc with trees in orchard-houses.

During dull weather, care must be exercised not to force the fruit-houses too rapidly, or elongated, spongy growth will be made at the expense of strength and fruitfulness.

Hotbed and Frame Cultivation.—Cucumbers in full growth require every attention. See that the heat of the beds does not fall below 70° : apply fresh linings as soon as this is the case. Attend to stopping and setting; allow no more than two or three cucumbers to grow at the same time on one plant; admit air in sunny weather, but not enough to produce a draught; give all the light possible, but cover at night with mats or straw, and add fresh earth if required. If it is desired to start more beds, the dung may be got ready, and during this time the seed may be sown in pots and placed in a bed in full operation. Good loamy soil is best to grow the seeds in, so that it is warm enough before planting. Place two plants on a mound, under each light; as they grow, add fresh soil till the bed is level. Peg the bines down as they grow: if a proper temperature and sweet dewy atmosphere pervade the frame, they will never be troubled with insects or mildew; but if they are chilled or over-heated, these will soon follow. If mildew attack them, sprinkle with water and dust with sulphur; if green-fly or thrips, fumigate with tobacco. The same directions apply to the culture of melons; but, before

planting, make the soil pretty firm. Melons require the same temperature as cucumbers, and great care as regards watering: too dry, they are apt to become infested with red spider; too wet, they are subject to canker: in the former case apply sulphur, or syringing; in the latter, soot about the collar. Set many fruit, but allow no more than two, or three at the most, to swell off at once; and cut away, or rather prevent, all superfluous growth, by pinching out every new shoot that is not wanted. Attend well to the application of fresh dung. Nothing can succeed unless the heat be maintained.

Water of the same temperature as the bed is absolutely necessary. Always water over the leaves, as well as at the roots, about twice or three times a week, which is as often as the plants are likely to want it. In watering forcing-beds use a fine rose, that the surface of the soil be not beaten down in the process; and take care that the water is of a temperature nearly equal to that of the bed—rather above than below: if liquid manure is used, it should be rather weak. For asparagus and sea-kale a little salt, about a teaspoonful to the gallon, may be advantageous: it is better to water effectually at once, than to water little and often, because the latter is apt to keep the surface slimy and soddened.

Frame Potatoes.—February is also a good time to put some potatoes in a little heat. An excellent plan is to pare the soil off an old cucumber- or melon-bed; add three inches of fresh earth, then set the potatoes fifteen inches apart, and cover with five or six inches more earth; put on the lights, and then give a good lining of prepared dung: this will cause heat; the potatoes will root into the dung of the old bed and be very fine: give them plenty of air, but never allow them to get frosted.

French Beans may still be sown: they may be placed in an old hotbed fresh lined. As the season advances, they will require less heat, but will not do out of doors yet. Radishes, if sown now on a slight hotbed, will come in much earlier than those in cold frames.

Now is the time for making a hotbed for sowing ridge cucumbers, vegetable marrows, tomatoes, capsicums, and such plants. Those who have hotbeds in operation may sow these seeds in pots, and put them in the frames; otherwise it is necessary to make a bed for them. The advantage of the pit made of fagots, described under the term Hotbed, will be apparent in raising things of this kind; the linings are more effective, and such beds will last several years, the fagots only sinking a little. Although it is advisable to get the dung, and begin to prepare it this month, it is not desirable to sow the seed till March; even the third or fourth week is time enough; for these things cannot be planted in the open air till quite the latter end of May, unless hand-glasses are used to cover them, and they are planted in a little heat, when they may be trusted out earlier; but March is quite early enough to raise them.

Early Carrots may be sown, for succession, on a slight hotbed; and very dwarf peas also, which may be treated in the same way as French beans, also mustard, cress, and lettuces, for succession. Some roots of mint, horseradish, dandelion, or chicory, may be potted and placed in a hotbed: some use them as salads. All but mint should be blanched, by covering from the light; for which purpose flowerpots will do: some parsley roots, potted and placed in heat, may also be useful.

Strawberry Plants in pots placed in heat now will fruit in April: they will want liquid manure occasionally, to keep them in vigour. Plants in cold pits or frames should be looked over often, dead leaves picked out, slugs and other pests destroyed. Cauliflowers, corn-salad, parsley, endive, lettuces, &c., in cold frames, should have the earth stirred between them occasionally; they should have every ray of sunshine, and be uncovered entirely in mild weather. Pick out dead leaves, and water if needful, but beware of too much moisture.

Seed-beds of cauliflower, lettuce, cabbage, brocoli, radish, carrot, onions, beet, &c., may be made in the cold pit or frame: they will not come on so quickly as those sown in heat, but will be earlier than those sown outdoors. It may be desirable now to commence raising flowering plants and tender annuals, for which purpose the fagot-pit will be useful. It is not well to begin too early, unless an abundance of manure is at hand; for the earlier it is begun, the more dung to maintain the heat will be required.

FENCES.

Fences for flower-gardens and shrubberies may be constructed of various materials and of many different patterns.

At one time, rustic fences were much used for separating the park from the pleasure-ground. While they are among the most beautiful, they are certainly the most expensive of all fences. They may still be used to separate one part of the grounds from another,—the rabbit-proof garden from the outside pleasure-ground, — where labour and expense are no object. The

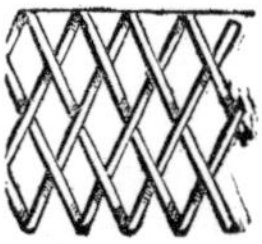

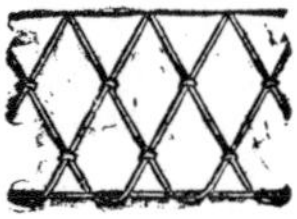

accompanying are pretty patterns, and can be made of hazel, larch, spruce,

and indeed any young trees. The bark should always be left on, and the more numerous and rougher the knots, the more rustic the fence will be. Wire fences, perhaps, look better, and their patterns and prices are endlessly varied, to suit the means and tastes of all.

FENNEL.

Fennel may be raised from seed in April or May. The seed should be covered lightly with fine mould, and, when the plants are strong enough, they may be set out in a bed about a foot apart. A good bed of fennel will last for years; but to insure fine leaves, the flower-stalks should always be cut off as soon as they appear, so as never to ripen seed.

FERNS.

Ferns are by many considered to be a remnant of the vegetation of a past era in the history of the earth, and the treatment they require would seem to confirm this view. Most of them delight in a loose soil, abundant moisture, and a warm humidity in the air. Many kinds are hardy: some are natives of our own climate; yet it is observed by experienced cultivators that those species which are found in temperate climates grow much finer in tropical ones, &c.: the sorts that live in England in the open air grow luxuriantly in a stove. However, in the cultivation of them, it is not necessary to go beyond what is ordinarily done. Hardy sorts may be grown out of doors, and those that will stand a greenhouse temperature are great ornaments in the house. Some kinds are naturally large, and the larger the more valuable,—as the Dicksonias or tree-ferns: these require a large house to grow them properly. Too much cannot be said in praise of this interesting class of plants. It is impossible here to give lists of the varieties and enter upon their merits. We can only advise our readers to consult the catalogues of Messrs. Williams, Messrs. Veitch, and others of our best growers, where they will find ample information on the subject, and to visit their nurseries, where they will see such specimens as may provoke envy without doing harm.

FERN-CASES.

In planting fern-cases, it is best to choose sorts of very dwarf, compact habit. This will allow for a little drawing up of the fronds from confinement. A mixture of loam, leaf-mould, and sand will be best for them to grow in; but it should be liberally mixed up with broken pieces of sandstone, or broken flowerpots, and small pieces of charcoal. These will hold a supply of moisture without stagnating; but water should not remain unabsorbed, so that the cases must be provided with suitable drainage; and although the confinement of the case will agree with many ferns, yet some ventilation is necessary to prevent damp and mouldiness, otherwise every frond or dead piece of leaf that touches the glass will cause a general decay.

FERNERIES.

Out-door ferneries are usually constructed in a shady nook, a damp situation on the margin of ponds, or in low-lying situations, where they would naturally receive that shade and moisture which agree with them: a shady bank, where water can be supplied artificially, makes a good fernery, and it requires a great deal of moisture to preserve the healthy greenness of them during a dry summer. If once allowed to flag, they get spotted, which diminishes the beauty of them, and they do not recover it the whole season. In building a fernery, make a liberal use of rough blocks of wood, gnarled roots, and blocks of stone, burrs, &c. Let there be no appearance of labouring to produce an effect, but let the whole be as natural as possible. Plant the ferns so that they show in niches and crevices, and not so thickly as to hide the burrs, &c. For out-door culture none can surpass hardy British ferns. Some of these grow much larger than others:—*Lastrea Filix*, *mas*, *Filix fœmina*, *rigida*, *osmunda*, *regalis*, are among the largest growers. The common brake should not be admitted. There are ferns, however, that have a similar habit to that on a much smaller scale,—various sorts of polypody; these are very useful for the front places. There are a great many ferns of dwarf habit, known as natives of this country, which require careful management to induce them to grow in a fernery; the Rue fern, for instance, seldom lives many years, except in the hands of very clever cultivators.

Greenhouse ferneries may be made in every way similar to those outdoors, only on a smaller scale, with the same view as to shade and moisture. If in an open spot, the top must be furnished with blinds, and the syringe be kept at work; but if close and warm, the ferns will grow most luxuriantly.

FIGS IN THE OPEN AIR.

Almost any well-drained soil will suit the fig-tree. Care, however, must be taken that it is not too rich, for if so, the tree will not produce fruit. Three sorts of figs are usually grown,—the Brown Turkey, Brunswick, and Black Ischia: all require a wall and a sunny situation. The best mode of training is perpendicular. Fix to the wall as many permanent leaders as are required at from 10 to 15 inches apart; get rid of all unnecessary wood by disbudding, and stop the fruit-bearing shoots at the end of August or beginning of September, according to the habit of the tree and the nature of the season. This operation is performed by merely pinching off or squeezing flat the terminal growing-point. This stopping, the object of which is to induce the formation of fruit for the ensuing season, is a matter of much nicety. A too early stopping with most trees will cause a too early development of fruit, the consequence of which will be that it will not stand through the frost of winter. The fruit for next year must not be much larger than a pea when winter sets in.

FIGS UNDER GLASS.

Instructions for the proper treatment of these will be found in the calendar for each month.

FIGURE-OF-FOUR TRAP.

This trap, which is formed with a common brick, supported by three pieces of wood placed in the shape of the figure 4, is very efficacious in the destruction of garden mice.

FILBERTS.

The trees may be introduced into orchards, shrubberies, plantations, or hedgerows. Planted close to each other, they form valuable screens or shelter in exposed situations. A filbert-walk is a great addition to any garden. Filberts are not merely ornamental but profitable. They will thrive almost anywhere, and are much improved by pruning. Webb's exhibition Cobb filberts are the best.

Plants may be had of Messrs. Barr and Sugden, Covent-garden, at 50*s*. per hundred, or 9*s*. per dozen.

FLEMING'S MACHINE.

This machine for cleansing gravel walks may be described as a large wrought-iron boiler, fitted upon wheels, with a fireplace in the centre, for the purpose of heating water to a boiling temperature. Connected with the boiler is a spring valve and delivery-pipe, similar to those used in the common watering-carts, through which boiling salt-water is delivered in a continuous and gentle shower, the salt being mixed in the proportion of two pounds of salt to a gallon of water. The same apparatus, in a more portable form, may, of course, be attached to any wheelbarrow. At Trentham this contrivance is found to be very effective, and much more economical than hand-weeding the paths, besides giving a freshness and brilliancy to the gravel.

FLORISTS' FLOWER-GARDEN.

The florist's flower-garden comprises the Dahlia, Hollyhock, Chrysanthemum, Tulip, Polyanthus, Auricula, Heartsease or Pansy, Ranunculus, the Anemone, Carnation, Pink, Picotee, Hyacinth, &c. &c., for florists have largely increased the objects of their care; but probably the present list includes all which can properly be called florist's flowers.

A florist's flower-garden is usually planted in formal and rather stiff-looking beds, the flowers in right lines, those of dwarf habit occupying the outsides of the beds, with the taller sorts in the centre. The garden itself should be very near to the dwelling of any one who has charge of it, for no plants require greater attention to grow them properly; they need all the air that can possibly be given to them, while a slight frost coming suddenly on after a warm April day—above all, heavy storms of rain, a hailstorm, or even a boisterous wind—will be destructive to many of them.

Heat is nearly as injurious. They should only meet the morning and evening sun: a shade of light calico for an hour before and after noon, during the flowering season, will much prolong their bloom.

The bed for the reception of auriculas, polyanthuses, carnations, and flowers of similar habit grown in pots, should be placed in an open airy situation, where they can readily receive shelter from rain and from a too ardent sun.

A useful bed or stage for the reception of these may be prepared by laying down about six inches of coal-ashes upon the natural soil, over which a platform should be made by a flooring of square tiles, closely fitting into each other. Over this are to be laid seven rows of bricks, equidistant from each other; and on these, at regulated distances, the pots may be ranged after the operation of potting has been performed in May.

Shelter and shade can be provided in the following manner:—A row of strong stakes, sufficiently close together to support a top rail without interfering materially with the pots which occupy the centre of the bed. These stakes should be six feet high, and five inches by four in size, and should be driven at least twenty inches into the solid soil; the top rail being sufficiently strong to receive and support the shutters. A similar row of stakes, with top rail, must be driven on each side of the bed, and about two feet and a half from it. Three inches on each side of the bed there should be another row of six stakes of equal strength, but only eighteen inches above the ground; the top being notched in the form of the letter V.—The use of these stakes will be obvious; they are to receive and support the lower end of the shutters—the central top rail when closed; and the outside rails are to receive and support them when it is desired to throw them open.

The shutters, each four yards long and three feet wide, when closed, form a span-roofed pit open at the sides, three posts supporting each shutter. They are made with feather-edged inch deal, forming a solid frame; the centre may be deal, felt, or any material impervious to heavy rains; if of glass, there should be an arrangement for shading with calico, or some other material; and the frames should lap one over the other at the sides, and meet at a proper angle at the top, so as to form a ridge.

Florists' Flowers, as we see them in their present state of cultivation, prove how immense is the field which Nature lays open to reward the industry and intelligence of man. Who can place the different flowers which have passed under the florist's hand for cultivation side by side with their wild originals without being struck with wonder at the almost marvellous results which follow from the ingrafting of nature and art? Compare the pansies of some of our recent prize-shows with the wild heartsease of the woods, and it is hardly possible to realize the idea that the two stand to each other in any sort of genealogical relationship; and the same is true of pinks, and hyacinths, and anemones. Nor, indeed, is the contrast yet at its height, for every year fresh progress is being made in symmetry, in richness and variety of colouring, or in size. Look at the dahlias and chrysanthemums of the present day, and think what were considered good flowers, and actually called forth admiration, some twenty years ago. The different varieties which come under the head of florists' flowers are so rich in beauty that most persons take delight in them. Indeed it is quite impossible for a garden to be really gay without its share of them, and with them any garden may be gay at all seasons, except in the depth of winter. Even as the year declines —late in the autumn months, though tulips, and carnations, and auriculas, and ranunculus, and hyacinths, &c. &c., are at rest, chrysanthemums and dahlias are in their glory; and these continue to enliven our gardens till an envying frost cuts them off. At all seasons of the year there is something to be done with florists' flowers, and the reader will find notices of them under each head. Instructions also for the management of particular flowers are to be found in the calendar of each month.

FLORISTS' FLOWER-SEED (Choice Varieties).

Carefully selected seed is absolutely essential where good flowers are desired. The following, supplied by Messrs. Barr and Sugden, at the prices named, may be relied upon:—

	Per packet. s. d.		s. d.
Calceolaria herbaceous,—saved from carefully hybridized flowers remarkable for their brilliant colours, fine shape, large flowers and beautiful markings. The plants from which this seed was saved were awarded the first prize at the Royal Botanic Gardens, Regent's Park, and Crystal Palace ..	2 6		
Ditto, very fine	1 0		
Ditto, half shrubby, habit remarkably compact, flowers beautifully spotted, saved from plants which were awarded the first prize at the flower-show of the Royal Horticultural Society	2 6		
Ditto, Cole's shrubby, very beautiful	1 0		
Carnation, — saved from bold finely-shaped flowers, bizarres, flakes, selfs, and fancy varieties	1 0	and	2
Ditto, perpetual, ditto, ditto ..	1 0	,,	
Cineraria,—saved from the most perfectly-shaped flowers, remarkable for size and rich colours	1 0	,,	
Mimulus,—saved from the most choice varieties	1 0		
Mimulus maculosa,—a superb variety, with beautifully spotted flowers, a hybrid between Mimulus cupreus and M. Gaiety. In sealed packets as received from Mr. Ball ..	1 6		
Pelargonium,— large-flowered English varieties	1 0	,,	
Ditto, French varieties ..	1 0	,,	2
Ditto, fancy varieties	1 0	,,	
Picotee, — from finely-shaped flowers	1 0	,,	
Ditto, perpetual, ditto, ditto ..	1 0	,,	
Primula, — extra fine	1 0	,,	

FLOWER-GATHERER.

By means of this simple instrument, flowers can be gathered from the interior of a parterre without treading upon the border, or from the top shelves of a greenhouse, without inconvenience. It is also admirably adapted for gathering fruit, not only cutting the flower or fruit off, but also holding it until relieved by the hand. To ladies fond of gardening, the flower-gatherer is invaluable, being extremely light, and entirely preventing the necessity of stooping.

FLOWERING GRASSES.

That splendid importation from the river Plate, *Gynerium argenteum*, or Pampas-grass, resists the cold of our ordinary seasons, but was in many instances killed during the severity of the winter of 1860. Old plants seem hardier than young ones, arising probably from the larger top affording more efficient protection to the roots. The old leaves should not be removed until the end of April, as they afford the best possible protection as far as it goes; experience, however, shows that of themselves they will not preserve life: hence the necessity of a little extra litter. This is decidedly the king of all the grasses, and deserves a place in every garden. As the centre group of a *grassery*, or placed in a rich shady dell, contiguous to rocks or water, it finds a congenial home, and imparts a charming effect. A rich alluvial soil, at least a yard deep, abundance of space to unfold its large, graceful leaves, and throw up its flower-stems, and an unlimited supply of water, are all the conditions its successful culture demands. Packets of seed can be bought at one shilling each, and plants that will flower the second year, from nine to twelve shillings a dozen. With liberal treatment, seedlings will flower the third or fourth year. By sowing thinly in February or March in pots, and planting out in prepared beds in May, a season may almost be gained in the growth of the plants. Like all the grasses, the seed should be barely covered with soil, and the surface kept moist, until germination is insured. There seem, however, to be several varieties of this grass, in addition to its sexual distinctions. When practicable, it is therefore best to purchase divided plants from those who have grown the finest flower-stems: it can be rapidly increased by division. Plants divided are more tender than others, and will require more protection, until they are thoroughly established. Few plants, however, are more worthy of attention, as they have a fine appearance when growing; and if the flower-stem is cut before it begins to fade, it looks almost as noble when dry. In addition to the localities here pointed out for them, they also contrast admirably with large masses of yews or other dark-foliaged shrubs. A companion grass to this, with broad-striped foliage and large feathery flowers, is the *Eranthis Ravenna*. The Tussack-grass, and some of the common reeds and rushes, also form beautiful features in connection with these. There are also eight or ten varieties of the *Holcus saccharatus*, or sugar-cane, whose elegant leaves, stately stems, and various-coloured heads of corn, are highly ornamental. These are half-hardy annuals, and should be sown in a gentle heat, and pushed rapidly forward to secure strong plants for planting out in May. The variegated, white-striped, and beautifully marbled *Zea*, or maize, requires similar treatment, and has a charming effect. The pretty millet-grass (*Milium effusum*), charming love-grasses (*Eragrostis elegans*, *E. Memaquensis*, and *E. Pursthi*), and the several varieties of *Briza*, or quaking grass, should be sown either in pots or on a rather sheltered bed out of doors. Two more beautiful annual grasses are the *Brizopyrum siculum*, whose branches rival in beauty the deciduous cypress, and *Bromus brizoporoides*, so useful for bouquets. The two feather-grasses, *Stipa pinnata* and *S. gigantea*, hardy perennials, and the hardy biennial *Hordeum jubatum*, are also most useful for mixing with other flowers, and very elegant in themselves. The smallest feather-grass almost rivals the *Festuca glauca* for edgings. The handsome silver foliage of the *Festuca* contrasts beautifully with red gravel walks, and is said to harbour fewer vermin than box or any other living edging whatever. Tufts can be purchased for 1*s*. 6*d*. a dozen or 15*s*. per hundred. It is neat, graceful, and easily kept, the only attention required being to cut off the flower-stems in summer, which maintains the leaves in health and beauty.

FOLIAGE PLANTS.

These have become very fashionable of late. For illustrations and for culture we refer the reader to Lowe's "Beautiful-leaved Plants," and a companion volume by Mr. Shirley Hibberd.

FRAMES.

No appliances are more useful than garden-frames, yet none are more generally misapplied in small gardens; many suburban gardeners considering them as proper only for the growth of the cucumber and melon, when, in fact, these should be considered but of secondary importance. There are three sizes of which garden-frames are usually formed, called one-light, two-light, and three-light frames: the last two are perhaps the most useful. The best dimensions for a three-light frame are 10 feet long and 4 feet wide; 15 inches deep at the back, and 7 inches at the front. The wood of which such a frame is composed should be one-and-a-half deal, well planed and dovetailed together at the joints; the back and front should be tied by two cross-pieces three inches wide, which should be dovetailed, one end into the back, and the other into the front, and so placed that they will come exactly under where the lights converge to each other. These cross-pieces should have a groove running the whole length of the centre of their upper surface, for the purpose of carrying off any water that may lodge between the lights. At each end of the frames there should be a slip of wood three-quarters of an inch thick, and about four inches broad, nailed on so that the upper edge will be level with the upper surface of the light. The object of this is to prevent the entrance of cold winds, which are apt to blow under the lights. The lights should be 4 feet long, and 3 feet 4 inches wide, and glazed with strong 16 oz. sheet glass at 3*d.* per foot. The laps must not be puttied, but left open, so as to admit of the steam being evaporated, and to allow the condensed moisture to escape. When all is complete, the frame should be painted white inside and dark lead outside. White paint inside gives some additional light, which is an advantage.

FRAXINEL'LA (nat. ord. Ruta'ceæ).

Handsome, free-flowering, hardy herbaceous plants, perennials, suitable for mixed borders; succeed in any common soil.

Fraxinella,—red, 2 ft., from South Europe.
" white, 2 ft. "

FRENCH BEANS.

Preparation of the Soil.—These delight in a deep, friable, and rich soil; and where the land is of a strong, tenacious character, it should be trenched and ridged as early in autumn as possible, well intermixing a liberal allowance of manure. Upon very strong soils a good dressing of leaf-mould may be added with advantage.

Time and Manner of Sowing.—The seeds being liable to rot if sown early in wet, cold soil, the first crop had better be planted in boxes or pans. Place these in a cold frame, or under the shelter of a south wall, and protect them from frost. When the plants are in the rough leaf, and the weather considered safe, transplant in rows about 2 feet 6 inches apart on a warm and sheltered border. Transplanting induces early fertility, and may be practised with advantage even where the plants are raised in the open border. Sow for the principal crops early in May, June, and July; and on light dry soils in warm localities a small quantity may be sown towards the end of July. Cover the seeds with about three inches of soil.

After-management.—When the plants are about four inches high, ridge the soil neatly up on either side. This will prevent their being blown about by rough winds: and while there is any danger of frost, the early crop should be sheltered by well-furnished branches of evergreens, stuck into the soil in a slanting direction on each side of the rows. Keep the ground between the lines well stirred and free from weeds. During dry, hot weather, if the supply threatens to fall short, an occasional soaking of water will be of service. The following are the best varieties. Cost, 1*s.* 6*d.* per quart:—

Canterbury White,—very prolific, well known, 1 ft.
Chinese Long-podded,—exceedingly productive, free-cropping variety, 1 ft.
Dun or Cream-coloured,—much esteemed for its earliness and free cropping, 1 ft.
Fulmer's Early Forcing,—a fine variety for forcing, very productive, 1 ft.
Mohawk, or Early Six Weeks,—a very good variety, 1 ft.
Negro Long-podded,—very fine cropper, with long pods, 1 ft.
Newington Wonder,—the best of all for forcing, very productive, 1 ft.
Speckled,—a well-known prolific variety, 1 ft.
Variegated Dun,—a very productive variety, very much esteemed, 1 ft.

FRENCH OR SPOTTED GERANIUMS.

The following list contains a most excellent selection, those marked * being the most expensive.—Average cost, about 18*s.* per dozen.

French or Spotted Varieties.

Admiration,—rose, edged with white; dark spots on upper petals.
Adam Bede,—deep pink, under petals crimson, margined with the bottom colour.
*Arthur Henderson,—very dark maroon; black spots; light centre.
*Archimede Rose,—crimson; maroon spots.
*Bertie,—deep rose; rich spots on lower petals; upper ditto carmine; fine good show variety.
Bracelet, — large rose-maroon spots; dark blotch on upper petals; fine.
Beadsman,—pale pink; maroon spots on centre petal.
Black Diamond,—dark crimson, margined with rosy scarlet.
*Constellation,—quite new; beautiful.

*Chevalier,—crimson; dark maroon spots and blotches.
Count Cavour,—rose-white centre; dark spots on all the petals.
*Criterion, — pure white lower petals, with rosy-purple spots at the base; upper ditto black.
Duchesse de Malakoff,—white ground; light purple blotches.
Dr. Andrey,—light crimson-rose; dark blotch; beautifully fringed.
Duc de Magenta,—deep rose; dark maroon spot; white centre.
Eclipse,—brilliant scarlet; fine dark spots.
*Edmond Bossier,—carmine-rose, lower petals; upper, black maroon; black spots; purple veins.
Endymion,—bright rose; all the petals spotted with black.
Eugène Duval,—fine purple.
Eole,—mulberry lower petals, upper ditto with dark blotches.
Fairy Queen, — rose-maroon blotch; white centre; fine.
*Fair Rosamond,—white, with purple spots; good.
Guillaume Peveryns,—lilac-maroon spots.
Gustave Odier,—crimson-lake; crimson blotch; good habit.
Géant des Batailles, — white, shaded with crimson-scarlet spots; fine large flower.
Hortense,—salmon-rose; crimson blotch.
Impératrice Eugénie,—pure white; dark violet spot.
James Odier, — bright carmine, tipped with rose; violet spot.
*Leo,—orange-rose spot on lower, and blotch on top petals.
Madame Furtado,—blush spot; rosy crimson.
Madame Pescatore,—rose-crimson spot; dark blotch on upper petals.
*Mara,—rose, with white edges; dark spots, shaded with violet.
Osiris,—rich crimson; dark spots on upper petals.
Oscar Lisible,—carmine; light maroon blotch; white centre.
Pandora,—scarlet, with light margin.
Perrugino,—superb pink, with large spots.
*Phiton,—deep crimson; dark maroon spots; white centre.
Painted Lady,—pink; white edges; maroon spots.
*Rupee,—purple lower petals; black upper ditto; fine purple margin.
Riflemen,—crimson scarlet; black spots; fine free-grower.
Rubens, — flower crimson; scarlet blotch; maroon spots.
Sanspareil,—bright rose; crimson spot; good form.
Salvator Rosa,—rose, shaded violet; brown spots; white centre.
Scaramouch,—fine exhibition variety.
*Senior Wrangler, — peach; maroon spots; shaded margin.
Spotted Pet, — lilac; maroon spots; large blotch on upper petals.
*Telegraph,— crimson lower petals; upper, bright maroon; deep habit; free bloomer.

FRITILLA'RIA.

Miniature Crown Imperials, with singularly marbled flowers. They are very interesting and pretty, succeeding in any common garden soil.

Twenty in twenty named varieties, 5*s*.
Choice mixed varieties, 1*s*. 6*d*. per dozen.

FRUIT-GATHERERS.

Several little contrivances have at different times been introduced to the public, in order to assist the fruit-gatherer; but these, as far as they have come under our own observation, are more remarkable for their neatness and ingenuity than for their general usefulness. Undoubtedly, the human hand is the best and safest of all fruit-gatherers; but when bunches of fruit grow at the extremities of slender branches quite out of reach, as is not unfrequently the case, some additional assistance appears requisite even when steps and light ladders are at hand. The little rack or cradle, represented in the following sketch, is much used on the Continent, and might, with advantage, be introduced among ourselves.

It is constructed thus:—1 is an oval piece of board; 2, a handle of any

convenient length, to which the board is firmly fixed; 3, 3 wooden pegs fixed in the oval frame. These pegs are about five or six inches long, and one and a half or two inches apart,—just wide enough, indeed, to allow the fruit-bearing twigs freely to pass through them. The application, of course, is obvious. The teeth act as a comb, and at the same time form a receptacle, by means of which the fruit may be safely conveyed to the basket; for, the rack being drawn over the twigs with the teeth upwards, the fruit is readily gathered into it. Another very simple, useful, and inexpensive fruit-gatherer may be made as follows:—

1 is a hoop of light iron rod; 2, a net-bag appended to it, after the manner of a landing-net; 3, three teeth set with a curve just a little higher than the hoop. These teeth may be made of the same wire as the hoop; but they should be covered with cloth or some soft material to prevent bruising the fruit; 4 is a wooden shaft or handle, which may be extended to any length,

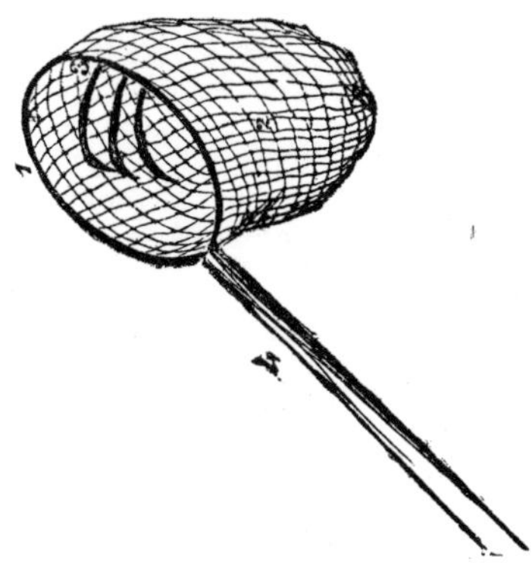

after the manner of a fishing-rod. In this case it is desirable that the teeth should be set at such an angle with the rim, and the rim at such an angle with the shaft, as to insure the fruit falling into the net. This, of course, though very easy of adjustment, cannot well be represented on paper. It would be well if the joint between the shaft and the rim could be made movable. With such an instrument, having a jointed shaft as described, fruit may be safely and expeditiously gathered from the ground off the very points of the outside branches, which otherwise are very difficult to be got at, and where, not unfrequently, the finest fruit is to be found.

Patent Fruit-gatherer, with Net.—The fruit-gatherers are fixed on rods of six or eight feet in length, having a net attached to catch the fruit when cut. By means of this instrument a tree may be cleared of its fruit in a very short time, without the necessity of using ladders; thus, the tree not being shaken, the ripe fruit is preserved; the instrument being very simple, any person can use it.—Price, 17*s.* 6*d.* each.

Another patent fruit-gatherer consists of two discs of india-rubber, which are so elastic as not to press injuriously on the ripest peach or the finest description of other fruits.—Price, 10*s.* each.

FRUIT-GATHERING.

Fruit-gathering is one of the most cheerful and agreeable employments connected with garden-management. It usually enlists every hand in its service, and in an abundant year finds all hands plenty to do. To the following plain and simple directions, those who are intrusted with the superintendence of fruit-gathering will do well at all times to attend. It is important, in the first place, to remark, that no fruit should be gathered for storing before it has arrived at maturity. By this we are to understand not necessarily its full flavour and ripeness, but the completion of its growth or size; and as all fruit, even upon the same tree, does not come to maturity at the same period, it will frequently be found the safest and most economical plan to make the gathering at two or three different times. It is very easy to ascertain when any particular fruit is ready; for ripe fruit always leaves the tree upon a gentle touch,—the fruit-stalk parts from the twig on which it grows without any signs of rending or violence. In a general way, with both apples and pears, several of the most forward fruit will have fallen before the general crop is in a fit state to be gathered; and this fallen or bruised fruit should never be mixed with that which is intended to be stored; all unsound fruit which may be found upon the trees at the time of gathering should also be rejected. Fruit, in fact, which ripens in summer and autumn, should be gathered a little before it is absolutely ripe: thus gathered, it is better in quality and higher flavoured than when absolutely ripe. But this must not be carried too far. A single day before they are perfectly ripe suffices for peaches and other delicate stone fruit; a week for apples and pears; but cherries are only gathered when completely ripe. Apples and pears, which arrive at complete maturity in winter, are best gathered at the moment when the leaves begin to fail, and the sap to withdraw from the branches in October. All gathering should take place in dry weather, and the fruit should not be handled or pulled about more than is absolutely necessary. The middle and afternoon of the day will usually be found the best time for gathering, as autumn mornings, even in the finest weather, are always more or less humid; and to avoid any risk in keeping, all fruit should be quite dry before it is taken from the tree. The most convenient baskets for fruit-gathering are peck and half-bushel baskets, with cross-handles. These should be provided with a line and a hook, by means of which they may be hung to the branches of the tree, and thus allow the gatherer the liberty of using both his hands: by the line, the baskets, when full of fruit, can be lowered to be emptied, and drawn up again.

With regard to the choicer sorts of pears, especially those growing on trees against walls, or on dwarf trees, it will well repay the little extra time and trouble it may cause, to gather these by their stalks without touching them with the hand, and to remove them at once to the fruit-room on the trays or in the drawers in which they are to be stored. There is on the skin of all fruit a secretion more or less marked, known commonly by the name of bloom. This, though less conspicuous on apples and pears than on plums and peaches, is nevertheless present, and its use is to protect the skin of the fruit from the ill effects of excessive moisture. While this bloom can be preserved, the fruit will never require wiping, and will retain its full flavour and freshness. The season of fruit-gathering must be considered to be the most important in the year. All other seasons are to be regarded as preparatory to this, which is to reward the cultivator for his past care and labour. Five or six weeks in autumn,—earlier or later according to the season, and according to situation also, are usually given to the gathering, collecting, and storing of the different varieties of apples and pears, which, in our country, are known as autumn fruits. In a commercial point of view, the result of this season has a most important bearing. The difference between a good and bad apple and pear crop is to be measured by many thousands of pounds; and what household is there, whether among rich or poor, which knows not the luxury of an abundant autumn, and the inconvenience—to say nothing of the pecuniary loss—when some of the many accidents to which our fruit-trees are liable, have deprived us of our autumn crops, or left us only a poor and indifferent supply for our winter wants? In some parts of the country, this loss, when it occurs, falls with far greater severity than in others. In most of the southern and western counties of England, cider is not only made for the consumption of the rest of the kingdom, but forms the chief drink of the labouring classes; and the quantity of apples consumed in its manufacture is something enormous. In Devonshire and Herefordshire the cider orchards are on a very extensive scale; and in these, and some other counties, a bad apple crop causes even far greater pecuniary loss than a deficient wheat crop in other neighbourhoods. The process of fruit-gathering for cider purposes is, for the most part, carried on in a very rude, and, we should consider, in a very wasteful manner. It is called "poulting," and consists in striking the different branches of the trees with a long pole to shake off the fruit, which is then gathered up from the ground. It can hardly be a matter of doubt that a more careful method would be less injurious to the trees, and thus, in the long run, be far more profitable to the grower.

FRUIT-ROOM.

With most persons the fruit-room is the great difficulty in the way of preparation for the keeping of fruit. They cannot follow out the plan which they themselves think best, because the chamber which they are obliged to make use of for a store-room does not admit of the necessary arrangements being made in it. A loft over the coach-house or stable, a spare room in the gardener's cottage, or what is even more generally the case, a top attic in the dwelling-house, is often converted into a fruit-room; not because it is well adapted for the purpose, but because it is the only place that can be spared. It was for this reason, among others, that it is deemed advisable to enumerate many of the different plans which are made use of for the storing of fruit, so that each one may adopt that which the circumstances of his case admit, rather than to attempt to determine what plan is abstractedly the best. Where, however, no such restrictions exist, and a fruit-room can be constructed and arranged in the manner most likely to accomplish the object desired, the following provisions should be carefully attended to:—

If the place to be built for a fruit-room be above ground, and not a dark, dry, well-aired vault, a north aspect must be selected; and if the room be on the top story, the roof of it should slope towards the north.

The best possible covering for a fruit-room is thatch; but if this cannot be managed, or from any cause is deemed objectionable, let the roof be double: also, the outer walls of the room should be hollow; for, with a double roof and hollow walls, the liability to injury from frost will be considerably diminished. Though the fruit-room should for the most part be kept dark, it is desirable that there should be one or two small windows in it, and some good and simple method of ventilation, so that on dry days, and whenever necessary, the atmosphere may be completely changed. This is most important; for though it is not desirable to admit air unless needed, ventilation must never be neglected when the exhalations from the fruit have in any degree tainted the air of the room. Whenever there is a strong smell in the fruit-room, we may be quite sure that something is wrong. Let us suppose, then, a fruit-room so situated as described, with a north aspect, properly roofed and ventilated, and of convenient dimensions for the size of the garden. We will say, that in shape it is a parallelogram, with its door or entrance in one of the shorter sides. A very important question now occurs. How can such a place be best and most conveniently fitted up? The centre should be occupied by a dresser running lengthways to the extreme end of the room. This will be useful for resting or landing the baskets of fruit, as soon as they are brought in from the orchard or garden. The underneath part of the dresser should be fitted up with drawers on one or both sides, according to the width of it; and the top provided with a ledge about two inches deep on all sides, to prevent any fruit that may be laid upon it from falling off. The depth of the drawers may vary according to circumstances—some may be deep for storing very dry fruit, one upon another; others shallow for fruit in single layers. The sides of the room also may be fitted up in the same manner, with dressers all round and drawers underneath. Over these dressers the side-walls may be filled with shelves of any convenient width, about nine inches or a foot apart from each other, according to the width of the shelves. These shelves must, in the same way as the dresser, be fitted with a ledge one or two inches deep to prevent the fruit rolling off; and in severe frosty weather the apples and pears on the shelves can be covered with fern-leaves.

FRUIT-STORING.

The following statement appears to embrace the best methods, and those that are most generally adopted, for the storing and preservation of fruit. It must be borne in mind that they are not arranged in order with any reference to their respective merits; some of them are decidedly objectionable; but the good and bad of each will be noticed as we proceed:—

1. Apples and pears may be sweated, *i.e.*, laid in heaps and left to heat, and then stored away in an apple-room on dressers, or in a dry dark vault in heaps, uncovered except during frost.

This plan, though very generally adopted where apples are kept in large quantities for sale, is always open to the objection of being more or less injurious to the quality and flavour of the fruit.

2. Fruit may be stored on open shelves and on the floor of a fruit-room, spread out upon straw, and covered, when necessary, with the same material.
3. In the same way, but upon dried fern-leaves, and with fern-leaves for a covering.

In our opinion it is by no means a good plan to store apples and pears upon straw, nor even to cover them with it; for straw always imparts an unpleasant flavour to the fruit. Fern-leaves, when properly dried, form an excellent bed for fruit to lie upon, and are not liable to the same objection. As a protection against frost, fern-leaves are decidedly a good covering.

4. In baskets or hampers, lined with straw or fern-leaves, but without any material between the layers of fruit.

If the fruit be dry when placed in the baskets or hampers, and the store-room of an even temperature, it keeps very well in this manner. However, for the reason assigned above, fern-leaves are preferable to straw.

5. In boxes or casks, with saw-dust.
6. In boxes or casks, with bran.
7. In boxes or casks, with wheat-chaff, or with oat-flights.

Sawdust is decidedly objectionable, even though taken from the hardest and most inodorous wood, for it is almost certain, after long keeping, to become musty and unpleasant; and so also does bran, which is naturally a fermenting substance, and soon heats if put together in any quantity, especially with fruit among it. In shallow trays, bran will answer for a time very well, but it will require attention. For packing fruit for conveyance, both bran and sawdust also may be used with good effect. Wheat-chaff, as well as oat-flights, is liable to produce the same mischief. It is quite impossible to be certain that the fruit will not become tainted by means of them, more particularly in closed boxes, and where there is no ventilation.

8. In boxes, with dry sand between the fruit.
9. In boxes, with powdered charcoal in the same way.

By adopting either of these methods, fruit may be preserved for a long period; but though sand and charcoal are good materials for keeping fruit sound, they are both open to the great objection of making the skin gritty and unpleasant.

10. In jars, without any material intervening between the fruit: the jars, when covered with a piece of slate or tile, to be buried in dry sand of a depth sufficient to exclude all air and to insure preservation from frost.

This plan will, undoubtedly, answer its purpose, as far as preservation is concerned; but it is attended with much greater trouble and inconvenience than most persons would deem desirable.

11. In deep drawers one upon another, without any substance between them.
12. In deep drawers, with sheets of paper or dried fern-leaves placed between the layers of fruit.

Both these plans are good, and if the fruit be stored sound and dry, there will be little need of any intervening material.

13. In single layers in shallow trays or drawers resting upon fern-leaves, and to be covered when necessary with the same.

This is the plan which we should recommend as the safest and best, under ordinary circumstances, to be adopted.

14. In heaps in dark, dry, well-aired vaults.

In this way both apples and pears, in large quantities, may be well and easily kept; and if the vaults be thoroughly dry and sufficiently beneath the surface to exclude frost, the fruit will require no further protection, and give but little trouble.

Filberts and walnuts, to be stored for winter use, should be gathered when full ripe, and on a dry day. The latter must be cleared of their husks. They may then be packed in glazed earthen jars, tied down with coarse brown paper, and kept in a damp cellar. Filberts keep best in this manner without their husks; but if the husks are to be preserved, the fruit must be left to stand for a night in open baskets, and be well shaken to get rid of earwigs. Many persons shake a little salt over the last layer of nuts before the jars are tied down.

All drawers, shelves, boxes, or jars containing fruit. should be labelled every year as soon as the fruit is stored, so that the different sorts may be easily and readily known.

FUCHSIAS (nat. ord. Onagra'riæ).

Whoever has a glasshouse two yards square, or a window free from dust, may grow one or more fuchsias. In fact they have become quite window-plants, and no plant is better adapted for the purpose. To grow them, however, in perfection, requires some judgment and skill. Cuttings should be inserted in pots filled either with loam and leaf-mould, or peat and silver-sand, in equal parts, to within an inch and a half of the top. Place over this three-quarters of an inch of silver-sand, and level the surface to make it firm; then insert the cuttings,—about one inch long is the proper length, and plunge the pots in a bottom-heat of 60°, either in a pit or propagating-house: if the latter, cover them with a bell-glass. In three weeks they may be potted in 3-inch pots, and replunged in the same bed, keeping them at a temperature of from 50° to 60°. As soon as the roots reach the sides of the pots, the plants should be shifted into fresh pots, until they receive their final shift into 6-, 9-, or 12-inch pots, towards the end of June. The size of the pot must be regulated by the period when they are wanted to bloom. If in July, a 6- or 9-inch pot will suffice; if in September or October, a 12 will not be too large. During the period of growth, the plants will require stopping at least six times, care being taken never to stop the shoots immediately preceding or directly after the operation of shifting into larger pots. If the pyramidal form of growth, which is the best of all forms for the fuchsia, is adopted, the plants, from the first, must be trained to a single stem, and all the side-shoots stopped, to make the pyramid thick and perfect. If the bush form is wanted, the whole of the shoots should then be stopped at every third joint, until branches enough are secured to form the bush, and then be trained into the desired shape. A regular moist, genial temperature must be maintained during the entire period of growth, never exceeding 60°. During bright sunshine, the glass should be slightly shaded with tiffany or other material: the delicate leaves are easily injured, and the plant should never receive the slightest check by being allowed to flag. Fuchsias will grow in almost any soil. Garden-loam and leaf-mould in equal proportions, with some broken charcoal and sand, do very well. It is better to feed them with manure-water than to mix dung with the soil. After they are well rooted, they should never be watered with clear water. A carefully-shaded conservatory, guarded against the ingress of bees, is the best place for them when in blossom. In such a situation, they will continue in bloom for three months if the seeds are constantly picked off. Most of the species are edible, and some of the green-coloured varieties really form a good dessert. Sir Colin Campbell is one of the finest fruiting kinds, and the best flavoured of the dark-fruited varieties; but its great attractions are the flowers. Nothing can be more graceful, either in form or flower, than noble plants of fuchsia, and their price is sufficiently low, and their culture easy enough to bring them within the reach of all.

FUCHSIAS (Hardy).

These make the best show when planted together in beds upon a lawn, the colours being judiciously blended. Those fuchsias which trail upon the ground should be grown with a wire hoop supported by three legs underneath them, so that their branches may be made to bend over the hoop. Several of the more hardy sorts may be trained on one stem, so as to appear as standards in the bed. Many large and beautiful varieties of fuchsias are hardy, and will stand our winters in the open ground, especially in a well-drained light soil having a large portion of peat in it; and a great many that are looked upon as tender varieties may be preserved if covered three or four inches with dry cinder ashes at the first approach of frost. The best plan is to cover the whole fuchsia-bed at that time with a good coating. The dead branches should not be cut off, nor should the ashes be removed until the fuchsias begin to shoot in the spring.

GAILLAR'DIA (nat. ord. Compos'itæ).

These strong flowers, natives of America, are both annuals and perennials. The former are splendid bedding-plants, remarkable for the profusion, size, and brilliancy of their blossoms, continuing in beauty during the summer and autumn: they thrive in any light rich soil.

Gaillardia alba marginata,—white-edged, half-hardy annual, 1½ ft.
Gaillardia grandiflora hybrida,—rich crimson and yellow, flowers remarkably large and attractive, half-hardy annual, 1½ ft.
Gaillardia grandiflora hybrida,—extra selected, half-hardy annual, 1½ ft.

Seed, 3*d.* per packet.

GALL-FLIES

(*Cynipidæ*) produce the large woolly galls upon various kinds of roses. The larvæ of *Rhodites Rosæ* are white fleshy grubs, destitute of feet, which are transformed into white inactive pupæ at their full size. They undergo their change to the perfect state within the gall, or *bedeguar*, as it is called, eating their way through it to the open air, and emerging in their winged state. Several species of these gall-flies are found together. No production of nature seems to have puzzled the old naturalists more than the galls produced by these creatures.

GARDEN TOOLS.

The different sorts of tools necessary for gardening purposes will be found described under their respective names, the most useful varieties pointed out, and prices given at which they can be supplied by Messrs. Barnard and Bishop, of the Market-place, Norwich, to whom the editor can with confidence recommend his readers.

GARDEN WALLS.

The materials of which garden walls are formed will always depend upon local circumstances; brick, stone, clay, chalk, and oak fencing, being all in common use. Of all these materials, brick seems to be the favourite, absorbing most heat, being the best for training and the most enduring. Forsyth says, "Where brick cannot be had, it is better to dispense with walls altogether and adopt wood." Whinstone, a species of basalt rock common in the northern counties, is reckoned next for these qualities, while its close grain rejects moisture.

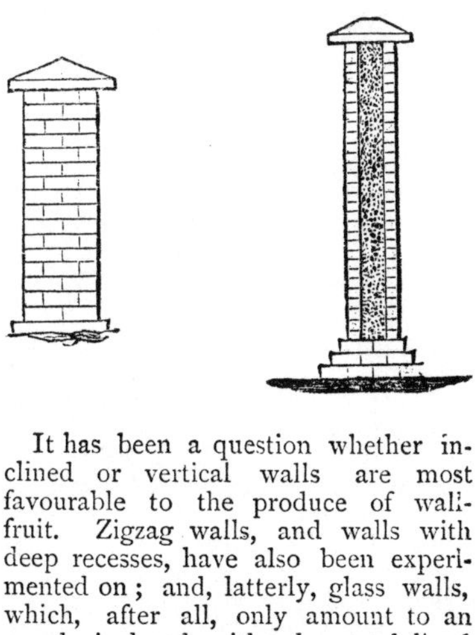

It has been a question whether inclined or vertical walls are most favourable to the produce of wall-fruit. Zigzag walls, and walls with deep recesses, have also been experimented on; and, latterly, glass walls, which, after all, only amount to an arcade inclosed with glass and lined with vines, fruit-trees, and exotics.

An economical wall is sometimes constructed of a brick in bed, or stretcher, on each side, the space between being filled up with concrete similar to that prepared for foundations. This concrete adheres to the brick-work; headers, or bricks across, being used occasionally as bonds, to hold the two sides together. A solid wall of fourteen inches, or even eighteen, which would require 3,620 bricks to the rod, would thus only require 1,210, while the cost of the concrete is comparatively trifling. In countries where brick is not easily obtained, a very good wall may be constructed with a brick in front and stone behind, where one front only is required for use.

The introduction of hollow bricks is supposed to be conducive to dryness and free ventilation, while it greatly reduces the pressure on the foundation; but it does not appear that we have any great experience as to its result on garden walls.

Stone walls for gardens should be built in courses of four or eight inches thick; the stones ashlar or hammer-dressed, the joints chisel-dressed, the mortar-bed not too thick, and the joints pointed and drawn clean.

Hollow walls are only found in gardens of lofty pretensions, where very high cultivation is adopted; and we have reason to believe that in many quarters where they exist they are rarely used.

Besides brick and stone, chalk and clay have been sometimes employed in erecting garden walls successfully. In each instance the process is pretty nearly the same. A foundation being obtained, a wooden frame is prepared and laid down on each side, of the exact thickness of the intended walls. Into this frame chalk or clay, previously worked into a thick paste, is thrown in layers about six inches thick all round. The layer thus placed is made level by raking, and left to consolidate, which it will do at one end before the workman has reached the other end of the wall, if it is of any extent. In this way the work proceeds layer by layer, until the intended height is attained, when a coping of stone or other material is bedded on it with cement or mortar.

GARDENER'S COTTAGE.

Almost every garden requires some buildings, the construction of which may serve to call into exercise the good taste of its proprietor. When the grounds are of sufficient extent, the gardener's cottage should be contained within them, and the proper situation of this will be as near as possible to the hothouses and melon-grounds. This cottage should be in keeping with the mansion and its lodges. It should be so arranged as to contain within it the fruit-room, of which a description has already been given under that title, and a store-room for seeds. In this store-room all seeds may be dried, cleaned, and put away. There should be a table in the centre, and dressers round the room; drawers and nests should be provided for the different seeds and bulbs. One or two cross-beams in the roof will be very handy, for, when provided with hooks, all pod seeds can be hung up and dried; onions also, in ropes or bunches, can be suspended from them. Sieves, bags, a quire of coarse brown paper, and a ball of string, with a packing-needle, are essential requisites in such a store-room; a small hand thrashing-machine and a small fanning-machine also will be found very convenient.

GARDENING FOR SMOKY CITIES AND LARGE TOWNS.

It is well known to every one that the vapour arising from substances in a state of combustion, which is usually termed smoke, is very prejudicial to vegetable life. Without taking into consideration the deadly effects arising from the diffusion of smoke generated in certain factories—more especially chemical works—which is fatal in proportion to the nature of the substances employed, and from which the smoke is evolved, it is sufficient for the gardener to have to combat smoke arising from ordinary coal-furnaces and the thousands of chimneys

Gardening for Cities and Towns.

for domestic use which surmount our crowded dwellings. Smoke of this sort is generally considered to consist of two parts—gaseous exhalations and certain minute particles of carbonaceous matter called soot. Both these constituents are capable of producing more or less injury to the bark, leaves, and blossoms of whatever trees, shrubs, and plants are brought into contact with them. Soot, applied as a manure to the soil, is a decided fertilizer, or perhaps it would be more correct to call it a stimulant to vegetation; but this is a very different application of soot from that with which vegetation is treated, when it is found struggling for existence against the dense masses of soot which are emitted from the chimneys of our populous cities and large towns. The gaseous vapours charged with soot form a black gummy coating over the stems and leaves, which prevents the respiratory organs of plants from performing their proper functions for the support of life. Still, so tenacious is Nature of her own rights, that even in the most murky and sooty atmosphere something green will be found growing. Indeed, the traveller through our coal districts is often struck with the luxuriance of the corn crops growing even up to the pit's mouth, and with the manner in which large trees have been able, at any rate, "to hold their own" in the severe struggle which they have had for years to maintain. We ourselves have vivid recollections of having seen, in the midst of "the black country" of South Staffordshire, at the foot of Dudley-Castle hill, several years ago, many very gay gardens in front of the cottages of the pitmen. Though Flora and her attendant train of Nature's beauties rejoice most in clear fresh country air and the pleasant places of the earth, it is a great mistake to imagine that they voluntarily banish themselves from, and cannot be invited to dwell in, the dark and sooty regions of mining enterprise and manufacturing industry, or where men densely crowd their dwellings together for purposes of business and professional intercourse. Of course it would be as useless as it would be foolish, under such unfavourable circumstances, to attempt the cultivation of all sorts of shrubs and plants indiscriminately; but it should be a matter of thankfulness that some sorts will grow, and that experience has pointed out those which will flourish and do best. It is the same with vegetable as with animal life; so varied are the gifts of Nature, that the same atmospheric conditions are not essential to the welfare of every individual, nor is the same food requisite for its support. The old proverb, "One man's food is another's poison," may be made to apply to both. It is not every constitution that can stand the extreme heat of the drying-rooms of some of our factories, much less the vitiated atmosphere of those stifling chambers to which our needlewomen and dressmakers' apprentices are too often consigned; and so it is with plants. Attempt to grow the delicate white China rose within the influence of London smoke, and it will not only disappoint you in flowering, but in a short time the plant itself will wither and die, while the common cabbage-rose, and even the maiden's blush, under precisely similar circumstances, will flower freely and live to a good old age. It is necessary, therefore, to know what trees, plants, and flowers will flourish best; and such knowledge, to begin with, will be the means of saving much trouble, disappointment, and expense. The following remarks are intended to be of service to those who are not unwilling to attempt what at all times must be regarded as "gardening under difficulties;" but with what good results the attempt may be made let the Temple Gardens testify. Greatly changed for the worse is the atmosphere of London since Warwick prophesied—

> "This brawl to-day,
> Grown to this faction in the Temple Garden,
> Shall send between the red rose and the white
> A thousand souls to death and deadly night."

Gardening for Cities and Towns.

Yet we venture to affirm that the great earl saw nothing half so gay around him as may be now seen in this same spot, notwithstanding dirt and soot. To Mr. Broome, the intelligent superintendent of these ancient gardens, all who live in smoky cities, and who still love flowers, owe a deep debt of gratitude. He has shown what may be done, and he has also left on record his own experience as to the best mode of doing it. "Fresh from the country," writes Mr. Broome, "having received initiation into the mysteries of my profession in the gardens of one of the wealthiest of our nobility, I was but little prepared for the difference which exists between the growth of plants in the country and in large towns. Those which in the pure air of the former grew almost spontaneously, would, notwithstanding the pains bestowed upon them, barely arrive at maturity in the smoky atmosphere of the latter. My previous experience availed me but little; I had almost everything to unlearn; however," continues he, "I set about my task with diligence, coupled with patience and perseverance, and have been rewarded by a complete triumph over all such difficulties as were not insuperable."

Some persons, perhaps, may imagine that outdoor gardening under such adverse circumstances can hardly repay the trouble that must be bestowed upon it, and that the subject loses its interest because there are not many persons who have much opportunity or convenience for availing themselves of it, so small a space in general being allotted in most cities and large towns to each house beyond the plot of ground which it actually stands upon. But why should even the smallest courtyard not be turned to the best account? Why should any open space be deprived of a green tree, a few shrubs and plants and flowers, to ornament it? Why should the back drawing-room, as is so often the case even in good houses, have nothing better to look out upon than bare walls and a dirty pavement? It should be observed that turf grows well under the influence of smoke, that trellis-work will hide any unsightly object, and the large quick-growing Russian ivy will soon cover a wall; a light verandah, also, at the drawing-room windows may be made available for creepers. The common nasturtium will do well, and so will the different varieties of tropæolum, also canariensis; but care must be taken that they do not suffer from drought, for drought in a smoky atmosphere is far more injurious to plants than it is where the air is clear and pure.

The following list will be found to contain most of the trees, shrubs, herbaceous plants, and annuals, at present introduced into this country, which are not so susceptible of the injurious influences of a vitiated atmosphere as many others, and which are consequently suitable for our cities and large towns:—

Acer pseudo-platanus.
,, rubrum.
Achillea lingulata.
Acuba japonica.
Æsculus Hippocastanum.
Ageratum.
Alyssum.
Ampelopsis hederacea.
Amygdalus communis.
Antirrhinum.
Aristotelia Macqui.
Artemisia Abrotanum.
Aster—varieties.
Betula alba.
Bignonia radicans.
Calceolarias.
Carnations.
Chronathes virgineum.
Chrysanthemums—varieties.
Clematis flamula.
,, montana.
,, vitalba.
Cornus mascula.
,, sanguinea.
Cratægus oxycantha, and varieties.
Crocus.
Cytisus Laburnum.
,, alpinus.
,, scoparis.
Dahlias.
Daisies.
Daphne Mezereum.
Dracocephalum.
Enonymus europæus.
Epilobium angustifolium (willow-herb)
Fagus sylvatica.
Foxglove.
Fraxinus—sorts.
Genista purgans.
German stocks.
Gladiolus.
Hardy phloxes.
Heartsease.
Hedera Helix, and varieties.
Helleborus niger (Christmas rose).
Hollyhocks.
Hypericum calycinum.
Hypericum elatum.
,, Androsæmum.
Ilex Aquifolium, and varieties.
Jasminum officinale.
Juglans regia.
Lavender.
Lily of the Valley.
Lycium barbarum.
Magnolia grandiflora.
,, conspicua.
,, glauca.
Mahonia aquifolium.
Mespilus germanica.
Mignonette.
Mimulus.
Morus nigra.
Negundo fraxinifolium.
Philadelphus grandiflorus.

Gardening for Cities and Towns.

Phillyrea—sorts.
Phlomis fruticosa.
Pinks.
Polyanthus.
Populus fastigiata and nigra.
Pyrus aucuparia.
Rhamnus Alaternus.
Rhododendron ponticum.
Rhus typhinum.
„ Cotinus.
Robinia pseud-acacia.
Rockets.
Rubus—varieties.
Salix—sorts.
Sambucus nigra.
Santolina chamæcyparissus.
Scarlet geraniums.
Snowdrop.
Sophoria japonica.
Spartium junceum.
Staphylea trifolia.
„ pinnata.
Sunflower.
Sweetwilliams.
Symphoricarpos racemosus.
Syringa—varieties.
Taxus baccata and fastigiata.
Thuja occidentalis.
„ orientalis.
Ulmus—sorts.
Verbenas—varieties.
Viburnum Opulus.
Vinca major.
Virginian stock.
Wallflowers.
Wistaria sinensis.

Dwarf Roses.

Maiden's Blush.
Provence.
Rose de Meaux.
And most of the common hardy annuals.

The above list is sufficient for every purpose of ornament and gaiety. In so long a list it must be obvious that some things will do better than others; but all are worth planting, as all have been known to live in a smoky atmosphere. Of trees, the plane, which sheds its bark annually, and the poplar in its different varieties, are decidedly the best where the air is most charged with soot.

Besides chrysanthemums, as we learn from Mr. Broome, a very fair display may be obtained throughout the year of other hardy flowers which will thrive in London smoke, and may be grown with success in most of the squares and small gardens in large cities and towns. And to those persons who take an interest in the vegetable kingdom, and wish to grow a few plants or trees for ornament in confined places, to save them unnecessary expense in purchasing what will not grow, "I here give," continues that great authority, "my thirty years' practical experience of what I have found to succeed, and keep up a succession of flowers through the year. As a winter flower, the Christmas rose (*Helleborus niger*) does very well. Snowdrops, too, bloom very freely. Next come the crocus and tulips, of different colours: these do remarkably well, and if planted in October, in beds or good-sized patches, will, in March or April, make quite a show, and form a pleasing mixture with the common primrose.

"In the middle of February sow round the crocuses a good quantity of Virginian stock, purple and white alternately: the leaf of the crocus shelters the young stock from the frost and cold March winds; and when the crocus has done blooming, either cut the leaves off or twist them round, and give them a tie to allow the Virginian stock fair play. This comes in succession to the crocus, and when sown in large patches in beds has a very pretty effect. I generally plant a large quantity of the common wallflower, choosing the darkest varieties. These flower a long time, and smell very sweet. They should be planted rather deep, and require a good quantity of water, or they soon flag. The gladiolus is a very excellent bulb for town borders, if planted in March in a strong loam, leaf-mould, and rotten dung, and plenty of water when the hot weather sets in. The daffodil and narcissus do very well. Next come the white candytuft and the yellow alyssum, which bloom at the same time. These strike from cuttings in the summer, and keep in a cold frame all the winter. Next come the *Iris germanica* and the rocket. Daisies and heartsease do well, and flower a long time. The calceolaria does exceedingly well, and flowers all the summer. Cuttings of these should be put in a cold frame in October, and merely require the frost to be kept from them. I peg them down like verbenas, instead of stopping them. The result of this is, that I obtain an earlier bloom: they throw out their laterals quite as well, and the wind is prevented from breaking them off. . . . When it is very hot, throw round the roots a little mulch or mould, to keep their flowers from drooping. Intermediate stocks do very well, and flower all the summer: these I sow in September, under a hand-glass. When old enough, prick out three or four plants in No. 48 pots, in a compost of loam and a little rotten dung, taking care they do not get too much wet. In November put them in cold frames for the winter, never watering except they flag, and plant out in February, as they will bear a little frost. Scarlet geraniums do very well. The *Ageratum mexicanum* does very well. I put in cuttings in October, which I manage to keep through the winter. You may also put in cuttings of this in the spring, which will flower very early. Verbenas flower well all the summer, but are difficult to keep through the winter, as they damp off in December and January for want of better air. The dark clove-carnation is very hardy and flowers beautifully. These I propagate by hundreds in the autumn, potting some in cold frames, and letting others remain out of doors. The sweet-william, lupinus, polyphyllus, scabiosa, antirrhinum, polyanthus, foxglove, and lily of the valley, do remarkably well. The fuchsia, if planted in a cold shady place in summer, flowers tolerably well, but must be attended to in watering, or the flower drops before opening. Plant them in leaf-mould, rotten dung, and yellow loam. If the weather is very hot and dry, cover the surface with a little rough rotten dung. The mimulus is a famous town flower, but requires plenty of water. Some of the hardy phloxes do pretty well. The double rocket flowers freely, and if the first bloom is taken off when faded, the plant will bloom again as freely as ever; but it requires a great deal of water. I would recommend nearly all the common hardy annuals, especially branching larkspur, the *Phlox Drummondii*, lupinus, coreopsis, &c. Balsams do very well if the seed is sown in a little hotbed, supposing you have the convenience to make one; it will also answer for china-asters, and when ready to be planted, mix plenty of leaf-mould and rotten dung in the borders for them, as they do not bloom freely without a rich compost, and being abundantly supplied with water. Have nothing to do with tender annuals: they are poor, sickly-looking plants

for town gardening. The common pinks do exceedingly well. The willow-herb (*Epilobium angustifolium*) is a very showy common flower, and will grow anywhere. Mignonette does well. Sow it for early blooming in January, in a little heat in 48-pots, in light mould to turn out. There are numbers of herbaceous plants that do very well; such as the Michaelmas daisy (*aster*), double sunflower, *Achillea lingulata*, *Dracocephalum speciosum*, sea-lavender (*Statice latifolia*), and all hardy plants of this class. The common English ferns thrive very well in shady parts, by watering every day in hot, dry weather. Plant them in leaf-mould, loam, and common sand, and mix with them a few plants of periwinkle and some rock-work; but be careful not to disturb them while forking up the borders. Hollyhocks do very indifferently, and are not worth trying. Dahlias do exceedingly well if well supplied with water, and carefully thinned as they advance in size. They ought to be planted very early in the spring to get an early bloom; as they are not required in September, the chrysanthemum taking their place, I generally cut them down in this month. Last year I pegged them down all the season, and kept them close to the ground by pruning, and they bloomed well. You ought to be particular in your selection not to purchase hard-eyed ones, as the ground becomes so hot and dry at the close of the summer, that they never bloom fully out. Among the best are, Beauty of the Grove, Richard Cobden, King of the Yellows, Mr. Glenny, Bees-wing, Brilliant, Empress, Annie Salter, Beauty of Slough, Fearless, and other free bloomers of this class.

"Respecting shrubs and deciduous plants," continues Mr. Broome, "few of these do any good. The lilac blooms very scantily, but does well for a screen, as it shows a little green in the summer. The *Aucuba japonica* answers in sheltered places. The euonymus does very well in smoke, and retains its foliage; but this year (1860) the severe winter has nearly destroyed

Gardening for Cities and Towns.

it. This shows it is not so hardy as many other shrubs, and requires to be covered with mats on very severe frosty nights. The box, holly, and privet thrive for two or three years; rhododendrons flower freely for a season, with plenty of water, all through the summer. The hibiscus rose, or *Althæa frutex*, grows and flowers remarkably well. The Daphne Mezereum does well, and flowers freely, both white and pink. The dwarf roses, such as Rose de Meaux, Cabbage, Provence, Maiden's Blush, York and Lancaster, are now doing tolerably well in these gardens, considering the murky atmosphere they grow in. I tried some dwarf standards, and they more than answered my expectation, as, after planting them in good maiden loam, and attending to their watering, some bloomed all the season. Madame Laffay, Jacques Lafette, Mrs. Eliot, Géant de Batailles, William Jessey, Duc d'Aumale, and several others, gave great satisfaction; but, of course, they require attention in taking off the seed and in watering. It is something to have a rose at all in this smoky town. Those grown as dwarfs on their own stocks do much better than those worked on the briars. The higher they are from the ground, the more smoke they get on the stems; consequently, dwarf plants near the ground are best.

"As respects forest-trees nothing does so well as the oriental plane, in consequence of its shedding its bark every spring: by so doing, it gets rid of the soot, which sticks to other trees like varnish, and which there is no getting off. You may train it to any habit you please by pruning, and the more confined it is, the better it does. The lime-trees do very badly; but the elm and thorn tolerably well. The Lombardy poplar is a capital tree for London. Irish ivy does very well where you want to cover a wall. The turf stands smoke as well as anything, and when the situation is open, looks remarkably well. Hundreds of children freak and play, and roll on the turf in the Temple Gardens every summer's evening, and when they are closed for the season, you would think it could never recover; but in a few weeks, with a little rain and rest, and a slight covering of fine mould, it springs up like a mushroom. Should there be any very bare places, I break it up three inches deep; sow a little mixed lawn-grass, cover it over, roll it down, and it is up in three weeks if there comes any rain. Under trees, I sow the Paris everlasting rye-grass, as that is stronger than the lawn-grass, and does better to trample on."

Such is the practice in the Temple Gardens, and every one who wishes to see what can be done in the way of gardening under the most untoward circumstances of atmosphere, will do well to pay a visit to them. It is strange that those who live in the noble squares, and about the inclosed crescents of our large towns, and especially of our metropolis, should have remained so long without profiting by the experience and example of Mr. Broome. Few places are worse kept than our London squares. Their cold, dreary, and comfortless appearance, is the remark of every stranger, and yet, in a general way, there is no lack of wealth in the dwellings around, and, doubtless, the means for their improvement would soon be found, if a few of the principal inhabitants would only spare the time, and exert a little energy and taste upon the subject. Let a garden committee be formed in each square, or wherever there is a space of ground needing cultivation, in which the surrounding inhabitants have an interest, and let funds be raised by means of rate or subscription. As soon as this is done, let a contract be entered into with some respectable nurseryman to keep the inclosure in good order, and gay with shrubs and flowers.

Many of our large nurserymen would take the contract for a much smaller sum than most persons would imagine, and would find it their interest to keep the place as gay and attractive as possible; for a square in London, or any of our large towns, would become an excellent advertisement, and tend greatly to increase the business connection of any respectable man. Beyond the trees and large evergreens, everything should be the property of the contractor, who would thus have the liberty of bringing in and removing whatever he might think fit. This must be regarded as the most important part of the engagement on both sides; for very many things, as the whole list of American plants, rhododendrons, kalmias, &c., will flourish well for one season in smoke, but if left longer they would not only cease flowering, but die. It would, therefore, be as much the interest of the committee as of the contractor, that these should be removed late in autumn, and replaced by others the following spring. The inhabitants would thus enjoy a succession of these most beautiiul spring-flowering plants, and the contractor would suffer no loss in the exchange, as such things, and many others, may be moved at their proper season without the slightest harm.

Mr. Broome's idea of conservatories for squares might then be carried out; for the contractor would, doubtless, find it his interest to erect some light ornamental building of iron-work for his own convenience, in keeping up a supply of bedding-plants, &c., for the square, and for the window and in-door decorations of the houses around, where all such things would, doubtless, find a ready sale. We accord fully with Mr. Broome's observation. "There is not a square in London that would not be much improved by its little conservatory. Glass is cheap enough now, and the cost of a light ornamental framework of iron would be a mere trifle among our rich citizens who reside in that locality, and they would have an ornamental object to look upon from their houses. A hot-water apparatus heated with coke would cause no nuisance by way of smoke: in fact, the artificial heat would not be wanted except on very frosty nights, as the air of London is much warmer than that in the country. Birds, gold-fish, and many interesting things, might be introduced to amuse the younger members of the family."

In the foregolng remarks we have said much about the necessity of well watering, and it must be remembered that deep digging and plentiful manuring are not less essential in the sooty atmosphere of our crowded towns. Every year the collected surface-soot should be buried by trenching about eighteen inches deep, and a good dressing of manure be worked in to renovate the soil.

GARLIC.

The finest garlic is imported. It is, however, grown in the country; seed, 8*d.* per lb.

GARNISHING HERBS.

These are handsome in growth, and useful for domestic purposes. Among them we may enumerate the ice-plant, the curled mallow, Melville's garnishing borecole, triple curled cress and parsley.

GATES.

These may be of wood or iron; and, as a general rule, they must always be in harmony with the character of the fence. Lodge- or entrance-gates are most effective in pairs. They should neither be too massive nor too light, and of sufficient width to prevent all anxiety about wheels and posts. The pattern must be determined by the character of the buildings to which they lead; the construction should be strong, and the colour such as can be easily discerned at night.

GENIS'TA (nat. ord. Legumino'sæ).

Exceedingly ornamental profuse-flowering hardy shrubs, equally valuable for the decoration of the conservatory, flower-borders, and shrubbery. They are grown freely from seed; price, 3*d.*

to 4*d*. per packet. The following are the best varieties :—

Genista bracteolata superba,—yellow, ft., from Teneriffe.
Genista candicans,—yellow, 2 ft., from Spain.
,, Canariensis,—yellow, 2 ft., from the Canaries.
Genista ephedrioides, — yellow, 2 ft., from Sardinia.
Genista mantica,—yellow, 3 ft., from South of Europe.
Genista multiflora alba,— white, 3 ft., from South of Europe.
Genista pendula,—yellow, 4 ft., from Italy.
,, racemosa,—yellow, 3 ft., from Italy.
,, ramosissima,—yellow, 3 ft., from Italy.
,, spinifolia,—white, 3 ft., from Italy.
,, umbellata,—yellow, 5 ft., from Barbary.

GENTIA'NA.

All the gentians are beautiful. *G. acaulis*, with its large deep mazarine-blue blossoms, looks well as an edging plant. It requires a pure air and rich light soil.

GERA'NIUM (nat. ord. Gerania'ceæ).

These well-known floral favourites are not less indispensable for outdoor than for indoor decoration. No plants are more universally cultivated, and of none are there greater varieties. Under the heads of Fancy and French and Spotted Geraniums will be found useful lists, and descriptions for the guidance of purchasers of these different sorts. With geraniums for the green-house, in order to secure profusion of bloom, early growth and under-potting are of the first importance. No matter how robust a plant is grown, one eighteen months old cannot be made to flower as freely as one four or five years old. Plants to flower in May should be cut down by the end of the previous June ; they should have broken, been reduced, repotted, and encouraged to grow two or three inches in a close cold frame, for a fortnight, and have received their final stopping by the end of July, and be placed in their blooming-pot by the 1st of November. Success depends upon their chief growth being completed before Christmas. No after-management can compensate for the neglect of early growth. Any size of plant or leaf may be obtained at any period ; but flowers will be scarce unless early growth is secured. Under-potting is the next great point. Plants in general, and geraniums in particular, flower best when they are pot-bound, and some varieties will scarcely flower at all unless their roots are in this condition. The reason seems to be, that whatever tends to check the extension of other parts, favours the development of flowers.

GERANIUM, BEDDING VARIETIES.

Of bedding varieties, the following list will be found to embrace the most useful. Strong healthy plants may be had at from 4*s*. to 6*s*. the dozen.

Auber Henderson,—white.
Baronne Souget,—fine scarlet.
Boule de Feu,—fine scarlet.
Boule de Neige,—white.
Brown's compactum.
Carmine,—mossy.
Cerise Unique,—cerise.
Christine,—rosy pink.
Comte de Morny,—rosy scarlet ; blush edges, suffused with pink ; fine.
Countess of Bective,—deep salmon, with dark brown zone.
Dawn of Day,—brilliant scarlet.
Defiance,—large.
Emperor of the French,—scarlet.
Frogmore scarlet.
Garibaldi,—bright scarlet, with white eye.
Harkaway, — deep habit ; perfect bloomer ; very distinct.
Henri de Beaudot,—very large ; salmon-coloured blossoms, belted with white.
Imperial crimson,—mossy.
,, Stella,—ditto.
Lady Middleton,—fine rose.
Madame Chardine,—salmon-rose, white centre; large.
Madame Vaucher,—white.
Minnie,—pink ; white spot on upper petals.
Paul l'Abbé,—clear rosy salmon ; fine.
Purple,—mossy.
Red,—ditto.
Richmond Gem,—light orange-scarlet.
Rose superbe,—fine rose.
Rubens,—fine salmon-colour.
Scarlet shaded and Spottishall,—varieties.
Shrubland,—scarlet ; fine large.
Silver variegated,—mossy.
,, Stella,—ditto.
Tom Thumb,—scarlet.
Tom Thumb's Bride,—good scarlet.
Trentham rose,—fine rose.

Silver and gold varieties, one thousand:—

Alma,—scarlet flower; silver lines.
Annie,—scarlet; sulphur-tinged.
Bijou,—strong-growing scarlet flower; silver leaves.
Brilliant,—slightly silvered; good scarlet; fine bedder; not a strong habit.
Cloth of Gold,—unique.
Countess of Warwick,—scarlet; white margin; leaves brown-white.
Culford Beauty,—scarlet flower; sulphur variegated.
Dandy,—a neat silver-edged gem.
Gold Ivy-leaved.
Golden Cerise,—unique.
Golden Tom Thumb.
Hendersonii,—like Flower of the Day, but scarlet flowers.
Lady Plymouth,—a neat silver-edged gem.
Miss Emily Domville,—salmon flowers, silver-zoned; good.
Perfection,—scarlet flower; white-margined leaves.
Pink-flowered,—ivy-leaved.
Rainbow,—scarlet flowers; silver, with red zone.
Scarlet-flowered,—ivy-leaved.
Silver Queen,—pink flowers; smooth foliage.
Silver,—ivy-leaved.
St. Clair,—pink flowers; silver habit.
White-flowered,—ivy-leaved, &c.

GERANIUM CUTTINGS.

Cuttings of all sorts of geraniums for bedding the following year should be struck early: from the last week in July to the end of the first week in August is very good time. They should be taken in dry weather, when the parent plant has had no water for some days, and they should be kept to dry twenty-four hours after they have been prepared for potting. The more succulent sorts, and any that appear difficult to strike, may with advantage be touched at the end with a small paint-brush dipped in collodion, which will serve to hasten the callus which the cutting must form before it will throw out roots. They may be potted four or six in a pot, according to size. It is essential that the pots be well fitted with drainers, that the soil be light and sandy, and that it be pressed tight round the joint of the cuttings, which should be buried in it as flat as possible. When potted, they may be sunk in the ground on a south border, and well watered in the evening, when the sun is off. They will require no shading, except the sun be very scorching; and, in this case, they must not be kept from the light, but merely screened from the scorching rays of the sun. They may flag a little, but this is of no importance; in two or three days they will recover, and put forth roots. If they grow too freely before it is time to take them in for the winter, the top shoots should be broken off, and in this way they will make strong bushy plants.

GERANIUMS, TO PRESERVE OLD ONES.

Take them out of the borders in autumn, before they have received any injury from frost; and let this be done on a dry day. Shake off all the earth from their roots, and suspend them, with their heads downwards, in a cellar or dark room, where they will be free from frost. The leaves and shoots will become yellow and sickly; but when potted about the end of May, and exposed to a gentle heat, they will recover and vegetate luxuriantly. The old plants, stripped of their leaves, may also be packed closely in sand; and in this way, if kept free from frost, they will shoot out from the roots, and may be re-potted in the spring.

GESNE'RIAS (nat. ord. Gesneria'ceæ).

Showy hothouse plants with scarlet flowers. They are propagated by cuttings, which require a little bottom-heat.

GLADIO'LI.

The varieties of Gladioli may be divided into two sections—summer- and autumn-flowering; *Ramosus* and its seedlings representing the former, *Gandavensis* and its seedlings the latter. The flowers of each are extremely beautiful, while the brilliancy and variety of their colours at once determine their importance and position for masses in the flower-borders. Planted alternately with roses, in large beds cut in the grass, or amongst rhododendrons and azaleas, the effective display produced by their long brilliant transparent spikes of bloom can hardly be conceived. When grouped in front of shrubs, the green background shows off their rich striking colours to great advantage. In suburban gardens they are great acquisitions, for they are not so much affected by a smoky atmosphere as many other flowers.

Where cut flowers are in demand for filling vases, &c., those of the Gladiolus are unsurpassed. The French frequently adorn their flower-borders, &c., with the cut spikes of gladioli, by placing the cut end of the flower in a bottle of water, and plunging the bottle into the soil, so that the uninitiated suppose the flower to be growing. In beds where there is a deficiency of brilliant colours, a few spikes treated in this fashion make them for the time look charming.

The *Ramosus* varieties bloom in July and August; the *Gandavensis* in August and September, and with a little management in successional planting, even the months of October and November may be enlivened with the brilliant colours of this floral gem.

Early-flowering Gladioli Seedlings of Ramosus.—Culture in Pots, for the decoration of the orchard-house or conservatory, and for an early summer bloom out of doors:—Plant in November, December, or January, three bulbs in a 6- or 7-inch pot, using a compost of equal parts of peat, leaf-mould, loam, and sand; make the soil somewhat firm about the bulbs, and withhold water till the plants appear; then give it very gradually. The pots should be plunged in ashes or cocoa-fibre in cold pits or frames, where they may remain till May, when the plants should either be planted out, or if intended for in-door decoration (*for which they are admirably adapted*), placed out of doors in a shady situation, the pots plunged in ashes or cocoa-fibre, and attended to with water till showing for bloom, when they should be placed in the conservatory, &c.

Culture out of Doors.—Plant for succession in December, January, February, and March. Should the soil be well drained, it will simply require deep digging and well working, adding as the work proceeds plenty of *thoroughly rotted* manure; should it be wet, or of an adhesive character, besides deep digging and well-working, it should be raised two or three inches above the general level. Plant the bulbs six inches deep and nine inches apart, surrounding each with an inch of river-sand or a handful of cocoa-fibre: when planted in February or March, three or four inches will be sufficiently deep. The first plantings should be protected by placing on the surface one or two inches of newly-dropped leaves or cocoa-fibre: the former must be removed in March or April. When the ground intended for these is occupied with spring-flowering bulbs, or is unusually wet and cold, first plant in pots, and when the time comes for turning the plants out, be careful not to disturb the roots. In dry seasons, it may be observed, much disappointment in the cultivation of these beautiful flowers would be avoided by mulching the plants with manure or cocoa-fibre.

Time of Purchasing the Seedlings of Ramosus.—The roots arrive from Holland early in November, and as soon after that time as possible they should be procured and kept in a cold dry place till wanted. Messrs. Barr and Sugden send out early-flowering gladioli, *Ramosus* section, for bedding, massing, &c.

	£.	s.	d.
500 in 30 splendid varieties	4	10	0
250 ,, ,, ...	2	10	0
100 ,, ,, ...	1	1	0
30 ,, ,, ...	0	8	6
500 in 15 splendid varieties	3	10	0
250 ,, ,, ...	2	0	0
100 ,, ,, ...	0	18	0
50 ,, ,, ...	0	9	6

Splendid mixed seedlings, 12*s.* 6*d.* per 100, 2*s.* per doz.

Gladioli, Autumn-flowering—Time of Planting.—On light well-drained soils the bulbs may be planted as early as the end of March; but on stiff soils, and such as are somewhat damp, the end of April or beginning of May would be early enough, unless required to be in flower early in July. To accomplish this, plant three bulbs in a 6- or 7-inch pot, and treat them as if they were intended to blossom without removal. In May, transfer them from the pots to the place in which they are intended to bloom, without disturbing the roots.

Time of Purchasing.—The bulbs arrive from France about the beginning of December, and should be procured as soon after that time as possible, and kept in a dry cool situation till wanted.

				£.	s.	d.
3 each of	50	splendid varieties	..	3	10	0
2 ,,	50	,,	..	2	10	0
1 ,,	50	,,	..	1	5	0
3 ,,	30	,,	..	1	10	0
2 ,,	30	,,	..	1	1	0
1 ,,	30	,,	..	0	12	6
1 ,,	20	,,	..	0	7	6
1 ,,	12	,,	3/6, 4/6, 6/, 7/6, or 9/			

Splendid seedlings of Gandavensis, the unnamed collection of an eminent gladioli-grower, per 100, 21*s.*; per dozen, 3*s.*

GLOXIN'IA (nat. ord. Gesnera'ceæ).

A superb genus of stove plants, producing, in great profusion, flowers of the richest and most beautiful colours; thrive best in sandy peat and loam. The varieties are

Gloxinia hybrida.
,, ,, erecta.
,, tubiflora,—white flowers in trusses, resembling the single tuberose; fragrance powerful and delicious, a single plant being sufficient to perfume a conservatory, 1 ft.

GODE'TIA (nat. ord. Onagra'ceæ).

This is the name given of late years to the purple-flowered kinds of Œnothera, or Evening Primrose.

GOOSEBERRIES.

Gooseberries bear on the young as well as on the two-year-old wood, generally upon small spurs rising along the sides of the branches. In autumn or winter, when digging between the bushes, sow fresh-slaked lime copiously over the whole ground, more particularly round the stems and about the roots, before forking it over. About the latter end of March repeat the operation, raking the ground afterwards. In a fortnight or three weeks this lining should be repeated, and, except under extreme circumstances, no future attacks from caterpillars need be apprehended. In pruning gooseberry-trees, for which January is a favourable season, keep the tree thin of branches; but let those left be trained to some regular shape, and never permitted to grow across each other, radiating in a cuplike form, so as to be six or eight inches apart at the extremities and hollow in the centre. Prune away all worn-out branches, retaining young shoots to supply their places, retaining also, where practicable, a terminal bud to each branch, while shortening stragglers. The same remarks apply to currant-trees. Young gooseberry-trees designed for standards should be pruned back to a clean stem for ten or twelve inches, retaining the best-placed shoots to form the head, and keeping these, as nearly as possible, of the same length and form.

In making new plantations, place the bushes eight feet apart each way, if in continuous rows; if into quarters, or to divide the ground into compartments, prune them up to a clean stem twelve or fourteen inches high; otherwise the foliage will impede the growth of the crops sown beneath them. Perhaps the best mode of growing gooseberries is as standards; in which case the bushes should be trained three feet high before they are suffered to form a head. According to the present system of training, the branches are often borne to the ground by the weight of the fruit, which is destroyed by being draggled on the soil and splashed by heavy rains.

GOOSEBERRY CATERPILLARS.

These pests have, of late years, become exceedingly prevalent, and in different parts of the country the gooseberry has been nearly destroyed by them. They come principally from a saw-fly, which lays its eggs in rows along the under-ribs of the leaves, and after having committed its ravage, falls to the ground, where it lives in the pupa state till the following season. The bushes should be carefully looked over once a week to watch the hatching of the eggs, when the infected leaves may be picked off. To prevent the fly from settling, the bushes should be dusted over with hellebore powder, or watered with a strong decoction of the Digitalis, or common foxglove. If the caterpillar has begun its ravages, the ground beneath the bush should be sprinkled with new lime, and a double-barrelled gun fired two or three times under it to shake the caterpillars down into it. The most effectual preventive, however, is to remove the top soil from under the bush during the winter time, and destroy the grubs in it by mixing it with salt or soot: the parings so mixed may be buried or entirely removed, and new soil placed round the roots instead of it. Layers of bark from the tan-yard, when used as a covering of the soil underneath the bushes, have been found very useful in destroying the insect in its chrysalis state. One of our very best practical gardeners, Mr. Ogle, at Erridge Castle, Kent, says, "In the autumn or winter, when digging between the bushes, sow the whole ground over with *fresh-slaked* lime, using a liberal supply of lime, more particularly round the stems and about the roots of the bushes, forking the ground over. About the middle or latter end of March repeat the application, more especially round the roots, and rake the ground in, repeating the operation in two or three weeks. Few caterpillars will survive this treatment."

GOURDS

All vegetables of this class, which produce an immense amount of food, may be profitably and easily cultivated by attending to the following directions:—The seed should be sown in April or May, in pots or pans of rich light soil, and raised in a warm frame. As soon as possible, the young plants should be potted off, and hardened in a cold frame for planting out in the end of May or early in June. Mr. James Cuthill tells us that marrows contain a rich sugary and farinaceous matter, and are a most excellent and nutricious article of diet when dressed in the following manner: —Cut the marrows into short pieces, take out all the pith and seeds, and boil them in plenty of water with a little salt. When well boiled, scrape out all the marrow, put it between two dishes, and squeeze out all the water; then mash it well, adding salt, pepper, and a little butter. It is then a dish fit for any table. The cultivation Mr. Cuthill recommends is to sow the seed about the first week in May in the open ground, in a warm corner, transplanted to moderately rich land. "I can grow," he adds, "twenty tons of the marrows to the acre easily; and when ripe, they can be stowed away anywhere, and will keep good for a very great length of time. In addition to their utility as a vegetable for the table, they form a most excellent and economical article when boiled for fattening pigs."

GRAFTING.

Gardening ingenuity has invented many kinds of grafting: we shall describe a few of these processes, in order to explain their principle. Select a suitable stock, whose height will be according to the purpose for which it is intended, also a graft, which should be from an early branch of the previous year's wood which has ripened under an August sun, so that the wood has been thoroughly constituted before the early frosts set in.

It should also be selected so that the graft is in the same state of vegetation with the intended stock. Where the texture of the wood is less advanced in the graft than in the stock, the latter intercepts the descent of the pulpy sap, and forms the bulging on the stem which is observable on so many trees; when the case is reversed, the swelling occurs in the branch above the graft; for the principle of the union is, that the pulp from the scion descends to the point of junction, where, being excluded by the ball of grafting-wax, which surrounds it, from the light and air, it forms woody fibre in place of the roots which it would have formed in the soil; in the mean while, the sap from the stock rises into the graft, where it is elaborated into pulp by the action of the leaves, and returns again, but in a more consistent state. It is necessary, therefore, where the graft selected is in a more advanced state of vegetation, to detach it from the parent stem, and bury it in the ground, under a north wall, until both are in a similar state: the graft will here remain stationary while the stock is advancing.

In gardening nomenclature, the term "stock," or "subject," is applied to the tree on which the operation is performed; that of "graft," and sometimes "scion," to the portion of the branch which is implanted in it.

Cleft- or Tongue-grafting.—In cleft- or tongue-grafting, the crown of the stock is cut across, and a longitudinal wedge-shaped slit, *c*, is made about four inches long, according to the size and vigour of the intended graft: this cleft is kept open by a wooden wedge until the scion is prepared. The scion is then selected, having a bud, *a*, at its summit; and the lower part of it is shaped with the knife so as to fit the slit in the stock. The double-tongue graft only differs from the first in having two grafts in place of one; and it is preferable, when the size of the stock permits of its use; the wound heals more quickly, and the chances of success are greater than in the single graft.

In placing the graft, it is to be observed that the top, whether single or double, should incline slightly inwards, as at *e*; thus leaving the lower extremity slightly projecting, as at *f*, in order that the inner bark of the

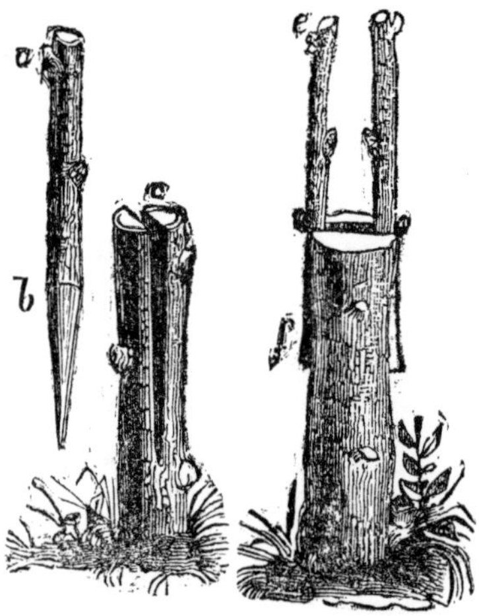

graft and stock may be in direct contact with each other. Finally, bind the whole, and cover it over, from the summit of the stock to the bottom of the cleft, with clay or grafting-paste.

Double Grafting.—In double grafting, where they both take, it is necessary to suppress the least vigorous as soon as the wound is completely closed, especially in the case of standard trees; otherwise the head gets formed of two parts completely estranged from each other. During the first twelve days after the operation, protect the head from the action of the air and the heat of the sun by some kind of shade. A square piece of paper, twisted into the shape of a bag, such as grocers use for small quantities of sugar, answers very well for this purpose, protecting it at the same time from the attacks of insects; and when they begin to grow, protect the graft from being disturbed by the wind, or by birds lighting on it, by attaching it to some fixed object. A perch formed of an osier rod, having both ends tied

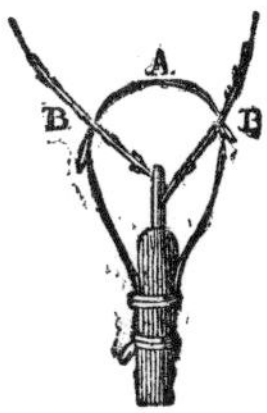

firmly to the stock, and having the young shoot attached to it, as in the engraving, will serve both purposes.

When the young scion begins to grow, it is necessary to suppress all buds which develop themselves on the stem, below it, beginning at the base, and upwards to one or two inches long.

The Bertemboise Graft.—A very neat mode of grafting, called by the French the "Bertemboise graft," is described and figured by M. Breuil. Cut the crown of the stock at a long bevel, leaving only about an inch at the top square, cutting out an angular piece to receive the graft, and operating in all respects as in the former instance. When the stock is not large enough to receive a graft on each side, this mode is preferred, as forming the neatest union, as well as the most rapid; for all the ascending sap is thus drawn to the summit of the bevel on which the graft is placed.

Theophrastes Graft.—A graft, honoured with the name of Theophrastes, is sometimes practised on trees having healthy roots, where it is desired to improve the fruit. Having cut the stem of the tree itself horizontally, or selected a single branch to be operated upon, about twenty inches from the principal stem, three vertical cuts are made in the bark, at equal distances from each other, about an inch long. Having selected three or more grafts, *a*, and shaped their lower extremities into a tongue somewhat like the mouth-

piece of a flageolet, with a neck or shoulder at the upper part, then introduce a graft under the bark of each vertical cut, raising the bark for that purpose with the spatula of the grafting-knife, and placing each graft in such a position that the inner bark of the graft is in immediate contact with the inner bark of the tree. When neatly arranged, bandage the whole, and cover with the grafting-paste.

Slit-grafting.—In place of the vertical cut through the whole of the stem, in this process a triangular cut is made in the side of the stock, as in the next engraving; the lower end of the graft is then cut so as to fit exactly into the gap made, so that the inner bark, or liber, meets in contact at all points: this done, it is covered with clay or grafting-paste, and bound up until amalgamation takes place.

A strong and efficient mode of grafting is represented in the second cut, next page. Make an elongated bevelled cut in the proposed stock from left to right; make another vertical wedge-shaped cut, three inches long, from left to right, leaving a narrow shoulder at the top on the left side, and terminating

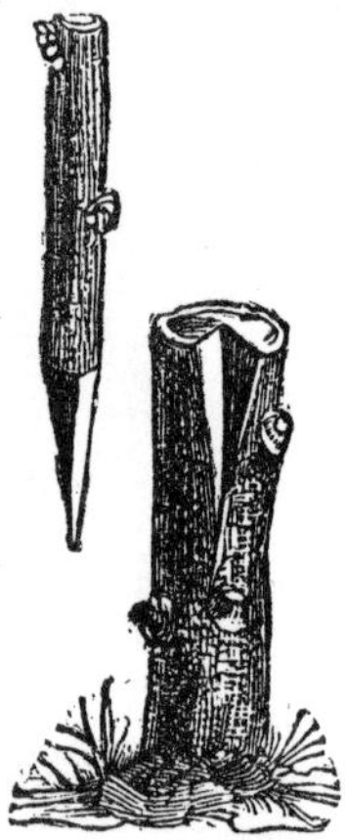

in the centre of the stock, so as to resemble that in the engraving. Take the intended graft, of the same diameter as the stock, and shape its lower extremity so as to fit into the cleft thus made; bind up in the usual manner,

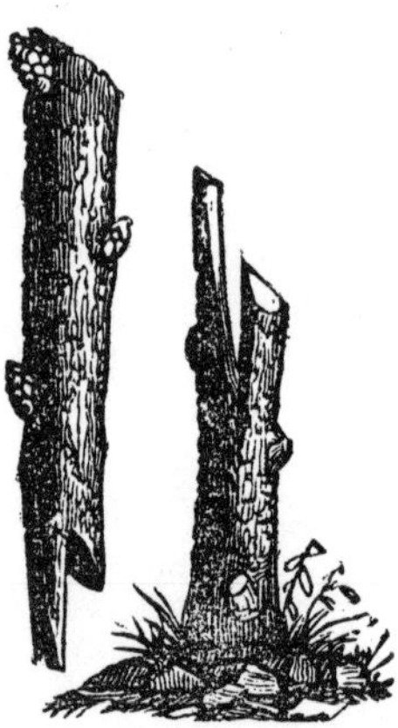

and cover the joint with grafting-paste. This forms a very strong and very useful graft in species which unite slowly.

Herbaceous Grafting, as initiated by Baron de Tschudy, consists in choosing branches still in active growth. Pines, walnut-trees, oaks, and other trees which are multiplied with difficulty by other processes, are easily produced by this one. The mode of operating differs slightly, according to the species. In the case of pines and resinous trees, when the terminal bud of the subject, *a*, has attained two-thirds of its growth, make an horizontal cut at *d*; then make a slit downwards to the point where it begins to lose its herbaceous character in the ligneous consistence of the tree; stripping the part of its leaves, and leaving only a bud or two at the top to attract the sap. The graft, *b*, is now prepared, having a cluster of young buds at its summit, and its lower extremity shaped to fit into the slit, where it is so placed that the upper part projects over the cut in the stock. It is now covered with grafting-clay and bound, beginning at the top, below the bunch of leaves left on the stock, so as to avoid disturbing the leaves, and working downwards. This done, break off, an inch or so from their axils, the branches *c c* of the

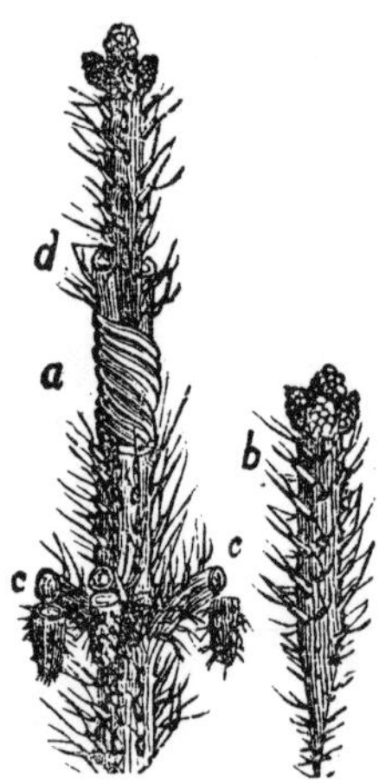

stock below the graft. When operating on delicate species, it may be desirable to envelop the graft in a covering of paper, to preserve it from

Grafting.

the over dry atmosphere or the heat of the sun, for ten or twelve days after the operation. Five or six weeks after grafting, the union will be complete, and the bandage may be removed, or at least relaxed; and when the suture is perfect, the leaves at *d* may be removed, otherwise they will originate buds and branches from the old tree.

In other species proceed as follows:—Towards the end of May, when the terminal bud of the tree is in a state of active vegetation, make an incision, crossing the insertion of the petiole of the third, fourth, or fifth leaf, as at *b*, penetrating half the diameter of the stem; the choice of the particular leaf depends upon its state of vegetation as compared with the proposed scion. If the axil of the leaf, *a*, is examined, it will be observed that it has three eyes, or *gemmæ*, the centre one being most developed: it is between the axis of the central eye, at *b*, and one of the lateral ones, that the oblique cut is

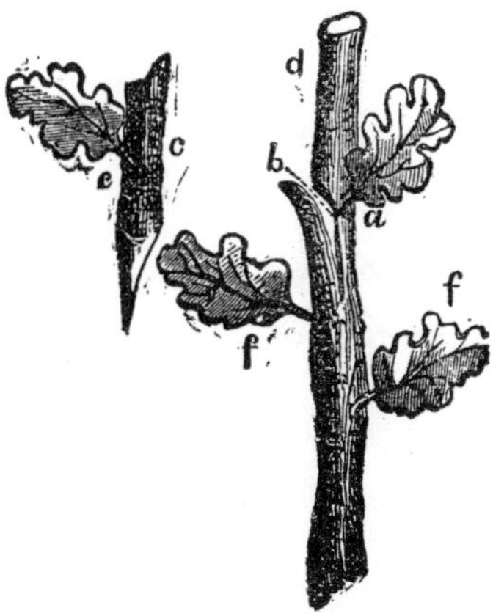

to be made, stopping in the centre about half an inch below the axil of the leaf. The graft, *c*, consists of the fragment of a branch of the same diameter as the stock, and in the same state of vegetation; it is cut to the same length as the prolongation of the stem, *d;* it is wedge-shaped, fitted to the slit into which it is inserted, bound, and covered with some grafting-paste. The leaf, *a*, is left on the stock to draw the sap upwards for the nourishment of the graft. The leaf of the graft, *e*, assists in the process by absorbing it to the profit of the young scion. The fifth day after the operation, the central eye, *a*, is suppressed; five days later, cut the disk of the leaf at *f*, reserving only the median nervure, rubbing off at the same time the eyes at the axil of these leaves, repeating the same suppression ten days later. At this time, also, that is twenty days after the operation, cut the disk of the terminal leaf, *a*: these several suppressions will force the sap progressively from the roots into the graft. Towards the thirtieth day the graft enters on its growth: at this time remove or relax the bandage, protecting it by a paper coronet from extreme drought and the sun.

Side-grafting. — In side-grafting it is not essential, as in other cases, to amputate the head of the stock, the graft being attached to the side, as its

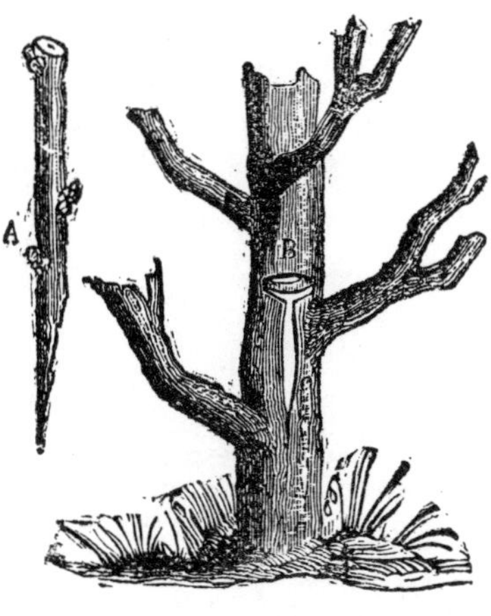

name indicates. Having made a cross-cut into the bark of a tree, as at B, and a vertical incision in the bark from its centre, thus marking a cut in the form of a T, each cut penetrating to the liber or inner bark; having also prepared the scion A by a longitudinal sloping cut of the same length, as B C, and raised the bark with the spatula of the grafting-knife, the graft is introduced, and the whole bandaged in the usual manner. This kind of graft is particularly useful in replacing branches on fruit-trees which are necessary to complete the symmetry of the tree for horizontal training.

Root-grafting.—In root-grafting the roots are operated on as the stems have hitherto been. Although it is by no means in common use, this mode of grafting is very convenient on some occasions. Having laid bare the roots

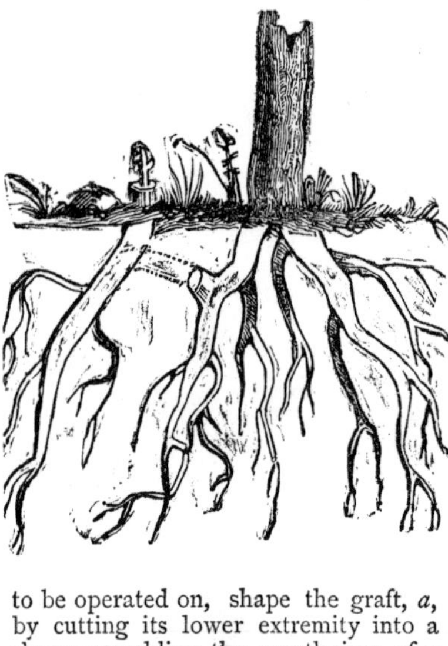

to be operated on, shape the graft, *a*, by cutting its lower extremity into a shape resembling the mouthpiece of a flageolet, with a tooth or shoulder, *d*, in its upper part. Cut the root across as at the dotted lines, and make a vertical cut in the separated part to receive the tongue of the scion, with an opening also corresponding to the tooth in the scion. Bring the scion and vertical cut together, so that all the parts cut meet and cover each other, meeting just below the last

bud on the scion. This root being already fixed in the soil, will serve to multiply plants which do not even belong to the same species.

Shield-grafting. — Shield-grafting is also usefully practised on the root in some cases even where the stock and scion are not of the same species. To discover the larger and best roots, trace them with the finger, and graft upon it in the spring, leaving the spot *a* (opposite) occupied by the cushion uncovered. In the following spring, when the graft has pushed forward, separate the root from the parent tree. We thus obtain a new individual.

Circle-grafting. — These grafts are composed of one or many eyes or buds, carried by a ring of bark including the liber. They are applied generally to the multiplication of certain large trees, —as the walnut, chestnut, oak, and mulberry. Towards the decline of autumn, as the sap returns to the roots, choose a mild day, free from rain. From the tree to be operated on, select a branch of the same size as the scion, having well-formed eyes. Upon this branch raise a ring of bark, *a*, without detaching the branch from the tree, making two circular incisions all round it, and making another vertical incision afterwards on one of its sides, and remove it gentl

Grafting.

Detach from the intended stock another ring of bark of the same size, and

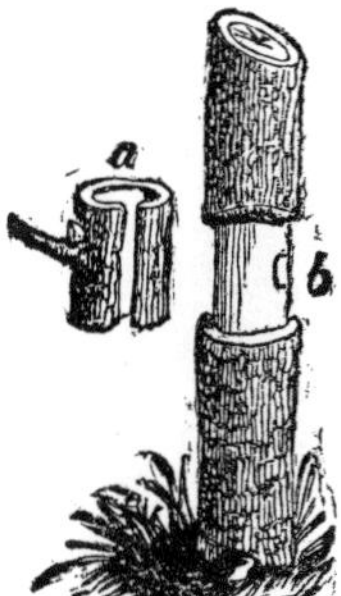

place the ring of the graft in its place at *b*, and the ring of the stock on the

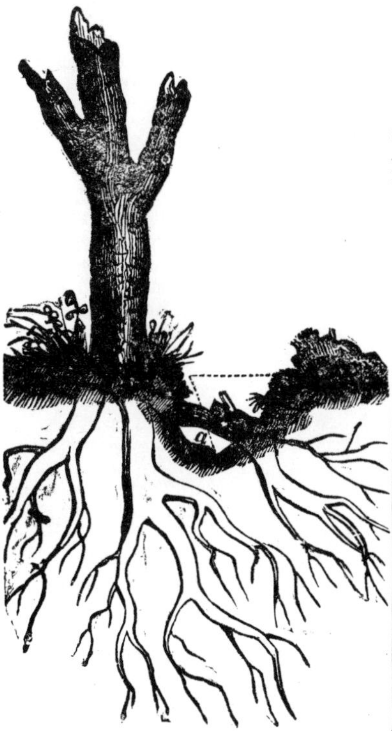

place whence the scion was taken; bind up and cover the joinings with grafting-paste. In the following spring, if the graft has taken, cut the head of the stock immediately above the rings, which will favour the development of the buds which they carry.

Another application of this mode is practised. When the spring sap is about to rise, cut the head from the tree to be operated on, and remove a ring *b* from the top *a*. Choose a tree of exactly the same size, on which the operation is to be performed; detach from it a ring furnished with two or three eyes, as *b*, and of the same length. Adjust this cylinder in the place of the ring detached, making it coincide exactly at its base with the old bark,

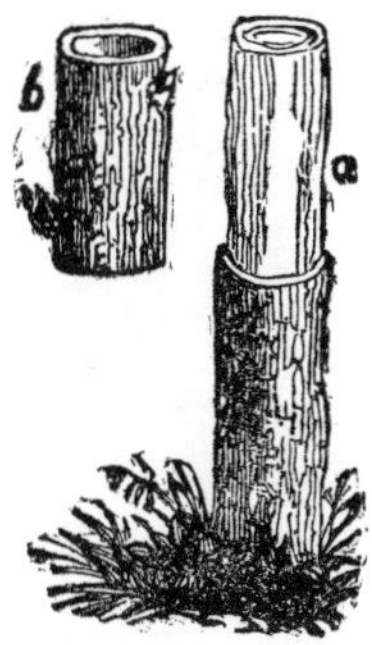

and cover the whole with grafting-paste. Of all these grafts this is the most solid, and least subject to be disturbed by the wind; but even this requires protection, so that it is not shaken in its place till complete suture has taken place.

Approach-grafting.—In approach-grafting, supposing the stock to be planted, and the scion in a pot, as in the engraving next page, make a longitudinal cut in the stock, of such extent as to reach the medullary canal at *a*, and leave a corresponding notch in the scion at *b*, but in such a way that in the scion it is less deep at the base, *b*; while, on the contrary, the cut in the stock is less deep at the summit, *c*. Bring the two cuts in contact, so that the liber, or inner skin, of each meets the other; then bind them. The consequence of these unequal incisions will be, that in

separating the head at the point *d* of the graft, and *a* in the stock, there will be less deformity left in the tree.

In the preceding examples of approach-grafting, the parts of the branch operated upon should be of the previous year's growth at least. It is sometimes desirable, however, to apply the principle to branches of the same year's growth. Accident may deprive a tree of the branches necessary to its symmetry, and a year's growth be saved by applying an herbaceous or green graft to supply the deficiency, if there happens to be a lower branch of the same tree available for the purpose. Let us suppose that a void exists at A A A, on an otherwise healthy peach-tree, and that side branches, or fruiting spurs, are required at these points to balance the tree and restore its sym-

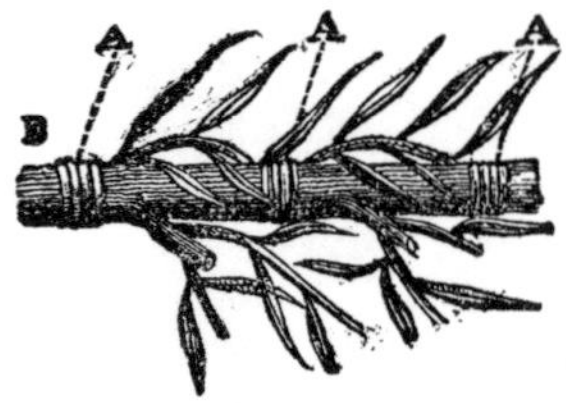

metry, and that a lower branch from B is available to supply them any time between June and August. Supposing the shoot to have attained sufficient length, an incision is made in the branch, about a quarter of an inch long, with a cross-cut at each extremity, deep enough to penetrate to the inner bark; the bark is raised from the wood on each side of the longitudinal cut by means of the spatula at the end of the budding-knife. A thin slice is now cut out of the shoot B, on the lower side, and opposite to a leaf-bud, corresponding in length with the incision on the branch. The parts thus laid bare are brought together, the lips of raised bark brought over the shoots, and the parts are again bound together. The process is continued as often as is deemed necessary, or the length of the shoots will permit, taking care that in each case a leaf-bud is left above the point of union, and that it is left uninjured by the ligature, but leaving eight or ten days between each operation.

In the following spring the union will be complete; but it is better not to separate the grafts till the second spring. At this time cut each shoot which has furnished the graft immediately below the ligature, and submit each of the new shoots to the usual training.

GRAFTING IMPLEMENTS.

The implements necessary for the operation are, a hand-saw, sometimes made with a folding blade, the peculiarity of which is, that the blade should be thin at the back, with very open teeth, A B; a grafting-knife, and a chisel and mallet bevelled on both sides, used where the graft is too large to be cut by the knife; also a supply of small quoins, or wedges of hard wood, to keep the slit open while the graft is preparing. The grafting-knife is furnished with a smooth spatula, of hard wood or bone, at its lower end. A bundle of coarse hemp, or worsted thread, or of willow bark which has been softened and rendered pliable by being soaked in water, and some composition which shall protect the graft from the atmosphere and from rain; these complete the appliances necessary in grafting.

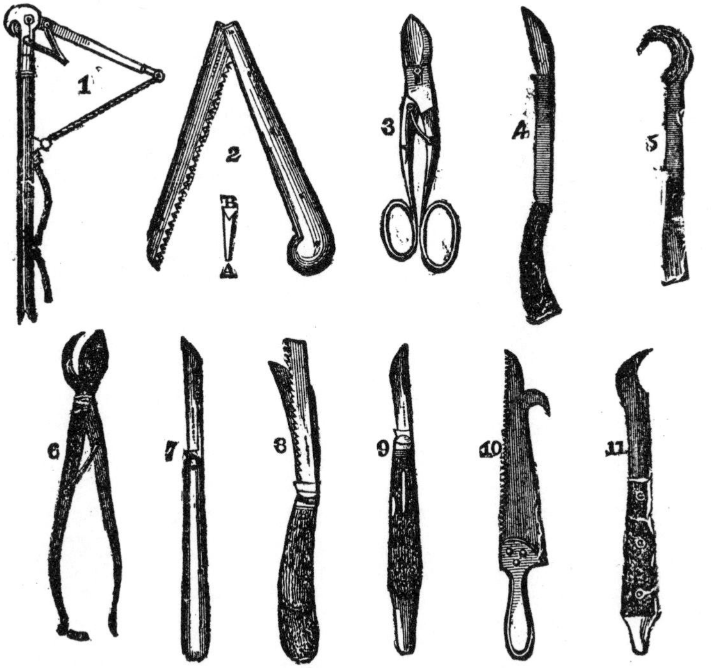

1. Averancators, six feet long. 2. Folding Pruning Hand-saw, with tooth, A B. 3. Bow-slide Pruning-shears. 4 and 5. Gooseberry Pruning-knife, straight and hooked blade. 6. Hand-sliding Pruning-shears. 7. Pruning-knife, with straight blade and smooth spatula. 8. Pruning-knife and Saw. 9. Budding-knife, buckhorn handle, with ivory spatula added. 10. Gentleman's improved Pruning-saw, with Billhook. 11. Grafting-knife, with strong curved blade serving as a chisel, with spatula added.

GRAFTING WAX (COBBETT'S).

Take of pitch and resin four parts each; beeswax two parts; tallow one part; melt and mix these ingredients, and use them for grafting when just warm.

GRAFTING WAX (FRENCH).

French gardeners use a paste composed of 28 parts black pitch, 28 parts Burgundy pitch, 16 parts yellow wax, 14 parts tallow, and 14 parts yellow ochre. This mixture is applied in a hot liquid state, but not so hot as to affect the tissues of the tree; it is laid over the graft in coatings by means of a brush, until sufficiently thick for the purpose.

GRASSES, ORNAMENTAL.

It is scarcely possible to over-estimate, for the adornment of the flower-garden and shrubberies, the decorative qualities of ornamental grasses: some are exceedingly graceful, others remarkably neat and compact in growth; there are some again wonderfully curious, while others are stately and majestic in appearance. The graceful and curious are best adapted for intermingling in the flower-borders, while the neat compact-growing kinds make beautiful edgings.

In large flower and shrubbery borders, select plantations, by the sides of rivulets, ravines, lakes, and on islands, the majestic-growing varieties relieve the monotony, and impart a charm of no ordinary character.

We therefore say to those who have not yet found a place for a collection of ornamental grasses, they are still without some of the most useful, attractive, and graceful of ornamental plants, whether for the purpose of gathering for summer and winter bouquets, or for imparting a light and graceful appearance to the borders.

That the plants may develop their true characters, thin out sufficiently to afford space for the growth of each, and this should be done as soon as the plants can be handled. All the varieties may be gathered and dried for winter decoration.

Collections suitable for flower-border decoration, 30 packets, 7*s*. 6*d*.; 20 ditto, 5*s*.; 15 ditto, 3*s*.
Ditto for edgings, 10 packets, 2*s*. 6*d*.; 6 ditto, 1*s*. 6*d*.
Ditto for shrubberies, &c., 30 packets, 7*s*. 6*d*.; 20 ditto, 5*s*.; 15 ditto, 3*s*.

GRATINGS.

Generally, it will be desirable to furnish gratings on the sides of walks for the removal of the surface-water; in no case, however, should these gratings communicate directly with the drains, as the sand soon chokes them up. They should consist of a well (C) formed

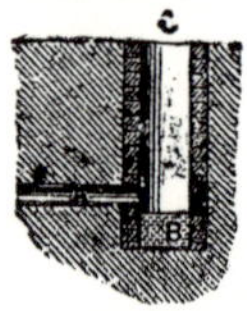

of brick, a foot or eighteen inches square, and of sufficient depth to leave a space (B) of one foot or eighteen inches below the level of the drain (A), for the deposition of sediment: this well cleared out occasionally, the drains will work for centuries.

GRAVEL WALKS.

Full instructions for the formation of these will be found under the term Walk: at present it is only necessary that we make some few remarks upon their management. Few things are more essential to a good garden than well-kept gravel walks. Leaves and all extraneous matter may be cleared away by frequent sweeping. Weeds also may be removed by hand-hoeing; care at the same time must be taken that the surface of the walk is hard and level, and for this constant rolling is desirable. When necessary, the colour may be refreshed by turning, and by the addition of a little fresh gravel; salt-and-water carefully used for destroying weeds will at the same time much improve the appearance of the gravel.

GREEN-FLY.

Fumigate with tobacco the plant infected, and syringe it well afterwards with clean water, or, if it is not possible to fumigate, wash the plant with strong tobacco-water, by means of a soft brush.

GREENHOUSES.

Glass structures of even the smallest kind would, a very few years ago, have been considered a piece of great extravagance for any but the affluent. We have lately, however, heard of the garden and greenhouse which paid the rent; and although we cannot promise our readers quite so desirable a result, we can promise them, if they will only debit the garden account with what strictly belongs to it, and give credit, according to the market value, for the luxuries as well as the necessaries of life they draw from them, they will find both garden and greenhouse prove not an expensive luxury, but a necessary adjunct, which need not be dispensed with on the score of economy; more especially, if either the master or mistress happens to have a taste for such employment, and does not disdain to undertake, with their own hands, some of the lighter portions of the labour so needful to keep all things in proper order.

In former times, greenhouses were not only costly to fit up, but inefficient when erected. The proper principle of their construction was not very well understood: heavy rafters, complicated sashes, at once costly and inefficient, encumbered many a fine garden, as well as gardens of smaller pretensions. To Mr. Fleming, the gardener at Trentham Hall, Sir Joseph Paxton, and some other well-known cultivators, the merit is due of breaking through the old system, and proving to the world that light inexpensive structures were not only cheaper, but actually better adapted to their intended purpose, than the old costly buildings.

GREENHOUSES, SMALL, TO FURNISH.

Among the thousands of villas and neat cottages which surround all our large towns and cities many have their small greenhouse or conservatory, and trim little garden, back and front, capable of growing a concentrated selection of the most choice plants on a small scale. It may be that the garden has to be planted with half-hardy plants. The greenhouse, however small, then comes in very useful for keeping a supply both for the garden in summer and the window and rooms during winter. A stock of geraniums, verbenas, petunias, lobelias, are struck in the months of July and August, and stored away for planting out the following season. After this is accomplished, a small collection of fuchsias will make the house lively; and as these are very easily cultivated, and may be stowed under the stage of the house during the winter, till the house is emptied in May, nothing is better for the purpose. The following sorts would give satisfaction:—

Dark.	*Light.*
Elegans.	Queen of Hanover.
Catherine Hayes.	Schiller.
Autocrat.	Fairest of the Fair.
Little Bo-peep.	Duchess of Lancaster.
Orlando.	Fair Oriana.
Excellent.	Clio.
Tristram Shandy.	England's Glory.
Crinoline.	Madame Sontag.
Big Ben.	Princess of Prussia.
Sir Colin Campbell.	Madame Corneilison.
	Mrs. Stury.

The three last have white corollæ, with red sepals, and make a pretty variety.

If it is desired merely to maintain a succession of plants in bloom during the year, it is advisable to select plants for the time in which they flower. Thus half a dozen azaleas, which flower in May; pelargoniums flowering in June; fuchsias in the three following months; then a few chrysanthemums, followed by *Primula sinensis* and heaths. A few dozen of bulbs will present a succession of flowers till May. By this simple process, which is easily managed, a continuous show of flowers can be obtained. Good plants for a small collection are—

Abutilon striatum, Venosum.
Acacia lophantha, Armata, Rotundifolia, Virgata.
Azaleas, — Indica alba, Model, Triumphans, Variegata, Halfurdiana.
Camellias,—Old white, Dunklaarii, Chandlerii, Imbricata, Genista racemosa, Alliance.
Clianthus magnificus.
Coronilla pentaphylla.
Corræa bicolor.
Daphne japonica.
Deutzia gracilis.
Diosma ambigua, Speciosa, Ericoides.
Epacris odorata alba, Hyacinthiflora, Impressa, and several other varieties.
Erica Bowieana, Cosma rubra, Gracilis, Hyemalis, Pulchella, Wilmorii.
Helichrysum proliferum.
Linum trigynum.
Metrosideros floribunda.
Myrtus communis tenerifolia.
Pimelea Hendersonii, Decussata.
Plumbago capensis.
Solanum crispum, Capricastrum.
Veronica Lindleyana.
Witrienia corymbosa.

A selection from such as these will give satisfaction. A few geraniums might be added; as—

Alba multiflora.
Gem of the West.
Madame Corbay.
Crimson King.
Multiflorum.
Viola.
Unique.

Also *Primula sinensis* and Cinerarias.

Calceolarias of the herbaceous kinds are well worth cultivating, and where grown in a small way, had best be sown in July, covering the seed-pots or pans with a piece of glass, and placing them in the shade. A few bulbous-rooted plants would be found very useful.—*Lilium album*, *punctatum*, and *rubrum; Oxalis tubiflora variabilis*, *Rosea-flava*, *Ixia aurantica*, *Lachenalia tricolor*, *Cyclamen coum*, *Persicum*, *Europæum*, are all very attractive in their season, giving them a season of dry rest soon after the bloom is over.

A few useful chrysanthemums for autumn-flowering might be named:—

Large Varieties.

Plutus.
Racine.
Alfred Salter.
Madame Lebois.
Mrs. Holborn.
Prince Albert.
Madame Cameron.
Annie Salter, &c.

Greenhouses, Small, to Furnish.

Pompones.

Andromeda.
Cedo nulli.
General Canrobert.
St. Thais.
Duruplet.
Adonis.
La Rousse.
Solomon.
Dr. Bois Duval.
Drin-drin.
Bob.
Mrs. Dix, &c.

These may be struck any time from November to June, or even later, and may be had of all sizes. Useful climbers for a small greenhouse are:—

Passiflora cærulea.
Ecremocarpus scaber.
Hibbertia volubilis.
Solanum jasminoides.

Maurandia Barclayana might be trained up the back or pillars. It is necessary to make a proper bed or border of earth for these to grow in.

Plant-culture is not the only use to which a small greenhouse may be put: the practice is not uncommon to grow fruit in them. For this purpose, small fruit-trees are grown in pots; the roots being confined, they are not liable to run to wood; but keep within bounds for the more certain production of flowers and fruit. Any one who can cultivate flowering-plants may grow fruit-trees in pots; the only points being to keep them well supplied with water while in a growing state, and to ripen the wood well in the autumn. A long list of fruit-trees suitable for the purpose might be named; but the following may serve as a guide. They are usually worked on quince or paradise stocks, which, in a great measure, serves to keep them within proper limits as to size:—

APPLES. — Braddick's Nonpareil, Cellini, Golden Pippin, Orange Pippin, New-town Pippin.
PEARS.—Beaurré, Hardy, Marie-Louise, Bon Chrétien, Winter Nelis.
PLUMS.—Victoria, Green-gage, Purple-gage, Topaz.
CHERRIES. — Bigarreau, Elton, May-duke, Morello.
PEACHES.—Noblesse, Royal George, Crawfurd's Early.
NECTARINES.—Impératrice, Newington Early, Stanwick.

GUERNSEY LILIES.

Without hesitation, we say to the floral amateur, if you have not yet seen the Guernsey Lily, you have a great treat in store. The flower is brilliant scarlet, with the appearance of being spangled with gold-dust when the sun's rays are upon it.

The bulbs of these lilies arrive from Guernsey early in September, with the flower-bud ready to expand, so that by the end of the month they are in full bloom. Orders should therefore be given early for them, as they are too advanced to travel safely when ordered late in September.

Culture.—Plant in moss, cocoa-fibre, or water, in any ornamental vase, &c., and they will bloom as well as if planted in the richest compost.

Guernsey Lily (Nerine sarniensis), 5*s.* per doz., or 6*d.* each.

GUMMING.

To get rid of gumming in fruit-trees, scrape the gum clear away, wash well the place where it has accumulated, and stop it with a compost of horse-dung, clay, and tar.

GUNNE'RA (nat. ord. Urtica'ceæ).

An ornamental foliage plant, with leaves of an immense size, particularly valuable for margins of lakes, islands, shrubberies, and pleasure-grounds; succeeds best in a rich loamy soil, and requires a slight winter protection. It is a half-hardy perennial.

Gunnera scabra,—flowers very remarkable.

HABROTHAM'NUS (nat. ord. Solana'ceæ).

Exceedingly handsome greenhouse evergreen shrubs, with bunches of brilliant-coloured flowers of a waxy appearance, especially useful for the winter and spring decoration of the conservatory or drawing-room; they may also be grown against a south wall in warm localities, with winter protection: succeed best in peat and loam. The varieties are,—

H. aurantiacus,—orange-yellow, 8 ft., from Mexico.
H. Bondouxii,—red, 5 ft.
H. elegans,—carmine, 6 ft.
H. fascicularis,—bright-crimson, 5 ft.
H. Hugeli,—rich claret, handsome, 5 ft.
H. Lutto de Comte de Rossi,—red, shaded violet, and tipped with white, 5 ft.
H. scaber.
H. zephyrinus,—shaded red, 5 ft., from Mexico.

HARMONY OF COLOUR.

To have a well-formed and well-filled garden is not enough,—it must also be nicely arranged as to colour; and this latter is even of much more importance than the former. It is of great importance that the outline of the beds and their relation to each other should be good; but it is of much greater importance that the colours with which they are filled should either harmonize or contrast well with each other.

The whole principle of effective grouping is based upon the fact, that all colours are more or less beautiful when placed in a certain relationship to other colours. Flowers are very much influenced by their neighbours. It is not good for them to be alone; but infinitely better to be alone than in bad company. All colours are strengthened and improved by harmonious contrast and congruous blending together. Certain flowers, when placed contiguously, appear to intensify each other's depth; others, equally beautiful in themselves, lessen or destroy each other's beauty when placed in juxtaposition. Hence has arisen the necessity of blending and arranging colours upon some generally-received philosophic principle.

HEARTSEASE.

The common *Viola lutea*, with *Viola grandiflora* and *Viola amœna*, are the joint parents of the many beautiful flowers known to us in these days under the general name of Heartsease or Pansies. The history of their cultivation is this :—In the year 1812 there was living at Walton-on-Thames the Lady Mary Bennett, daughter of the Earl of Tankerville. The common heartsease was her favourite flower, and a large space in her garden was devoted to the growth of it. Her gardener, Mr. Richardson, with praiseworthy assiduity, selected the best seed each year, and was pleased to find that he could thus obtain some remarkably good varieties. These seedlings were shown by Mr. Richardson to other florists, who became interested in his experiments, and in a few years the culture of the Heartsease became popular; it soon took rank among florists' flowers. Heartsease require little attention during the autumn months; indeed, those not intended for propagation may be dug up as soon as flowering is over. The choicer varieties must be taken care of, in order that their roots may be divided, or cuttings taken from them in April or May; for it is only by such an annual renewal that degeneration can be prevented.

About the first week in October is a good time to make a selection of plants for potting. These should be vigorous, healthy plants. The bed for their reception may be prepared by digging out the soil for about 18 inches, and filling it up, after providing proper drainage, with compost properly mixed: a better plan is to make a raised bed for the purpose. This may be done by placing a row of bricks, 18 inches high and four feet wide, or wood, supported by stakes at each end, of the same height, and of a length suited to the number of plants required. This bed should be filled with compost, consisting of well-decomposed turfy mould, leaf-mould, and thoroughly-decomposed cow-dung; or, failing that, stable-manure, in the proportions of a bushel and a half of the first to half a bushel each of the two latter: where the loam is stiff, a little well-washed river-sand should be added; where it is light and sandy, equal parts of earth should be added.

Set the plants in rows 12 inches apart, and protect them from frost, which is easily done in the raised bed: occasional examination for their great enemy the wire-worm, and the removal of dead leaves, is all the care they require during winter; in the spring, copious watering, and in summer, mulching, to prevent radiation. The plants may either remain to bloom in the bed, or be used for bedding-out purposes.

HEATHS.

Under the term Erica will be found an account of the best varieties of greenhouse heaths. Our remarks now will be confined to the hardy sorts. No collection of shrubs, and no garden, should be considered complete without an assemblage of hardy heaths. They flower chiefly at the end of summer and during the autumn; the species Carnea, however, blooms early in the spring. For beauty of habit, delicacy of tint, sweetness of perfume, usefulness and durability of bloom, they have few rivals. They are also cheap. Good strong bushy plants, of many varieties, can be supplied by most of our leading American nurserymen at less than a shilling apiece in hundreds. In many parts of the country several good sorts can be collected from the hills for nothing. They can also be increased by cuttings, layers, and seed. The one great drawback to their culture is, that generally they must have peat-earth to bring them to perfection, and even to maintain them in health. Carnea, and several other varieties, do very well in a mixture of loam and leaf-mould. As a rule, however, all thrive best in a hard, sandy, gritty peat. Bog-peat is hardly fit for their growth, unless it is liberally mixed with sharp sand and the *débris* of freestone rocks. Dryness and hardness of soil seem to be essential to their maintenance in health. No one can have traversed heath-clad mountains without being convinced of this. From six inches to a foot of soil is more than most of them find in their natural habitats. It must be borne in mind, however, that in such situations the whole surface is covered with plants; consequently the evaporation of moisture from the soil is checked by the leaves and branches. For their culture in the garden, from 18 inches to two feet of such soil, resting on a dry bottom, would be desirable. Beds or groups of hardy heaths make a charming display. Such groups harmonize well with the different fir-trees. Nothing can exceed their beauty, congruity, and adaptability, as furnishings for rock-work. Peat-earth could easily be placed among the crevices, and the heaths introduced there. They thrive admirably in such situations, and contrast well with ferns and other rock plants.

The following are the varieties most generally cultivated :—

Erica australis.
,, cinerea alba.
,, ,, rosea.
,, ,, rubra.
,, herbacea.
,, ,, carnea.
,, lanceolata.
,, mediterranea.
,, ,, hibernica.
,, Mackaiana.
,, stricta.
,, Tetralix rubra.
,, ,, alba.
,, vagrans carnea.
,, vulgaris alba.
,, ,, ,, minor.
,, ,, coccinea.
,, ,, decumbens.
,, ,, Hammondii.
,, ,, pumila.
,, ,, pygmæa.
,, ,, variegata.
,, ,, rigida.
,, ,, variabilis.

HEDGES.

Hedges, if properly managed, undoubtedly constitute the cheapest and most lasting, as well as the most ornamental, of all the artificial divisions of land. Few persons will object to the opinion, that the country where fields are divided by the common white thorn or may, presents a far more agreeable appearance at all seasons of the year, and especially during spring, when the thorns are in blossom, than those parts where dwarf stone walls are made to answer the same purpose. The White Thorn, however, though most commonly employed, is not the only plant that can be made use of for separating one piece of ground from another. Though for fields it is, perhaps, as useful as any, still, for park and garden purposes, there are many other plants which may be advantageously employed. The different kinds of thorn certainly embrace all the constituents of a good hedge : they are of easy culture, quick growth, and capable of being trained in any direction; they branch out and thicken under pruning, and are not over particular as to soil; but there are many other plants far more ornamental which will fulfil all these conditions equally well. However, there is one objection to the general introduction of most of these, at any rate up to the present time ; and this is the price, a very great objection, most people will say ; still, it is one that need not exist, and one, we fondly hope, that is rapidly being got rid of. Hollies, and several other evergreens, can be raised at almost as small an expense as thorns. Upon every large estate the woodman should have his seed-bed of hollies, evergreen oaks, and other things that can be used for hedge purposes. We shall presently have to mention several sorts of evergreens and deciduous shrubs from which good hedges can be made, and if these were in demand for the purpose, there is little doubt that a supply would soon follow, for nurserymen would find it to their interest to grow them in large quantities and sell them at greatly reduced rates. We are happy to find that there is a decided tendency to this result, for white thorns for hedges have remained for years at about the same price, while hollies and other evergreens are becoming cheaper every year.

Few things have a better appearance than a well-kept holly hedge. The best variety for the purpose is *Ilex Aquifolium*, the common holly. In forming a holly hedge, the ground should be prepared by trenching, and, if the soil be poor and sandy, it will be well to let it have a dressing of manure. The best plants are those of three years' growth, which have had one shift from the seed-bed. They should be taken up carefully with as much soil on the roots as possible, and planted soon after midsummer, if possible, during the rains of July. A broad trench should be dug, capable of receiving the plants, which should be placed in it singly, with their roots well spread out. If the weather be dry at the time, the best plan is to water the bottom of the trench and to give no water afterward, unless a severe drought should set in. The next season, if they be well rooted, the young plants may be moderately pruned with the knife, after which they will branch out and form themselves into a good hedge.

Next to holly for forming a compact and durable hedge is the Yew. It bears close clipping, takes up but little space, and is a good shelter throughout the year. The yew, however, must only be used for garden purposes, or, at any rate, in places where cattle can be kept from it, for horses and all cattle are very fond of the yew, and will eat greedily the young spring leaves, though they are very injurious, and often fatal, to them. The same objection attaches to two other plants, which make very useful and ornamental hedges—the Box and the Privet. Both these should be kept out of the way of cattle. In gardens and pleasure-grounds they may be used with very good effect, for they bear clipping almost better than anything else, and are very neat and compact. The privet mixes well with the thorn, where greater strength is required than can be had by using privet alone.

Those persons who have travelled in Holland and Belgium have no doubt noticed the neat manner in which small enclosures of land are separated from each other by their thrifty and industrious owners. The hedges are trained along stakes and rods placed for the purpose, and to these, the plants of which they are composed are tied with pieces of osier. In this way every slender branch is laid in, and, as they are made to cross each other frequently, a regular network is formed. These hedges, when in leaf, are very close and tight, they take up very little room, and form scarcely any harbour for small birds. It has often occurred to us that in this way many of our ornamental shrubs might be trained to form hedges; the *Pyrus japonica*, for instance, which is close, quick-growing, and bears a most beautiful flower. This plant is as hardy as any native British plant, and very easily propagated. There can be no doubt that if young plants were wanted for ornamental garden hedges, they would soon be produced at a very reasonable rate.

The Cotoneaster, again, may be employed for the same purpose and in the same way. Cuttings of cotoneaster taken in August and put into the shade, will be rooted well enough for planting out next spring. When planted, they should be about one foot or a foot and a half apart, and have a trellis of stakes or hazel rods to support them. This hedge will require, at first, a good deal of attention in training and entwining the branches; but when three or four feet high, it may be clipped and kept in shape.

The different Veronicas also make firm hedges, and are very handsome when in flower. Strong bushes may be planted three feet apart and trained to stretched wires, which, in this case, are better than stakes. We have seen in Guernsey the Purple Hydrangea forming a hedge to a grass field, and nothing could be more beautiful. Both this and the Veronica, however, are not sufficiently hardy to admit of their being used except in the extreme south. Such, however, is not the case with the Aucuba, which is so hardy that we imagine it might be used in most parts of England. We have never seen it planted as a hedge, but it is of easy culture, and as we have raised a large number of strong cuttings, we are about to make the experiment: we shall train it to stretched wire.

An American writer recommends the common Barberry, *Berberis vulgaris*, as a hedge-plant. "A hedge-plant," he says, "to become popular, must be perfectly hardy and easy to propagate. It should also be vigorous enough to grow well in ordinary soil without manure. It should be thorny to keep cattle off, and low enough to require little or no pruning. The common barberry combines these qualities better than any plant that I am acquainted with. It is remarkably hardy, thriving well in a great variety of soils, and is said to live for centuries. It has a shrubby habit, growing from six to ten feet in height, yellowish thorny wood, leaves in rosettes, yellow flowers on drooping racemes, and scarlet oblong berries, very acid, but making delicious preserves. We have a barberry hedge," he continues, "in our grounds at Wallingford, Connecticut, twenty-four rods long, and nine years old, from the seed. Two rows of plants were set, the rows one foot apart and the plants one foot apart in the rows, and set alternately to break joints. This hedge has been clipped a little two or three times to keep it even, and is now six or seven feet high, with a firm, compact base, perfectly impervious to the smaller animals, and stout enough to turn ordinary farm stock. An important item, as regards this plant, is its habit of sending up suckers from the bottom, by which, in a few years, it comes to have a base six to twelve inches in diameter."

We have no doubt that many conifers would make excellent hedges, all that is required being that they should be supplied at a suitable price. At present they are a great deal too dear to be used for such purposes, except, perhaps, on a very small scale. But as most, even of the choicest varieties, grow very freely from cuttings as well as from seed, there is no question that a great reduction could and would be made if the demand were such as to warrant a more extensive culture. We know that the common Scotch fir is used, with very good effect, both as a fence and shelter along many of our lines of railroad. When headed down, this fir throws out strong laterals, which, interlacing each other, make a very substantial and lasting hedge. The young plants should be set closely, and as they grow up, any weak places can easily be stopped by rails crossing the stems. Like all other hedges, these require occasional training and attention.

In forming any hedge, it is of course necessary to take into consideration the aspect, the quality of the soil, and all other particulars that conduce to the healthy state of vegetable life. The skill of the gardener is hardly anywhere more discernible than in the exercise of that statesmanlike quality which consists of putting the right thing in the right place. All plants will not suit all climates, all situations, and all soils. It is wise, therefore, to consider that though there are many ornamental plants and shrubs that will make good hedges, it is not all of these that may choose to flourish where we wish our hedge to grow. As a general rule, the knife may be used unsparingly in all things suitable for hedges, and the hedge itself will be greatly improved by its use. All hedges, but especially those that bear the shears or clippers, should be cut upwards to a narrow ridge, for, by this means, the lower part not being overshadowed by the upper, will be kept thick, and the hedge will last sound much longer. After they have been planted several years, hedges of most materials will require to be cut down, the soil renovated, and, perhaps, new plants introduced. This necessity, however, is very generally the result of neglect in early years, for where proper care has been bestowed and annual pruning given, hedges will last as long as brick walls.

HELIAN'THUS (nat. ord. Compos'itæ). Hardy Annuals.

A genus of plants, known as Sunflowers, remarkable for their stately growth and the brilliancy and size of their noble flowers; they are eminently adapted for dispersing in shrubbery borders. Round the margins of lakes, ponds, and wherever plants of this character are required, this genus will be found extremely effective; some of the varieties, as *H. Californicus* and *H. Californicus striatiflorus*, are particularly adapted for mixed flower-borders and large beds in conspicuous situations. They grow freely in any rich soil.

HELICHRY'SUM (nat. ord. Compos'itæ). **Hardy Annuals from N. Holland.**

Very beautiful everlastings; they are exceedingly effective in mixed flower-borders. The flowers, if cut when young, make pretty winter bouquets. *H. compositum maximum*, fl. pl., and *nanum* make valuable pot plants for in-door decoration. A collection of these was exhibited at the 1862 autumn flower-show of the Royal Horticultural Society, and was greatly admired. Succeed in any rich garden soil.

HELIOTRO'PIUM (nat. ord. Boragina'ceæ). **Half-hardy Perennials.**

Profuse-flowering and deliciously fragrant plants, valuable for bedding, ribboning, rustic baskets, and pot-culture; seeds sown in spring make fine plants for summer aud autumn decoration; succeed in light rich soil. The best plants are obtained from cuttings in the same way as verbenas and bedding calceolarias. All the heliotropes are very sensitive of frost.

HERBACEOUS PLANTS.

The modern bedding system has well-nigh banished herbaceous plants from our gardens: nevertheless many of them are very beautiful, and a collection containing Phloxes, Asters, Campanula, Delphinium, Aconitum, Pentstemon, Helleborus, Aquilegia, Cheiranthus, Gentiana, Iberis, Lathyrus, Lupinus, Monardia, Pæonia, Potentilla, Primula, Salvia, Saxifrage, Sedum, Silene, Spiræa, Iris, Statice, Chelone, Lychnis, Alyssum, Acanthus, Fraxinella, Achillea, Orobus, Yucca, Scabiosa, Œnothera, Dianthus, Dielytra, Veronicas, Myosotis, Sachys, &c. &c., arranged according to their height, colour, and time of flowering, and intermixed with bulbous-rooted plants, such as the Crocus, Narcissus, Hyacinths, Cyclamen, Oxalis, Tulips, Ornithogalum, Scilla, Fritillaria, Lilium, Cypripedium, Gladiolus, Allium, Anemone, Ranunculus, Galanthus, Tritonia, Orchis, Colchicum, Pancratum, and Tigridia, make a very fine display.

Most herbaceous plants are easily increased, by dividing the roots, by offsets, by cuttings from the side-shoots or roots, and by seeds. Many of them, from their rapid growth, require taking up and dividing every second year. To insure good flowers, a few strong stems of such plants as Phloxes, Asters, &c., must be secured, in preference to a multiplicity of smaller ones. Consequently, they require frequent and severe subdividing; the early months of the year, up to April, being the best period for performing this operation. Others, again, such as Gentians, Iberis, Alyssums, Achilleas, and similar flowering plants, thrive best without being often disturbed, and must be increased by small-rooted offsets. These should be planted in the reserve garden for the summer, and transferred to their flowering quarters next year. Double rockets, scarlet lychnis, hollyhocks, and other double-flowering plants, are often increased by cuttings. These can generally be obtained either by thinning the young shoots in the spring, or by securing all that appear at the bottom of the flowering-stems in the autumn. Whenever taken, they should be inserted in sandy soil, covered with a hand- or bell-glass, and receive a gentle warmth until rooted. If in the spring, they will of course be transferred to the reserve garden as soon as the rooting and gradual hardening processes are completed. If in the autumn, they will be safer under shelter until the end of April. In either case, with liberal treatment, they may flower the following summer. To induce autumn-struck cuttings to do this, however, they must be potted off in rich soil as soon as rooted, shifted into separate pots, and receive the stimulus of a genial atmosphere and shelter from the weather. All the mints, galiums, and other plants with running or creeping roots, are so easily and obviously increased as to require no instructions.

All single-flowering herbaceous plants may be increased readily by seed. This may either be sown as soon as ripe, or after September in pots. If sown in early spring, on beds of light soil, and the plants carefully transplanted two or three times during the summer, they may be transferred to their blooming quarters in November: if they have been properly treated, they will flower profusely the following season.

HERBARIUM.

Plants intended for the herbarium should be gathered in flower, and when small, they should be taken with the root. The plants, in this state, are placed between leaves of paper prepared for the purpose, and between two boards, or under one, from which they are not removed until they have become perfectly flat. Where there are conveniences for so doing, the packet may, with great advantage, be placed in an oven. When dry, change the paper. Some plants, as orchids and bulbs, will sometimes vegetate for months in the herbarium after they have been placed there. If plunged into boiling water for a minute, and immediately afterwards placed between paper, their drying will be more rapid. If the plants are unknown or new, indicate their popular names, the height at which they were procured, and their habit; also their size, as well as their odour.

In order to be prepared for collecting, provide some sheets of paper of a suitable size (16 inches by 12 is a good size) and several boards of the same proportion. These should be formed of two thin boards glued together, the grain of the one transverse to the other. These may be connected together by means of straps, so as to communicate considerable pressure. A large book of blotting-paper between two other similar planks will complete this temporary herbarium.

Insects are the bane of all collections; and great care is required in order to preserve the plants that have been collected. Sir James Smith used a wash composed of corrosive sublimate two drachms, spirits of wine, in which a small piece of camphor was dissolved, one pint. This wash should be lightly applied, so that all the raphidès of the flowers, and the fleshy parts of the plant, are saturated with it.

Beautiful specimens are prepared by an apparatus to which the name of M. Le Coq, professor of natural history at Clermont-Ferrand, has been given. This apparatus consists of two open covers made of strong iron-wire network, having an iron frame round them, in which the plants are placed between thick blotting-paper. After they have been kept under pressure for a few hours, the covers are compressed by means of straps; and the open network of the frame allows the moisture to escape freely while the plants are gradually dried.

HERB-GARDEN.

The *olitory*, or herb-garden, is a part of horticulture somewhat neglected, and yet the culture and curing of simples was formerly a part of a lady's education. All the sweet herbs are pretty, and a strip of ground halfway between the kitchen and the flower-garden would keep them more immediately under the eye of the mistress. This would probably recover, for our soups and salads, some of the neglected tarragons, French sorrel, purslain, chervil, dill, and clary, which are only found now in the pages of the old herbals. Laid out after a simple geometric design, the herb-garden might be rather ornamental than otherwise. Most of the herbs are propagated by slips in the autumn. *Basil*, *burnet*, and other herbs, require to be sown early in spring, on slight hotbeds of about two feet in depth; but many cultivators leave them later, and sow in the open ground. Thyme, marjoram, savory and hyssop, chervil, and coriander, may be sown in dry mild weather, to be transplanted afterwards. Sow in shallow drills about half an inch deep and eight or nine inches apart, and cover in evenly with the soil. *Mint* may be propagated by separating the roots, and planting them in drills drawn with a hoe six inches asunder, covering them with an inch of earth, and raking smooth. They will quickly take root, and grow freely for use in the summer. This method may be applied to the several sorts of spearmint, peppermint, and orange mint.

The whole family of borage, burnet, clary, marigolds, orach-root, carduus, dill, fennel, buglos, sorrel, and angelica, may be sown about the middle of March, when the weather is open. Sow them moderately thin in drills or beds (each sort separate), in good light soil; if in drills, six inches apart; some of the plants may remain where planted, after a thinning for early use; others may be planted out in the summer.

HIBIS'CUS (nat. ord. Malva'ceæ).

Beautiful and showy plants. Whether the hardy sorts be planted in mixed or shrubbery borders, or the more tender varieties be grown for in-door decoration, they are all alike characterized by the size and varied colours of their flowers.

Hibiscus Africanus,—cream-colour, rich brown centre, hardy annual, $1\frac{1}{2}$ ft.
Hibiscus ochroleucus grandiflorus, — yellow shaded rose, greenhouse shrub, 2 ft., from Africa.
Hibiscus pedunculatus,—rosy pink; beautiful; greenhouse shrub, 3 ft., from the Cape.
Hibiscus puniceus,—dazzling scarlet, shaded purple, enormous size, blooming profusely during autumn and winter; greenhouse shrub, 4 ft.
Hibiscus roseus pallidus grandiflorus,—pale pink, 3 ft.; greenhouse shrub.
Hibiscus splendidus, — carmine, 3 ft., half-hardy perennial.

HINTS ON SOWING SEEDS.

There are two points in connection with seed-sowing which are of paramount importance to the success and vigour of germination, and the regularity, strength, and luxuriance of the crop, besides that of having good and perfect seed. These are the proper mechanical condition of the soil, and the regular and uniform depth at which the seed is sown. The presence of air, moisture, and a certain degree of warmth, is essential to the germination of seeds. In the absence of these agents, the process of germination will not go on. The soil is the medium by which a supply of air, moisture, and warmth is kept up; but, unless the soil be in a proper condition, it cannot supply these. If it be very dry, it contains too much air and too little moisture. The proper condition of the soil is when it is neither very dry nor very wet; it is then moist, but not wet; it has the appearance of having been watered, and is easily crumbled to pieces in the hand, with its particles adhering together.

A state of too much dryness seldom occurs in this country; but the presence of too much water is not uncommon; it is, however, remedied by drainage. The grand point is to get the soil thoroughly well pulverized, by means of which, with proper drainage, it will be in a condition favourable to germination of seeds. Temperature exercises a powerful influence over the time required for germination; and, within certain limits, the higher the temperature is, the more rapidly does germination go on. The soil receives its heat through the medium of the air; consequently the surface-soil is more quickly heated than that lower down. Whenever the air is warmer than the soil, the surface will be warmer than that below; when, on the other hand, the air is cooler, the surface will, by contact, cool much more rapidly than that below the surface. From this it follows, the more rapid germination will occur at about one inch below the surface, to which depth the heat will soon penetrate, and which, nevertheless, will not be so readily cooled during the night. Seeds on the surface will generally grow most rapidly, and the germination of others will occupy more time as the distance from the surface is increased. It is owing to this fact that seeds too deeply sown do not grow at all, the temperature not being sufficiently elevated, and the supply of air being too limited to set the chemical process at work, which is essential to germination.

HOLLYHOCK.

There is no finer ornament of the autumnal flower-garden that the Hollyhock: its noble tapering spike-like stem and rich rosettes of flowers clustering round the footstalks of the leaves, its pannacled head and luxuriant massive leaves, render it the most effective occupant of a gap in the shrubbery, or in the back row of an herbaceous border. In rows in the flower-garden, or in beds by themselves, their variety of colour renders them also most attractive objects. Hollyhocks may be propagated by seed and by cuttings.

The seed of the Hollyhock should be gathered only from the most perfect plants, in which the flowers have been round, the florets thick and smooth on the edge, the colour dense and decided, and the flowers close to each other on the stem. About the middle of March, or not later than the first week in April, the seed-bed should be prepared, four feet wide, with an alley on each side. The soil should be rich and in good heart: such soil as would suit a cabbage will grow the Hollyhock in tolerable perfection. Trench the bed two feet deep, throwing the top spit to the bottom, and bringing the second spit to the surface, breaking up the surface thoroughly. On this bed, raked smooth, sow the seed so thickly as to come up an inch apart, and sift over the seeds some rich dry soil, so as to cover them for about an inch. When they come up and begin to grow, the weeds must be kept down, and vigorous growth encouraged by watering in dry weather. In June the plants will bear removal to a nursery-bed, prepared in the same manner as the seed-bed. If the seedlings have been growing vigorously, the roots will be strong, and must not be broken in taking up: this may be prevented by soaking the bed thoroughly the night previous to removal, and lifting the plants cautiously with a fork inserted under them, as in lifting potatoes. Plant them in the new bed six inches apart each way, using a dibber, making a hole large enough to receive the roots, and pressing the earth round them by making another hole on each side with the point of the dibber, watering the bed thoroughly when planted. When dry and somewhat settled, rake the bed smooth, giving the same care as to weeding and watering when dry, as well as to destroying slugs, earwigs, and insects. In the autumn the plants will be strong and fit to put out where they are to bloom. If they are intended to bloom in rows where they stand, every other plant must now be removed, so as to leave them one foot apart all over the bed; here they may be supported by strong stakes placed at both ends of each row, and a strong cord carried from one to the other, to which the plants are to be tied.

As they come into bloom, in the second year, every single flower which does not exhibit some desirable character of habit or colour, should be thrown away before they begin to ripen seed: the majority will be in this category. Those selected for further experiment should be cut down to within three inches of the ground, the earth round them stirred with a fork, to loosen the soil and let in the air, having previously named or numbered them in your book, and described the qualities for which they were selected.

In propagating by cuttings, as soon as the first flowers of an old plant open sufficiently to judge of the flowering, the superfluous side-branches having no flower-buds should be taken off, with two or three joints and leaves. Cut the shoot through with a clean cut, just under the lower joint, leaving the leaf entire; cut it also at about two inches above the joint: either joint will do, provided they have growing eyes, with a leaf and piece of ripened wood to support the bud until roots are formed. These cuttings, planted in a light sandy soil, placed under a hand-glass, and watered occasionally, and shaded from the sun, will require little further care except keeping clear of weeds and dead leaves. When rooted, pot them off in 60-sized pots, and put them in a cold frame where they can remain during the winter. In spring plant them out in the open ground, where they are to flower, taking care to furnish the roots with the proper soil.

The old plants in autumn furnish another source for new plants. When the flowers are becoming shabby, cut the plants down, and, beginning at the bottom joints, continue to make cuttings, as described above, until the fibre gets too soft for the purpose,—each joint having eyes will furnish a plant: these struck under a hand-glass, on a very slight hotbed, will grow vigorously, the soil being gritty sand, loam, and leaf-mould, in equal proportions. Sprinkle the cuttings slightly with water every day in fine weather.

Mr. W. Paul, of Cheshunt, who has made the Hollyhock his peculiar study, finds that the season of flowering may be greatly extended by striking and transplanting at different seasons. "There is," he says, "a difference of six weeks in the period of flowering between plants removed early in autumn and late in spring; and of this we may avail ourselves to lengthen the succession. Early-rooted cuttings and old plants may be induced to bloom in July, and late-rooted cuttings and spring-sown seedlings in November: hence there is no difficulty in obtaining flowers for four successive months."

Mr. Paul attaches much importance to a free supply of water in the spring months, when the plant has just been turned out of the pots, and when it is most desirable to have rapid and vigorous growth.

Three flowering-spikes should only be allowed to the strongest plants,—to weakly ones only one. When a foot and a half high, stake them, placing two to each plant, one of these stakes being driven in on each side of the plant, the stakes being five feet long and driven 2½ feet into the ground. "Pass the bass round the stem of the plant," says Mr. Paul, "drawing it first to one of the stakes, and tie it;" then perform the same operation on the other side a few inches higher up, tying it in the opposite direction, "until the plant is rendered quite secure. When there are two stems to one root, three stakes will be necessary, placed in a triangle, tying the stems alternately as before;" care, however, should be taken that the stakes are covered with the foliage of the plant as much as possible.

The following selection from Messrs. Paul's numerous list of plants is particularly worth notice, towering, as many of them do, with spikes ten feet high:—

White and blush-colour,—Vista; Celestial; Lady Tarlton.
Buff, fawn, and salmon,—Empress; Mr. Oakes; Queen of the Buffs.
Lemon,—Walden; Masterpiece.
Pink,—Lady Franklyn; Perfection.
Rosy carmine,—Beauty of Cheshunt; Beauty of Walden.

Crimson,—Memnon; Sir Colin Campbell; Red Rover; Waterloo.
Claret,—In Memoriam.
Purple,—Perfection.
Plum-colour,—Plutarch.
Sulphur and Yellow,—Sulphur Queen; Queen of the Yellows.

HOTBED.

To make a hotbed, let a quantity of stable-dung be got together, proportioned to the size of the frame: two double loads for a three-light frame are usually allowed for the body of the beds; but it is as well to add an additional load if the bed is required to last some time.

The dung should be turned over four or five times during a fortnight, and wetted, if dry. This preparation is most important; the inexperienced operator, unless he would run the risk of destroying his plants at the beginning, should follow it to the letter; for, unless the material has been well worked before the bed is made, it is apt to heat too violently, and burn the roots of plants. An equal quantity of leaves mixed with stable-dung may be used with advantage: the leaves give a sweeter and more moderate, as well as more lasting heat.

When the material is ready, measure the frame, length and breadth, and mark out the bed, allowing a foot or 18 inches more each way than the length and breadth of the frame. At each corner of the bed drive a stake firmly into the ground, and perfectly upright, to serve as a guide to build the bed by; then proceed to build up the bed, shaking up the dung well and beating it down with the fork. The whole should be equally firm and compact, so that it is not likely to settle more in one part than in another. The frame and lights may now be placed in the centre, but the lights left off, so that the rank steam which always rises from a newly-made hotbed may escape.

This is the usual way of making a hotbed; there is, however, another which is very effective, and greatly economizes the manure. The trimmings and prunings of trees may be tied up into fagots, and with these the walls of a pit should be built, the exact size of the frame: on this the frame rests. The fagots are fixed by means of stakes driven through them into the ground, the walls being about four feet high. After the frame is put on, the mixture of dung and leaves is thrown in and well beaten down. The dung is piled nearly up to the glass, to allow for sinking; in other respects, the management is the same as for an ordinary bed. The advantage of this plan is, first, it requires a trifle less manure; secondly, the heat from the linings penetrates through the fagots under the bed, and is found more effective.

When the bed is made, the frame and lights put on, and the rank steam passed off, which generally takes five or six days, let a barrowful of good loamy soil be placed under each light; by the next day this will be warmed to the temperature of the hotbed, which will now be ready for use.

The heat of the manure is not lasting; consequently, the bed will require watching. It is advisable to have a thermometer in the frame, and as soon as the heat gets below 70°, apply a lining of fresh dung, which has been prepared as the body of the frame, to the front and one side of the bed; and when this again declines, add another to the back and the other side. The bed can be kept at a growing heat for any length of time by this means, removing the old linings, and replacing them by fresh.

In covering the lights, during frosts or rough winds, it is advisable to avoid letting the mats, or what not, hang over the sides, as there is often danger of conducting rank steam from the linings into the frame. Straw hurdles which exactly fit the lights are better than mats. The covering should be used just sufficiently to protect the plants from frost or cutting winds, without keeping them dark and close.

HU'MEA (nat. ord. Compos'itæ).

A remarkably handsome plant, invaluable for decorative purposes, whether in the hall, the conservatory, or dispersed in pots about the lawn, pleasure-grounds, or terraces. Planted in the centres of beds or mixed borders, its majestic and graceful appearance renders it a most effective and striking object; in long mixed borders, if placed at intervals in irregular positions, it breaks that monotonous appearance which most persons so much dislike. Indeed, in any position, this plant stands unrivalled as a garden ornament. The leaves, when slightly rubbed, yield a powerful odour. When well grown, we have seen it eight feet high and four feet in diameter. Succeeds best in light rich soil.

Humea elegans,—red, 8 ft., half-hardy biennial, from New South Wales.

HY'ACINTH.

The Hyacinth is a most delightful and valuable flower. In the conservatory or sitting-room it is equally at home, and its well-being is less dependent upon the mysteries of the gardening art and the pure atmosphere of the country than that of almost any other exotic in cultivation. In the most confined streets of London the Hyacinth may be seen blooming as magnificently as if surrounded by all the advantages of the open country, and displaying ungrudgingly for the delight of its city cultivators charms which most other plants, even though indigenous to our own soil, cannot be induced to reveal.

Time of Planting.—This must to a considerable extent be regulated by circumstances. Nature has undoubtedly declared herself in favour of planting the Hyacinth in October and November; yet, without disputing her authority, we would say to the lovers of this flower, make your first planting as near the 1st of September as possible, and your last about the 31st of December; should an opportunity, however, afterwards offer of purchasing sound bulbs at half price as late as the middle of January, plant them too. You may then have your sitting-room and conservatory adorned with the glowing beauty of the hyacinth from Christmas till April or May.

In the open ground we have planted hyacinths as late as the beginning of March, and have been rewarded by some very good blooms; others planted early in February blossomed beautifully. We do not, however, recommend planting later than the beginning of January.

After the early part of December, hyacinths intended to bloom in glasses would flower better if first planted in pots, and there allowed to remain till half grown or even in bloom; the removal into the glasses being readily performed (especially if Messrs. Barr and Sugden's new collar glass be used), by simply turning the plant out of the pot, placing the ball in a basin of tepid water, and gently washing away the soil from the roots.

The first selection of hyacinths, as of most other bulbous roots, arrives in London from the 20th of August to the 5th of September; orders should therefore be given for them as soon after that time as possible. If it be inconvenient to plant them immediately, they may be placed on a cool dry shelf till wanted.

Hyacinths in Moss.—In the new rustic jardinets "Alexandra," "Prince of Wales," and "Rustic Robin," introduced by Messrs. Barr and Sugden, china bowls, glass dishes, jardinets, and any other elegant contrivance having no means of drainage, moss, or better far, amalgamated cocoa-fibre and charcoal, can be used with great advantage: this latter is always sweet, and bulbs strike their roots freely into it, and are less subject to decay than if planted in any other medium with which we are acquainted.

If clean moss is used, at the bottom of the vessel lay a handful of charcoal, on which place the moss and firmly press it down; on this plant the hyacinth bulbs, and cover them with nice green flat moss, which is to be found in most localities. If the amalgamated cocoa-fibre and charcoal be used, press it down moderately tight, and cover the bulbs over with the same material; this again may either be covered with flat moss or a variety of Lycopodium. Water with tepid water overhead two or three times a week, through a fine rose, till the plants are in bloom; thus the freshness of the moss will be maintained, and the plants freed from dust, which, if allowed to remain, would prove injurious.

Hyacinths out of Doors.—If the soil be light or medium, it simply requires to be deeply dug and well worked; if heavy, besides deep digging and well working, the bulbs should be surrounded with sand, or, better still, two good handfuls of cocoa-fibre; if wet or subject to occasional floodings, drain the ground with a series of drains, three feet deep and ten feet apart, or raise the bed six inches above the general level. When manure is added, thoroughly rotted cow-dung or leaf-soil is best; and when winter protection is given, long straw laid loosely on the bed, and hooped down to prevent its littering the garden, or cocoa-fibre,—both are unequalled; but they should be removed as soon as the plants begin to show.

In planting, the crown of the bulb should be four inches under the surface, and to produce a very effective display the bulbs should be planted six inches apart, but many persons plant them eight or ten inches from each other.

Where the beds are required for the summer occupants before the bulbs have matured themselves, they may either be removed to the reserve garden, and carefully planted in a north border to ripen, or the following plan adopted:—Take as many 4-inch pots as you have bulbs, plant one in each, using the best compost you can possibly command, and place the bulbs on the top of the soil. Prepare the ground as already recommended, then bury the pots as thickly as you please, keeping the top at least three or four inches under the surface; as soon as the blossom fades, remove the flower-spike, dig up the pots, and replant them in the reserve garden, or place them on a north border, surrounding them with moss, cocoa-fibre, or whatever will assist in keeping the roots cool.

Here we may suggest how, on the same bed, two distinct displays of floral beauty can be secured. At the time of planting, groups of crocus, snowdrops, winter aconites, or *Scilla sibirica*, can be planted in masses—these will bloom before the hyacinths; or in spring, autumn-sown annuals can be pricked in all over the bed—these will succeed the hyacinths.

Hyacinths in Pots.—To secure a regular succession of hyacinths, to develop their beauty most fully, and to employ them for the various styles of decoration, this is by far the most important method of cultivation. At any stage of growth the plants can be removed from their pots without injury, and arranged, either in jardinets, flower-baskets, vases, or into hyacinth-glasses; so that from the beginning of January to the end of April, with a little management, the beauty and delightful fragrance of this spring favourite may be enjoyed, either in the sitting-room or conservatory.

To cultivate the Hyacinth successfully in pots, a free porous soil is indispensable, and one composed of equal parts of turfy loam, rotted cow-dung, and leaf-soil, adding about one-eighth part of silver-sand, and thoroughly incorporating the whole and passing it through a rough sieve, is undoubtedly the best compost for the production of handsome flowers. As this, however, cannot always be commanded, use, instead, road-scrapings a year or two old, or good garden loam (not of a retentive nature) mixed with silver-sand. Amalgamated cocoa-fibre and charcoal, mixed with rotted cow-dung and loam, makes a fine mixture if used in equal parts.

The size of the pot must be regulated by the accommodation and requirements of the cultivator; for one bulb a

4- or 4½-inch pot will grow the Hyacinth well; for three bulbs a 5½-inch pot will be sufficient (and here we would remark, hyacinths cultivated in groups are much more effective than grown singly). At the bottom of the pot place over the hole a piece of potsherd and some charcoal, and on this some rough pieces of turfy loam to insure good drainage; then fill the pots with the prepared soil to within an inch of the top, placing the bulb in the centre, or if three, at equal distances apart, pressing them well into the soil, and filling up, leaving only the crown of the bulbs uncovered; moderately water, and place them anywhere out of doors, on coal-ashes or anything that will secure good drainage and at the same time be objectionable to worms; then with coal-ashes, leaf-soil, or old tan, or better still, common cocoa-fibre, fill up between the pots, and cover over two or three inches. In five or six weeks the pots will be full of roots, and may then be removed at pleasure. For a few early blooms some may be removed at the end of three or four weeks and placed in a gentle hotbed, warm greenhouse, forcing-pit, or vinery, but they must be kept close to the glass, to prevent them from growing tall and unsightly. At first they should be forced very gently.

To maintain the succession, a portion of the newly-potted bulbs, intended for late blooming, should be placed under a north wall, while those for early blooming should be arranged under a south wall, and every fortnight a part of these should be brought in-doors. As the season advances, the leaves, and even the flowers, will burst from their prison; so that when the plants are removed from under the ashes, &c., they must be placed in the shade for a few days, till the leaves, &c., become green.

Hyacinths in Sand.—Besides the advantage which sand offers in being independent of drainage, it may be procured in various colours. The different shades may be arranged either in geometrical figures or fanciful designs, with very charming effect. As soon, however, as the plants appear, the surface should be covered with green moss, the best for this purpose being found near the roots of old trees.

When the Hyacinth is cultivated in sand, it is assumed that one of the new drawing-room jardinets, a glass dish, china bowl, or the new rustic hyacinth jardinet, or "Rustic Robin," &c., is used. These being without the usual means of drainage, a handful of charcoal should be placed at the bottom, and over it the sand. Should the vessel be shallow, raise the sand to a point in the centre, placing one bulb upon the apex, and three, six, or more, according to the size of the basket, at equal distances around.

To insure an effective display, it is necessary to plant thickly. Push the bulbs into the dry sand, leaving only the top visible, and to fix the sand, the vessel should be immersed in a pail of water; also, to prevent any subsequent displacement of the sand, and to secure for the plants a sufficient supply of moisture, this operation must be repeated once a week, or oftener if required, a bath of two or three minutes' duration being sufficient; and if the water used be tepid, it will be all the better, as it encourages the development of the flower. An occasional watering of tepid water overhead, through a fine rose, will free the plants from dust, and keep them healthy and vigorous. The amalgamated cocoa-fibre and charcoal is a much better medium than sand.

Hyacinths in Water.—The hints we offer for the cultivation in water are simple but ample, and if followed cannot fail to insure success, provided the roots be sound, of the proper age, and the right varieties for glass-culture. Never use spring water if you can get clean rain-water. Place the bulb on the glass, and let the water just touch its base; for three or four weeks keep it in a dark, cool situation, but avoid a damp, close atmosphere.

When the roots have grown two inches, remove the water half an inch from the base of the bulb. All disturbance of the roots should be avoided; therefore never change the water while it remains sweet: as a purifier, place a piece of charcoal in the glass. Avoid a close, hot room, or you will have long stems and small flower-spikes. Choose an airy situation, and place the glass or Ne Plus Ultra in the lightest and sunniest position, turning it once a day. Never allow dust to remain either on the bulb, leaves, or flower; once a day, or oftener, remove it with a camel-hair brush and water.

Carefully guard against changes of temperature, especially from heat to cold, and never remove the plants from a hot room to a cold one; and when the water is changed or the glasses filled up, the chill must always be taken off the water. Never use a support till the plant requires it.

A preference is generally given to dark-coloured glasses over clear ones, on the supposition that the Hyacinth grows better in them; but it is our opinion that the Hyacinth will do as well in the one as in the other; therefore those who delight in watching the growth of the roots, as well as the development of the flower, should buy the clear glasses.

HYDRAN'GEA (nat. ord. Saxifra'geæ).

The common Hydrangea is a Chinese shrub, half-hardy, imported into England about the year 1790, by Sir Joseph Banks. It thrives best in a rich soil, and requires plenty of water. When the plant has done flowering, its branches should be cut in. Blue hydrangeas are much admired. It is some peculiarity in soil and situation which produces this variety. Blue flowers may in general be procured by planting in a strong loam and watering freely with soapsuds, or, what is better, with a solution of alum or nitre.

HYDROPULT.

No garden tool-house can be considered furnished without this useful instrument. For sprinkling shrubs and plants under glass it is invaluable. Price two guineas and upwards.

IBE'RIS (nat. ord. Crucif'eræ).

The Iberis is better known as Candytuft, and will be found described under that name.

ICE-HOUSE.

A large house in the country can hardly be said to be properly provided unless it has, somewhere in the grounds, an ice-house. Ice is a very inexpensive luxury to those who live in the country, and who have the means of keeping it. The construction of an ice-house is very simple, and the management of one extremely easy. On any dry spot of ground, under shade of trees, on the slope of a hill, or where drainage can be obtained, let a well be sunk of any convenient size. It is a mistake to suppose that it need be very deep, for ice keeps best in a broad, solid mass, as we may prove by examination of any ice-house, where we shall find that melting always begins next to the side walls. At the bottom of this well fagots should be laid to form a drainage, and upon these a bed of dry straw or reeds to receive the ice. From the bottom of the well, under the fagots, there should be a brick drain, trapped on the outside with a siphon, so that all water may be carried off and no air admitted. The walls of the well are best built hollow, and the top arched. The ice-house should be provided with two doors—an inner one on the top of the well, and an outer one some few feet from it. The interval between these doors should be filled up with straw, and the entire outer covering of the whole building should be a mound of earth. This mound may be planted with John's wort, periwinkles, and other creepers, and in this way it will be rendered a pleasing object. It hardly comes into our present design to explain how ice may be best kept;

we may, however, observe that the thinner the ice is the better; for to keep well, it must be broken into small pieces and thoroughly rammed down, so as to form a solid mass.

ICE-PLANT (nat. ord. Ficoida'ceæ).

Preparation of the Soil.—As the leaves are ornamental in proportion to their size, the soil should be of the richest possible description; and the few plants that will be necessary should be placed in a warm sheltered corner. Unless the soil is in itself suitable, dig pits about 2 feet 6 inches apart, and fill them with very light rich compost, allowing about a barrowful to each couple of pits.

Time and Manner of Sowing.—Sow the seeds in a pot filled with rich light soil early in April; cover lightly, and place in a gentle heat. As soon as the plants are strong enough, pot them in small pots and replace in the warmth. When the plants are well established, gradually harden them for planting out.

Planting and After-management.—Plant out about the end of May, or as soon as the plants are strong and properly hardened, and all danger of frost is over. Keep them well supplied with water until the roots get hold of the soil. When once fairly established, they will only require to have the ground kept free from weeds, and the shoots pinched out, so as to prevent their being overcrowded. In hot, dry weather weak manure-water may be given frequently with advantage.

IMITATION SCENERY.

Attempts have sometimes been made to imitate or make models of real Alpine scenery, but generally with indifferent success, as may be supposed. Lady Broughton chose a model of the mountains of Savoy for imitation in the rockery at Hoole House. With great trouble she succeeded in preserving the outline, imitating the Mer de Glace in grey limestone, quartz, and felspar. After labouring for six years at this rocky boundary to the flower-garden, it is described as an exquisite piece of workmanship, completely covered with rare and beautiful Alpine plants, except where snow, glaciers, and the pinnacles of rocks are present; the first two are represented by glittering spar and white marble. Each plant is placed in a bed of soil of suitable character, and protected by broken fragments of stone, clean-washed gravel, moss, and other suitable materials; stones being selected for certain subjects, according as they reflect or absorb the heat. Among the plants which abound in this rocky bed are saxifrages, sedums, rock pinks, anemones, myosotis, heaths, violas, *Lychnis alpina*, campanulas, oxalis, hepaticas, anagallis, cyclamens, calceolarias, dwarf veronicas,—in short, every gem of the garden that will grow in such soils is to be found in this choice spot.

IMPA'TIENS (nat. ord. Balsamina'ceæ).

Handsome border plants, called also *Noli me tangere*, from a curious property in the seed-vessel, which springs open as soon as touched. *I. flaccida* is a fine species, with vinca-like flowers and broad leaves. They thrive in rich loamy soil.

Impatiens tricornis,—yellow and crimson, half-hardy annual, 2½ ft., from East Indies.
Impatiens flaccida,—lilac, very handsome, 2½ ft.

INDIAN AZA'LEAS.

The Indian azaleas require more delicate treatment than their more hardy congeners. They live and grow in a low temperature, however, and are not materially injured by a few degrees of frost; but while growing, a moist warmth and equable temperature are essential to their flowering properly.

INDIAN CORN.

Preparation of the Soil.—Select a warm sheltered situation, and trench, deeply, adding a liberal dressing of well-rotted manure.

Time and Manner of Sowing.—Sow in pots in April, or in the open ground in May, but, except in very favourable localities, the plants succeed best if raised under glasss and planted out when the weather becomes warm and settled. If raised in pots, be careful to keep the plants strong and stocky, hardening them by giving air freely on fine days.

After-management. — When planted out, water freely till the roots have got hold of the fresh soil, and also in dry, hot weather. Keep the surface of the ground free from weeds, and in an open state by frequent hoeings. The ears, if cut when green and young, make a delicious vegetable. They should be cooked and served up as asparagus.

INOCULATING.

This term in gardening is usually confined to a peculiar process of creating grass lawns by distributing over the surface of the ground small pieces of turf, rolling them in, and leaving them to take root and get together. The process, if properly carried out, is a very good one. The pieces of turf should be free from weeds and the surface made level to receive them.

INOPSID'IUM (nat. ord. Crucif'-eræ).

Charming profuse-blooming hardy annuals, growing freely, in any damp rich soil, or upon the shady side of rock-work; they make remarkably neat edgings in shady situations, and are valuable for pots, vases, and rustic-work.

Inopsidium acaule, — sky blue, ⅛ ft., from South Europe.
Inopsidium album,—white, ⅛ ft., from South Europe.

INSECTS.

As all insects are produced from eggs, and as a natural instinct enables the mother to place the eggs in a spot where they will not only be safe, but where the young grub will find food to support itself until its first transformation takes place, a knowledge of the habits of the more destructive species is absolutely necessary to the gardener; the most effective remedy being to destroy the egg; for the caterpillar or larva state is that most destructive to vegetation. In this state the name of caterpillar is applicable to lepidopterous insects or moths, and butterflies, and some of the Hymenoptera, or bees. Grubs are the larvæ of beetles, generally with three pair of feet, strong jaws, and fat mis-shapen bodies; maggots are the larvæ of flies, moving along the ground by the muscular action of the rings of the body; the larvæ of bees and ants being also generally called maggots.

When the larvæ of these creatures have exhausted the food near which the provident care of the mother has placed them, they are generally prepared for their second transformation —viz., the pupa or chrysalis state: winding themselves in their cocoons, they bury themselves in the earth, or in some other obscure place, and emerge in a few hours in forms as various as were their larvæ, the beetles with rudimentary feet, which are developed in their perfect state; the butterflies naked, suspended by the tail, or attached to the branch of some tree or wall; the moths enveloped in a bag or cocoon, which they have spun round themselves, as in a shroud; the flies and two-winged insects, smooth oval substances, are fixed to the plants or trees which have supported the larvæ. At length their last metamorphosis occurs: the caterpillar becomes a moth or butterfly, gaily painted in its garb of summer; the grub becomes a beetle, with its diaphanous-coloured, hard, shining shell; the maggots develop themselves in thousands of shapes, floating and humming in the air,—the two-winged insects, or Diptera.

All the mischief, however, has been done, so far as the garden is concerned, and the gardener has only to look forward, as he ever must, to the next season. The insects humming and buzzing around him are short-lived: one object of their creation has been attained; they have performed, so far, their office of scavengers; their next is, to perpetuate their species; and the object of the gardener must be to circumvent them here, by destroying their eggs as they are deposited.

INSECTS ON ROSES.

There is no class of flowers so much exposed to the depredation of insects as roses, and no remedy can be applied to their depredations without a precise knowledge of their habits and different states of transition. St. Pierre, when he had studied the economy of the different insects which infest the rosetree for thirty years, still found something new to note. Moths, beetles, and gall-flies, and other insects hardly known to the initiated, seem to unite their forces in order to attack the queen of flowers. During June and July, the rose-beetle (*Cetonia aurata*) may be seen wheeling round the rose-tree, with its low hum, its wing-cases and elytra erect, instead of being extended from the body. It feeds upon pollen and honey, and in doing so bites off the anthers of the flowers, while its larvæ feed upon decaying wood and vegetable matter, burying themselves in the ground like the cockchafer.

Among the moths, the bell-moth (*Argyrotoza Bergmanniana*) is distinguished by the rich golden yellow of its breast and fore-wings, slightly clouded with orange, and bars of purple-brown with silvery scales. This moth, in the caterpillar state, is very destructive round London to roses. The moths deposit their eggs in the summer in the incipient buds, and they commence their operations on the leaves as soon as they appear, attaching them back to back by their silk-like thread-fibres. Round these leaves others grow in distorted shape, while the caterpillar revels on its core, "a worm i' the bud," devouring the petals of the flower as well as the leaf. When disturbed, the caterpillar drops down, suspended by a thin web which it spins, and by which it is able, when the danger disappears, to resume its former position. The only method of destroying these insects is by sharply pinching the buds where they are suspected to be in the early spring: this will relieve the plant, and enable it to throw out fresh leaves. If allowed to arrive at maturity, the moths

should be destroyed as soon as they appear, and before they can deposit their eggs. The ashy-white bell-moth (*Spilonota aquana*) is another moth of the *Totricidæ*, which has been reared from the leaves of the rose, and of habit similar to the preceding. The yellow-tail moth, which has usually been found on the oak, the elm, and the blackthorn, Mr. Westwood has also found on the Scotch rose in his garden, feeding upon the petals, and afterwards attacking the leaves. This moth appears at the end of July, and the caterpillar (which is thickly clothed with long black hairs) feeds also on the pear.

INSECTS ON PEAR-TREES.

Pear-trees are subject to the attacks of several species of lepidoptera, saw-flies, and aphides. Among the lepidoptera, the beautiful moth *Zeuzera pyrena*, with its antennæ feathered on each side, is furnished with an elongated telescope-like ovipositor, with which the female deposits the eggs to a considerable depth in the crevices of the bark of the tree. The perfect insect appears in July, and the caterpillars in August, when they immediately burrow into the wood of the tree. In September they moult, and in the following June they are full-grown. Sparrows are the gardener's best ally in destroying this insect in the perfect state. Several other small lepidoptera are injurious to the pear: *Argyromyges scitella*, one of the Tincidæ, deposits its eggs on the under surface of the leaves towards the end of May. The young larvæ penetrate the under cuticle, and feed on the fleshy parenchyma, leaving the surfaces untouched, giving the leaf a flabby and blistered appearance. The chaumontelle is said to be particularly subject to the ravages of this creature, especially in the beginning of autumn.

INTERMEDIATE STOCKS (Matthi'ola, nat. ord. Crucif'eræ). Half-hardy Biennials.

The Intermediate Stock is entensively cultivated for Covent-garden market; it is dwarf and branching, and in the early summer months constitutes the principal feature in furnishing jardinets, &c., during "the London season." It is also of great value in filling flower-beds for an early summer display.

Stock, Intermediate,—the true Covent garden scarlet variety, three-fourths of which, say Messrs. Barr and Sugden, may be depended upon to flower double, 1 ft., from 1*s.* per packet.
Stock, Intermediate,—purple, very fine, 1 ft., 6*d.* per packet.
Stock, Intermediate,- -white, very fine, 1 ft., 1*s.* per packet.

IPOMŒ'A (nat. ord. Convolvu-la'ceæ).

Beautiful climbing plants of various colours. The seed should be raised under glass in April and the young plants set out in May. They look very well over the handles of baskets and in contrast with canariensis. They require a rich light soil. In some situations the plants will shed their seed and come up from year to year in the open ground.

I'RIS (nat. ord. Irida'ceæ).

Amongst the many forms of floral beauty which adorn the flower-borders in June, few assert their title to admiration more effectively than the Iris; the flowers are large and handsome, the colours extremely rich, varied, and beautiful. The height of the plant is from 18 to 24 inches, while its cultivation is unusually simple, succeeding in any ordinary light rich garden soil. The Iris should be planted in clumps of three or more, and if allowed to remain undisturbed, they will each succeeding year become more effective: planted in rose or rhododendron beds, they are most valuable. Time of planting and purchasing the same as that recommended for the Hyacinth.

Messrs. Barr and Sugden say of their Paxtonian section of English iris, that the varieties enumerated have been selected an account of their special adaptation for producing *en masse* a display of some of the richest and most striking combinations of colours to be met with in flowers.

Twelve each of ten magnificent varieties, 21*s*.
Fine mixed, per 100, 6*s*. 6*d*.; per dozen, 1*s*.

IRISH IVY.

The Irish Ivy, *Hedera canariensis*, or, as it is sometimes called, the Giant Ivy, is very ornamental. It is also extremely useful, as its growth is so rapid that a screen may be formed of it in a very short space of time. It requires to be clipped once or twice a year freely.

IRISH YEW.

This is an upright shrub with very dark foliage. It has a very good effect when standing alone on a lawn, and may be introduced with advantage into shrubberies in contrast with other shrubs of lighter foliage.

IRON IN WATER.

Carefully avoid for gardening purposes all water impregnated with iron. No plants thrive well that come in contact with it.

ISME'NE.

A genus of free-flowering handsome sweet-scented summer-blooming plants, which should be cultivated in every garden. They grow freely on a south border in a mixture of light loam and rich vegetable soil; they make also handsome plants for in-door decoration.

Culture the same as recommended for hardy and half-hardy amaryllis. The best varieties are:—

Ismene calathinum (Peruvian Daffodil), — large white cup flower.
Ismene Illyricum,—white.
,, maritimum,—white.
,, undulatum,—white.

IX'IA (nat. ord. Irida'ceæ).

An exceedingly pretty Cape flowering bulb, producing its graceful flowers in long slender spikes, and in the greatest profusion; succeeds well on a warm south border, in a mixture of sandy loam and leaf-mould, or peat.

Ixia,—choice mixed, half-hardy bulb, from Cape of Good Hope; may be purchased at the seedsman's for about 7*s*. per 100.

JACOBÆ'A ((nat. ord. Compos'itæ).

A useful and exceedingly showy class of gay-coloured, profuse-blooming plants, remarkably effective in beds or ribbons; delight in a light rich soil. The garden Jacobæa is of many colours, the purple is much admired. It may be raised form cuttings, as verbenas, &c. All the sorts grow freely from seeds; price, from 3*d*. to 6*d*. per packet.

JANUARY.

January is the first month of our year, and the second of winter. The average temperature is 39° during the day and 32° during the night, and the mean temperature, during an average of many years, does not fall below the freezing-point; severe frosts, and frosts of long continuance, occurring in January, are therefore exceptional occurrences in our climate.

The gardener's attention must now be concentrated on the future, rather than diverted by the past. All arrears of labour due to the past year must at once be discharged. Nothing tends more to mar the success of gardening operations than dragging through the necessary work three weeks or a month behind the time proper for its performance. The peculiar fickleness of our climate renders gardening precarious and difficult enough with every advantage of judgment and foresight. It will be well, therefore, to bear in mind that the work can only be done "weather permitting." For instance, it is impossible to dig, plant, or sow when the frost has set its strong seal upon the earth. It is bad practice to dig in snow, and worse than useless to attempt anything on the surface of the ground when an excess of moisture has converted it into mud. It may thus occasionally happen that a part or the whole of the work prescribed for one month, may have to be deferred to another, and thus a double portion fall upon one or any of the winter or spring months. In such cases, extra labour must be employed, or diverted from other departments, until the whole of the work indicated is completed. There is a difference of several weeks in the climate of different parts of the country; operations that should be performed at once in the South, may thus generally be deferred for several weeks in the North. The term flower-garden seems almost a misnomer at this season. But now is the time to consider what can be done to prepare the garden for the return of flowers.

The moment that flower-beds are cleared of their summer occupants, they should be dug up as roughly as possible. But rough-digging, while it can never present a smooth, may always exhibit an even surface, and in this way is not unsightly. It would be difficult to say whether the mechanical or chemical influence in enriching the quality of the soil is the most important. Certainly both are of the highest value, and their influence will be powerful, or the reverse, in exact ratio to the quantity of fresh surface exposed to atmospheric influence. Hence the importance of rough-digging, of forking over ground in frosty weather; resulting in that finely pulverized, mellow, genial soil in spring, in which plants delight to grow.

Next in importance to draining, trenching, and manuring, and often of greater moment than any or all of them put together, is the frequent digging, forking, and scarifying of the surface; and from December to April are the months specially adapted for these operations.

Shrubberies on poor soils would be much benefited by manuring during this month. The usual practice of raking every weed and leaf off the surface, and cruelly disrooting the plants by a deep winter or spring digging, may be designated barbarous. When once shrubberies are properly established on good soil, no rake should ever cross their surface; and every leaf that falls upon them should be merely dug in, any time from December to April,—the earlier the better. Leaves are Nature's means of maintaining the fertility of the soil; and whenever or

wherever art removes them, without applying a substitute, the soil rapidly tends towards sterility.

All newly-planted shrubs and trees should have their roots protected during the first winter with long litter. When placed close together in nursery lines, plants shelter and protect each other, and the massiveness of their tops, and possibly their summer leaves, shield their roots from the frost. Their condition is widely different when placed thinly, in newly-formed shrubberies. Hence the propriety, and in many instances the necessity, of what is termed mulching, that is, covering the surface with some good non-conducting material. The next point of most importance in planting trees or shrubs, especially of large size, is to secure firmly the top to a strong stake, or by any other method, so as to keep it immovable, for when trees, both top and root, are the sport of every fresh breeze, the probability is, that after the roots have made a feeble effort to grow, and been forcibly wrenched from the soil, they will perish.

During January, plant crocuses and any other hardy bulbs for succession: the main crops should have been planted in October or November.

Place old verbenas that are to be used for propagation into a gentle heat, and prepare a slight hotbed for cuttings. All bedding-plants will bear a much stronger heat while they are striking in the spring than in the autumn; verbenas will root in a week, placed in a close pit, with a bottom-heat of from 80° to 90°.

Place scarce varieties of dahlias in heat, for the purpose of securing plenty of cuttings. Proceed with potting-off singly all cuttings in store pots, using 48-sized pots for geraniums, and large 60 for verbenas, &c., where abundance of space is available. Where this is not the case, the potting-off must be deferred till another month.

Prepare a good stock of soil, clean pots, sticks, labels, stakes, &c., in bad weather, so that there may be no hindrance during the busy season. No soil is better for the majority of bedding-plants than equal parts of loam and leaf-mould, and a sixth part of sand.

Keep all cuttings free from green-fly, thrip, and other insects; cover up, water, and give air with caution and judgment, and ever bear in mind that the beauty of next summer's garden is dependent not only upon the quantity, but the health and the cleanliness of your stock.

In the reserve garden, in very severe weather, autumn-sown annuals should be protected by having some boughs stuck among them, or by being covered with mats, canvas, &c. Dig and ridge all vacant ground, and get the beds intended for the main sowing of hardy annuals prepared. Give beds intended for choice ranunculuses a liberal dressing of two-years-old cow-dung, and lay them up rough, ready for planting next month. Protect beds of hyacinths and tulips during severe weather, as they are often injured when coming through the soil.

In the rose-garden, proceed with planting and pruning hardy roses, and protect tea and China roses with boughs, covering the roots with old tan, cinder-ashes, &c. Procure stocks for budding; liberally manure all the ground occupied with roses, and take care that their roots are not injured during the process of digging. Florists' flowers require attention. Water auriculas, polyanthuses, pinks, carnations, &c., in frames, with care; remove early blooms from polyanthuses; examine pinks in beds, and if any of the plants are heaved up by the frost, press them firmly down in the soil.

Collect materials, and form new rock-works. Stone is the only really legitimate basis for scenery of this description; but as this is not to be found everywhere, and as the taste for rock-works is universal, we must submit to have rocks of clinkers, débris of pottery, bricks, cement, chalk, concrete, and timber.

A collection of hardy heaths should be found near the rockery. Sweep up leaves; roll grass and gravel; remove all litter of dead or dying plants; and let the impress of neatness and the stamp of order be everywhere apparent.

January.

Kitchen-Garden.—The work to be done in the kitchen-garden in January depends altogether on the weather. In open frosty weather no opportunity should be lost for wheeling manure on the vacant ground. All the refuse about the grounds should be collected and added to the manure-heap, and that burned or charred which will not readily decompose.

Now the forethought of the gardener may be exhibited. He has to lay down his plan of operations for the year, or at least for the next three months; and on his judgment in doing this much of the successful cultivation depends. If he cover too much ground with early crops in these three months, not only will great waste arise, but he will have forestalled the space required for the main crops in April, May, and June, when some of the most important crops are to be sown. He should make his calculations, so as to secure a constant succession of the various products as they are required, leaving little or nothing to run to waste. It is a good practice, in going through the orchard, bush-fruit, and trees generally, to cut off all spare wood at this season, and to tie it up in bundles ready to be used for peasticks and other purposes.

The crops to be got into the ground this month are peas and beans, in the open ground or in cold frames; also in frames, radishes, lettuces (the black-seeded cos does well if sown early), Walcheren or early Cape brocoli, cauliflower; on a slight hotbed, early horn-carrot and potatoes: of course, these will be earlier and better for the assistance of a slight hotbed of two feet or so in height. A little parsley sown now on a slight hotbed will be useful for planting out early. A little celery for an early supply, and a little cabbage also, should these be scarce, so as to fill up the main crop, if thinned out by severe frosts.

At this season it is necessary to be

provided with mats or litter to cover the glass, in case of sharp frost; for, though most of these crops are hardy, yet, when young and growing, they are not unlikely to be cut off by frosts. They are also much strengthened and hardened by exposure to the air in mild weather. A warm shower, if it can be had, is beneficial; but too much wet is injurious.

Early peas may be got in any time that the weather permits. Where the ground is tolerably porous and well drained, and a warm border, well sheltered on the north, is available, nothing more is required than to sow in rows, five, six, or more feet apart, the rows running north and south: for dwarf peas, five feet will suffice. About London it is the custom to sow spinach between the rows of peas, the spinach coming off in time to be replaced with brocoli before the peas are over; it is better, however, to sow spinach apart, and leave the spaces between the peas till the time for planting potatoes, French beans, and other open-ground crops.

Lettuces may be sown in a warm border under a south wall or fence: they are better sown in a frame at this season, if one can be spared, or even under a hand-light. Wanting either, it is advisable to cover the seed, when sown, with straw or light litter, taking it off sometimes to give a dusting with lime, in case of slugs; the ground should be well dug one spit deep, a dressing of manure being turned in.

For the purpose of growing very early potatoes, nothing is more suitable than a broad roomy melon-pit. The potatoes will be fit for use about the time for planting out the melons. About the beginning of January, let some middling-sized tubers be laid in a warm and moderately dry place, well exposed to the light: here they will make short plump shoots by the time the bed is ready. Prepare a quantity of dung sufficient to make a bed three feet six inches in depth. When the bed is in order, lay on three inches of soil, and place in the potatoes fifteen inches apart, covering them with six inches more of soil. Some seed of the scarlet short-top radish may be scattered over the surface. As these begin to grow, give abundance of fresh air in mild weather, so that neither potatoes nor radishes be drawn up; and as they come up, remove the radishes which happen to be immediately about the crowns of the potatoes: earthing up will not be required. The radishes will be ready in March; the potatoes early in May. Sow mustard and cress.

Plants under Glass.—Without protection of some kind during the winter months, no collection of plants can be kept together; but when mere protection is all that is sought, it is easily obtained; a trench two feet deep, dug in the ground, if the soil is dry, and a drain at hand to carry off surface-water, will suffice, if covered with frames, straw, hurdles, or other efficient covering; for it is ascertained by numerous experiments, that the earth at two feet deep is warmer by two or three degrees than the surrounding air in winter. A vacant frame, a cold pit, a greenhouse, or a conservatory, will also either of them serve the purpose. On the other hand, where plants of a warmer climate are to be forced into early bloom, artificial heat must be applied, not only to keep out the cold, but to assimilate their native climate and atmosphere.

Forcing-houses.—The routine business here during the month commences in earnest in January; a few plants of all kinds for ornamenting the house and conservatory should be introduced and started gradually; Indian azaleas, bulbs, roses, and lilacs, if already somewhat advanced, should have others brought forward to succeed them. Towards the end of the month, a good stock of pinks, sweet-williams, and lilies of the valley, should be started in pits or frames. The temperature of the forcing house should not be suffered to fall below 50°; and as the days lengthen, the temperature should be increased 4° or 5° until it attains a minimum temperature of 60°, and a maximum of

70°, by artificial heat, and an increase of 10° by sun-heat; giving air daily, even if for a short time only, and keeping the atmosphere always moist and genial by syringing or watering the pipes and flags.

Greenhouse.—With the opening year and the lengthening days the busy season in the greenhouse commences; plants of all kinds begin to move, and most of them may be assisted with a little heat. Soft-wooded plants may be stimulated by it; and, when they begin to grow, moved into the larger pots in which they are to flower; while those which are more advanced and showing bloom, may be introduced into a warmer place. Many cinerarias are now in bloom, and may be removed to the window or conservatory; those reserved for blooming in May and June should still be kept in cold pits or frames, taking care to guard them from severe frosty weather, and especially from moisture. If large cinerarias are required, shift a few into larger pots, and pinch off the tops to produce a bushy head, tying or pegging down the side-shoots to keep them open: keep them moderately supplied with moisture, and give air on every possible occasion.

Fuchsias may be started, and large early-flowering specimens produced by cutting down the old plants and shaking the roots out of the old soil as soon as they have broken, re-potting them in a good rich compost, with sufficient drainage. Strike cuttings for bedding-plants as soon as the shoots are long enough. Calceolarias require great attention as to watering. Remove all decaying leaves as they appear, peg down the shoots to the soil, that they may root up the stems, and thus strengthen the plant. As seedlings advance, shift them into larger pots, and prick off those sown for late blooming. In potting, use a compost of light turfy loam, well-decomposed manure and leaf-mould, and a liberal portion of silver-sand, with an ample drainage of potsherds and charcoal, and keep them free from insects.

January.

Pelargoniums which are strongly rooted may be shifted into larger pots, with stronger soil, using silver-sand freely, and taking care that the pots are clean and dry and the drainage good. Stop some of the plants required for succession, remove decaying leaves, and thin out weak shoots. Stake and tie out the shoots of those sufficiently advanced, to admit air to the centre. In plants of dwarf habit, peg the shoots down to the edge of the pot, to encourage foliage. Stir and top-dress the soil from time to time, if required: a watering once or twice with lime-water and soot imparts a rich dark colour to the foliage, and destroys worms in the soil.

Where early flowers are required, and a stove or hothouse or other forcing convenience is at hand, remove a few plants, such as Admiral Napier, *Alba multiflora*, Amas, Jenny Lind, or any more recent early-flowering sort, for forcing.

Should frost appear, or the weather prove damp, light the fires in the afternoon, and shut up the house before the sun disappears, keeping the heat as low as is consistent with keeping out frost and dispelling damp. Water those plants which have become dry, but water them copiously. The fancy varieties, being the most delicate, should be kept in the warmest parts of the house, and their foliage thinned out occasionally. Use fumigation, to prevent the appearance of the green-fly.

A constant and ample supply of compost, well turned and thoroughly dry, should now be prepared for spring potting, and pots washed and dried for use when wanted.

It is usual, where circumstances permit, to grow hard-wooded plants, such as heaths, azaleas, camellias, and others of similar habit, in a separate house; and some cultivators go so far as to recommend those having limited accommodation to confine their culture to one family, contending that it is better to have a houseful of finely-grown heaths, geraniums, or camellias, as the case may be, than a miscellaneous collection of indifferently-cultivated plants.

Care should be taken that hard-wooded plants do not suffer from the absence of moisture at the roots. After severe frosts, when fires have been used, evaporation by the sides of the pots is very great, while the surface seems to be moist enough : this should be seen to. To camellias and other plants of similar habit advancing into bloom, occasional doses of manure-water in a tepid state should be given, and the plants syringed with tepid water every other day, until the flowers begin to expand.

Among the hard-wooded plants, the same remarks respecting heat are applicable ; a temperature of 40° should be aimed at during the night, rising a little by natural causes during the day. Air should be given from above or by means of ventilators, without exposing the plants to cold draughts, and moisture encouraged by sprinkling the floor, flues, and pipes, when warm, with water.

With heaths, guard against mildew, and water moderately. Avoid artificial heat if possible, but keep out frost : if heat becomes necessary, remove such plants from its influence as are required for later flowering.

Camellias should be advancing into full bloom, and the young expanding buds should be protected from cold currents of air, but without much fire-heat.

Azaleas should be growing freely, if they were shifted and promoted to a warm place last month. To get early-flowering plants, some of the more advanced specimens should be introduced to greater heat, while others may be retarded for a succession, to supply the conservatory or window-cases. *Indica alba* is a fine early-flowering variety.

The conservatory, being only a more ornamental variety of the greenhouse, the same directions apply to it. Being generally a lofty building, the conservatory is not so well calculated for growing plants unless they be of a climbing habit, when they may be displayed to great advantage. Everything should now look fresh and healthy. Acacias should be advancing into bloom. Camellias are either out or advancing rapidly into bloom : to promote this, see that they do not want for water. If there is a stove in the establishment, many orchids, hyacinths, arums, tulips, and other bulbs, with heaths, epacridæ, from the greenhouse ; and if only a frame is available, cinerarias, violets, and mignonette, will render the conservatory both gay and fragrant.

To preserve all these in bloom for the longest possible period is now the object. Keep the atmosphere moist and genial, but not wet ; water regularly when necessary, especially the bulbs, giving as much water, of the same temperature as the house, as they can assimilate ; keep the temperature about 40°, rising a few degrees from sun-heat during the day, ventilating daily, if only for a short time, but avoiding cold draughts of air.

Vines, where they form a feature in the cultivation, are usually cultivated on some principle of succession, either by dividing the house by partitions, or by having a succession of houses. Supposing the plants to have been started in October, they would break last month with a temperature in houses of about 70°. This should now be the point aimed at, the minimum being 60° during the night. The actual heat, however, should be regulated by the state of the external border. If the heat is falling, then fresh heating materials must be applied ; for on that depends the result. Later sections may follow for succession, beginning at a lower temperature, and increasing the heat gradually as the vines break and advance. Vines in pots, if started in October, and exposed to regular heat, will now be setting their fruit ; they may be pushed on vigorously ; for, the roots being entirely under control, there is less danger of the plants being injured by over-forcing. Fresh plants should be brought forward. This may be done by plunging them into a hotbed and frame, and adding linings to keep up the heat until they break, when the heat of the vinery will be found sufficient. The plants showing fruit should be assisted by occasional applications of manure-water in bright weather.

JASMI'NUM (nat. ord. Olei'neæ).

Of the fragrant free-flowering shrubs called Jasmines, there are many hardy varieties. The most common are *Jasminum officinale*, which has white blossom, and *J. revolutum*, yellow. There are several hothouse varieties extremely beautiful, as *J. grandiflorum* and *J. odoratissimum*. All the jasmines are easily propagated by cuttings in sandy soil, covered with a hand-glass.

JERUSALEM ARTICHOKE.

Preparation of the Land.—These useful vegetables will grow and yield plenty of tops in almost any soil or situation; but to secure an abundant crop of large and good-flavoured tubers select a deep light sandy loam. The ground should receive a moderate allowance of manure in autumn, and be trenched to a depth of two feet at least, ridging it up roughly for the winter.

Time and Manner of Planting.—Plant early in March, in lines three feet asunder, and about eighteen inches apart in the lines. The tubers may be dibbled in, as is often done with potatoes; but we recommend the making of a narrow trench, about six inches deep, in which the tubers can be placed at equal depths with greater certainty; the soil placed over them should be left in a loose open state.

After-management.—Some growers practise topping the stems when they are from three to four feet high, but we believe this only causes the formation of an extra quantity of shoots, and is decidedly injurious to the crop: it would be a much better practice, especially where the soil is strong and damp, to thin out the shoots when a few inches high, not leaving more than two or three from a tuber. This, however, will be unnecessary where the soil is light and somewhat dry. Keep the ground free from weeds by frequent deep hoeings. The tubers may be left in the ground till wanted for use, or they may be taken up towards the end of November, and stored in sand or soil; but they must be so covered that the light and air may be effectually excluded, otherwise they will be of a dark colour when cooked.

Jerusalem artichokes,—2*s.* per peck of 14 lb.

JONQUIL.

The Jonquils admit of the same culture as the other Narcissi. They are hardy bulbs, and may be left in the ground several years without any injury; care, however, must be taken not to shorten or cut off their leaves. Planted four or six in a pot, they are very useful in a conservatory.

Price of bulbs in Messrs. Barr and Sugden's catalogue, per dozen :—

	s.	*d.*
Double,—largest roots, rich deep yellow, very fragrant	2	6
Double,—second size	2	0
Single,—sweet-scented	1	6

JULY.

The month of July is the hottest of all, the mean temperature being 61°, although the thermometer ranges from 82°, and sometimes falls to 42°. This high temperature is chiefly occasioned by the increased radiation of heat at the earth's surface: in consequence, the nights are much warmer than those of June. A period of rainy weather usually occurs about the middle of the month, accompanied by thunderstorms.

Flower-Garden and Shrubberies.—All strong-growing plants, such as asters, helianthuses, and solidagos, should be attended to. Hollyhocks planted on the lawn, whether singly or in groups, should be staked in time: in fact, they should be staked when planted, and the leaves and plants kept in a healthy state by watering and syringing in hot and dry weather. Tie up œnotheras neatly. Speciosas, planted pretty thickly over the beds, will produce a fine mass of white flowers, if trained so that they have plenty of light and air, and watered abundantly in dry weather; metrocarpa and *Matricaria grandiflora* will well reward any labour bestowed on them. Beds of verbenas, and similar plants, require occasional syringing with weak tobacco-water.

The first week or so in July will be chiefly occupied by the usual routine of pegging-down plants intended to be kept dwarf, tying others up, and keeping the surface of the beds free from weeds until it is covered by the growing plants. If pinks are attacked by wireworm, place pieces of potato just below the surface of the soil. Examine them every morning, and a great number can be thus caught and destroyed. Pinks should now be propagated; cuttings may likewise be put in of tea and China roses, selecting wood of the present year when it becomes a little firm at the base. Roots, bulbs, anemones, tulips, crocuses, scillas, fritillarias, &c., which have been out of the ground for some time to dry, may now be re-planted.

Fuchsias, *Geraniums*, and other plants in flower, will require regular supplies of water.

Florists' Flowers.—Take up tulips whenever the weather will permit. When lifted, do not separate the offsets from the parent bulb, nor remove the roots or skin: these had better remain till a later period. When lifted, ridge up the soil of the beds for exposure to the air. In taking up seedlings, great care must be used, as their bulbs will often strike down from four to six inches. If possible, keep the stock of each separate; this will save an immense deal of trouble hereafter. Tie carefully the spindling shoots of carnations and picotees—not too tightly; keep the pots free from weeds, and in dry weather do not let them suffer from drought. Attend to the fertilization of pinks: a very little attention to this interesting operation will insure a good crop of seeds, and by selecting only excellent varieties instead of trusting to chance and gathering promiscuously, abundant success will be the result.

By the end of the month, seedling ranunculuses should be taken from the pans or boxes in which they may have been grown; but as many are so minute, and so like the colour of the soil, that without great precaution, they may be overlooked, the best way is to put soil and roots together in a fine wire-sieve, and by holding it under a tap, or pumping into it, the soil will be washed away and the roots left; they must then be placed in the sun for an hour, and afterwards removed to an airy shady place to dry gradually. The large roots of named varieties must be taken up at once, for should they start again, which they are very apt to do previous to removal, death is inevitable. Continue to put in pink pipings; disbud carnations and picotees, giving occasional doses of liquid manure. Attend sedulously to dahlias; tie as they require it, and give a good supply of water.

Rose-Garden. — Autumn-flowering roses now require a liberal supply of liquid manure; guano sown on the ground, and thoroughly soaked with rain-water, will serve the purpose. Remove faded flowers and seed-capsules every morning; plants which have flowered in pots keep growing freely, as the future bloom depends on their vigorous growth at this season. Climbing roses should now be pushing out strong shoots from the roots and main stem; if not required for future training, these should be taken off entirely, or have their tops pinched off a foot or so from the stem. Budding should be in full operation, watering the roots and plants freely in dry weather, both before and after budding. Cut back perpetual-blooming roses, and water them with the richest manure-water to encourage a second growth and bloom.

Baskets, vases, &c., will require an occasional regulating; those having plants in them which require to be tied up, should be examined. Convolvuluses, maurandias, lophospermums, &c., after being pegged over the surface of the soil, should be left to grow over the sides of the vases, or allowed to ramble among the more formal plants which fill up the centre. Baskets, cases, or other contrivances containing plants in bloom, will require frequent attention to keep them fresh. Remove everything in the shape of decayed bloom or leaves, and take advantage, when fresh plants are wanted, to effect a change in the arrangement, which will be found more pleasing than adhering to one plan.

Kitchen-Garden.—Probably this is the busiest month of the year in the kitchen-garden, both on account of everything growing so fast, and because many crops have ceased to be useful, and must be removed and give place to others. We have to look forward to a long winter and spring, when vegetation is stationary or very slow; yet at that time it is necessary to have suitable crops, and to prepare the ground and get them in their places. It may be observed, that where rows of vegetables have previously grown, the ground is usually dry and hard. However moist the season has been, it will always be found different to that eighteen inches or so on either side; it is not, therefore, advisable to crop immediately over the same spot; the difference will soon be observable between the rows planted exactly where peas have grown and those planted at the distance indicated. It is best not to plant winter crops on ground that has been newly-dug or trenched. All brassicæ are far more liable to club on loose or newly-trenched ground; much may depend on the nature of the soil; it is, however, proper that stiff soils be dug some time previous to cropping,—especially in sowing small seeds, as turnip. The soil will dry in hard lumps at first; but advantage must be taken of the first shower that wets it through, as it will then readily fall to pieces under the rake. On light soils this is of less consequence, and it is as well to sow immediately after digging, as the seeds vegetate quicker. Keep the weeds down at this season, as their growth is very rapid in showery weather.

Asparagus.—Cease cutting early this month, unless some part of the bed can be spared for late use, in which case it must have a rest the following season. Late cutting has the effect of weakening the roots, but they will recover after a season's rest, if they have not been cut too closely. Hoe frequently between the rows.

Artichokes will now be in bearing. Cut when the heads are about three parts open. These root deeply, and scarcely require water.

Seakale should have an abundance of water, particularly young plants. Soot or wood-ashes strewn about them will, in a great measure, prevent the attacks of insects.

Beans.—Pull up early crops as soon as they have done bearing; those advancing will produce better for being well watered. Make a groove each side of the rows, and give enough to soak the ground to a considerable depth.

Runner-beans.—Apply strong sticks, if not already done. These beans may be kept dwarf by picking off the runners as fast as they appear; but it is much better to let them have full play by providing supports: the produce is tenfold greater.

Peas.—If any are sown this month, let it be sorts that bear equally, or the shortening days will prevent their bearing at all. Dwarf early sorts are best. Clear away any that have ceased to be productive, and stake those that are just above ground. Copious waterings will greatly benefit those coming into flower, but may be discontinued when they begin to pod, excepting for tall sorts, which continue bearing and flowering at the same time.

Celery.—The main crop should be got out directly. If this is planted where peas had previously grown, make the trenches *between*, not *on* the rows where the ground has been heavily drawn, or the crop will not be so good. It is very proper to give early crops plenty of room, so that, should they not be ready to clear away, other crops may be planted between, while they are growing.

Cardoons, like celery, should be got out in the trenches, remembering that they require a soil highly enriched with manure; they should also have plenty of room and abundance of water: be not hasty in earthing-up.

Beet.—See that this crop is properly thinned, and keep the ground well hoed between.

Carrots may be sown any time this month; they will be useful in winter and spring. Sow on an open spot, and do not dig the ground deep; look over the main crop, and pull up any runners: they will be of no use if left. Take care that no weeds are allowed to grow.

Onions may be sown now for salad in the autumn. Towards the end of this month some of the main crop will be showing signs of maturity, when they may be pulled up and laid on their sides, and thick-necked ones may be pinched.

Leeks.—Plant out the main crop on well-manured ground in deep drills or shallow trenches, for the convenience of earthing. Leeks are strong feeders, and should be well watered.

Potatoes.—Pick off the flowers, if possible: if allowed to seed, they diminish the produce, the tubers growing less in proportion to the quantity of seed allowed to ripen. Some advise cutting off the haum as soon as any disease appears.

Turnips.—At the beginning of this month, a principal sowing should be made for autumn and early winter use, and again, towards the end, another sowing should be made. These will be useful in winter and following spring. Some prefer broadcast, and using the large hoe continually, till the plants meet. Some recommend sowing in drills a foot apart, and sowing soot, wood-ashes, superphosphate of lime, and other ingredients at the same time. The seed must be protected from birds.

Surface Crops.—*French Beans.*—A late sowing of these may be made now any time: dwarf kinds, as the Newington Wonder, are best. Sow on unmanured soil; thin out sufficiently above ground to four or six inches apart, and draw plenty of earth up to the stems, which will stay them in windy weather.

Lettuce sown now do well on a shady border, provided the spot is not too much overhung by trees. An open well-manured spot is best for them, if kept well watered.

Endive.—Two sowings should be made this month; one at the beginning, another towards the end. Sow in the same way as lettuce, and plant out as soon as large enough to handle.

Tomatoes should be carefully trained, and stopped as tney grow. Stop just over a bunch of flowers, and leave no more shoots than can be conveniently trained. Unless the ground is very dry, they do not require watering.

Vegetable-Marrows will be in active growth; and, planted on a manure-heap, they will grow freely enough without watering; but if on the common soil, they should be freely watered in the morning.

Spinach.—It is not advisable to sow this month; but the ground should be prepared for sowing next month.

Brassicas (*Brocoli*, *Brussels Sprouts*, *and Savoy*).—The principal crops of these should be got out. Plant them in drills two feet apart, and 18 inches in the rows. If liable to club, dip the roots in a puddle of clay and soot before planting, or fill up the holes with wood-ashes, which will prevent it in a great measure.

Cabbage.—Sow for coleworts early in the month, and for early cabbaging about the end of it: strew lime in soot over the young plants, to drive away the fly. This should be done in the morning, while the dew is on them. Plant out for autumn use.

Cauliflower sown now may be useful late in the autumn.

Mint, and such-like herbs, should be cut for drying just as they begin to flower; *Savory*, *Sage*, and others, may be now propagated by cuttings or division; *Parsley* and *Chervil* may be sown for winter use.

Fruit-Garden.—Peaches and Nectarines should receive their final thinning. Some prefer allowing them to get large enough to use for pies, &c., before doing so; but the sooner the surplus fruit is taken off the better for the crop. Some little judgment must be exercised in thinning both wood and fruit; the object being to regulate both, so that a fair balance be maintained: if too much fruit is left on, the present year's crop will not be so good, nor will the strength of the tree be maintained for future bearing; if too much wood is left, the fruit is unduly shaded, and the wood itself becomes weak: regulate both, so that the present crop of fruit has a fair chance of doing well, and just about enough wood is left to furnish the tree for another year, without having recourse to much pruning in the winter. Nail in neatly all the young wood, and give the fruit the slightest shelter of the leaves; and no more: too much shade deteriorates the flavour of the fruit; no shading at all is apt to produce a premature ripening of it.

Apricots, Plums, Cherries, and Figs, on walls, should be carefully looked over, and all shoots that are not really useful, or any that are ill-placed and cannot be properly nailed in, should be removed. It is important to do this in time, because, if neglected till the fruit begins to ripen, the real advantage of doing it is lost: disbudding ought in no case to be deferred. Figs, especially, are apt to make strong superfluous wood, the leaves of which throw a dense shade over the fruit and impede the ripening. The garden-engine should be played freely over wall-trees about two or three times a week, to wash off dust and insects, and maintain that cleanliness so conducive to health.

Espaliers and dwarf fruit-trees should receive the same amount of attention. The summer training and pruning is of the greatest importance, since, when a bud or small shoot is taken off now, the wound is small, and no harm need be apprehended: this is not always the case as regards the cuts produced in winter pruning.

Standard trees are usually left to take care of themselves and their fruit during the summer time; but good gardeners attend well to them, as to wall-trees; nor is there any reason why they should not. Judicious pruning, stopping, and removing superfluous wood at this time, prevent, in a great measure, gumming, canker, and immature decay in standard trees. Time will also be well spent in thinning out the fruit if too thickly set.

Vines out of doors should be closely stopped and trained in. All the heat of the sun is necessary to the well-doing of this fruit, which cannot be expected to ripen in our short seasons, unless every care is taken to secure it all the light and warmth of the sun.

Gooseberries, Currants, Raspberries, and other bush-fruit will require some protection from birds. Nothing is better for the purpose than tanned netting or old herring-net, spread over and round the tree, completely covering it in. Caterpillars are often abundant on gooseberry and currant bushes; and various ways are propounded for destroying them; as spreading old tan under the bushes, and after a time burning it to destroy the larvæ; picking them off, or shaking them on to a cloth or sheet.

Strawberries.—This is by far the best month of the year for making new plantations. There are various methods of doing it: perhaps the best is as follows:—The earliest runners are laid in 3-inch pots, fixed in their place by means of small pegs; in three weeks they have rooted into the soil with which the pots are filled. During this time they require an occasional watering, but may be planted out permanently as soon as rooted, placing them eighteen inches apart in rows three feet apart. This is a clean and expeditious mode; the plants bear the following year better than old plants. It is also the best mode of obtaining potted plants for forcing the following winter or spring; for this purpose, however, they should not be dissevered from the old plants till they are well rooted. They should then receive good culture till the autumn, when they may be stored in frames. Strawberries are sometimes grown on permanent beds four feet wide. Another method is to have them in narrow beds, two feet wide, with two-foot alleys between. When they have ceased bearing, the runners are allowed to trail over the alleys, and when they are well covered, the old beds are dug in. Next year the same process is repeated: thus a succession of young plants is kept in bearing with very little trouble.

In hot summers the earth about the roots of fruit-trees, &c., often becomes so parched, that the fruit is not properly nourished in the process of swelling or stoning. The following mode of remedying this evil, especially in the case of vine borders, cannot be too strongly recommended:—Perforated pipes are laid about a foot or eighteen inches below the surface of the soil,—in the case of strawberry-beds, about six inches; from these a tube is carried to a convenient place for filling with water or liquid manure, with which they are charged twice a day, or as often as it is considered necessary. By this means a thorough moistening of the roots is effected, greatly to the improvement of the crop and flavour of the fruit.

Flower-cultivation under Glass.—Conservatory.—The "sere and yellow leaf" is now apparent here: the work of decay has commenced; exotic bulbs have nearly finished flowering, and require a state of rest; those whose stems are still green should have water, in order to mature the bulbs. When done flowering, keep them in dry earth

or sand, and in a warm situation, to ripen. Cinerarias and calceolarias require as cool an atmosphere as the house admits of; those which have flowered may be cut down and planted out in a light loamy border: seeds of both for flowering in spring should be sown. Cuttings of geraniums and most greenhouse shrubs may now be struck, and forwarded by plunging in a gentle hotbed, taking as cuttings only strong and healthy shoots three to five or six inches long, according to the size of the plants. These cuttings should be planted in pans, boxes, or pots of rich light compost, a few inches apart, moderately watered, and placed in a frame shaded from the midday sun till they are rooted. Soft-wooded plants like the geranium hardly require such delicate treatment, although they strike sooner under it. Cactuses, euphorbias, and other succulent plants of similar habit, can now be struck in beds or pots of light compost without the help of artificial heat, but they root more readily in bark or hotbed and frame.

Fuchsias, geraniums, achimenes, and salvias, requiring larger pots, should be shifted, removing the entire ball, and placing them in the centre of the new pot, properly drained and half-filled with fresh compost. Having first trimmed the roots when the pots are filled up with compost, let them be well watered, and put away in an airy but shaded situation, to settle. All pots and tubs, especially orange and lemon plants, require stirring on the surface of the soil, and to be top-dressed and watered. Oranges, camellias, azaleas, and other hard-wooded plants, can now be budded or grafted: in the beginning of the month, myrtles, oleanders, and jasmines may be propagated by layers.

The stocks for budding orange-trees are raised from seeds sown in March or April in pots of rich earth, and plunged into a hotbed. In five or six weeks the plants will come up, when they may be planted singly in thumb-pots, and plunged into a fresh hotbed; the

July.

frame should be raised as the plants increase in height, to encourage their growth. In August they will be eighteen or twenty inches high, when they may be removed into the greenhouse, placing them near the lights. In March or April shift them into larger pots, and plunge again into a hotbed, gradually exposing them to the air towards the end of May, to harden them, and turning them out from June till August. In the third summer they will be fit for budding, for which they are best prepared by removal into the greenhouse, giving them plenty of air and light, and turning the side on which they are to be budded from the sun. Three weeks before budding, the plants may be plunged into a moderate hotbed of tanner's bark, where they can have free ventilation.

Hard-wooded plants, including most of the genera from New Holland, which bloom early in the spring, will about the middle of the month be so far advanced in their new growth that any requiring re-potting should at once have a shift. After turning them out, loosen the outside roots before placing them in their new pots, to enable them to take up the fresh soil more readily. Keep them close for a few days, especially if the roots have been much disturbed, and damp them once or twice daily overhead.

Attention at this season should be directed to the stock of plants intended to furnish the supply of bloom through the winter, as it is requisite plants should complete their growth early for this purpose. Of heaths, those which flower through the winter should also be encouraged to complete their growth. Keep epacrises under glass till their growth is complete; but more air and light must be allowed them as the wood gets firmer. Towards the end of the month they may be placed out of doors in an open situation, where they can be protected from heavy rains. Young specimens should be carefully trained, the shoots neatly tied down or pegged, to insure a compact habit; the flowers of heaths, &c., dying off should be removed. Stop all straggling branches.

Such stove-plants as are intended to flower in the winter, as justicias, *Eranthemum pulchellum*, euphorbias, jasmines, &c., should be looked to. Many of these things require to be kept in small pots, and should be watered with liquid manure, to grow them on without getting into too large pots.

Balsams, thunbergias, and other annuals intended to decorate the conservatory and show-house for the next two months, should be finally potted, using soil of a light and rich description. Keep down spider with the syringe. Ipomœas, thunbergias, and other creepers, should be neatly trained to their respective trellises as they advance, keeping them fresh and healthy by frequent watering, and by picking off all decaying leaves; and, where the plants are flagging, water them with very weak liquid manure.

Brugmansias, and similar plants of vigorous habit, should be frequently assisted with manure-water: as they are often troubled with red spider, the engine and syringe must be kept constantly at work, taking care, however, not to injure the fine foliage. Succulent plants, as cactuses, euphorbias, cereuses, sedums, and others of similar habit, require to be abundantly supplied with water, and also a full exposure to the sun, in order to obtain a fine bloom.

Remove from the conservatory all plants which show, by their faded blooms, that they are past their best: their prolonged presence would detract from the freshness essential to beauty and good order.

Achimenes, gloxinias, &c., out of bloom should be removed to a pit to ripen their bulbs. Clerodendrons, &c., in the same way may be transferred to vineries, or any place where there is a dry cool atmosphere.

At no period of the year do heaths and hard-wooded plants require more care than the present, particularly such as have been recently potted. To keep the old ball sufficiently moist to preserve the plant in health in the high temperature without getting the new soil in a sour state, requires great nicety in watering, supposing the plants to be under glass. At this season all the air possible should be given to the greenhouse and stove plants, keeping it on all night.

Greenhouse plants, after they have done blooming, should have a comparatively cool temperature, and no structure presents so many advantages for this purpose, as well as for growing delicate-leaved plants through the summer, as houses having a north aspect; while for the purpose of retarding plants and for preserving them in bloom, it is indispensable. Such plants, therefore, as epacrises, leschenaultias, pimeleas, aphelexis, and others of similar habit, which have been kept for late bloom and are now over, should be placed in a house of the above description, or in deep frames, with the sashes turned towards the north, having first picked off the old remaining blooms : here, with gentle syringing once or twice daily, the plants may remain till the new growth commences, and afterwards be placed in a more favourable situation for ripening their wood.

Camellias, whenever the young wood appears getting ripe, may be removed to the open air: they thrive best in the shade; they must be placed on a dry bottom to prevent worms from getting into the pots.

Chinese azaleas should also be turned out. Unlike camellias, they require full exposure to sun and air, and should be placed in an open situation, that their wood may become thoroughly ripened. It will, however, perhaps be necessary to place them for a week or two in a partially-shaded situation, to harden their foliage sufficiently to bear the full sun; otherwise the sudden change from a house to full sunshine might cause their leaves to turn brown or burn.

Orange- and lemon-trees will now be in bloom, and should be supplied with water at least three times a week in dry weather, and occasionally supplied with liquid manure after stirring the surface of the soil and top-dressing. Orange-trees when too full of bloom should have the flowers thinned out. They are always in request for drying or distilling. The young fruit when too thickly set should also have a thinning. To procure dark glossy foliage, water with clear soot-water.

Fruit-culture under Glass.—Vinery.—Ripe grapes, if required to be kept, must be shaded during hot sun, to prevent shrivelling. The Cannon Hall, Muscat, Sweetwater, and Frontignans, having tender leaves, are most liable to burn, either from bad glass or imperfect ventilation. They must be well watched, as the injury done to the foliage not only affects the present crop but the succeeding one. Any heat given now should be given during the day, to forward them before the season gets too far on.

As the houses are cleared of their fruit and the wood is ripened, the vines will be much benefited by having the lights off, and by being freely exposed to the atmosphere. Air must be given in abundance by night as well as day, and the necessary stopping of lateral growths and thinning of the fruit in the last house proceeded with. Watch for mildew. Vines in pots, intended to fruit next season, should now be well supplied with manure-water, to swell out and perfect their buds.

Peaches and Nectarines.—Any tendency to the leaves decaying, when the fruit has been gathered, should be prevented by syringing and watering the roots. Fruit coming to maturity will be the more delicious for a comparatively cool temperature while ripening. Examine daily and gather before it is over ripe. The great object now is to get the wood properly ripened; and that will be best promoted by a full exposure to the sun, the air, the rain, and the dews, by removing the sashes and top-lights.

Pinery.—Still continue to supply swelling fruit with water, and syringe frequently, but not during bright sunshine, unless the shading is immediately put on. Young plants growing fast will require liberal watering, in addition to air in large quantities by day: the temperature will allow them to have a good portion by night. During hot weather forced fruits of all descriptions will be benefited by this practice.

About the second week, the plants selected in the spring for autumn and winter fruiting will be showing fruit; and if they are in a pit by themselves, will require, if a steady bottom-heat is kept up, but little attention for some time, except slight shading, plenty of air, and a liberal allowance of water. On no account let the plants be wetted while in bloom. Some pines having large flowers, as the Jamaica, &c., frequently cut up with black spots in the middle, although apparently sound outside, which arises from a small quantity of water passing through the bloom to the fruit-cells, and causing the latter to decay.

Let succession plants have abundance of air day and night, to encourage a stocky growth. Where it is intended to plant out the fruiting stock for next year, a sufficient quantity of loam, peat, and sand should be in readiness for use. Directly the present crop is cut, the stumps should be cleared out, and either all, or part of the soil, removed, according as it may appear exhausted.

As soon as the principal part of the present crop is ripe, the pit will most likely be required either for fruiting the winter stock, or for the succession intended for next season. Whatever fruit, therefore, may yet remain to ripen, should be carefully removed to one end of the pit, unless it can be transferred to a house devoted to fruiting the autumn and winter supply. The bottom-heat must be freshened up by the addition of fresh material, and made ready for plunging the new stock of plants as they are placed in their fruiting-pots.

Advantage should be taken of this change to put the house in repair, if requisite, and the heating apparatus in a state of efficiency: no such favourable opportunity will occur again for a twelvemonth. Give air liberally to successions, and water freely when the pots become full of roots. Keep the bottom-heat steady. At this season young plants may be potted whenever they require a shift.

Figs swelling off their second crop should be assisted with liquid manure, more especially if growing in pots or tubs. As the fruit ripens, care must be taken to preserve it from damp, which the frequent syringing to keep down insects induces; it should be a rule, therefore, to look over and pick the ripe fruit every morning, and syringe directly afterwards: admit air freely, and pinch out the points of the young wood when grown sufficiently long. This will assist the swelling of the fruit, and produce useful spurs for bearing next year. Figs should be so managed during the summer, that nothing further than a slight thinning-out should be wanted in the winter.

Proceed to pot strawberries for forcing: as soon as the pots in which the runners were layered becomed filled with roots, pot them in 6- or 7-inch pots, using rich loam of medium texture, and well-rotted dung, with plenty of drainers. The kinds intended for early forcing need not have quite such large pots as those intended for a later supply. When potted, place them in an open situation exposed to the sun, on boards, or a prepared bottom, to prevent worms from getting to the roots.

Melons.—Keep a steady bottom-heat and free ventilation, more especially in wet weather. Watch for red spider and mildew; for both of which, sulphur, properly applied, is the best remedy: also keep the roots in action by a well-adjusted bottom-heat. Sow Lord Kenyon's, or any other good house cucumber, for autumn supply, following the same directions as for melons.

Orchard-house.—Ventilation is now the greatest care; fasten back and front shutters down, so that they cannot be closed; syringing night and morning, and watering copiously when dry. If any trees are growing too rapidly, tilt up the pots, and cut off all the roots on that side which are making their way into the soil. A week later, serve the other side in the same way. If the surface is getting hard from watering, place some fresh compost loosely on the surface. Pinch in all lateral shoots to within two buds of their base. On the 10th and the 25th lift the pots, in order to break off the roots. Remove all trees into the open air, to ripen their fruit in a sheltered sunny spot. This will greatly increase the flavour of the fruit.

Hotbed- and Frame-Cultivation.—The purposes of hotbeds are limited at this time of the year, at least in most places. Cucumbers, melons, &c., are usually grown in houses and pits that are otherwise unoccupied at present; and as their culture is more cleanly in this way, hotbeds may be dispensed with; those, however, already in operation will require attention. The weather is usually hot this month and next, but is often changeable, and the manager of frames must be ruled by it. We sometimes have sudden aud heavy showers, which would drench the plants and beds if they were uncovered, probably to their destruction. Plenty of fresh air is necessary; and the sudden changes produced by clouds obscuring the sun for a time, and then bursting forth hot and fierce, must be provided against: it is in such cases that a little shade may be advantageous; but it must be very slight, and not be left on a moment longer than is really required.

Many gardeners make hotbeds at this time for propagating plants—as roses and greenhouse plants,—and also for other purposes connected with the flower-garden, &c. Hotbeds made in the ordinary way, where the material is plentiful, are probably the best; but a very useful bed for propagating and raising seeds, &c., is made as

follows:—Having prepared the dung as usual, lay the foundation as for an ordinary bed, but commence from the bottom an opening which leaves the bed hollow; the sides and ends of the bed are narrowed at an angle from the bottom, and drain-pipes are laid to conduct the heat from the linings into this hollow, which is covered by boards laid across, on which the frame rests; the boards are then covered with soil, ashes, tan, or dung: while the heat of the bed lasts, the pipes must be plugged up, but opened when lining is applied, to conduct the heat into the bed.

Cucumbers in bearing should be watered. If the soil is not sufficiently moist, take care to water plentifully, as at this time of the year there is less danger of overwatering. If the weather is hot, and not too dry, the lights may be pulled quite off for an hour or two before 8 a.m. and after 5 p.m.; but be careful that the plants are not chilled before closing. Pickling cucumbers may be planted in the open ground at the beginning of this month. The soil should be well dug, and made pretty firm again, and well mulched after the plants are put in. Choose a warm sheltered spot for them, and place hand-glasses over them if they can be spared.

Melons planted at the beginning of this month may be put out in the ordinary manner in a common melon-pit, with a good body of dung; but, if planted later, it must be so that heat can be applied to ripen the fruit, which will be required, as the days are short. Plants that are ripening their fruit must have very little water.

Capsicums, &c., in fruiting condition, should remain in the pots, and be plunged in the bed; the roots will ramble through the pots, but they are more likely to bear than if planted in the bed.

Mushroom-beds.—These may yet be made out of doors, providing plenty of clean straw and mats to protect them. Some gardeners make a practice of spawning melon-beds, either while the fruit is ripening, or after they are cleared off. It is done in this manner:—Clear off the old soil, break the spawn into small pieces, lay it regularly over the bed, and cover it with about two inches of horse-droppings, or very short dung. Let this again be covered with two or three inches of good loamy soil, and all trodden down and made firm. Heat may be applied by means of fresh linings of well-worked dung.

JUNE (Monthly Calendar).

Aspect of the Month.—The direct power of the sun's rays indeed is now at its maximum, although the radiation of heat from the earth's surface, which decides the temperature of our atmosphere, does not attain its highest point till August. The variation of the temperature is still great, ranging, according to local circumstances, from a few degrees above freezing to 90°, the mean heat being 58°. The average mean temperature at Chiswick, for a period of ten years, at one foot below the surface, was 60°; at two feet, 58°; and on the surface, 60° 45′; the mean maximum and minimum being respectively 64° 13′, 63° 10′; 81° 13′, 45° 10′. The dryness of the atmosphere is also at its height in our moist climate, and vegetation now depends on the "Orient pearl;" the dew, with which the atmosphere is laden, is condensed, and every blade of grass and leaf saturated with it an hour or two after sunset and sunrise. Beautiful indeed are the mornings and evenings of June, when the dew hangs upon leaf and blossom, and beautiful the economy of Nature as displayed in this arrangement; for the formation of dew is an illustration of the law of attraction.

Flower-Garden and Shrubberies.—As soon as the beds, borders, &c., of the flower-garden are finished, the baskets and vases filled, and the general spring planting-out brought to a close, the remaining stock of bedding-plants should be looked over. A portion will be required for stock; and as a considerable number of plants will in all probability be required to make good failures, or to replace beds now occupied with short-blooming plants, and other demands through the season—these, with few exceptions, had better be kept in pots; and therefore, if any unpotted cuttings yet remain, let them be potted off into clean pots. Re-pot others, also, getting too full of roots, plunging them afterwards in ashes, in a cool shady situation, and pinching off all early or premature blooms: they will soon be ready for turning out. A few kinds of annuals should also, for the same purpose, be sown on a light soil and shady border. By frequently transplanting and stopping, their tendency to bloom will be encouraged, and the formation of roots promoted, and they will soon bear removing to the permanent beds without injury.

The newly-planted beds require constant watching. All failures should be instantly made good, and the tying and staking of everything requiring support attended to. Where an early display of flowers is not wanted, the buds may be pinched off. Cuttings of *Iberis saxatilis* root readily under a handglass at this season: when placed in a shady situation, they form a beautiful edging, and may be cut like box for a week or two, to encourage the plants to cover the ground. Pansies, anemones, double wallflowers, and other spring plants, should be removed as they go out of bloom, to make room for autumn-flowering ones, the beds being made up with fresh compost, in planting the later. Creepers against walls or trellises should be gone over and tied or nailed in.

Rose-Garden.—Standard and pillar roses should likewise be looked over to see that they are properly secured to their stakes. This being the month in which roses are in their glory, care should be taken that their effect is not destroyed by imperfect buds or deformed flowers. Weak-growing shoots should be tied up and regulated, and all fading flowers and seed-vessels removed, cutting back the perpetual or autumn-flower kinds, as soon as all the flowers of the branch are expanded, to the most prominent vertical eye, stirring the ground and saturating it with manure-water, or sprinkling the ground with guano and watering with soft rain-water.

Towards the end of the month many shoots will be firm enough for budding, and some sorts work best on the flowering shoots, provided the buds are taken before the flowering is over.

Watch the different annuals as they come into flower, and mark those varieties whose superior habit of growth, size of flower, and brilliancy of colour, make it desirable that seed should be saved from them.

Florists' Flowers.—*Dahlias.*—Dahlias already planted out should be watered in the evenings with soft water overhead, the soil being previously stirred, and others planted out for later bloom, taking care, in hot weather, to mulch round the roots, where it can be done without being unsightly, with short well-decomposed dung. As the shoots advance, train and tie them up carefully, and search for earwigs and slugs in the mornings.

Ranunculuses will be making rapid growth. Always water in the evening, and with water which has been exposed to the rays of the sun. When they begin to show colour, the awning, or other shade, should be placed over them.

Carnations, *Picotees*, and *Pinks*, as they advance, should be tied to their stakes, reducing the number of the shoots according to the strength of the plant. Care should be taken that the flower-pods of pinks do not burst; and those having ligatures round them will require easing and re-tying. Shade any forward flowers, giving plenty of water and liquid manure.

Auriculas and *Polyanthuses* should be removed into a northern aspect, all decayed petals taken away from the seed-pods, and as the capsules turn brown, they should be gathered. Water as they require it, and keep the pots free from weeds.

Pansies struck from cuttings in April and May will produce fine blooms if planted in shady situations, or potted into 6-inch pots, and shaded in very bright weather. Cuttings may still be taken from promising plants. Mark all seedlings having good or singular properties.

About the second week, the awning may be taken from the tulip-shed, and the foliage of the plants exposed fully to the action of the sun and rain. Offsets in warm situations will require taking up before those on the main bed: as soon as the foliage turns yellow, they may be removed with safety. Seedlings which have grown one year should be allowed to remain in the ground during the first winter; when two years old, they may be lifted and kept separated.

Reserve-Garden.—A shady piece of ground in the reserve-garden should now be prepared for cuttings of double wallflowers, rockets, sweetwilliams, pansies, and other plants required for next spring's bloom. Alreetias and many other spring-flowering plants may also be divided and planted out this month; and beds of annuals for autumn-flowering should be sown in the space left by the zinnias, China asters, and marigolds planted out.

Kitchen-Garden. — Many principal crops come in this month, and, following suddenly upon a time when the supply from the kitchen-garden is somewhat scanty, show the real effect of cropping too abundantly in the early part of the year. Peas, beans, cauliflowers, carrots, potatoes, and many other vegetables, come in all at once, that could not be produced earlier in the open ground. All show the propriety of dispersing the crops more regularly through the season. The young gardener should make a note of it, and endeavour to manage so that there is no flush of vegetables at one time and a dearth of them at others. Particularly let it be borne in mind that we have long cold springs, in which the weather is exceedingly variable and mostly ungenial, when vegetation makes very slow progress indeed; it is then that root-crops and brassicæ come in so useful; then that Brussels sprouts, kale, and brocoli yield a succession of sweet wholesome sprouts, that grow almost in the coldest weather, and form the principal supply from Christmas to May. It is now the time to look forward to that time and be well prepared for it, so that available space should have been left, in which a plentiful supply of the above-named can be grown. Ground that has been lying fallow since the winter can now be turned to good account; and be it remembered that fifty firm stocky plants of brocoli will yield a better supply than a hundred plants that have been drawn up between other crops, or been crowded. This month being generally a dry one, the watering-pot must not remain idle; many kitchen crops will not do well if kept dry. Most kinds of salads are worthless if stinted of water; and as a rule, a judicious application of it will amply repay the time and labour; but let it be applied copiously, for mere surface-watering only attracts the roots to the surface, to be burnt up by the sun.

Asparagus. — Water newly-planted beds, and keep clear of weeds. Beds in bearing will be benefited by an application of liquid manure.

Seakale.—Thin out the crowns where they are at all thick. A few strong heads are better than many weak ones: young seedlings will be benefited by a sprinkling of wood-ashes. It being a marine plant, salt may be strewn between the rows. Keep the young plants well watered, and hoe frequently between.

Beans.—The last sowing of these should be made for the season: they seldom pay for sowing later. Top those in bloom before they become infested with aphis. Mulching will increase the quantity and quality of the crop.

Runner Beans do well sown any time before midsummer. On light ground they may be dibbled in—an expeditious method. Some recommend soaking them in water for a day before sowing, which may be advantageous in hot, dry weather; but it is as well to water the drills or holes at the time of sowing. Those sown last month should be earthed and staked before they begin to run. This vegetable is often used by cottagers to form or cover an arbour, or fence, or screen, for which it is well adapted, except on account of its ephemeral character.

Nasturtiums may still be sown, being very quick at this time. Those already up should have their supports about four or five feet high.

Peas.—After the second week this month, it is not advisable to sow strong-growers,—such sorts as Auvergne or Champion of Paris. The time from sowing to bearing is less, and there is more certainty of a crop.

Celery will probably be in condition for final planting towards the end of this month: the main crop had better be deferred till next month. Celery is generally considered a gross feeder, requiring a rich, highly-manured soil and abundance of water. It certainly cannot be grown to perfection without both.

Carrots.—Thin without delay, but not too closely, as some are apt to run, even under the best culture. From nine inches to a foot is a good average. A succession may be sown any time before midsummer.

Onions should receive a final thinning, allowing eight or nine inches for the main crop. Use the small hoe as often as possible, and keep them clean. Onions for salading may still be sown. A shady border on the north side of a wall will suit them. Tree-onions, potato ditto, and those planted for seed, will require some support.

Leeks.—Plant in deep drills, to admit of earthing-up: give an abundance of water in dry weather. Soot dredged over them will stimulate them, and prevent the attacks of insects in a great measure.

Potatoes.—Earth up before they get too tall, but leave the top of the ridges nearly flat, so that the tubers are not buried too deeply. It is a great error many fall into of drawing the earth as high as possible up the stems. They do not bear so well, from the greater exclusion of air from the roots. Potatoes that have been retarded may be planted this month : they will yield new potatoes in the autumn.

Turnips.—Sow a good breadth of these—they will come in well and be very useful in the autumn. Sow immediately after rain, or, if the ground is light, immediately after digging. They grow very quickly ; but some slight protection from birds will be necessary the short time they are germinating. White worsted will generally be found efficient. Tread the seed in well, or use the wooden roller after sowing, but finish off with a rake.

Scorzoneras, &c.—Thin to about ten inches or a foot, and stir the ground well between them.

French Beans.—Sow a few rows of these for succession. There are many varieties; but it is immaterial what sort is sown, except on the question of flavour or productiveness. The larger-growing sorts are considered the best to sow now. The Royal Dun, the Negro and Cream-coloured, &c., unlike dwarfer sorts, continue in bearing a long time. Thin to four or six inches, and earth up, but give no manure.

Lettuce.—Sow on a north border, but plant in an open situation. It is necessary to sow often to insure a succession. Water the ground thoroughly, or not at all: surface-watering is very injurious.

Endive may be sown this month, as it is less likely to run now than formerly. The seed grows very quickly, and birds do not seem to care about it; it may therefore be merely sown broadcast, trodden and raked. Plant out early to insure a good curl in the leaf.

Vegetable-Marrows and Pumpkins should be got out early this month. If good strong plants, they may be merely planted on a sunny border ; but they are much better for having a little dung-heat ; or dung without heat will suit them, for they delight in a loose bed of light but well-rotted dung that they can root into easily. Give plenty of water if the weather holds dry.

Capsicums and Tomatoes the beginning of this month.—Plant these against a south wall if possible—otherwise against a sloping bank : the full sun is necessary to induce them to bear well. Any vacancies under and between wall-trees may be well filled up by them.

Cress.—Sow American and Normandy for succession.

Brocoli.—Defer not later than the middle of this month the final sowing of late sorts. Walcheren sown now will very likely come in during the winter. Plant out those that are ready, and never allow them to draw up in the seed-bed; but prick them out temporarily : they will pay for it. If there is no room for them otherwise, transplant in drills made for the purpose.

Brussels Sprouts, Borecole, and Savoys.—Get these planted for good as early as possible ; plant in drills two feet apart, and water freely. Puddling the roots in clay and soot mixed with water may be good for them and prevent clubbing in a great measure. Plant between rows of peas and beans that will soon be off the ground—no matter how firm the ground is. Judging from experience, this group do best if the ground has not been dug for several months before planting. Watering once a day, or oftener, will be necessary in dry weather.

Cabbage and Cauliflower should also be planted out when strong enough. The latter will prove very useful in August and September. A succession of these is an important matter.

Fruit-Garden.—If the fruit seems setting thickly, let it be partially thinned, reserving the main thinning, however, till after it has stoned. The trees will have been mulched last month to prevent evaporation, and should now be watered, and that so copiously that it does not require frequent repetition, pouring the water into the roots. *Apricots* will now require their final thinning, and stopping, and watering, also followed by mulching, which is important at this time for all fruit-trees where evaporation is active.

The beginning of the month is a busy period in this department, and much vigilance and perseverance will be requisite to keep pace with the advancing growth, in preventing and keeping down the different pests.

In disbudding pears, plums, and cherries, the fore-right shoots, and those not wanted for laying on, should remain for the present, as stopping them at this time would only cause a fresh breaking into wood, either of the eyes at the base of the stopped shoot, or some portion of the spurs; as they, however, look unsightly on well-regulated trees, it will be better to tie them slightly to the main branches for the present: this will give a better appearance to the trees, and bending the shoots will in some measure stop the over free flow of the sap, and so help the object in view. The precise time at which shoots should be shortened must be regulated according to the vigour of the tree, and should be deferred till all danger of the remaining eyes again breaking into wood is over. Cherry-trees now progressing towards maturity should be gone carefully over, the shoots stopped and laid in, and the trees netted, to save the fruit and protect it from birds. If the black-fly appears, cut off the ends of the shoots, unless it is more convenient to wash them in tobacco-water.

Where a large number of strawberries are yearly forced, the plants, after the fruit is gathered, will be found valuable for planting out, producing a most abundant crop the following year: the later-forced ones will answer best, as they are not so liable to bloom again in the autumn. Turn the plants into rich soil, and if they are only to remain one year, they may be planted pretty thick: water them till they get established. Place straw, or some similar material, between strawberries now in bloom, to preserve the fruit clean in heavy rains, and to keep the ground moist.

Figs.—Stop all except the leading shoots, when they have made three or four joints, and lay on leaders and shoots required for filling up. Watering the roots with soap-suds is found greatly to benefit the fruit.

Vines will require going over. Thin out what wood is not wanted for bearing, and stop the bearing shoots at one joint above the shoot: nail in the leading shoots close to the wall. Where the long-rod system of pruning is adopted, a shoot must be selected and carried up from the bottom of each stem, to furnish bearing wood for next year. By careful attention to the vine-border and to pruning, the vine on open walls may be made much more productive, as well as ornamental, than it usually is.

Remove useless suckers from raspberry plantations, to admit more sun and air to the fruit. Begin to layer strawberries in 60-pots directly runners can be obtained for next season's forcing. Let the soil used be rich and rather light, to encourage the runners to root freely: when layered, do not let them suffer for want of water.

Flowers under Glass—The Conservatory.—The difficulty of furnishing the conservatory is now one of taste and selection. Every floral tribe will now be ready to furnish its quota, and discrimination only is required in selecting and arranging them. Avoid crowding; encourage variety and harmonious contrast in colour; remove all decayed or decaying blossom, and guard against insects of all kinds by cleanliness and timely fumigation. Regulate the luxurious growth of creepers and border-plants, watering copiously, occasionally using liquid manure.

Ventilation is now of the utmost importance. Air should be admitted night and day, except in cold gloomy weather, and shading from the burning sun attended to for an hour or two daily.

Large orange-trees grown for the flower-garden or grounds during the summer months may now be moved to the places they are to occupy. If they have been kept cool and airy, they will not have commenced their new growth, which should not take place till they are out of doors.

Fruit-culture under Glass.—Houses where the grapes are ripe should be kept dry, and succession crops encouraged by a little heat, according to their several stages. Although the nights are now getting warm, it will still be necessary to apply artificial heat, both in houses ripening and in later crops now in bloom, especially where Muscats, West's St. Peter's, and other shy setters are grown, as they rarely form perfectly-shaped bunches without a warm and dry atmosphere, which in our climate requires fire-heat. Stop all lateral shoots in the succession-house after thinning the crop, that nothing may interfere with the swelling of the fruit. As the season advances, air must be given in abundance, the ventilators being left partially open by night. To prevent the atmosphere from becoming too dry during hot weather, keep the floors, interior walls, paths, and pipes damp by sprinkling several times a day. This will also assist to keep in check the ravages of the red spider. Where new vine borders have been made in the spring, the present is a favourable time for planting if the vines have been started sufficiently long to have a shoot of moderate length. In planting, liberate the roots freely, and spread them in the direction of the border, giving a slight watering, and mulching the surface. The house should be kept rather closer for a few days, shading the newly-planted vines, if disposed to flag, until they show indications of starting, when the usual routine must be followed, preserving the young vines from injury by tying and training the leader up the roof.

Vines training in pots for next season's fruiting require daily attention and stopping: when they have attained a proper length required for fruiting, stop the laterals and expose the principal leaves to the light. Water with liquid manure when the pots are full of roots.

Pinery.—The principal crop of summer pines, now swelling their fruit, must be encouraged by frequent waterings, using liquid manure alternately. Support each fruit in an upright position, and remove useless gills and suckers, reserving only sufficient of the latter for stock. Shade with some light material during the middle of bright sunny days, unless vines are grown over them; bearing in mind that the more light they get the better will be the colour and flavour of the fruit. Give air early, increasing it as the day advances, and close early in the afternoon, at which time the plants, beds, and interior walls should be damped over. When the nights become warmer, a little air may again be put on, which will assist the colouring of the fruit. To insure strong sturdy plants, maintain a uniform bottom-heat of 90° during the season of active growth. The frosty nights which occasionally occur, and cloudy or rainy days, require that this temperature should be kept up by fire-heat.

Peach-house.—The ripe fruit should be looked over each morning, to gather such as are likely to ripen in a day or two. The fruit will be higher in flavour than when allowed to ripen on the tree, and will be saved from getting bruised in falling, to which heavy fruit of the peach is very liable, with the best contrivances to catch them. As the crop is gathered, the young wood should be so exposed as to ripen well.

Melons.—As soon as the fruit is cut (if it is intended that there should be a second crop), prune back the shoots to where the fresh growth commences. Two or three inches of fresh loam should be spread over the surface of the bed, which should at the same time have a good soaking with manure-water, to assist the plants to make a fresh growth; an additional stimulus at the same time should be given to the roots by slightly increasing the bottom-heat. Bring forward the succeeding crops.

Cucumbers at this season of the year do best with a considerable amount of shade: this should be attended to, and the necessary bottom-heat and moisture kept up. Keep the vines thin and regular by frequent stopping. In planting out at this season, use a rather poor, in preference to a rich soil, which in cold wet seasons produces canker.

Orchard-houses.—In hot and dry weather trees will require watering abundantly every evening; in all weathers syringe morning and evening, at seven a.m. and six p.m. If the surface of the soil in the pots or border be dry, a new top-dressing may be added. Thin the fruit, pinching in all shoots to the third leaf.

Remove plum-trees and apricots into the open air to ripen their fruit. On the 10th, and again on the 25th, lift up the pots in order to break off the roots which have protruded through the drainage-holes, and attend to summer-pinching of pyramid and bush trees.

Ventilation and watering as in last month, syringing till the fruit begins to colour. Pinch the laterals, and at the end pinch off all leading shoots. The ripening of peaches, apricots, and nectarines may be retarded by removal into the open air. Summer-pinch pyramidal peaches.

Hotbed- and Frame-Cultivation. — Making hotbeds is seldom deferred till this time of the year; yet it may be done advantageously. Both cucumbers and melons, if started this month, will pay for cultivating; the directions for doing so being the same as in former months, it is unnecessary to repeat; but common brick pits will be very suitable for the purpose. Cucumbers in an advanced stage will want clearing of dead leaves, and the soil stirred about them, and probably fresh earth added. A toad kept in a frame will destroy a great many woodlice and other insects, and keep the plants cleaner than they otherwise would be.

Cucumbers are sometimes allowed to trail over a trellis; by this means the fruit is suspended, and no glass tubes are required to keep them straight: some even when grown on a bed are tied up with sticks for the same purpose. When tubes are used, it is sometimes necessary to watch them, in order that, during the swelling of the fruit, it does not get wedged into the tubes so tightly as to be difficult to withdraw. Care should be taken that the bloom which adorns the fruit is not removed in cutting. In the application of lining to maintain the heat, in watering and giving air, &c., proceed as before.

Plants intended for open-air culture, if sown last month, will be ready for ridging out. A south border, or between rows of tall peas or scarlet runners, ranging north and south, will suit them. Open a trench four or five feet wide, and fill with prepared stable-dung, to the thickness of three feet; cover this with a foot of soil; place the plants five or six feet apart, two or three together, and cover with hand-glasses.

Melons may be started for succession. As these are not generally continuous bearers, nothing is gained by endeavouring to induce old plants to bear again: it is more satisfactory to raise fresh plants and make new beds for them, unless, indeed, they are planted on old beds newly lined. With a tolerable bottom-heat, the growth of these plants is very rapid at this time of the year; and though they may be grown without it, still, for the production of fine fruit, heat is indispensable.

KALE.

Preparation of the Soil.—To secure heavy crops of this hardy useful winter vegetable, a deep rich soil is essential.

The ground should be trenched two feet deep and liberally manured.

Time and Manner of Sowing.—For the main crops, sow about the middle of March, covering the seeds thinly and evenly. Another sowing may be made about the middle of May, which will furnish plants for filling spare ground in August.

Time and Manner of Planting.—The Cottager's Kale, which is one of the best and most useful of this tribe, should be planted in rows not less than two feet six inches apart, allowing the same distance between the plants. Unless these are properly cared for, and planted out as soon as they are sufficiently strong, they will not, in cold localities, furnish sprouts until spring. A moderate breadth of the Dwarf Feathered, and any other esteemed sorts, should be got out as early as circumstances will permit.

Spare ground may, however, be planted with these as late as the middle of August, and although the crop will not be so abundant as from the June planting, they may yield a fair produce at a time when vegetables are scarce, particularly if they have previously been transplanted with a little care into nursery lines, about four inches apart, so as to have them strong and stocky. Keep the ground between the rows open and clear of weeds, by frequent stirrings. The tall-growing varieties will be benefited, particularly in exposed situations, by ridging the soil up about their stems. If the weather is dry at the time of planting, water occasionally until the plants get fairly established. The best varieties are :—

Asparagus, or Chou de Milan.
Buda Kale,—sometimes called asparagus.
Cottagers' Kale.
Feathered, or Fine Dwarf Curled German Greens.
New Imperial Hearting.
Melville's Garnishing.

KAL'MIA (nat. ord. Erica'ceæ).

This pretty shrub, known also by the name of the Calico Laurel, is a native of North America, and should be treated as rhododendrons, &c., with bog earth. The Kalmias are quite hardy. They may be propagated by seed or by layers, and with care may be transplanted at almost any season.

KAULFUS'SIA (nat. ord. Compos'itæ).

These little free-flowering plants, of good compact growth, are, when well grown, exceedingly effective in beds or mixed borders : they grow freely in any soil.

Kaulfussia amelloides,—bright blue, ½ ft., from Cape of Good Hope.
Kaulfussia rosea,—rose, with mauve centre, ½ ft.

KENNE'DIA (nat. ord. Legumino'sæ).

There are many species of this beautiful plant, and all of them, we believe, natives of Australia. In habit they are climbers, and in our climate must be grown under glass. They require a sandy loam or peat, and admit of easy propagation by cutting.

KIDNEY-BEAN.

Kidney-beans may be grown in the open ground or forced by heat. In an ordinary hotbed, as if made for cucumbers, place as many 6-inch pots as will stand fifteen inches apart. These pots being filled with good loamy soil, plant in each, triangularly, three Newington-wonder beans, a sort which is of small dwarf habit and a great bearer, and, as they grow, give them regular waterings; but they need not be removed, and the heat should never fall below 60°. They are very susceptible of frost, and will require careful protection. Nothing can be better for covering the lights than hurdles made of lath and straw. If sown in January or February, they will bear in April or May. They sometimes require supporting with sticks.

KITCHEN-GARDEN.

No better form can be devised for a kitchen-garden than a square, sub-

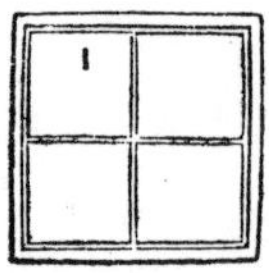

divided by two centre walks, as in fig. 1, or a long parallelogram, as fig. 2.

Something like fig. 3 has been recommended by Mr. Loudon and others, the rounded part being a fruit-garden.

The same figure might also be rounded at both ends. The centre walk should pass through close at each end. *a* represents the wall; *b*, fruit-tree border, ten feet wide; *c*, walk, six feet wide; and *d*, border for dwarf trees or bushes, or the culture of strawberries, &c., six feet wide. Whatever shape be adopted, borders should always be introduced on each side of the main walks. Nothing tends more to relieve the heavy appearance of large masses of vegetables than such borders. They are separated from the main vegetable compartments by small walks, from 18 inches to two feet wide. These walks can be edged with pebbles, and have a sprinkling of gravel, or simply cut off as alleys, and left solid earth. If formed of some hard substance, all the wheeling can be performed on them instead of on the main walks.

Perhaps the nearer to a level a kitchen-garden can be formed, the better. A slight inclination to the south-east, south, or west, might be an advantage; on no account should it incline to the north. Some gardens, however, are formed on the side of a hill, and prove very productive. Where the garden is nearly level, it may often be desirable to give fruit-tree borders a considerable inclination, to get the benefit of the sun's rays and insure thorough drainage. Borders against the wall may be sloped in directions opposite to those which line the inner side of the walk. These borders have also a good effect laid on in round ridges. It is also in kitchen-gardens a good plan to throw up sloping banks or zigzag ridges for early and late crops. The south front of such banks, especially if a thatched hurdle or some other check to the wind is placed on the top, is equal to a south border; and the north side is equally useful for late strawberries, salading in hot weather, &c. Such banks are also most useful for training peas, &c., on table-trestles, within one foot or 18 inches of the surface. Some of the borders at the side of the walk might also be occupied by iron wire for training trees. One should be devoted to raspberries, planted three feet from the walks, and trained to a hand-rail at the side of the walk, from three to four feet high.

The size of the kitchen-garden must depend upon the demands upon it, and the mode of culture adopted. It is bad policy to have it too large. It should be kept in the highest state of cultivation, and its productive powers stimulated to the utmost by liberal dressings of manure. The soil should be trenched at least four feet deep, and drained a foot deeper. All the coarse vegetables, such as Jerusalem and globe artichokes, horseradish, rhubarb, &c., should be grown outside the walls, if possible, in a slip by themselves. Herbs should have a border devoted to them, and be grown in beds three feet wide. Thus cultivated, the back-garden becomes a source of interest and an object of beauty.

If the soil in the kitchen-garden is naturally good loam, no more is required than to mix a quantity of well-rotted dung with it before throwing it back into the trench, making the borders slope gradually towards the paths. If the soil requires improving, get a quantity of friable loam, mix rotten dung with it in the proportion of one part dung to three parts loam, and mix this again with the soil of the border where the trees are to stand. Plant healthy young trees of peach, nectarine, and apricot, and, if desirable, with grape-vines and figs : these ought to be placed 12 or 15 feet apart. We have seen a very convenient plan of growing grapes on a wall between the peaches. The latter were placed 15 feet apart, and a vine planted in each space halfway between ; the vine was carried in a single stem to the top of the wall, where it divided into two stems, which were trained right and left under the coping; and as they were pruned on the spur system, they took up little room, and did not interfere with the other trees. On the east and west walls plant trained trees of plums, cherries, pears, and mulberries, after the same rule, but without the same precaution as to soil, as these are not so particular.

In draining the kitchen-garden, one of the drains ought to run the whole length of the south border; for where peaches, nectarines, and especially apricots, are to be cultivated, the ground should be thoroughly drained.

KITCHEN-GARDEN SEEDS.

In most large kitchen-gardens seeds of all the different vegetables in use are saved from year to year. This practice is recommended not only by economy, but by every consideration of good management ; for, in this way, sorts that have been found to suit the soil and situation are effectually preserved. To save seeds, however, is a work of some trouble. It causes a great waste of ground, exhaustion of the soil, and also involves much labour. Moreover, in a thickly-wooded country, the birds are generally so troublesome, that, if they do not prevent the saving of seeds, they add much to the expense of it. Wherever, therefore, ground is limited, birds troublesome, and there are no spare hands, we should be inclined to give up the practice, or, at least, to limit the saving of seeds to a few favourite sorts. Good seeds can now be purchased at a very reasonable rate, and novelties in every kind of vegetable are continually being introduced.

But whether seeds are saved or bought, great care must be taken in storing them. They should be kept until wanted for use in some dry, airy situation. It is not well to commit seeds to boxes and drawers ; the safest plan is to hang them up in small paper or muslin bags. Peas and beans, which are subject to maggots, should be looked over occasionally and kept clean. Seeds of some sorts of vegetables will keep good for years ; but, of course, it is best to use new seeds ; and there is always a saving of time in so doing, for old seed, when good, does not germinate as quickly as new. Most seedsmen publish lists of seeds with prices, suitable in quantity to gardens of all sizes, and as the demand for seeds is an annual one, no man of character will venture to hazard his reputation and his interest by sending out bad seed. It is very easy to test the growing qualities of seeds, and this should be done before they are packed up and offered for sale. We are assured that it is done with all seed supplied by Messrs. Barr and Sugden, of 12, King-street, Covent-garden, London. Their collections of kitchen-garden seeds are so varied in sorts, and so moderate in price, that the gene-

Kitchen-Garden Seeds.

rality of gardeners may well be spared the trouble of saving seeds, and use their land for some useful crops. The following is a year's supply, with quantities and prices to suit gardens of six different sizes.

Collections of Seeds for One Year's Supply.

	No. 1.	No. 2.	No. 3.	No. 4.	No. 5.	No. 6.
LEGUMINOUS SECTION.	12/6	15/6	21/0	31/6	42/0	63/0
Peas, including those best suited for succession, the earliest, most productive, and the finest flavoured ..	3 pt.	3 qt.	5 qt.	7 qt.	10 qt.	18 qt.
Broad beans, best sorts, for succession	1 pt.	1½ qt.	2 qt.	3 qt.	4 qt.	7 qt.
French Beans, including Dwarf and Runners	1 pt.	1½ pt.	1½ pt.	3 pt.	3½ pt.	6 pt.
EDIBLE-LEAVED AND EDIBLE-FLOWERED SECTION.						
Borecole, or Kale, including Cottager's Kale	2 pkt.	2 pkt.	3 pkt.	3 pkt.	4 pkt.	5 pkt.
Brocoli, the best successional varieties	2 pkt.	4 pkt.	5 pkt.	6 pkt.	7 pkt.	9 pkt.
Brussels Sprouts, imported Seed	1 pkt.	1 pkt.	1 pkt.	1 pkt.	1 pkt.	1 pkt.
Cabbage, the best varieties..	1 pkt.	3 pkt.	5 pkt.	6 pkt.	7 pkt.	9 pkt.
Cabbage, Savoy, best sorts..	1 pkt.	1 pkt.	2 pkt.	3 pkt.	3 pkt.	4 pkt.
Couve Tronchuda, or Seakale Cabbage	1 pkt.	1 pkt.	1 pkt.	1 pkt.	1 pkt.	1 pkt.
Cauliflower, including Covent Garden early	..	1 pkt.	1 pkt.	1 pkt.	2 pkt.	2 pkt.
Spinach, summer and winter	2 oz.	3 oz.	4 oz.	1 pt.	2 pt.	3 pt.
EDIBLE-ROOTED SECTION.						
Beet, the best varieties	1 pkt.	1 pkt.	1 pkt.	2 pkt.	2 oz.	3 oz.
Carrot, best for forcing, and general crop	1 oz.	2 oz.	3 oz.	7 oz.	10 oz.	16 oz.
Leek	1 pkt.	1 pkt.	1 pkt.	1 pkt.	1 pkt.	1 oz.
Onion, including White Spanish, syn. Reading ..	1 oz.	2 oz.	3 oz.	6 oz.	8 oz.	13 oz.
Parsnip, including selected Hollow Crown	1 oz.	1 oz.	2 oz.	3 oz.	4 oz.	6 oz.
Salsafy, syn. Vegetable Oyster, an excellent vegetable	..	..	..	1 pkt.	1 pkt.	1 pkt.
Scorzonera, — a most valuable and fine-flavoured vegetable	..	..	..	1 pkt.	1 pkt.	1 pkt.
Turnip, including best varieties for succession crop ..	2 oz.	2 oz.	3 oz.	6 oz.	8 oz.	16 oz.
EDIBLE-FRUITED SECTION.						
Capsicum and Chili	..	..	..	1 pkt.	2 pkt.	2 pkt.
Cucumber, including Barr's Pearl Gem	1 pkt.	2 pkt.	2 pkt.	3 pkt.	3 pkt.	4 pkt.
Melon	..	..	1 pkt.	2 pkt.	2 pkt.	3 pkt.
Tomato	..	..	1 pkt.	1 pkt.	2 pkt.	2 pkt.
Vegetable-Marrow	1 pkt.	1 pkt.	1 pkt.	2 pkt.	2 pkt.	2 pkt.
SALAD SECTION.						
Celery, including Covent Garden variety	1 pkt.	1 pkt.	2 pkt.	2 pkt.	2 pkt.	2 pkt.
Corn Salad, valuable for winter use	1 pkt.	1 pkt.	1 pkt.	1 pkt.	1 pkt.	1 pkt.
Cress, including Curled, Plain, and Australian ..	3 oz.	3 oz.	4 oz.	6 oz.	8 oz.	12 oz.
Endive, best kinds	..	1 pkt.	1 pkt.	1 pkt.	2 pkt.	3 pkt.
Lettuce, including Covent Garden Giant White Cos ..	2 pkt.	2 pkt.	3 pkt.	3 pkt.	4 pkt.	6 pkt.
Mustard	2 oz.	3 oz.	4 oz.	½ pt.	1 pt.	1 qt.
Radish, suitable sorts for succession	3 oz.	4 oz.	6 oz.	9 oz.	14 oz.	16 oz.
POT, SWEET, AND GARNISHING HERB SECTION.						
Herbs, Pot and Sweet	2 pkt.	2 pkt.	2 pkt.	3 pkt.	4 pkt.	6 pkt.
Herbs for Garnishing	..	..	1 pkt.	2 pkt.	2 pkt.	2 pkt.
Parsley	1 pkt.	1 pkt.	1 oz.	1 oz.	2 oz.	3 oz.

	£.	s.	d.
No. 7. Extra large Collection of Vegetable Seeds for One Year's Supply..	4	4	0
,, 8. ,, ,, ,, ...	5	5	0
,, 9. ,, ,, ,, ...	6	6	0
,, 10. ,, ,, ,, ...	8	8	0
,, 11. ,, ,, ,, ...	10	10	0

KOLREUTE'RIA (nat. ord. Sapinda'ceæ).

A handsome plant, with graceful acacia-like foliage, requiring a rather sheltered situation to produce its flowers freely and in perfection; succeeds in any common garden soil.

Kolreuteria paniculata,—yellow, a hardy tree, 10 ft., from China.

LABELS.

Labels, called also Tallies, are made of wood, earthernware, or metals, and bear the names of the plants. Yeates's strong metallic labels are perhaps the best. These labels may be written upon with Yeates's indelible ink, or may be painted white, and, while wet, written upon with a common lead-pencil, or, when dry, with black paint. Prices per box of 100 and of 50, including suitable pens, ink, &c., as annexed, also price per 100 for the labels alone:—

No.	Size. Inches.	Per box of 100.	Per box of 50.	Labels per 100.
1. The "Paxton" Conservatory Label	$3\frac{1}{2}$ by $1\frac{1}{2}$	5/	3/6	4/0
2. The "Hampton Court" Border	$2\frac{5}{8}$,, $1\frac{1}{8}$	4/6	3/0	3/6
3. The "Bushy Park" Pot	$2\frac{3}{4}$,, $1\frac{1}{4}$	4/6	—	3/6
4. The "Glenny" Garden	5 ,, 1	4/	—	3/
5. The "Hogg" Fruit	$3\frac{1}{2}$,, 2	4/	—	3/
6. The "Rivers" Rose	$2\frac{1}{4}$,, $1\frac{1}{2}$	3/6	—	2/6
7. The "Barron" Specimen tree	$2\frac{1}{2}$,, $\frac{7}{8}$	3/	—	2/

LANTA'NA (nat. ord. Verbena'ceæ). **Half-hardy Perennials.**

A genus of dwarf bushy shrubs, from 12 in. to 18 in. in height, thickly studded with pretty miniature verbena-like blossoms of varied colours and changing hues,—from *snow-white* with *primrose* centres to delicate *pink* and *rose* with *white* discs, and from bright *rose-lilac* to *orange* and *scarlet* with *creamy* centres. For the conservatory and flower-garden they are alike valuable. Seeds sown in March make fine summer and autumn blooming plants. They succeed best in dry, warm situations, and in light rich soil.

Seed, from 4*d*. to 1*s*. per packet.

LARKSPUR (Delphi'num, nat. ord. Ranuncula'ceæ). **Hardy Annuals.**

One of the most generally-cultivated and ornamental genera of plants, combining unusual richness with an endless variety of colours, all extremely beautiful and pleasing; the flowers are produced in the greatest profusion, and the plants in beds, masses, or ribbons are strikingly effective; indeed, few plants are so generally useful and valuable for their decorative qualities either in the garden or, when cut, for vases. For the guidance of amateurs, we may simply notice, that the stock-flowered Larkspur is of the same habit as the old Dwarf Rocket, but has longer spikes and much larger and more double flowers. The tall stock-flowered variety is of the same style as the branching, but with more compact spikes and larger and more double flowers. The tall-growing varieties scattered in shrubbery borders produce a charming effect when backed by the green foliage of the shrubs.

LAVATE'RA (nat. ord. Malva'ceæ).

Very profuse-blooming showy plants, which are exceedingly attractive as a background to other plants, or for woodland walks and wilderness decoration, growing freely in any soil.

Lavatera trimestris,—rose, pink-striped, 3 ft., hardy annual, from Armenia.

Lavatera trimestris alba,—white, 3 ft., hardy annual.

Lavatera arborea (Tree Mallow),—violet, 5 ft., hardy biennial, from Italy.

Lavatera Armeniaca,—lilac, 4 ft., hardy biennial.

LAWNS.

During spring, and the early summer months, all garden turf and lawns will require very great attention. If they are to look well for the rest of the year (and we must remember that the general appearance of the whole garden depends much upon the state of the turf), it is at such times that the broom and the roll must be kept in constant use. If the grass, from the nature of the soil, is inclined to grow rank and coarse, it will be much improved by a good dressing of sand all over it; if, on the other hand, it has a tendency to scald and burn up, it will receive great benefit from a sprinkling of good guano or soot just before a shower of rain. Before regular mowing commences, it will be well to go over all grass, carefully removing rank and unsightly weeds, daisies, dandelions, the little buttercup, &c. &c. Wherever the turf is mossy, it is a very good plan to rake it well with a sharp five-toothed rake; but it must be borne in mind, that under-draining is the only effectual cure for moss. Daisies should never be allowed to flower: a good daisy-rake, with a little trouble, will remove all flowers as they come out; but the only plan to clear a lawn effectually of these disagreeable weeds is to take them out with the *daisy-fork* wherever they are found. This clever little tool, which consists of a wooden shaft of any length, shod with a cleft iron prong, having a half-round of iron at the back to act as a fulcrum, may be used by any lady or child; and in process of time the most hopeless pieces of grass may be cleared by it. We have known turf, quite white with daisies in the spring, cleared entirely in the course of a season. The neat appearance of the garden will well repay the time and trouble spent in the continual use of the daisy-fork. We know a rectory garden in the east of Norfolk, where there is a piece of turf of about a quarter of an acre, which a year or two ago was one mass of weeds and daisies, and which now is as fine and beautiful as any turf can be. This change was entirely brought about by the children of the village school, who had each a yard or two measured out to them on half-holidays, which they cleared, some with daisy-forks, and others with two-pronged table-forks, receiving some little present as their reward. A few showers of rain and a heavy roll soon obliterated the holes they made; and fine grass was not long in filling up the spaces hitherto occupied by weeds.

LAYERING.

Layering, which consists in arresting the circulation of the sap on its return to the roots, is one of the most useful methods of propagation. In this operation an upward slit is made half across a joint; and by fixing the part so cut in favourable soil, the latent fibre expands into a root, and the branch becomes an independent plant. The process is well adapted for pinks, carnations (the example illustrated in the engraving), roses, and many other plants. It is, indeed, a very important operation in gardening, and should be neatly executed. Choosing the suitable branch of the carnation, for instance,

which is first stripped of all branches below the joint selected, and being furnished with a very sharp knife, the operator begins his incision a quarter of an inch below a joint, passing the blade through it in an oblique direction to a quarter of an inch above, taking care that the cut terminates as nearly as possible in the centre of the stem:

the tip of the tongue thus made is cut off with a clean sharp cut, and the layer pegged down in a little fine rich mould, but not more than an inch under the soil. In the case of carnations, the plant is in a fit state for the operation as soon as the flowering season is over; and no stem which has already produced flowers should be employed for the purpose.

In the case of roses, and other shrubby plants, all that is required is to run the knife sufficiently through a joint to make an opening or crack near it, and peg down the wounded part three inches below the surface of the soil, pressing the soil lightly round it, and leaving that part of the branch above the soil as erect as possible. The roots will soon form, and then the new plant may be separated from the parent tree.

LAYING OUT A GARDEN.

This subject being far too extensive

Laying out a Garden.

to be fully discussed in these pages, our observations had better be confined to a moderate-sized garden, such as is generally attached to villa residences. We will therefore treat of a garden of a single acre. Here about two-thirds should be devoted to lawn, flower-garden, and shrubberies, and one-third to kitchen-garden, exclusive, we will suppose, of the melon-ground.

The melon-ground ought to be about twenty yards square, walled or fenced round to the height of six feet, with a gateway leading into it large enough to admit a horse and cart. The drainage of the melon-ground should be perfect, the water from the pits and houses falling into a tank placed sufficiently deep in the ground to receive all the drainage from the dung-beds and compost-heaps. If this tank is within the kitchen-garden, it will be invaluable in the cultivation of flowers and vegetables. Here also are placed the potting-sheds, and sheds for the preparation of composts, which should always be prepared under cover; and as the yard is by no means ornamental, it should be placed as far as possible from the house.

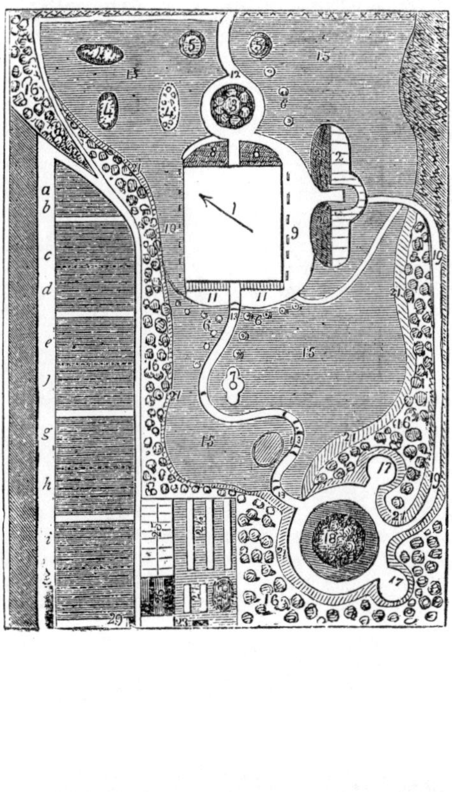

In the plan, 1 is the house; 2, the conservatory; 3, clump of American plants, consisting of some rhododendrons, ledums, and heaths; 4, roses; 5, flower-beds, with coniferæ in the centre; 6, flower-beds; 7, jardinette, with fountain; 8, borders planted with Alpine plants; 9, vines or ornamental climbers; 10, pears, cherries, &c., trained against the wall; 11, verandah with climbers; 12, carriage-drive; 13, arches over path for climbing roses and other ornamental climbers; 14, fernery; 15, turf lawn; 16, shrubberies; 17, summer-house; 18, flower-beds, with deodars in the centre, surrounded by turf; 19, shady walk; 20, flower-border fronting conservatory; 21, flower-border fronting shrubberies; 22, melon-ground and

Laying out a Garden.

compost-yard; 23, back entrance, wide enough for carts to enter; 24, range of three forcing-pits; 25, vinery and forcing-house; 26, tool-house; 27, frames; 28, manure-bed; 29, garden entrance. The kitchen-garden being thoroughly drained, trenched, and manured, and the walls in order, the following will be its first order of cropping:—*a*, Jerusalem artichokes; *b*, gooseberies: *c*, raspberries; *d*, red, white, and black currants in rows; *e*, strawberries, seakale, rhubarb, and globe artickokes; *f*, a row of plum-trees, asparagus, horseradish, and more strawberries; *g*, pot-herbs, potatoes, and peas; *h*, a row of pyramid apple-trees, parsnips, carrots, and turnips; *i*, cabbages, celery, broad beans, scarlet runners; *k*, pyramid pear-trees, scarlet runners, broad beans, cauliflower, and early brocoli. On the south border, plums and cherries.

In all theoretical gardening it is forbidden to crop the border on which wall fruit is planted; but this is rare in practice: the crops indicated here generally occupy such borders; but probably a line might be drawn beyond which such crops should not approach the wall. Supposing such a border to be 16 feet, 12 feet might be devoted to such crops in the kitchen-garden as require a warm sunny border.

The following is another illustration of a convenient villa garden.

Where it can be so arranged, the garden should be an oblong square; 100 yards from east to west, and 70 yards from north to south, about the proportions laid down in the accompanying plan. This allows the vegetables to range from north to south, which is always to be preferred, otherwise they get drawn to one side by the side-light of the sun.—1, The site of the house; 2, the conservatory; 3, a clump of trees and shrubs fronting the main entrance; 4, coach-house and stables; 5, tool-house; 6, manure- and frame-yard; 7, flower-borders and shrubberies; 8, ferns and American plants; 9, rose clumps; 10, circular beds for hollyhocks, dahlias, and other free-blooming plants in summer, and thinly planted with evergreens to take off the nakedness in water; 11, arbour; 12, flower-beds; 13, lawn; 14, paths; 15, beds for placing out flowers in pots; 16, kitchen-gardens; 17, peach wall; 18, east wall for plums, cherries, and pears.

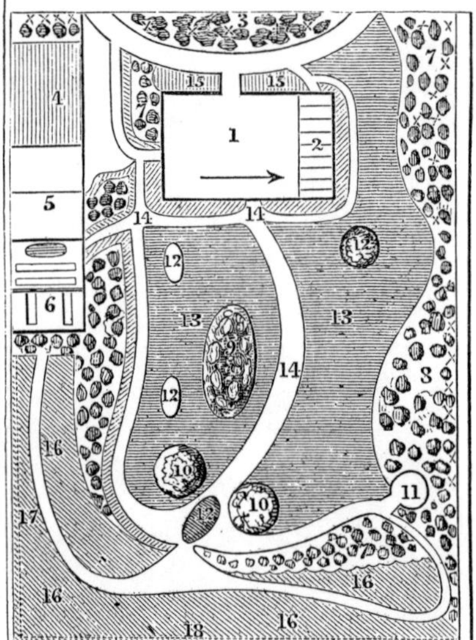

It is sometimes advantageous to nave buildings and even groups of large trees contiguous to gardens. Where these are situated to the north, they not only break and turn aside the cold winds, but concentrate the heat of the sun; they also preserve the crops during winter. Buildings have this advantage over trees, that they afford the shelter without robbing the soil of the food necessary for its legitimate crop. In the accompanying plan it will be observed that the whole frontage north of the house is laid out as lawn, and to the south, that the breadth of the house and offices is disposed in the same way; a single winding path running through it. East of the house lie the conservatory and offices, sheltered by a belt of shrubbery, which runs round the whole lawn. The kitchen-gardens occupy the north-west side of the ground, and adjoining, at the southern extremity, are vineries, forcing-houses, and orchard-houses. The northern boundary is a dwarf wall with green iron railings.

LEAF-MOULD.

Leaf-mould is a substance complex in its nature, and its functions, except so far as its heating properties are concerned, are imperfectly known. The substance of any flowering plant, or leaf, being taken and comminuted by rasping or cutting, and exhausted of its specific secretions by means of solvents, all that remains behind is lignum and cellulose; the components of which are, carbon 24, hydrogen 16, oxygen 16. All bodies of this class yield by slow decomposition results of the highest importance in the cultivation of the soil. When exposed to a sufficient amount of heat, and under the full play of atmospheric air or oxygen, they burn, yielding water and carbonic acid, leaving only a trifling amount of organic matter behind. Natural decay or *eremacausis*, as the chemists term it, is just such a slow combustion of moist organic matter as is required; it is decomposed when freely exposed to the oxygen of the air by slow burning, and the elements dissipated in gradually evolved gaseous combinations. The result is, that the gaseous fumes are given off, and a blackish-looking mass remains, consisting of bodies of the humic acid series. When reduced to this state, they are, to all physical appearance, like dark-brown soil, or earth; and it is to their presence that garden-soils owe their peculiar colour. On ultimate analysis, these brownish bodies are found to consist of humic, ulmic, and leic acids, and a substance called humine; neither of them soluble in water, but all soluble in alkalies, with which they have a strong affinity. Hence their tendency to unite in the ammonia, and their value as manures in connection with alkali. "Not only do they absorb such of this alkali as they come in contact with," says Dr. Scoffern, "but it is suspected that they actually, like many other porous bodies, promote the combination of oxygen and hydrogen, and *form* ammonia by catalytic agency,—a term used by Berzelius to express the result of the contact of a third body upon two others, without being itself changed in its character,—a beautiful provision of nature, by which the products of natural decomposition are endowed with the properties necessary to render them fit for assimilation as food for vegetables." These remarks will show how important it is that no leaves should be suffered to run to waste, but should be swept up as they fall, and conveyed to a heap, taking care to keep them by themselves, and apart from other manures, until they are in a state fit for mixing into composts.

LEEKS.

Leeks, for the main crop, are usually sown in April, about the same time as onions. Some gardeners sow them with a small sowing of onions, the latter being drawn young for salading, and the leeks being left on the bed, or planted out. Some sow them in drills 18 inches or even two feet apart, and thin them to a foot or so apart in the row, planting the thinnings at the same distance. This gives room to draw earth up to them for the purpose of blanching the root and stem. Sow very shallow, tread, and rake, provided the ground admits of it: thin before the plants interfere with each other, and water in dry weather. This crop delights in a light rich soil, and in moist seasons grows very large. The London Flag is the sort most usually grown; but the Scotch or Musselburg is esteemed by many, as growing larger.

LEPTO'SOPHON (nat. ord. Polemonia'ceæ).

A charming tribe of hardy annuals. *L. densiflorus*, with its pretty rose-lilac flowers, and *L. densiflorus albus*, with its pure white blossoms, are exceedingly attractive in beds or ribbons. *L. hybridus*, *L. aureus*, and *L. luteus* make pretty low edgings, and are very suitable for rockwork; they all make nice pot plants, and succeed in any light rich soil. Seed, 3*d.* to 4*d.* per packet.

LETTUCES.

Preparation of the Soil.—A rather strong and highly-enriched loamy soil is best; but ordinary garden soil, with plenty of old rotten manure, will produce very fine lettuces.

Time and Manner of Sowing.—For an early crop sow under glass in February, and transplant on a well-prepared bed, in some sheltered corner, in April. For successional crops sow, in beds of well-pulverized soil, early in March, and at intervals of about a fortnight until the end of July. The crop intended to stand the winter should be sown in the second week of August and first week of September, using some approved hardy sort. Make the surface of the beds fine, sow thinly, and cover the seeds lightly with fine soil. The plants for the main summer crops may be transplanted with advantage into nursery lines, in beds of light rich soil, and if not transplanted, they must be thinned out in the seed-bed early, so as to afford them ample space to grow strong and stocky. They must be lifted carefully in transplanting, injuring their roots as little as possible. The August and September sowings should be planted about two or three inches apart, in sheltered situations, transplanting them again early in spring. In many localities it may be necessary to winter them under frames or hand-glasses, planting them out in sheltered situations in the spring.

Planting and After-cultivation.—Plant in lines about a foot apart, allowing the same distance between the plants. In hot, dry weather give a good soaking of water immediately after planting, and keep the ground moist afterwards. A north border is a good situation in which to plant during the summer months, as the plants are less exposed to the sun, grow stronger, are more succulent and crisp, and are longer before they run to seed. Keep the surface of the ground loose and open by frequent hoeings. Some varieties require tying up in order to get them properly blanched, and this should be done when the plants are a fair size, and a week or ten days before they are wanted for use, selecting first the strongest plants, continuing to do this as they are wanted. Where lettuce is wanted for the winter, a portion of the plants from the sowing made at the end of July should be covered with glass. By thus protecting them from frost and wet and giving air freely, they will, if not too large, keep in good condition for a long time. The following are the best varieties:—

Cos Lettuces.

Covent Garden Giant White,—the best white Cos lettuce known; it is less affected by hot weather than other varieties, and does not readily run to seed.
Covent Garden Giant Brown,—large, crisp, and fine-flavoured.
Butler's Fine Summer White,—very fine variety.
Carter's Giant White,—very excellent.
Carter's Giant Brown,—very fine.
Dunnett's Giant Black-seeded Bath,—a most desirable variety.
Paris White,—a very superior variety.

Cabbage Lettuces.

Covent Garden Winter,—the best winter cabbage lettuce.
Drumhead,—the best summer cabbage lettuce.

LEUCOJUM, or SNOWFLAKE.

Very pretty hardy bulbs, with spikes of snow-white blossoms resembling a large snowdrop. *L. æstivum* (the Summer Snowflake) flowers in May, and blooms freely in an aquarium, while *L. vernum* (the Spring Snowflake), which is the most valuable, blooms in March, but if forced will flower earlier; it is much prized for the sitting-room. Roots, 10*s.* 6*d.* per hundred.

LEVELLING.

For levelling extensive tracts of country, a theodolite, which is a spirit-level raised on three legs and furnished with a telescope, is the instrument employed. A quadrant is also frequently used for the same purpose, and for determining the level of drains, &c. The following diagram and remarks are taken from Loudon's "Self-Instruction for Young Gardeners":—"Suppose it were required to run a level through the ground indicated, AB, from the point A. Provide a few staves proportioned in length to the work in hand, and let them have cross-pieces to slide up and down; then, having firmly fixed the staff in the ground, to which the quadrant is attached at the point A, set the instrument in such a position that the plumb-line shall hang exactly parallel to the perpendicular limb of the quadrant: the upper limb will then be horizontal. This done, direct the eye through the sights, and, at the same time, let an assistant adjust the slides on each staff so as exactly to range with the line of vision. Then suppose the height AC to be five feet downwards from the upper side of the slide upon each staff, so shall the dotted line AB represent the level line required. Suppose the operation had been to determine a cut for a drain, to have a fall of 3 inches in every 20 feet, the distance between each staff in the above figure may be supposed to be 20 feet; then 5 feet 3 inches would have to be measured down the first staff, 5 feet 6 inches down the second, 5 feet 9 inches down the third, &c. &c. The dotted line AB would then represent the line parallel to the bottom of the intended drain."

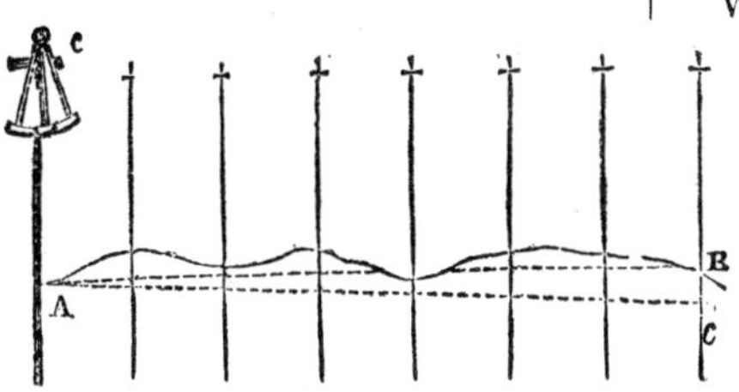

Where hills or mounds are to be thrown up, stakes should be inserted of the desired height, and a line stretched across their tops to show the conformation of the surface, as in the cut. These stakes, in all garden operations, should range from 10 to 20 feet apart, 15 being a good average: they are not only necessary for ascertaining the levels, but enable the men to perform their work with the utmost ease and certainty as to the result.

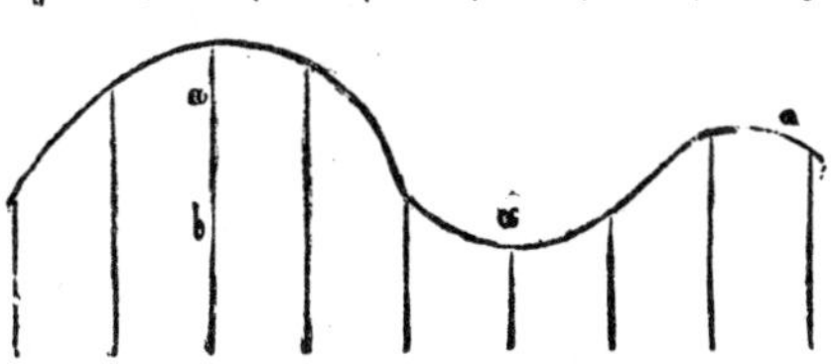

One of the chief things to be attended to in levelling, is to retain all the best soil for the surface: this increases the labour and expense, but is of the first importance in all garden operations. However, if judgment is exercised in the performance of the work, the surface-soil can generally be passed over on to the new level without the intervention of carts or barrows. This will be obvious from the opposite section, in which *a* is the desired level, *b* an open trench to get rid of the worthless subsoil,

and *c* the section of the next ground to be levelled. Of course, the surface-soil would be thrown from *c* into the trench *b*, up to the level of the line *a*; the subsoil would then be carted or wheeled where it was wanted, and the same process be repeated throughout the entire section. The new level would then be furnished with a depth of from two to three feet of good soil, fit for all cultural purposes.

LILIUM.

The Lily in all its varieties is equally adapted for ornamenting the conservatory and the sitting-room as it is for the flower-borders.

Culture in-doors. — Use a good mellow soil, composed of equal parts of leaf-mould and loam, with a little peat, and one-sixth of silver sand. A 12-inch pot, with six bulbs planted in it, will furnish a group of no ordinary beauty: smaller-sized pots will require fewer bulbs. Place at the bottom of the pot a piece of potsherd, and over it some pieces of wood charcoal and rough fibry soil to secure good drainage, then fill up with the compost. When planted, the bulbs should be covered one inch, and the soil made close by pressure: they should be treated in their first stage of growth precisely as hyacinths grown in pots, except that they should remain buried in ashes or cocoa-fibre till they begin to indicate a top-growth. Those intended to flower early should be placed under glass, while such as are for late blooming should remain out of doors in a sheltered situation, the pots plunged to the rim in ashes or cocoa-fibre.

Culture out of Doors.—If the land be of an adhesive nature, it should be removed to the depth of two feet, and replaced with a rich free soil, or else the bulbs should be planted in 5-inch pots, and early in May turned out where intended to bloom. Light or medium soils will only require deep digging and well working, with the addition of some thoroughly-rotted manure. Plant the bulbs five inches deep, and for the first winter place on the surface a few dry leaves. The bulbs should not be disturbed oftener than once in three years, as established patches bloom much more profusely than those taken up and divided annually.

The varieties best adapted for in-door culture are *Atrosanguinium maculatum*, *Lancifolium album*, *L. punctatum* and *roseum*, *L. rubrum* and *longiflorum*. These vary in price from 20*s*. to 5*s*. per dozen. The Martigon varieties are very effective in borders; so also are the common White Lily and Chalcedonicum, or Scarlet Turk's Cap. These can be purchased for 5*s*. to 3*s*. 6*d*. per dozen.

LILY OF THE VALLEY.

To grow these spring favourites to perfection, the roots should be set in bunches one foot apart and covered with a dressing of well-rotted manure before the winter sets in. They can hardly be treated too liberally. If grown in pots for the greenhouse, by a little management a succession may be kept in bloom till June. Keep the pots perfectly dry and in a cool shady place until their natural season is past, and by watering they soon come into foliage and flower.

LIME.

Chalk, marble, and limestone are carbonates of lime. Under heat, the carbonic acid is driven out, and pure or caustic lime remains. In its effects on animal and vegetable matters it resembles potash and soda, is slower in action, and is used most beneficially on peat land: its excess of organic matter is thus gradually destroyed, and converted into nutritious food for plants. Quicklime sprinkled with water absorbs it; heat is evolved, and the lime falls to powder, or is slaked. Slaked lime is a white powder, dry to appearance, but contains, in reality, water in an invisible form, chemically combined with lime. If exposed to the air, it attracts carbonic acid from the atmosphere, and becomes partially changed into carbonate of lime. Salts of lime are found in all ashes of plants; soils, therefore, capable of sustaining vegetable life, must contain lime in some form or other.

LI'NUM (nat. ord. Lina'ceæ).

A fine genus of free-flowering plants, among which stands distinguished for its beautiful saucer-shaped flowers of rich crimson-scarlet with crimson-black centre, *Linum grandiflorum coccineum*, one of our most effective and showy bedding plants; its habit of growth is slender and delicate, and it produces flowers in profusion for many months. *L. flavum*, with its golden-yellow blossoms, profusion and duration of bloom, forms a valuable contrast and companion to the above. *L. corymbiflorum luteum*, with its beautiful straw-colour blossoms, also forms a pleasing contrast with *L. g. coccineum*. *L. campanulatum*, *L. flavum*, and *L. grandiflorum coccineum* do well in pots. The plants succeed best in a light rich soil.

Seed, 6*d.* to 1*s.* per packet.

LIQUID-MANURE TANK.

In anticipation of a hot dry summer, every garden should be provided with a liquid-manure tank, and this may be easily and inexpensively made of an old tar-barrel either standing on the surface or sunk into the ground. The barrel should be filled about one-third with well-rotted cowdung and two-thirds pond or rain water, and occasionally stirred. As the liquid is used up, more water may be placed upon the sediment, which, as it becomes exhausted, can be replenished from the cow-yard and the stable-drain.

LOBE'LIA (nat. ord. Lobelia'ceæ).

Exceedingly pretty profuse-blooming plants: the low-growing kinds make the most beautiful edgings. *L. speciosa* forms a delightful contrast to *Cerastium tomentosum* and the variegated alyssum; *L. gracilis erecta compacta*, from its bush-like habit and profusion of celestial-blue flowers, is equally beautiful in pots, beds, or used as an edging: all the varieties of *L. Erinus* are valuable for hanging-baskets, rustic-work, or vases, over the edges of which they droop in the most graceful and elegant manner. The perennial species, with their handsome spikes of flowers, are exceedingly ornamental, and are valuable from their blooming in autumn, along with gladioli, *Cilium lancifolium*, tritomas, &c. All the varieties grow freely from seed, and most of them from cuttings.

LO'TUS (nat. ord. Legumino'sæ).

The hardy varieties of this plant are well suited for ornamenting rockwork or dry banks. *L. Australis*, with its splendid spikes of rose-coloured flowers and dwarf habit, grows freely in light soil. Other varieties are :—

L. corniculatus multiflorus,—trailer, from Levant.
L. Jacobæus,—dark brown, 2 ft., from Cape de Verd Islands; half-hardy perennials.
L. Jacobæus luteus,—yellow, 2 ft., from Cape de Verd Islands; half-hardy perennials.

LUPI'NUS (nat. ord. Legumino'sæ).

Free-flowering garden plants, with long graceful spikes of bloom, colours rich and beautiful. Many of the varieties are of a stately, robust growth, which makes them exceedingly valuable for mixed flower and shrubbery borders, while the dwarf varieties make neat, trim bedding-plants. Amongst the most distinguished, we may mention *L. Hartwegii* and varieties, *L. hybridus* and varieties, *L. Menziesii*, *L. magnificus*, *L. pubescens elegans*, and *L. subcarnosus*.

Seed, 3*d.* per packet.

MAGNESIA.

This ingredient is never wanting in fertile soils. Magnesian limestone, which is a natural compound of the carbonates of lime and magnesia, contains 30 to 40 per cent.; and in this form it exists in all dolomite and many other solid rocks. Soils containing much carbonate of magnesia absorb moisture with great avidity, and are generally what are termed cold soils.

MANGANESE.

Manganese is a metal, which, in combination with oxygen, associated with oxide of iron, occurs naturally in many soils. In the ashes of plants traces of it are also found; but iron usually predominates. The ash of the horse-chestnut and oak bark is rich in manganese, with no trace of iron.

MANURE.

Collecting and preparing manure, and transporting it where it is wanted, are operations that should be attended to when other operations become impossible. The waste, not only of liquid, but solid manure, in this country, is enormous. Everything that has ever been endowed with life, and all the excrements proceeding from them, are available for manure. Their nature, qualities, influence, and the mode of their application, may be endlessly varied; but all alike possess a power of enriching the earth. The hard texture of bone or wood fibre may render it desirable to subject them to chemical action, or the influence of fire, to render them more speedily available to the wants of plants; but these hard substances possess the elements of plant-food in common with the soft constituents of plants and animals. The influence of sulphuric acid upon bones is well known. When fire is used to break down or soften woody fibre, it should be applied so as to char, and not to burn it. Charring is effected by covering the heap of wood to be operated upon with turf or earth, so as almost entirely to exclude the air, and thus insure slow combustion. Almost any vegetable refuse, including roots of weeds, can be charred; and this charcoal, saturated with urine, is one of the best fertilizers. It may be usefully drilled in with seeds, in a dry state. The scourings of ditches, scrapings of roads, decayed short grass and weeds, half-rotten leaves, soot, and every bit of solid manure that can be got, should be collected and thoroughly mixed together. The excrements of most animals are too rank and strong for flower-garden purposes, applied in a pure state; by mixing, however, the bulk of the manure may be quadrupled; it will be sooner available, and much more valuable. There are some very useful fertilizes sold under the name of Portable Garden Manures, in canisters at 2*s.* 6*d.* each.

Genuine Peruvian Guano
Rape Dust.
Sulphate of Ammonia.
Cubic Petre.
Genuine Peruvian Guano, 4*d.* per lb.
Bone Dust, 3*d.* per lb.
Wood Charcoal, 3*d.* per lb.

MARCH (Monthly Calendar).

This is generally a busy, but by no means a genial month. Trees, plants, and shrubs that may have borne the rigours of winter with impunity, often succumb beneath the chilling blasts of March. The increased temperature during this month is chiefly observable during the day: it is still very variable, advancing, as it were, by starts; but the mean temperature of the month is about six degrees higher than February; the thermometer ranges from 28° to 53°, including the night and day temperature, the mean maximum being 49° 9′, and the mean minimum 40° 49′.

Flower-Garden and Shrubberies.—Magnolias, delicate roses, and other scarcely hardy plants on walls, should receive some shelter from the stern bite of March frosts and winds. Care must be exercised not to keep them too close and warm, or the remedy will prove more disastrous than the evil. For walls, nothing answers better than a thin layer of straw, covered over with a mat, and kept as dry as possible. Protection against the exciting energy of the sun's rays during this month is almost of equal importance to warding off the effects of extreme cold. The later in the season tender plants can be kept in a dormant state the better, and nothing secures this object more effectually than a thin covering of dry non-conducting material, such as straw. The utmost caution must be exercised in removing protection. Uncover by degrees.

Every day of genial weather imparts strength and inspires confidence, and a number of flowers, either in embryo or further advanced, greet us with their gladdening look of beauty. The Snowdrop, that has so cheerily nodded its head for the last month or six weeks, is now putting off its vestal robes and going into widowhood and desolation for ten long months; but the crocuses are in full glory, and a brilliant display they make; while tulips, narcissi, crown imperials, cyclamens, ixias, scillas, and hyacinths hasten forward to uphold the matchless supremacy of bulbs as the most beautiful of all spring flowers. The double-blossom furze, deciduous yellow jasmines, scarlet ribes, almonds, heaths, daphnes, snowy mespilus, *Magnolia conspicua*, holly-leaved berberry, saxifrages, orobus, calycanthus, &c. &c., weave a floral garland of which any month, not excepting June even, might be proud. This increase of beauty points out our duty, and defines the routine work for the month. The more beauty in the garden, the better it must be kept. Grass lawns must be frequently swept and rolled; gravel walks turned, fresh-gravelled, raked, rolled, and swept, edgings cut, planted, or altered; and all planting, pruning, and digging finished as soon as possible. This is also a good season to remove plantains and daisies from the turf, and to sow grass-seeds for new lawns. Fork over flower-beds on frosty mornings, to expose a fresh surface to the atmosphere, and provide a finely-pulverized soil for the roots of bedding-plants. Stir the surface by flat-hoeing or deep-raking among borders of annuals and bulbs. Complete pruning and training clematises, jasmines, bignonias, and other creepers on trellises. Remove all prunings and winter rubbish, to be either rotted or charred, and see that the entire garden has a neat appearance.

This is the proper month for planting all the hardy gladioli. If they were taken up in November and kept in a proper temperature, they will now be starting, and should be planted at once. They grow well in any rich garden soil. Drills are drawn on beds or borders about four inches deep, the bulbs inserted, and covered over with the soil. Stakes about two feet high should be put in at the same time, for, if inserted afterwards, they might injure the bulbs. The distance between the bulbs should be from nine inches to a foot.

In addition to the sowing of the annuals named in February, the following should be at once sown, either in the reserve-garden or on beds, or in rows where they are intended to flower :—

Adonis Flos.
Calandrinia.
Calliopsis.
Campanula Lorei.
Centauria.
Chrysanthemum.
Clarkia.
Collinsia.
Convolvulus minor.
Erysimum
Larkspurs.
Linum.
Love lies Bleeding.
Lupines.
Malope.
Œnothera.
Poppies of different kinds.
Saponaria.
Sweet Peas.
Venus's Looking-glass.
Veronica.
Virginian Stock.
Viscaria.

Half-hardy annuals, which require a frame, are perhaps better left till April.

Proceed with the potting-off of all bedding-plants; keep them close for a fortnight after potting. No place is so good for them as a frame, with a hot-water pipe run round it to exclude frost: in the absence of this, the frame must be kept quite close for a few days, partially shading it at noon rather than giving air. Where there is not room in the pits, they may be placed in vineries, or other houses at work. In cold-pits they will still require protection on frosty nights. Use light rich soil for potting. A single crock or a hard bit of manure over the hole will be sufficient drainage for bedding-

March.

plants at this season. The whole of the pot will then be filled with food for the roots. Keep the propagating-house at a temperature of from 60° to 70°. Pot as soon as rooted, and urge the cuttings on to a vigorous growth, in a genial temperature of from 50° to 55°.

This is also the best month for increasing dahlias by cuttings. If the old stools were placed in a warm pit or house last month, cuttings three or four inches long may now be secured. Cut them off close to the stem, if you can find as many as you want; if not, leave one or two eyes on the old stool, and in another week these eyes will furnish two, four, or six more cuttings. Place them in light sandy soil; plunge the pots in a bottom-heat of 80° and a top-heat of 60°: in a week or ten days they will be rooted. The white, scarlet, yellow, and purple bedding sorts should be placed into heat where an increase of stock is required.

Shrubberies.—Let all planting and alterations cease for this season at once. Top-dress rhododendron-beds with equal parts of cow-dung (thoroughly decayed) and leaf-mould. On poor soils this imparts a rich gloss to the foliage, and causes luxuriant growth. Where such material is not procurable, a thick layer of leaves may be *pointed* in with excellent results. Finish digging and clearing. Attend to staking, tying, and mulching all newly- or recently-planted trees and shrubs, before the March winds tear them half up by the roots. Choice specimens, recently moved, would be much benefited by a copious syringing with the engine, on the evenings of dry, pinching days, to check perspiration and husband the scanty juices of the plants. The usual routine of sweeping and rolling turf and gravel must be assiduously attended to: if the weather is mild, the grass must have a first mowing during the month.

Reserve Garden.—Stir the soil among winter-sown annuals; transplant them to their blooming quarters in the flower-garden. Sow ten-week stocks on a sunny bed for succession to those raised in heat. Prepare a piece of ground for sowing anemone-seed: Hortensis, Coronaria, and Rectifolia are the most useful varieties for shrubberies. Rub the seed clean in sand; sow in shallow drills nine inches apart, and cover with fine sifted leaf-mould and sand. Get ground in readiness for a general sowing of all biennials and perennials next month. The oftener it is forked over the more thoroughly pulverized it will be; consequently, the better adapted for raising seeds of every description. Protect seeds from birds, which are often most destructive just as the seeds are vegetating. Enrich the hooped beds, designed for the temporary protection of bedding-plants next month, with a liberal dressing of manure.

Rose-Garden. — Finish planting all hardy roses, if bloom is expected this season. The excited state of the shoots from a mild winter must not make you impatient to finish pruning. The more excited they are the greater the necessity for delay, as the expenditure of the sap in the terminal buds will preserve the buds near the base of the shoots longer in a dormant state; and it is upon these buds we are dependent for next year's blossom. In pruning roses, every bit of old wood, loose bark, &c., should be carefully removed, as it is exactly amid such *débris* that the larvæ of caterpillars, aphides, &c., are deposited. Whenever trees have been much affected with these pests, they might be dressed with a paste, equal parts of sulphur, soot, lime, and cow-dung mixed up with strong soap-suds. This would remove all moss, &c., from the stems and branches, and is less troublesome than hunting all the summer for green caterpillars, buried deep in fine rosebuds, or wrapped up in glossy leaves. When the green-fly makes its appearance, a strong infusion of carbonate of ammonia (smelling-salts) is the only remedy that ought to be admitted among choice roses in bloom. This will not only destroy the aphis, but supply the plants with useful food. A number of trees may quickly be cleaned with the aphis-brush, which is made in the shape of a pair of large sugar-tongs, with a pair of soft brushes at the ends. The shoot, with its living freight, is firmly grasped by the tongs, which are gently drawn along, removing the insects.

Florists' Flowers.—As the power of the sun increases, if the weather continues mild, auriculas might have the benefit of warm showers. The lights should be drawn off daily on fine days. Avoid cutting draughts. See that the plants have plenty of water, as they will now be throwing up their flower-stems. The material in which they are plunged may be sprinkled, to keep up a moist, genial atmosphere. Plants intended for show should have seven pips as level as possible, round and well-shaped : any ill-shaped small pips may be cut off. Cover up securely from frost, and shade for a few hours on bright days : take off offsets, insert them in a close frame, and water with care until rooted.

Carnations and picotees should now, if the weather is mild, be placed in their blooming-pots, and sheltered under glass during bad weather : they should be potted firmly, care being taken to keep the soil out of the axils of the leaves. Pinks in pots or open borders should be top-dressed with a mixture of the fine loamy soil and half-rotten manure.

Kitchen-Garden.—During this month most of the principal crops must be got in. Hitherto, warm and sheltered spots and borders have been appropriated, while the larger quarters have been dug up into ridges, and exposed to atmospheric influences. Now the whole garden is to be cropped upon a carefully-considered plan, so that no crop of the same character should follow on the same spot ; for instance, where any of the Brassicæ, or deteriorators, were grown the previous season, follow them with preparers, which are mostly root-crops, as potatoes, carrots, parsnips, onions, scorzoneras, salsafy, &c. These, again, should be followed as far as possible by surface-crops, which are mostly the shortest-lived of any, and include all saladings. We may go further, and include pot or sweet herbs, and also medicinal herbs, besides some of the shorter-lived vegetables, as spinach, coleworts, French beans, and early carrots. Map out the garden, and give each crop its proper position and space, and note the time of its duration, as a guide for selecting its successor : this applies to kitchen-gardens of any extent, but more particularly to those which must economize room. Those crops called deepeners, on account of the depth and richness of soil they require, and their long occupation of the same spot, comprise but a small portion, comparatively, of the occupants of the kitchen-garden, and cannot be used in the same proportion, although their office in respect of deepening the soil is important ; but where bush-fruits are grown largely in the kitchen-garden, they may be added to the group, and managed in the same way ; that is, plant a certain number every year and remove an equal number of old ones : by this a fresh piece of soil can be devoted to grosser-feeding crops, which has long been free from them. The principal point of culture for the deepeners is that the ground must be deeply worked, both at planting and taking up. For the preparers the ground should be trenched two spades deep, chiefly bastard-trenching, with plenty of manure of good sound quality, or mixed with maiden earth. For the surface-crops merely pointing or forking manure into the surface or top six inches of soil, will suffice ; after which, if again trenched two spits deep, adding no fresh manure, the ground will be in excellent condition for the most scourging of all crops,—the exhausters ; viz., brocoli, savoys, Brussels sprouts, cabbages, borecole, &c. By working on some such principle as this, the soil may be kept in a state of fertility for ages.

Having laid down a well-devised plan, the operations become comparatively easy ; assuming, therefore, that the soil was turned over in autumn, that it has been frozen, the surface turned over and frozen again, and dried by the winds which generally occur early this month, it is now ready for cropping.

Seakale still requires some covering, but less than last month, blanching being now the main object of it; and sand ashes, or leaves, will effect the object. When the kale is past blanching, its use does not end: the leaves may be eaten all through the summer and autumn while they are green, merely dressing them in the same way as winter greens. It will be found a very profitable crop for cottagers: it grows well in shady places, is not particular as to soil, and will stand a cold, bleak climate. A top-dressing of very rotten dung, of any kind, may be improved by addition of a little salt, —about a pound to the barrowful of manure: wood ashes are also beneficial, and may be added in any quantity.

Celery.—It is too soon to sow the main crop of celery, but a little may be sown for early use. First sowings may be in seed-pans; but for the main crop shake together a small heap of stable-dung, just sufficient to give a slight heat; spread three inches of soil on it, sow the seed, and cover with a hand-glass. Seed sown in this month will be ready to transplant in April.

Jerusalem Artichokes should be planted. The ground for them should be rather deeply worked, for, the plants growing tall, are exposed to rough winds, which they resist better where they root pretty deeply. Almost any part of a tuber will grow and form a plant; but it is advisable to select middling-sized tubers, planting them a foot or ten inches deep. This may be done as the ground is dug or trenched; or they may be planted with a spade or trowel, making a hole for each set. They should be not less than a yard apart—four feet is better. The more open the spot, the more likely they are to prosper. No other treatment is required than to keep the ground well stirred about them, and prevent the growth of weeds. Cut them down when the leaves are decayed, but not before; otherwise the tubers will cease to grow.

Globe Artichokes will be making offsets which should be taken off for propagation.

Cardoons are not so generally cultivated now as formerly, especially in small gardens, on account of the space they require. The seed is sown in March, in a warm sheltered spot, or under a hand-glass or frame. When large enough, they are planted eight or ten inches apart, in rich or well-manured soil. Then again they are planted in rows or trenches, after the manner of celery, only at a much greater distance from each other. During the autumn, earth up to blanch. The plant grows very large, after the manner of the globe artichoke.

Potatoes.—About the beginning of this month is the time to get in early potatoes. Some recommend planting them in October, placing them deep enough to be out of the reach of frost. In porous well-drained soils this answers admirably; but the advantage is not so great as to recommend it for general practice. To insure a good crop, the ground should be bastard-trenched in October or November, and left in ridges; in February levelled, and some thoroughly decomposed manure forked in. In March the frosts will have left it well pulverized, and ready to receive the sets. Some prefer middling-sized potatoes for setting, planting them whole, scooping out all the shoots except one or two; others choose large ones, cut in two or more, assuming that a large potato makes stronger shoots, capable of standing erect in full light of day.

Carrots may be sown now, but the main crop should be deferred till the first week in April. Such sorts as the intermediate may be sown in the four succeeding months: they will be useful to those who like to have this vegetable fresh from the ground. The ground should be deeply dug or bastard-trenched in autumn, left at first in a rough state and when it has been well frosted, stir and level it in January or February. For this, the Canterbury hoe (that is a hoe having three prongs instead of a blade) is a very useful implement. This treatment of the soil applies in all cases of spring-sowing, especially if the ground is heavy or retentive: in that case it will not fall to pieces, unless it has been frosted and dried by winds. In preparing the ground for carrots, no manure should be applied, as it induces them to fork and to become grub-eaten. A dressing of sand is advantageous.

Cabbages.—It is advisable to sow some cabbage-seed of a quick-hearting sort, to follow those raised in January, or that have stood the winter. They will be of great service in July and the following months. The Early York, Large York, Nonpareil, Matchless, indeed any sort, will do. Sow broadcast on a warm sheltered spot, and protect from birds with light litter or netting; but, if covered with litter, it must be uncovered to admit light and air, or the plants will be drawn up weak. Avoid planting cabbages when the ground is soddened after heavy rains. The soil is best when tolerably dry, and the state of the weather most favourable is a dull day preceding rain. It is an excellent plan to mulch the roots of the young plants in a compost of soil and soot, wetted to the consistency of thick paste. This saves a great deal of trouble in watering afterwards, and in the driest weather will generally prevent flagging. Brocoli-plants so treated will be found very free from clubbing. All young plants should be set deep, certainly to within an inch of the first leaf.

Cauliflower-seed sown now will furnish plants to be set out in May and June: it may be sown in the open ground, or in a frame or hand-glass. Sow on the surface, tread and rake, and protect with litter or netting.

Brocoli.—Such sorts as Walcheren, Purple Cape, or any sort that heads in autumn, should be sown at this time in the same manner as cabbage or cauliflower. They will be ready to plant out in May or June, and will be very useful at a time when summer crops are over, and winter crops not ready.

French Beans may be sown towards the end of this month, choosing an early dwarf sort; but the principal sowing should be deferred till next month: those sown this month should be in a border, sheltered from cold winds, but open to the sun.

Radishes may be sown thinly between the rows of the more enduring crops, such as onions.

Peas should be sown this month in succession, and coal-ashes scattered at the roots of those coming up, to prevent their destruction by slugs: sow a row of many-leaved spinach between the peas.

Fruit-Garden.—If there are any fruit-growers who still doubt the efficacy of protecting the blossoms of apricots, peaches, and other wall-fruit, this month will test their faith. Protection cannot be dispensed with in our uncertain climate. The best protection will probably be found in temporary wood copings, projecting ten or twelve inches from the wall, with canvas curtains attached, which can be readily removed in fine weather; next to the coping, worsted netting is, perhaps, the most efficient defence against severe weather, and causes the least obstruction to the necessary circulation of air, light, and rain. Those who have curtains will do well to use them, not only against frost, but against the extreme ardour of the noonday sun, to retard and strengthen their blossom. Generally speaking, pruning and nailing will be finished, but the trees should be washed with the garden-engine or syringe, using tepid water, with solution of sulphur and soot, or lime-wash, against scale and other insects. The apricot has a great tendency to die prematurely,—first a branch, then a side, until scarce a vestige of the tree remains; this generally occurs on fine sunny days in spring and early summer, supposed to arise from the sap-vessels being excited too early and rising too rapidly, so that they are in too watery a state to resist the severe frosts which sometimes follow. Every possible protection should be given to these delicate trees, and, perhaps, planting them in a border, where they would be less exposed to the action of the sun, would help to retard the rising of the sap till the season is more advanced. Trained trees not already disposed of should now be pruned and dressed at once: to delay till the buds swell, is to endanger them.

Apples and Pears.—Pruning should now be finished, and this is the last month for planting until the autumn; the various operations of grafting and budding are now in full progress. This is especially the season for crown-grafting, where it is desired to use some vigorous old tree bearing an indifferent fruit. In this case, the grafts should be taken from the trees before the buds begin to swell.

One of the chief causes of unfruitfulness in trees is over-luxuriant growth, and this must be overcome by root-pruning. In the case of old trees, this is best carried into effect in August, and the readiest means is to dig a trench a few feet from the stem, according to the size of the tree, and to cut all those roots which appear to penetrate deeply into the soil, and which grow beyond the range of the others. This will induce the growth of a number of small fibrous roots at the extremities, which roots, in some way or other, appear connected with the fruitfulness of the tree. Another means of checking too gross a habit is to bore a hole with an auger completely through the stem of the tree, about six inches from the ground, and before the sap begins to rise, filling up the hole so made with a piece of thorn. This will prove an outlet for superabundant sap, and by checking growth will be found frequently to throw the tree into bearing. When one or both of these methods fail, it may be useful, especially in the case of pear-trees, which send out an abundance of tall upright shoots, to bend all the leaders down by tying weights to their extremities. But if none of these expedients is found to answer, and the tree continues vigorous in growth without forming blossom-buds or bearing fruit, all that can be done is to cut off the head and work the stem over again, carefully selecting scións from good bearing trees.

Strawberries.—British Queens, hitherto protected, should be uncovered, and the beds weeded, and the plants trimmed; the soil stirred round the roots with the fork without disturbing the dung. Runners placed in a nursery-bed last autumn should be removed to the spot where they are to remain for fruiting. Where fruit of a large size is required, open a trench, as if for celery, filled half up with well-rotted dung, and dig it well into the bottom of the trench, and fill in the soil previously taken out, and plant immediately. Where they are planted between dwarf fruit-trees, it is good practice to keep each plant or stool separate for the first two years, and then allow them to cover the ground. Where plants have been growing in the same place for several years, weed the beds well before they begin to grow, stir the soil, and sow some guano over them in showery weather.

The Culture of Flowers under Glass.—The Conservatory.—The interest and beauty of this house will now increase day by day. Let a minimum temperature of 45° be maintained, allowing for a rise of 10° from sun-heat, and give as much air as the state of the weather and the maintenance of a kindly genial atmosphere will permit. The less fire-heat used the longer the flowers continue in blossom; therefore, in very cold weather, suffer a depression of 5° from the above, rather than increase by artificial heat. Keep the heating apparatus cool in the morning if there is the slightest chance of bright sunshine. Nothing destroys flowers so fast as the sun shining upon a house while the pipes or flues are in operation: this remark applies to all heated flue-structures, although specially so to conservatories. Flowers reveal its effects sooner, but it is doubtful if they suffer more from this cause than other plants in full growth: in the one case, the effect is apparent at once, in showers of dead flowers; in the other, it is hidden for months, but not the less potent. Except on dull, wet days, when fires are necessary to expel damp and maintain the temperature while air is admitted, lay it down as a rule, that the conservatory fire is drawn right out, or shut off by the valves every morning which promises sunshine.

Camellias in full flower must be liberally watered at the roots: during the expansion of a heavy crop of buds, the demand on their roots is very great. Clear weak manure-water will excite them gently; it must, however, be both clear and weak, or it will do harm rather than good, for camellias seem to have no power of assimilating gross food. The blossoms must on no account be rubbed, touched, or wetted: they show at once any bruise or spot of water on their clear and delicate petals. Two buds can scarcely be held in the hand at the same time without injury. In cutting the flowers, each should be placed separate in a basket divided into small compartments, or in pots filled with sand. Immediately after camellias have flowered is the best time for inarching any indifferent or worthless variety with a good sort. This operation is very simple: partly cut through the bark into both stock and branch, and unite the wounded parts, binding them tightly together, and fix them securely in one spot, excluding the air from the united part: in two months they will be united. Cut off the head of the stock, and leave it a few weeks longer to make sure that the junction is perfect; then cut off the branch, and place the stock with its new head amongst the others as an independent plant: the operation is now completed. Large branches from three inches to three feet high can be attached in this manner in the course of three months, and most valuable plants secured at once. The stock and branch must always, however, bear a proper relation to each other, and the latter, as a rule, should never exceed the former in thickness.

The Greenhouse.—Proceed with the shifting of all plants requiring it. Free-growing plants, such as lischenaultias, boronias, &c., may be treated on what is termed the one-shift system, provided they are very healthy. They require turfy peat, well coloured with gritty silver-sand, and a fourth part of clean sweet leaf-mould. Dirty putrid water is certain death to hard-wooded plants. Therefore, unless the leaf-mould is really good, add none to your compost for them. In shifting any of these from a 48- to a 16- or 12-sized pot, the soil should be used in a much rougher state than for ordinary potting. The draining must also be more liberal, say at least four inches deep, besides mixing pieces of broken potsherds or charcoal freely with the soil in the process of filling up. The soil should be so dry as not to stick to the fingers, but by no means quite dry. It should also be well consolidated as the work goes on, rammed in with a small rammer, or the bottom of a pot of about the same size, before the plant is inserted. If the soil is of the proper texture, and in a right condition in reference to moisture, it will be almost impossible to make it too firm in potting. The roots of hard-wooded plants seem unable to get hold of loose soil. To secure plenty of roots, thorough drainage is the first desideratum, proper compost the second, firm potting the third, careful watering the fourth, and proper top-management the very last point for consideration. Keep the new soil level with the top of the old ball. All plants, however hardy, should be kept warm and moist for a few weeks after repotting, especially if they have received a large shift. The growth of the roots is thus promoted—a point of great importance at this stage. At first it only occupies the hall of its new dwelling, whence it is easily expelled by accident or disease; but after it has taken possession of the whole house, and fills every available space with its large family of roots, the plant is no longer a tenant at will, but a tenant for life, and it requires a violent wrench to remove it.

Heaths.—The potting of the entire family should now be proceeded with.

Pelargoniums will require careful training. Remove every dead leaf, thin out superfluous shoots, and keep the plants scrupulously clean. Maintain a temperature of 50° ; syringe on fine, bright mornings. If the weather is fine towards the end of the month, sprinkling may be repeated in the afternoon, and the house shut up about four o'clock. Keep the plants close to the glass, and admit air in quantity proportioned to the mildness of the external air. Stop and shift plants for the latest bloom, and put in the toppings for cuttings. Fancy pelargoniums require the same general treatment, but even more care in ventilation and watering.

Cinerarias.—Keep clean, remove decayed leaves, and throw away all but the most choice varieties as soon as they have finished flowering. Save the best sorts for seed or suckers, and sow seed at once for the earliest plants.

Calceolarias.—Thin out the worst of the crowded leaves ; peg down the shoots to increase the strength of the plants, and sow seed for next year.

Forcing-pit.—Introduce fresh batches of azaleas, lilacs, rhododendrons, roses, &c. Remove pinks as soon as they fairly show flower, to a cooler house. Hydrangeas introduced now will force well, and make useful plants for the conservatory. Part of the pit should now be devoted to sowing tender annuals in pans or boxes, a first sowing of balsams, amaranthus, egg-plants, mesembryanthemum, ipomœa, thunbergias, *Primula sinensis*, humea, &c.

Stove.—Keep a nice growing temperature of from 65° to 70°. If the sun continues very bright throughout the day, houses containing variegated plants will require shading for a few hours about noon. This will be the more necessary after repotting. Clerodendrums, allamandas, stephanotis, ixoras, &c., should be pushed forward in a sharp bottom-heat. They may receive a liberal shift, and be allowed to grow rather loosely for a time, to encourage a rapid extension of parts. Ferns should be thoroughly overhauled, examined, shifted into larger pots, or reduced, as circumstances may require: nice fibry peat, leaf-mould, sharp sand, and broken sandstone suit them well.

Now is the time to destroy scale.

Fruit-culture under Glass.—March is a peculiarly trying month for forcing. The extreme changeableness of the weather, varying almost every hour, from the fiercest sunshine to the bitterest cold, renders the utmost attention necessary. This is the more essential, as at this season the young foliage and fruit are so easily injured. Perfect ventilation may be said to constitute the main feature of successful cultivation throughout the month. The powerful rays of the sun compel us to give air,—the keen withering wind forbids it. Both must be obeyed ; a skilful balance, resulting in a genial atmosphere, must be struck between these contending forces. The moment that one ceases to act, the other must be checked. Hence the extraordinary attention required, and labour involved in ventilating houses during March.

March winds are not only cold, but dry. This renders it of the utmost importance that every space in forcing-houses should be kept damp during bright weather. The inside air is not only to be warm, but it must be kept moist. Every particle of outside air admitted, becomes charged with it, exhausting the moisture so necessary to the existence of the plants, extracting the water out of the leaves, and leaving them thin, dry, and parched. Lay it down then, as a principle of universal application, that the less of the cold air admitted this month (consistent with the maintenance of a proper temperature, and a change of atmosphere in the house), the better, and that the more you are compelled to admit, the more water must be used to supply the demand that cold air makes for water.

Vineries.—The above remarks are peculiarly applicable to grape vines in the early stages of their growth. When fully expanded, the leaves will bear the strongest sun, and exposure to a cold air in the autumn, without inconvenience; but when young they are very easily injured. The earliest grapes may now be stoning. Don't attempt to hurry them during this process; for you will certainly weaken the vines. Stoning occurs when the grapes are about three parts grown, and often causes vexation and disappointment to young beginners. The grapes make no *visible* progress for six weeks or two months. They are, however, progressing within, forming their seeds, or stoning, as it is technically called. A temperature of 60° at night is enough until this work is completed.

The Pinery.—Many of the fruiting plants will now be showing flower. Maintain a minimum temperature of 70°, allowing a rise of 10° or 15° in the sun, and a rather dry atmosphere, until the blooming period is over. Drip, or too much water on the blossom, will prevent it setting. Unless it set, that pip will not swell, and one pip vacant in a pine destroys the beauty and symmetry of the finest fruit. Use water at 80° immediately after potting, to prevent the roots receiving a check from the cold soil, and maintaining a nice growing heat of 65° to 70°.

Peaches.—Guard against sudden or great variations of temperature, and cutting draughts, and syringe morning and evening as soon as the fruit is set. Begin to disbud the more forward woodbuds, leaving the strongest and best-placed shoots. This disbudding should be done very gradually; say at five or six periods, during the early stages of growth. Early peaches, after they are stoned, will bear a temperature of 70° with safety. They should be exposed to all the light and air possible, consistent with the principles enunciated in the preface to these instructions.

Strawberries.—There is no better position for these plants during winter than the floor of an orchard-house, cool, dry, and free from frost, which preserves them in a healthy dormant state. They may now be looked over, top-dressed, raked, and plunged in a pit with a bottom-heat of 50°, giving air in sufficient quantity, dry and bright, to keep the top for another fortnight at 40° to 45°. This will secure a root-action in advance of the top; so that, when the top moves and the trusses appear, plenty of active roots may be ready to support them. The temperature in the pit may be raised from 45° to 55°; and this should not be much exceeded until the fruit are set. They will then bear ten degrees more heat during the ripening period. Plants may also be introduced upon shelves in vineries, &c.; but a pit for themselves is the best place for them. For succession, introduce a fresh batch of plants every fortnight. Cuthill's Blackfriar is a useful early sort. Nothing, however, is better than Keen's Seedling for the early, and British Queen for the late crops.

Hotbed- and Frame-cultivation.—Cucumbers.—Where cucumbers have not already been started, it should be done now. Let the manure be shaken and turned over three or four times: on this everything depends; the heat lasts longer, and the plants are not exposed to violent and irregular action. When the bed is made, some gardeners recommend its being left a short time to settle, before putting on the frame and lights, in order to prevent violent heating and rapid sinking, from the additional weight of the frame; but if the bed has been well turned and beaten down in the process of making, this will hardly be necessary. If the frame is not put on at once, however, it is advisable to cover the bed with litter or mats, in case of heavy rains, which would reduce the temperature of it. After the frame is on, place about a bushel of loamy soil under the centre of each light: too much soil at once would induce too much heat. It is an old-fashioned but safe plan to thrust a pointed stick into the bed. By drawing it out occasionally, the temperature of the bed can be ascertained by feeling it: if more exactness be desired, a ground thermometer might be plunged into it. If the plants have been raised in a temporary bed, they may be planted five or six days after the bed is made: they will thus be ready to start into active growth at once. If no plants are ready, sow two seeds each in 3-inch pots, only half-filled with soil at first, and add fresh soil as the plants grow. The soil in which they are to grow should be rather coarse, and by no means sifted. The after-treatment is the same as that described in January.

Melons.—This is also a good time to make up hotbeds for melons to ripen in June and July. The soil should be put into the frame at once to the depth of eight or ten inches, and trodden or pressed rather firmly, if the dung has been carefully turned and the bed well beaten down in the making. Two plants should be planted under each light, the vines radiating from the centre; or place them further apart, and train the vines back and front, picking off all superfluous soil, and leaving only sufficient to nourish the fruit. Where a cucumber or melon-bed is in full operation, the other seeds may be sown in pots, and placed in them; and when up, repotted, and grown till the beds destined for them are ready: a great saving of time and material is thus effected. Where a good sort is growing, which it is desired to increase, it may be done either by plunging some pots filled with soil, and laying shoots of the vines into them, or by taking off cuttings, and placing three or four round the edge of a pot: they will strike root readily in about the time it takes to raise plants from seed, and bear rather quicker than seedlings.

At this time, as in previous months, hotbeds must be lined with prepared dung, to maintain the heat; for any decline below the point of safety, which is about 70°, will check the growth of the plants, and throw them back considerably. This applies to the culture of cucumbers and melons, and all forcing plants; but, in the case of plants which are to be turned out later in the season, it is necessary to inure them, by a gradual decrease of heat in the frame, to the natural temperature of the air.

Vegetable Marrows may be sown thickly in pots, and placed in a cucumber- or melon-frame. When up, they should be separated and planted out, two or three in a 4-inch pot, where they may either continue till their final planting-out, or separated again, and potted singly, to prevent their getting pot-bound. At the end of March, or early in April, plant them out on a bed of manure of sufficient heat to start them, covering them with hand-glasses. In May plant them out, without any such stimulus, on ridges in the open ground. *Tomatoes* and *Capsicums* are raised in the same manner. They may be planted out under a south wall, or grown in pots, in frame, pit, or greenhouse, during the summer.

Asparagus.—Slight hotbeds should still be made for forcing *Potatoes, Asparagus, Seakale, French Beans, Strawberries,* and *Radishes,* or any of these may be sown or planted on an old bed; the old lining removed and fresh but prepared linings applied to give the necessary heat. If they are forced in a pit, let the dung be well worked, laid in carefully, levelled and beaten down, and filled high enough to allow for sinking. At this time of the year, no other heat than that supplied by the dung in the pit will be necessary; for late spring forcing, brick pits are preferable, on account of their cleanliness.

Salading.—For a supply of *Mint* or *Parsley,* some roots planted now in a hotbed will produce young shoots or leaves. Some roots of *Horseradish* and *Chicory* may be planted in the same way, and blanched by excluding the light. A succession of *Mustard-and-Cress* should be sown every week. *Radishes* may still be sown in frames, or in the open air.

MARIGOLD (nat. ord. Compos'itæ).

Well-known, free-flowering plants, with handsome double flowers, of rich and beautiful colours, producing a splendid effect, whether planted in beds, borders, or ribbons. The African, the tallest, are also the most striking in large beds, mixed flower and shrubbery borders. The dwarf French, in beds, or used as a foreground to taller plants, are invaluable, while the new brown and new orange miniature French varieties make splendid compact edgings to beds or borders.

MATS FOR FRAMES.

As a substitute for the Russian garden-mats, which are expensive, and often not warm enough for protection against frost, a very durable and efficient mat may be made of the long stout reeds which are used by thatchers and plasterers, and which, in the parts of the country in which they are grown, may be bought for about 10*d.* or 1*s.* a fathom of six bundles.

Cut the reeds into lengths of four and a half feet for the width of the mat; work them in bunches about one and a half inch thick, the bunches to be tied tight together with strong cord, in three places, each with a single tie: the mat will thus present a succession of rolls of reeds strongly tied together, forming a strong warm covering for frames and pits.

The mat can be made of any length that may be required, and if rolled up and stowed away in a dry place, will last for years.

MAY (Monthly Calendar).

The average temperature of this month is nearly ten degrees above April, but it presents even an increased variation in its extremes of heat and cold, which renders it very dangerous to the tender flowers and fruits of spring, which now, in consequence, require increased care in protecting them from cold frosty nights, and shading from the sun's heat. The maximum average of heat in May for the ten years ending in 1853 was 65·36°, the minimum 41·73°, and the average mean 53·54°.

Flower-Garden and Shrubbery.—When autumn-plantiug has been neglected, Portugal laurels, evergreen oaks, red cedars, arbor-vitæ, &c. &c., and hollies, have been found to take root more freely now than when planted earlier in the spring. Continue to prick off annuals raised in frames into small pots, and harden such as are established preparatory to turning them out into the open ground. Those which have been potted some time should have another shift, rather than allow them to become stunted in their pots. Another sowing of annuals may now be made either in an open border for transplanting, or on small squares of turf, grassy side downwards. When the plants are up, the pieces of turf with the plants may be removed to their final quarters. As the season advances, have everything ready, by hardening the plants, that they may experience no check by removal. Turn over and well work the soil to get it into a proper state for planting.

Large plants of some genera, as phloxes, asters, &c., generally throw up too many flowering-shoots: where such is the case, thin them out at once, so as to obtain not only fine heads of bloom but increased strength to the remaining shoots, to enable them to need less assistance from stakes. Hollyhocks for late blooming may still be planted. It is better, where they are grown extensively, to plant at two or three times to insure a succession of bloom. As the soil and weather will now be in a fit state to commence bedding-out, a start should be made with the hali-hardy plants first; as antirrhinums, pentstemons, &c., which may be followed by calceolarias and verbenas; reserving heliotropes and the more tender kinds of geraniums for the latest planting.

Where bedding-out is practised, this is a busy month: let all be done according to a well-digested plan, in which the height and distance, as well as the colour of every plant and size of every bed, are previously determined; for the next few weeks will be devoted to filling up the flower-garden with beds and clumps intended for the summer and autumn display. Every exertion should be made to get the planting-out completed with all possible despatch; and, premising the plants intended for each bed have been previously determined and hardened off, no great difficulty will now be met with. If an early display be wanted, they must be planted rather thicker, and need not be stopped; if they are to bloom not before a later period in the summer, plant somewhat thinner; the flower-buds also should be pinched off as they appear, till the plants have filled the beds.

Select a shady border, and give it a good dressing of rotten dung or leaf-soil; slightly fork in for planting with the runners of the different kinds of violets for forcing. The Neapolitan is the best for frames or pots, and the runners will now be found in a proper state for removing: plant them eight or ten inches apart, water them abundantly in dry weather, and pinch off the runners as they appear: if the soil be rich and open, they will grow into stout bushy plants by the autumn, and may then either be potted or planted into pits for forcing.

Stake or peg down such plants as require it, as planting proceeds, or the wind will break many of them. Plant out in rich soil a good supply of stocks and asters for the autumn, and sow a succession of annuals for making up any vacancies which may occur, and likewise another sowing of mignonette in pots for rooms or for filling window-boxes.

Bulbous Roots and Tubers intended for removal should be taken up as their leaves decay. Even those which are usually left in the ground should be taken up every two or three years, and their offsets, which will have grown into large bunches, should be separated, if large and handsome flowers are desired. When the offsets are detached from the principal bulb, it is desirable to give it a season of rest. This treatment is necessary for all bulbs. The principal one, planted in its season, flowers with renewed vigour; and the offsets, in time, form new plants. The proper time for removing the various narcissuses, jonquils, irises, tulips, and hyacinths, and all other bulbs, is the season when the leaves and stems begin to decay; for then the roots are in a state of rest: if left in the ground three or four weeks later, they put forth fibres and buds for the following year's bloom, thus wasting their strength.

Tender Annuals, such as cockscombs, balsams, amaranthus, egg-plants, and others, wanted early, should now be shifted to another hotbed previously prepared for them, either on the surface of the ground or in a trench of the size of the frame. When ready, plunge the pot into the soil, cover the bottom with the proper drainage, and half-fill it with fresh compost; then take each plant from the old pot with its ball of earth, and place it in the centre, filling it in all round with fresh earth to within half an inch of the top, and water moderately. When the lights are put on, tilt them a little for ventilation, and to let the steam escape, also shade from the noonday sun. As the plants increase in height, raise the frame gradually; expedients for doing this will readily present themselves.

Half-hardy Annuals for beds and borders should now be planted out in the ground, others potted or pricked out on a slight hotbed, and those pricked out last month will be fit to transplant, having been gradually inured to the open air. For this purpose let them be taken up with the roots entire, and carefully planted with their ball of earth in the places where they are to remain. Ten week-stocks, mignonette, and China asters, may still be sown in a bed or border of rich soil : a gentle hotbed will bring them forward so as to flower a fortnight earlier.

Hardy Annuals.—Lupines, Adonis, lychnis, mignonette, and many others, may still be sown in beds or patches, where they are to flower, watering them after sowing and in dry weather. Perennials may be increased by cuttings of the young flower-stalks.

Grass Lawns and Gravel Walks should be in high order, the grass well mown once a week if possible, and kept clean and orderly ; gravel walks kept free from weeds, well swept and frequently rolled, especially after heavy rains ; borders, beds, and shrubberies free from weeds, and where vacancies in the beds occur, let them be supplied ; let the earth be clean and well raked, and the edgings, whether of turf or box, be in perfect order.

Florists' Flowers.—Hyacinths and tulips, ranunculuses and anemones, are now in full bloom. The more valuable hyacinths and tulips should be planted in beds defended by hoops, which, in hailstorms and heavy frosts, are covered with mats. These protecting coverings may now be only kept at hand ready to throw on when their shelter is required. By this means the blooming season for these gems of the flower-garden may be prolonged for a fortnight or three weeks, and their brilliancy increased.

When these choice bulbs are past flowering, and the leaves begin to decay, let the roots be taken up and spread out to dry and harden, in some dry shady place for a fortnight or three weeks ; the roots may afterwards be trimmed, cleaned, and deposited upon shelves or in boxes, till required for replanting in autumn. Some recommend that the bulbs should be recommitted to the earth, not planted out, but placed on their sides in a bed of dry soil, and the roots covered for two or three weeks, during which the moisture of the bulbs will gradually exhale, and they will dry and harden without shrivelling or rotting. From this bed they can be removed in a dry day, the stalk-leaves trimmed off, and the bulb well cleaned, then spread out in a shady place till perfectly dry, when they can be put away till required.

Spring crocus, snowdrops, crown imperials, and all other flowering bulbs, should also be taken up when the leaves decay. This should especially be practised in the case of bulbs which have remained in the ground two or three years and increased by offsets into large bunches. These offsets can be detached from the principal stem, and each planted separately. The larger roots, planted again, bloom the following year, and offshoots will probably bloom the year after. This month, or the following, it will be proper to remove the autumn-flowering bulbs, such as the colchicums and autumnal crocus, which have now ceased to grow. All these removals must be made in dry weather, the offsets carefully separated, and either planted again immediately, or spread out to dry, and stored till August, when they are to be planted again.

Dahlias potted off last month, and hardened by exposure, may be planted out about the third week. If the pots are getting too small for the growing plants, it is better to re-pot them in larger pots than to plant out too early.

Auriculas going out of bloom should be placed in a shady place, if in pots, and receive shade from the sun, if in beds.

Carnations and *Picotees* in pots should have every assistance given them ; sticks should be placed to support the stalks towards the end of the month, the plants watered in dry weather and kept clean, the soil occasionally stirred, and kept free from dead leaves, and a sprinkling of fine fresh soil added occasionally. All the side-stalks rising from the stem should be taken off, leaving none but the top buds ; shading the pots from the midday sun. Pinks, as well as carnations and picotees in beds, require the same treatment.

Pansies may be planted for success sional beds in a north border ; for this spring seedlings may be used. Plants in bloom should be shaded at noon in sunny days, and well watered in the evenings. Blooms not required for seed should be cut off as they fade, and side-shoots taken off and struck.

Ranunculuses should have the soil pressed round the collar and watered when it becomes too dry.

Tulips beginning to show colour should be shaded by an awning, but not too soon ; neither should it remain on after the sun has begun to decline. Watering round the beds will keep the bulbs cool, and protract the blooming season.

Phloxes, whether in pots or beds, should be watered occasionally with liquid manure.

Kitchen-garden.—Asparagus.—New plantations of asparagus may still be made, but it must be well watered, unless rain occurs. Sow asparagus-seed where it is to grow, and thin the plants to the proper distance. Beds that are in bearing should be kept clear of weeds, and the ground stirred occasionally, adding a sprinkling of salt, which improves the flavour. In cutting, use a rough-edged knife, and insert it close to the head to be cut, to avoid cutting others in the process.

Artichokes.—Stir the earth well about them, and reduce the shoots to three, and draw the earth well about the roots. The offsets taken off may be planted in threes, four feet apart one way and five another, giving a copious watering till they have taken root.

Seakale should be cleared of the litter used in forcing, and the ground forked between the rows, keeping it clear of weeds till the following December, unless the season should prove a dry one, when one or two copious waterings should be given, especially to newly-raised plants, the roots of which are yet shallow. If the leaves are used, they must not be thinned too much.

Rhubarb roots may yet be divided and planted four feet apart : it is a good practice also to sow the seed, which may be done at this time. Sow broadcast, and leave the plants till the following spring, so as to judge of the earliest, so that thinning is unnecessary till this is ascertained. Roots for forcing may be raised thus in abundance.

Horseradish.—Pinch out the tops where running to seed, and use the hoe freely all the season through—it will require little other attention the rest of the season.

Beans may still be sown : about the end of this month some will be in full bloom ; pinch out the tops of such, to hasten the setting of the flowers.

Celery.—Prick out that sown in March, giving six inches' distance from plant to plant : in order that they may get strong, let plenty of good rotten manure be worked into the soil. An excellent plan is to cover a hard surface with four inches of rotten dung, over this three inches of soil, which having trodden and raked even, prick out the young plants the same distance apart, and water plentifully : they will form a mass of fibres, and may be cut out with a trowel for planting in the trenches. A little shade will benefit them in sunny weather.

Cardoons may be treated in a similar manner ; they may still be sown—they will grow large enough for every purpose : there is no advantage in having them over large.

French Beans.—These may be sown plentifully this month ; they will be found exceedingly useful, as they follow the main crops of peas. Sow in drills three inches deep and three feet apart. Earth-up those that have made a pair of rough leaves, after thinning to four or five inches. They should have no manure, as it is likely to make them run all to haum.

Runner Beans may also be sown ; being of a climbing habit and very quick growth, they must have plenty of room. Sow in rows seven feet apart, or sow 10 or 12 feet from row to row, which will allow of planting ridge cucumbers between : drill them in four or six inches deep, or dibble them in clusters or circles, of five or six beans in each cluster; these being six feet apart, they may be grown with fewer sticks, and are ornamental. The Giant White, the Case-knife, and other varieties, have all the same habit; but that most usually grown is the scarlet runner, which is unsurpassed either for flavour or productiveness.

Nasturtiums are often grown for salad, and also for the seeds, which in the young state are useful for pickling. Sow in drills, the same as peas: they are ornamental as covering for rustic fences, hurdles, &c.

Peas.—To sow now, use such sorts as Knight's Dwarf and Tall Marrows, Mammoth, or British Queen, in good soils, and even in poor soils, if mulched with good sound manure, the atter sort yields immensely. Observe the same rule in sowing these as in scarlet runners, as regards distance. Earth-up and stick any that may be advancing, as they grow quicker now than in former months: this must be done in time, or they will fall over. Dwarf sorts will not require sticks, and are very useful on this account.

Carrots that are advancing should have the small hoe employed between them; nothing benefits them more than continually stirring the surface of the soil: thin them to the proper distance. Fresh sowings may still be made. Horn carrot sown now will be useful in the autumn; they should be sown thicker than larger sorts.

Onions may still be sown, more particularly for salading, for which purpose thin out the earliest sowings and clear from weeds: drenching the soil with liquid manure occasionally will benefit them. Give a dredging with soot occasionally.

Leeks.—Thin where forward enough, and plant the thinnings a foot apart, in rows two feet from each other; give liquid manure to those that remain, and stir the ground between.

Parsnips.—Thin out to a foot apart at least—18 inches is not too much.

Potatoes.—Continue to plant if desirable: no fear need be entertained of their doing well. Several good late sorts do as well planted this month as earlier. Earth-up those that are forward enough, but not too much: more earth than is just sufficient to cover the tubers is likely to prove injurious to the crop.

Turnips may do well sown now, if wet or showery weather occur: sow broadcast, tread the seed in, and rake soot in with it. This seed germinates very quickly at this time, especially if sown on fresh-dug ground. Such as are up should be hoed between and thinned out immediately: doing this early will be of great advantage to the crop—the oftener it is done the better.

Scorzoneras, *Salsafy*, and *Hamburg Parsley* may still be sown, the treatment of these being very much the same. Sow in drills 15 or 18 inches apart, and thin to about nine inches when up. Their culture is very simple, merely requiring the hoe between them during the summer. It is as well not to give manure before sowing.

Lettuce.—Sow in drills a foot or more apart, especially on light ground: let as many as possible continue where sown. Those transplanted had better be in drills, for the greater facility of watering, an abundance of which they must have in dry weather, to insure crispness and milky flavour, which indicates a well-grown lettuce. The soil for lettuces cannot be too rich. The large-heading kinds of cabbage-lettuce are proper for this month, but cos lettuces do equally well. Tie up cos lettuces about a fortnight before using.

Endive.—The Batavian may be sown now: it may be used in the same manner as spinach: treat in the same way as lettuce.

Sow the white as a substitute for spinach, and also silver beet to be used as seakale: treat as the red.

Rampion. — Sow broadcast or in drills, and thin to about 10 inches. This being a very small seed, the ground should be raked over before sowing, to prevent the seed getting buried too deeply: tread it in and rake afterwards.

Spinach may be sown; but as it is apt to run very quickly, it is advisable to sow on a north border. Give plenty of room: it is less likely to run than when crowded.

Chervil and *Parsley* sown now on a sunny border will be useful in winter. Sow either in drills or broadcast; tread the seed in before raking; thin out that which is sufficiently advanced to nine inches; plant out the thinnings at the same distance—they curl better when planted out.

Radishes. — Sow for succession. These must be well protected from birds, as they are immoderately fond of pulling them up as they begin to grow. They must be well watered, to prevent their becoming hot and woody. A good retentive soil suits them best at this time.

Cress.—American, Normandy, and Australian cress, and corn-salad, to come in in August, should be sown now in shallow drills or broadcast, treading the seed firmly in before raking: they will all require copious watering.

Cabbage.—To hasten the hearting of those that have stood the winter, tie them in the same way as lettuces. Plant out early-sown ones, and sow again for succession.

Cauve Trouchuda is much esteemed in some families for the midrib of the leaf, which is used as seakale. Treat as Brussels sprouts. All the members of this group like a retentive soil, highly enriched with manure, which is best given in the form of mulch. They then fibre on the surface of the ground and grow luxuriantly.

Brussels Sprouts and *Borecole* may still be sown: treat in the same manner as brocoli.

Savoys.—Sow again this useful vegetable, since moderately-sized heads of good colour are better than large white ones, the result of too early sowing. The main point in their culture, in common with the rest of this group, is an open situation and plenty of room,—two feet each way is not too much; they must also receive their final planting before they are drawn up in the seed-bed.

Cauliflower.—Plant out early-sown 18 inches apart. Those that have stood the winter should have liquid manure, or, at least, plenty of water, unless they were previously mulched, which prevents evaporation, and also feeds the plants. Break the centre leaves over any that may be heading.

Brocoli.—This being a good time for sowing late sorts, as Purple Sprouting, Miller's Dwarf, &c., care should be taken to have a good supply of them: they are invaluable in the early spring time. Give them an open situation; sow broadcast, each sort separately, and rather thinly. Walcheren sown now will be very useful in the autumn: plant out early sorts that are large enough before they get shanky.

Herbs, as Balm, Mint, Marjoram, Savory, Thyme, &c., may be increased by slips, offsets, or divisions of the roots: at this time they grow quickly after the operation: they must be well watered.

Other herbs, as Basil, potted Marjoram, Fennel, Dill, &c., may be sown on the open ground. They are not generally subject to the attacks of birds, as many other seeds are.

Flowers under Glass.—Conservatory.—A watchful eye must now be kept on all house plants for insects, or the labours of months, perhaps even years, will be lost. Ply the syringe diligently upon all plants not in actual bloom, to keep away the red spider; wash off the scale with soft soap, and fumigate for aphis and thrips. Where fumigation is necessary for a few plants only, they can be removed to a close room and subjected to that process.

The occupants of the greenhouse are now being transferred, rendering the conservatory gay and lively. Roses will be coming forward from the forcing-houses. Camellias, their season of bloom being past, are now in their full growth, and will be benefited by being shaded from the bright sunshine. An application of weak manure-water will be of great use to them if the surface soil is getting dry.

The *Camellia* is, perhaps, the most beautiful flowering shrub which enters the conservatory; its dark glossy leaves are beyond description magnificent when well-grown, and are almost as attractive as the plant in flower. Every year collections are enriched with some new variety which surpasses its predecessors; it is, however, important to preserve the few old favourites, by inarching them on strong, vigorous plants bearing inferior sorts, a process which is best performed while both are in vigorous growth after flowering. According to Mr. Glenny, a perfect camellia should be round in outline, the petals smooth on the edges, and thick and firm in texture; each row of petals should rise sufficiently above the other to form a globular face; and perfect symmetry, uniformity, and order should pervade the plant. To secure these points, the plant should be grown bushy and short-jointed, shrubby, and with foliage compact, and close down to the rim of the pot; the blooms encouraged at the end of the shoots fairly beyond the foliage, which should conceal the stems and present a bright surface of dark green.

Climbers must be trained, and the house kept thoroughly ventilated and moist.

Azaleas as they go out of bloom should be attended to, the old flowers and seed-vessels picked off. Should they require re-potting, it should be done when the new growth begins; the strong shoots of young plants stopped, except one, to form a centre for a tall pyramidal-shaped plant, the best form for this beautiful tribe of flowering-plants.

Pelargoniums trussing up for flowering require watching: tie out the shoots as far apart as possible, to admit air freely to the heart of the plant, keeping the pot covered to its rim with foliage: give liquid manure two or three times a week, and fumigate for protection from the green-fly: give all the ventilation possible, and water sufficiently to prevent the lower foliage losing colour.

Scarlet Geraniums should be encouraged to grow by liberal shifting; and when established, water them freely, giving liquid manure to those fully rooted. Stop those growing too rank, that they may become compact and bushy plants.

Fuchsias, shrubby *Calceolarias*, *Heliotropes*, and *Alonsoas*, like the geraniums, require liberal shifting in order to grow them properly. Select strong plants of all, and shift them into sufficiently large pots filled with a good rich compost, and, if convenient, place them in a gentle bottom-heat. Shade them from the sun, and syringe occasionally, to keep up a moist atmosphere. If they are required to be large plants, pinch out the first flower-buds and place stakes a foot higher than the plants, to tie them to as they grow. When well established, give liquid manure and ample ventilation during the day; but shut up early to promote vigorous growth. Pick off all decayed leaves from calceolarias and other shrubs, and peg down to furnish the surface of the pots.

Fruit under Glass.—The great enemies of fruit-forcing are insects. Strict watch must now be kept for the red spider; if allowed to establish itself on the vines now beginning to ripen their fruit, it will seriously compromise next year's crop. The thrip is a still more insidious enemy, and its destruction is both difficult and expensive. On large-leaved plants, such as the vine, if not very numerous, it may be kept down by carefully washing the infected leaves with weak tobacco-water, using a soft sponge for the purpose, that the leaves may not be injured; but on peaches, strawberries, and even when numerous on the vine, nothing will serve to destroy them but repeated fumigations with tobacco. The brown scale is sometimes troublesome to peaches, and should be brushed off with a small painter's brush dipped in strong soap-suds; but this pest seldom occurs if the proper dressing is applied to the trees before forcing. French beans, strawberries, and the like, must be removed from houses occupied by other crops as early as possible, as they are generally the means of introducing some of these pests.

Vinery. — The earlier crops now coming forward will be colouring: they must be kept perfectly dry, and have as much air as can be given safely, keeping the house at the temperature of 65° or thereabouts. The most important part of the vine's growth is between the breaking and the setting of the fruit: for the formation of sound, healthy wood and perfect bunches, they should be assisted by artificial means during that stage of their growth. Hamburgs, and the more hardy grapes, will require to be kept near 65° as a night temperature as they approach the time of flowering; but the Canon-Hall and the common Muscat, the Damascus and West's St. Peter's, will require an additional 5° as they get into bloom; and this heat should be maintained till the berries are wholly set, when a slight diminution of temperature may take place, according to the time when the crop is wanted. Regulate the growing vines so as to keep them as evenly balanced as possible. To effect this, keep the lower spurs on a par with the upper ones, and allow them to grow for some time before they are stopped: this will help to counteract the flow of sap upwards, and to balance the growth of the tree.

Thinning, stopping, and tying in should now be done daily; water freely, and some sorts with more delicate foliage shade for a few hours about noon. About the middle or end of the month remove any fermenting material which may have been left on the borders of the early houses, and give a dressing of decayed turf or rotton dung, spreading it over the surface to preserve the roots. When the grapes in the early house are cut, great care should be taken to preserve the foliage in a healthy condition for the next three months, by frequent syringing, to keep down the red spider, which the dry air of the house during the ripening of the fruit will have encouraged. The success of next season's crop will mainly depend on this after-treatment. If the foliage is unhealthy, or the vines weakly, and new wood is required to furnish healthy leaves, the growth should be stopped when three or four joints are formed. Abundance of air and light are indispensable auxiliaries. Keep the houses containing grapes ripe or ripening very dry, and admit air liberally.

Vines in Pots.—Where it is intended to grow vines in pots, select the necessary plants now; those raised from last year's eyes are best for forcing. Cut them down and pot them in 12- or 14-inch pots, using a compost composed of good turfy loam mixed with a little rotted dung. Place them in a cool house or pit to break; afterwards remove them to a house where they can be trained near to the glass.

Pinery. — Keep the atmosphere of the swelling fruit humid, and the earth about the roots moderately moist, using occasionally weak manure-water. Where extra heavy fruit is desired, all suckers should be removed as they appear. On warm afternoons syringe copiously, and close up with a temperature of 90°, giving air again towards evening. When there are indications of changing colour, withhold water, and see that the bottom-heat is kept steady at about 85°. The plants intended for autumn-fruiting should now be shifted into their fruiting-pots. The best pines for swelling their fruit in winter are the smooth-leaved Cayenne, the Black Jamaica, and Queens. To insure these showing fruit within the next two months, it will be necessary either to remove them into a house with a drier atmosphere, or to apply it to them where they are growing. They should now have filled their pots with roots, and should have larger pots without delay. Let the pots be large enough to allow a good portion of turfy loam round the ball; pot them firmly, and rather deeper than at the previous potting. On plunging them afresh, allow them considerably more room, and bring them near the glass. Pines planted out in open beds must also have their roots kept in a moist state by waterings, which at this period may be given overhead, provided the pits are closed up at a high temperature.

Peach-house.—The fruit on trees put forward in December will now be approaching maturity, and the house should be kept rather dry, giving all the air possible. At this stage they will bear forcing freely; keep, however, the syringe at work twice or thrice daily; tie in the shoots as they advance, and expose the fruit to the free action of light, if a high colour is wanted. In the succession-house the borders should be kept well watered. British Queens are very subject to red spider: to keep this down, ply the syringe well; the inside walls of the house should be washed with a sulphur mixture. The fruit of the "Queens" will require some kind of support, owing to the length of the footstalk. That the ripening fruit may enjoy all the advantages of light and air, tie close in the shoots intervening between the trellis and the glass, and take off any leaves shading the fruit from the sun. Give air freely to peaches during their last stage, to improve the colour and flavour, and allow them plenty of time to ripen, which will improve both their size and appearance. A net should be suspended loosely underneath the trees before the crop is ripe, to collect any fruit which may get overlooked in gathering.

Figs will now be ripening, and in this stage watering should be discontinued, as it injures the flavour of the fruit. When in tubs, however, and a second crop is coming on, manure-water may be given in moderation.

Melons now swelling will require a moderate amount of water; if the plants are growing in mere loam, liquid manure should be given. Be particular that the bottom-heat is maintained at a steady point: a deficiency or excess of heat at this stage would most materially interfere with the swelling of the fruit. To preserve the soil in a medium state of dryness, and to save frequent waterings, the surface of the bed may be covered with common flat tiles or broken brickbats. Great attention must be paid to preserve the principal leaves from injury. The fruit of plants growing on trellises should be placed on a thin piece of board suspended under the plants. After the fruit is three parts swelled, a fresh growth may be permitted if the plants are intended to produce a second crop.

Orchard-house. — Ventilation must still be strictly attended to. Open all ventilators during the day, except in fierce north and east winds. Worsted netting of half-inch mesh may be placed over the ventilators with advantage in severe weather. If the caterpillar attacks the young shoots of the apricot, the ends must be pinched off and crushed. Summer-pruning of trees to be so treated to commence early this month. Apricots in pyramids, as soon as the shoots have made six or seven leaves, must have the sixth leaf with the end of the shoot pinched or cut off with a penknife, leaving only five main leaves. From this leading shoot two or three will break: in like manner when they break, all but one of these is to be pinched down to five leaves. When this one has made ten leaves, pinch down to nine. With pyramidal peaches and nectarines, as soon as the shoot has made three leaves, pinch off the third leaf with the end of the shoot, leaving two principal ones. These pinched shoots will soon put forth fresh shoots, which, with all succeeding ones, must be pinched off to one leaf as soon as three are formed.

Hotbed and Frame-cultivation.—Hot-beds may be made for starting cucumbers and melons with greater certainty of obtaining fruit, and also with far less labour and material than earlier, the weather being much warmer, and the sun aiding by his rays the efforts of the cultivator. Give plenty of air to growing plants, particularly in sunny weather. Neither cucumbers nor melons should be shaded—it is necessary that the stems be matured and ripened, in order to secure a good bearing condition: plants that are vigorous and healthy will bear the full light of the sun, if air is admitted proportioned to its influence. Attend well to pinching back under-growth and pegging down the stems: they will root at every joint by so doing, and continue bearing much longer. Water must be given more freely as the weather gets warmer; but see that the plants are not chilled, which will be the case if the water is not of a temperature nearly equal to that of the bed. Shut up about 4 or 5 p.m., and open as early in the morning as the weather will permit. Water before closing in preference to other times; as during the night the plants revel in a moist, dewy atmosphere. The principal summer crop of melons should be got out this month; and here the ordinary melon-pit will be brought into requisition. Let a good quantity of well-prepared dung be ready: the pit should be about four feet deep in front, rising at an angle of 45°, or thereabouts, of the most simple construction, — no other appliances being necessary; but it should be broad and roomy, so as to hold sufficient dung to maintain a lasting heat, and also that the plants may have sufficient room to trail. Keep them within bounds by stopping and pinching; let the dung be thrown in evenly, and worked about with the fork, so that it may not sink more in one place than another; allow it to settle; throw on six or eight inches of good loamy soil, which tread over. When of the right temperature (about 80°) the plants may be put in, settled with warm water, and afterwards watered about twice a week, but not overhead when about setting the fruit. Bees will find their way into pits and frames at this time of the year, and fertilize the fruit-blossoms, although some growers, to make doubly sure, still perform that task. Melons in full growth must have plenty of fresh air to insure that dark healthy greenness in the foliage indicative of vigour in these plants. Close before the air cools too much, and open in the morning before the steam shows on the glass: both are important, because, if the lights are left open late, the air inside is chilled, and rendered unsuited for healthy respiration; whereas, in the morning, if kept closed too long, the plants sweat, and are less able to bear the sunlight. Shading is unnecessary, except in case of fresh planting: if properly treated in other respects, the plants will be able to bear the sun's rays.

Cucumbers and melons may be grown under hand-glasses, if managed in some such method as the following. The plants are supposed to be raised in March or April, potted singly or in pairs, and kept growing till the beginning of this month; a trench is marked out, four feet wide, and dug out to the depth of 15 or 18 inches, throwing the earth equally on each side; then throw in dung which has been previously prepared, sufficient to form a bed at least three feet deep; on this throw a hill of soil (if good garden soil, that thrown out of the trench will do) at intervals of four feet from each other. The only reason for making small hills, of eight inches high or so, is to avoid the rapid sinking consequent upon adding too great a weight all at once, which would cause a proportionate rise in temperature, a circumstance to be avoided, because the greater the heat the sooner it is over. Place hand-glasses one on each hill (those with iron frames and portable tops are best) when the rank heat has passed, put in the plants, two under each hand-glass, and shade if necessary. When the fibres begin to appear through the soil, add more earth till the whole is level. The heat is maintained by placing more dung, first on one side and then on the other. By that time the weather will be sufficiently warm to keep them growing. As they begin to trail, lift the lights on bricks, or inverted flower-pots, before they run any length. It is advisable to mulch with light litter: watering will be sometimes necessary; but it should be administered warm, and not too often; stopping and pinching must also be attended to. If several ridges are ranged together, leaving four feet clear between, this can be filled in with proper dung, and the whole levelled for the plants to trail on.

Vegetable-marrows and gourds may be planted in somewhat the same manner, if done before the last week in this month; but let the bed be broader, and not quite so high, placing about a foot of soil on it; all that is necessary is a slight heat to start them, and covering with hand-lights.

Frame potatoes, carrots, cauliflowers, &c., will be fit for the table this month, and the frame may be used for any of the above, taking out the old soil and replacing it with fresh, and applying new linings. Such are also very useful for growing capsicums and tomatoes, either for fruiting or preparatorily to planting them under a wall: in either case, they should be grown in pots. They may be used for other tender annuals,—celosias and cockscombs, which always do best when plunged in heat, and grown in a frame or shallow pit.

Frames are also excellent for hardening off all sorts of bedding-stock for the flower garden; the lights can be pulled quite off, and the plants are thus inured gradually to the open air.

MELIAN'THUS (nat. ord. Ruta'ceæ).

Known as the Honey-flower; a native of the Cape of Good Hope. It is a shrubby plant, with bluish-green leaves, and in our climate mostly found in greenhouses. If grown in the open air and slightly protected from frost, it will attain some eight or ten feet in height, and produce abundantly large spikes of flowers of a brownish-red colour. It requires a rich light soil.

MELONS.

The culture of the Melon is very similar to that of the Cucumber. The preparation of the manure, making the bed, raising the plants, the stopping and setting, are the same; but the soil in which they are finally planted should be trodden down rather firmly; and as the fruit appears all nearly about the same time, it is advisable to have the melons swell off as nearly as possible together; otherwise, the most forward will take the lead, and become much larger than the other. Two melons on a plant are as much as can be expected to do well; but never more than three should be allowed to remain: pinch off all the rest, and every other unnecessary growth. It is important that the plants be not allowed to ramble after the fruit has begun to swell; for this will require the whole strength of the plant. The fruit takes some four or five weeks, occasionally more, from the time of setting to the time of ripening, which is indicated by the stalk appearing to separate from the fruit. They should be cut and used on the day this takes place, or very soon after.

Both cucumbers and melons, it is known, are sometimes grown in pits heated with hot water. The superiority of this plan is so fully established, that none would be troubled with dung-beds after having tried it. The diminution of labour, the cleanliness and comfort, and last, but not least, the ornamental appearance of the suspended fruit, have a decided advantage over the many inconveniences attached to the management of hotbeds.

MESEMBRYAN'THEMUM (nat. ord. Mesembrya'ceæ). Half-hardy Annuals.

A brilliant and profuse-flowering tribe of extremely pretty dwarf-growing plants, from the Cape of Good Hope, strikingly effective in beds, edgings, rock-work, rustic baskets, or vases in warm sunny situations; also for in-door decoration, grown in pots, pans, or boxes: succeed best in a dry loamy soil. Seed, 3*d*. per packet.

MICE.

There appear to be three sorts of mice, all doing more or less injury to gardens,—the common house-mouse, and two descriptions of field mice, the short- and long-tailed. They are all very destructive to newly-sown peas and beans, also to crocuses and other bulbs. To preserve peas and beans from injury by mice, let them be well saturated with a solution of bitter aloes before they are sown, or, having soaked them in salad-oil, let them be rolled in powdered resin, which will answer the same purpose. Chopped furze, also, may with great advantage be placed in the drills over the seed. The most effectual remedies, however, are poison and micetraps: of the latter, that usually termed the figure-of-four trap, formed with three pieces of stick and a tile, is perhaps the most simple and efficacious.

MIGNONET'TE (nat. ord. Reseda'ceæ).

A well-known fragrant favourite, which forms a pleasing contrast to the more showy occupants of the parterre. If well thinned out immediately the plants are large enough, they will grow stronger, and produce larger racemes of bloom: the seed should be scattered about shrubberies and mixed flower-borders, where it grows readily.

Mignonette,—½ ft., from Barbary.
" grandiflora,—½ ft.

MIGNONETTE-TREE.

The tree mignonette is formed by training a vigorous plant of common mignonette for about three years. Sow the seed very thin in April, draw out to a single plant. Next autumn remove all the lower shoots and shape the plant into a tree. Somewhat later shift into a larger pot in good loam. Keep it in a warm greenhouse and in a growing state, carefully removing all flowers. In the spring, it will appear woody. Treat it in the same manner the next year, removing all branches except those that are to form the head of the tree. By the third year it will have bark on its trunk, and form a handsome shrub; and by stopping the flowers as they appear during summer and autumn, it may be made to blossom freely during winter and spring for many years in succession.

MILDEW.

Syringe the plant upon which the mildew has begun to make its appearance, with a strong decoction of green leaves of the elder; or use in the same way a solution of nitre, made in the proportion of one ounce of nitre to one gallon of water. A mixture of soap-suds and sulphur will, in many cases, answer the same purpose.

A composition made by Mr. Bell, of Exchange-street, Norwich, is the most valuable of all remedies for mildew. It may be safely used anywhere, and is indispensable for wall fruit-trees.

MIMO'SA—Sensitive Plant (nat. ord. Legumino'sæ). Half-hardy Annuals and Perennials.

Very curious and interesting plants: the leaves of *M. pudica* (the Humble-plant) and of *M. sensitiva* (the Sensitive-plant) close if touched or violently shaken. They succeed out of doors in a warm situation, growing freely in peat and loam.

MIM'ULUS (nat. ord. Scrophularia'ceæ).

A genus of extremely handsome profuse-flowering plants, with singularly-shaped and brilliantly-coloured flowers, which are distinguished by their rich and strikingly-beautiful markings. Seed sown in spring makes fine bedding plants for summer blooming, and seed sown in autumn produces very effective early-flowering plants for greenhouse decoration, &c.

Mimulus cardinalis,—scarlet, 1 ft., from California.
Mimulus cardinalis atrosanguineus maculatus, —dark red, 1 ft.
Mimulus cardinalis Lehmannii,—bright rose, 1 ft.
Mimulus cardinalis Napoleon III.,—rich purple, 1 ft.

MISTLETOE.

To many persons the cultivation of the mistletoe is looked upon with as much doubt as we are told the ancient Romans looked upon the cultivation of mushrooms. It may, however, be very readily cultivated by attending to the following directions :—Make an incision in the bark of an apple-tree (many other trees, as the pear, oak, whitethorn, and even laurels, will answer equally well), and into this incision, in the spring of the year, insert some well-ripened berries of the mistletoe, carefully tying the bark over with a piece of bass, mat, or woollen yarn. This experiment often fails, from the birds running away with the berries from the place where they have been inserted, for they are very fond of them. To prevent this, the incision in the bark should be made on the underside of a hanging branch, where birds are not likely to rest.

MIXED GARDENS.

There are thousands of good old English gardens where it would not only be contrary to the genius of the place, but practically impossible, to separate altogether the kitchen- and flower-garden. Most gardens attached to farmsteads, and many vicarage gardens, fall under this category. But there are many others of greater pretensions, where it would be a great mistake to leave what is called the kitchen-garden entirely devoid of floral ornaments. Without at all interfering with the proper and profitable culture of vegetables and fruits, the kitchen-garden, with a little taste and far less labour, may be made extremely ornamental. Let the walks that need it be kept well gravelled; and as box-edging is always getting out of order in a kitchen-garden, substitute for this a thin tile, one foot long and one inch thick, and about six inches deep, scalloped at the top, which may be purchased in various patterns; or a row of fine bricks, laid at an angle, makes a good edging. These, which are very inexpensive, and last a long while, should be inserted half their depth in the soil, and form a very useful and ornamental division between the walk and the border: a small movable wooden step should be used whenever it is necessary for the barrow to pass over them. A broad grass-walk, also, down the centre, or elsewhere in the kitchen-garden, may be made to contribute much to the beauty of it, by having rows of well-trained pyramidal pear-trees planted on each side, with standard rose-trees in the intervals between the pears, and in a line about two feet nearer than they are to the centre of the walk; wire arches, with roses over them, may in different places be thrown across the gravel walks without at all interfering with the general purpose of the garden, and with a very pleasing effect. Crocuses, narcissi, and daffodils near the edging-tiles will make the walks gay in the spring. The piers of the walls also, without at all interfering with the fruit-trees, may have many pretty flowering-shrubs, &c., trained up them.

MOLES.

These troublesome intruders may be driven out of the garden by placing the green leaves of the common elder in their subterranean paths, for the smell of these is so offensive to them, that they will not come near it; or they may be poisoned by placing in their paths worms, which, for some time, have been left in a place with a small quantity of carbonate of barytes.

MOSS ON FRUIT-TREES.

Wash the branches of the trees

wherever moss appears, with strong lime-water: strong brine will also answer the same purpose.

MOSS ON GRAVEL WALKS.

Sprinkle the walks and yards over with refuse salt, but be careful to keep the salt from box-edgings and the sides of the grass. This sprinkling should be done in dewy or damp weather, but not during rain.

MOSS ON LAWNS.

All remedies are useless until the lawn is well drained; when this is done, rake the grass with a sharp-toothed rake in different directions to drag out the moss, and roll with a very heavy roller in wet weather. Nitrate of soda, at the rate of one and a half to two cwt. per acre, should be sown in the spring, over the mossy grass. Very fine coal-ashes, also, may with great benefit be spread over those parts of the lawn where moss abounds, especially if done in wet weather, or before a soaking rain.

MOSS-ROSE.

The origin of the Moss-rose is buried in obscurity, and all that can now be said of its past history is, that it was introduced into England from Holland; the general belief being that it is an accidental sport of the Provence rose.

The moss-rose above all others requires a warm rich soil, with an airy exposure; moisture and shade also seem essential to preserving the mossy character; but this moisture must not partake of the stagnant nature. To insure a fine autumnal bloom of moss-roses, Mr. Rivers tells us, the soil should be deep and rich; if not so naturally, the roses should be lifted annually or biennially, and replanted with some rich fresh compost at their roots. When grown as standards, they should be budded on the dog-rose; but they do best budded on short stems or on their own roots, and pruned close. Grown on deep, rich, and warm soils, the more vigorous sorts may be fashioned into "pillar-roses." "What will our readers say to a pillar formed of the old red moss reaching to the height of fifteen feet?" says Mr. Paul. "Such a one exists, I confidently assert, in the garden of Mr. Anderson, Ball's Cross, Cheshunt, growing within a few feet of the road. When I examined it, some of the shoots of last year's growth were above six feet long, and extremely robust, and the main stem had swelled to a considerable size."

The following list gives a few of the best moss-roses, selected from Mr. Paul's list and Mr. Rivers's catalogue:—

A feuilles luisantes,—flowers delicate, pink-blush on the circumference; of medium size; full and globular; blooming freely in clusters, with shining leaves.

Alice Leroi,—flowers lilac-blush, shaded with rose, the centre a deep rose; large, double, and well massed and cupped; thrives as a standard, pruned close.

Celine,—flowers deep rosy-crimson, shaded with purple, a streak of white occasionally tracing the centre of a petal; colour brilliant when nearly opened. Thrives well as a standard.

Old Moss,—flowers pale rose; very large and full, well massed and globular; very beautiful. Thrives as a standard.

Comtesse de Marinais,—flowers pale flesh-colour when newly opened, changing to white; large and very double. The only white moss (according to M. Vibert) ever raised from seed. A fine standard.

Comtesse de Noé,—very brilliant crimson, changing to lilac as the flowers go off. Flowers in clusters of fifteen to twenty blossoms each, with a dark green shining foliage.

Eclatante,—flowers deep pink; well massed, large, and double. Thrives as a standard.

Etna,—flowers brilliant crimson, with a purplish tinge; large and very double. A beautiful rose.

La Diaphanie,—flowers rosy-blush; large, and very double; of pendulous habit; a free bloomer. Raised by M. Laffay between the moss and French rose.

Panachée Pleine,—flowers white or flesh-colour, occasionally streaked with rose; of medium size, cupped, and very double. To bring out the streaks, plant in rather poor, but fresh soil, as turfy loam, giving a very little manure.

Pompon, or de Meaux,—flowers blush, pale pink, centre small; full and cupped. The Taunton rose.

Princess Royal,—flowers purple and crimsom, beautifully mottled; large and double, cupped, and very showy. A fine standard.
Princesse Royale,—flowers rosy-flesh; large, full, and globular; well massed.
Uuique, — flowers pure white, occasionally tinted with lake after expansion; large, full, cupped, and well massed.

MOWING-MACHINES.

These useful machines are fast supplanting the scythe both on large and small lawns. Their use is too well known to need description. They may be had to cut from eight inches to twenty-two inches, to be worked by hand, at prices varying from £2. 10*s*. 6*d*. to £7. 10*s*. These are the prices of Messrs. Barnard & Bishop's patent noiseless lawn-mowers, which are decidedly the best we have seen.

MULCHING.

This operation consists in spreading a layer of stable-dung over the roots of trees or plants, and in times of drought watering through it. After a time the dung may be forked into the soil.

MUSHROOMS.

Mushrooms may easily be had at any season of the year by adopting an artificial process, and spawning, with Milltrack or other artificial spawn, a bed made after the following manner:—The best situation for the artificial growth of mushrooms is a cellar or underground tool-house, or any other place where the atmosphere is of that close, damp, foggy character which is always so peculiarly favourable to the growth of fungi. The antechamber or passage to an ice-house is an excellent place for a mushroom-bed, and is frequently made use of for this purpose: any shed, however, whether underground or not, may be made available; and, indeed, with a little more care, mushrooms may be grown in the open air, without any roof to cover them at all; but a cellar or underground hole has a decided preference. The foundation of the bed must be well-rotted manure from the horse-yard, which has been sweetened by being turned over two or three times: it may have a little good loam mixed with it, in the proportion of about two barrows of loam to twelve of manure. The bed is best made on a gentle slope, and the manure should be well and firmly beaten down with a spade. When the heat has fallen to about 75°, the spawn may be put in. This artificial spawn, which is usually made up in cakes, must be broken up into pieces about two inches square, and placed all over the bed, upon the surface of the manure, about ten or twelve inches apart. A covering of one inch, or one and a half inch, of good garden loam is then to be placed all over the bed, and the surface again beaten firm with a spade. The whole must then be covered well over with straw or other material, to exclude all light. The growth of the mushrooms will, of course, depend somewhat on the state of the atmosphere; but in a temperature of 45° to 55° they will usually begin to appear in about six weeks. Little or no water should be given to the bed until the mushrooms begin to come up, as its own moisture and heat ought to be sufficient to start the spawn; but as soon as mushrooms appear, a plentiful supply of water may be given, and it will be found that a little common salt, or, better still, saltpetre, will have a great effect upon the crop. It is essential that the surface of the bed be kept quite dark. If the bed be made in the open air, it may be necessary, after a time, to give to the spawn a fresh start, by placing a lining of hot manure around it; but on all occasions great care must be taken that the heat of the bed is not so excessive as to burn up the spawn. This, however, can never happen at a temperature of 75°; and when a bed is above this, no spawn should ever be inserted.

MUSTARD.

If a supply is required in winter, or when the weather is too cold for the seed to vegetate out of doors, sow in shallow boxes or pans, placing these in a warm house or pit. During the heat of summer a shady border will be the most suitable situation. Make the surface of the soil fine, level, and smooth, then water it and sow the seed very thickly. Press it gently into the soil, but avoid covering it with soil, else the earth and sand will adhere to the leaves and be with difficulty removed by washing. Exclude the sun's rays, and keep the seeds moist by coverings; but these must be removed as soon as the seeds have fairly germinated. To furnish a regular supply, sow at intervals of a few days, and never allow the plants to get too old before being cut for use.

NAILING.

This is a difficult operation, for nailing is no ornament, and the less it shows itself the better. The gardener's skill must be exerted to conceal his nails and shreds as much as possible. List is generally used; but strips of leather or black tape are preferable. They not only have a neater appearance, but afford less harbour for insects. Fruit-trees should be nailed close on to the wall; ornamental shrubs, &c., merely fastened in for the sake of support.

NARCIS'SUS (nat. ord. Amarylli-da'ceæ).

This genus is a very extensive one, embracing Jonquils, the Polyanthus, Narcissus, the Hooped Petticoat, the Poet's Narcissus, and many others.

The Double Roman Narcissus, planted early in September, would bloom in-doors before Christmas, while the Paper-white, combined with the other varieties for in-door culture, if planted in succession from the 1st September to the 31st December, would maintain a rich floral display till the end of April.

Culture in-doors is similar to that recommended for the Hyacinth. The bulbs of the Polyanthus Narcissus being large, a 5-inch pot will be needed for one bulb, and a 6-inch pot for three; a group of six in an 8-inch pot will produce an exceedingly beautiful effect.

Culture out of doors is exactly the same as that for the Hyacinth, except that the crown of the bulb should be at least five inches under the surface, and for winter protection should be covered with about an inch of newly-dropped leaves, or three inches of cocoa-fibre.

September is the time for sowing seed, in order to obtain new varieties. For the mode of proceeding we cannot do better than quote the words of Mr. Leeds, of Manchester, who has been one of the most successful amateur cultivators of the Narcissus. Mr. Leeds says: "To obtain good varieties, it is needful, the previous season, to plant the roots of some of each kind in pots, and to bring them into the greenhouse in spring to flower, so as to obtain pollen of the late-flowering kinds to cross with those which otherwise would have passed away before these were in flower. With me the plants always seed best in the open ground. When the seed-vessels begin to swell, the flower-stems should be carefully tied up, and watched until the seeds turn black. I do not wait until the seed-vessels burst, as many seeds in that case fall to the ground, and are lost, but take them off when mature, with a portion of the stem, which I insert in the earth in a seed-pot, or pan, provided for their reception. I place them in a north aspect, and the seeds, in due season, are shed, as it were, naturally, into the pot of earth. I allow the seeds to harden for a month on the surface before covering them half an inch deep with sandy soil. The soil should be two-thirds pure loam and one-third sharp sand; the drainage composed of rough turfy soil. In October, I plunge the seed-pots in a cold frame facing the south, and the young plants begin to appear in December and throughout the winter, according to their kinds and the mildness of the weather. It is needful, in their earliest stage, to look well after slugs and snails."

NASTUR'TIUM (nat. ord. Tropæola'ceæ).

The dwarf improved varieties of Nasturtium are amongst the most useful of garden flowers for bedding, massing, or ribboning; and rank with the Geranium, Verbena, and Calceolaria; their close, compact growth, rich-coloured flowers, and the freedom with which they bloom, all combine to place them among first-class bedding plants. The scarlet, yellow, and spotted Tom Thumb are distinguished favourites, as are also the old crimson, and the new Crystal Palace Gem.

Seed, 3*d.* per packet.

NEAPOLITAN VIOLETS.

These are the best for forcing. Place a frame over a small well-prepared hotbed, and cover the bed a foot thick with prepared soil, consisting of the remains of an old cucumber-bed with a little leaf-mould added. The violet plants should then be carefully removed, with as large a ball of earth round the roots as possible, and planted in rows close together, but not touching each other, and so arranged that the foliage may be close to the glass without touching it, as the bed will settle an inch or two after the lights are put on. When planted, give them a copious watering, and in warm showers take the lights off: this will give them a clean, healthy appearance. The lights may be kept off all night with advantage when there is no appearance of frost, and all dead, decayed, or turning leaves, should be removed as soon as they appear. Plants thus treated will yield a supply of violets from November to April.

Where it is desired to have violets in summer and autumn, runners should be laid either in pots or on a hotbed where they are growing, in February, selecting the strongest runners, and pegging them down, with a little soil over the runner, and keeping them moist: these will be ready to plant out early in April, each with its bundle of roots, and will come in a month or six weeks earlier than the others. But they must be placed in their winter quarters early in September.

NECTARINES.

Full directions for the treatment of Nectarine-trees will be found under the head of Fruit-Garden in the calendar for each month. It will be necessary here merely to mention that the following will be found very useful varieties, and form a good succession in ripening:—Fairchild's Nectarine, Violette hâtive, Elruge, Marry, and Red Roman.

NEMO'PHILA (nat. ord. Hydrophylla'ceæ).

This is perhaps the most charming and generally useful genus of dwarf-growing hardy annuals. All the varieties have a neat, compact, and uniform habit of growth, with shades and colours the most strikingly beautiful, so that ribboned, sown in circles, or arranged in any style which the fancy may suggest, the effect is pleasing and very striking. *N. maculata* and *N. phacelioides* are distinct; the latter is a beautiful hardy perennial; the former is more robust in growth, and has larger flowers than the other varieties. They all grow well from cuttings and seeds,—the latter from 6*d.* to 3*d.* per packet.

NEPEN'THES (nat. ord. Cytin'eæ).

The curious plants of this class are well known under the general name of pitcher-plants. They are mostly natives of China and Ceylon. Many very choice and beautiful varieties have been introduced of late years. The following are some of the most choice. *N. distillatoria*, very graceful pitchers, moderate-sized, dark green, mottled. *N. phyllamphora*, a robust species, producing bright green pitchers in great abundance. *N. Rafflesiana*, fine grower, with pitchers beautifully coloured.

NE'RIUM (nat. ord. Apocy'neæ).

The best known of this class is the common Oleander, which usually requires a greenhouse in England, but which flowers beautifully out of doors in Southern Europe. All the oleanders require a mixture of equal parts of peat, loam, and sand.

NETTING.

Netting is extremely useful for many gardening purposes, to protect blossom from frost and fruit from birds. It may also with very good effect be suspended beneath both wall and standard trees to catch any falling fruit. Netting of a fine mesh may be used successfully to keep off the attacks of wasps and flies. Old fish-netting mended up can be purchased at 1*d.* per yard.

NOISETTE ROSES.

This beautiful group of roses was originally a hybrid between the Bengal rose (*R. indica*) and *R. moschata*. It was sent from North America in 1817, by M. Philippe Noisette, to his brother, Louis Noisette, of Paris; and the letter which accompanied it states that it was obtained by the artificial fecundation of the former with the pollen of the latter, applied by camel-hair pencil. M. Boitard thinks this statement may be doubtful, pointing out how easily the hybridizer may deceive himself in carrying out the details of his operation. "Our cultivators," he adds, "obtain every day new varieties resembling the Noisettes by merely sowing the seed of *Rosa indica*, without any attempt at artificial fecundation." It is not very obvious, however, why this doubt is raised: it is quite certain that the original type of the Noisette is becoming scarce, while the new sorts approximate to other groups.

NORTH BORDERS.

A north border under a south wall in a garden is generally much undervalued. In the flower-garden, a north wall, if it happens to exist, is frequently looked upon as a nuisance, and covered with ivy; in the kitchen-garden it is only more profitably occupied by Morello cherries and red currants, while, in both cases, the border is kept as shallow as possible, and turned to little or no account. Many plants and shrubs, however, will flourish upon a north border and against a north wall, and show themselves hardy there, which in any other situation would not outlive a winter's frost. In the flower-garden let the north wall have a good deep border of bog, and against the wall all the hardy sorts of camellias will flourish and blossom freely. The green and the black tea-plant also, not having their bark exposed to the scorching sun of summer, will survive our severest winters in such a situation. Rhododendrons will also do well, and so will chrysanthemums. All our hardy indigenous ferns do better upon a north border than under any other aspect. Those persons who wish to acclimatize any tender plants should, by all means, make their first experiments upon a north border or against a south wall. The shady side of a south wall is decidedly the best position for all cuttings during spring and summer, to enable them to stand the severity of winter.

NOVEMBER.

The atmosphere during this month is saturated with moisture; dense mists and fogs abound, and gloomy boisterous weather, as a rule, prevails. The leaves of the beeches are changing their green hue for the purplish chestnut autumnal shade. The mean temperature is about 42° Fahr., but the thermometer ranges between 23° and 62°. The mean temperature of the earth one foot deep is 46·01°; at two feet, 47·28°; that of the air being 42·98°, on an average of the years 1844 to 1853.

Flower-Garden and Shrubberies.—The glory of the flower-garden is waning, and it will soon be desolate, in spite of the gardener's care. Meanwhile, keep the beds neat by the timely removal of decaying foliage, and the grass and gravel walks clean and smooth by frequent rolling. Plants to be taken up and potted should be attended to immediately, or at least protected during the nights, for fear of sudden frosts. Pelargoniums, calceolarias, and similar plants, are greatly benefited by being placed in a gentle bottom-heat until the fresh roots break. Now is an excellent time for propagating cuttings of calceolarias and most herbaceous and shrubby plants, if placed in a cold frame. Chinese, Bourbon, and hybrid perpetual roses will now root freely under the same treatment.

When the beds are cleared, trench them up; manure and add new soil where necessary, and plant the bulbs for spring flowering. Hardy annuals sown last month, if large enough, may be transplanted at once to their permanent beds, with pansies, alyssums, phloxes, primulas, and other herbaceous plants from the reserve-garden.

Where alterations are contemplated, they should be determined on without delay, and proceeded with when the plans are thoroughly matured,—not before. To render the grouping system permanently interesting, occasional changes, both in form and arrangement of beds, are necessary; and a retrospective glance, with a view to future arrangements, will be useful now, while the whole effect is fresh in the memory, and when next year's bloom is about to be provided for. In the selection of plants, it is to be borne in mind that duration of flowering should be the first consideration, for few gardens will afford the time or the cost necessary to carry out the plan of a changeable flower-garden, in which the beds are decorated in early spring with scillas, bulbocodiums, erythroniums, hepaticas, sanguinarias, and other precocious flowers, to be succeeded by autumn-sown annuals, in masses, in the summer months, and autumnal bulbs, dahlias, hollyhocks, and chrysanthemums, bringing us again to the verge of winter. This system of gardening, however attractive when attended with high keeping, is too costly and entails more trouble than proprietors of the ordinary run of gardens will incur; therefore the gardener must have an eye to the means as well as to the end, and arrange his plans accordingly. In the survey recommended, he will probably remember that, in proportion as the prevailing colours are warm or cold,—that is, scarlet or purple,—so the distance which separates the beds will be apparently diminished or increased. "Warm colours," according to Mr. Caie, "like light, irradiate the atmosphere to a greater distance with their peculiar hues; of some colours, as those of the verbena called Hamlet and *Campanula carpatica*, it may be said that subdued light is the condition in which they are seen to the greatest advantage, since they become really beautiful as the sun passes the horizon." If the distribution of colour has engaged the attention of the cultivator, many expedients will probably occur to him by which the angularity, which is now the distinguishing feature of the flower-beds, may be rectified. *Erythronium Dens canis*, *Allium Moly*, *Anemone apennina*, *Sanguinaria canadensis*, *Scilla italica*, *Phlox verna*, and a vast number of other hardy plants introduced now, will add interest to the flower-garden by-and-by.

Now is the best time to collect leaves from lawns and drives, and to stack them in some out-of-the-way place for use Oak and beech are the most valuable to the gardener, affording the most durable heat. Tread them firmly in the stack, and afterwards thatch them to keep them dry; the remainder may be thrown together for rotting, when they form a valuable auxiliary for potting and composts. The principal lawns should be swept when leaves are numerous, as well as to remove worm-casts, &c. An occasional rolling will keep the surface in good order.

The stock of cuttings should be looked over, and additional heat applied, when the roots are not fully formed. Late geranium-cuttings may be removed to the kerbs of the pine-pits, to make roots. In storing the stock away for the winter, endeavour to keep all those plants together which require similar treatment. Some kinds will stand more damp than others, and may be wintered in common frames; but the better kinds of bedding-out geraniums, and some other tender things, will require a moderately dry house or pit. To preserve verbenas, petunias, &c. &c., properly through the winter, they must be kept dry to prevent mildew, to which they are very liable in frames during wet weather. As it is desirable to protect the recently-struck plants from rains, and yet to give them a large portion of air, the sashes must be daily tilted up back and front, to cause a complete circulation. Where room can be found for the bedding stuff in empty vineries, they should be allowed to remain there as long as possible, as in dull weather they become better established than when kept in frames, more especially those only recently rooted.

The herbaceous ground will now require a thorough cleaning, cutting down the stalks of plants done blooming, and seeing to the support of the few things still in flower, as the Michaelmas daises, and rake and hoe the borders neatly.

During this month the flower-beds should be enriched with manure or

fresh loam, and the soil turned up before frost sets in; the edges of beds in grass should be gone over with the edging-iron to preserve the form. All flowering plants standing in pots or frames should be fully exposed to the sun on every favourable occasion, so as to harden their tissues; and all growing plants, like the verbenas, stopped back to secure a bushy habit by-and-by. Most of the verbenas may be kept in a cold pit, dusting a little slaked lime over the soil in the pots or boxes; applying the same treatment to the shrubby calceolarias. Pot-up and cut back the dwarf lobelias and *Œnothera prostrata*, sprinkling a little silver-sand among the roots. Lophospermums, maurandyas, and the tropæolums, require a dry and airy situation in the frame or greenhouse when taken in doors.

Shrubberies should now be thinned out, alterations completed, and the formation of new shrubberies brought to a close during the month. For the purpose of renovation, the necessity of a reserve-garden cannot be too strongly urged. Most herbaceous plants blossom incomparably finer from young plants propagated betimes than from old and exhausted ones. With a reserve-garden in which the best shrubs are coming forward, alterations are easily made: where overgrown branches have to be cut back and thinned, the operation must be performed gradually, and a portion headed down every season until the whole is renovated and covered with young foliage.

Among the shrubby flowering-plants which are only to be met with in the best gardens, but which might be cultivated everywhere, we may mention the magnolias: they are natives of North America, China, and Japan; have a noble foliage and wonderfully beautiful flowers, and some of them a powerful and most agreeable fragrance. They flourish well in a compost made of good loam, peat, and decomposed leaves. The grandifloras,—all three American, are perfectly hardy, flourishing luxuriantly in the open border even

November.

when exposed to cold and cutting winds. No garden should be without them.

Aralia japonica is another splendid shrub from Japan, of rich foliage, and throwing out numerous expanded clusters of bloom of whitish-green colour, each cluster being composed of several spikes of bloom 18 inches long, diverging from a common centre : it requires a sheltered spot in the garden, however. The spiræas again are a highly ornamental family of shrubs, some of them adapted for rock-work, as *S. prunifolia;* others for planting behind smaller shrubs, when the long spikes of bloom bend gracefully forward, like *S. Lindleyana;* others are dwarf, of good habit, and bloom in rich spikes both of white and pink flowers, in great abundance.

Rose-Garden. — Planting and transplanting are now the chief employment : if very dry during the month, give a good watering to each plant before the soil is fully filled in. Stocks should also be collected and planted for budding on next season. The true dog-rose makes the best stock, and may be distinguished from sweet-brier by the large white thorns which thickly cover the stem of the latter towards the base; and from those of climbing habit, by the dark green colour of the bark and weakness in the stem. Prune the old roots close to the stem, cutting all strong shoots close off. When planted, some growers cut the head down to within four or six inches of the height at which they are wanted, and, having levelled the soil, leave them till spring. The best growers prefer leaving the head full until the plant is thoroughly rooted.

Florists' Flowers.—At this season of the year the amateur cannot do better than get together those soils, &c., which are indispensable for the proper growth of his favourite flowers. Turf, pared two inches thick from a loamy pasture or a green-lane side, stacked together to decompose, will be the foundation of his composts. A large heap of melon-bed manure should also be secured, not forgetting as large a quantity of fallen leaves as possible. A cartload of sharp river-sand is an indispensable adjunct, and the florist should look out for willow-dust and decayed and rotten sticks. A quantity of excellent food for plants may be scraped out from hedge-bottoms. Allow auriculas to have abundance of air, but little or no moisture : the plants being in a state of rest, require but little. Tulips out of the ground now suffer every day.

Auriculas are in their winter quarters; they require abundant air, and occasional inspection to see that no worms are in the pots; the indications being castings on the surface : if such appear, water them with lime-water, or remove them by repotting.

Carnations and Picotees, layered in previous months, should be potted off, and placed in their winter quarters, protection from dampness being the chief consideration : in fine weather let them be fully exposed. *Pinks* planted last month must be protected from the wind.

Dahlias are still fresh and gay, if the weather has been tolerably mild : should frost appear, no time should be lost in taking them up. Store them away carefully labelled, stalks downwards, in some place where they can be secured from damp. Seedlings that have bloomed late, and weak plants, are benefited by being potted and kept dry through the winter.

Hollyhocks.—Cut down and propagate from the old stools. Take eyes from the flowering stems, but without forcing.

Pansies should be potted off as reserves for filling up vacancies, and for new beds in the early spring : the beds should be examined to see that the worms have not attacked them.

Polyanthuses in beds will be benefited if the surface of the soil is stirred, and a top dressing of equal parts of maiden loam, leaf-mould, and well-decomposed cow-dung, applied.

Tulips, not yet planted, should be got in without delay, taking care,

November.

however, that the soil is not wet: hoop them over, and let matting be prepared against rainy weather.

Kitchen-Garden.—Approaching winter bids vegetation prepare for a rest. In the kitchen-garden the crops will make little progress for the next four months. Now will be apparent the amount of forethought displayed in summer and autumn cropping. If a fair amount of Brussels sprouts, savoys, and other winter vegetables have been provided—which is the main point,—and supposing herbs, salading, and minor crops have been attended to, then, if any ground is unoccupied, lay it up in ridges, having first trenched it or dug it deeply. For planting early potatoes, the advantages of ridging are great: heavy clayey ground does not pulverize easily: the action of frost is wanted on the surface. Of course the thicker the surface acted upon the better. In digging heavy ground, give the men to understand that they must lay the soil in solid spits as they are cut out with the spade: the spits should not be broken, but laid roughly together, with plenty of openings for the air and frost to act on them. Ground managed in this way is easier to crop in the spring-time than that which has lain in ridges, because, when the ridges are levelled, a new surface is turned up, and the pulverized surface is buried. Ground ridged this month, therefore, should be levelled again in February, and another surface exposed and pulverized. At this time it is very necessary to give attention to the state of the drainage: unless surplus water can get away readily, great inconveniences may result, for heavy rains will make the garden a swamp, and spoil the crops already put in, besides preventing others from being sown or planted.

Asparagus, if not already done, should be cut down, and the beds receive a dressing of very rotten dung, which may be forked in or not; it signifies but little, as its fertilizing qualities will be washed into the ground during the winter; but, previous to manuring, all weeds should be removed. If it is intended to make new beds, no better time can be chosen than the present for trenching the ground. If done now, the new surface will be exposed to atmospheric influences the whole winter long, and, if frequently turned, will be in fine condition for planting the following April.

Artichokes.—A good mulching of leaves will be of considerable benefit to these in protecting the crowns from the frost. Let the ends of the leaves be exposed, and be killed. If a good cordon of leaves grows round the collar of each, they will stand better and come in earlier.

Seakale.—As the leaves decay and detach themselves, they may be removed; but, unless pots and hot dung are soon to be applied, it is not necessary to remove them.

Beans.—On light ground and sunny borders, these may be put in without fear of failure. Without such advantages, autumn-sowing of them is not recommended; the true purpose of it is to have crops a trifle earlier than they would be by deferring the sowing till February; but the loss during the winter counterbalances the advantages, and sowing now may be left to those who have plenty of room.

Runner-Beans.—Pull up these, as they will produce nothing more this season; the haum may be pulled off the sticks; or, if all pulled up together, the leaves will soon drop off and the haum dry, when all may be chopped up together for firewood, or tied in fagots.

Peas, like beans, may be sown, and with the same proviso as to the nature of the ground. Crops are so often lost during damp winters, that we would not recommend autumn-sowing to those who have not an abundance of room. Early sorts are of course best for sowing now.

Celery.—It is advisable to give the final earthing-up during this month: it grows much slower now, and must be allowed time to blanch. Besides, should severe frost set in, it might be

November.

injured by exposure. Even that grown merely for soups, &c., had better receive a little earthing for protection; and if dusted with lime to destroy slugs, before earthing, so much the better.

Cardoons.—Treat in a like manner.

Beet.—Get this crop housed or pitted at once; it will not stand frost. Cut off the leaves not too close to the roots, which should lay a couple of days to heal or callow; then stow them where they will not mould or damp till pitted.

Carrots.—Treat in a similar manner to beet. It is advisable to get them housed before there is any danger of very severe frost. Young crops to stand the winter should be carefully thinned and hoed between.

Onions.—The autumn-sown should be treated in a similar manner.

Leeks ought to be earthed up, if not done before, when they can be taken up as wanted: they will continue to grow in mild weather.

Parsnips are as well left in the ground till wanted.

Potatoes, if any are left in the ground, should be taken up without delay, and stored: they keep well in the ground by taking up every other row, and placing an additional layer of earth over each ridge left.

Turnips should be hoed and kept clean.

Scorzoneras, &c., are best left in the ground till wanted.

Lettuce, if tied up for blanching, should be kept dry, if possible, or they will soon rot. The advantage of good cabbaging sorts will be apparent at this time. Some may yet be planted out to stand the winter.

Endive.—Continue to blanch in succession. If this is done with flower-pots, these, as they are removed, can be placed on others.

Spinach.—If this has been properly thinned and kept clean, it will continue to grow, the leaves alone being picked for use. If the plants stand nine inches or a foot apart, it will be all the better.

Brocoli.—Such as are coming in now should be watched. Remove dead leaves, and use the hoe between them.

Brussels Sprouts, *Borecole*, and *Savoys* are best kept free from dead leaves, which in damp weather become unpleasant.

Cabbage may still be planted out for the next summer's crop; but the earlier it is done now the better. Use the hoe freely amongst those planted last month: they will be much better for it.

Cauliflowers.—Stir the soil about those in hand-glasses, and keep the lights off unless there is fear of frost.

Fruit-Garden.—Let the bulk of kitchen and dessert apples in the fruit-room be often looked over to remove decaying fruit. In doing this, be careful not to bruise the others. Clear off the remaining leaves from wall-trees; and, now that the greater part of the fruit-tree leaves have fallen, the whole should be cleared off the ground preparatory to pruning and turning up the borders for winter. Figs against walls should have any odd remaining fruit taken off. Thin out superfluous shoots, and pinch out the points of the wood selected for bearing, when the branches should be tied together and matted, or protected by haybands, fern, &c., for the winter.

Towards the end of the month is the best time to commence pruning dwarf apples and pears. Make up your mind what particular form the young tree should assume when at its full size, whether pyramidal, globular, or spreading. Shoots to form the skeleton of the tree should next be selected. How far these require shortening will depend on their strength and the shape of the tree. The remaining shoots must be cut back so as to fill up the figure. Orchard-trees, where covered with lichens and mosses, should have them scraped off, and a wash of hot lime and water applied to the branches. Apples, pears, plums, and cherries may be taken in the order in which they are named. Remove all the old shreds where they are used: those that will do another season should be boiled to destroy the eggs of insects before using them again. The large wood looks better neatly tied in with osier twigs. Before tying or nailing, examine the trees, and if infested with scale or other insects, dress them with soft soap dissolved in hot water, to which add sulphur, quick-lime, and tobacco-water; mix the ingredients well together, which should be of a consistency to adhere well; dress the branches with this, but not during frost.

Apricots, peaches, nectarines, and vines may be left till February or March, taking apricots first, as they are the first to open the flower. Young plantations of strawberries should have some short dung spread between the rows, to preserve their shallow roots from frosts, which otherwise might lift them out of the ground. Look the beds over, and head the ground firmly round the plants. This is more necessary where the soil is light and rich, as the frost will make such ground more porous.

Plums.—All late sorts should be gathered before the frost sets in, and either wrapped in paper or hung by the stalk in the fruit-room. Pruning should follow.

Currants and Gooseberries.—Plant and prune both while the weather is favourable. For the production of large gooseberries, short pruning is necessary. Where quantity is required, and the trees are young, shorten the young shoots one-half or two-thirds. If they are of full growth, only take the points off the young shoots, and when the branches are thinned out, cut back to a bud on the upper side of the shoots. When the trees are pruned, lime the ground, and, if necessary, add manure and dig it slightly.

Strawberries.—Continue as last month, unless inclined to adopt an expedient which has sometimes produced enormous crops: it is, to take up the old plants in spits and plant them again immediately in the same ground. The reason for this, or for its results, does not appear, unless it is analogous to the root-pruning of dwarf trees as recommended by Mr. Rivers.

Flowers under Glass.—During the continuance of *characteristic* November weather, every glass-house should be looked upon and managed as a huge Wardian case, the use of which is to keep *November out*, while *we*, the proprietors, are enabled to enjoy spring, summer, and autumn, at our pleasure, *within*. It is the height of folly to allow a November fog to inundate a conservatory under the pretence of *giving air;* such air is not wanted by the plants. This is emphatically the *dead season*. Plants under glass, though in the best possible health, would rather sleep just now than grow; and if a dry atmosphere and rather a low temperature is maintained, houses may be kept shut up close for a fortnight or three weeks together, not only with perfect impunity, but with positive benefit to the plants; this, however, supposes that the external atmosphere is ungenial; but such is not always the case. Embrace every opportunity of admitting the external air to conservatories and greenhouses when it is of a temperature of 45°; also change the air of stoves, &c., during the few hours of sunshine that often come to chase away a November fog. In fine, the more fresh air the better, provided it be warm and genial;—the less the better when it is otherwise. Plants will live and thrive for weeks in the same atmosphere, when adverse circumstances render a change dangerous, and they will bear this treatment better now than during any other season of the year; and yet, as a general rule, we repeat, the more fresh air the better.

As the quantity of external air admitted may now be safely reduced to its minimum, so may also be the quantity of water. The fact is, the power of a plant to use water to any good purpose chiefly depends upon the intensity of light and heat to which it is exposed.

November.

In watering thirsty roots, see that the flowers and succulent leaves are kept dry. This is a point of considerable importance at almost any season,—at this, it is a question of life or death to many plants. Chinese primroses, for instance, double or single, will speedily fog off and perish if the needful water is poured into the centre, or permitted to trickle down wet leaves to the same vulnerable point. Other plants suffer in the same manner, although few, perhaps, to the same extent. The water given to plants should always be 5° or 10° higher than the house in which they grow. Never water a plant until it is dry, and then water thoroughly. Regulate the quantity given by the state of growth and drinking capabilities of each plant. A chrysanthemum coming into flower will require three times as much as a camellia in the same state.

Greenhouses occupied by heaths, azaleas, &c., not in flower, must be kept cool, dry, and clean. They may also have more air than the conservatory, and a temperature of 40° will suffice.

Camellias.—Where these have a house devoted to them, they require careful management. The buds will just be swelling, and a sudden change of temperature, a scarcity or excess of water, or a cutting draught of cold air, will often cause the buds to drop. Be extremely careful not to give an excess, when fire-heat becomes necessary, on account of frost, and maintain a genial growing atmosphere of 45°.

Pelargoniums.—The same temperature will suit these during the month. If worms make their appearance in the pots, water three or four times in succession with *clear lime-water.* The repetition is necessary to insure their destruction, as these pests seem to have the power of casting their skins when injured, and so escape. But as they cannot carry on this evasive system indefinitely, a few repetitions of the lime will effectually destroy them. Remove every dead leaf; thin out and train the shoots; shift late-flowering plants into their blooming-pots; keep pansies at the warmest end of the house, and give fire-heat enough to drive out damp and enable you to change the atmosphere during mild days or gleams of sunshine.

Orchids.—See that they are clean; keep them in a dry temperature of 65°, and let them sleep.

Plant-stove.—Here the *Poinsettia pulcherrima*, *Euphorbia jacquiniflora*, *Begonia nitida*, *Gesneria cinnabarina*, will be lighting up by their dazzling beauty, masses of ferns, palms, and variegated plants. Late caladiums must now be watered with great care, as the bulbs are impatient of damp during winter. Those beginning to go off must have scarcely any water, and as soon as the leaves are matured, water should be entirely withheld, and the pots turned on their sides for the winter. Remove dead leaves and flowers as soon as they appear; water in the morning for the next three months; keep a temperature of 65°; frequently change the arrangement of the plants, and only admit air in fine weather.

Fruit under Glass.—One of the chief duties here is fruit-preservation. This is just the very worst month in the whole year for keeping ripe fruit of any kind, and especially trying for ripe grapes: one speck of decay or mildew will soon increase under the influence of a November fog. Houses of ripe fruit must therefore be examined daily, and every specked berry or decayed leaf removed. Brisk fires must also be lighted in the morning, to enable you to give air both at front and back, to agitate the atmosphere and expel damp. No plant must, on any account, be placed in the house, nor a drop of water be allowed to fall on paths, &c.; neither must the house be shut up close until the heating apparatus is cold.

An increase of temperature in the absence of a current of air is most injurious to ripe grapes, and causes them to decay almost sooner than anything: unless during very cold weather, a current of air should always be maintained through vineries containing ripe grapes. Better that the grapes should be slightly shrivelled than that they should be altogether decomposed. In fact, the toughness of rind induced in the process of shrivelling is one of the surest preservatives against decomposition. If the houses are not waterproof, or plants must be placed in them, the best plan will be to cut and store the grapes as recommended in October.

Another great point in preserving late grapes, is to keep the rain off the borders in which the roots are growing. This is sometimes effected by thatching with straw, sometimes by the use of boarding or tarpauling, and often by spreading a layer of concrete, formed by mixing six parts of coarse gravel to one of quick-lime over the surface of the border. If the border has a pitch of three or more inches from back to front, and this concrete is put on about three inches thick, it will furnish a cheap and efficient waterproof covering: it may be removed in the spring or not, at the option of the cultivator. The best grapes have been produced from vines in a border thus covered for three whole years. During that period they were never watered, and never showed any symptoms of needing it: the surface of the concrete in summer was sometimes so hot one could scarcely touch it. It never cracked with the sun's rays, however, and early in October it was always covered with strawy litter, to prevent the dispersion of that heat which its absorptive powers had husbanded in the border.

After taking care of the grapes that we have, let us look after those that are to come. The vinery started last month will now be breaking, and a genial temperature of 50° to 55° must be maintained. This should not be exceeded during this month: the absence of the sun renders rapid growth dangerous. What is gained in rapidity will be lost in solidity and strength. If the sun should shine, however, an increase of 10° or 15° will do no harm, but much good. See that the heat of the outside borders is kept regular, avoiding all extremes: it may continue 3° in excess of the inside temperature. If maintained by the aid of dung and leaves, frequent examinations and turnings will be necessary to keep it right; sometimes fermenting material is also used to aid other means of keeping up the internal temperature. It makes a good deal of extra labour, but has the great merit of both feeding and warming at the same time. Where it is used, it must be partially sweetened before it is introduced, as too much rank ammonia would prove destructive to the tender foliage of the vines. When this is properly attended to, perhaps no food is so grateful to, nor so speedily available for, vines as this.

Vines in pots may be started in a bottom-heat of 53° in hotbeds, unless means are found for giving them bottom-heat over flues, &c., in the houses in which they are to be fruited. After they have fairly started, they can be carefully moved to their fruiting quarters; in many places the first vinery will now be started. Proceed as recommended last month.

Peaches.—If these are wanted next May, trees in pots must now be started. They should already have been untied, pruned, washed, &c. Examine the borders thoroughly; water, and top-dress with good maiden loam, if necessary. See that the house, as well as the trees, is scrupulously clean, so that you do not have to battle with vermin as well as dark skies and inclement weather for the next six months. The Royal George, Noblesse, Galande, and Vanguard peach, and the Red Roman and Violette hâtive nectarine, are best for early forcing. Proceed slowly; give no fire unless compelled, and do not exceed 45° by fire-heat during the month.

Orchard-houses.—If these are either open or unroofed, see that the hungry birds do not destroy your next year's crop. They seem fond of model standard trees, and in a single day will often mar the hopes of a twelvemonth. The lights should be placed on these houses, it is a dangerous practice to allow standard trees to be much frozen. The cold is also much more intense here than on the surface of a south or west wall.

Fig-trees grown under glass should never be frozen. The embryo fruit will most likely be destroyed, and a whole month's or six weeks' forcing lost in consequence. This is a good time to examine the wood thoroughly for scale, &c., and to paint the trees over with the composition recommended for vines.

Pines.—Those swelling off must be assisted by a warm genial atmosphere of 75°, and be watered when necessary. Bottom-heat will require to be examined, and fermenting material renewed, possibly. Plants intended to fruit next spring and summer must be guarded against any sudden check, be kept rather dry, and *rest* for the next three months in a temperature of 60° to 65°.

Similar treatment, except the *resting*, will suit the general stock of succession plants. They must be kept slowly moving in a dryish atmosphere.

Much attention will be necessary to renewing linings, &c., to those in pits, to maintain the requisite temperature. Coverings of mats or reed-frames must also be applied in severe weather, and all sudden changes guarded against. Occasionally, too, some of the strongest succession plants will require water at the roots, although the air may still be very damp.

Cold Frames.—Plants in these are often treated as if they were more tender than they really are. The object is not so much to stimulate them into growth, as to protect them from such injury from frost and storms as they would be exposed to in the open air. Corn salad, endive, lettuce, cauliflower, parsley, carrots, radishes, onions, and many more light crops, are not so tender but that they will stand out of doors; but then they keep so much better and fresher under the protection of frames, that it is well worth while to have a few lights devoted to them. They also begin to grow rather earlier in the spring, and continue growing later in the autumn, than they would do if quite exposed; but it should be strictly observed not to keep them in any way close, so as to breed mould. If any mouldiness accrue, it is a sure sign that they are kept too close. Let the plants have full exposure as much as possible, just as if they were growing out of doors, with merely the aid of the lights to protect them in case of sharp frosts, heavy rains, snow, fog, or winds, should these be more than ordinary. Water should be given rather carefully. Avoid giving enough to chill the roots; a medium state, rather approaching dryness, is better than the least overwetting, especially in frosty weather.

Seeds of radishes, lettuce, and small salading may be sown any time during the month, or any time in the winter. They will germinate slowly, but may come in very useful in the spring; the latter will be ready in about a month. In frosty weather the protection of a mat will, in addition to the lights, be sufficient for most of these things.

Garden-frames are very useful for protecting other plants than those above named. Many plants, as pinks and pansies, stocks and chrysanthemums, and indeed many plants generally accounted hardy when planted in the borders, will, when in pots, require the protection of a frame, or, if planted in a bed of soil placed within the frame, they will flower earlier and stronger.

NYMPHÆ'A (nat. ord. Nympha'ceæ), the Water-lily.

The yellow British variety is generally classed under the name Nuphar. Of Nymphæa there are many species. Those from Egypt, which are very beautiful, require a hothouse in this country. They vary in colour; some are blue and others pink.

OCTOBER.

Flower-Garden and Shrubberies.—The mean temperature of the month is nearly 7° lower than that of September, and frost is by no means uncommon towards the end of it. The moisture in the atmosphere increases, and evaporation diminishes considerably; the mean average temperature being, at one foot below the surface, 51·52°; at two feet, 52·78°; and at the surface, 49·35°.

Maintain scrupulous cleanliness in the flower-garden, and continue the beauty as long as possible. Prepare pots and space for potting or boxing the chief stock of geraniums, calceolarias, jasmines, &c. If frost should come, get everything you intend to save under cover directly, and proceed to store them away at leisure. There is, however, no necessity for destroying the beauty of the garden before the frost.

The great business of propagating for next year should now be completed. Nevertheless, such things as verbenas, calceolarias, &c. &c., may still be put in with the certainty of success.

We will now take a rapid run through the shrubbery and pleasure-ground, and note if any and what changes are to be effected there. Beeches, &c., 20 or 30 feet high, are to be moved, to break the prevailing east wind, on the other side of the lawn. Lose no time, then, in preparing the holes, and getting all perliminaries arranged for a heavy job of transplanting. The sooner all deciduous trees are moved, the greater is the chance of success. If the weather continues mild, they will form fresh roots before the winter; and by the time that the spring excites to renewed growth, the roots will be sufficiently restored to perform their important functions without let or hindrance. Large evergreens may also be safely removed this month. Space forbids us to enter into details. Turf-laying, and ground-work generally, will be proceeded with. Where much has to be done, a great deal will be gained by beginning early.

Reserve-Garden.—Keep annuals, and other plants in beds, quite clear. Plant off primroses, polyanthuses, violets, iberis, and arabis. Wall-flowers may now be removed to flower-beds and borders, if these have been cleared of their summer occupants. Increase by division of the roots, such herbaceous plants as rockets, lychnis, &c., and plant them in beds in this department. Plant beds of narcissus, hyacinths, crocuses, &c., either for permanent flowering here or for removal to the flower-garden afterwards.

Florists' Flowers.—Place auriculas, polyanthuses, pinks, carnations, &c., if not already done, in their winter quarters. Give all the air possible to induce a quick growth. Gather hollyhock and dahlia seeds if ripe. Pot choice varieties of hollyhocks, and winter under glass. Pot up pansies for stores and flowering in pots. Plant out seedlings and put in cuttings. Prepare beds of good, light, fibrous, sandy loam for tulips, and have all in readiness for planting the main stock early next month.

Kitchen-Garden.—Towards the end of the month the asparagus-beds may be cleared of their haum, but not till it is yellow and the seed ripe, and a portion of the soil forked into the alleys; then mix some good manure with a little salt, and lay a good coating of it over the plants, covering the whole with the soil thrown into the alleys.

Celery.—Earth-up as often as it becomes necessary, not only for blanching, but to preserve the plants from frost.

Seakale will be ready to force towards the end of the month, either by removal to a forcing-bed or by covering the plants with pots, and these with stable-manure on the beds.

Cardoons should now receive a general earthing-up, choosing dry open weather for the operation, first gathering up the leaves and tying them together with a hayband. Peas and beans are past: let the ground be cleared, and, where vacant, dug or trenched, or ridged up, so that it may have the advantage of fallowing.

October.

Carrots, Potatoes, and Parsnips are now at maturity. Dig them up and store for the winter, so as to protect them from frost. The three-pronged potato-fork, with broad tines, rounded and blunt at the points, is a well-known implement. It is usual, where the haum is strong, to cut off the tops, and by inserting the fork under the plant, turn the whole up in a mass, the potatoes being collected after the digger in baskets: they may either be kept in a suitable room, or stored away in pits in the open ground, properly drained and covered, first with a layer of earth, then with a thatching of clean straw, and then with soil sufficiently thick to protect them from the severest frosts.

Small crops of *Mazagan Beans* may be planted, with a chance of their standing the winter, and coming in in May or June. A crop of *Early Peas* may be sown at the same time, either on a warm south border or under a fence; the early Hotspur pea being the best for the purpose. If the border is eight or ten feet broad, let the drills run across, and sow an inch and a half deep, and three or four feet asunder, and so placed as not to come in front of the stems of the trees on the wall.

A little *Carrot-seed* may also be sown on a warm border, with a chance of young carrots in spring.

All the *Cabbage* tribes require the greatest attention this month in weeding and warring with caterpillars, which infest them.

Cauliflowers sown in August will require pricking out, not less than four or five inches apart, where some kind of protection can be given, either under a frame or hand-glasses: those formerly pricked out and hardened off require planting out under hand-glasses to stand the winter, keeping the glasses close till rooted, and then supporting them on props two or three inches thick for air. Transplant *Cabbages* at the end of the month, choosing the strongest plants. *Coleworts* should now be planted out for spring use, and all the late-planted *Brocoli Cabbages*, &c., hoed, to loosen the soil and destroy weeds.

October.

Lettuces for a spring supply may be pricked out under a frame: the hardier kinds will frequently stand the winter on a warm border. *Lettuce* and *Endive* formerly planted out now require tying up. Small supplies of small salading sow weekly in boxes. Keep winter spinach free from weeds, and thin off where requisite, leaving the strongest plants. Sow also a small patch of Short-top and Salmon *Radishes* in the beginning, and again towards the end, of the month. If the weather proves mild, they will advance, and be ready for drawing in November and December.

Fruit-Garden.—The planting of fruit-trees should be proceeded with if the necessary preparations have been made. These preparations consist in draining and preparing stations, where planting in the open ground is intended, and in digging and manuring the border where the wall-trees or espaliers are to be planted. The most important point in planting, next to soil and subsoil, is to keep the collar of the stem at the surface of the soil, removing all diseased or bruised fibres, spreading the roots out carefully, and putting fine soil over them; keeping the young tree firmly in its place by stakes, without lifting or treading upon the roots: the autumn rains will settle the earth about the roots better than any other means. Root-pruning should now be performed either by lifting the trees altogether, and replanting, or by digging a trench round them, and removing or shortening old roots of over-luxuriant or perpendicular growth.

Apples and Pears are now ripening fast. Gather on fine days, taking care that pears especially are tenderly handled. When laid in the fruit-room for a week, they should be carefully looked over: more fruit decays in the first week than for many weeks afterwards, and if not removed, it soon affects others.

Peaches and Nectarine-trees should have all superfluous shoots removed, and the young wood left exposed to as much sun as possible, to ripen the shoots, on which the hopes of the following year depend. As soon as the leaves part readily from the branches, sweep them off, but not violently, with a new birch-broom. The trees will be benefited by passing a light broom over the foliage in the direction of its growth. It will detach the ripened leaves, and admit air to the heart of the tree and branches. Root-pruning, if thought requisite, perform towards the end of the month. The sign of its being required is found in over-luxuriant foliage, with an absence of fruit; but it requires to be done with caution. Dig a trench round the tree, one, two, or three feet from the stem, according to its size, so as to lay open all the roots. All old roots which have ceased to throw out rootlets or spongioles, should be pruned away close to the stem, the young roots trimmed, and all having a tendency to tap-root should be cut away. This done, fill up the trench with suitable fresh soil or compost. Where extensive root-pruning is necessary, it should be done partially in two or three years, removing a portion of the objectionable roots on each occasion.

Plums.—In wet seasons gather the late sorts, with their stalks attached; suspend them in the fruit-room, or wrap them in thin paper, and they will keep for several weeks. Quinces, medlars, and all sorts of nuts, are now fit to gather.

Raspberries of the autumn-bearing kind should be bearing a good supply of fruit. If the weather be fine, the canes which have fruited should be cut out, and the young ones left three or four to a stool. Manure, and dig between them, leaving the young shoots their full length until the spring. New plantations may now be made; the improved mode being to plant single canes about 18 inches apart, and attach them to espaliers.

Strawberries.—Remove all runners from the plants, and manure and dig between the rows; using the three-

tined fork, so as to avoid injuring the roots. Runners may be bedded out for new plantations, the formation of which had better stand over till the spring.

Flowers under Glass.—The chief duty of the month is to see that all tender and all hardy plants intended to be bloomed in winter are placed under requisite shelter. Nothing injures the former, or prevents the perfect inflorescence of the latter, more than being exposed to the chilling drenching rains that often fall at this period of the year.

It is good practice, in fine weather, to place out, in sheltered situations, many of our heaths, azaleas, camellias, &c. &c.; but better far to keep them entirely under glass than leave them out too late in the season.

Plants that have stood for months in the free air of heaven are most impatient of confinement. Unless the wind is very cutting, or the thermometer is under 40°, the houses should stand open night and day for several weeks after the plants are admitted; otherwise the sudden change of temperature will either cause flower-buds to drop or excite to premature wood-growth, perhaps both.

All plants are liable to injury from this cause,—camellias perhaps more than any other. Sudden transitions from an open and free to a close, confined atmosphere; rapid alternations of temperature, and extremes of wet or dry at root or top, are the main, if not the only, causes of flower-buds dropping in this beautiful species. But the causes that influence this plant so powerfully and suddenly affect all others in a greater or less degree. Hence the importance of adopting, in all changes with plants, the gradual process. The change from a low to a high, or a high to a low temperature, —from a dry to a moist, or a moist to a dry atmosphere, must be moderate and easy.

The Conservatory.—The conservatory is always dependent for three-fourths of its charms upon the taste and skill

October.

displayed in its arrangement. Beautiful objects beautifully placed, lovely climbers neatly festooned or gracefully trained, and the preservation of all this beauty as long as possible, are the grand desiderata here. As a cool atmosphere is one of the chief means to this end in summer, the mistake is sometimes made of maintaining this structure at too low a temperature. It should never, unless in the severest weather, be lower than 45°. Comparatively few blossoms will expand in perfection, or continue very long, at a lower temperature than this. From 45° as a night temperature to 55° as a day, is a safe range for the next four months with fire-heat, 50° being a safe day medium and 55° the maximum by artificial means. If the sun is genial enough to raise the temperature to 60° a few hours in winter, and air is admitted, it will do no harm. In managing the house, two things must be equally guarded against,—a moist, stagnant atmosphere and a sharp current of frosty air. Although directly contrary in their nature, both are almost alike destructive to flowers. The proper balancing of air at rest and air in motion, and the right proportion of moisture to be suspended in it, constitute the true secret of successful conservatory management. In general terms, it may be stated that the more light that can be secured for the next four or five months the better. All shading may now be dispensed with, and the foliage of the climbers gradually reduced, however beautiful they may be. They should be gone over two or three times until they are finally cut in to the smallest compass by the middle of November. Every ray of light at this period is alike necessary for the health of the plants and the colour of the flowers. Little or no syringing or sprinkling of paths will be necessary, except over chrysanthemum and camellia leaves for the first week or fortnight after their introduction from out of doors. Generally a sufficiency of vapour will rise from the surface of pots and borders,

without having recourse to either sprinkling leaves or paths. Care must be taken not to wet the latter in performing the necessary watering. Chrysanthemums will require a liberal supply of clear manure-water every day in bright weather, and must never be allowed to droop from want of it. Chinese primroses will require the next largest supply of water; then early-flowering epacrises, camellias, heaths, &c. &c.

Plants in full growth coming into bloom always require more water than plants past their meridian. Therefore all those already named, and early cinerarias, &c., will require much more copious supplies than late-flowering fuchsias, geraniums, begonias, &c. &c. Semi-stove plants, such as gesnerias, gloxinias, globe amaranths, achimenes, &c., which it is desirable to keep in bloom throughout the month, will now require very little water.

In reference to all such, and stove-plants in general subject to conservatory treatment, it is of immense importance to bear in mind that the lower the temperature in which they are placed the less *water* they require, and *vice versâ.* Cold, which stimulates man's assimilating organs to the utmost, paralyzes those of plants in the exact ratio of its intensity. Hence the necessity of a stinted regimen in cold weather, if vegetable life is to be preserved in full vigour. These remarks are applicable to all plant-structures, but are particularly applicable to a house where luxuriant health should ever appear adorned with floral beauty. Heaths, epacrises, late pelargoniums, fuchsias, scarlet and other geraniums, arums, petunias, salvias, Chinese primroses, Japan lilies, and chrysanthemums, will now constitute the chief display

Greenhouse and Heathery require similar general treatment, but should be kept five or ten degrees cooler than the conservatory. They will also bear sharper currents of air with impunity. Leschenaultias, chorizemas, &c., in this house, must be carefully examined for green-fly. This pest is very prevalent among, and very fatal to, the first-named plants. Sometimes it also suddenly attacks heaths, pimeleas, &c. As soon as one is discovered, fumigate instantly with tobacco-paper. This is also a good time to eradicate scale—white, black, or brown—from acacias, clianthus, and any other infected plants. Hand-picking is the most effective remedy.

Stove Plants.—Vincas, clerodendrons, &c., that have finished flowering, should now be cut back, and after they have slightly started, be shaken out of the pots, and inserted in pots as small as possible, for they seldom winter well in large pots. Water liberally poinsettias, justicias, begonias, gesnerias, &c., coming into bloom,—other plants going out of flower water scantily. All watering should now be done in the morning; and sprinkling, &c., unless on very bright days, entirely dispensed with. Drips of water must not be allowed to stand on variegated begonias, or other fine-foliaged plants, after this period: their impaired vitality, combined with the decrease of solar heat, renders them peculiarly liable to be injured from this cause; the leaves speedily become decomposed, and large blotches or holes appear, in consequence. Climbers on roofs, and all artificial shade, must be gradually and finally removed during the month. From this time to the middle of January the utmost amount of solar light attained in our climate is all too little for the natives of tropical climes that generally find a home in our plant-stoves. During cold nights a temperature of 60° will be sufficient, rising to 70° during the day, which must be the maximum of fire-heat permitted for the next four months: five or ten degrees higher from solar influence will be very serviceable. However, air must in such cases be given at once. Few plants are proof against the disastrous shrivelling influences of being placed between two fires,—artificial heat and the sun's rays. Often, for a week together, a sweet genial atmosphere may be maintained within, when the outside air is totally unfit for admission. Nothing requires greater practical knowledge and sounder judgment than the ventilation of tropical plant-structures in winter; a happy medium between the close glass-case and cutting-wind systems is the grand desideratum, and nothing but experience can confer the necessary qualifications for the performance of this important work. It should ever be borne in mind, that plants are endowed with the power of purifying their own atmosphere within certain limits; and that, consequently, the incessant admission of ungenial, harsh, external air, is not essential to their healthy existence. On the other hand, they rapidly exhaust the supply of carbonic acid gas present in a given quantity of air, and, therefore, an occasional change of air is essential to furnish them with food. Not only that,—the quantity of oxygen liberated bears a relative proportion to the amount of carbonic acid gas consumed; consequently, the less of the latter appropriated by plants, the less of the former is given back to the air, and it becomes the sooner deteriorated in consequence. It therefore follows, that while for a limited period plants may thrive in the same atmosphere, their constitution and necessary wants demand a change sooner or later. The frequency of the change required will very much depend upon the energy with which the vital force is being expended. In other words, the faster the plant grows, the more fresh air will be necessary. Now, as winter is the dormant period, less external air is requisite in winter than at any other period of the year. The fact thus elucidated is of immense practical importance to the cultivator; for just when it is well-nigh impossible to admit such air, we discover, both by science and experience, that its presence may be largely dispensed with. This remark is equally applicable to the cultivation of orchids; it even applies with double force to them; for, as most of these will now be comparatively dormant, the orchid-house may often remain for a month without fresh *air* with impunity. The great points are a dry atmosphere and a comparatively low temperature,—from 65° to 70°, and the maintenance of all in a dormant state.

Forcing-pit. — Introduce the first batch of rhododendrons, kalmias, Ghent and Indian azaleas, &c.; also some tea and hybrid perpetual roses, and early-flowering and sweet-scented geraniums, white and Anne Boleyn pinks, perpetual carnations, and lily of the valley; also *Salvia gesneraflora*, late gesnerias, and *Euphorbia polygonifolia*. Towards the end of the month, some hyacinths, tulips, &c., potted late in September, should now be pushed forward. Procure, and pot forthwith, the whole stock of hyacinths, crocuses, narcissuses, tulips, jonquils, and other hardy bulbs.

Cold Pit and Frames.—Give all the air possible, unless it actually freezes; guard against damp and over-crowding; carefully examine mignonette, stocks, &c., and remove every bit of mould the moment it appears. Provide mats or reed covers against frost; keep the glass clean, and let vigilant attention to the minutest details be the keynote of your successful culture of flowers under glass in "brown October."

Culture of Fruit under Glass.—In our climate, fruit must be cultivated under glass, if at all, at this season of the year; and those who wish for peaches or grapes on their table in May must begin this month.

Early work calls for early rest; and where this call is refused, the work will either be badly performed, or the machine will speedily be worn out. Hence, if plants are required to move to any good purpose *early* in the autumn, they must rest early in the summer. If, however, they have had a good long rest, and if they have first of all finished their summer work well by thoroughly ripening their wood, it is astonishing what an influence a warm house and syringing with warm water have in arousing them to vigorous exertion. Only it must not be too warm;—water, at a temperature of 50°, applied at first with a syringe all over, in the form of a shower-bath, will suffice. A temperature of 45° or 50° being maintained at the same time, and the bath repeated twice a day, the plants will begin to expand their buds. No sooner does this occur than they must be kept growing; one of the greatest mistakes in forcing is to allow them to go to rest after they have begun to break.

Peach-house. —Supposing that the fruit was gathered in May or June, the lights removed in July, the trees pruned in August or September, they may now be thoroughly painted over with a composition consisting of equal parts of sulphur, clay, cow-dung, and soot. The borders should also be forked up, six inches or one foot of the old soil removed, and the same quantity of turfy maiden loam substituted in its place. Every bit of trellis and woodwork should also be thoroughly washed with soap and water, unless the house has just been painted, the walls whitewashed, coloured, or painted, and the hot-water pipes painted over with a mixture of equal parts lime and sulphur. Perhaps it will be as well to omit the painting from the first 12 feet from the boiler on the flow-pipe. If the roots of the trees are at all dry, water with manure-water at a temperature of 60°, which will not only moisten, but gently excite them, by considerably raising the temperature of the soil. Having thus laid the foundation of success in cleanliness and suitable food, place the lights on, and, if the weather is mild, leave them half-down night and day for the first week. If the roof is a fixture, give all the air possible at front and back, and leave the door open. Sprinkle the trees overhead several times a day; sprinkle paths, &c., and maintain an atmosphere like a cool April morning. Proceed thus during the entire month, varying, of course, your treatment,—the quantity of air, &c., according to the nature of the external atmosphere. A temperature of 50°, however, should

October.

never be exceeded by fire-heat, if fire becomes necessary, which is not often the case, during the month.

Vinery. — All preliminary matters may proceed here exactly on the same principle as for the peach-house. In all forcing, either of flowers or fruit, let cleanliness be your first care. Before the painting, &c., let every bit of loose bark that will rub off with your hand be removed; severe barking,—scraping it off with knives, &c., is not desirable; for although vines have endogenous stems,—that is, increase from the inside, and not from the out, and their bark is consequently not essential to their healthy existence,—still it is useful in retaining moisture about their stems; and certainly nature never intended that vines should present the appearance of so many *peeled sticks.* Both tidiness of appearance and the destruction of insects require the removal of that which is loose and easily removed; to go beyond this, if not injurious, is obviously unnecessary, and a loss of time. The varieties best for early forcing are the Dutch White-water, Royal Muscadine, Joslin's St. Albans, and Black Hambro. Give them the same general treatment as that recommended for peaches during the month.

Prune other vines as soon as the fruit is cut, if the leaves are thoroughly matured, the wood almost as hard as bone, and they are required to start afresh in January. If these conditions are not complied with, defer pruning for another month. Carefully look over grapes twice a week, removing every dead berry and leaf that may have fallen on a bunch.

If late grapes, such as Muscats and West's St. Peter's, are not ripe, they must be ripened off with a brisk fire as speedily as possible. If not ripened forthwith, they will not only be deficient in flavour, but will not keep. When bunches of grapes have to be cut at once, either to make room or to prune the vines, nine inches or a foot of the branch should be cut with them, and the bunches be suspended in a cool dry room: they will often keep better in such positions than on the vine. In all cases where orange-trees or other plants are compelled to be placed in houses containing ripe grapes, the grapes had better be cut and thus stored away. Grapes may be so kept for three months; Muscats keep best, Hambro and West's St. Peter's next, and Frontignacs worst of all. Grapes cut for this purpose must never be *laid down.* Cut them carefully, leaving all the leaves on the branch; hand a couple of bunches, one at a time, to an assistant, and proceed to hang them up. The slightest bruise by laying them on their side, or allowing two bunches to be carried in one hand, would prevent their keeping. The riper they are, the more care is necessary. If slightly shrivelled, they keep all the better. Shrivelled Muscats would hang in this way for six months without injury. This mode of clearing a house at once is often of the greatest consequence to the cultivator, and may be adopted with the utmost confidence.

Pineries.—It is a good plan to cover the pots of succession and other pines two inches thick with partially decayed tan or leaves for the winter. This obviates the necessity of watering through the winter months, and maintains the roots in that medium state of dryness so favourable to the health of the plants during that period. Pines planted out in beds might be mulched over in a similar way. The less water given in any stage during winter, consistent with health, the better: they are especially liable to injury from the accumulation of moisture in the axils of the leaves. Whenever it is necessary to water for the next four months, the water must be applied to the *soil only.* It is often necessary to use a bent tube, with a funnel at one end, to prevent it falling upon the leaves. If the atmosphere of the house, from the continuance of bright sunshine, or any other cause, becomes too dry, it will be better to secure the necessary humidity by evaporation from the surface of the floor and heating apparatus, rather than by syringing overhead. After this period maintain a temperature of from 60° to 70° to all pines, the maximum being applied to the fruiting plants. The bottom-heat may range from five to ten degrees in excess of the atmospheric temperature. Give a little air when sufficiently genial; guard against sudden changes, and maintain a growing atmosphere to fruit swelling off. Cut pines in winter a week before they are ripe, and place them in a hot dry place (near the kitchen fire will do), in a temperature of from 80° to 90°. This will prevent all risk of the fruit decaying, and vastly improve the flavour.

Melons.—A second or third crop may occasionally be well ripened during this month. If in pits, renew linings, &c., to maintain a brisk heat; if in houses, keep the fires moving to secure a bottom-heat of 80°, and a surface one of 70°. Beware of watering to excess, as less can be thrown off by the leaves now than earlier in the season; consequently, more must be absorbed by the fruit, which is apt to burst, and often becomes insipid in consequence. With care upon this point, melons may often be ripened as successfully in October as in August.

Figs.—These may possibly be ripening their third crop; if so, a brisk temperature of 65° or 70° must be kept up. If the second crop is gathered, and a third is not wanted, reduce the supply of water and the temperature to a minimum, to induce rest or hasten maturity.

Orchard-house.—This house, unless used to ripen fruit that has been retarded behind a north wall, must now stand open night and day, or the trees be removed outside, and the house be devoted for three months to storing bedding plants, &c. If the trees are planted in the borders, then the lights may be stored away for three months. In all cases secure a season of perfect repose for the trees.

Strawberries.—These ought to have completed their growth for the season: the sooner they go to rest the better. The floors of orchard-houses are the best possible wintering-places;—to be kept as cool as possible, without being frozen, is all the winter treatment they require. Properly placed, it is seldom indeed that they require any water until they are wanted to grow. Lacking the floor or stage of any cool house or cold pit, the next best mode of keeping them is to stack them one upon another sideways. The stack can be built on any dry bottom; the best possible position being the south side of a wall or fence. In such a position mark out a place a yard wide or so, and of any convenient length, according to the quantity of plants, and spread upon it a layer of ashes three inches thick; place a row of pots on their sides at the distance indicated from the fence, or nearer, in proportion to the number of plants or height of stack contemplated. Fill up all between the pots, and the space between the bottoms of the pots, with dry ashes or old tan, keeping the side next the wall a little the highest. Then place another layer of plants on the top of the first, about two inches further back than the other. Fill up as before, and repeat the filling-up and layers of pots until this space is occupied, or all the plants provided for. The whole will then present a sloping surface to the sun. A boarded roof, six inches wider than the bottom rows, should then project over the top, and slightly incline to the back: the front may be supported on stakes driven in at intervals of six feet. Always excepting the floor of a cool house, there is no better mode of protecting and treating plants than this. They are kept dry, the frost has little or no influence upon them; for if it is very severe a thatched hurdle may be laid against them, and both pots and plants are preserved in safety.

ŒNOTH'ERA (nat. ord. Onagra'ciæ).

A genus of most useful and beautiful plants, for beds, borders, edgings, or rockwork. All the species are free-flowering, and most of them perennials. The most remarkable of the perennial kinds are *Œ. grandiflora Lamarkiana*, *Œ. macrocarpa*, *Œ. taraxacifolia*, *Œ. campylocarpa grandiflora*, *Œ. macrantha grandiflora*, *Œ. biennis hirsutissina*, *Œ. biennis alba*, and *Œ. prostrata*: most of these, if sown early, flower the first year. Of the annual varieties, the best are *Œ. Drummondii nana*, *Œ. bistorta Veitchii*, and *Œ. rosea Mexicana*. They all succeed in any good rich soil, and grow well from seed, to be bought at 3*d*. to 6*d*. per packet.

OLD AMERICAN PLANTS.

It not unfrequently happens in gardens once famed for the luxuriance of their plants on bog or peat borders, that a period of decay arrives. Rhododendrons become sticky, moss accumulates about their roots, and their leaves flag and look sickly at the slightest drought. Kalmias, also, have continually dead branches to be removed, and azaleas do not make the new wood they ought. These are undoubted evidences that renovation is required, and should be forthwith attended to. A top-dressing of the soil, with a mixture of well-rotted manure from the cow-yard, and fresh peat or bog, may do some good; but if evidences of decay are very striking, it will be far better to take up all the plants and dig in a good change of soil. Bog-earth which has been kept for a season, and turned two or three times, is, of course, the best; but, in the absence of this, leaf-mould and cow-dung may be used. Those rhododendrons which have run too far from home, and bear leaves only at the extremities of long sticky branches, must be cut down. The season of the year best suited for pruning rhododendrons is immediately after the flowering season, that they may have all their growing period of the year before them to make fresh shoots. Rhododendrons of any size may be taken up and removed, and not unfrequently with great benefit, as far, at any rate, as flowering is concerned, if care be taken that the mould about the stem and roots be not disturbed. In cases, however, where bog-plants come up very easily, having no hold in the ground, and with a hard ball of earth about the roots, which appears disinclined to blend with the surrounding soil, it is frequently of great advantage to loosen this ball and open the roots a little before the plants are placed in their fresh bed.

OLD APPLE-TREES.

Open a deep and wide trench all round them, remove the soil, and fill in with fresh rich loam with a good top-dressing of well-rotted manure that can be washed into it with every shower. It will do no harm to cut through a few of the roots, especially at some distance from the stem. After this, in early spring, scrub the bark of the stem and larger branches with a strong brine.

OLD BOX EDGING.

Nothing gives a more neat and agreeable appearance to a garden than well-kept box edgings. The sort of box in use for this purpose is a dwarf variety of the common box-tree, or *Buxus sempervirens*, which, with a little attention, may be kept in order for several years; but, if neglected, as is too frequently the case, it very soon gets out of order. In old gardens, the box edgings often look coarse and bushy, and full of gaps; for this there is no remedy but to take all up, and replant. The plan is this:—Fork up the old box, and pull it into small pieces, with not more than one or two stems each, selecting the youngest and freshest pieces for immediate planting. These should be cut with a sharp spade or garden-shears, so as to be even at the top and also at the roots, leaving each piece about three or four inches in length. The old wood may be served the same way; but, before these are used to form box edgings, it will be better to plant them out in the reserve-garden for a season, in a rich light soil, to give them a start, without which they cannot be considered fit for edgings, as they will certainly not recover from their rusty and shabby appearance for a year or two. As box edging, under the best treatment and greatest care, can hardly be made to last and look well longer than eight or ten years, it is very desirable to have a reserve of young fresh plants always on hand. At the time of planting, the surface of the soil should be levelled and flattened with a spade, and a trench cut sloping towards the gravel walk, so that the roots of the young plants may rest in gravel, and not in the garden soil. This will prevent a rank growth, and make it an easy matter, by an annual clipping, to keep the edging within due bounds. This clipping should never be omitted, and the best time for it is towards the end of June; for the box, after this, will soon recover its freshness at this season.

OLD EVERGREENS AND HEDGES.

Few things afford stronger indications of the necessity of renovation and reform in a garden than the state of the evergreens and hedges. These are so easily and so insensibly suffered to grow wild, and are so seriously injured by want of care and the proper use of the knife, that neglect cannot go on very long without its ill consequences becoming manifest. Portugal laurels and many other evergreens may be cut in; but with the common laurel it is a saving of time to cut it down at once; so also with the arbutus and sweet bay. Thorn, privet, and holly hedges, which from years of neglect are found to be occupying too much space, must be cut in. The two former may often be cut down with advantage to within a few inches of the ground, and the latter cut close on all sides to the single stems. In a few years new and fresh wood will fill up all vacant spaces, provided the soil is enriched and kept free from weeds.

OLD GARDENS.

In a long course of years, from the sameness of cropping and over-working, most gardens show signs of decay. Where the evil arises from over-manuring, the remedy is to clear a good portion of the richest earth away. "Generally speaking," says a correspondent of the *Gardener's Chronicle*, "there are few places where an exchange of fresh earth may not be made; for this garden soil forms one of the most valuable dressings for pasture or meadow land which can be met with. It is not always possible to get turf, or even soil, from pasture land, which is the very best for garden purposes; but failing this, that from arable land, if moderately fresh and loamy, will form no bad substitute. When the rich top-soil has been removed, spread a good dressing of quicklime over the lower surface and fork it in: if the lime is an inch in thickness it will not be too much. Afterwards road-scrapings or old mortar may be added when the soil is heavy, and marl or a dressing of the scourings of ditches when it is light. When this is well mixed with the lower spit, bring in the fresh earth and thoroughly incorporate the whole together. Rather than do this imperfectly, it will be better that only a small portion should be done at once, commencing with those portions on which peas, cauliflowers, cabbages, onions, and carrots are to be grown, leaving the parts appropriated to asparagus, seakale, and rhubarb for after-consideration. Above all, the fruit-tree borders, if they cannot be entirely renovated, should only have one half of the old soil removed and replaced by fresh loam, having previously made a good rubble bottom one foot deep, over which two feet of the above compost should be placed for the trees. Many kinds of fruit-trees may safely be lifted, if done carefully, and the roots laid in any spare piece of ground while the borders are being renewed,—more particularly pears, plums, and apricots, which will grow on richer soils than the peach and cherry." Thorough draining is indispensable in all these improvements both in the garden and fruit borders. In the latter, intersecting surface-drains are recommended for aërating the soil as well as for removing moisture.

Where it is found impracticable to remove any portion of the over-rich earth, the next best thing is to employ those materials which are found by practice to counteract soils containing superabundance of organic manures. Lime is the best and most readily procurable. A mixture of 64 bushels and 2 cwt. of salt is a valuable compost for old gardens, and is sufficient for one acre. Superphosphate of lime mixed with a small quantity of nitrate of soda is the next best; but it is more expensive. Both these applications should be forked in directly they are spread over the ground. A dressing of hot lime given every third year, adding phosphate of guano occasionally, would be a great improvement on stable-dung, no opportunity being lost of applying road-scrapings and marl, or calcareous soil, where much manuring is necessary. Liquid manure is a better material than stable-manure for these gardens, as it is more easily taken up by plants; and with chalk or lime occasionally added, it will tend to form a better and more productive soil, and one that will keep in good heart for years, without the danger of getting over rich.

OLD GARDEN-WALLS.

Troublesome things to a gardener are old garden-walls, where years of nailing have loosened the mortar-joints, and left even the bricks full of holes; but they are even more troublesome as harbours of refuge for insects and all sorts of garden pests. When garden-walls get into this state, the first convenient opportunity should be taken for thorough cleansing and repair. In autumn, after the fruit is gathered, or in early spring, the weather being dry but not frosty, let every tree be unnailed, the branches tied carefully together with hay-bands to prevent injury from the wind, and the stem of each tree drawn gently away from the wall as far as can conveniently be managed without injury to the roots, and kept there by means of a rope placed round it about two-thirds of its height, which rope can be made fast by a stake driven round the border, at a little distance from the stem. The wall, being cleared, should be scraped to remove all moss and every kind of parasite that may be growing upon it. After this, if the weather be quite dry at the time, it will be found a very good plan to give the wall a thorough dressing with very thin size, put on boiling hot with a large plastering-brush: this will effectually destroy all larvæ and eggs of insects that may remain after scraping. The wall can now be pointed in the usual way, using either cement or mortar made of newly-slaked lime and river-sand, great care being taken that all the old loose mortar in the joints is removed; otherwise the new jointing will not bear the nailing to which it is to be subjected.

OLD SHRUBBERIES.

In old gardens, it is no unfamiliar thing to find the lawn and borders skirted by long, unbroken belts of shrubs, intermingled in pell-mell fashion, the lower part of most of the deciduous shrubs lean and naked, long since denuded of their smaller twigs. Confusion rather than order seems to have been encouraged. Stems bare and naked at the roots show only straggling wiry branches towards the summit. When a shrubbery has acquired all or any of these characteristics, renovation, in whole or part, has become indispensable.

Shrubberies skirting winding paths,

either as a screen to unsightly objects or as shade and shelter from sun and wind, are perhaps the most agreeable portions of a garden; but in order to be so the shrubs must be cultivated with much care. Evergreens should be selected for their close habit of growth, and this habit increased by high dressing, judicious pruning, and pegging down. This compact habit, however, can only be maintained in beauty for a number of years by planting the shrubs so far apart that they may not touch each other; the ground between being kept clear by frequent raking and hoeing. There are some exceptions to this rule of planting. Rhododendrons do well planted in masses, and where the shoots are pegged down, they soon present a broad mass of green on the margin of the clump or shrubbery, when the turf can be carried up to their lowest branches. Behind these dense shrubby evergreens, the taller thorns, Turkey oak, the sophoras, and other trees of moderate height, and of the fancy arboretum varieties, might be planted for shade and breadth of effect.

Shrubberies on the verge of the lawn would naturally be planted with the best small flowering shrubs on the margin, either in masses or singly: if in masses, the shrubs should be pegged down, so as to present a continuous mass of vegetation along the whole margin, relieved as before with a background of ornamental trees; leafy masses of rhododendrons, touching the margin of the turf, form an admirable connecting link between the grassy sward and the shrubs and dwarf trees behind them. Where the shrubbery is planted for individual effect, those of an enduring growth and elegant habit should be chiefly used. Where there is space for such display, the lawn adjoining the shrubberies may be advantageously dotted with single evergreens and some of the more elegant-flowering deciduous shrubs. An occasional hemlock-spruce, with its weeping plumes; a holly whose lower boughs, still fresh, sweep the turf on which it is planted, or the graceful Cedrus Deodar, or Araucaria, in order to break the outline. Hardy flowering plants may also be introduced with excellent effect until the lower branches of the shrubs have made sufficient growth to admit of the surface being turfed up to meet them.

In planting or renovating lawn and shrubberies, due attention should be paid to their different seasonal effects. There are a few shrubs which herald in the spring; such as *Chimonanthus fragrans* and *Cornus mascula*. Mezereon, *Ribes sanguineum*, *Corchorus japonicus*. In conjunction with these, the strongly-characterized *Cryptomeria japonica*, *Abies canadensis*, and some trees of the Sumach family, deciduous cypresses, purple beech, and weeping laburnums, might be planted with effect. There are so many noble trees which present rich gradations of tint in autumn, that it is almost needless to name them. The old Virginian creeper is more beautiful in its autumn costume than in its vernal hues. The scarlet and other American oaks, the wild cherry, *Kölreuteria paniculata*, and many others, have a splendid effect either by themselves or in the skirts of the shrubbery; and, judiciously planted, well-selected and arranged, possess great interest. It is the tendency of many of the herbaceous plants to become crowded, and to exhaust themselves. Phloxes, asters, monardas, delphiniums, and other free-growing plants, soon choke their delicate companions, leaving little room for the more graceful. The plants of coarser habit expel the more delicate flowers, and with it all idea of order and proportion, on which so much of the beauty of the garden depends.

Supposing this state of things has gone on until entire renovation has become necessary; that the border is exhausted by continually growing the same things for years, and a radical remedy is required, there is only one which is effectual. Remove the plants to a place of safety, and after that exchange the soil to the depth of two feet before planting again.

OLD WALL-TREES.

How frequently do we find the inheritor of an old garden praising loudly bygone times in reference to some noble pear-tree against a wall, or covering perhaps one whole side of his house, calling to mind the bushels of fruit borne by it when he was a boy, and lamenting its present diminished produce. What is to be done with it? is the inquiry. The tree is, to all appearance, full of vigour, and it would be a shame to cut it down; besides, it must take years for another to fill up the space it occupies. Perhaps, also, there is some little fruit on it each year, though nothing to what a tree of the size ought to produce, for the centre never has a single pear or blossom-bud upon it. Look to nature! is the only answer to be made to one so inquiring; and you will find that all the fruit and all the blossom of the fine old pear-tree is upon the young wood, at the extremities of its branches. The case is clear, then: young wood must be encouraged, and old wood got rid of. Let any one try the following plan, and he will not be disappointed. Cut out, at pruning-time, all the lateral branches within one eye of the stem; but, in order to balance the tree, and give employment to the roots, let this be done by degrees; let every alternate lateral, on either side, be cut out each year; and in a year or two, when fresh wood is filling up the bare spaces, the whole tree will be covered with bearing wood. Old and exhausted Chaumontel pears will well repay any one who will bestow this treatment upon them. It may also, with benefit, be applied to all espaliers, whether apples or pears, which are found to fall off in bearing, especially when they are found to bear, as is so often the complaint with old trees, only at the extremities of their shoots. Where the vigour of the old tree is expended in producing wood and leaves, with an inadequate supply of fruit, it probably arises from over-vigorous root-action. The remedy of root-pruning may be applied with advantage.

ONIONS.

Selection and Preparation of the Land.—A rather strong, deep, and rich loamy soil is most suitable for this crop: where very large bulbs are desired, soil of this character is indispensable. Onions grown in a strong soil are much less liable to be attacked by the fly or maggot than in light, dry, sandy soils. The ground should be heavily dressed with rich well-rotted manure, trenched deeply, and ridged up early in autumn. If the soil is light and sandy, cow manure will be most suitable.

Time and Method of Sowing.—The main crop should be sown as early as the ground may be in working condition, and whether this occurs in February or early in March, a favourable opportunity for putting in the seed should not be suffered to pass. After levelling down the ridges, if the soil is light, tread the ground regularly and closely over, then rake and well pulverize the surface, making it as fine as possible. Set out the ground in four-feet beds, with alleys a foot wide between; draw drills half an inch to one inch deep, six inches from each alley, and nine inches apart. Sow the seeds thinly and regularly, and cover with the soil displaced in making the drills, or, where this is too lumpy, with other fine soil. A sowing should also be made about the middle of August, to furnish a supply of young onions during winter, and bulbs for use in summer before the main crop is ready. Where small bulbs, such as are used for pickling, are required, sow the Silver-skinned thickly early in May, upon the poorest soil, and in the driest situation at command, and thin out very sparingly.

After-management. — The ground

must be kept clear of weeds by frequent hoeings, and the plants thinned early, to from six to nine inches apart. In dry, warm situations, strong manure-water may be given freely during the summer; but where there is any danger of the crop running to "thick necks," or not forming bulbs, watering should not be practised, except when the weather is very warm and dry, and then not after July. Towards the end of September the bulbs should be well formed, and the tops show indications of ripening; where this is not the case, go over the crops, bending or breaking them down with the back of a wooden rake, and repeat this as often as may be necessary to check the growth of the tops effectually. As soon as the bulbs seem to be properly matured, which will be known by the decay of the leaves, &c., take them up, spread them in an airy shed, or sunny situation in the open air, until thoroughly dried, and then store in a dry, cool place till wanted for use. The Lancashire method of wintering onions is, perhaps, the best. There they tie up the bulbs in what are called ropes, and hang them on an outside wall, not facing the sun, and protect them from wet by placing a board against the wall overhead. They keep sound longer by this than by any other method. The best varieties are :—

White Spanish (true Reading),—the mildest in flavour, and most useful for main crop.
Deptford, or Brown Spanish,—similar to the above, but brown; a useful and good keeping variety.
Brown Globe,—a hardy useful kind.
White Globe,—a mild-flavoured good keeping variety.
Giant Madeira,—grows to a great size, and particularly mild-flavoured.
Blood-red,—a very useful hardy kind.
James's Long-keeping,—keeps longer than any other variety.
Silver-skinned,—the best for pickling.
Tripoli Large flat Italian,—the best variety for autumn sowing.
Tripoli Large Globe,—very fine for autumn sowing.
White Lisbon,—the variety sown in autumn by market gardeners for spring onions.

Seed from 4*d.* to 1*s.* per ounce.

OPUN'TIA (nat. ord. Cacta'ceæ).

This is the Prickly-pear of South America. They are ornamental and interesting greenhouse shrubs, with edible fruit, and succeed best in sandy peat.

ORCHARDS.

The grafting of most of our fruit-trees upon stocks being calculated to produce short, stunted growth, has considerably modified the practice of hardy-fruit culture; and unless the demand for fruit is very great, we would not generally recommend the formation of orchards. Should an orchard be deemed necessary, the spot selected should be entirely sheltered from the north and north-east, and it should have a gentle inclination, and full exposure to the south. The best soil is a good loam, four feet in depth, resting upon chalk, thoroughly drained by tiles inserted six inches beneath the chalk-level, the tiles being covered over to that depth with broken stones. The permanent trees, which, if it is intended to lay the orchard down in grass, must be standards and half-standards, with from four to six feet of clear stem, should be planted in rows, from 30 to 40 feet apart, and in what is termed the *quincunx* style, thus :—

*   *   *   *   *
   *   *   *   *

The north or coldest side of the orchard should be planted with walnuts, cherries, medlars, chestnuts, &c., to provide shelter for the others. These might be succeeded by the hardiest plums and apples, to be followed by the tender pears on the south or warmest side. If a gradation of height were also followed, the shelter provided would be more efficient, and the general effect more pleasing. Filberts, mulberries, and service-trees may also be introduced. But these temporary trees should be inserted as nurses between the permanent trees. Firm-growing varieties that come early into bearing should be chosen for the purpose, and they will not only encourage the growth of the permanent trees, but pay their own cost a dozen times over before they require removal. They must, however, be carefully watched, lest they weaken the energy or destroy the symmetry of the permanent trees. The rows should run east and west.

Though, from the introduction of dwarf trees, upon which, in a good kitchen-garden, as much fruit may be grown as will be required for the consumption of a family, an orchard is not now so necessary as it was some years ago, still we are not inclined to see this useful appendage of the country-house wholly neglected. A piece of pasture where the soil is good may be very profitably employed as an orchard. It will yield both a crop of fruit and a crop of grass, and if the former be not required for consumption, there is at all times a ready sale for it. Apples, pears, and cherries are the fruits properly cultivated in orchards; but plums, walnuts, and filberts are not unfrequently considered as orchard fruit, and in cases where there is only one orchard, all these fruits may, with advantage, be included in it.

Upon the nature of the site and soil best suited for an orchard, Abercrombie observes, "Land sloping to the east or south is better than a level; a sheltered hollow, not liable to floods, is better than an upland with the same aspect, and yet a gentle rising, backed by sufficient shelter, or the base of a hill, is eligible. A good loam, in which the constituents of a good soil predominate over those of a hot one, suits most fruit-trees; the subsoil should be dry, and the depth of mould thirty inches or three feet. Before planting, drain, if necessary; trench to the depth of two feet, manure according to the defects of the soil, and give a winter and summer fallow; or cultivate the site for a year or two as a kitchen-garden, so that it may be deeply dug and receive a good annual dressing."

In forming an orchard, Dr. Lindley recommends, and we quite agree with him, the early transplanting of the different trees. "They cannot," he says, "be removed from the nursery too soon after the wood has become ripe and the leaves have fallen off, for between this time and the winter many of them will make fresh roots, and be prepared to push forth their young shoots with more vigour in the spring than those whose transplanting has been deferred to a late period of the season." All young trees should be carefully staked and protected from the wind, and, if a dry spring should succeed the autumn of their planting, they will require to be watered, or, what is better, to have manure laid round their roots and be watered through it. Pruning and training are necessary; but, as a general rule, the knife should be avoided, if it is possible to bring the tree into a good shape without it. Pear-trees will thrive in a lighter soil than apples, and they are generally more hardy, and bear the wind better. In a good soil, the distance at which trees should stand from each other is from twenty-five to thirty feet; if all free-growing varieties are planted, it may perhaps be desirable to give from thirty to forty feet between them, and in all cases the quincunx mode, as we have already stated, is the best.

In selecting apples and pears for planting, and, indeed, all fruits that admit of sorts, it is of the greatest importance to take into consideration not only soil but climate. Very little good is gained by selecting the best varieties if they, or any of them, are not suited to the locality. Disappointment too often follows want of judgment in this respect. Whoever intends to plant an orchard, especially of apples and pears, should ascertain, in the first instance, what sorts flourish best in his part of the country. He should then select the best of these, and introduce such other sorts as, from their resemblance to them, may seem likely to answer. The following lists are taken from the fourth volume of the "Floral

Orchards.

World." The sorts are undoubtedly all good, and the descriptions accurate; but it would be quite wrong to imagine that they are all adapted to every locality.

Twenty-four Orchard Apples.—*K.* kitchen purposes; *D.* dessert.

Alfreston, K.—Large, round, skin light orange next the sun, greenish-yellow in the shade; flesh yellowish, crisp, sharply acid. November to March. A fruitful variety and showy grower.

Bedfordshire Foundling, K.—Very large, pale green when ripe; flesh yellowish, acid. November to April. A handsome kitchen apple, but rather fitful in productiveness.

Bess Pool, K., D.—Large, conical, handsome, yellow suffused with red next the sun; flesh white, sugary, vinous. Good from November to May. Rarely fails to give a good crop, and fit for any purpose.

Blenheim Orange, K., D.—Very large, ovate, yellowish, red next the sun; flesh yellow, sugary. November to June.

Court of Wick, D.—Medium size, very handsome, greenish-yellow, orange, and russety; juicy, high-flavoured.

Dumelow Seedling, K.—Large, round, yellow and light red; flesh yellow, first-rate. November to March. Also known as Wellington and Normanton Wonder.

Devonshire Quarrenden, D.—This is the famous "sack apple" of the western counties. Medium size, deep crimson; flesh greenish-white, juicy, subacid. August.

Dutch Codlin, K.—Very large, conical, and ribbed, greenish-yellow, with light tinge of orange; flesh white and firm. A first-rate kitchen apple, always bears, and will keep till Christmas.

Fearn's Pippin, D., K.—Full medium size, round, and handsome, greenish-yellow, russety, and bright red; flesh greenish-white, sweet, and rich-flavoured. November to March.

Forge, K.—Medium, golden-yellow mottled with crimson, and dark red next the sun; flesh tender, juicy, and perfumed. Always bears well. September to February.

French Crab, K., D.—Large, dark green, brownish next the sun; flesh green, firm, subacid. Bears immensely, and will keep any reasonable length of time.

Gooseberry Pippin, K.—Large, roundish, bright green; flesh greenish, tender, gooseberry flavour, which it retains till May or June, and it may be kept to the following August.

Hawthornden, K.—Large, ovate, yellowish-green, reddish blush next the sun; flesh white, juicy, almost good enough for dessert. This never fails to give a large crop: it is not a strong grower. The new Hawthornden is more robust, and produces a finer fruit, but is scarcely so prolific as the old. If but one apple-tree could be planted in the garden, we would have the Old Hawthornden in preference to any other. September to February.

Hanwell Souring, K.—Medium size, greenish-yellow, red blush; flesh firm, crisp, acid. No orchard should be without it. November to April.

Kerry Pippin, D.—Small, pale yellow streaked with red; flesh yellow, firm, juicy, and sweet. First-rate in every respect. September to November.

Loudon Pippin, K.—Large, roundish angular, with five protuberances round the crown, deep yellow; flesh white, subacid. Very fruitful. October to February.

Melon, D.—Large, lemon-yellow and light crimson; flesh white, tender, juicy, vinous, perfumed. One of the best American apples, generally fruitful. December to February.

Nonpareil, Old, D.—Small, greenish-yellow, one of the hardiest; pale russet and brownish-red; flesh tender, juicy, rich. January to May.

Norfolk Bearer, K.—Large, green, yellowish, and crimson; flesh tender, brisk flavour. A prodigious bearer. December to February.

Northern Greening, K.—Medium, dull green, brownish-red; flesh greenish, subacid. First-rate. November to May.

Sturmer Pippin, D.—Medium, yellowish-green and brownish-red; flesh yellow, firm, sugary, and rich. January to June.

Skye-House Russet, D.—Small, roundish, greenish, aromatic, and highly-flavoured. One of the best dessert apples. November to March.

Winter Pearmain, K., D.—Large, conical, handsome greenish-yellow and deep red; flesh juicy, sweet, and brisk-flavoured. October to April.

Yorkshire Greening, K.—Large, roundish, irregular, dark green striped with dull red; pleasantly acid. October to February.

For very exposed situations on the east coast and north of the island the following varieties are recommended:—

Dessert.—Devonshire Quarrenden, Early Julien, Kerry Pippin, Nonesuch, Summer Strawberry, Franklin's Golden Pippin.

Kitchen.—Carlisle Codlin, Hawthornden, Keswick Codlin, Loudon Pippin, Manx Codlin, French Crab, Tower of Glammis, Yorkshire Greening, Winter Colman.

From the same excellent authority, the "Floral World," we extract the following list and description of pears suitable for orchard cultivation.

Alexandre Bivort.—Medium size, melting, rich, and exquisite; prolific bush. December and January.

Bergamotte d'Esperen.—Medium, late, melting. Forms a handsome prolific pyramid or bush; but in wet or cold climates it requires a wall. March to May.

Beurré, Brown.—Large and excellent. End of October.

Beurré d'Aboise.—A hardy variety of Brown Beurré.

Beurré d'Aremberg.—Medium, delicious, melting; forms a handsome prolific pyramid. Orpheline d'Engheim is a variety of this pear, equally good, less vigorous habit, a most prodigious bearer as a dwarf bush. December and January.

Beurré d'Amanlis.—Very large, melting; one of the best autumn pears, not particular as to soil. End of September.

Beurré Rance.—Large, late, melting, insipid from a wall; but on the quince, in the open grounds, its flavour is quite exquisite. Requires double working, and forms a better bush than a pyramid. March to May.

Beurré Easter.—Large, melting, perfumed, insipid from a wall; best on the quince, and forms a beautiful bush. January to May.

Beurré Goubaut.—Medium, melting, excellent; wonderfully prolific when worked on the quince; better as a bush than a pyramid. Middle of September.

Bon Chrétien (Williams's).—Large, perfumed, melting; should be gathered before it is ripe. September.

Broom Park (Knight's).—Medium size, melting pear; partakes of the flavour of the melon and pineapple; on the quince must be double-worked; a prolific bush. January.

Chaumontel.—Large, well-known, melting. December. This is the pear which grows so fine in Jersey and Guernsey.

Comte de Lamey.—Medium; one of our most delicious autumn pears. October.

Dr. Trousseau (Van Mons').—A new, excellent, and most delicious hardy melting pear, which succeeds well on the quince, and forms a prolific bush. December.

Duchesse d'Angoulême.—Very large and handsome, insipid from a wall; forms a fine pyramid. November.

Forelle, or Trout Pear.—Medium; a very handsome speckled pear, melting and good. Forms a prolific bush, or a pyramid of moderate growth. December.

Josephine de Malines.—Medium size, delicious melting pear, aromatic. On the hawthorn it forms a spreading, fruitful tree; succeeds well on the quince, but does not form a handsome pyramid; as a bush or espalier it is very prolific. February to May.

Louise Bonne of Jersey.—Large. Mr. Rivers says: "When cultivated on the quince stock, this is the most beautiful, as well as the most delicions, melting pear of the season. Every one possessing a garden of six square feet should plant a tree on the quince stock of this variety; it forms a most ornamental pyramid, and a compact fruitful bush." It is worthy of the orchard-house. October.

Marie Louise, or Marie Louise Nouvelle.—Large, melting, excellent; on the pear it forms a prolific pyramid, on the quince, double-worked, a prolific bush. October, November.

Monarch (Knight's).—Medium, excellent; forms a handsome pyramid on the pear. Deserves a wall, and may always be relied on. January till February.

Peach, or Poire Pêche.—Medium, early, melting, slight aroma, very juicy; a prolific bush. September.

Seckle.—Small, highly-flavoured, melting; bears profusely as a pyramid on the pear. October.

Urbaniste, or Louise d'Orléans.—Medium size, a delicious melting pear; succeeds well on the quince, and forms a handsome pyramid. November.

Winter Nelis.—Small, roundish, buttery and melting, rich and aromatic; an abundant bearer, and a beautiful bush. November to February.

Yat.—Medium or large, a hardy Dutch pear, melting and juicy, highly-perfumed; forms a prolific bush. September.

The following pears are also suited to orchards and well worth growing:—Aston Town, Autumn Bergamot, Beurré de Capiaumont, Bishop's Thumb, Grosse Calebasse, Hacon's Incomparable, Napoleon, Swan's Egg, Lusette de Bavay.

There are several sorts of baking and stewing pears, but the best are, Catillac, Vicar of Winkfield, Summer Compote, and Uvedale's St. Germain for a wall.

The following pears are best adapted for a cold climate:—Alexandre Lambré, Gansel's late Bergamot, Beurré d'Amanlis, Williams's Bon Chrétien, Calebasse d'Eté, Colmar d'Eté, Citron des Carmes, Hessle, Jargonelle, Louise Bonne of Jersey, and Thompson's Pear.

As we have spoken of cherries and plums as orchard fruit, it may be well to give a small list of each for the guidance of those who are intending to plant an orchard. The earliest cherries are the Black Tartarian, the Early Purple Guigne, and the Early May. These are succeeded by the May Duke, the Bigarreau, the Elton, and Black Eagle; the Late Duke is the latest of sweet cherries. For cooking purposes, there is the Kentish; and for brandy, the Morello; for drying, the Belle de Choisy, the Flemish, and the Kentish. Waterloo is a good cherry, ripening in July, so are Werder's Black Heart, Adams's Crown, and Archduke.

Of plums the varieties are infinite. Among the best may be classed, Cloth of Gold, Coe's Golden Drop, Denniston's Superb, Denyer's Victoria, Rivers's Early Favourite, Old Greengage, Goliath, Guthrie's Late Red and Guthrie's Late Green, Jefferson's Yellow, Kirke's Dark Purple, Magnum Bonum, Mitchelson's Large Black, Early Black Orleans, Purple Orleans, Oullen's Goldengage, Reine Claude de Bavy, Rivers's Early Prolific, Sharp's Emperor, Violette Hâtive, Walshington, Winesour, and Woolston's Blackgage.

Of filberts we have already spoken under that head.

ORCHARD-HOUSES.

Mr. Rivers, who is our best authority upon orchard-houses, describes as a convenient form of house, a lean-to structure, 30 feet long and 12 feet 6 inches wide, made in the following simple manner: Six posts of yellow deal, 5 inches by 3 inches, or oak posts, 4 inches by 3 inches, and 9 feet 6 inches in length, are firmly fixed, and driven 2 feet into the ground, the lower ends being previously charred and coated with coal-tar. This is the back line of posts. Six other posts, exactly similar, but only 4 feet 6 inches long, are fixed 18 inches in the ground, forming the front posts of the house,—the one rising 3 feet and the other 7 feet 6 inches above the ground-level. Two posts at one end occupy the centre, and form the door-posts. On the six posts, both in back and front, a wall-plate is nailed to receive the rafters, one of which springs from each of the six front posts, resting on the corresponding back post.

The rafters are 14 feet long;—a 9-inch deal, 3 inches thick, will make four of them. On the upper side of each rafter is nailed a slip of ½-inch deal, 1¼ inch wide, which will leave half an inch on each side as rebate to receive the glass. The rafters so prepared are fixed in their place to the wall-plates by having a piece cut out at each end to correspond with the angle of the back and front plates. They are then firmly nailed, at back and front, by a strong spike-nail, leaving a space between each rafter of 5 feet, which is called a bay: this is filled up by smaller rafters or sash-bars, of a size proportioned to their length and the use they are to be put to,—vines trained to them requiring stronger bars. A piece of ¾-inch deal board, 6 inches wide, nailed along the top of each rafter, so as to be even with their upper edges, forms the ridge-board, leaving a groove to receive the upper end of the glass. A similar piece of inch deal, 6 inches wide, let in by sawing a corresponding piece out of each rafter, will receive the glass and carry off the water. The placing the glass is a very simple process: beginning at the top, a plate of glass, 20 inches wide, is laid in the groove, and fixed in its place by a brad driven into the rafter, a bed of putty being first laid; and so on till the whole is covered in,—open joints in the glass being rather advantageous than otherwise, if not too wide. No putty is used in the laps. The ends of the houses are fitted up to correspond with the roof, only that above the doorway a large sash is fitted in for ventilation. These sashes at each end, and the front or side sashes, are said by Mr. Rivers to be quite sufficient; indeed, he pronounces the ventilation perfect. Well-seasoned ¾-inch deal, planed and jointed, nailed outside the posts, forms the lower part of the house.

In the back wall, sliding shutters, 3 feet by 1 foot, will afford ventilation to the roof; and about 3 feet from the surface of the ground, two similar sliding shutters will ventilate the lower part of the house behind, and on a level with them. Ventilation is secured by sashes 2 feet 6 inches wide, and running the whole length of the house under the wall-plate: below these sashes the space is filled in with boarding, well painted. In summer it is impossible to give too much air. The house is now complete, except the door, which must open inwards for obvious reasons, and may be half glass, or otherwise, at the proprietor's discretion.

Within the house, a trench, 18 inches deep, is formed, to which two steps from the outside will lead. This leaves a platform or border on each side of 4 feet 9 inches; the back border requires to be raised 18 inches, and Mr. Rivers suggests that it would be improved by a second terrace behind the first, of 14 inches, supported by a 4-inch brick wall, so that the back row of trees need not be shaded while they are brought nearer to the glass.

Now, everything depends upon these borders; their surface loose and open, formed of old lime-rubbish and road-sand, mixed with manure, may be laid 4 inches deep, the whole forked over, and well mixed with the soil 9 inches deep. The estimate for this house, as given by Mr. Rivers, is £28. 5*s*. A handy person with his tools could probably do the whole for much less; at least, the material and glass, calculated at the prices in Montgomery's list of sash-bars and rafters, are under £15. Here is Mr. Rivers's description of a span-roofed house, which comprises the advantage of border as well as pot-cultivation:—Height at sides, 5 feet; height of ridge, 9 feet; width, 14 feet. The roof rests on oak posts 5 inches by 3 inches. The rafters are 20 inches apart; it is glazed with 16-oz. glass, in 20-inch squares. Under the eaves-boards, the sides, back and front are filled in with glass 15 inches deep, joined without putty. Under this is a ventilating-board, on hinges, opening downwards; below this are ¾-inch boards, to the ground; the two ends are glazed to the same level as the side-lights; the doors with glass sash, opening inwards. Over the door, an angular space, 9 inches deep, is found sufficient for roof-ventilation; the rafters, 3-inch by 1½-inch stuff, are tied at the top with a light iron tie screwed to the rafters. No putty is placed in the laps of the glass, which serve every purpose of roof-ventilation found necessary in this house. The only ventilator is the shutter 1 foot deep on each side, and 2 feet 6 inches from the ground, and the angular opening over each door.

The borders in such a house need not be raised, nor the path sunk, except as a matter of choice; they should have a dressing of manure and sand, or manure and burnt soil, or any loose material well forked over, and mixed with a dressing to the depth of 6 inches, composed of the top spit of a pasture of tenacious loamy soil, which has been exposed to the air for the summer months, mixed with one-third of well-rotted manure, chopped up into lumps as big as an egg. In the border thus composed, two rows of trees may be placed; the front row 3 feet apart, the second being in the rear, zigzag-fashion, but halfway between, so that they are each 3 feet from stem to stem, and none shading the other. Such a house as this, without artificial heat, is intended for protection only, and not for forcing; but it would, Mr. Rivers thinks, grow oranges and camellias successfully, if the house could be heated in very severe weather so as to prevent it falling at any time below 26°. The most severe frost would not injure tea-scented roses so sheltered; but the house is essentially intended for the protection of fruit-trees, whether planted in the borders or in pots, and has the effect of bringing us, without artificial heat, to the temperature of Angers, in the south of France, where the royal muscadine grape usually ripens in the open air on the 25th of August.

The use Mr. Rivers proposes to make of the first structure is the culture of peaches, vines, and figs, in pots. Selecting a straight-stemmed maiden peach or nectarine, well furnished with lateral buds, and not more than four or five feet high, it is planted in an 11-inch pot, and each lateral shoot is cut in to two buds. As soon as the shoots have made three leaves, the third is pinched off, leaving two, not reckoning, however, one or two small leaves generally found at the base of each shoot. These pinched shoots soon put forth a fresh crop of buds, each of which, and all succeeding ones, must be pinched off to one leaf as soon as two or three leaves are formed.

"This incessant pinchiug off the shoots of a potted pyramid-tree, in the climate of an orchard-house, will, in one season, form a compact cypress-like tree, crowded with short fruit-spurs." In spring, these will require to be thinned, and every season the shoots will require to be pinched off as above described.

Dwarf pyramidal peach- and nectarine-trees may also be planted in the border, two feet apart, with excellent results. They require the same incessant pinching, and must be *lifted and replanted* annually in October; but the span-roofed house is better adapted to the culture of trees planted in the borders.

The chief details of culture are as follows:—Miniature peach-, nectarine-, and apricot-trees, grafted on the black damask plum stock, should be placed in a garden frame in January. As soon as their young shoots have made four leaves, their ends are pinched off, leaving their leaves, and all succeeding shoots, pinched off to one leaf. In January, the house must be closed day and night. If at any time the registering thermometer indicates a night temperature of 20°, some dry hay or litter should be placed among and over the pots or borders. If the trees are inclined to shrivel from drought, give a quart of water in the morning. If snow falls, clear the glass of it. In bright sunny weather, open the ventilators to check early buds from swelling. Paint every bud and shoot, before it swells, with Gishurst's compound, half a pound to the gallon of water, to destroy eggs of insects.

Continue the mode of culture recommended by Mr. Rivers from the autumn after grafting till the fourth or fifth year, when the graft is beginning to show fruit-buds: these, which it is the object of this training to promote, are distributed along the branches, in their whole length, in spur-bearing fruit, as the apple and pear. In the peach tribe, short spur-like shoots appear towards the end of August, bearing triple buds,—a plump silvery one on each side, and a thin one in the centre. This central bud is the terminal leaf-bud, the two others blossom-buds, which, in March, will have opened their silvery coat, showing the bright pink of the blossom. These indications appear in the third year after planting. Their development is promoted by carefully watching every branch, checking the more vigorous shoots by pinching off the terminal buds, or by breaking or half-breaking them, so as to check the flow of the sap. The work of pruning begins with the second year's growth. In the winter following, the terminal branches will present a series of small shoots more or less vigorous, and the pruning required will be according to their vigour; repressing the stronger as early as possible by pinching off the leading shoots, and encouraging the weaker shoots; thus balancing the growth of the tree, and suffering no more branches or leaves to be produced than can properly perform their function of elaborating and storing up matter for the production of fruit,—a function for which a full exposure of every part of the tree to light and air is quite essential. It is the pruner's work to remove all shoots which do not fulfil this condition, by rubbing them off, and arresting the over-luxuriant ones by timely pinching off the terminal bud. Others suited for his purpose he leaves at their full length, merely depressing their points, which will induce them to push from every bud fruitful twigs of moderate growth, or he prunes back a weak shoot to two or three buds, raising the point in a perpendicular direction, knowing that the sap may thus be concentrated so as to produce a more vigorous growth. If he wishes to increase the vigour of his trees, he will prune them early in autumn, so that the sap they may accumulate in the winter is not thrown away; he studies, in fact, the ways and means of the tree; nor does he forget that the roots should be under control as well as the branches. The treatment should be preventive as well as remedial; the latter, indeed, as Mr. Rivers tells us, "is out of place in a well-ordered garden,—the finger and thumb, and a moderate-sized penknife, should do all the pruning required."

ORCHARD-HOUSES, FURNISHING OF.

Full directions for the management of the orchard-house will be found in our calendar every month; we need not, therefore, repeat them. It will be well, however, to give a list and description of such trees as may be introduced into an orchard-house without fear of disappointment, for it is hardly necessary to observe that all sorts of trees do not bear the confinement of glass, nor ripen their fruit under such circumstances equally well. All the sorts we shall mention are of course suited to the table; for no one would take the trouble which an orchard-house involves to grow in it any sorts of fruits which are fitted only for cookery.

Apples.—Ribstone Pippin, Blenheim Orange, Cox's Orange Pippin, Sturmer Pippin, Golden Reinette, Coe's Golden Drop, Melon, the Nonpareil, Margil, Newtown Pippin, Northern Spy.

Apricots. — Early Sardinian, St. Ambrose, Shipley's Early, Kaisha, Grosse Pèche, Royal Orange.

Cherries. —Archduke, Belle de Choisy, B. Magnifique, Bigarreau, B. Napoleon, Black Eagle, Coe's Late Carnation, Early Amber, Governor Wood, Kentish, Kirtland's Mary, Knight's Early Black, May Duke, Ohio Beauty, Royal Duke, Young's Black Tartarian.

Figs.—Early Violet, White Marseilles, Brown Turkey, White Ischia (for forcing).

Grapes.—Early Malingre, Prolific Sweetwater, Grove End Sweetwater, Muscat St. Laurent, Royal Muscadine, White Romain, Purple Fontainebleau, Black Hamburg, Chaplat, Muscat de Sarbelle.

Grapes (for forcing in the orchard-house).—Chasselas Musqué, Black Frontignan, Purple Constantia, White Frontignan, Bowood Muscat.

Nectarines.— Downton, Elruge, Early Navington, Rivers's Orange, Violette Hâtive, Prince of Wales, Victoria, Pineapple.

The Orange Tribe.—Maltese Common Oval Orange, Maltese Blood Oval Orange, Citron, Lemon, Persian Lime, Silver Orange, St. Michael's, Tangerin, Egg Orange.

Peaches.—Acton Scott, Late Admirable, Barrington, Bellegarde, Chancellor, Claremont, Crawford's Early, Early Albert, E. Newington (Smith), E. Savoy, E. Victoria, E. York, French Mignonne, Galande, George the Fourth, Grimwood's Royal George, Grosse Mignonne, Malta, Millett's Mignonne, New Royal Charlotte, Noblesse, Red Magdalen, Royal George, Téton de Vénus, Violette Hâtive, Admirable Warburton.

Pears.—Doyenne d'Eté, Jargonelle, Duchesse d'Angoulême, Seckle, Louise Bonne of Jersey, Josephine de Malines, Passe Colmar, Williams's Bon Chrétien, Winter Nelis, Gansel's Bergamot, Cressane, Marie Louise, Beurré d'Amanlis, B. d'Aremberg, B. de Capiaumont, B. Clairgeau, B. Diel, B. Easter, B. Giffard, B. Goubault, B. Hardy.

Plums.— Angelina Burdett, Belgian Purple, Green-gage, Guthrie's Aunt Anne, Guthrie's Late Green, Huling's Superb, Ickworth Impératrice, Jefferson's Kirk's New Blue, Mitchelson's Orleans, New Orleans, Oullen's Golden-gage, Pond's Seedling, Prince Engelbert, Prince of Wales, Reine Claude de Bavay, Reine Claude Hâtive, Rivers's Early, Victoria, Washington, Woolston's Black-gage.

OR'CHIDS (nat. ord. Orchida'ceæ).

The plants of this extensive genus are generally divided into four classes: orchids from the tropics, which require a stove; orchids from the Cape of Good Hope, which are suited to a greenhouse; those from the south of Europe, which need only a slight protection during winter; and our own native varieties. We need hardly add that the more tender sorts are the most curious and beautiful. Full directions as to treatment will be found in the calendar of operations for each month.

Those who take an interest in the cultivation of orchids, and do not grudge expense, will do well to add to their collection some of the following latest varieties, which have been introduced by Mr. B. Williams, of Holloway.

Anæctochilus Turnerii.—This is one of the most beautiful of the genus, possessing the advantage of being a strong and free grower; the leaves are broad ovate, of a rich bronze colour, freely marked with golden reticulations.

Anæctochilus nobilis (Physurus). — A very pretty and distinct variety, with ovate-lanceolate leaves, of a rich bronzy-green colour, distinctly traced with silvery markings on upper surface. This also has a good robust habit.

Calanthe Turnerii.—This will prove a useful addition to our winter-flowering orchids; the petals or labellum are of the purest white, with centre of a clear flesh-colour; it continues flowering from the same spikes for several months.

Cypripedium concolor.—A very distinct and beautiful stove species from Moulmein, remarkable for its large yellow flowers, which are borne upon chocolate-red stems, and its beautiful variegated leaves, which are richly mottled in two shades of dark green.

Cypripedium Dayanum.—This is undoubtedly one of the most beautiful additions to the charming class of cypripediums. The foliage is beautifully variegated, and the flowers are very large, exceeding six inches in diameter. The upper petal white, with lines of lively green; the two lower are of a reddish-brown, intermixed with green and mauve; lip large, two and a half inches in length, of a reddish-brown colour; upper part mauve, spotted with white. It blooms during the winter and spring months, and continues in perfection from six to eight weeks.

Epidendrum erubescens.—A magnificent new species from the mountain regions of Mexico, forming large branching spikes of sometimes as many as fifty lovely rose-coloured or rosy-purple broad-petalled flowers, each one and a half to two inches across, having also the advantage of a very free-growing habit.

Odontoglossum Bluntii.—A magnificent species, allied to *O. Alexandræ* and *O. crispum*; the sepals and petals, acutely lance-shaped and wavy, white, tinted with blush, and conspicuously spotted with rose; the lip oblong and fringed, and marked with a yellow blotch.

Odontoglossum gloriosum.—A fine variety, with the habit of *O. nævium majus*, and producing large panicles of flowers, richly spotted; the sepals and petals oblong-ligulate acuminate, and the lip nearly of the same form, with a hastate base and denticulate margin.

Odontoglossum Hallii. — This is one of the finest species of this grand genus of epiphytes. The flowers are large, star-like; the sepals and petals almost wholly chocolate, with yellow margins and blotches; and the lip white, with chocolate-brown blotches, acuminate and finely fringed.

Odontoglossum radiatum.—A splendid stove epiphyte from New Granada. The sepals and petals of its large flowers are chocolate-brown, with the margin and some slight blotches yellow; the lip nearly white, panduriform, and finely fringed on the dilated anterior portion.

Phalænopsis Luddemanniana.—This beautiful and remarkable species is a most welcome addition to the universally admired genus to which it belongs; the leaves are light-green, same size and form as those of *P. rosea.* The flowers are white, with the sepals and petals barred transversely with amethyst-purple, and the front of the lip violet.

OSTEOSPER'MUM (nat. ord. Compos'itæ).

An ornamental greenhouse evergreen shrub, with pretty yellow flowers; thrives in any light rich soil.

Osteospermum niveum,—yellow, 5 ft., from Cape of Good Hope.

OX'ALIS (nat. ord. Oxalida'ceæ).

A genus of exceedingly pretty bulbous plants, all of which have beautiful green foliage, which forms a fine contrast to their richly-coloured blossoms. They are admirably adapted for pots, borders, and rock-work, succeeding in any light soil.

Messrs. Barr & Sugden offer the following varieties from 1*s.* 6*d.* to 3*s.* 6*d.* per dozen :—

Oxalis bipunctata,—lilac.
,, Bowieii,—crimson, large trusses.
,, cernua,—yellow
,, ,, fl. pl.,—double yellow.
,, floribunda rosea,—rose.
,, grandiflora alba,—white.
,, hirta rosea,—rose.
,, hirta rubra,—red.
,, rubella,—red.
,, speciosa,—rosy-purple, very showy.
,, tetraphylla,—purple.
,, versicolor,—scarlet and white.
,, fine mixed, per 100, 10*s.* 6*d.*

PACKING FRUIT.

Many of our readers have, no doubt, been struck with the fine appearance and rich flavour of the Newtown pippins and other apples and pears which now reach this country annually from Canada and North America. Much of their fine quality is owing to the manner in which the fruit is gathered and preserved. We believe we are correct in giving the following as the process of preservation which it undergoes:—As the fruit-gathering season approaches, tin canisters of a proper size are prepared and carefully soldered; the usual size being seven inches in height by five in diameter. "Select the finest fruit, — peaches, strawberries, pears, apples,—what you please," says a writer in the *American Horticulturist.* "It should be just ripe, but not beyond that stage, and perfectly free from bruises. Fill the canisters, place the tin lids in their places, and solder them down, leaving only a small hole the size of a pin in the centre of the lid for the escape of air. The next point is to drive all air out of the canister. In order to do this, take a broad flat-bottomed boiler pan, place the canisters in it, and fill the boiler with water to within about three-fourths of an inch of the tops of the canisters; place the boiler over a gentle fire until the water boils. This will drive all the air from each canister; but to make sure that it is all expelled, when the temperature of the water in the boiler is about 200° Fahr., let a drop of water fall on the hole: when the bubbles of air cease to rise through the water thus dropped, the air is all expelled. You may now pass a dry cloth over the top, and solder the holes by letting a drop of solder fall on each. This seals the canister hermetically, provided it has been properly made, and the fruit will remain perfectly unchanged for years. The immersion of the canisters in boiling water does not impart the slightest taste of having been cooked to the fruit; but the canisters should be left to cool gradually in a dry place."

This is probably too expensive a process, except for the more delicate fruits. We believe the main supply of apples and pears which reach us from America come in casks, in which layers of cork sawdust alternate with layers of fruit, which has previously undergone a drying process by exposure in a dry and shaded room.

In respect to peaches, apricots, and nectarines, we need not tell our readers that their handling must be of the most delicate nature. As the fruit approaches the ripe state, nets or mats stretched on short stakes should be suspended beneath, each having a lining of dry moss or lawn-grass, not to supersede hand-picking, but to guard against accidental falling. When a gathering is to take place, a shallow basket should be selected, covered with a layer of moss or leaves, and each fruit as it is removed from the tree should be deposited in it, separated from those already in the basket by a leaf placed under it, and covered with another, to protect it from contact with the next.

With such delicate fruit as the peach and its congeners, no mode of preservation for winter use will be effectual, unless it be the American process which we have given in detail; but even packing it for short journeys requires much care. Let us recommend for this purpose a box sufficiently deep to hold two tiers of fruit, and no more, and pack these with the following precautions:—The box being ready, and a quantity of well-beaten and dry moss, or dried lawn-grass in the absence of moss, being provided, wrap each fruit, with the bloom untouched, in a piece of tissue or other equally soft paper, and pack them pretty closely with moss until the first layer is completed, then make it perfectly level by filling up with moss, placing an inner lid over the tier; make a second layer in the same manner, and put on the lid in such a way that the fruit, without being exposed to pressure, will nevertheless remain steadily in its place.

PÆO'NIA (nat. ord. Ranuncula'ceæ).

For late spring or early summer flowering few plants are more useful than Pæonias. Every flower-garden should have some of them. They are mostly very hardy, and in colour vary from pure white, blush, salmon, and rose, to the most intense and brilliant scarlet. The Chinese tree varieties (*Pæonia Moutan*) are also hardy and early flowering. Bedded upon lawns they have a beautiful effect. In a shrub-like form they rise from three to five feet in height, and branch out in a good rich soil to ten or eighteen feet in circumference. There are many varieties, and the colouring is extremely rich. They are most of them profuse flowerers.

PARSLEY.

Full crops of parsley should be sown in the spring along the edges of one of the borders. In order to grow this useful herb in perfection, it is necessary that the roots and stem should be kept in a perfectly dry state : this is indispensable to the health and freshness of the plant. In preparing the beds, therefore, remove the soil to the depth of six or eight inches, and fill in the bottom with the same depth of stones, brick-rubbish, and similar loose material. Over this prepare the bed of light rich soil, which will thus be raised considerably above the level of the ground, the bed being raked smooth and level. Towards the end of May, sow some seed of the most curly variety, either in shallow drills, slightly covered with fine soil, or thin broadcast raked in. If the weather continue dry, water frequently : in five or six weeks the plants will have appeared ; when large enough, thin them out, so that they may be four or five inches apart. By the end of autumn they will be large and vigorous plants. At this time, drive a row of stakes or hoops into the ground, on each side of the bed, so as to form arches strong enough to support a covering of mats, which should be laid over them as soon as frosty or wet weather threatens to set in. During intense frosts, increase the protection, removing it on fine days, and removing it entirely in mild weather. The soil should be kept dry, and all decayed leaves carefully removed : in this manner this useful vegetable may be available all the winter.

PARSNIPS.

Preparation of the Soil.—Parsnips succeed best in a deep, free, rich soil, and as the application of fresh manure tends to the production of forked and badly-formed roots, ground in high condition (having been heavily manured for the previous crop) should be selected. If manure *must* be applied, let it be well decomposed, or use guano. The ground should be trenched 2 feet 6 inches, and ridged up as long as possible before sowing.

Time and Method of Sowing.—Sow in lines 15 to 18 inches apart, as early in spring as the ground can be found in fair working condition, scattering the seeds thinly, and covering them half an inch to one inch with the finest of the soil.

After-management.—When the plants are about two or three inches high, thin them out, leaving six or eight inches between them. Keep the ground free from weeds, and the surface open by frequent deep stirrings with the hoe. Towards the end of November take up the roots, and, after cutting off the tops, &c., either store them in damp sand, in a cellar, or pit, as is done with potatoes. The roots being hardy would be quite safe in the ground.

Sutton's "Student."—This variety has been ennobled from the wild parsnip of Great Britain, and is considered an important acquisition : the flavour is very superior and the roots are clean and handsome. We confidently recommend it.

Hollow Crown Improved,—the most useful for main crop.
Jersey,—a large valuable sort.
Chervil Parsnip.

PASSIFLO'RA—Passion-flower (nat. ord. Passiflora'ceæ).

A genus of magnificent ornamental twining shrubs, with flowers at once interesting, beautiful, and curious, which are produced in the greatest profusion and in succession during the greater part of the year under glass, and out of doors during summer and autumn. They are among the most important and effective of plants for training in conservatories or covering the fronts of cottages and villas in town or country. For in-door culture, P. Contessa Clara Gigliucci is one of the most important, and for out-door decoration *P. cærulea*.

PEACHES.

In the calendar of the different months will be found full instructions for the growing and management of peach-trees, whether out of door or in the orchard-house, and lists of the best sorts.

PEA-PROTECTORS.

These are made on an arched frame, covered with galvanized iron wire netting, to protect peas when sown from birds. They are a yard long, and may be bought of Messrs. Barnard and Bishop, Norwich, at 15*s.* per dozen.

PEARS.

These are best grown dwarf. The varieties of the Pear are very numerous, there being upwards of 500 varieties known. Of these 500 the following is a selected list of table pears :—

Beurré Giffart,—ripe in July; suitable for a standard.
Citron des Carmes,—ripe in July.
Epargne,—in July and August, suited for espalier on an east or west aspect. Does not make a good pyramid.
Beurré d'Amaules,—a standard; August and September.
Professeur du Breuil,—suited for espalier and east or west aspect.
Beurré d'Angleterre,—grafted on a stock as a standard; ripe in September.
Louise Bonne de Jersey,—an espalier on free stock; east aspect; ripe in October.
Beurré Gris,—an espalier on free stock; east and west aspect; ripe in October.
Beurré de Capiaumont, — espalier on free stock; east and west aspect; ripe in October and November.
Duchesse d'Angoulême, — as an espalier on east, west, or north aspect; ripe in October and November.
Bon Chrétien Napole,—espalier on free stock; east or west aspect; ripe in October and November.
Beurré Beaumont,—as a standard; ripe in August.
Jargonelle,—ripe in August.
Bon Chrétien, Williams's,—a standard, grafted on a free stock; ripe in August and September.
Seckle,—ripe in October.
Beurré Diel,—an espalier on east, west, or north aspect; ripe in November and December.
Beurré passe Colmar,—espalier on free stock, for east, west, or north aspect; ripe in November and December.
Althorpe Crassane,—ripe in November.
Hacon's Incomparable, — in December and January.
Glou Morceau,—in December and January.
Knight's Monarch,—in January.
Easter Beurré,—in March; keep till March.
Beurré de Rance,—espalier for east, west, or south aspect; ripe in February and March.
Ne plus Meuris,—in March and April.

PEAS.

Selection of Soil and Situation.—For heavy crops of this prime esculent a deep loamy soil must be secured; but ordinary garden soil, if properly prepared and well manured, will yield abundantly. For an early crop, plant in the warmest and most sheltered situation; but for the main crops choose an open airy situation; and instead of devoting a portion of the garden to peas alone, as is usually done, plant them in single lines amongst other crops: the plants will thus get more sun and air, and bear much longer and more abundantly.

Preparation of the Land.—Trench to the depth of two feet, and ridge up roughly, exposing as large a surface as possible to the action of the weather;

and this should be done as long before sowing as convenient. The summer and autumn crops will require abundance of well-rotted manure; but the early crop will come sooner into bearing if planted in poorer soil, which should be deep and well pulverized.

Time and Manner of Sowing.—Sow the first crop about the middle of November, the second early in January, putting in a small breadth of a second early variety at the same time; and to secure a constant succession, sow once a fortnight from this time till the end of June, or yet later. After the beginning of March sow the best kinds of Wrinkled Marrows; but for the last two sowings use a free-cropping early, or second early variety, and when the ground is sufficiently dry to work kindly, sow in drills two inches deep and four inches wide, covering the seed with friable soil. If sown in successive lines, let the intervening space exceed the reputed height to which the variety grows by six or twelve inches. As the seed for the earlier crops will be some time in the ground exposed to the depredations of mice, &c., it should be sown thickly. The strong-growing branching kinds, which are used for the main crops, succeed better if sown thinly, but it is prudent to guard against loss from various causes by sowing all rather thickly. If the plants are found to be too close when fairly started, they can easily be thinned out.

After-management.—When the plants are about two inches high, draw the soil neatly towards them, and apply stakes of about the height to which the variety grows. Spruce fir or other evergreen branches will afford a useful shelter to early crops. Keep the ground between the rows well stirred and free from weeds. In dry weather mulch with manure for eighteen inches on each side the rows, giving a liberal supply of water when necessary, to keep the plants vigorous, and to prevent mildew: the growing crops should never be allowed to feel the want of water.

For the selection of sorts best suited to the different periods of sowing, and prices, see Messrs. Barr & Sugden's "Guide to the Kitchen Garden."

PEAT-GROWING PLANTS FOR GREENHOUSE.

Many choice varieties have recently been added to the stock of peat-growing plants for the greenhouse. We name some few of these:—

Azaleas.

King of Spots,—orange-scarlet, fine form, beautifully spotted on the centre: a very effective variety.

Snow-white,—a beautiful flower of pure white ground, marked with rosy pink streaks, and of a velvet-like substance.

Lord Derby,—rich pure rose, spotted with crimson on the centre top lobe: a fine exhibition variety.

Queen of Roses,—a charming variety of warm rose-colour; growth free and compact.

Queen of Scarlets,—a very effective variety; flowers brilliant scarlet, and of model form.

Salmon Queen,—a fine variety, with rich salmon-tinted rose-flowers, of good shape, large, and an abundant bloomer.

Camellias.

Madame Ambroise Verschaffelt,—a very fine white variety, with a blush rosy tint, fine form, and handsome foliage.

Elvira Bianchini,—an effective flower of a cream-white tint, elegantly marked with rose-coloured bars and streaks.

General Cialdini,—bright shaded carmine; very attractive.

Zoraidi Vanzi,—blush-white, with very picturesque bars of rosy-red, petals large and rounded.

Etoile Polaire,—bright carmine-scarlet, each petal marked with a central white bar or stripe.

Bonomiana,—fine large white, with double stripes of red; very uncommon.

Epacris.

E. andromedæflora has flowers like the Andromeda.

E. densiflora, with blush and white flowers, is very effective.

E. miniata splendens,—vivid crimson tube, with pure white bulb.

E. nivalis, with snow-white flowers.

E. purpurescens,—purple; and E. variabilis.

Ericas.

E. Hibbertiana,—a fine orange-flowered species, of small growth, and very pretty.

E. echiiflora, E. vestita rosea, E. echiiflora pulchella (this latter is dwarf in growth, and shows its rich rosy-red flower-tubes from January to April), E. Albertii, E. rubens, E. Thomsoniana, and E. odorata.

PEGS FOR BEDDING-PLANTS.

Various expedients are resorted to by gardeners to peg down the different sorts of bedding-plants,—verbenas, petunias, &c. &c. Some use ladies' hair-pins, and some use small pegs made of hazel or other wood; but the neatest, the cheapest, and most efficient pegs which have come under the writer's notice, are cut from the brake, a wild fern which grows freely in every lane and on almost every common in England. Many a poor boy might earn an honest penny by cutting these in autumn, when the wood is tough, and selling them in bundles for next summer's use. Galvanized wire pegs are very durable, and may be bought at 3*s.* per thousand.

PELARGO'NIUMS.

June and July are the best months for increasing pelargoniums for ordinary purposes. Cuttings struck at this season from plants which have been forced, and the wood thoroughly ripened, produce fine plants for autumn flowering and early spring forcing, supplying the want of flowers in the conservatory in winter and spring. The pots being prepared in the usual manner, and well supplied with drainage and other loose material for one-third of their depth, fill up with a compost composed of equal parts turfy loam and silver-sand well mixed and sifted, so as to keep back the large lumps. Select cuttings from strong short-jointed shoots three or four inches long, removing the lower leaves so as to leave the base of the cuttings clear; place them round the edge of the pot about an inch or an inch and a half deep. When planted, water freely to settle the soil round them, and place them in a cold pit or frame. Sprinkle them occasionally overhead till rooted; afterwards give air gradually to harden them for potting off into 3-inch pots.

For autumn flowering, the most desirable are the free-blooming and strong-growing kinds, as Lyne's Forget-me-not. Beck's Meteor, Negress, and Sultana are better adapted for spring forcing; and, among scarlets, General Ayres, the Queen, Royal Dwarf, and Compactum will stand the high temperature well.

When well established in the small pots and about six inches high, stop them, that they may throw out lateral or side shoots. When they have made their shoots, repot them in 48's, in equal parts turfy loam, peat, and decomposed cow or stable dung, with a good proportion of road or river sand, the pots being thoroughly drained with potsherds or oyster-shells: thin out the leaves and small shoots occasionally, to throw the whole sap into the shoots which are to produce flowers. When plunged into the border to flower, these plants will be benefited by being lifted occasionally to prevent them from rooting through the bottom of the pots. Those for spring forcing will require a further shift in September; and the fancy varieties, being more delicate growers, will require more drainage; and a little charred cow-dung in rough pieces over the potsherds will be found beneficial.

Fancy Sorts for Specimens.—When autumn-flowering plants are required, take cuttings in early summer, when they will strike freely; fill the pot half full of broken potsherds, then add a compost of equal parts of good turfy loam, peat, and well-decomposed cow-dung and leaf-mould, with a good portion of silver-sand. By the end of July the plants will require to be re-potted: take care that this is repeated as often as roots fill the pots. As the season advances, a little heat will make them expand their blossoms more freely. For large fine-grown specimens select a strong plant, and pot in a compost consisting of two parts good turfy loam, one of leaf-mould, one of well-decomposed cow-dung, and a good portion of silver-sand. After a summer's free growth, assisted by frequent watering, about the beginning of July begin to diminish the quantity of water, so that the wood may be thoroughly hardened before cutting down. By the end of July the plants should be shaken clean out of the soil, the roots pruned at the points, and repotted in a similar compost. In November they should be potted again; and in February they will require another shift, when each shoot should be stopped at the fourth joint, to induce lateral shoots. When these laterals are of sufficient length, they must be stopped again. If intended to flower in May, stop in July; if in June, stop in January; and if in July, stop in February.

PERENNIALS.

Those plants are called perennials which do not require annual cultivation. They are not woody, and generally die down to the ground every year, and spring up again the year following. Some, however, do not die down, but retain their leaves, as pinks, carnations, saxifrages; and these, on this account, are called evergreen perennials.

PERPETUAL ROSES.

These have been so crossed that their real origin is very indistinctly known. A French author, quoted by M. Boitard, traces their wood and spines to the old Damascus roses, their leaves and foliage to the Bengal, their clustering flowers to the Bourbons, and their odour to Centofolio; proving, as M. Boitard observes, if all these characteristics be true, the correctness of his opinion on the question of species. Mr. Paul divides them into groups; founded—1. on the Four Seasons rose, "a branch of the Damask now little known, and chiefly valued as the type of the lovely Damask Perpetuals." 2. The Trianons, a group formed by M. Vibert, of Angers, "obtained," as he tells us, "from several varieties which acknowledge the Rose de Trianon as their type." The flowers of this group are produced in small clusters, flowering in the summer; the leaves gathering in tufts near the end of the shoots. A third group—3. the Damask Perpetuals, "chiefly descended from the old monthly and Four Seasons rose; the varieties being more remarkable for the delicious fragrance of their flowers than for their size or symmetry of form; but which," he adds, "are more properly described as Damask roses blooming in autumn." The fourth group—Hybrid Perpetuals. These lovely additions to the rose-garden have been raised in great part by M. Laffay, between the Bourbons, the Chinese, and the Damask. "Princess Helena was the first introduced in 1837; Queen Victoria followed; and in 1840," says Mr. Paul, "there were above twenty varieties enumerated in the rose catalogue, one-fourth of which, however, were Bourbons. The others might be called," adds Mr. Paul, "hybrid Chinese blooming in autumn." They are, indeed, fine roses, quite hardy, and very sweet. They thrive under the common treatment, and are suited alike for standards and dwarfs, for pot-culture and forcing.

The following lists give a few of the best varieties of Hybrid Perpetual Roses:—

Earl of Derby,—scarlet, flowers deep rose, tinted with purple; large and semi-double.

Baronne Prevost,—bright pale rose-colour; glossy; a very large, full, and compact flower; free grower, blooming freely from June till November.

Dr. Marx,—rich glowing carmine colour; large full-cupped flower, and very fragrant. A very beautiful rose.

Géant des Batailles,—dazzling crimson, the nearest approach to scarlet in this class; very free grower, and one of the most abundant bloomers, flowering from June till December.

La Reine,—brilliant glossy rose-colour, shaded with lilac, and sometimes with crimson; cupped and very large; has the appearance of a true perpetual cabbage, but much larger.

Madame Laffay,—bright crimson, inclining to

purple; large, cupped, and very double; very fragrant; free, vigorous grower, and an abundant bloomer from the end of May to the middle of December.
Standard of Marengo,—brilliant crimson.
William Jesse,—light crimson, tinged with purple; very large, double, and cupped; a large and fine flower; strong grower: forms a splendid mass.

PETU'NIA (nat. ord. Solana'ceæ).

Highly ornamental and profuse-flowering half-hardy perennials, easily cultivated both from seed and cuttings. The brilliancy and variety of the colours, combined with the duration of the blooming period and the capability of the flowers to bear the atmosphere of large towns, render petunias invaluable. Seed sown in March or April makes fine bedding-plants for a summer and autumn display: they succeed in any rich soil.

In growing petunias, it is best to adhere to a few distinct, well-defined varieties; such as the Bride Rose, with white eyes; the Countess of Ellesmere, and Lady Emily Peel, for violet rose. The following are also good:—

Brilliant,—fine velvety rich crimson.
Eclipse,—distinct and novel.
Rosy Circle,—good rose-coloured bedding variety; better than the Queen, which is also good, and of similar character.
Prince Albert,—crimson.
Prince of Wales,—crimson, often blotched, and edged with white.
Crimson King,—a good bedder.
Fascination,—white circle; bright rose; good habit for bedding.

PHLOXES (nat. ord. Polemona'ceæ).

This magnificent genus of plants, both annual and perennial, is unrivalled for richness and brilliancy of colours, and profusion and duration of blooming. The *P. Drummondii* varieties make splendid bedding and pot plants; the *P. decussata*, French perennial varieties, produce a fine effect in mixed borders; no garden should be without them. They succeed best in light rich soil.

Seed from 4*d.* to 6*d.* per packet.

PICOTEES' (nat. ord. Caryophylla'ceæ).

These are a kind of carnation, distinguished by a narrow dark-coloured edging to the petals, or by the petals being covered with very small coloured dots. The cultivation is in every respect the same as the carnation.

PILLAR ROSES.

There is no form in which the Rose grows so gracefully as when rambling over rocks and climbing up trees or trellis-work, or over the alcove. In the garden, well-planted pillars may become objects of great beauty. To make roses grow with the necessary luxuriance, "each plant," says Mr. Rivers, "should have a station at least two feet in diameter to itself. In the centre of this space a stout stake of yellow pine, tarred at the bottom, should be driven two feet into the soil, and stand eight feet above the surface; the upper part painted green. If the soil be poor, it should be dug out three feet in depth, and filled up with rotten manure and loam, laying this compost about a foot above the surrounding surface to allow for settling. In wet soils they will grow the better for being on a permanent mound; but such soils should be well drained. In the centre of this mound plant a single rose, or, if a variegated pillar is desired, place three plants in the same hole,—a white, a pale-coloured, and dark variety. Having replaced the soil, cover the surface with manure, keeping the manure replenished, as it is drawn in by worms or washed in by rain. Water with liquid manure in dry weather, and there will be shoots, probably eight or ten feet in length, the first season. Three of the most vigorous should be fastened to the stake, and the spurs from them will, for many years, give abundance of flowers. "I scarcely know," says Mr. Rivers, "whether to recommend grafted roses on short stems for pillars, or plants on their own roots. This will depend in a great measure upon the soil, and perhaps it will be as well to try both. Most roses acquire additional vigour by being worked on the dog-rose; but some of the robust kinds grow with equal luxuriance when on their own roots: finally, for dry and sandy soils, I am inclined to recommend the latter, unless plants can be procured budded on the Manetti stocks, which, of all others, are the best adapted for dry soils." Of these roses, Brennus is a superb pillar-rose, its long flexible shoots adapting it for training up a column, or as a drooping standard rose. Roses of this character, throwing out long vigorous shoots of eight or ten feet in a season, require little shortening in the winter pruning: when cut in, they produce abundance of wood the following season, and few flowers. If only tied up to a wire, or trained on a pillar, they will be full of bloom. Blairii is of similar habit; Chênedole and General Jacqueminot, and Triomphe de Bayeux, the only white Chinese hybrid, are all vigorous growers, and well adapted for large standards or pillar roses, the only drawback being their fleeting bloom.

PINES.

At one time pines were the great luxury of the upper ten thousand; now, through the numerous quantities imported, they are brought within the reach of all: perhaps chiefly for this reason, they are not so generally grown as formerly. There is also a very prevalent idea that their cultivation is both difficult and expensive. The formidable treatises published on their culture have frightened many from undertaking it; and yet few plants are more easily cultivated. There is also no comparison between a well-ripened English-grown pine and an imported one. The former is generally a luscious fruit; the latter is very often not equal to a sweet turnip. Occasionally, however, good foreign pines may be had; but they can never compete with English ones; and there is no reason, in cultural difficulties nor expense of production, why every lover of this fruit should not grow his own. Houses for their culture are easily made. No peculiarity of structure is necessary. Doubtless the nearer the light they can be placed the better, although excellent pines may be grown under the shade of vines at least a yard from the roof. The most convenient, and ultimately the cheapest mode of supplying bottom-heat, is by hot water: pipes, and a hot-air chamber under the bed, are best, and least liable to accident. The bed to grow pines in should *be four feet deep*, to allow of a sufficiency of plunging material to cover the highest pots, of sufficient soil to plant the pines out in the bed. This latter is the best, cheapest, and most efficient mode of growing pines. Prepare the bed thus:—Place six inches of rough brickbats for drainage, then a layer of broken bones two inches thick; on this a layer of rich loam, in whole pieces, with the turf inverted on the drainage in solid pieces one foot square and two to three inches thick. Then fill up to within eight inches of the top, with this soil chopped into pieces about four inches square, mixed with broken bones and pieces of charcoal, and broken freestone instead of sharp sand. The charcoal or bones give a sort of enriching power to the loam, and all other food is supplied afterwards, just and only when it is wanted, in a *liquid state.* Secure some good Queens of any approved variety—a Sugar-loaf or two,—and some black Jamaicas or black Antiguas for winter; as many Providences as you can find room for; a few Montserrats, Envelles, and gold and silver-striped for variety: these are all you require. For the general crop nothing equals the Queens. Providences are the next best, and by far the noblest of all. See that your plants are perfectly clean and healthy, rather than large, when you purchase them. When pines once get infested with scale or bug, they are useless. Turn the plants carefully out of the pots, plant from three to five feet apart, according to the sorts, size of plants, &c. Providences require most space. Unwind as many roots as possible without breaking the ball too much; earth-up the stem as high as the good sound healthy leaves (those that are otherwise should be removed) will allow you; leave a hard smooth surface, water with water at a temperature of 80°, and the work is complete. Plants thus bedded out will not require watering nearly so often as those in pots; and if the entire sarface be mulched over with cocoanut-fibre refuse, a good soaking once a month, in the growing season, will probably suffice. It is probable that, with generous treatment, most of these plants will fruit within eighteen months of the time of planting. When the fruit is cut, let the leaves be as little injured as possible. With amazing strength and rapidity, two or three suckers will spring up, and grow with the greatest vigour. One only should be left, the others may be either potted for suceession-plants or be thrown away. From a period varying from six to twelve months from the time of cutting one fruit, another will be ripe on the same stool. As the young plant on the stock advances, the old leaves on the latter may be reduced until all, or nearly all, are removed. At the same time the roots should receive a rich top-dressing of the same material in which they grow; thus nearly eight inches will be left on the surface at planting, so as to allow two or three inches of fresh dressing to every new crop. This is essential, as, from the suckers possessing a self-elevating power and proceeding from a few inches of the bottom of the stool, they could not have an independent support from the soil unless it was raised up with them. After a few years it may be necessary to remove the entire bed *bodily*, and begin at a lower level afresh. There can be no question that this is the cheapest, most rapid, and most profitable system of management.

The entire trouble of succession plants may be avoided. No one now scarcely ever thinks of propagating pines by *crowns* and *gills*, when a sucker can be had strong enough to fruit in from six to nine months. The great feature is to make part of the supply that went to produce the old fruit available to the young plant. The stem is to it a magazine of the best food, laid up in the best form, in the most easily accessible place. Old routine said, Wrench this away, and force the young plant to nurture its babyhood on it own resources. Common sense and analogy demand that it should continue to live beneath its mother's fostering wing until its meridian strength is attained. The two systems are not incompatible. The pot and bedding-out practices can be readily combined thus; only allow the same stool to fruit once, and pot, in place of planting out the stronger suckers.

When the suckers are thoroughly rooted (which is often the case before the fruit is cut), and the fruit is cut, remove the stools, separate the suckers, make a new bed, and plant the latter singly, as at the beginning. Whatever plan be adopted, it will often be necessary to pot quantities of the best suckers to keep up a good stock, form new beds, &c. When the beds get too thick, or the soil gets exhausted, begin as at the beginning. In growing pines in pots, there will generally be two potting seasons,—March, and June or July. Ten- or 12-inch pots will fruit the largest plants, and as soon as the first are cut, and the suckers large enough for removal, the stools may be destroyed.

In all work among pines, remember their leaves are their very life. Appearance also requires that they should never be bruised or injured in the least. Practice alone can enable one to perform the necessary operations without bruising or breaking the foliage. The roots, too, must be carefully preserved. The facility with which pines emit roots up the stems, made the old gardeners reckless about those they already possessed: hence the wholesale disrooting once so common. But the emission of fresh roots does not necessarily supersede the use of those already formed. Neither do pine-roots die naturally annually; the longer they can be preserved the better. The more mouths, provided there is food to fill them all, the more nourishment and strength will be imparted. It is the business of the cultivator to supply this food in a liquid state when and where it is wanted. Healthy roots and leaves convert it into pine fruit; consequently, the greater the quantity used, the heavier and the better-flavoured the pine will be.

PINE'TUM.

A place where pine-trees are grown. In the pinetum, if space permits, plant every pine that will endure our climate. If space be limited, and economy to be studied, the following will prove good varieties :--

	FEET.		
Araucaria imbricata	50	to	100
Abies Smithiana	50	,,	—
,, Douglasii	100	,,	180
,, canadensis	30	,,	50
,, nigra	60	,,	70
Cedrus Libanus	30	,,	100
,, deodara	50	,,	100
,, ,, robusta			
Cryptomera japonica			
,, Lobii	30	,,	40
Cupressus sempervirens (the common cypress)	30	,,	40
,, horizontalis	30	,,	40
,, lusitanica	15	,,	20
,, torulosa	15	,,	20
,, McNabiana	6	,,	10
Fitzroya patagonica			
Juniperus compressa			
,, pendula	5	,,	—
,, canadensis	1	,,	2
,, communis	3	,,	10
,, virginiana (the red cedar) ..	30	,,	40
,, Sabina (the savin)	2	,,	4
,, foliis variegatis			
,, prostrata			
,, recurva	5	,,	10
,, excelsa	20	,,	30
Larix europæa (common larch) ..	80	,,	100
,, pendula	15	,,	20
Picea pectinata (silver fir)	80	,,	100
,, cephalonica	50	,,	60
,, Pinsapo	30	,,	60
,, Nordmanniana	80	,,	90
,, picta	10	,,	—
Picea grandis	100	,,	—
,, nobilis	80	,,	[illegible]
Pinus sylvestris (the Scotch fir) ..	60	,,	80
,, Pumillio	10	,,	20
,, austriaca	60	,,	80
,, Pinaster	40	,,	60
,, Pinea (the Stone pine) ..	15	,,	30
,, ponderosa	50	,,	100
,, Sabiniana	40	,,	100
,, insignis	30	,,	40
,, radiata	30	,,	50
,, Cembra	30	,,	50
,, Strobus (Weymouth pine) ..	50	,,	80
,, Lambertiana	100	,,	—
,, excelsa	90	,,	100
,, Hendersonia	40	,,	50
,, macrophylla	30	,,	50
,, Segnoia sempervirens ..			
,, Wellingtonia gigantea ..	300	,,	—
Taxodium distichum (the deciduous cypress)	30	,,	70
,, pendula	20	,,	—
Thuja occidentalis (the American arbor vitæ)	20	,,	30
,, siberica	20	,,	30
,, orientalis (the Chinese arbor vitæ)	13	,,	20
,, filiformis	10	,,	15
Cephalotaxus Fortunii			
Taxus baccata (the common yew)	20	,,	30
,, elegantissima			
,, canadensis	3	,,	5
,, erecta	13	,,	—

PINKS (nat. ord. Caryophylla'ceæ).

Pinks are closely allied to picotees and carnations, and admit of very similar cultivation. New varieties may be obtained from seed, and old plants may be increased by pipings.

Pipings, as the grass is called when it is pulled out of the joint in the parent stem, should be struck under a hand-glass, and when well rooted should be planted in a bed, in rows six inches apart, and three inches between the plants: here they should remain till September, when they may be planted in a bed or pots, in a compost, consisting of two-thirds of loam from decayed turf, and one-third well-decomposed cow-dung. If in pots, let them be 48's, having a few crocks in the bottom, and filled with compost. Lift the plants carefully, without breaking the fibres, adjusting the soil so as to place the plant in its proper position, spreading out the roots on the soil, and filling up the pot to the surface. The roots must not be sunk too deep, but the soil on the top must be on a level with the collar of the plant. When gently watered, the pots may be placed in a common garden-frame, and the glass closed for four-and-twenty hours. Throughout winter the plants give very little trouble, seldom requiring water, but all the air which can be given them. In March they should be repotted in the pots in which they are to bloom, which should be 24's, with an inch at least of crocks for drainage;—the soil as before.

The soil best suited to receive the young plants is a mixture of good hazel-loam, with well-rotted manure from old cucumber- or melon-frames. This mixture should be made some months before it is required for use, and at the time of planting or potting the layers, a little white sea-sand should be added. Where layers of carnations and picotees are potted, the best plan appears to be to place them singly into small pots for the winter months. In this way they can be packed closely under common frames in old tan or cinder-ashes. Let the newly-potted layers have all the air possible in fine weather; but if the winter prove severe, it will be necessary to cover the glass with mats, straw, or pea-haum.

Pink pipings properly rooted should be planted out in October; avoid the old system of shortening the grass. Where seed is required, the decaying petals should be picked off.

PIT FOR CUTTINGS.

To preserve cuttings from frost where there is no greenhouse, dig a pit about four feet deep, strew the bottom well with ashes, and sink the pots in the same. Over it place a common garden-frame, bank up the outsides with straw and a coating of earth. In such a pit, verbenas, calceolarias, ageratums, fuchsias, &c. &c., may be preserved during winter, provided the pots be kept in the dark by being well covered with matting in severe frost.

PLANTING.

The season for planting may be from September to March. Many arguments may be brought forward in favour of the month of November, if the weather be open and free from frosts. Spring is always a busy season in the garden; digging, sowing, grafting, and pruning are then in full operation. "And why should planting be added to the number?" asks the Rev. Mr. Lawrence "It makes part of the wise man's pleasure and diversion to have always something to do, and never too much. Amusements and recreations of all kinds should come to us in regular and orderly succession, and not in a crowd; besides, some intervals of time for meditation between different kinds of work in a garden are very desirable to a good and thoughtful man."

The Pear loves a silicious earth, of considerable depth; Plums flourish in calcareous soils, and the roots seek the surface; the Cherry prefers a light silicious soil; and all cease to be productive in moist, humid soils. The Apple accommodates itself more to clayey soils, but does best in a loamy soil of moderate quality, slightly gravelly. In preparing stations, therefore, suitable soils should be supplied to each. The station is prepared by digging out a pit about three feet square, and the same depth, in ground that has been well drained. In the bottom of this pit lay 10 or 12 inches of brick or lime rubbish, the roughest material at the bottom, and ram it pretty firmly, so as to be impervious to the tap-root: the remainder of the pit is filled in with earth suitable to the requirements of the tree. When the surrounding soil is a tenacious clay, the roots of the young tree should be spread out just under the surface, and rich light mould placed over them, forming a little mound round the roots; but in no case should the crown be more than covered: deep planting is the bane of fruit-trees.

The stations being prepared, the trees require attention; it is necessary to prune the roots, by taking off all the small fibres, and shortening the larger roots to about six inches from the stem; if there be any bruise, the root in which it occurs should be removed entirely, by a clean sharp cut. Two or three spurs are sufficient: but if there be more good ones, they may remain, after careful pruning. The roots may be laid in milk-and-water or soap-suds, a few hours before the trees are planted. The process of planting will differ, according as the trees are intended to be dwarf, standard, pyramid, or wall-trees. With dwarf, standard, or espalier, place the tree upright in the centre of the station; spread the roots carefully in an horizontal direction, and cover them with prepared mould to the required height, supporting the young plant with a strong stake, driven firmly into the ground, and tying the stem to it with hay, or something that will not bruise; press the soil gently, but firmly, over the extended roots, having first cut away the tap-root. Then mulch the place. This process, called mulching, consists in spreading a layer of short half-rotten dung five or six inches thick round the stem, in a radius six inches beyond the extremity of the roots; the mulch spread evenly with the fork, and gently pressed down by the back of the spade, or, if exposed to the wind, pegged down to prevent its being blown away. In the case of a wall-tree, let the root be as far from the wall as convenient, with the stem sloping to it, the roots being extended and covered in the same manner with the soil.

The nature of the soil is to be regarded, and the tree planted at a greater or smaller elevation above the level of the surrounding soil accordingly: where the subsoil is a stiff clay, the mound in which it is planted should rise from nine to twelve inches; in a warm dry soil, a very gentle elevation suffices. The roots should be planted in the richest mould; and various expedients may be used to keep them moist and cool, and free from canker. The mould requires to be pressed gently round the roots with the hand, so that the soil may be closely packed round them: with these precautions, no fear need be entertained of productive fruit-trees being obtained.

PLUMS.

The most useful varieties for small gardens are, for early fruiting, the Goliath, Greengage, Victoria, and Rivers's Prolific; for late fruiting, Purple-gage, Magnum Bonum, Coe's Golden Drop, and Damson. The Reine Claude de Bavy is an excellent plum upon a warm wall or under glass.

POLYANTHUS.

Divide the roots of the best plants intended for preservation. This operation must be performed every year, or the flowers will soon degenerate. Fresh soil and continual division is the only plan with all florists' flowers which give out offsets. The single varieties of polyanthus alone are looked upon as florists' flowers; and as these seed freely, an infinite variety of polyanthuses may be obtained by those who will take the trouble to select and sow seed. Late in autumn is the time for sowing; for moderate sunlight only is required to bring up the seed, and the young plants will not stand the scorching sun of summer. Sow in boxes, or pans well drained, filled with light rich mould. The seed must be very lightly covered,—indeed, it may almost lie upon the surface. The boxes should be placed under glass, and sparingly watered. They require no artificial heat.

POMPONES.

Pompones, or Lilliputian Chrysanthemums, form a very valuable addition to this tribe of flowers. Mr. Broome says of them, "The introduction of this little favourite has tended in no small degree to resuscitate the cultivation of the chrysanthemum, which of late years has much fallen off. Beautiful, though small, it will bear any amount of looking into, yet it seems more specially designed to set off and act by way of contrast to its larger rivals, whether it be in the *parterre* or in the vases of the drawing-room." There is no difference in the method of cultivating these small varieties, so that our observations apply to both kinds. With regard to the character of the flowers of the chrysanthemum, three kinds are enumerated. The reflexed petals mark the older and less-esteemed varieties, the petals turning back towards the calyx. The incurved petals turn inward, so as to give rather a cup-like appearance to the flower. The anemone-flowered chrysanthemums have a centre of short compact petals, arranged in a globose form, around which the larger petals radiate. They are very beautiful, but it is somewhat difficult to get them to bloom perfectly. The following is a list of really good sorts :—

Large Varieties.—Louisa lucida; Madame Leo; Vesta,—white: Aimée Terrière; Eugénie; Hermione; King,—blush and pale pink: Admirable; Baron Scalebert; Phidias; Leon Leguay,—rose and lilac: Grand Napoleon; Progne; Rantonette,—rose and carmine: Changeable,—yellow: Cloth of Gold; Gold Queen of England; Persanne,—yellow: Agustie Mie; Madame Poggi; Pluton; Lothario,—red and crimson: Alcibiade; Cassy; Poudre d'Or; Ruth; Zephyr,—bronze and orange.

Large Anemone-flowered.—Eclipse; Reine Marguerite,—yellow: Fleur de Marie; Madame Sentir; Nancy de Sermet,—white: George's Land,—red, with yellow centre: Louis,—lilac: Marguerite d' Anjou,—nankeen.

Pompones.—Berrol; Ida; Solfaterre,—yellow: Bijou de l'Horticulture; Cedo Nulli; Nelly,—white: Duke de Rouen; La Promise; President Decaisne,—rose: Attila; Marceau; Surprise; Zebra,—pink and lilac: Mustapha; Pandore; Sainte Thais,—bronze and orange.

POMPON ROSES.

These beautiful little gems are admirably adapted for bedding-out purposes, from their singularly pleasing and distinct colours, and the admirable contrast they present. The beds for these delicate roses, where they are confined to one variety, should be small, as should be the garden. They are best adapted for a fairy garden, which should be well drained, otherwise they could not survive the winter. Whatever the soil, the beds will be improved by its being removed to the depth of 18 inches to two feet, and replaced with a layer of stones and brick and lime rubbish, for drainage. If the natural soil is pretty good, it may be returned, after mixing it with a portion of decomposed cow-dung, adding a little sand, the whole thoroughly blended together: rich vegetable mould full of fibre will do.

These roses are recommended to be on their own roots and planted in autumn. The stocks on which they are usually budded are too gross for their delicate structure. Plant them 15 inches apart if it is intended to peg them down, so as to cover the bed; if they are to stand apart, 18 inches will be better. In March, or early in April, when all danger from frost is over, they may be pruned. Use the knife sparingly; cut out all dead wood, and regulate the branches: this is all that will be required.

As the season advances, water them from time to time with weak liquid manure, removing all decaying leaves; and where they have bloomed in clusters, cut back to the next bud, from which they will again break, and bloom in the autumn. Short shoots, showing no bloom, should have the terminal buds pinched off on attaining the length of five or six inches; the lateral shoots thrown out will probably bloom freely.

During the winter keep the buds as dry as possible; they are even worth protecting from the cold rains. We venture to class a few of the most favoured suitable for bedding :—

ROSE-COLOUR, *Clémentine Duval*,—flowering from May to November, every shoot terminating with a bunch; *General Merlin*,—flowering the whole summer and autumn; *Léonie Verger*,—rather delicate, but a free flowerer; *Pompon*,—small, but extremely pretty; blooming in clusters; *Psyche*,—bright pink; blooming freely in clusters; very neat and pretty.

CHERRY-COLOUR, *Coquette de Montgomery*,—shaded with violet; a very free bloomer.

PURE WHITE, *Pauline Bonaparte*,—small, but distinct and pretty; contrasting admirably with all the others.

CRIMSON, *Nemesis*,—very deep colour, blooming in clusters through summer and winter; *Crimson*,—a miniature China; the best we possess for edgings, being perpetually in bloom; *Jenny*,—miniature China, continually in flower, and very pretty.

CARMINE, *Pompon de St. Rudegonde*,—brilliant purplish; a strong grower, and good-sized flowers.

BRIGHT YELLOW, *Pactolus*,—a tea-scented rose, blooming in clusters very freely; an admirable rose.

All those roses may be grown in pots with advantage for blooming in spring. In March they require a moderate shift, using good fibrous turfy loam and cow-dung. Protect them in a cold frame; water occasionally with manure-water, and pinch off all buds and shoots when about four inches long, and give another shift during the summer. In September they will become bushy plants, ready for shifting into their blooming-pots, which must not be large, using the soil already recommended. Keep them in a cold frame through the winter, giving very little water. In spring, apply manure-water, and prune as recommended for out-of-door culture.

POTATO.

Selection and Preparation of the Soil.—A deep, thoroughly drained, light sandy loam, or peaty soil, is most suitable for the potato. The application of manure is now generally held to increase the liability to disease, to bring it on at an earlier period, and to produce large crops of imperfectly matured tubers, which if they escape the disease while in the ground, are more liable to be attacked after they are lifted. The ground selected, therefore, should be in fair condition, from having been moderately manured for some exhausting green crop in the previous season. But if the only land to be had is so poor as to render it necessary to apply manure in order to insure a fair crop, then use charred vegetable refuse, or a very light dressing of well-decayed farm or stable-yard manure. The ground should be trenched two spades deep, and ridged up early in autumn; if manure is applied, this should be well mixed with the soil. Charred vegetable refuse, however, may be applied about the sets when they are planted. We believe that a slight sprinkling scattered along the trench before planting, and then used in covering the sets, has proved a partial preventive of disease.

Time and Manner of Planting.—We have no hesitation in saying, that early planting has hitherto proved the best preventive against the attacks of disease; for, as the crops sooner arrive at maturity, they frequently escape altogether, or suffer comparatively little. Plant, therefore, as early in January as the ground can be found in fair working condition. A small breadth of the ash-leaved kidney should be planted on a south border, or in the warmest and most sheltered situation at command, to furnish an early supply. In planting, let the ground be neatly levelled, then, beginning at one side, dig it over about six inches deep, and put in the sets in the openings at proper distances, which must be regulated by the growth of the variety. The lines for the early kinds, as ash-leaved, &c., which form but small tops, may be about twenty inches apart, leaving about nine inches between the sets, but for the second early varieties two feet should be allowed between the lines, and ten inches between the sets. The late kinds will require an additional six inches between the lines. The sets should be covered about six inches, leaving the soil over them as open and loose as possible. On strong heavy land the ash-leaved and other weakly growers should not be covered more than four inches. Planting in autumn has been strongly recommended, and on light, well-drained land, it may safely be practised—the crop will probably be both earlier and more abundant than from spring planting; but the plan has not answered the expectations which were entertained respecting it as a means of enabling the crop to escape disease. All things considered, we think that planting early in spring is to be preferred.

After-management.—When the tops are four to six inches above the ground, ridge the soil up neatly about them. In the case of the early varieties, which may be in danger of suffering from the frost, the soil should be kept ridged up round the shoots as soon as they appear above the ground, keeping them covered until they are four to six inches high, and all danger of frost is past. Before earthing up, fork the ground lightly between the lines, so as to pulverize the soil, then draw it to the plants with a hoe or spade. Keep the ground clear of weeds. When the crop attains maturity, lift and store; or if the disease is troublesome before the tubers are ripe, lay the shoots down along the top of the ridge and cover them with soil. This seems to be the most suceessful method known at present of checking the ravages of the disease. The crop should be taken up, however, as soon as possible after disease makes its appearance, and the tubers stacked and temporarily covered in some place where they can be examined occasionally. When the disease appears to have done its worst, pit them in the usual manner, covering them sufficiently to protect against severe frost.

The following varieties are most worthy of cultivation:—

Round Potatoes.

Early Covent Garden Prolific,—a first-class variety, very early, an extremely heavy cropper, fine-flavoured, with a dwarf compact top. We highly recommend this variety.
Early Oxford.
,, Shaw.
Regents.
,, Pink-eyed.

Kidney Potatoes.

Early Ash-leaf,—for forcing or very early use. A very fine stock.
Early Myatt's Covent Garden Prolific Ash-leaf,—a handsome and most desirable potato; an abundant cropper, but not quite so early as the above, nor so well adapted for forcing.
Webb's Imperial,—a great cropper, resists the disease better than most others, is very handsome, and may be cooked from July to June.
Daw's Covent Garden Matchless,—a very handsome and desirable variety, fine-flavoured and very prolific, ready in August, and much in demand in Covent Garden.
Flukes.
Lapstone.

POTATOES IN FRAMES.

When potatoes are grown in a frame, the treatment is much the same as before; but they are also grown very successfully in this manner:—The frame being placed on a level piece of ground, the soil within is dug out to the depth of two feet, and banked round the outside of the frame. The pit thus formed is then filled with prepared dung; and on this three inches of soil is placed; then the potatoes; then six inches more soil. The potatoes, when planted, should be just starting into growth; but the shoots should never be more than half an inch from the tuber, or they do not grow so strong. It is advisable to pick off some of the shoots: three on each tuber are sufficient. They may also be forced under the stand in a greenhouse or hothouse, the potatoes being planted singly in large pots of very rich light soil. Each pot ought to yield a good dish.

POTTING.

This is one of the most important of gardening operations. Adapt the pots to the size of the plants as near as possible,—or rather, to what the plant is expected to be,—as allowance must be made for growth of the root as well as the plant. Let the pots be perfectly clean. Effectual drainage of the pots does not consist so much in the quantity of drainage, as in the arrangement of it. A potsherd should be placed over the hole: some pieces of pot, broken rather small, over that; and these again covered with a layer of peat-fibre or rough earth. This gives efficient *drainage*, and need not occupy more than an inch and a half of the pot. Hard-wooded plants should be potted rather firmly; soft-wooded should be left rather loose and free.

PRI'MULA (nat. ord. Primula'ceæ).

This genus is a very large one, including, as it does, some of the most popular florists' flowers; viz., the Auricula, the Polyanthus, and the Primrose. We cannot here do more than call the reader's attention to the greenhouse varieties of Primula so useful for winter decorations. Mr. Williams, to whom the public are so much indebted for the care he has bestowed on these beautiful plants, says, "Taking them all in all, these are the most valuable winter-flowering plants in existence." His directions for sowing and culture are as follows:—"Sow in March, April, May, June, and July (with great care, for although so easily raised in the hands of some, it is nevertheless a great difficulty to others, who, in many instances, too hastily condemn the quality of the seed), in pots filled to within half an inch of the top with sifted leaf-mould, or, what is better, with thoroughly-rotted manure, which has been exposed to all weathers for a year or two. Leave the surface rather rough, and sprinkle the seed thinly upon it, not covering with soil. Tie a piece of paper over the top of the pot, and leave it in a warm house or hotbed. When the seed becomes dry, water the paper only: the seed will then germinate in two or three weeks. After this remove the paper and place in a shady place, potting off when sufficiently strong into small pots: place the pots near the glass in a frame or greenhouse . . . . One caution is necessary—never use peat mould or any soil liable to cake on the surface or turn green, as the loss of the seed is a certain consequence."

PROPAGATION.

In a state of nature all plants are propagated from seed, and the multifarious form of the seeds and envelopes with which they are provided is one of the many interesting subjects of investigation to the lover of nature. For our purpose it is sufficient to state that most seeds are covered with a hard shell or envelope, which protects them from external injury; that within this envelope lies the embryo plant. All seeds in this latent state contain an organ, or Germ, which, under favourable circumstances, shoots upwards, and becomes the stem of the plant; another, called the Radicle, which seeks its place in the soil, and becomes the root; and the Seed-lobes, which yield nourishment to the young plant in its first stage of growth. Moisture, heat, and air are necessary conditions for the development of all seeds; and most of them require, in addition, concealment from the light.

It is found, however, that except in the case of annuals (as plants raised from seed, which grow, produce their seeds, and ripen their fruit in one year are called), much time is lost by following this mode of propagation; it is also found that the seed does not always produce the same identical plant; above all, it is found that none of the double-flowering, and few of the herbaceous-flowering plants, with which our gardens are furnished, ripen their seeds in our climate. This has led to other methods of multiplying; for, besides the roots properly so called, which attach themselves to the soil, and draw from it the principal nourishment of the plant, it is found that each branch conceals under its outward covering a bundle of fibres or tissues, which, under favourable circumstances, develop roots, and become the basis of an independent plant, identical with that from which it sprung. Many plants have also a crown with buds or eyes, each capable of propagating its species. Every plant with roots of this description may be divided into as many portions as there are eyes, taking care that a few fibres are attached to the root, and each will become an independent plant. The potato, and all the bulbous and tuberous plants, are familiar examples of this principle of propagation; so are the Dahlia and Pæony, which grow better when the set is confined to a piece of the tuber with one eye attached, than when planted whole. So conspicuous is this in the potato, that, where it is planted *whole*, all the eyes except one, or at most two, should be scooped out with a sharp knife, because the young plant will thus be supplied with more of its natural pabulum while it is rooting, and will increase its vigour.

Other plants throw off short stems, like the daisy and house-leek, by means of which they are propagated. Others again, like the strawberry, throw off runners, each of which is furnished with its root-fibre already elaborated, only requiring soil in which to root itself. But there are others, where nature requires the aid of art, and this has given rise to the operation which will be found explained under the article *Layering*.

PROTECTING BEDDING-PLANTS.

It is always desirable to get bedding-plants out as early as possible, and yet there is much danger both from wind and frost in so doing. It is an excellent plan to stick sprays of evergreens, Scotch and spruce firs, in different parts of the bed as a protection. By this means the force of the wind is broken, and the plants take hold of the ground sooner: the tender leaves also are saved, which otherwise not unfrequently turn brown and fall off, retarding the growth of the plants.

PRUNING.

The pruning of fruit-trees is performed at two seasons,—winter and summer. Winter pruning should be performed while vegetation is entirely at rest,—the period which follows the severest frosts, and which precedes the first movement of vegetation, that is to say, the end of February or the very beginning of March, in ordinary years. If trees are pruned before the strong frosts of winter set in, the cut part is exposed to the influence of the severe weather long before the first movement of the sap takes place, which is so necessary to cicatrize the wound, and the terminal bud is consequently often destroyed. Equally troublesome are the wounds made during frosts: the frozen wood is cut with difficulty; sometimes the cuts are ragged, and do not heal; mortality attacks the bud, and it disappears. To prune after vegetation has commenced, except summer pruning, is not to be thought of; therefore let all chief pruning be done in February, if the frost has disappeared, especially for the peach, whose buds, placed at the base of last year's shoots, are particularly exposed to the action of the ascending sap.

The implements required in pruning are a hand-saw, a pruning-knife, a chisel, and a mallet. For garden trees the knife is the most important: it should be strong and of the best steel, with a considerable curve, so as to take a good hold of the wood. The manner of operating is far from indifferent. The amputation should be made as near as possible to the bud, but without touching it; the cut should begin on the opposite side, and on a level with its lower part, made at an angle of 45°, and terminate just above the bud.

If it is necessary to cut away a branch altogether, a small portion of it should be left on the stem, and the cut should be a smooth and bevelled one, presenting the smallest possible extent of wounded surface. If made with the saw, it should be made smooth with the knife or chisel, and covered with grafting-paste.

The first object in pruning a standard

Pruning.

tree is the formation of its head. The first pruning must take place at the end of the first season after grafting,

Fig. 1.

when the scion has made its growth, as represented in fig. 1, when two shoots have sprung from the graft. To

Fig. 2.

Pruning.

form a full round head, the two shoots should be pruned in to *a*, *a*. The year after the tree will present the appearance represented in fig. 2; or, if three shoots have been left the first year, and the whole three headed in, in the following year they will appear as in fig. 3, each shoot having thrown out two new branches. The one tree now presents a head of six, and the other four shoots. At the end of the second year both are to be headed back, the one to the shape indicated by the

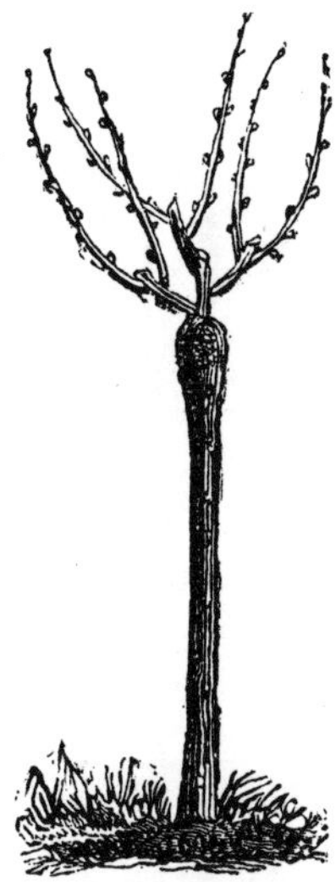

Fig. 3.

crossing lines, *a*, *a*, *a*, *a*, the other as nearly as possible to the same distance from the graft.

Another year's growth will, in each instance, double the number of main shoots, which are now eight and six respectively, as represented in fig. 5. If a greater number of shoots appear, or if any of them seem badly placed, their growth should be prevented by pinching off the tops when young, and pruning them clean off when the tree has shed its leaves. The time for pruning is any of the winter months between November and February before the sap begins to stir. Those trees which have produced six shoots should be pruned exactly like those with eight, to form a compact head, as in fig. 4; and when the standard tree has acquired eight main branches by these various prunings, it has attained its full formation, and with a little care may easily be kept in shape.

When a standard tree has reached its bearing state, the object of the

Fig. 4.

pruner is the production of fruit. If the branches are well placed, let them have free course, and they will throw out bearing-spurs at the extremities. Little more need be said on the subject, except that all unproductive wood, crowded sprays, and decayed branches, that cross each other, should be cut out, the tree kept open in the centre, and the open cuplike form rigorously maintained. These remarks apply chiefly to apples, pears, and other trees which bear their fruit on spurs: where their habit is different, it will be noticed in treating of them specifically. These spurs will in time become long and scrubby, with many branches, as in fig. 6, where we see a spur with many branches getting fur-

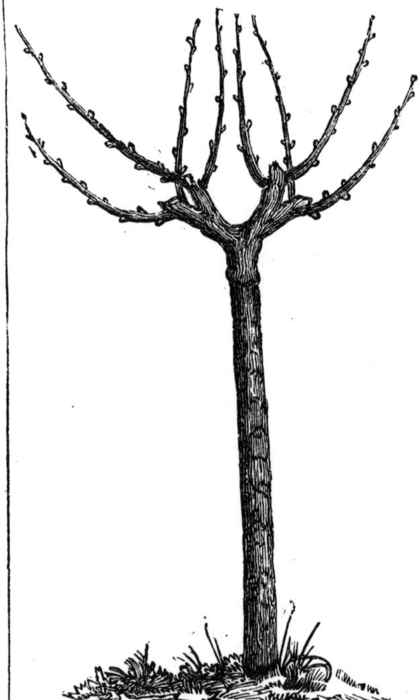

Fig. 5.

ther and further away from the main branch. To bring it back to its proper position, cut away, neatly, the upper shoot at *a*, and the side-shoot at *b*, cutting out, also, the central shoot, when the small bud, *c*, will push out and form blossom-buds the following year.

When a tree is very vigorous, the buds will break strongly and run into wood too strong to form blossom-buds,

The remedy in this case is to break the young shoot near the third bud from the main branch, leaving the broken part hanging down. The time for this operation is about the middle of March. The broken part,

Fig. 6.

while it droops, nevertheless draws up a portion of the wood-sap. The following winter, when the buds are turned into blossom-buds and become fruitful, the hanging shoot should be neatly pruned away, when a fruitful bearing-spur will be formed.

PUMPKINS.

These are used, when young, as a vegetable. When ripe they form a valuable esculent for soups and "pumpkin pies" in winter. The young shoots in summer are an excellent substitute for asparagus.

The varieties enumerated below constitute a portion of that magnificent collection of edible and ornamental gourds which was awarded the three principal prizes at the Great International Gourd Show, held at the Royal Horticultural Gardens.

Big Ben of Westminster, Blondon, Dr. Lindley, Emperor, Giant's Punch-bowl, Mammoth, Monster, Portmanteau de Naples, Victor Emmanuel.

Seed, from 4*d.* to 1*s.* per packet.

Messrs. Barr & Sugden offer seed, of twelve splendid varieties, at 4*s.* 6*d.* per packet.

QUAKING GRASS.

This curious plant should find a place among the ornamental grasses. It is easily dried, and in this state becomes useful for winter decorations. There are several varieties, all hardy annuals, growing freely from seed. *Briza major*, the large quaking grass, is the favourite.

Seed, 3*d.* per packet.

QUERCUS, the Oak.

The species are chiefly forest trees; still there are many extremely ornamental. *Q. Ilex*, the evergreen oak, is very useful in shrubberies. The American oaks are very handsome, particularly for the tint of their leaves in winter. *Q. Mirbeckii*, from Algiers, is also noted for its glossy, variegated, and picturesque foliage and its majestic growth.

QUINCUNX.

This is the name given to a system of planting very extensively adopted by gardeners and with very good results. It consists in arranging trees or plants in such a manner that those in one row stand opposite spaces in the next. Thus :—

```
*    *    *    *    *
   *    *    *    *
     *    *    *
        *    *
          *
```

RADISH.

Preparation of the Soil.—Deep, light, and rich soil—not made so, however, by the application of manure—should be chosen. It should be carefully dug or forked deeply, making the surface soil fine and level before sowing.

Time and Manner of Sowing.—Sow early in January, on a warm sheltered border, and at intervals of three weeks until May; afterwards every fortnight during the summer, and at longer intervals when the weather becomes cold in autumn. Radishes are often sown much too thickly, and this causes the roots to be small, hard, stringy, and disagreeably hot in flavour. Sow broadcast, in beds of convenient size, and cover the seeds evenly and lightly with fine soil. The early sowing will require to be protected from frost by a covering of litter, but this must be removed every mild day, as soon as the plants appear above ground. When the weather is hot and the ground dry, well water before sowing; and some days before drawing, water the beds well, and keep the soil moist until the crop is finished. With the convenience of a frame and a little fermenting material, a supply may be obtained considerably earlier than in the open border, and with much less trouble. If grown in this way, cover the manure with six inches of light rich soil, and sow when there is no risk of the bed overheating. Give air on every favourable occasion, so as to secure stocky growth, and cover up at night when frosty. The Spanish varieties should be sown in drills, about a foot apart, and thinned out when sufficiently strong to draw, so as to stand from four to six inches apart in the rows. For a winter supply of these, sow from the middle of July to the middle of September, regulating this by the locality, and the size at which the roots may be most esteemed. Fair-sized roots, however, will be obtained in most localities from sowings made about the middle of August. These may be taken up before severe weather sets in, and pitted or stored in damp sand, in a cool cellar or shed, for winter use.

Seed, 2*s.* 6*d.* to 3*s.* per quart.

RAMPION.

This is a campanula, and very good as a vegetable, to be used like radishes.

Preparation of the Land.—This plant will be found to thrive best in well-pulverized, deep, rich soil, such as is recommended for carrots; well decomposed manure may be added, if necessary. If grown in a warm, dry situation, the roots are liable to be hard and stringy; therefore the main crop should be sown in a cool situation, and if this cannot be done, water liberally during droughty weather.

Time of Sowing, &c.—If to be used for salad or for cooking, in a small state, sow at intervals, to be regulated by the size at which the roots may be most esteemed. For winter use sow in April or early in May, in lines a foot apart, covering the seeds very lightly with fine soil, and thin the plants out, so that they may stand four inches apart in the lines.

Seed, 2*s.* per ounce.

RANUNCULUS.

Next to tulips these are the most beautiful of all bulbs or tubers, if, indeed, their claw-like roots deserve these names. They rival the tulip in brilliancy of colour, and many prefer the beautifully-arranged balls of the ranunculus to the stiff formal cups of the tulip; both, however, have their distinctive features of beauty, and deserve a place in every garden. They may be planted from October to the end of March, some preferring one period and some another: perhaps no better time could be chosen for planting than the beginning or middle of February. As soon as the beds are in a fit state, lose no time in planting, if the weather be favourable; waiting a day, or even a week, is nothing in comparison with placing the roots in soil in an unfit state to receive them. They are best cultivated in 4-feet beds of rich loam mixed with one-fourth part of decomposed cow-dung. The soil should be dug from 2 to 2½ feet deep, and if the situation is moist and partially sheltered, so much the better. A constant supply of moisture is essential to their beauty and growth, although an excess of water would destroy the tubers during the cold of winter and early spring: after their blossom-buds are formed, however, the surface of the beds must never be allowed to become dry; a daily soaking of water will then be necessary in dry weather, not only for the sake of the flowers, but to preserve the roots from injury, these being very near the surface. The roots should be planted about two inches deep and six inches apart; their claw-like extremities should be pressed firmly into the earth, and the crowns be covered with an inch of sand previous to another inch of soil being spread over them; the beds may then be covered with a layer of spruce branches, straw litter, or leaf-mould, to protect them from the frost: this will, of course, be removed before the appearance of the plants above ground.

Ranunculuses are increased by offsets, dividing the tubers, and seed. Offsets is the usual mode of increase, and they are generally sufficiently strong to flower the first year. Choice sorts may also be divided into several plants; every little knot that appears on the top of a tuber will form a plant if carefully divided, so as to insure an accompanying claw. Unless, however, for choice sorts, this mode of increase is not desirable: by seed is the most rapid mode of increase, as well as the only way of securing new varieties. It is said by some persons that ranunculuses never come true from seed, so that variety is certain. Perhaps the best time for sowing is the month of January, and the best place a cold frame. Sow either in the frame or in pots or boxes, on a smooth hardish surface, and barely cover the seed with soil. Exclude the frost, and keep the frame close until the plants show two seed-leaves; then gradually inure them to more air, until the light may be entirely removed in May. The little tubers may be taken up when the foliage is quite ripened off: they will require the same, or even more attention, in watering than the old roots.

Some prefer sowing the seed on beds out of doors in the autumn or spring months. Generally ranunculuses will have died down, and be fit for taking up and storing, by the end of June or beginning of July. The place for storing should be dry; a drawer with a bed of sand being the most convenient. The following are good named varieties :—

Abbé d'Elugne,—dark brown.
Amazon,—light purple.
Argus,—velvety brown.
Belle Forme,—white, red-spotted.
Bergère Blanche,—white, rose-spotted.
Black Prince,—black.
Blanche Amiable,—white.
Ceres,—purple variegated.
Clothilde,—rose variegated.
Comte d'Artois,—white.
Comte de Gloire,—blood-red.
Comtesse de Pompadour,—deep yellow.
Dictator,—scarlet.
El Dorado,—yellow and brown.
Eleonora,—rose.
Fireball,—fire-red.
Formosum,—brown and yellow.
Genevra,—citron.
Gloria Florum,—brown.
Habet Electoral,—golden yellow.
Hasdrubal,—deep rose.
Herculaneum,—purple-spotted.
Horatius,—dark grey.
La Céleste,—violet.
La Charmante,—light rose.
La Pucelle de Paris,—yellow.
Mathilde,—purplish blue.
Mont Blanc,—white.
Nosegay,—yellow-brown spotted, sweet-scented.
Œil-noir,—true black.
Penelope,—rose and yellow.
Polydore,—velvety blackish purple.
Princesse d'Orange,—orange.
Quintinianus,—rose-spotted.
Reine des Violettes,—velvet.
Rinaldo,—velvety black.
Rose sans égal,—white, rose-feathered.
Temple van Apollo,—dark purple.
Valois,—dark brown.
Vocabule,—white and rose.

RASPBERRIES.

Under the article *Bush Fruit* will be found such ample instructions for the cultivation and management of raspberries, that, to avoid repetition, we think it best to refer the reader to that article for any information he may require.

RED BEET.

This should be sown at the beginning of April. Let the ground be fully exposed to the sun, and quite open and away from trees. Sow the seed in shallow drills 15 inches apart, and drop three or four seeds at intervals of 10 inches or a foot apart, or sow thinly along the drill: cover, tread, and rake the ground roughly with a wooden rake, drawing off large stones, &c., that may be on the surface. Sowing this seed in drills is preferable to sowing broadcast, because it not only gives greater facility for thinning out and using the hoe between, but it insures a regular crop without wasting the seed, the plants being at regular distances. When they are about a foot high, thin them to not less than a foot apart, leaving the best-coloured rather than the strongest plants; for the better it is, the less likely it is to grow strong and large. Large roots are not esteemed, being deficient in flavour. One of the best sorts for ordinary culture is Cottell's blood-red: it is of fine colour, and not apt to grow too large. Of equal merit is Henderson's pine-apple.

RED SPIDERS.

The free use of the syringe, and an occasional washing of walls, &c., with lime or sulphur, is the best method of getting rid of these troublesome pests.

REGENERATING FRUIT-TREES.

It frequently happens that grafted fruit-trees, some at one period of their age and some at another, cease to assimilate themselves with the stocks upon which they have been worked. This is to be seen by a thickening of the tree just about the place where it has been worked. This thickening, which in some parts of the country is called a burr, is always to be regarded as an effort of nature to throw out new roots and preserve life, and should be treated accordingly. If the tree has originally been worked, and the burr consequently shows itself at some distance above the ground, a large box should be provided, and placed round the burr, in such a way that it may contain a quantity of soil, into which the tree can strike out its new roots. This soil should be a light loam, and always kept moist. In the second or

third year, new roots will have been formed, and the tree may safely be separated by a saw from the old stock, and let down into the earth beneath. When the tree has been worked close to the surface, a place about a yard square may easily be built up with bricks or tiles, and filled with light soil a few inches over the burr, to receive the new roots. In this way the writer has preserved two small trees of the Sturmer pippin, which he found fast dwindling away, the stocks on which they were worked not having power to sustain them. By a somewhat similar process, the healthy branch, *b*, of a favourite tree may be preserved by layering it in a box or pot, *a*, as in the engraving.

Another operation, the object of which is to utilize the roots and stem of the old tree, is connected with the foregoing.

The final cause of the languishing state of these trees being the absence of vigorous young shoots and the imperfect organization of the cambium and liber, and, finally, the abortion of root-fibres in consequence, the tree can only be restored to health by the production of more healthy and vigorous organs; and this may be done by concentrating the whole energy of the tree on certain points. Amputate the principal branches, *A* (*see* the engraving given in illustration), about seven or eight inches from their base at *c*, the branches *b* being left entire for the present, the amputations being so made that the branches left are not required to carry out the new system of training to be adopted, passing, in all cases, the four largest branches. These branches are retained for the present, it being doubtful if the tree has strength to develop upon the old bark the new buds necessary to fulfil the functions of the roots; for if the buds perish, and there is no outlet for the rising sap, the tree dies. By preserving these branches, their leaves and shoots provide against such accidents. To facilitate the issue of buds on the tree, the hard dry bark should be removed by a plane, and its place covered by a coating of chalk and water, a covering which will stimulate the vital energy of the living bark, and protect the tree from the sun's rays.

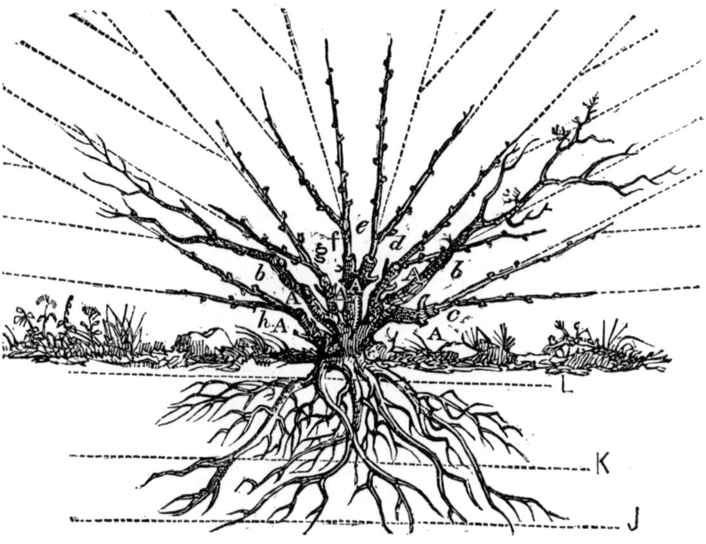

Regenerated Pear-tree.

Following this operation, we shall find that the sap concentrated on only a few branches acts with great energy upon the cellular tissues of the bark nearest to the summit of the cut branches. It determines towards these points the formation of buds, which soon develop vigorous branches. Towards the middle of June, choose such shoots as are best suited to form the principal branches for horizontal training; such would be *c d e f g h* in the accompanying engraving. The others must be cut towards the middle of their length.

The year following, in the spring, train the principal branches according to the plan laid down; for example, in the fan shape, as in the engraving, break the tender branches close to their junction with the stem or main branch, and, during the summer, pinch the leading shoots off, so as to convert into fruit-spurs the shoots not intended to form main branches.

In the following spring the tree will be as represented above. At this time, the branches *b*, left for precaution, may be entirely suppressed, the several cuts being covered with grafting-paste. These new suppressions increasing the energy of the young branches, they will henceforth grow with great vigour, and will soon replace the ancient tree.

In the same proportion in which the stem is operated upon, so must the roots be. As soon as buds begin to appear upon the portion of the branches left, the leaves which are developed send towards the roots a quantity of ligneous fibre and corticle, or wood-fibre. In its course towards the roots, this sap meets with beds or layers of cambium and liber, through which they extend themselves in a languishing state (since it is now deprived of the fluid which facilitated its passage), taking their natural direction, and penetrating the cells in the bark upon the roots, they give place to new organs, at once more nourishing, more healthy, and more vigorous than the old roots. If, after three or four years, a tree operated upon as we have indicated is transplanted, it will be observed that the lower half of the old roots, comprised between the lines J and K, is decayed, and that young roots, comprising those between K and L, have been thrown out. The tree has reached the state represented in the engraving, and is supplied with young, healthy, and vigorous roots, as well as more vigorous branches, with new layers of cambium and liber. It is, in reality, a new tree, which has taken the place of the prematurely old one, whose organs have ceased to live.

Analogous treatment to that which we have indicated for espalier trees may be followed with standards and pyramid trees; removing the objectionable branches eight or ten inches from the stem, and placing a crown or cleft graft on each, if it is considered necessary, but taking care to leave a fourth of the old branches, till the branches cut down have thrown out young shoots. In the second year, the remaining branches may be removed altogether, the extremity of the severed cuts, when made perfectly smooth, being covered over with grafting-paste.

By these processes, it is possible, except in cases of complete decay, to restore the tree to its first vigour, especially in the case of pip fruit, as the apple and pear. In stone fruit, the success is less assured; above all, it is doubtful in the peach, which scarcely ever produces buds on the old wood; and the application of grafting is had recourse to when it is desired to regenerate the tree, or to substitute an improved variety on an old but healthy stock. In this case, crown-grafting is adopted, and a graft placed at the extremity of each branch, which is cut down in the manner already described, favouring, in the mean while, the development of young wood at the base of the tree, by short pruning, and pinching off the buds at the summit.

RESERVE GARDEN.

Utility must be the principle embodied in laying out a reserve garden; this, however, is quite compatible with neatness and order.

No better system can be adopted than making a few good walks through the ground, and forming the latter into beds four feet wide, and any convenient lengths. Part of the ground can be left without division for raising hollyhocks and other large-growing plants, or for growing dahlias, &c., for exhibition or other special purposes. The beds can be used for raising annuals or biennials, for propagating choice varieties of pinks, carnations, polyanthuses, &c.; and for providing a reserve stock for verbena borders and flower-beds, &c. &c. Roses might be budded, choice shrubs layered, seedling rhododendrons, &c., nursed up here; new varieties of all bedding-plants preserved—seedlings, flowers—and experiments to find out the capabilities of any given plant, made in this department. Rich beds can also be provided for growing and layering chrysanthemums, salvias, &c., for potting in the autumn. We would not advise the beds to be divided by gravel walks; alleys cut with the spade, from one foot to 18 inches wide will suffice. The position of beds and paths can then be changed every second year, and the whole ground enjoy the benefit of the highest culture. In wet weather, a few boards may be thrown down on the earth-paths when much used. A dry soil—of great importance everywhere else—is essential here; as the three great agents in the germination of seeds are heat, moisture, and air. An excess of moisture, by reducing the temperature and excluding the air, decomposes the seed before the vital principle can develop itself. Hence, on wet soils, the frequent complaint of bad seed.

As its name imports, the reserve garden is not meant to be a special object of beauty in itself, but to provide the means of upholding a continuous display of beauty elsewhere. Many plants that are totally unfit, from the short duration of their bloom, to enter the flower-garden as permanent occupants, may, with perfect safety, be transplanted there for the display of their floral beauty, and be returned, as they fade, to the reserve garden. Of this class is the whole race of polyanthuses, hepaticas, hardy auriculas, primroses and violets. The winter aconite, *Helleborus hyemalis* and *niger*, *Arabis verna*, *Alyssum saxatile*, all the saxifrages, sedums, the campanulas, early-flowering phloxes, adonis, orobus, and other similar plants, should also be found here. All these, and any other plants of similar habit, may be moved into the flower-garden after the bedding-plants are cleared off in October or November, and taken back to the reserve garden in April or May, to make room for the more permanent flowering plants. Most of them are propagated by division of the root; and at the time they are transferred back to their summer quarters in the reserve garden will be the best period thus to increase the stock. When they are severally subdivided, it may be necessary to shade them for a time, as the profusion and perfection of next year's blossoms are dependent upon the healthy growth of their summer leaves. In no case, however, should shading be resorted to if the plants will bear full exposure to light and air without it; as direct sunlight is the great agent in elaborating the sap and inducing the production of flowers. The roots of some of the species, of which the Russian violet may be accepted as a representative, should be divided, and young plants formed annually. Others, of which the *Alyssum saxatile* is a type, flower better, and are much more effective as large plants or patches.

The reserve garden is also the proper place for sowing hardy annuals in the autumn, for embellishing the flower-garden in the spring. They should be sown thinly broadcast in beds, in September or October, and the oftener they are pricked out or transplanted the better. The checks incident to such operations insure profusion of bloom and hardiness of constitution.

In rapid-growing plants the sap is not only more abundant, but more watery, or thinner, than in those of slower growth. The affinity of frost for water especially exposes plants in this state to the full force of its blight-ing power. The thicker or more highly elaborated the sap, not only the more profuse the bloom, but the greater the power of the plant to resist cold. Hence the safety of brocoli that has been heeled over, and of stocks that have been transplanted, when both, left to grow freely, are killed by the frost; and hence, too, the benefit of transplanting those annuals that are intended to withstand the severity of the weather.

The following are among the best for this purpose:—*Calliopsis Drummondii*, *C. tinctoria*, *Clarkia pulchella*, *C. p. alba*, *Collinsia bicolor* and *grandiflora*, delphinums or larkspurs of sorts, *Bartonia aurea*, *Erysimum Perovskianum*, *Eschscholtzia californica*, *Gilia capitata* and *tricolor*, all the annual varieties of *Iberis* or candytufts, *Leptosiphon androsaceus* and *densiflorus*, white and pink Virginian stocks, *Limnanthes Douglasii*, and all the varieties of *Neomphila*, *Schizanthus humilis*, *porrigens*, and *Priestii*, and *Viscaria oculata*, will also stand through ordinary winters, and be useful in furnishing the flower-garden in spring or early summer.

Many of the spring-sown hardy annuals could also be raised here, although in most gardens where they are extensively grown, the majority of them are sown either in patches or lines, where they are intended to flower.

The reserve garden is also the proper nursing-place for the whole race of half-hardy annuals. Stocks, asters, marigolds, clintonias, calandrinas, lobelias, mesembryanthemums, portulacas, œnotheras, *Phlox Drummondii* (varieties), salpiglossis, maurandyas, tropæolums, &c., raised on a slight hotbed, must be gradually hardened off, and planted in rich soil in a warm corner, to be finally moved to their blooming quarters. Hardy biennials, such as wallflowers, Brompton stocks, sweetwilliams, foxgloves, &c. &c., should be sown here in May or June, and receive their proper culture throughout the summer. Any perennials, such as hollyhocks, that are raised from seed, should likewise be sown in the reserve garden, and treated the same as biennials. Cuttings of any plants that will root in the open air should also be inserted; and a corner should be devoted to shrubs that are intended to be increased by layering. Provision should also be made in this department for affording temporary shelter, and the means of gradually hardening off the whole stock of bedding-plants.

In places of any extent, the reserve garden should be furnished with ranges of cold and partially-heated pits and frames; and beds of rich soil, with raised edgings, of brick, stone, or wood, spanned over with hoops, to support mats, canvass, reed coverings, &c., in cold weather.

In most gardens there is a sad lack of means for the gradual transferring of plants to the open air, and several months of beauty in the flower-garden are often lost in consequence. These raised beds, which may be protected at pleasure, will also be the best possible positions for growing the choicest sorts of tulips, hyacinths, anemones, and other favourite flowers of early summer. It is generally considered better to plant hardy bulbs, such as crocuses, snowdrops, and the commoner tulips, say from one foot to 18 inches deep, and leave them permanently in the flower-beds or borders, than to remove them out of the way of the bedding-plants annually. Those, however, who object to this treatment will of course provide space for them in the reserve garden, and remove them thither when they plant out regular bedding-plants in May. All surplus stock, to fill blanks or repair accidents, should be neatly plunged in pots, ready to be moved when wanted. Others, that root more freely, and bear moving better, may be planted in rich soil for similar purposes; if not required to fill up gaps in the flower-beds, they will furnish strong early cuttings and cut flowers throughout the season. When the reserve garden is of sufficient dimensions, the whole of the cuttings and cut flowers should be derived from it, thus leaving the flower-garden in full perfection throughout the season. For want of such a reserve to fall back upon, some gardens have no sooner arrived at perfection than they are fearfully mangled, and their beauty marred, by the imperious demands of the propagator and decorator. Choice collections of pinks and carnations, dahlias, roses, and chrysanthemums, for show flowers, should also be grown here. The arrangements and special culture that some of these flowers require to produce them in the highest perfection, are hardly consistent with the high finish and refined enjoyment which should be the leading characteristic of every well-kept garden. When the flower-garden is furnished with shrubs for winter, space must be found for them in the reserve garden in summer. Small plants of hollies, laurels, box, acacias, berberries, sedums, kalmias, rhododendrons, and other flowering shrubs, are very effective and useful for this purpose. They may be either grown in pots or carefully moved without pots. After a few years' transplanting in good sound loam, they will be furnished with such compact balls of roots as to be moved with impunity at almost any period of summer or winter. Living plants are much better than branches of shrubs for relieving the bald outlines of flower-beds in winter. By studying the various shades of green, intermixing variegated varieties, and edging the shrubs with bulbs or other plants, to increase the effect, the garden may be made almost as interesting in winter and spring as at any other period.

The soil in the reserve garden should be varied, to suit its special uses. That most generally serviceable will be a rather heavy loam, which, by the addition of sand, leaf-mould, &c., will produce almost every conceivable variety best adapted to the varied purposes of this department. Some beds of peat should also be provided, and composts of various kinds laid up within easy distance. The size of the reserve garden will entirely depend upon the demands upon it. A plot a yard square may suffice for an amateur; a quarter or half an acre may be needful for some of our largest places. No garden, large or small, can be complete without one; for what the propagating, store, and growing houses are to the conservatory and drawing-room, the reserve garden is, or should be, to the flower-garden. It should not only be a great manufactory of raw material, but an inexhaustible warehouse, filled to overflowing with finished goods ready to be delivered whenever and wherever a supply is demanded.

RHODAN'THE (nat. ord. Compos'itæ). Half-hardy Annuals.

Everlastings of great beauty; valuable alike for the decoration of the conservatory and flower-garden; their neat compact growth renders them suitable for flower-beds and ribbons, while their rich-coloured flowers, elegant habit of growth, and profuse blooming, make them objects of universal admiration: the flowers, if gathered when young, are valuable for winter bouquets. Succeed best in a light rich soil and warm sheltered situation.

Rhodanthe Manglesii,—bright rose, with silvery calyx, 1 ft., from Swan River.

Rhodanthe maculata, — flowers nearly two inches in diameter, and of a bright rosy-purple, with yellow disc, surrounded by a conspicuous dark crimson ring. A first-class novelty.

Seed, from 4*d.* to 1*s.* per packet.

RHODODENDRONS.

Since the rise of the great Bagshot and Knaphill nurseries, rhododendrons have not only increased and multiplied, but improved so rapidly by crossing, that they are now, without exception, the most magnificent of all our hardy shrubs. They are also so cheap as to be brought within the reach of all, and yet many fine specimens are so valuable as to continue the luxuries of the rich. They vary in price from 15*s.* a hundred to 15 guineas a plant. Nothing equals the common Ponticum for underwood in plantations, or furnishing cover for game. There are about eighteen or twenty varieties of this class alone, including almost every shade of colour. The splendid Catawbiense variety has been almost equally fruitful in hybrids, and presents its formidable list of albums, roseums, purpureums, splendens, &c.

Amidst hosts of other hardy hybrids, from the scarlet arboreum, perhaps the following dozen are as good as any :—Blandyanum, Aclandianum, Atrosanguineum, John Waterer, Nobleanum, *Maculatum grandiflorum*, *Roseum picturatum*, Mrs. John Waterer, Victoria, Towardiana, Duchess of Sutherland, and Parryllianum. Doubtless there are a hundred more almost as good. Unless you have considerable experience, it is best to leave the selection to the nurseryman, stating the price per dozen or hundred. Fine plants of the above will range from 5*s.* to two guineas each. All rhododendrons require bog. They bear frequent removal ; but care must always be taken not to break the ball of earth or loosen the soil from the stem.

RHUBARB.

Directions for the cultivation of rhubarb will be found in the monthly calendars. It will grow without forcing; but is far better forced. The best kinds for early forcing are the Prince Albert and Linnæan, which force with less heat than most other kinds. If rhubarb be forced on the ground where it grows, nothing more is required than to cover with large pots and stable manure,—by this method it is blanched; but when forced in a frame, or otherwise, it is unnecessary to exclude the light, as there is no advantage in blanching it. Rhubarb may be planted at any time of the year, although mild weather in autumn or early spring is best: it should be planted on a clear open spot on good soil, which should be well trenched three feet deep. The plants should be not less than four feet apart ; or, where it is intended to take up some every year for forcing, a distance of three feet will be sufficient. Before planting, a good substance of very rotten manure should be worked into the soil. When the plants are to be increased, it is merely necessary to take up large roots and divide them with a spade : every piece that has a crown to it will grow ; and as it grows very quickly, this is a good method of propagating it. To insure fine rhubarb, a large dressing of well-rotted manure should be dug in about the roots, as soon as you have finished pulling the leaves. It is not right to wait till the winter before the plants are dressed.

RIBBON-PLANTING.

The ribbon style in border-planting is very effective. As an illustration of it take the following arrangement :—Supposing there be room for five or six rows, each row a foot or 18 inches wide,—a double row of *Lobelia speciosa* next the edging, followed by a row of verbenas,—Mrs. Holford's Snowflake, or any other white sort ; these, again, followed by *Calceolaria aurea*, this by Tom Thumb geranium. If there be room for more rows, the above may be followed by *Salvia patens* (blue), *Coreopsis lanceolata* (yellow), a row of white phlox, and a back row of dahlias. These should graduate in height and colour. This is merely given as a sample of what may be done. There are many plants that may be used in the same way, as *Kœnigia variegata*, isotomas, *Phlox Drummondii*, which are all dwarf, and suitable for front row; petunias, heliotropes, lantanas, &c., might form a second ; ageratums, galardias, salvias, a third. Again, mirabilis, still taller ; then dahlias and hollyhocks, tallest of all. Ribbons are also very pretty planted with annuals, as *Phlox Drummondii*, stocks, asters, zinnias, xeranthemums, and sweet peas, all which graduate in height and vary in colour. These may be raised in frames in March and planted out in May, or sown in the open ground in May. Hardy annuals may be sown early in spring, and be allowed to flower, and then followed by bedding-plants or by biennials, which are best sown in May and planted out. Hardy herbaceous plants alone may keep a border perpetually gay, but are not well suited for massing. They should, however, be arranged with regard to height and colour. Pansies, daisies, primroses, selines, &c., being dwarf; pinks, cloves, carnations, veronicas, &c., taller; phloxes, various sorts of campanulas, chrysanthemums, &c.; starworts, rudbeckkias, &c., being tallest of all. Plants of this class flower at various times of the year, from early spring to late in the autumn. Where spring-flowering bulbs are mixed up with them, it is not advisable to plant them near the edge of the beds. Plant them far back; as they flower when the borders are comparatively bare, they are sure to be seen to advantage; and the long grassy leaves do not disfigure the borders after they have flowered. Late bulbs, as gladiolus and lilies, being tall, should be placed far enough back to correspond with the other plants. A very good effect may be produced by planting a ribbon border or clump with plants of ornamental foliage. These look better than most people would imagine. The very commonest and cheapest of plants may be made use of; for instance, a front row of variegated arabis, which is a very common, hardy, herbaceous plant; second row, Henderson's beet, treated as an annual. This is a dwarf, and very bright crimson-coloured sort, and grows about eight or 10 inches high; third row, antenaria, or variegated mint; fourth row, *Perilla nankinensis*—annual; fifth row, ribbon-grass; sixth row, purple arack, *Atriplex rubra*. These graduate in height and colour, have a very pretty effect, and last the whole summer and autumn.

RI'CINUS (nat. ord. Euphorbia'ceæ).
Half-hardy Annuals.

A magnificent and highly ornamental genus. The picturesque foliage, and stately growth (6 to 10 feet in height), combined with the brilliant coloured fruit of the Giant varieties, impart to select plantations, shrubbery, and flower-borders, quite an oriental aspect. In the gardens around Paris they form one of the principal features of attraction, and if planted out and grown as single specimens on our lawns and pleasure-grounds, ornamental foliage plants would form a new and striking feature. The dwarf varieties (three to four feet in height) are of a compact growth, with rich and beautiful-coloured foliage, stems, and fruit: these are peculiarly adapted for breaking the monotony and giving a picturesque effect to the flower-borders of suburban gardens: succeed best in rich soil.

Seed, from 3*d.* to 1*s.* per packet.

ROCKETS (nat. ord. Crucif'eræ).

Very pleasing early-spring-flowering hardy perennials, with deliciously fragrant flowers; grow freely in any soil.

Rocket, Sweet,—purple, 1½ ft., from Europe.
" " white, 1½ ft., "
" " mixed, 1½ ft., "

Seed, 2*d.* per packet.

ROCK-WORK.

Few ornaments of a garden have a better effect than rock-work properly disposed; while at the same time it is also very useful. By means of it, not unfrequently, an ugly corner may be turned to very good account, and very many plants will be found to flourish and do well upon rock-work which can hardly be kept alive elsewhere. Sometimes, when the garden or pleasure-ground is very extensive, a piece of rock-work may appear to be needed on its own account, to form a break in the scene; in which case it will be desirable that the work be constructed of the stone of the country, to give to it as natural an appearance as possible; but, in a general way, for rock-work which is intended to be covered with plants, any material that comes most readily to hand may be made use of. The flint stones from the chalk and marl pits, where they can be had, form excellent rock-work; and so, of course, do the different spars of Devonshire and Derbyshire also. As a general rule, rock-work should never be raised on grass, but on gravel, or on a concrete foundation. It is also well placed around a pond or water-tank. In the centre of a square gravelled plot, a tall piece of rock-work is a very pleasing object.

It may be constructed by using the roots of old trees piled one upon another as a basis, which should be well covered with a good coating of fine loam. On this the stones may be built up, in any form that good taste may suggest, interstices, with more or less of surface, being left, which will in this way form beds for the different plants. The spring of the year is the best season for making rock-work, since the soil will have time to settle, and the stones to become fixed in their position before the next winter's frost. Almost every county in England has some material natural to it from which rock-work can be formed,—even the larger stones of the gravel-pits may be used for this purpose; and, in the absence of anything else, blistered clay from the brickyards and clinkers from the smith's furnaces are not to be rejected. The seashore also, all along the coast, affords plenty of material out of which a little taste and good judgement will soon arrange something both agreeable to the eye and useful as a bed for many different classes of plants. On the tall piece of rock-work which has just been described may be planted almost every variety of hardy or half-hardy creepers,—lophospermums, *Maurandya canariensis*, the different sorts of periwinkle, &c. &c.; while lower down, between the stones, cistuses, saxifrages, and sedums may be grown. The wild sedums of our different counties form most interesting collections when placed by themselves in a separate piece of rock-work; and so also do the wild ferns. The writer of these remarks has formed on a piece of rock-work under a north wall in his garden, what to himself is a most interesting collection of seventeen or eighteen different varieties of ferns, gathered with his own hands in different places in Norfolk. Many other counties in England are much richer in these natural beauties, which, when arranged in rock-work as county collections, will well repay any one for the time and trouble spent in searching for them.

ROLLERS.

Rollers for garden purposes are best made of cast iron, with wrought iron mountings. The most useful sizes are from 20 to 24 inches. The cost of them at Messrs. Barnard & Bishop's works, Norwich, is from 50*s.* to £3. 10*s.*

ROOT-PRUNING.

This is an important operation in gardening: it is performed by laying bare the roots three feet from the stem of the tree; then with a sharp axe, or chisel and mallet, cutting through a portion of the strongest roots, according to the requirements of the tree. If the tree is extremely vigorous, without producing fruit, two-thirds of the stronger roots cut through in this manner will probably restore it to a state of perfect bearing; the trench being filled up with fresh virgin mould, and the tree left at rest for a year. The proper season for root-pruning is the autumn, when the roots will send forth small fibrous spongioles, which elaborate the sap, and form blossom-buds. Should this operation fail to check the superfluous vigour of the tree, the roots may be again laid bare in the following autumn, and the remaining large roots then cut away, avoiding, as much as possible, all injury to the smaller fibres which have pushed out from the previous operation. Should the tree still present an over-vigorous growth, it must be taken up entirely, and all the strong roots pruned in, then re-planted, taking care that in re-planting, the tree is raised considerably above its former level,—a severe operation, but certain to be successful in reducing a tree to a fruitful state.

ROSA MULTIFLORA.

Of this there are many varieties, chiefly of Italian origin: it is a delicate rose, and often killed to the ground by the frost. Covered with mats, it shoots so early that it cannot endure the spring frosts. Grevillea, or Seven Sisters rose, is a vigorous climber of this family, blooming in clusters, of shades varying from rose to purplish crimson; the flowers change from crimson at first coming out, to pale rose and purplish crimson. The protection recommended by Mr. Rivers, is to thatch over the pillar in November with green furze, which admits air and keeps off the severity of the frost; continuing this covering till March, and then removing it by degrees, so as to inure the plant to the cold before full exposure to it. In this way, Alba, or Double White, a pretty pale flesh-coloured rose; the Double Red, and Hybrida, or Laure Davoust, a most elegant and beautiful hybrid, with large flowers and beautiful foliage, will bloom in perfection.

ROSE-CULTURE.

The Rose is propagated by seeds, by cuttings, by layers, by budding, and by grafting, and new varieties are produced by hybridization,—that is, by transfusing the male pollen of one flower into the stigma of another, with the object of producing seed which shall reproduce the best properties of both the parent plants.

Botanists apply the term hybridization to a plant produced from two parents of different species; and of all products of vegetation the Rose has, perhaps, yielded the most numerous varieties to cultivation: this has also occurred, in all probability, in a state of nature. A plant is in flower, and the wind, an insect, or the industrious hand of the gardener, conveys the pollen or powdery matter which accumulates on the ripe style of the male flowers, to the equally ripe stigmata of the female flower. The stigma absorbs the moisture from the dusty particles of the pollen, and it fructifies; the seed which results from the operation produces a new variety, partaking of the more prominent properties of both parents.

The great obstacle to hybridizing in our climate is the difficulty found in ripening the seeds. Tea-scented and Chinese roses must be grown under glass to do so. Many other varieties, however, ripen their seeds sufficiently out of doors, and Mr. Paul gives a list of twenty kinds which ripen their seeds perfectly in this country in ordinary seasons. These are:

Hybrid Chinese,—Chénédole; Marshal Soult; Duke of Devonshire: General Allard.
Hybrid Bourbons,—Athelin; Great Western; Charles Duval.
Moss,—Du Luxembourg; Celina.
Hybrid Perpetuals,—Madame Laffay: Comtesse Duchatel; William Jesse.
Austrian Brier,—Harrisonii.
Bourbons,—Bouquet de Flore; Malvina; Ceres.
Rosomène,—Gloire de Rosomène.
French,—Rosa Mundi.
Multiflora,—Russelliana.
Ayrshire,—Splendens.

Having chosen suitable varieties for experimenting upon, and decided the several questions which bear upon the object of the operation, such as the qualities to be obtained from each parent, bearing in mind that colour is supposed to belong to the female and foliage and habit to the male, "they should be planted," Mr. Paul says, "in the sunniest spot in the garden, in a soil not too rich, for this promotes a vegetation too vigorous for the perfect development of the seeds. In pruning, the branches should not be shortened very closely; while growing, the soil ought to be hoed occasionally during spring, and watered in dry weather, caterpillars sought by hand, and aphis got rid of by syringing with soot or tobacco-water. As the flower-buds increase in size, secure a good portion of the earliest and boldest buds, but not all; leave some in different stages of forwardness, and remove all buds forming imperfectly, or in places where the branches will shade them."

Having selected the plant to be impregnated, as well as that from which the pollen is to be taken, and having removed the stigma of the female flower with a pair of round-pointed scissors, just as the flowers begin to expand, both flowers being in a fit state for the operation, the flower of the male parent is brought just over the seed-bearing tree. If the weather is calm, the petals of the former are cut away, the operator holds a finger over the flower of the latter, while the tree deprived of its petals is struck a sharp blow. This sudden shock drives the pollen into the other flower, and the work is done. When the wind is high, it is better to collect the pollen on a camel-hair pencil, and convey it to the styles of the female flower. It is of much importance that both plants are grown in the same temperature. The stigma is known to be in a fit state for fertilizing by a viscous exudation of its sutures; when this is the case, no time should be lost in completing the operation.

When the flowers have disappeared, and the seed-pods begin to swell and ripen, they should be protected from birds; they should remain on the trees till perfectly ripe, and turning black, when they should be gathered to be sown, and buried in the earth, either in pots or in the ground, taking care that proper numbers are attached to them, so that there may be no doubt as to the origin of the expected progeny.

The operation of cleaning the seeds is performed by rubbing them out between the hands, preparatory to sowing in February or March. As soon as the seed-pods are broken up, lay the seeds out in the sun to dry, so that the pulp and husk may be entirely removed, and the seeds sifted and winnowed ready for sowing. Some prefer sowing the seed immediately on its reaching maturity, and this M. Boitard considers the best plan. In this case they come up the following spring, with all the fine growing season before them.

The hardier kinds may be sown in the open borders, selecting a sunny spot, with an eastern aspect, and sheltered from the afternoon sun: the more tender varieties require a frame and glass.

The beds for the hardier kinds should be dug 18 inches deep, the soil light and rich, the top spit broken up fine and raked level. In sowing, let the seed be laid on the top, spread pretty thick, as only a third or fourth will come up. Beat the beds smooth with the back of a spade, water, if dry weather, and sift over the whole about half an inch of light sandy soil. If the sowing takes place in spring, keep the seeds in water for three or four hours before sowing, taking care that the germ of the seed, now developed more or less, is not injured. The more delicate roses should be sown in pans thoroughly drained and filled with equal parts of leaf-mould and yellow loam well mixed together. Water, when sown, as directed above, and cover with half an inch of the same soil mixed with a little sand. In each case a sprinkling of soot or lime scattered over the bed will be a necessary precaution against insects and worms. About May some of the seeds will germinate, and others will come up from time to time till autumn; they now require constant care in shading, weeding, and watering when when the soil is dry.

Roses may be increased by budding, by cuttings, by grafting, and by suckers. Special directions for budding will be found under that head, and need not be repeated.

By Cuttings.—Most roses may be increased by cuttings; but all are not alike calculated for being thus propagated, bottom-heat being indispensable for the more tender varieties. Where it is necessary to propagate a number of plants from one, however, the method is invaluable; it is especially useful in the case of Chinese and Indian roses, where the young branches are inclined to be woody. Summer and autumn are the best seasons for cuttings. The shoot made in spring is taken with a small portion

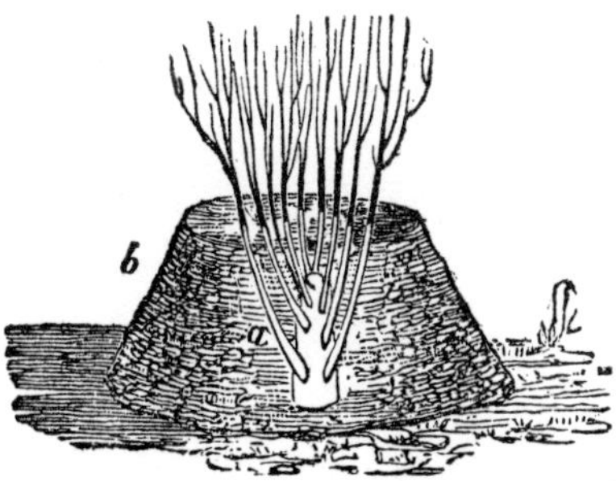

of last year's wood attached, and cut into lengths of five or six inches, selecting such as have two lateral shoots, with five or six leaves to each. An inch of the old wood should be inserted in the soil, leaving at least two leaves above. From four to six of these cuttings may be placed round the inside of a 60-pot, in soil consisting of equal parts of leaf-mould, turfy loam chopped fine, and silver-sand, watering them well with a fine rose-pot, to settle the earth round the roots. When the water is drained off, and the leaves dry, remove to a cold frame, or place them under hand-glasses, shade them from the sun, excluding the dew, and sprinkling them daily for a fortnight. If threatened with damping off, give air and sun. In a fortnight *callus* will be formed. At this time they are greatly benefited by bottom-heat; they root more rapidly, and may soon be shifted singly into 60-pots, and removed back to the cold frame for planting out in August, without bottom-heat. They must be kept in the frames till the spring.

Grafting is performed by cutting the top of the stock to a proper height by a clean horizontal cut; then make a longitudinal V-shaped cut down the centre, one, two, or three inches long, according to the size of the stock. In this slit place the graft, after having cut the lower end of it to fit the cut in the stock. Having inserted it, bind the whole up with clay or grafting-paste, as directed in budding.

It has been asked whether roses *grafted* are equal to budded ones. Mr. Paul says, when the junction is perfect they are quite as good; but the scion and stock do not always coalesce, owing to which, more imperfect plants are raised in this way than by budding. The best time for grafting roses in pots is January; and July, in ordinary seasons, is the best month for budding; but that depends upon the season. Some operators prefer a moist gloomy day for the operation.

By Suckers. — Roses — some kinds much more than others—push their roots in a lateral direction under ground, and throw up young shoots or suckers from them; these suckers, separated from the parent root by the cut of a sharp spade, form flowering plants the same season, if separated in the spring and transplanted to suitable soil. When a rosetree is shy with its suckers, it may be stimulated by heaping earth round the roots.

ROSES IN POTS.

The best compost for roses in pots is a good stiff loam one bushel, rotten dung from an old hotbed one peck, and half a gallon of pigeon-dung, or double the quantity of sheep-dung, well decomposed. Another good soil is a turfy loam, rather stiff, and well-decomposed cow-dung in about equal parts. These, with good drainage in the pots, gentle forcing, careful examination for insects, and keeping the trees well balanced and neatly trained and tied down to their supports, with constant attention to watering with liquid manure, as well as pure water, will produce abundance of bloom. All the strong-growing varieties, such as Hybrid Provence, Hybrid China, Hybrid Bourbon, French, Moss, Alba, Hybrid Perpetuals, and the strong-growing Bourbons and Noisettes, should be potted in autumn; the delicate Bourbons and Noisettes, together with the Tea-scented and Chinas, should be left till the spring. In the autumn, before potting, examine the stocks minutely, particularly among the roots, cutting out any decayed parts, all knots, and the remains of suckers; lop any wounded or bruised roots, and clean all well, as no such opportunity will again offer. When potted, cut back the head about a third, and at the end of February or the beginning of March cut back to from two to four eyes. In potting, let the pots be well drained with from one inch to an inch and a half of broken crocks, used in large rough pieces, having the concave side downwards. The pots should not be over large,—from six to eight inches inside the rims will be sufficient, according to the size of the plant, condition of its roots, &c.

The pots should be plunged to their rims in coal ashes, or any garden soil, on an inverted flowerpot, leaving a cavity underneath each to prevent the ingress of worms. In this state they should remain till about the middle of May, when they will require a shift. The same soil as before should be used, but, if possible, more rough, and they should be again plunged to the rim. During summer they will require constant attention as to watering; they should have liquid manure at least once a week, using soft water at other times. The best liquid manure is the drainage of dunghills, and sheep or cow-dung steeped in water and drawn off clear. Guano is excellent, but it requires great caution in using, owing to its variable quality. If, therefore, it is used, err on the safest side, and give it weak,—half a pound of guano to eight or ten gallons of water. During summer the plants require constant attention in taking off all suckers as they appear, as well as all flower-buds, as they are not intended to bloom this season. If the plants are too crowded with wood, they should be thinned out moderately, so that the remaining shoots may perfect their growth. All strong, gross, or watery shoots should have their extreme points pinched off before they get long,—say at six or eight inches: they will soon break out afresh, and add to the bushiness of the plant. If all goes well, these plants will, about the beginning of August, require another shift, which should not be over large. They must be treated in every respect as before until the end of September, when they should be shifted into their blooming-pots.

RUSSIAN VIOLETS.

To have an abundance of fine flowers in the autumn and early spring, these should be planted in beds under a wall, in a warm aspect. The soil should be light, but very highly manured, with a large quantity of sand about four inches underneath the top soil. The roots should be planted in rows about three or four inches apart, and well watered. Every year, about Valentine's day, immediately after they have done flowering, the beds should be broken up, the soil renewed, and fresh plants set for another year. Even if the old beds have not done flowering, fresh beds should not be delayed beyond the last week in February.

SAGE.

This useful garden herb is a salvia, which is a very extensive genus in botany. All the kinds should be grown in a light rich soil, and are propagated by cuttings, the division of roots, and seed.

SALSAFY.

This may be sown about the end of April or beginning of May. It is best to sow this seed in drills 15 inches apart, or thereabouts, and thin to six inches in the row. The roots of the plant are usually eaten in the same way as radishes, being often a substitute for them during the winter; in the spring-time, the young shoots are blanched and used as seakale.

SAPONA'RIA (nat.ord. Caryophylla'ceæ).

Of these charming little plants it is impossible to speak too highly; they carpet the ground with their pretty little star-shaped flowers during the summer and autumn months. For edgings they are unequalled, bearing cutting back, if necessary, for a late autumn bloom; in beds they produce a fine effect, while in ribbons, the pink, rose, and white make a striking combination. *S. ocymoides* flowers so profusely in the spring and early summer months as literally to present to the eye a sheet of rosy pink: a fine rock-plant.

Saponaria Calabrica (true),—rich deep pink, ½ ft., from Calabria, hardy annual.
Saponaria Calabrica rosea,—rose, ½ ft., hardy annual.
Saponaria Calabrica alba,—pure white, ½ ft., hardy annual.
Saponaria ocymoides,—rose-pink, ¼ ft., from Europe, hardy perennial.

Seed, 4*d.* per packet.

SAVOY.

The Savoy has been in cultivation in this country since the times of Gerarde, by whom it is described. It is distinguished by its curly leaves and deep green colour from the cabbage; it grows a compact, well-shaped head, and it is propagated by seed in the spring. Sown on a hotbed in February, or on beds in the open ground early in April, plants will be ready for planting out permanently in May, June, and July.

In all respects the treatment is the same as with cabbages, removing the plants to a nursery-bed when two inches high, selecting the strongest plants first. When planted out permanently, they should stand two feet apart in the rows and 20 inches between the plants; but it is not unusual to plant them between standing crops of peas or other less permanent crops, whose place they thus occupy when removed.

SAW-FLIES.

Among the saw-flies, so called from the females possessing a saw-like apparatus at the extremity of the body, *Cladius difformis*, which is very destructive in gardens, measures a sixth of an inch in length, black and shining in body, with dirty yellowish-white legs. It feeds upon the leaves of various kinds of roses; the caterpillars are found feeding on them in the beginning of July, remaining in the pupa state a fortnight or three weeks, when they appear as perfect insects.

SCARLET RUNNERS.

These may be planted at any time from April to late in July. The seed should be dropped about four inches apart, and if a line be selected along the two sides of a walk in the kitchen-garden, a very pretty shady avenue may be made. Plant stakes seven or eight feet high in the row where the beans are; set two or three stakes to the yard, and bend them over at the top to form arches. In the spaces between the stakes place pea-sticks, to which the runners may at first be trained. The stakes should be tied together by wands arranged longitudinally, one along the top and one halfway up each side. When this framework becomes covered with scarlet runners, a very pleasant shady walk will be formed. With a little care in manuring and watering, the runners may be kept green and in bearing till killed by the autumn frosts. The runners will blossom and bear much more freely if the old beans are all removed, and they are not allowed to ripen seed. A mixture of the white Dutch runner with the scarlet runner gives to the avenue a very pretty effect.

SCORZONERA.

This is sown in the same manner as salsafy, and, by some, is much esteemed. To have it large, it should remain over the second season. It seldom grows large enough for use the first year, but is none the worse for remaining two or even three years before using.

SCREENS.

If a screen be needed in the garden, it may easily be managed, and with a very good effect, by means of hollyhocks and chrysanthemums. Hedges of either of these flowers will serve to shut out from view anything that may be required, and at the same time produce a beautiful effect. Hollyhocks can be staked separately in the line where they are wanted; but with chrysanthemums the best plan is to stretch a rough wire fence to which they may be trained. This may be made of a few rough stakes supporting three or four rows of wire, over which on both sides the plants may be trained after the fashion of espaliers, so as to cover all the framework. Many other plants also there are which will suggest themselves to every gardener as capable of forming a pleasing and effective temporary hedge.

SEAKALE.

This useful vegetable may be grown from offsets and from seed.

Preparation of the Soil.—To grow seakale in the highest perfection, the ground must be deep and rich, and should be trenched two or three feet deep, working in a very liberal dressing of the richest manure. In strong tenacious soils, two or three inches of sharp sand or finely-sifted ashes, well mixed in, will be of service. The readiest method of propagation is by offsets, but it may be raised from seed.

Time and Manner of Sowing.—Sow in lines, as early in April as the ground is ready. Scatter the seed thinly, and cover it with about an inch of free soil. The distance which should be allowed between the lines will depend upon whether the plants are to be transplanted the following season, or used for forcing, or are to be cut where they grow. In the former case the rows should be 15 to 18 inches apart, and the plants thinned out to a foot apart; in the latter, 2 feet 6 inches should be left between the rows, and from 12 to 15 inches between the plants. In peculiarly favourable soils, roots of a useful size for forcing may be obtained the first season, but in most cases it would be advisable to sow in lines 12 or 15 inches apart, and transplant in the following spring, allowing 2 feet 6 inches between the rows, and 1 foot 3 inches between the plants.

Cultivation.—Destroy weeds as they appear, and keep the surface open by frequent deep stirrings. During the growing season give a liberal soaking of manure-water when the ground is dry, or a light sprinkling of salt, washed in with clear water, which will answer equally well. Keep the plants to one crown, or shoot, cutting off others, and removing seed-shoots as soon as they appear. After the second season's growth, the roots will be in the best possible condition for taking up and forcing, or for producing a crop of fine large kale where they stand.

Seed, 4*d.* per packet; 6*d.* per ounce.

SEED-SOWING.

The following observations upon the

sowing of garden flower-seeds have the advantage of the experience of Messrs. Henderson, of Wellington Nursery, St. John's Wood, London, and, if closely followed, they will generally insure success. Too frequently good seed has to bear the blame of bad management.

Preparation, or Mode of Sowing Seeds.—In the majority of instances, the treatment recommended is the best in such situations where soil, locality, and other causes require care; for, in more favoured sheltered positions, the plants may succeed with more hardy treatment. Small seeds should only be lightly covered with soil, and if unusually dry weather prevail, a slight surface protection with moss or similar material is beneficial until the seeds have well germinated. The scale of humidity and temperature adapted to the germination of seeds and rearing of young plants is regulated by the temperature plants are capable of bearing in their mature growth. The hardier the species, the lower the average temperature required for germination, and *vice versâ*, allowing for the artificial stimulus naturally required for establishing young plants in their primary stages of growth. The absence of surface- or bottom-heat may in some measure be compensated by early ventilation, if required; and, where compatible, closing up pits or houses with a high degree of sunheat and artificial moisture. As a uniformly modified degree of moisture in the soil is indispensable to the successful germination of seeds, it is important that the seed stores or pots should never remain parched or dry overnight: such omissions, when repeated often, prove injurious to the vital germs, and cause the eventual loss of the produce.

The following may very well serve as types of the different sorts of seeds. Martynia, abroma, and tropæolum generally require peeling previously; cobœa is best planted edgeways; geranium pricked in, leaving the feathery tail or pedicle out. Calceolaria germinates best without heat. Ipomœa and convolvulus, when very dry, or as old imported seed, often refuse to vegetate. They should be taken up and slightly cut on the surface, or on the edge, apart from the eye or vital speck (where it exists outwardly), which should be preserved from injury. Rhodanthe, and other seeds of similar character, should be well soaked in water before sowing. Cyclamen should be sown as soon as ripe. Orchid seed may be sown on a rough-barked block, and suspended in the shady, humid atmosphere of a tropical stove or orchid-house: warmth and continued moisture are essential. Ferns should be sown on the surface of rather coarse heath-soil, without further covering them. Place over a flat square of glass, or a bell-shaped one; place the pot in a dish, and keep the surface-soil uniformly moist and covered until the plant germs are well developed, after which very gradually admit air. Seeds of *Clianthus Dampieri* should be sown singly, each in a small pot. Mistletoe seeds should be inserted within the bark, on the underside of the branches, to prevent the birds from feeding upon them.

In the sowing of exotic seeds in pots, especially those of a small and delicate structure, and those in which germination is slow and irregular, one very essential point consists in obtaining the most suitable quality of soil for surface-covering. Whilst it is important that the bulk of soil used in such operations should be well pulverized, and proportionately porous throughout, in order to admit of a free and quick growth during and after germination (which a too retentive and close quality is unfavourable to), it is still more important that the soil with which the seed is covered should not only be well pulverized but also rendered less retentive of moisture. For effecting this, where prepared soils are not at hand, that which is intended either as a mixture or otherwise should be passed through a suitable sieve, and also be thinly spread in the open air, or exposed to the influence of artificial heat until thoroughly dry or parched.

In making use of the soil thus dried for covering seeds, it is best sprinkled with pure water, and passed through the hands until it admits of being easily spread. By thus reducing the retentive quality of the soil, it admits of a more uniform and healthy circulation of moisture during the first growth of the young seedlings, and, moreover, preserves the surface soil from becoming stagnant by the incipient germination of moss, &c., brought on in unprepared soils by repeated after-waterings. Two very important benefits arise from using a less retentive quality of soil for covering seeds: first, it admits of a proportionately greater depth of soil upon the seeds, while being equally pervious to the atmosphere; thus acting as a preserving medium in the case of small and delicate seeds exposed to extreme alternations of temperature; secondly, it dispenses to a great extent with the excess of sand in mixture, which is too often used in covering seeds generally. Beyond the requisite amount of it as a mechanical agent or force in modifying too retentive soils, sand only impoverishes in proportion to its bulk. The more nutritive the elements of soil for the growth of plants, the less they are subject to injury by extremes of temperature, other conditions being equal, and *vice versâ*. In all cases where rare or delicate-bodied seeds, uncertain in their periods of germination, are covered with prepared soil, as described in the foregoing remarks, it is requisite that the pots or seed-pans thus sown should be carefully well watered immediately to settle the soil down to a uniform surface, suitable for after-waterings. As all seeds lie dormant in the soil for given periods previous to the swelling of the inner substance, which is the first evidence of their fermentation, it is not safe to give successive heavy waterings for a short time after the first application, as referred to. Even the softest seeds should be but gradually moistened, and not repeatedly gorged with water, before they are able to digest or decompose it through the medium of living organs; and from this fact it is legitimately inferred that there should always be a due period allowed between the first repeated waterings of seeds, to admit of a healthy evaporation from the surface soil at each watering, especially where the material for covering seeds has been indiscriminately applied, without previous exposure to the ameliorating and purifying influences of sun and air. Daily or alternate waterings are essential, when required, first by the gradual upheaving of the surface soil, and secondly, by the bursting or expansion of the seed-lobes above the soil. Water may always be given more freely with advancing growth to the most delicate germs, admitting a healthy evaporation or dryness of surface as the test of a further supply. The importance of uniform attention to watering may be best learnt by experience and observation; but the inexperienced cultivator may be reminded, that to omit a single watering overnight of young plant-germs from seeds, when in a parched state, often leads to the eventual loss of the whole, and, in many individual instances, is the incipient cause of constitutional debility throughout the entire life of the plant.

SEPTEMBER.

The reduction of temperature begins to be felt this month, less, however, by night than by day, the mean temperature of the air being 66·14°; one foot below the surface, 57·54°; and two feet, 57·89°; being, from this month till April, warmer at two feet than at one foot. The average fall of rain is also increased considerably, falling more in the night than in the day. It abounds, however, in delicious autumnal days, when the air, the sky, and the earth seem lulled into universal calm,—softer and milder even than in May.

Flower-Garden and Shrubberies.—Now that the beds are thoroughly covered, nothing contributes more to a high style of keeping than the removal of every dead flower and leaf as fast as they appear, the maintenance of neat edgings, and sharply-defined lines of coloured or ribbon borders, or beds planted on the ring principle. Generally, it would be bad taste, except in beds planted on the pincushion system, to allow one colour to run into the other.

Regularity of height is also another proof of high keeping. Not that every bed, or every part of a bed, should be of one dead uniform height, but it should either present a level or an even surface. Suppose, for instance, a bed is raised in the middle, as a rule it should gradually fall towards the sides, and the same parts of the bed should be of the same height. If the edging is six inches high, it should be this height all round; if the second row is nine inches, it should be nine inches throughout, and so on. Nothing is more indicative of a want of judgment in planting, or of slovenly keeping, than a row or bed six inches here, 12 there, and 10 at another point, without regular gradation. Second only in importance to the blending of proper colours, is the arrangement of plants according to their proper heights. Of course the appearance of a weed, great or small, on either beds or ground, is quite inconsistent with high keeping. Closely-strewn well-rolled turf has a powerful influence in exhibiting floral beauty in the best light. In harmony with all this the walks must be scrupulously clean, hard, smooth, and bright. While enjoying the present beauty of the flower-garden, we must, especially during this month, have regard to the wants of another season.

All trimmings of verbenas, ageratums, geraniums, calceolarias, &c. &c., that are cut off to maintain sharp lines, clearly-defined edgings, &c., must be inserted as cuttings. Where enough cannot be thus secured, the thickest parts of lines or beds must be thinned for this purpose; or, better still, plants that were placed in the reserve-garden for this object must be cut down and divided into small morsels for cuttings.

Dahlias will require careful tying, disbudding, and thinning off the shoots, where first-rate flowers are required; a good soaking of manure-water in dry weather will also be most serviceable to them. The blooms of hollyhocks may be much prolonged by similar treatment. All offsets of the best varieties ought to be inserted as cuttings, and previously-rooted cuttings planted in the reserve-garden.

Roses.—Perpetuals may still be cut back with the hope of a third bloom; and late-budded plants will require looking after, watering, and training to stakes.

Pot off layers of carnations as fast as rooted, water sparingly, and place in a cold frame for a few days until they make a fresh start.

Plant out in beds early-rooted pansy cuttings, insert a succession of cuttings, and prick out seedlings in the reserve-garden. Here also let seedllng polyanthuses, offsets of these and auriculas, be planted on rich shady beds. Stocks sown in pans, or in the reserve-garden, in August, will now be fit either to pot off and place in frames until established, or to prick out on shady beds in this department. The first sowing of hardy annuals to stand the winter in the open air should also be made towards the end of the month. Prepare beds for, and plant out, pinks for next year's blooming; hunt for and destroy earwigs on dahlias, hollyhocks, &c., and see that everything is being prepared by a season of healthy growth to meet the trials and storms of winter, as well as to add to the loveliness and increase the glory of this delightful autumnal month.

Kitchen-garden.—To secure a supply of vegetables in the winter and early spring, all arrangements not already completed should be made without delay; the growth of those already planted must be encouraged by hoeing and stirring the earth round the roots, and where slugs abound, their ravages counteracted by sowing soot or lime on the soil.

Celery.—The earthing-up of this useful vegetable now demands special attention. The sowings made in July and August will be ready for transplanting.

Cauliflowers may still be sown in some situations, and those sown last month pricked out under hand-glasses, or in frames, as they advance: if the season is mild, they may be planted out under a south wall. Those plants advancing and heading should have the large leaves broken and turned over them, to give shelter from sun and rain, and the earth drawn round the stem. The plants sown in May will now be ready for planting out in rows two feet and a half asunder: give them a copious watering.

Cabbages.—Prepare a piece of ground by deep trenching and heavy manuring, for spring cabbages, savoys, and winter greens, and keep it forked over regularly until the plants are sufficiently advanced for planting out. When ready, plant in rows two feet apart, watering well to settle the earth at their roots. Savoys and spring cabbages, in particular, require a rich soil thoroughly manured.

Brocoli also require a good soil richly manured. Plant them out from the beds in rows where they are to grow, two feet apart each way: water till the plants have rooted. Mr. Errington finds an advantage in dibbling a large hole to receive the plants, and filling it up with calcined wood or vegetable ashes. This crop may follow peas with advantage, or be set between the rows of late sorts.

Brocoli seeds may be sown to stand the winter, and come up for a late spring crop.

Brussels Sprouts and Winter Greens.—Plant out for autumn use.

Endive seeds sown now will come in to supply plants for winter use; the green curled being the best for main crops. Water the beds in dry weather, and tie up to blanch plants advancing to maturity.

Small Salading.—Sow cresses, mustard, radishes, and other small salads, every seven days, choosing a shady border and sowing in very shallow drills: water daily.

Lettuces. — Sow cos and cabbage lettuces in a bed of rich mellow ground; in the first, second, and fourth week, prick out on nursery-beds the plants last sown, and plant out the strongest plants in the open ground. Dig neatly and rake evenly, and put in the plants by line 12 inches apart each way: continue to water till rooted.

Spinach, for winter use, sown late in July or early in August, should now be planted out. The prickly-seeded or triangular-leaved is the hardiest for winter use.

Turnip-radishes (black and white) should now be sown for winter use; also some small Italian (white and red) for autumn use.

Onions may be sown of the Strasburg and Welsh sorts, early this month; the former to transplant in the spring, the latter for use in salads. The general crop will be ready for harvesting.

Carrots should be sown in an open situation, and on light soil, sowing them as soon as the bed will work after digging.

Turnips may still be sown for autumn and winter use, the Early Stone being a good sort: sow immediately after digging. Hoe the crops sown in May and June in dry weather, and thin out till the plants are seven or eight inches apart.

Fruit-garden.—The chief work to be done in the fruit-garden and orchard is harvesting the fruit and preparation for planting. Let it be understood with regard to the latter, that while something of the future success depends on soil, subsoil, and situation, perfect drainage is the main point. Soil and subsoil may both be corrected by properly-prepared stations, if the drainage be sufficient; without this success is impossible.

Early apples and pears should be gathered a day or two before they are ripe: it is a very good plan to make two or three gatherings from the same tree, for, if gathered too soon, the fruit shrivels, and if suffered to remain on the tree after maturity, much of the best fruit will fall and get bruised. As they are gathered, lay the pears singly, and the apples in tiers, not more than two deep ; and separate carefully all bruised fruit.

Peaches and Nectarines require to have the future bearing-shoots nailed in closely, and all laterals not required removed, so that the fruit may have the full benefit of the sun, from which it derives colour and flavour. A few of the leaves may also be removed where they shade the fruit too much. As the fruit approaches its ripened state, nets should be extended beneath it to catch any that fall. To protect the fruit from wasps, use Haythorn's hexagon netting ; it admits of perfectly free circulation of air, and at the same time keeps off wasps and flies. Should mildew appear at any time, dust the shoots with flour of sulphur : an occasional washing with soap-suds and syringing with pure water will also be useful, avoiding, of course, contact with the fruit.

Gooseberries.—Mat over where necessary, to retard ripening.

Strawberries. — Alpines and other late sorts are now in full bearing. This is also the season for saving seed, if seedlings are desired for planting. Selecting a few of the finest bearers, let them be fully ripened, and the seed saved. Take the fruit and rub it on a piece of glass or slate, so that the pulp may dry up, when the seed may be rubbed off and preserved till the season for sowing in the spring. Runners, which are the only means by which plants are obtained true to the sort, should also be encouraged to grow, but not more than are required for new beds, as the fruit is always largest and best where the runners are trimmed off.

Flower-culture under Glass.—Conservatory.—For several months past the great difficulty here has been one of selection. It is not flowers merely that must be had ; but what flowers shall we accept ?—Azaleas, geraniums, fuchsias, balsams, globe amaranths, achimenes, liliums, gloxinias, begonias, &c. &c., have been contending with each other for the best place, and each form or type of beauty has been striving by turns for supremacy. The house can hardly be kept too cool at this season, though it should be free from all draughts upon stove-plants. Good arrangement is a main point. Too many beautiful things crammed together without order or system are never so satisfying as a very few disposed to the best advantage. Good specimens must also have plenty of space if they are to continue good. During this month the climbers on the roof must be gradually thinned and the shading partially withdrawn, to allow the wood of both permanent and temporary occupants of the house to ripen well. Much of next season's success depends upon this. Well-ripened wood will also enable plants to pass through the winter better, and to bear a greater amount of cold with impunity. To most plants, except balsams and fuchsias in small pots, liquid manure must now be given but sparingly, if at all.

The object now is not rapid growth, but abundance of flowers and matured wood ; therefore, even pure water must be given as sparingly as is consistent with good health. All sprinkling of paths, and other summer expedients to maintain a humid atmosphere, should be abandoned. Perfect cleanliness will of course be maintained, as beauty and dirt are not only irreconcilable, but the latter neutralizes and destroys the influence of the former.

Greenhouse.—This house must at once be got ready for its winter occupants. Many of these, such as ericas, epacrises, azaleas, camellias, have probably been in cold pits, or sheltered situations out of doors, for the last four months. In ordinary seasons they will be safe enough there until the end of September. Meantime, however, if the house requires painting or cleaning, the sooner it is done the better. Probably the fumes of paint do not injure plants, but

September.

they are very unpleasant to plant-owners; and the paint stands much better if it has time to become quite hard before the house is used. Green-houses that have no climbers on the roof should all be fumigated with burnt sulphur several days before any plants are brought into them. This is certain death to all animal life, if the outer air is cut off, and insures, if the plants are clean when brought from their summer quarters, perfect freedom from insects for some time.

Pelargoniums.—The grand secret of profuse bloom is early strong autumnal growth. "I would have given ten times the value of this entire work to have known this fifteen years ago," writes a very successful gardener. "I have worked my way to this fact by many failures and dear-bought experience." The moment pelargoniums begin to fade, they should be placed out of doors in the full sun to ripen their growth. When the wood becomes slightly browned, cut them down to within two, three, or four eyes of the old wood. Leave them in the same position, or place them in a house or pit to *break.* When the young shoots have advanced from 1½ to 2 inches, shake them entirely out of the pots, slightly pruning the roots; pot them in any light soil in as small pots as the roots can be got into; return them to a close house or pit, and the reduction, re-potting, and re-starting are finished. Remember the immense importance of getting the plants underweigh as early as possible. All plants intended to flower next May or June should now be ready for removal to their blooming-pots. Harden-off, cut down, and start afresh, plants for late summer and autumn blooming as soon as they are ripe enough.

Cinerarias.—Pot-off suckers from old shoots; prick-off, pot, and shift seedling plants, and push forward the first batch for flowering from November to February. Calceolarias require the same general treatment. Shift chrysanthemums, liberally water at top for late blooms, and stake. Likewise primroses, pansiés, &c., shift into larger pots, in order to maintain them in health.

Provide plenty of linums, *Salvia splendens*, oxalis, &c., for winter or spring; likewise hyacinths, narcissus, tulips, &c. &c.; pot the first batch, as early rooting is the only certain foundation for good flowering.

Stove.—To a certain extent all that has been said about comparative dryness in connection with the conservatory is equally applicable here. However, the higher temperature and the difference in the nature of the plants occupying this house render a greater amount of moisture necessary; still an autumn temperature must be maintained. Plants with succulent leaves must be gradually inured to as much sunlight as they will bear. This, while it will injure the appearance of some variegated and fine-foliaged plants, will improve others. Some of the caladiums, such as pictum, Newmanii, and bicolor, assume their most vivid hues when fully exposed to the light. Others, such as argyrites and Belleymei, look most beautiful and delicate when considerably shaded. It is best for the strength and vigour of the roots of all caladiums to have their leaves fully exposed to the sun and gradually matured in the autumn. This must, however, go on gradually, and the greatest care must be exercised in getting a plant like *Cyanaphyllum magnificum*, for instance, in full vigour, to bear the full blaze of an autumnal sun. The smallest drop of condensed water on such a leaf, or on almost any begonia leaf, will in half an hour do irreparable damage. The heating rays of the sun convert each drop into a burning lens, which quickly parboils the delicate texture of their leaves. Caladiums are not so often injured in this way, as their composition and structure seem specially adapted for throwing drops of water off their surface. Clerodendrons, poinsettias, justicias, euphorbias, begonias, &c., must be grown on freely for winter flowering.

September.

Stephanotis, passion-flowers, jasmines, &c., on the roof, must be carefully trained, cleaned, and regulated. Allamandas often make a splendid display when trained as semi-climbers on the roof of a stove. The new violacea would look well near to the cathartica or other varieties. Achimenes and other plants, suspended from the roof in elegant wire baskets, have a charming effect among climbers, and make the roof at least as showy as shelves and beds. Gloxinias and gesnerias will also make a splendid display here during the month. A proper arrangement of flowering and variegated begonias, intermixed with marantas, musas, palms, ferns, caladiums, and a few other fine-foliaged and flowering plants, will give the house an air of oriental grandeur and magnificence.

Orchid-house.—More light and air, and less water, must be the rule here. Those plants, however, that are in full growth must not be stinted, by any means, as the natural growing season of most orchids is the rainy season,—the season when it rains every day and night, for perhaps six weeks, without ceasing. Rapid growth, long seasons of perfect repose, and sudden excitement, seem to be the essentials of successful orchid-culture.

Fruit under Glass.—Orchard-houses cannot have too much air. Where no fire is used, sometimes late varieties of peaches, &c., are grown here, to come in after the fruit out of doors. Fruit on the north side of an orchard-house, with a thorough draught through the house, will be a month or six weeks later than the same varieties on a south or west wall. Maintain all the trees in the most perfect health, and liberally water those in pots with manure-water.

Vines.—Care must be taken, in preserving the foliage of grape-vines, not to allow too many leaves on the lateral shoots. It is the large leaves at the base of the fruiting-branches, near to the main stem, that are of most consequence. The buds at their base will

September.

yield next year's crop, and the fuller, rounder, and more plump they become, the larger that crop will be. The great point is to maintain these leaves in health without *inducing new growth* or causing the buds to break. A comparatively dry atmosphere and cool temperature are the chief things necessary for this. These are also the main desiderata for preserving grapes as long as possible. An excess of drought and sudden alternations of temperature are almost as injurious as too much water. If the latter induces decay, the former causes the fruit to shrivel, and robs them of their lusciousness.

Ripe grapes must be frequently looked over, and every specked berry be at once removed. If mildew makes its appearance in the late houses, paint the pipes with a mixture of equal parts lime and sulphur, and sprinkle the infested parts with dry sulphur. Prevention, however, is much better than cure. "I have invariably painted," says a good grape-grower, "all my pipes annually, and have never had any mildew. The fumes of the sulphur from hot pipes can do no harm; they are not disagreeable, and I believe they are a certain preventive of mildew." Flues, however, must not be painted over near the fire, as the slightest ignition of sulphur produces sulphurous acid, and would destroy every leaf. Leave air on all vineries, night and day, except where the air is admitted by the roof-lights in wet weather; but where the ventilation is given by openings in the wall, a little air should be constantly left on the house, and fire used in rainy weather to maintain the requisite temperature. Sixty degrees is high enough for all ripe grapes; but late Muscats, now ripening, should enjoy a minimum of 70°, rising to 85° or 90° with sun-heat. See that grapes intended to keep till January, February, or March, are well thinned: the Muscat of Alexandria and West's St. Peter's are the best adapted for this purpose.

Peach-house.—The lights may now

be removed for six weeks from the early peach-house; or, if this is not practicable, as much air as possible should be given night and day.

Figs require plenty of water when in full growth: in fact, in this state they may be treated almost like aquatics. The second crop of fruit will now be ripening, and those who wish for a third crop in November and December should have stopped the shoots in the middle of August; but where a very early crop is required, the shoots must not be stopped after this period. Great care must be exercised in ripening the wood, and seeing that the embryo fruit-buds are formed in the axils of the leaves. Water must be gradually withheld, and a dryish atmosphere maintained for this purpose.

Pines.—Keep a genial atmosphere of from 70° to 83° among fruiting plants; water them with clear manure-water, and refrain from syringing plants in flower and ripe fruit. Providences, and the black varieties for winter fruiting, would be best in a house by themselves from this time. Maintain a steady bottom-heat of 85° to fruiting plants, and 75° to succession plants. Where hot water is used, this is easily managed; but dung, tan, or leaves require greater caution. Pines, however, grow better when the bottom-heat is derived from fermenting material than from hot water. All the succession plants should already have received their final shift for the winter: those planted out in beds, either fruiting or succession plants, must be sparingly watered from this time; for if the soil becomes too wet, it will dry slowly at this season of the year. Attend to the making of linings; give as much air as is consistent with the maintenance of a proper temperature; gradually withdraw all shade, and endeavour to secure a firm indurated growth before the approach of winter.

SHOW GERANIUMS.

Of the cultivation of all fancy and other geraniums full particulars will be found in the monthly calendars.

The following is a list of excellent show, French or spotted, and fancy varieties. Those marked thus * are the most expensive; but fine selections from this list can be had from 12*s.* to 60*s.* per dozen :—

Ariel,—nearly white, with dark carmine spot on top petal.

Amy,—pink; deep spot on upper petals; excellent flower.

Aurelia,—purple; white centre; upper petals maroon.

*Bride (the),—pure white; rosy carmine blotch; fine rose.

Blink Bonny,—crimson lower petals; black blotch upper; fiery margin; free-blooming.

Bianca,—white lower petals; upper ditto carmine; margin white.

Belle of the Season,—lower petals white, tinged with pink; upper, cherry; white edges.

*Celeste,—rich orange lower petals, white centre; upper petals maroon, edged with orange-scarlet.

Candidate,—rose lower petals; white centre; maroon and orange top.

Carlos,—rose lower petals; white centre; maroon top, edged with carmine.

Conspicuum,—fine show variety.

Delicata,—rose lower petals; maroon blotch on upper.

Desdemona,—pure white; maroon top petals; fine show variety.

*Destination,—chocolate: deep maroon spot on lower petals; upper, maroon blotch, with an even margin of the ground colour.

*Eclipse,—deep scarlet; maroon blotch on top petals.

Emperor,—crimson lower petals; dark upper petals; showy and fine.

Etna,—scarlet lower petals; maroon top; margin scarlet.

*Euphemia,—bright rose lower petals; dark top; carmine margin; white centre.

Eastern Beauty,—orange-rose lower petals; upper, maroon; white centre.

Fairest of the Fair,—white; pink blotch on upper petals; free bloomer; first-rate for exhibition.

Fair Helen,—white; dark blotch on upper petals; margin white.

*Fairy,—lower petals pink, with maroon spots; upper, deep maroon; free bloomer.

Fire-Queen,—fiery scarlet; dark blotch on top.

Glow-worm,—crimson-scarlet; maroon blotch on upper petals.

*Garibaldi,—rose lower petals, white centre; top dark maroon; strong habit.

Governor-General,—deep rose, tinted orange; maroon top; first-rate show variety.

General Havelock,—lower petals bright rose; white centre; upper petals dark crimson; fine show variety.

*Hyperion,—rich scarlet lower petals; maroon, upper; fiery margin.
*Hesperus,—bright salmon; dark blotch on upper petals.
Jacques,—orange-rose lower petals; dark top.
Jessica,—salmon lower petals; rich top; orange margin.
King,—scarlet; tall grower.
*Lady of the Lake,—delicate pink shaded lower petals; upper, maroon; fine form; good.
Lady Alice Peel,—soft pale lilac; maroon blotch; white centre.
Leviathan,—purple; large blotch on upper petals; very large; splendid show variety.
Lady Canning,—large rose; white centre; dark spot on upper petals.
*Mrs. Hoyle,—violet-rose lower petals; black spot; good.
Mrs. Benyon,—deep rose; white centre; upper petals rich maroon.
Mars,—deep crimsom; very constant; fine and good.
Mr. Foster,—rich lake lower petals; upper dark crimson, shaded rose; pure white centre.
*Patroness,—large white; shaded crimson on upper petals; white margin; fine form.
Perdita,—crimson lower petals, white centre; black upper ditto.
*Prince of Hesse,—deep rose and red lower petals; top ditto rich maroon; carmine edge; white centre.
*Princetta,—rose and dark red lower petals; upper crimson; white centre.
Princess Beatrice,—white lower petals; maroon top; white margin; good.
*Prince of Wales,—rose lower petals; dark maroon top; white centre; fine.
Queen of Scarlets,—rosy scarlet; black spot.

SILVER SAND.

Silver or grey sand is an indispensable ingredient in all composts for plant-culture. In its purest state, silica or sand is the *dêbris* of quartz, or rock-crystal, which is composed almost entirely of silica, hard sand being the result of the disintegration and decomposition of rocks by the chemical agency of the atmosphere, assisted by the mechanical powers of the winds, of rain, and abrading waters. It varies much in its composition; oolitic rocks, granite, limestone, and red and green sandstone, all furnishing their quota. As an impalpable powder, it occurs in all soils. In its chemical character silica is an important constituent of organic life, being found, on analysis, in most plants. Mixed with soda, and heated to redness in an iron ladle, silica dissolves to a fused mass: if thrown into water, it will desolve; and if nitric acid be added, it becomes gelatinous,—indications of the means by which silica is treated in the great alembic of nature, and adapted for absorption into the tissue of plants.

In preparing it for the more obvious mechanical purpose which it serves in plant-culture, sand is divested of the other constituents of the soil, by washing and sifting through a fine sieve. In this way, all soils will yield a portion of this element, which may be dried; but the best mode of procuring it, is to proceed to some stream running through any of the sandstone countries. In such a stream there are few places where winding eddies have not formed a sand-bank, and one of these will generally furnish an ample supply.

When thoroughly washed, and all particles of clay extracted, let it be thrown into a heap, sheltered from the rain, and turned until it is thoroughly aërated; it should then be harvested in a dry place till wanted for use. Silica is a constituent of all the grasses, and is absolutely necessary for all those cultivated in our hothouses and gardens: it is also a necessary ameliorator in all clay soils. Its value, therefore, is beyond calculation to the gardener.

SKIZAN'THUS (nat. ord. Scrophularia'ceæ).

A genus of extremely beautiful and strikingly effective plants, if well grown, combining with elegance of growth a rich profusion of beautiful flowers. For flower-beds and borders all the varieties are desirable, but for single specimens, either for conservatory decoration or the centre of beds and vases, *S. carneus*, *Grahamii*, *retusus*, and *retusus albus*, are the most useful, producing in such situations a splendid effect. Valuable for in-door decoration during the winter and spring months; they succeed best in a rich soil. Those just named are half-hardy annuals, but all the other varieties are hardy annuals. Seed, 4*d*. per packet.

SLUGS.

Of slugs there are several varieties, but the most destructive in gardens are the small white and small black slugs, which bury themselves in the ground or under leaves, and come out in the night-time to feed. To destroy these, take fresh lime in a powdered state, put it into a coarse bag, and after nightfall or before sunrise, dust the ground where slugs are about: every slug touched with the smallest particle of the lime will die at once. If the weather be wet, the power of the lime will soon be destroyed: but if the ground be strewed in the evening with fresh cabbage-leaves, the slugs will hide under these, and may be destroyed in the morning.

SMALL FLOWER-GARDEN.

Arranging flowers in small gardens being a matter of taste, must be left to the proprietor. We can only give general directions for his guidance. In planting beds with half-hardy plants, which is generally done at the end of May, the plants should be ready to start into flower. Much time is lost by using small and late-struck plants. The best effect is produced by massing, every bed being planted with one distinct class; viz., one with verbenas, another with geraniums,—and these, again, arranged according to their various colours, either in groups or ribbons, with due regard to height.

Verbenas are very much of the same habit and height; but a very fine effect is produced by planting beds entirely with them, they combining all colours but yellow.

Geraniums are much the same, but vary in height. Thus, Little David is very dwarf; Tom Thumb, rather taller; Punch Queen (perpetual), taller still. The Zonale, or horseshoe-leaved, are mostly of tall habit; Cerise and pink-flowering sorts are generally dwarf.

Calceolarias embrace all shades of yellow and orange: some are very dwarf, as *aurea floribunda;* others are taller, but rarely exceed 18 inches in one season.

Blue Lobelias are all of very dwarf habit, and are very effective for frontage, being continuous bloomers.

Cupheas grow about eight or ten inches high.

Petunias are much the same in habit as verbenas, being dwarf and trailing: this tribe embraces many colours.

Heliotropes are mostly of lilac colour, but some are darker: they are mostly dwarf and spreading; but they are chiefly valued for their perfume.

Lantanas are much the same in habit, growing about 15 inches high.

Ageratums grow still taller, and some are variegated: all these, and many others of a like nature, may be raised from cuttings in heat, in February and March, and hardened off in frames before planting; or they may be struck from cuttings in July and August, and wintered in a greenhouse, pit, or even in a window, it being merely necessary to guard against frost and damp.

SNAILS.

To prevent snails crawling up walls and trees, they must be looked for, picked off by the hand, and killed. Make a thick paste with train oil and soot, and daub the bottom of the wall with it: this will form an effectual barrier, over which no snails will attempt to pass.

SNOWDROP.

This is one of the most elegant and interesting of spring flowers: it may be had in bloom in-doors at a very early period; its swan-white blossoms contrasting beautifully with the rich hue of the Crocus, &c. A row of snowdrops is often very effective in juxtaposition with a row of blue crocuses. October is the best month for procuring and planting them, although they may be inserted much later. The following are among the best varieties of this charming bulb.

Aletta, Wilhelmine, Argent, Bride of Albion, Blucher, Bride of Lammermoor, Charles Dickens, Caroline Chisholm, Cloth of Silver, David Rizzio, General Todtleben, La Plus Belle, Lord Raglan, Mrs. B. Stowe, Prince of Wales, Passelonto, Sir J. Franklin (very large, but loose), Sir W. Scott, and Victoria Regina.

For in-door culture select extra large roots. The varieties are

Double-flowering, per thousand, 18*s*.
Single-flowering, „ „ 18*s*.

SNOWFLAKE, or LEUCOJUM.

Of all our early spring flowers few

can excel the Snowflake. The very early variety is greatly superior to *L. æstivum.* To insure a fine display of blossom, the roots should be well manured as soon as they have done flowering.

Leucojum vernum (spring Snowflake),—pure white, tipped with green; blooms in February or March.

Leucojum æstivum (summer Snowflake),—white; a pretty snowdrop-like flower, which blooms readily in aquariums, fountains, and small fishponds early in May.

SOILS AND COMPOSTS, HARVESTING OF.

All who have examined this question admit that the value of manures is in proportion to the nitrogen or phosphates which they contain, more especially the former; for nitrogen is almost synonymous with ammonia, that being the chief source of nitrogen for plants. "Let the cultivator," says Dr. Scoffern, "take care of his ammonia; let him take care of his phosphates; let him prevent the loss of all soluble matters from his compost-heap."

The first and most important source of these elements is farm-yard manure, which, in its fresh state, consists of the refuse of straw, of green vegetable matter, and the excreta of domestic animals. Horse-dung varies in its composition according to the food of the animal; it is most valuable when they are fed upon grain, being then firm in consistence and rich in phosphates. Sheep-litter is a very active manure, and rich in sulphur and nitrogen; for if a slip of white paper, previously dipped in a solution of lead, be exposed to the fumes of fresh sheep-dung, the paper will be blackened; a sure test of the presence of sulphur.

Cow-litter is cooler, and less rich in nitrogenous or azotized matter; but it is rich in salts of potash and soda, and thus better adapted for delicate and deep-rooted plants. Swine's dung is still less azotized and more watery, and full of vegetable matter; but the most important of all manures is the urine from the stables and drainings of the dung-heap, which is wasted daily to an enormous extent. "The urine of carnivorous animals," says the authority we have already quoted, "is rich in the principles urea and uric acid. In herbivora, hippuric acid takes its place; but in all cases it is rich in nitrogen, and, when allowed to putrefy, ammonia is evolved. Urine is thus one of the most important constituents of farmyard manure."

The composition of manure is a very heterogeneous mixture. It may be broadly viewed as a mixture of humic acid bodies fixed in alkaline salts, and nitrogenous bodies capable of yielding ammonia; and it becomes an important question how is its strength best economized. Some advocate the practice of allowing the compost-heap to be entirely decomposed into an earthy mass,—thus permitting the whole of the ammonia to escape; others have gone so far as not to permit of any fermentation at all, stopping all action by continual turning. "It must be a bad practice," says Dr. Scoffern, "to allow so valuable an agent as ammonia to go to waste; and this is the inevitable result of permitting manure to undergo its last degree of fermentation. In the second place, it is doubtful whether the full and immediate virtues of the manure can be brought into play if it has not been submitted to incipient decomposition." There are means, however, of fixing the ammonia and retaining it in all its strength, while the manure containing it is reduced to a state suited for assimilation as food for plants. It may be absorbed by gypsum or sulphate of lime, which, being cheap, is often mixed with the compost-heap for the purpose; the ammoniacal salts thus formed being afterwards decomposed by the vegetable organism, or by its agency combined with atmospheric influences.

SPANISH BEET.

This is usually sown in March, and allowed to grow large: the leaves are eaten in the same way as spinach. It is a useful summer crop, because spinach soon runs to seed in that season, when this beet makes a very good substitute, and may be grown advantageously by those who desire to have a continuous supply of vegetables throughout the season.

SPINACH.

Preparation of the Land. — The ground for a summer crop of spinach cannot be too rich, and should be heavily manured and trenched deeply: a rather strong loamy soil is to be preferred. For the winter crop, however, a light and sandy soil is the most suitable, but this also should be deeply trenched, and in unfavourable localities a sheltered situation should be chosen. In wet, undrained soils, or those of a very strong tenacious nature, it may be advisable to sow the winter crop on raised beds, for spinach is very impatient of ground saturated with wet in winter, and under such conditions will not stand severe frost. The spring and summer crops are often sown between the rows of other crops, as peas, celery trenches, &c.; and there can be no objection to this practice, save the injury which may be done to the ground by treading it, when wet, in gathering the spinach. Crops sown in this way should be cleared off as soon as done with, and the ground forked up. If the soil is not moderately rich, a slight dressing of well-decayed manure should be applied; but this should be kept some distance under the surface.

Time and Manner of Sowing.—For the summer crop sow early in March, and at intervals of three weeks or a fortnight, until the middle of July, in quantities according to the demand. The round-seeded varieties are the best for summer crops. The winter crop should be sown from the middle of August to the beginning of September. The prickly-seeded is the hardiest, and should be partly used for this crop. All the crops should be sown in drills, from one to two inches deep, and from 12 to 18 inches apart, scattering the seed thinly, and covering with the finest of the soil. When the ground is dry, the drills should be well soaked with water before sowing. If the seed is steeped for twenty-four hours before sowing, it will germinate sooner; but this should be done only when the ground is hot and dry.

After-management.—The winter crop should be thinned as soon as the plants are strong enough to draw, so as to leave them about nine inches apart in the row; but the summer crops soon run to seed, and need not be thinned to a greater distance in the line than three inches. Some growers recommend a liberal use of manure-water for the summer crop, and this doubtless increases the size of the leaves; but it must not be depended upon to prevent the plants running to seed for more than a few days; and while the weather is hot a succession should be provided for, by making frequent sowings. Keep the ground between the lines free from weeds, and in an open state by frequent deep hoeings.

Seed, 2*d.* or 3*d.* per oz.

SPRING FLOWER-GARDEN.

To those who wish to know how a rich floral display can be maintained from the blossoming of the snowdrop till the planting out of geraniums and verbenas, we recommend the following remarks by Alpha, the intelligent correspondent of Messrs. Barr & Sugden.

There is literally no reason why every possessor of a garden should not have it yielding him as much beauty and enjoyment during the early months of the year as in summer and autumn. There are flowers which are willing to display themselves to the doubtful advances of the March and April sun, whose rich and glowing colours are not outrivalled by those which flaunt themselves in the full fire of the solstitial rays, and which possess a grace and elegance peculiarly their own.

Amongst the many showy plants which, if properly treated, will fill the parterre with beauty during the spring months, in addition to annuals, we may name tulips, hyacinths, crocus, winter aconites, snowdrops, scillas, narcissus, dog's-tooth violets, anemones, ranunculus, &c.; so that neither upon the score of difficult management, interference with subsequent occupants of the beds, nor cost, is there sufficient ground for leaving the garden during so many months bare and unattractive, with the dull soil and unrelieved masses of evergreens repelling by their sombreness and monotony.

From January, when the snowdrop and winter aconite timidly offer their simple charms to our gaze, until May, when the ranunculus and anemone are ready to make way for the plants then fit for bedding out, the whole tribe of spring-flowering bulbs are waiting to delight us with their choice and varied beauties. At a singularly small cost and with very simple treatment, they offer a means of decoration which in exquisite effect cannot be surpassed at any season of the year.

To secure a fine spring display from bulbs, it is necessary that the most suitable sorts for the purpose should be selected; the ground, moreover, must be properly prepared, and the bulbs planted in November, or as early as convenient. Having given in our lists cultural directions for each section of bulbs, we need not repeat them here. We would, however, observe that ground to be planted with bulbs should be well manured, dug deep, and well pulverized, and ought also to be thoroughly drained. This attention will be especially necessary for hyacinths, anemones, and ranunculuses, which delight in a rich deep soil, and are impatient of stagnant moisture during the winter.

For assistance in making a selection, we will name the classes of bulbs which we have found by experience to be the most suitable for spring decoration, and indicate how we think they can be arranged in planting, so as to secure the best possibe effect.

Beginning with the snowdrop, which is the first to make its appearance, is universally admired, and very cheap, let us say that it should be largely used, both for edging beds filled with other things, and for planting in clumps and masses; but as it blooms too early to flower at the same time as tulips, hyacinths, &c., it should not be planted with a view to its forming any combination with these; and the same warning must be given respecting the pretty little winter aconite. The crocus also blooms too early to allow of its being successfully used in combination with tulips, &c. But there are so many varieties of this flower in different colours, that a very effective garden might be produced with it alone. It is also very cheap, and should be largely planted as edgings to beds, in clumps about shrubbery borders, or in any desired arrangement in the beds. The lovely scillas bloom shortly after the crocus, but as they last many weeks, they may, if desirable, be planted in any arrangement with the later-blooming bulbs; but these are so beautiful that we recommend that they should be planted where there will be no necessity to disturb them until their leaves decay. The dog's-tooth violet is also a beautiful little plant, with prettily-speckled leaves, blooms early, and may be used as an edging, but, like the scillas, is well deserving to be grown in a bed by itself.

The most effective display will be obtained from hyacinths, the various sections of tulips, ranunculuses, and anemones. The hyacinth and tulip bloom before the ranunculus and anemone; but by planting the latter early in November, and the former towards the end of the month or early in December, they may generally be had in flower at the same time. Both the hyacinth and tulip furnish so many colours that a varied and effective display may be produced from each; and the same is nearly true of ranunculuses and anemones. We have known persons plant flower-gardens with the various spring-flowering bulbs, and arrange them according to height and colour, but with a total disregard of the time of flowering, and then expect the bed of blue crocuses to be in bloom at the same time as the one of scarlet anemones. We trust, however, that our remarks on this subject will prevent any of our readers from making a similar mistake.

We recommend all to plant bulbs without stint, nay, to plant them profusely for a spring display in the open garden; and if they will act upon our recommendation as to treatment, we answer for it that they will be amply recompensed. To our taste the most suitable arrangement for spring-flowering bulbs in the borders is the ribbon planting; the taller growers, as Crown Imperials and fritillaria, being placed at the back, then tulips, &c. But if the error of expecting all to bloom together is avoided, the display will be satisfactory whatever arrangement of planting may be adopted.

In addition to bulbs, the reader must remember that there are many plants and shrubs which flower so early that they contribute to the floral decoration of spring. Among them we may mention the yellow alyssum, the purple arabis, and the early sorts of hardy rhododendrons.

STANDARD ROSES.

These roses are used to decorate the lawn. Sometimes they are placed irregularly; at others they are planted at regulated distances round the walks; at others, again, they occupy the centre of the flower-beds; and in some instances they form separate beds in the rosarium, the different sizes being either planted in separate beds or in rows, rising towards the centre; the tallest standards forming the central row, while dwarf bushes pegged down occupy the edges of the bed. In all cases the effect they produce will depend upon the skill with which they are arranged, as to colour, continuous blooming, and general cultivation.

They may be divided into—

1. Dwarf standards, having a stem varying from six to twelve inches.
2. Half-standard,—a foot and a half to two feet and a half high.
3. Standards,—three feet high.
4. Tree and weeping roses,—four to five feet.
5. Pillar roses,—eight feet and upwards.

Standard roses are grafted or budded, generally on the stock of the dog-roses, budding being the neatest process, as well as the most certain, inasmuch as, in grafting, unless it is very carefully done, the head is not always secure. In budding, although two buds are inserted, one well placed is better, and it is not unusual to cut off the upper one if the lower one produces a vigorous shoot. Much of the success, however, depends on the choice of the stock. Where it is intended to form a collection by preparing stocks and budding, November is the best month for laying them in: they should be selected of sufficient thickness to support a good head, and of vigorous growth, removed to the place they are to occupy, with their roots uninjured, and as much of the soil attached as possible, and planted in soil rich enough to promote a vigorous growth before budding. "About six years ago," says Mr. Rivers, "I received, among others, some short dog-rose stocks, not more than two feet in height, but stouter than a broom-handle, the bark thin and grey with age: they were planted, and grew most luxuriantly. All stout and old rose-stocks require to be worked with very strong-growing sorts of roses to take off the abundance of sap and keep them in a healthy state. I had them budded with some varieties of the evergreen rose: they grew most luxuriantly, and not being adapted for sale, they were planted in a sloping bank of strong white clay, and left to bloom as nature dictated; not a shoot was ever touched with the knife. One of these, the *Félicité perpétuelle*, has been for three summers past a picture of beauty. When in full bloom, the ends of its shoots rest on the ground, and it then forms a perfect dome of roses."

Where the collection is to be procured from the nursery, the proper way is to go over the nursery-grounds while the roses are in bloom, and select plants of the kind desired, bearing in mind that the foliage, as well as the flowers, should be healthy, for no after-care will compensate for a sickly growth and dwindling habit.

In removing them, some care should be taken to see that they are transplanted without lacerating the roots; above all, that they are not suffered to bleach in the sun, while others are being removed. Let them be taken up with as much soil at the roots as will cling to them. When they reach their destination, let them be laid in a trench by the heels until they are required for planting; and when all is ready, the roots trimmed and all decayed ones cut off, lay them out horizontally, so that they radiate all round the stem; and while the tree is firmly held in its proper place, sprinkle the compost over them gradually, pressing it gently into the roots; the hole being filled up, so as to form a slight mound round the stem, and a coating of mulch placed over all, take care that the crown of the stock is level with the surface of the mound, neither planted too deep nor too shallow; drive a stake of sufficient strength into the ground, and tie the stock firmly to it, in such a way, however, as to avoid galling. Where the rose-tree is planted on a lawn, the turf should be neatly replaced, and the mulching rendered inoffensive to the sight by a covering of moss, held in its place by a neat layer of pebbles arranged round the stem. Whether in beds or otherwise, standards should never be nearer than three feet to each other.

In order to obtain large standard rose-trees, a judicious system of pruning is necessary. "Having pruned some large specimens," says Mr. Paul, "I watched for the bursting of the buds, with the view of practising disbudding. When they had shot forth about half an inch, I took a knife with a sharp point, and commenced my search at the heart of the tree. From here I rubbed off a great number of buds close to the bark, leaving such only as, from their position, promised to increase the size or improve the colours of the head. If a bud were pushing where there was a gap, or which had a lateral or outward growth, it was left; the others thinned out. Proceeding upwards, I cleared the centre of the tree pretty freely towards the top and circumference; and the buds, where crowded or likely to cross each other, were removed. A month later they were looked over again,—and this was done again and again, watering them once a week during the growing season with liquid manure, the soil in which they grew having become impoverished. The growth was, in consequence, more vigorous than in the previous year, and the flowers fine. On the fall of the leaf in autumn, the trees were pruned as usual; little thinning was required. The second and third year the same plan was followed, and the trees are now of handsome form, large, and healthy, producing an abundance of good flowers." By pursuing this practice, and not by age and soil alone, some of the large trees which surprise the visitors to their nursery have been produced; "for the oldest tree," Mr. Paul tells us, "cannot number more than twelve years, while there are others much older and not half the size."

STOCKS—Mathi'ola (nat. ord. Crucif'eræ).

The Stock Gilliflower is one of the most popular and important of our garden favourites; its delicious fragrance, brilliant and diversified colours, profusion and duration of its bloom, make it invaluable for flower-beds and borders, for edgings, ribbons, and pot-culture.

The 10-week Stock (*Mathiola annua*) is the most universally cultivated; it usually blooms ten or twelve weeks after being sown, grows from 6 to 15 inches high, and when cultivated in rich soil and occasionally watered with very weak guano-water, throws out an immense quantity of lateral spikes of bloom, so that a plant forms a perfect bouquet: it would indeed be very difficult to surpass the grand effect produced by these exquisite floral gems.

The Imperial or Emperor, sometimes called Perpetual Stocks.—They are half-hardy biennials, hybrids of the Brompton, growing 18 inches high, and of a robust branching habit. Sown in March or April, they make splendid "autumn-flowering stocks," and form a valuable succession to the summer-blooming varieties. Should the winter prove mild, they will continue flowering to Christmas. Sown in June or July, they flower the following June, and continue blooming through the summer and autumn months.

The Brompton and Giant Cape are generally called winter stocks, on account of their not flowering the first year: the former is robust and branching, the latter possesses the characteristic so much esteemed by some, viz., an immense pyramidal spike of bloom. These are half-hardy biennials.

The Intermediate Stock is extensively cultivated for Covent-garden market; it is dwarf and branching, and in the early summer months constitutes the principal feature in furnishing jardinets, &c., for "the London season." It is also of great value in filling flower-beds for an early summer display. Half-hardy biennials.

STOCKS, TO SELECT DOUBLE FLOWERS.

Reject from the seed-bed all those plants which have a long tap-root (these will almost invariably prove single), and reserve for bedding only those which have the largest quantity of delicate fibres at the roots: experience shows that these, in general, prove double.

STORING SEEDS.

In collecting seeds, the greatest care is required to have them ripe, and that the bags into which they are put are correctly marked. All that is known of the parent plant should be added, if it is other than a common kind, including the soil in which it is found. When collected, before packing away, the seeds should be carefully dried. When they belong to pulpy fruit, separate the grains from the pulp as soon as decomposition begins, and dry before placing them in bags.

STORING VEGETABLES.

There are several sorts of vegetables which require storing for winter;—potatoes, carrots, beet, and onions are the chief of them. Potatoes do best when harvested in clumps in the open ground, care being taken to protect them from rain and frost. A long ridge is the best form. The ground should be dry and thoroughly drained. The potatoes should be heaped on a ridge, tapering from a base of three feet to a foot and a half, or less, at the top, separating the different sorts by divisions in the ridge. It is usual to cover this ridge with a thatch of wheat-straw, and then with six or eight inches of mould; but some authorities highly disapprove of this. McIntosh recommends the tubers being covered with turf, and afterwards with soil; and in the absence of these, laying on the soil at once without any litter. After having laid on nine or ten inches of soil, thatch the whole over an inch and a half thick, with straw, fern leaves, or any similar non-conducting material; "the object being," he says, "first to exclude frost and wet, and, secondly, to exclude heat; for which purpose earth is not sufficiently a non-conductor of heat and cold."

If the weather is fine when the tubers are taken up, and the potatoes are required for early use, much of this labour may be dispensed with; but if for spring and early summer use, the precautions will be found necessary.

Carrots, beet, and other similar root-crops should be taken up before the frosts set in: they may either be stored in a dry cellar, covered with dry sand, or after the manner of the potato. The London market-gardeners winter their beet and carrots in large sheds, in moderately damp mould, and banked up with straw; "for," says Mr. Cuthill, "it is a mistake to pack them all in dry sand or earth for the winter; and the same may be said in regard to carrots, parsnips, salsafy, scorzonera, and other similar roots; and by this means," he goes on to say, "the roots retain their natural sap, and the colour is preserved."

It is probably unnecessary to add that in roots and tubers, as with fruit, all cut or bruised ones should be thrown aside: when the skin is cut, or a bruise exists, the elements of decay are soon introduced, and all others within reach contaminated. A dry day should be chosen for lifting them, and they should be exposed a few hours before collecting into heaps, that the soil adhering to them may dry.

Onions should be lifted a little before they have altogether ceased to grow: the leaf turning yellow and beginning to fade will be the sign. As they are taken up, they should be placed in a dry airy place, but without being exposed to the sun. If they are thinly spread out on a dry floor or shelf covered with sand, or on a gravel walk partially shaded in fine weather, they will do very well. As they dry, the roughest leaves should be removed; when dry, they should be removed to a warm dry loft, where they can ripen more thoroughly. When in a proper state for storing, they should be gone carefully over and separated, the smallest ones for pickling, the ripest picked out, as likely to keep longest: those with portions of leaves to them are best stored by stringing and suspending them from the ceiling of the room, which promotes ripening. The stringing is done by twisting a strong piece of matting or twine round the tails of each in succession, so that they may hang as close together as possible without forming a cluster, until the string is about a yard long; when they are hung up, they occupy very little room, and have a good opportunity of ripening.

STRAGGLING PLANTS.

To preserve a neat appearance in the flower-borders, all perennials that have a tendency to run about or stray,—and there are many of which this is the habit,—should have their roots confined under the surface with tiles. Old chimney- and seakale-pots are very good for the purpose. By this means they may be kept within due bounds, but, of necessity, will require every few years to be transplanted into fresh soil.

STRAWBERRY-BEDS.

The proper time to make new strawberry-beds is the month of August; but if space of ground cannot then be had, or the time spared, it is an excellent plan to take the runners at that time, and set them only a few inches apart in peat soil, on a north border, where they will soon make good root, and become strong plants. In the early spring they should be taken up separate, with a ball of earth, by means of a trowel, and planted a proper distance from each other in the bed intended for them.

STRAWBERRY-BEDS (Novel Method).

An American writer, Hiram W. Buckley, New York, gives the following novel method for forming new strawberry-beds:—"Whenever I wish to make a new strawberry-bed, I allow the old bed to run into mass. Then, at any time during the autumn or early spring, I line strips about 7 inches wide and 20 inches apart through the length of it, and cut them into squares. These squares I take up with a spade, about 3 inches deep, and set them 18 inches apart in furrows previously made 2 feet apart, in a new bed. As the roots are not disturbed, they bear a full crop the first season, and this pays well for the heavy labour of removing so much earth. I make no account of the large number of roots required, since they spread so rapidly as to cover the ground in a single season, even when runners are kept back till after fruiting. The trenches made in the old bed are filled with rich earth and manure, and the bed is soon covered with plants again, when other trenches may be made and filled; thus renewing the whole bed by degrees, as occasion requires." It is of so recent a date that this American plan cannot have been tested in this country. It seems, however, very likely to answer, and to be a saving of time in the formation of new beds. Still it must be remembered that when fine fruit is required, the plants should be kept single—quantity undoubtedly is gained by allowing the beds to run into mass.

SUMMER-HOUSES.

Summer-houses and seats add much to the comfort, as well as the ornament, of pleasure-grounds and gardens. Almost any clever carpenter can put up a rustic arbour, at any rate with the assistance of a few hints. Arbours, however, as well as seats, can be bought ready-made. Very neat buildings may be formed with young oak stands, ornamented with pieces of oak billet and thatched with reed; also of Scotch fir poles split, showing the bark on the outside. Such summer-houses as these may be boarded inside and lined with matting, or made more ornamental by a panelling of split hazel worked into different patterns. The flooring can be of brick or stone. More substantial houses can be built wholly of flint or stone, and fitted up accordingly. Of garden-seats the variety is infinite. In the wilder portions of the plantations and shrubberies, the more simple and rustic these seats are the better. The stump of a tree, or the stem placed lengthways, may be fitted up for the purpose. We have seen three or four seats shaped like large mushrooms placed here and there under trees, and they are not only very comfortable, but they have the great advantage, from their peculiar shape, of always being dry. In all matters of rustic ornament, Mr. Curry, of Upper Clapton, London, is a great authority, and those persons who cannot design such things for themselves will no doubt find all they want by applying to him. Of late years cast-iron garden furniture has been introduced. We have seen some very good imitations of oak chairs and tables in this material; but we give the preference to wood. The price, however, of this cast-iron furniture is so moderate that many persons may be inclined to adopt it, especially as it is so durable that unless broken by a sudden blow or fall, it will last for ever. For gardens and pleasure-grounds near the house, what is called the Leicester garden-seat is well adapted. It is a combination of wood and wrought iron, and forms by no means an uncomfortable seat. It is light, and, being fitted with bolts and nuts, it can readily be taken to pieces and put away during winter. We have seen some garden-seats by Barnard & Bishop, of the Norwich Iron-works, which, in our opinion, are superior to all others. These chairs have frameworks of wrought iron and seats of a chain or network of galvanized wire. They are very elastic, and almost as comfortable and soft as a stuffed cushion. These chairs are made of various shapes and sizes; single chairs can be folded up, and are so light that a child can carry them.

SWEET HERBS.

A convenient spot in every kitchen-garden should be appropriated to the growth of such herbs as are useful for culinary purposes. With a little care and management, the herb-garden may be made not only useful but ornamental also. It should, in general, be situated as near the kitchen premises as possible; and each kind of herb should have its own separate bed. If a square piece of land be set apart for the herb-garden, the beds may be arranged in some fanciful form, or separated by gravel walks, and having neat box or tile edgings. The most useful and best worthy of cultivation are the following:—Parsley, sage, thyme, mint, fennel, rue, basil, marjoram, balm, and rosemary.

SWEET-WILLIAM — Dianthus barbatus (nat. ord. Caryophylla'ceæ). Hardy Perennials.

A splendid free-flowering garden favourite, producing an unusually fine effect in flower-beds, borders, and shrubberies. Amongst these, Hunt's auricula-flowered varieties are remarkable for their rich, varied, and beautiful colours and immense heads of bloom, which surpass in effect even the handsomest of the perennial phloxes.

Sweet-William, Hunt's magnificent auricula-flowered, choice mixed, 1 ft., 1*s*. per packet. Ditto, in 12 splendid colours, 2*s*. 6*d*.

TACSO'NIA (nat. ord. Passiflora'ceæ).

A grand genus of the Passiflora family, yielding to no twining shrub in cultivation for the dazzling brilliancy, size, and beauty of its flowers, which are produced in great profusion for months in succession. As some difficulty has been experienced in this country in blooming the varieties of this magnificent genus, the Sardinian correspondent of Messrs. Barr & Sugden has supplied the following information:—"To flower the Tacsonia successfully, it should be frequently stopped, as the flowers are produced upon the lateral shoots; it should be grown in rich soil, and frequently syringed during warm weather, to induce a vigorous growth: thus treated it will cover a large space in an incredibly short period, and bloom most profusely." He adds, "I have had *T. ignea* with from 150 to 200 gorgeous scarlet flowers open at the same time."

TANKS.

In gardens where fountains are not attainable, tanks are not only useful, but may be made exceedingly ornamental, either in flower- or kitchen-gardens. The position in the latter should be in the centre of a broad grass walk lined with pear-trees and standard roses. It should be made with an asphalte composition, and surrounded by rockwork covered with sedums and the different kinds of saxifrage. In the flower-garden its position must be determined by circumstances. It forms a useful and beautiful centre to a hardy fernery, and, if near enough to the house, may frequently, at a very small expense, be provided with a fountain by means of a small gutta-percha tube in connection with the cistern, which is supplied by the force-pump of the house. This tube should be so managed as to be removable in winter, for fear of frost. The position of the tank in the kitchen-garden should be in the centre of the broad grass walk. A simple tank of this kind may be made by digging out the soil in a circle four feet deep, and puddling it all round with tempered clay, that is, clay thoroughly washed and kneaded, until divested of all silicious soil, and nothing but pure clay remains: this well rammed round the whole excavation for nine or 10 inches, is impervious to water. Large stones, or boulders of handsome shape, placed with apparent irregularity, but real symmetry, all round, will form a handsome and useful basin; and if some of the more delicate water-plants, as *arums* and other *nymphææ*, are planted in large pots in the bottom of the tank, a good effect will be produced.

TARRAGON.

This is the *Artemisia Dracunculus*, the leaves of which are so much used in France for salads and flavouring vinegar. The plant is a native of Tartary.

TEA ROSES.

The Tea-scented Chinese Roses form undoubtedly the most desirable group which has come under our notice. Their odour is delicious, and closely resembles the flavour of high-class tea; their colours are generally subdued in tint, being white, creamy-white, flesh-colour, and yellow, except where they have been hybridized with others of more brilliant colours. The blush tea-scented rose was introduced from China in 1810; ten years afterwards, the yellow was imported; for we find Mr. Williams, a corresponding member of the Horticultural Society, reporting upon it in 1823, after he had cultivated it for three years. "Three years ago," he says, "I had buds of the double yellow, as well as some of the dark and of the sweet-scented Chinese roses, inserted on strong shoots of a musk cluster-rose, which is trained on the east front of my house. Last year both Chinese varieties flowered in great beauty during the whole season, the dark Chinese particularly well, the flowers being much larger than when grown on its own roots. My buds," he adds, "were inserted 10 feet from the ground; and Mr. Knight thinks the large size of the blossoms is owing to the distance the sap has to pass before it reaches the flower-buds."

It was long said by writers, both French and English, that the yellow Chinese produced few hybrids worth cultivating; and this opinion prevailed pretty generally until the finest of the whole group was raised by Mr. Foster, of Plymouth. This was Devoniensis, a fine creamy-white, with buff centre: others from the same parent soon followed, partaking of the Noisette roses, with some of which probably Mr. Foster had hybridized.

Mr. Paul divides tea-scented roses into two classes,—the Ligneous, which form good standards, and the Herbaceous; not that they differ in fibre, but because these latter are more tender and require more delicate treatment. "If trained to a south-east wall," he says, "the tea-roses grow vigorously, and flower in great beauty, much earlier and much finer than in the open ground, producing a constant succession of flowers during one half of the year. They also flower freely in pots plunged in the open gronnd, so as to be removed to a cold frame for protection during winter."

To grow this group in perfection requires considerable knowledge of their habits as well as care; they are peculiarly adapted for that kind of pot-culture which has so flourished of late years under the fostering care of the Royal Horticultural and other societies. In the open ground they all require a rich well-drained soil, close pruning, and the means of protection from frost in winter. As ornaments to the conservatory they are unsurpassed. "At Orleans House, Twickenham," says Mr. Paul, "the vigorous growers are trained up wire pillars to the height of 12 feet; the flowers, drooping with their own weight, are displayed to greater advantage; their elegant and shining foliage is kept on during the greater part of the winter, and nothing could be more appropriate,—nothing more beautiful."

The following is a list of the hardier tea-scented roses.

Belle Marguerite,—flower rose, shaded with crimson; large, double, and well-expanded.

Bride of Abydos,—white, delicately tinged with pink; large and double; a free-bloomer.

Caroline,—blush, suffused with deep pink; large, cupped, and full.

Comte de Paris,—flesh-colour shaded with rose; full and cupped.

Corinna,—delicate wax-like flesh, sometimes fawn in the centre; very double.

Gloire de Dijon,—fawn, tinted with salmon and rose; small, fragrant, and of vigorous growth.

Goubault,—bright rose, the young buds opening a rich deep crimson as the sepals open; very large, double, and expanded.

Mansais,—rose, shaded with buff; very large, full, cupped, and sweet.

Niphetos,—creamy-white, approaching to lemon, the centre lemon-colour; magnolia-like; large, full, and globular; a beautiful rose.

Nisida,—rose and fawn; shaded, double, cupped, and very sweet.

Original,—creamy white, centre salmon-buff; large and full.
Pauline Plautier,—white, tinged with lemon; globular and full.
Princesse Hélène,—white, yellowish centre; large, full, and cupped.
Safrano,—saffron-yellow to apricot-colour in the bud, changing to pale buff; cupped, large, and double.
Taglioni,—creamy white, centre flesh and lemon; large, full, aud cupped.

Of the more tender varieties, the following list contains those most worthy of cultivation:—

Adam,—rosy salmon-colour; very large, full, globular, and fragrant, with camel-like petals; suitable for a small mass.
Ajax,—yellow, colour deepest in the centre, outer petals spotted with rose; large, full, and globular.
Aurora,—cream-colour, centre yellowish; large and double; of vigorous growth.
Bougère,—glossy bronze rose-colour, approaching to deep salmon; cupped, large, and full; a robust grower.
Canary,—true canary-colour; semi-double, charming in bud, but forces very pale.
Cant's Aurora,—a rich cream-coloured rose, tinged with buff in the centre, with full and finely-formed petals, supposed to be an old kind generally lost; although Mr. Cant, of Colchester, has grown it for twelve years. Beautiful blooms exhibited in 1861, cut from a south wall.
Clarisse,—pinkish white, changing to creamy white; full, and medium size.
Devoniensis.—creamy white, tinted with rose-buff, sometimes yellow in the centre; very large, full, cupped; a splendid rose, beautiful in the clump.
Eliza Sauvage,—cream-colour, approaching to pale yellow, sometimes with deep orange, inclining to buff in the centre; large, full, and globular: a delicate rose, of dwarf habit. The best yellow for a small bed.
Hamon,—flesh-colour, variable up to crimson; large, double, and very sweet.
Homer,—white, tinted with rose and fawn; very large, and somewhat variable.
Jeanne de Gironde,—yellow petals; very thick, sometimes bordered with rose-colour.
Josephine Malton,—rich cream-colour, centre often inclining to buff; tops of the petals sometimes tinged lake-colour; large, double and cupped; of exquisite fragrance, but delicate.
Julie Mansais,—straw-colour, margins white; large, full, and cupped; sweet, and rather delicate.
La Renommée,—white, centre pale lemon-colour, sometimes mingled with flesh; cupped, large, and double.
Louise de Savoy,—pale yellow; globular; very large and double.
Madame de Hardelay,—clear sulphur-yellow; large, full, and cupped; of vigorous growth.
Madame Villermoz,—white, salmon-colour in the centre; a recent and very fine rose.
Marie de Medicis,—flesh-colour, tinged with rose and carmine; large, full, and globular.
Moiré,—flesh-colour, shaded with pale fawn; very large and beautiful rose.
President,—flower blush, tinged with salmon-buff when young, becoming blush when older; a large, well-cupped, and newly-formed rose, of free growth and hardy character.
Prince Esterhazy,—flesh-colour, centre rose; very large, double, and globular, and delicately sweet.
Rêve de Bonheur,—yellowish, shaded with rose; very double.
Souvenir d'un Ami,—salmon and rose-colour, shaded; cupped, large, and full; a fine rose.
Triomphe du Luxembourg,—flesh-colour, tinged with fawn and rose-colour; very large, full, globular, and fragrant.
Vicomtesse Decazes,—yellow, deeper in the centre; shaded copper-colour; very distinct and beautiful; large, double, and cupped.

TE'COMA (nat. ord. Bignonia'ceæ).

Magnificent ornamental greenhouse evergreen twining shrubs, with large and beautiful flowers; require the same cultural treatment as Bignonia.

Tecoma stans,—yellow, from North America.
,, jasminoides grandiflora,—white flowers, with beautiful crimson throat.

TENT BEDS ON LAWNS.

These are very ornamental; they may be formed in a variety of ways, which good taste will suggest. The usual shape is round or oval, having a pole in the centre and chains or ropes directed to the sides, to be covered with creepers,—evergreen or annual, or both, on alternate wires.

THU'JA (nat. ord. Conif'eræ).

A splendid genus of hardy ornamental shrubs; the beautiful colour of their foliage, combined with their symmetrical growth, renders them desirable objects for lawns or shrubberies: they succeed in any garden soil. *Thuja aurea variegata* is an especial favourite.

THUNBER'GIA (nat. ord. Acantha'ceæ).

A genus of slender and rapid-growing climbers, with extremely pretty and much-admired flowers, which are freely produced, either when grown in the greenhouse or in a warm situation out of doors: they delight in rich loamy soil. All the varieties are half-hardy annuals, except *T. coccinea*, which is a greenhouse perennial, and blooms in clusters.

Thunbergia alata,—orange, rich brown eye, from East Indies.
Thunbergia alata alba,—brown eye, rich, from East Indies.

TOMATO.

An admirable vegetable by itself,—it enters largely into a great number of our best and most wholesome sauces. It may be cooked and brought on to table like other vegetables in several different ways. Moreover, those who have analyzed its properties say that the tomato is singularly wholesome, and very useful, especially in cases of bad digestion: however, it is not appreciated or cultivated as it ought to be. There is, undoubtedly, some little difficulty in our climate in fruiting and ripening tomatoes to perfection; but the following directions, if attended to, will generally be found to succeed:—Sow the seeds in pots in very rich light mould in March or April, and place them in a cucumber-frame, or other gentle heat. When the second leaf appears, re-pot the plants either singly or at most two or three together, keeping them near the glass and well watered. In May remove them to a cold frame for the purpose of hardening them before they are planted out, which should be done as soon as the fear of spring frosts is over, and the earlier the better. The best situation for tomato-plants is against a south wall fully exposed to the sun. The plants should be well watered with liquid manure to keep up a rapid growth. As soon as the blossom-buds appear, watering should cease. Stop the shoots by nipping off the tops, and throw out all those sprays that show little signs of fruit, exposing the young fruit as much as possible to the sun and air, only watering to prevent a check in case of very severe drought, of which the state of the plant will be the best index. In a very dull, wet, cold autumn, even with the greatest care, the fruit will sometimes not ripen as it ought; but in this case it may frequently be made fit for use by cutting off the branches on which full-grown fruit is found, and hanging them in a warm dry greenhouse or elsewhere to soften and ripen: a cool oven may be used advantagenusly to effect this.

TOOL-HOUSE.

The tool-house may be attached to the gardener's cottage or placed at the back of the hothouses, if such a situation be found more convenient. In every well-planned tool-house there should be contrivances of different sorts for hanging up the tools,—rakes, hoes, spades, &c.,—which should all be well cleaned before they are put away. If many men are employed in the garden, each one should have a proper place for his own tools. Watering-pots, syringes, garden-engines, should have their movable parts separated, and be reversed, in order that they may drain and dry. The mowing-machine should be kept thoroughly clean and oiled, and so should all clippers and pruning instruments. A bench with a vice attached to it will be found very useful in a tool-house; also a grindstone and hones for the sharpening of different tools.

TOOLS.

The tools required in a garden may be divided into implements, instruments, and tools; the former comprising the pick, spade, fork, hoe, and rake, all of which require the use of both arms, and some of them the whole muscular force of the frame. They generally combine the principle of the lever and the wedge, the blade of all of them being employed to separate particles of matter by the application of lever power, which lies in the shaft or handle. Where the implement is intended to be grasped and held firmly at one spot, as in the spade, a handle is provided adapted for that end; where the hand is to slide along, the handle should be smooth and round : such is the form of the handles of the rake, the hoe, the pick, and all similar tools. Ash is the best material for handles requiring strength, willow being lighter, and strong enough for others, such as the rake, the Dutch hoe, &c., where the handle is required to be of some length.

From the catalogue of Messrs. Barnard & Bishop, the Walk, Norwich, we select the following tools, with their prices.

The Pick is a compound lever, the blade of which ought to be of the best wrought iron edged with steel, the handle of well-seasoned sound ash. The pick is made in various shapes; for garden use, one end is usually pointed, the other wedge-shaped, to adapt it for cutting through roots when they are met with in the soil. That called the mattock, having the edge axe-fashion, is used to chop up hard grassy surfaces, and to stub up whins, heather, and other wild shrubs.

The Spade is a broad blade of plate-iron, attached to a handle of tough root-cut ash. Two-thirds of the blade ought to be of steel, and the other of the best scrap-iron, well welded together. In some, the blade is perforated for the purpose of cleaning itself when employed on adhesive soils. The semi-circular spade, used by "navvies," is useful in hard close soils and new ground. The shovel, having a broader blade, is useful in throwing up the loose soil at the bottom of a trench. Cast-steel spades, 3*s*. 6*d*. to 5*s*. each; shovels, 3*s*. 6*d*. to 4*s*. 6*d*.

The Fork, of which there are several kinds, is used for filling in dung litter and haum, and for levelling the surface, or stirring it round the roots of plants which might be injured by using the spade. The form of the fork is generally three-pronged,—those used for litter, and for forking up the earth round roots of trees, have only two prongs; but Parker's fork has five prongs, and in many cases supersedes the use of the spade. The three pronged fork with broad tines is used for digging potatoes, and is otherwise a very useful implement in the garden. Three-pronged forks, 4*s*. to 4*s*. 6*d*.; five-pronged, 5*s*. 6*d*.

The Hoe, also, is of many forms. Its use is to stir the surface of the soil and destroy weeds in their first leaves. The draw-hoe is set at the end of a long handle at an angle, so that when drawn to the operator, it sinks also into the soil. In the other, generally termed the Dutch hoe, he thrusts it from the angle formed by the height of the hands from the ground, carrying it gently into the surface of the soil. This is used where the weeds are merely cut up and left in the soil. Hoes, 6*d*. to 1*s*. 6*d*. each; Dutch hoe, 9*d*. to 2*s*. 6*d*.; Prussian hoes, 1*s*. 6*d*. to 2*s*.

The Rake is a row of small tines inserted in a bar of iron from six to eighteen inches long, and fixed by a socket placed at right angles to the bar, to a handle five or six feet long. This is a most important implement to the gardener, being used to make his beds smooth and trim, and to remove loose weeds. It is also used in raking the lawn before rolling. Garden rakes, from 1*d*. to 2*d*. per tooth; daisy rakes for lawns, 5*s*. to 7*s*. each.

The common Garden-knife consists of a blade of prepared steel, fixed in a handle of horn or bone, without a joint, and carried in a sheath. It generally has a hooked blade, and is used for cutting cabbages and other vegetables, trimming the roots of turnips, and similar purposes.

The Pruning-knife has the blade quite straight on the cutting side: it may be either with or without a joint. 1*s*. 6*d*. to 4*s*. each.

The Grafting-knife has a thinner and

narrower blade, and is generally made with a folding joint. 1*s*. 6*d*. to 4*s*. each.

The Budding-knife has the sharp edge of the blade rounded off, backwards; while the handle, of bone or ivory, is brought to a fine point at the end opposite the blade, so as to form a spatula for lifting up the bark of the stock for the insertion of the bud. Goodsall's budding-knife has a heart-shaped termination to the handle, which is found more convenient for lifting the bark. 1*s*. 6*d*. to 2*s*. 6*d*. each.

The Grafting-saw.—This has a blade of steel with double teeth, so that it may pass through green wood without choking up. For larger branches the forest-saw, having a handle six or eight feet long, is used to enable the operator to reach the loftier branches. When this instrument is used, the end left on the tree must be smoothed with the chisel or pruning-knife, and the wounds covered with some composition which will exclude the air. Saws, from 3*s*. to 5*s*. each.

The Chisel.—There are two sorts in use,—the garden and the forest chisel: the first is chiefly used in grafting, and differs from the carpenter's chisel in being wedge-shaped, or bevelled on the edge on both sides; thus tapering to a central point. It is used with a mallet, to slit stocks for grafting when they are too large for the grafting-knife, and to smooth branches cut with the saw. 1*s*. to 1*s*. 6*d*. each.

The Bill-hook: a hooked blade sharpened on both sides, with a handle about a foot long; a useful instrument for cutting away branches too thick for the knife. With a long handle and sharpened on the hooked side, it is used to cut hedges, in place of clipping them. 2*s*. 3*d*. to 4*s*. each.

The Axe is a steel wedge, attached at right angles to a strong handle of ash timber, about two feet and a half long. The axe varies much in form: the long and narrow one, known as the American axe, is the most useful. It is used for cutting roots of trees which cannot be conveniently reached with the saw. 6*d*. to 6*s*. 6*d*. each.

The Scythe: a long blade of steel, attached to the end of a crooked wooden handle. Boyd's scythe is much used in gardens where the grass is kept under by mowing. Lawn scythes complete, 6*s*. 6*d*. to 7*s*. 6*d*. each.

Shears of various kinds are in use in the garden, both for clipping hedges and dressing the edgings of the beds. The turf edges are kept smooth by using those with long handles, moving upon a single wheel: shorter shears are used for cutting box-edgings and quickset hedges. Shears, 2*s*. 9*d*. to 7*s*. 6*d*. per pair; with wheels, 7*s*. 6*d*. to 8*s*. 6*d*.

The Garden-engine is of essential service where water cannot be distributed from a tank to all the garden by means of a hose. These vary in price according to contents—from 12 gallons to 30 gallons, price from £3. 10*s*. to £5. 15*s*.

With the Syringe, which is essential in the greenhouse, the garden-engine may be made to produce the nearest possible approach to a natural shower of rain, preceded by a misty dew. Price of syringes, 6*s*. to 13*s*. 6*d*. each.

The Garden-line consists of an iron reel turning on a spindle, terminating in a peg and a cord. The cord is wound round the reel, and, having a peg at the other end, the beds are trimmed and the rows directed by the line. Price 2*s*. 6*d*. to 3*s*. 6*d*.

The Level, as its name implies, is to guide the workman in all operations where either a perfect level, or, as in draining, a regulated fall, is required. The most useful is half a square, with an iron index, marked out with ninety degrees or divisions. Where a slope is to be laid out at a perfect level, the plummet will hang in the centre, or 45°, and on a slope it may hang at any lesser number, in ascending at any higher number, according to the steepness of the slope.

The Measuring-rod is made of wood, generally 10 feet long and an inch square, on which the feet are marked, the last foot having the inches also.

The Wheelbarrow, though last is

not least; indeed, it is the most indispensable implement in the garden next to the spade, hoe, and rake, and is too well known to require description.

The Ladder, of various sizes, will be required in the garden.

TRAINING FLOWERS.

When training is required, it snould be done neatly and tastefully, using thin and pointed sticks, and very fine fibres of matting or soft twine; avoid anything like stiffness or formality, which is the opposite extreme to the graceful habit of plants.

TRAINING FRUIT-TREES.

Various modes of training fruit-trees are in use among gardeners, but none are more graceful than the pyramidal form; and it is profitable as well as graceful, inasmuch as double the number of trees may be planted in the same space without crowding. This mode of training is extensively adopted in continental orchards, chiefly with

Fig. 1.

pear-trees, but it is equally applicable for apples, cherries, and plums. The form is, of course, the result of pruning as well as training; and the commencement is from a young tree with a single strong leader, which may be obtained at any of the nurseries; though the best and surest way is to plant stocks where the trees are to stand, and graft them with suitable varieties for the purpose, taking care that one shoot only is allowed to spring from the graft. If they are procured from the nursery, plant them in properly-prepared stations, supported by a strong stake driven firmly into the soil, and leave them for a year, in order that the roots may have a secure hold of the soil, and send up plenty of sap when growth commences, to push the buds strongly. We will assume that the young trees have plenty of buds nearly down to the graft; then, in the following autumn, cut off the top of the shoot at *a*, fig. 1, with a clean cut.

Fig. 2.

At the end of the second year it will have made several shoots, and will probably, in many respects, resemble fig. 2; but as we still require vigorous growth, it will be necessary to cut in again severely at *a* and *b*, *b*. The summer following, the side-shoots will spring forth with great vigour, spreading on all sides; and now the first foundation of the pyramidal form is laid, by extending the shoots horizontally, and tying them firmly to stakes so placed that the range of branches forming the bottom of the pyramid should project from the tree at nearly right angles, and at equal distances from each other. If they are too numerous, the superfluous shoots should be cut off. The third summer, if it continues in a healthy state, the tree will present the appearance of fig. 3, with this exception, that the lower branches will be more horizontal than they are here represented, in consequence of being tied to the stakes. If some of the branches have grown more vigorously than others during the summer, such shoots should be pruned in

Fig. 3.

to where the lines cross the branches. On the other hand, should others develop themselves feebly, they should be left at their full length, so that the descending sap, elaborated by the leaves, should deposit a larger amount of cambium. Strong shoots may also have their vigour modified by making an incision immediately below their junction with the stem, just before the sap rises in the stem; and if a desirable bud remain dormant, it may be forced into growth by making an incision just above it. Where a large vacancy occurs between the branches, then a side-graft should be inserted to fill up the

Training Fruit-trees.

space. The branches should again be cut at *a*, and the fourth year will present the appearance of fig. 4. It will then most likely begin to throw out fruiting-spurs: these should be carefully encouraged, for it depends on the number of spurs which a branch exhibits whether the tree is to bear a good show of fruit or not.

The tiers of branches, as they advance in height, should be regulated, so that every side is furnished with an equal number of branches. In the autumn of the year the tree will re-

Fig. 4.

semble fig. 5. The pruning is now confined to shortening the leading shoots and the laterals where the lines cross (fig. 5) the branches. The spurs should be carefully examined, and if any of them get long and branching, prune them in, as described and illustrated in fig. 6. If any of them promise to be unfruitful, follow the method described in figs. 1 and 2.

The fifth year the tree, continuing its progressive growth, presents the appearance of fig. 6. It is now a tree of considerable size, and requires, besides the regular annual pruning of the

Training Fruit-trees.

leading shoots and spurs, that the lateral branches should be cut in a line as nearly as possible to that indicated between *a* and *b* in fig. 6. We see in the figure some short lateral shoots crowding towards the centre: all these, if present, should be pruned away. After this, careful pruning is all the tree requires, taking care that the lower branches are not shaded by the upper ones, which is attained by pruning

Fig. 5.

them at greater length than those above; for it is one of the great principles on which this mode of training has been advocated, that the trees should be so managed that the advancing tier of branches shall not interfere with the swelling and ripening of the fruit on the lower tier by overshading them. During every summer all superfluous shoots should be rubbed off as they appear, and all strong shoots in the spurs should also be stopped during that season, in order to insure vigorous action in the remaining buds, while the base of the pyramid is to be extended as far as is consistent with the development of fruit-bearing habits: and this will probably be best attained by making it a rule, that as soon as

Fig. 6.

a shoot has extended from eight to ten inches, the point should be cut. By this practice the more powerful shoots are checked, and the weaker shoots encouraged. The advantages derived from this system of training may be stated as follows:—

1. An increased number of trees in the same space.

Training Fruit-trees.

2. The trainer has his trees more directly under control.

3. Increase of crops.

4. Ornamental and uniform appearance.

Some years ago, M. Cappe, a gentleman of very great experience in the management of fruit-trees, and curator of the gardens belonging to the Museum of Natural History in Paris, devised a modification of the pyramidal form, which secures a more complete diffusion of light and air in the interior of the trees, causing the centre of the tree to be more fruitful, and the fruit to ripen and colour more perfectly. He terms it the winged pyramid, and certainly a tree so managed exhibits the highest skill in pruning and training, and is, independently of its fruit-bearing qualities, a most beautiful object. In adopting this system of training, a long pole of oak, or some other imperishable wood, some thirty feet in length, and charred at the lower extremity for about four feet, is employed. The charred end is driven firmly into the soil, close to the stem of the tree. At the upper extremity of the pole is fixed a strong iron ring or hoop, perforated with five holes equidistant from each other ; five strong stumps of oak, charred like the pole, are driven into the earth, at spots corresponding with the holes in the hoop, the tops being four inches above the ground and having a strong staple attached to them. Five iron rods with hooks are attached to the staples at one end, and to the holes in the hoops at the other : this is the framework of the winged pyramidal tree. These preparations being completed, the tree is planted in the soil, and on a station previously prepared for it, and pruned annually, so as to produce lateral branches in the manner already described. The branches are to be trained in right lines, slightly rising at the points towards the iron rods. It is evident that there will be regulated lines or openings between each of the five rods, into which light and air penetrate without obstruction, the openings, also enabling the operator to reach every part of the tree with great facility; for the radiating branches should not

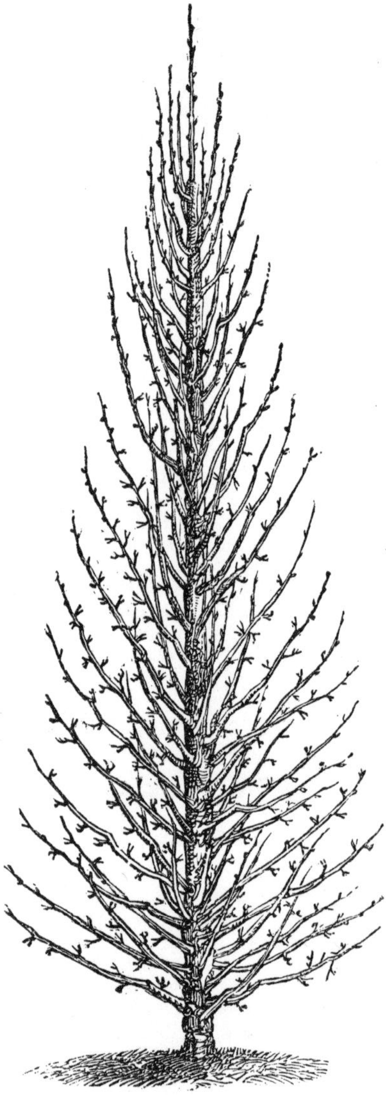

Fig. 7.

be too close together in trees trained in this manner: 20 inches would be a proper distance, though that would greatly depend upon the habit of the tree. In one of vigorous growth, that distance would not be too great; but for one of delicate growth 16 inches would probably be better.

Any large and straight tree that has

Fig. 8.

been allowed to grow in a wild manner, may, by grafting, be converted into the pyramidal form, like that illustrated in fig. 7. By a process of this kind, following the directions already given for side-grafting, fine new varieties of fruit may be raised in a comparatively short period, and a comparatively lifeless tree converted into an object of great beauty.

Fig. 9.

Another method of training the pear-tree, which has obtained some reputation with our French neighbours, was first practised by M. Verrier, chief gardener at Saulsaye, by whose name it is known. The tree is subjected to this training when it has attained a central stem and two lateral branches, as in fig. 8. In the autumn or winter pruning of the following year, the two

Training Fruit-trees.

side-branches are trained horizontally, as in fig. 9, and pruned back to about two-thirds of their length, with a bud immediately below the cut. The stem itself is pruned back to about 18 inches above the side-branches, taking care that there are three buds immediately below the cut,—one on each side, well-placed, and a third in front to continue the stem. With the fall of the leaf in the following year the tree

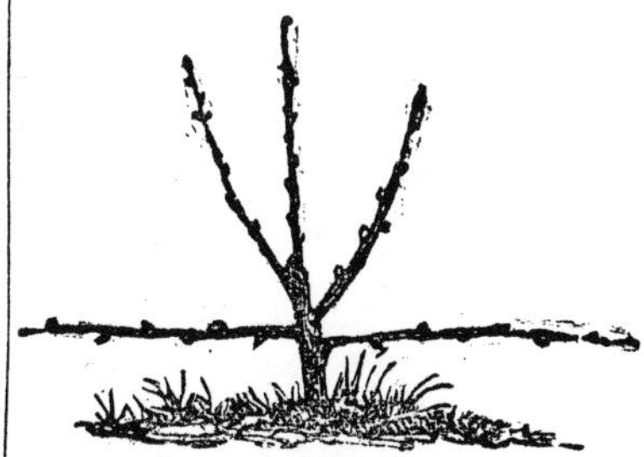

Fig. 10.

will be as represented in fig. 10, with two horizontal shoots, a central stem, and two other untrained side-shoots. When the pruning season arrives, the same process of cutting back takes place, each of the new side-shoots being cut back to two-thirds of its length, the two lower branches to two-

Fig. 11.

thirds of the year's growth, and the stem to within 18 inches of the second pair of laterals, leaving three well-placed buds immediately below, as before, to continue a third pair of side-branches and the stem. With the fifth year's growth the lower side-branches will have atttained as much horizontal extension on the wall or espalier as it is intended to give them.

Having, therefore, nailed or tied them to the trellis, give the end of the shoot a gentle curve upwards.

Continuing this annual process of cutting back after each year's growth, in some eleven years from the graft the tree will have covered a wall 12 or 14 feet high, and 6 feet on each side of the stem ; each side-shoot, when it is within 18 inches of the one immediately below it, receiving an upward direction, until the tree is as here shown. The stem, as well as the side-shoots, having reached the top of the wall, the extremities of the branches are pruned back every year to about 18 inches below the coping, in order to leave room for the development of the terminal bud, which is necessary to draw the sap upwards for the nourishment of the fruit. After 16 or 18 years, a healthy tree, properly trained on this system, presents a surface of upwards of 60 square feet of young fruit-bearing wood. The symmetry of the tree is pleasant to look at, and it is said to be admirably balanced for vegetation, and consequently for fruit-bearing.

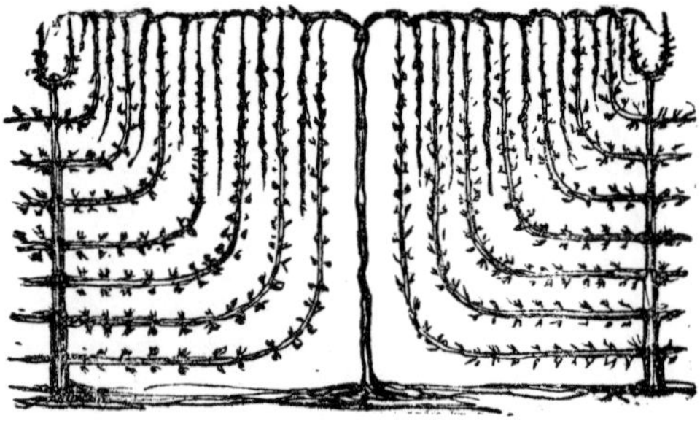

Fig. 12.

One objection to this mode of training is, that the buds do not always occur at the right spot for projecting new side-shoots. When this is the case, the process of shield-budding is had recourse to in August. In other respects, the same principle of pruning is adopted as in pyramid-trained trees, the only modification being the removal of the spurs thrown out between the tree and the wall. Another objection to the system is the time which must elapse before the wall is covered; but this is inseparable from any mode of growing apples and pears on walls, and may be met by planting vines between each, running a central rod of the vine to the top of the wall; stopping it there for the first year, and carrying a shoot on each side under the coping, with descending rods at intervals, calculated not to interfere with the side-shoots of the pear-tree.

TRAINING-WIRES, Novel Mode.

We have recently had introduced to our notice a very neat and efficient mode of training trees against walls; also of training all sorts of espalier trees, raspberries, and indeed all bush fruit, by means of stretched galvanized wire. By this system nails and shreds are entirely dispensed with, the walls are not injured, and no harbour is afforded for insects, and the tying of the branches is effected in much less time than nailing. The wire, together with a very ingenious contrivance for stretching and tightening it, and full instructions both for wall-trees and espaliers, may be had of Messrs. Barnard & Bishop.

TRANSPLANTING.

In transplanting any tree or shrub, especially evergreens, be careful to preserve the same aspect; that is, keep the same sides to the north, south, east, and west, as before. This will greatly facilitate the speedy establishment of the plant in its new situation.

Transplanting is an important operation, and in a general way November is the best month for it. To save time, it is frequently desirable to transplant large trees and shrubs. The effect of ten or twenty years' growth is gained on any given spot at once. This is of immense importance in the lifetime of a man, and the practice of transplanting large trees is therefore popular and highly to be commended; neither is there much risk of failure, with proper caution and skill, and it is not so expensive as many imagine. With the aid of McGlashin's patent transplanting machines, trees of almost any size may be safely and expeditiously removed: in fact, these machines forcibly remove earth and roots, and all, with the minimum risk of failure. But even very large trees and shrubs may be safely moved with no other machinery than a few strong planks nailed on a harrow sledge. In this mode of transplanting, a trench is dug round the plant at a distance from the bole of two-thirds the diameter of the top, and to a depth of two to five feet, according to the age and size of the tree, character of the soil, depth of roots, &c., leaving a space of from two to three feet at the back of the tree untouched. At the same time, the front, or part where the tree is intended to come out, should be approached at an easy angle of inclination, extending from two to three feet beyond the circumference of the trench already begun. The earth is rapidly removed from the trench; the roots carefully preserved as you proceed. The size of the ball in the centre must be determined by the nature of the soil and size of the plant. Its size is of less consequence than the preservation of the roots.

As the removal of the earth proceeds, a fork must be used to separate the

roots from the soil, and they should be carefully bent back and covered over until the work is finished. After excavating from one to three feet beyond the line of the bole of the tree or shrub, according to its size, introduce into the vacant space a sledge or low truck; cut through the solid part at the back line, and the tree will rest on the machine. This should be furnished with four rings at the corners, through which ropes or cords should be fastened and firmly fixed to the bole of the tree. Of course, some soft substance, such as hay or moss, will be introduced between the bole and the cords, to prevent them chafing the bark. The tree is then ready for removal; the necessary horse or manual power can be applied: the plant will slide gently up the inclined plane, and may be conveyed any distance desired with facility. Sometimes it may be impossible to fix the cord through the back rings until the tree is out of the hole. In that, and indeed in any case, cords had better be attached to the top, and carefully held by men, lest a too strong vibration of the top should upset the machine, or topple the tree over. The hole destined to receive the tree should have an inclined plane on each side to enable the horses to walk through. When the ball arrives towards the centre of the hole, the horses stop. If the tree is not too heavy, the truck or sledge is prised up by manual strength, and the plant gradually slid off. If very heavy, a strong chain is passed under the ball, attached to a couple of strong crowbars; the horses are applied to the other end of the truck, and the tree drops off into its place. The roots are carefully undone, and spread throughout the whole mass of soil as the process of filling-up goes on; three strong posts are driven in to form a triangle, and rails securely fixed to them across the ball to keep it immovable; the top reduced in proportion to the mutilation the roots may have suffered; the whole thoroughly drenched and puddled in with water and covered over with four inches of litter to ward off cold and drought, and the operation is complete. If this operation is well performed, the loss will not average more than from five to eight per cent. The principle involved in all planting is the same, and only of secondary importance to securing as many healthy roots as possible. The stability or immovability of both root and top comes next; for, if not attended to, every breeze that blows is analogous to a fresh removal. No sooner do the roots grasp hold of the soil than they are forcibly wrenched out of it again, and the plant lives, if at all, as by a miracle. The planting of young trees and small shrubs is so simple as scarcely to require instructions. Always make the hole considerably larger than the space required by the roots, whether few or many, so that they may find soft recently-moved soil to grow in; and yet the soil must not be left too loose. If so moist as not to need watering, which will moisten and also consolidate the soil, it may be gently trodden down round the roots.

In reference to the proper distance at which shrubs should be planted, much depends upon the object in view. A safe rule, however, is to plant thick, and thin quickly: from three to four feet is a good average for small shrubs and trees. In three years, two out of three plants should be removed; and in planting it is well to introduce rapid-growing common things amongst choice plants, to nurse them up; only the nursing must not continue too long.

TRELLIS-WORK.

This may frequently be introduced with good effect in the mixed flower and kitchen-garden, to shut out buildings or unsightly objects. Small oak stands, or small larch poles, about five or six feet apart, and having the intervals filled with thin iron wires crossing each other, form the most durable trellis-work. Against the walls of a house a very nice trellis-work may be made with a lacing of copper wire over nails of the same. This may be worked in any pattern and carried in any direction; to this wire the creepers may be tied when necessary; and in this way the walls of houses may be covered with flowers or evergreens, without any injury to the brick-work from continual nailing.

TRITO'MA.

An exceedingly showy free-flowering plant, with long graceful leaves and majestic flower-spikes, three to seven feet in height, crowned with densely-flowered spikes of bloom, which are produced during the autumn months, 18 to 27 inches long.

Culture.—Dig and well work the soil to the depth of two or three feet, adding plenty of rotted manure. The crown of the plant should not be more than an inch and a half in the soil; for winter protection surround the plant with two inches of sawdust, firmly trodden. Remove this early in May: from then till the plant is in bloom, weak liquid manure must be applied in large quantities, especially during dry weather.

Tritoma glaucescens,—rich scarlet.
,, J. grandis,—bright scarlet, tall and late.

TROPÆ'OLUM (nat. ord. Tropæola'ceæ). Half-hardy Annuals.

A tribe of elegant-growing, profuse-flowering, and easily-cultivated climbers, combining with these important qualities great richness and brilliancy of colour, with finely-formed and beautifully-marked flowers. For pillars and rafters, in the greenhouse or conservatory, they are invaluable; for covering trellises, verandahs, and bowers out of doors, they are of equal importance; while for bedding purposes we have only to remind our readers of the important part they annually play on the terraces of the Crystal Palace. When used for bedding, they should be regularly and carefully pegged down, interlacing the shoots, and occasionally removing the large leaves. In pleasure-grounds, where the beds are sometimes protected with fancy wire-work against the depredations of rabbits and hares, the tropæolums are invaluable for covering it: they grow rapidly, are easily trained, and continue flowering the whole summer and autumn.

We may remark that all the "Lobbianum" varieties bloom beautifully through the winter months in the greenhouse or conservatory, so that where cut flowers are in demand they will be found an invaluable acquisition. Grow freely in light rich soil.

TU'BEROSE (nat. ord. Hemerocallid'eæ).

A bulbous-rooted plant from the East Indies; flowers white, very odoriferous. They require to be started in a pit. In January plant the bulbs singly in very small pots in sandy loam; plunge them in a pit of moderate heat; give little or no water till they have made a start, then water sparingly. When they have filled their pots with roots, shift them and re-plunge them until they show bloom, when they may be removed to the greenhouse, where they will last in flower about two months.

TU'LIPS (nat. ord. Tulipa'ceæ).

There is a peculiarity belonging to tulips which does not, so far as we are aware, belong to any other flower. The seedlings, in their first bloom, generally produce flowers without any stripes or markings, all the upright portions of the petal being self-coloured, flowering for years without any such variegations, when they are called breeders. After some years they break out into stripes: if these are liked, they are named; but they have multiplied in the breeder state, and may have been distributed in all directions, each person possessed of one which has broken using the privilege of naming it; hence many, with different synonymes, are one and the same thing. It is another peculiarity, that of twenty of a sort in the same bed, scarcely two may come up alike, although good judges can recognize them. These particularities interfere with their cultivation, though, as Mr. Glenny surmises, they may be one of the charms of tulip-cultivation.

The perfection of soil for tulip-culture would be three inches of the top of a rich loamy pasture, the turf of which, cleared of wire-worm, grub, and insect, has lain by till thoroughly rotted, and which has been repeatedly turned and picked: the decayed vegetable matter will suffice without other dressing. The tulip-bed should run north and south, with drainage perfect, but without stones or rubbish at the bottom. The bed may be dug out four feet wide and 2 feet 6 inches deep, and the compost previously prepared filled in till it is a few inches above the path, the centre being two inches higher than the sides. All water must be withdrawn from the bottom of the bed: it is not enough to give drainage, unless an outlet is found, so as to avoid stagnant water. Giving a few days for the bed to settle, rake all smooth, leaving the bed three inches above the path. On this the tulips are placed in seven rows across the bed, and six inches apart in the rows. They are pressed in a little; soil is then placed upon them, three inches above the crown of the bulbs, so that the bed being raised in the centre, the middle row will be covered four or five inches. The bulbs are planted, of course, according to their height and colour,—those growing 15 or 18 inches occupying the outside rows; the second rows on each side are those growing two feet, and those growing 2 feet 6 inches occupy the three centre rows. When planted and covered, they may be left until the leaf-buds begin to peep through the ground. Of course the sides of the bed must be protected by edgings either of wood or tiles.

As frost approaches, while giving as much air as possible, they should be protected against it by mats or other shelter, but not longer than is necessary; otherwise they get drawn up weakly. In February they begin to appear, when the ground should be stirred, all lumps broken, and pressed close round the stems. As the spikes begin to open, they form a receptacle for the wet, and the frost must not then be allowed to reach them. When the colours begin to show, in order to protect their bloom, a top-cloth must be provided to shelter them from the sun, taking care that no more air than is absolutely necessary is excluded, the cloth being let down on the sunny side only, and that only when the sun is powerful.

By the end of June the stems will have turned brown or yellow. As soon as the leaves begin to decay, the bulbs may be taken up, dried, and stored away in drawers provided for them, which are usually marked in seven compartments, so that each row in the bed occupies a similar place in the drawers.

The best time for planting is the last fortnight in October, or early in November. Tulip-seed may be sown either in spring or autumn, and in the soil already described; it should be saved from the best flowers only, and those grown by themselves, where no inferior pollen can reach them. The small offsets should be planted by themselves and labelled, in similar soil to that already described. Breeders such as we have described may be grown in any soil.

Tulips are divided into Roses, Byblomens, and Bizarres. Roses have a white ground, and crimson, pink, or scarlet markings.

Byblomens are those having a white ground, and purple, lilac, or black markings.

Bizarres have a yellow ground, with any coloured marks that present themselves.

Self-tulips are those which are of one colour, such as white or yellow, showing no inclination to sport into other colours.

Early Tulips.—For the purposes of winter and spring gardening, early-flowering tulips, double and single, are even more indispensable than the hyacinth, narcissus, and crocus. Their rich, brilliant, and diversified hues constitute, for the sitting-room, conservatory, and winter garden, a charm of no ordinary character, while in the beds and borders of the spring flower-garden their picturesque effect and glowing combination of colours exceed those afforded by any other section of garden favourites. Their extreme hardiness, certainty of blooming, and the absence of all difficulty in their cultivation, distinctly entitle them to a preference in the choice of occupants for the spring flower-garden.

For the development of spring gardening, where tulips are made to form a leading and prominent feature, the country is deeply indebted to her Grace the Dowager Duchess of Sutherland; and no small credit is due to Mr. Fleming, her gardener. The spring flower-garden at Cliveden, with its annual display of tulips, &c., and the attention given to these bulbs at the Crystal Palace and the Royal Botanic Gardens, Regent's Park, have done much to stimulate the extended cultivation of spring flowers. Their influence has been felt not only around London, but in the most remote parts of the island; so that grounds which at one time possessed little or no attraction till the bedding plants or spring-sown seeds commenced blooming, are now as rich with floral beauty during April and May as in August and September.

Tulips do well in the shade, and there they remain long in bloom.

Early Single Tulips.—No section of tulips displays so great a variety of delicate, striking, and attractive colours. Of Selfs, there are beautiful scarlets, crimsons, whites, and yellows; of parti-colours, snow-white grounds, striped and feathered with purple, violet, crimson, rose, puce, and cerise, and yellow grounds, with crimson, scarlet, and red flakes and feathers; so that only those who have cultivated the varieties of early single tulips systematically can form any just idea of their beauty, either as regards the shape of the flowers, the brilliancy and variety of their colours, or their general value for decorative purposes.

"For the encouragement of those who possess small town gardens," say Messrs. Barr & Sugden, "we may just mention that in 1860 we had a collection in a little London garden, with a due north aspect, and there the colours came out with as much brilliancy as if the plants had been cultivated under infinitely more favourable circumstances."

Culture in ornamental vases and other elegant contrivances should be the same in every respect as that recommended for the hyacinth.

Culture in pots is also the same as that of the hyacinth, except that three bulbs should be planted in a 4- or 5-inch, and five in a 6-inch pot. To produce an effective display, they should be grown close to the glass, and during fine days have abundance of air. Those intended for early blooming should be forced as soon as the shoot appears.

Culture out of doors precisely that of the hyacinth, except that the bulbs should not be planted more than four to six inches apart, when an effective display is desired, though many persons plant them six to eight inches from each other.

In beds they can be very advantageously arranged in distinct colours, either in circles, diamonds, or with the colours intermixed: we have seen charming beds where the tulips have been planted in geometrical figures, the double tournesol, which flowers simultaneously with the single varieties, being used to define the figures. These suggestions are merely thrown out to show how capable the tulip is of being used for fanciful designs, &c. The crown of the bulb should be three inches under the surface, and should the weather be severe, a few branches placed on the bed will be found ample protection.

Time of Planting for out-door Decoration.—The early part of November, or as soon after that period as convenient. We have planted the tulip as late as January, and have had a splendid display. We do not, however, recommend keeping the bulbs so long out of the ground.

Early Double Tulips.—The massive form, brilliant, diversified, and beautiful colours, which are leading features in double tulips, admirably adapt them for beds on the lawn, terrace, or flower-garden, and for edgings to rhododendron, azalea, and rose beds, or for planting in the flower and shrubbery borders in groups of three or more.

In pots the varieties of this section are very attractive, but as a rule they are better adapted for out-door than in-door decoration.

Parrot Tulips.—The parrot tulip has a singularly picturesque appearance; the flowers are large and the colours brilliant, so that when planted in flower-borders and the front of shrubberies they produce a most striking effect. When grown in hanging baskets, and so planted as to cause their large gay flowers to droop over the side, the effect is remarkable and unique.

The following are the best varieties, price 1*s.* 3*d.* per dozen:—

Admiral de Constantinople,—red, streaked wlth orange.
Coffee-colour,—yellow, green, and brown, mottled.
Large Yellow,—slightly striped with red.
Markgraaf Van Baden,—crimson striped yellow.
Monster Rouge,—crimson.
Perfecta,—yellow, scarlet, and green.
Fine mixed, 1*s.* per dozen.

TURF.

The appearance of a garden depends greatly on the quality of the turf and the way in which it is kept. Close cutting and continual rolling is the secret of good turf. On good soil little else is requisite; but on poor sandy soil the verdure must be maintained by occasional waterings with liquid manure and a dressing with guano or soot, if the lawn be not so near the house as to render such applications objectionable.

TURNIPS.

Preparation of the Land.—A somewhat light, sandy, but deep rich soil, is most suitable for turnips, and is indeed essential to secure bulbs of mild and delicate flavour. If the summer crops sustain any check during their growth, they are apt to be stringy and high-flavoured. Select, then, a deep light soil, manure it heavily, and trench to a depth of two feet, early in autumn. If ground must be used for the summer sowings which was not trenched in autumn, this should be done before putting in the seed.

Time and Manner of Sowing.—Sow a small breadth of the early Dutch, for the chance of a crop, upon a south border, or in a warm, sheltered situation, early in March; and as this sowing is liable to run to seed soon, put in a small quantity of the same variety about the middle of the month, and again early in April, sowing a small breadth of the American Strap-leaf at the same time; afterwards sow at intervals of three weeks or a month till July, and for a winter supply from the beginning to the middle of August. On light warm soils, in favourable localities, useful-sized bulbs may be obtained from sowings made early in September. The Orange Jelly is one of the best varieties for autumn sowing; but if a white-fleshed turnip is required, use the red-top American Stone. All the sowings should be made in shallow drills from 12 to 18 inehes apart, regulating the distance by the size of bulbs which may be most esteemed: 12 inches will be sufficient for the early and late sowings. Scatter the seed very thinly and evenly, and cover it lightly with the finest of the soil. In summer, when the ground is dry, the drills should be well watered before sowing, and if the seed is steeped in water for 24 hours, this will hasten germination.

After-management.—Thin out the plants as soon as they are sufficiently strong to draw, so that they may stand from six to nine inches apart in the row. If fly makes its appearance—and this is generally very troublesome during summer in warm localities, dust the plants over with quick-lime early in the morning, while the leaves are moist with dew. Repeat this operation as often as may be necessary. Keep the surface of the ground open and free from weeds by frequent stirrings with the hoe.

U'LEX (nat. ord. Legumino'sæ).

This is the botanial name for the Furze, of which there are several varieties. All are free-flowering evergreen shrubs with yellow blossoms: they may be propagated by cuttings, and most of them from seed, which they produce and ripen freely. The double-blossomed furze is singularly beautiful and very useful for hedges. Where furze of any kind is used for this purpose, the best plan is to raise a bank the height desired, wider at bottom than at top, and along the ridge to plant the cuttings, or sow seed, as may be preferred. The Irish furze, *U. stricta,* is an upright variety and has no spines; like the double-blossomed kind, it is said never to ripen seed, but must be propagated by cuttings.

UL'MUS (nat. ord. Ulma'ceæ).

The Elm is very ornamental in parks and pleasure-grounds. It requires a deep rich soil. The Weeping Elm is a very beautiful variety.

UMBI'LICUS (nat. ord. Crassula'ceæ).

Navelwort; a class of plants allied to the houseleeks; mostly natives of the Cape of Good Hope. They grow well in any light sandy soil mixed with lime rubbish.

UMBRELLA-TREE.

A name given by the Americans to one species of the Magnolia,—*M.*

tripetala—from the size of its leaves. The flowers are white and very fragrant. Single specimens are very handsome objects on lawns; they flourish best in peat.

URTI'CA, the Nettle (nat. ord. Urtica'ceæ).

The common nettle, *U. dioica*, is known to every one as a wayside weed. There are, however, some beautiful varieties well worthy of garden cultivation. *U. reticulata*, from the West Indies, is remarkable for its dark green foliage and red and yellow flowers. *U. nivea*, from China, is a half-hardy perennial, with fine leaves, the under side of which is silvery white; a fine plant for flower-borders or the centres of beds; grows in light rich soil: blooms freely the first year. This plant yields the fibre called Chinese grass.

US'NEA (nat. ord. Cryptogam'ia).

This is one of the lichens common on oak and other trees.

UVULA'RIA (nat. ord. Melantha'ceæ).

Hardy North American perennials, bearing flowers of a pale yellow. Like most American plants, they succeed best in bog earth. They produce an abundance of suckers, from which their propagation is very easy.

VACCIN'IUM (nat. ord. Erica'ceæ).

This is the Whortleberry, a pretty little heath-like shrub with drooping flowers and showy fruit. The Cranberry and the Bilberry belong to the same class of plants.

VALE'RIAN (nat. ord. Valeria'neæ).

Perennial plants suitable for rock-work.

VALLISNE'RIA (nat. ord. Hydrocharid'eæ).

A curious and most interesting water-plant, so named after Antonio Vallisneri, an Italian botanist. It should be potted in turfy loam, and the pot sunk in the water-tank of a greenhouse or conservatory. The male and female flowers are on different plants;—the latter rise on a spiral stalk to the surface, while the former are produced at the bottom. "Before the anthers burst to discharge the pollen," says Mrs. Loudon, "the male flowers detach themselves from their stalks and rise to the surface, on which they float like little white bubbles. After the pollen has been distributed over the stigmas, the male flowers wither, and the spiral stalks of the females coil up again, so as to draw the seed-vessel under the water, that it may ripen at the bottom and burst when just in the proper place to deposit its seeds. Nothing can be more beautiful than the whole arrangement: and nothing can show more strikingly the admirable manner in which the economy of nature is carried on." This plant is very suitable for aquaria.

VANIL'LA (nat. ord. Orchida'ceæ).

This little creeping parasite will flower best in the strong damp heat of the orchid-house. It throws out roots at every joint, and requires plenty of pieces of bark, &c., to which to attach itself.

VANTHOL'S TULIPS (nat. ord. Tulipa'ceæ).

These are dwarf varieties which flower in early spring. There are two sorts, double and single; the latter are the most beautiful. Both, however, are very effective as edgings for beds. The cultivation they require is that of tulips generally.

VARIEGATED PLANTS.

Much attention has been paid of late years to plants of variegated foliage, and certainly they are a great success. Few things are more attractive than the different sorts of caladiums, begonias, *Coleus alocasea*, &c. For a plant to be truly variegated, that is, able to retain its different colours under propagation, the edges of the leaves must be well defined. We frequently meet with party-coloured leaves which are mere sports, and which revert to their original hue if any attempt is made to increase the plants by cuttings, &c.

VASES.

These may be introduced into pleasure-grounds, especially upon terraces, with very good effect. They can be filled with soil and planted, or pots of choice flowers can be set in them and changed as soon as the blossom begins to fade.

VEGETABLES.

There are several processes, most of them of French origin, by which vegetables of the more delicate varieties, as French beans, green peas, and cauliflowers, may be preserved in their green state, and be nearly as fresh as when first gathered. In the *Revue Horticole*, the following is given as the method employed by M. Gohen, of Montigny, for preserving French beans in a fresh and green state, so as to keep sweet till the following season, when new crops are fit for gathering. The beans for the purpose are gathered in dry weather, and after the dews of the night have been evaporated. They are plunged into boiling water, taken out again immediately, and allowed to stand till they are cool, when they are put into a small cask, a layer of vine-leaves being placed at the bottom; over this is laid a layer of beans six inches thick, then another thin layer of vine-leaves and then beans; and so on alternately, until the cask is nearly full, when the whole are covered with a layer of vine-leaves. A board is now fitted to the cask, neatly fitting into it, and a weight placed over it, sufficient to press the contents of the cask into a compact mass. When the pressure has been on it some few hours, a sufficient quantity of salt and water should be poured over it to saturate the whole mass freely, and the board and weight replaced. As the salt and water evaporate, it should be replenished from time to time, to keep the whole contents of the cask moist, taking care that the board is always replaced immediately after portions of the vegetable have been removed for use.

VEGETABLE MARROW.

Preparation of the Soil.—These require a very deep, light, rich soil, and if planted in the open ground, a sheltered and warm situation. Dig pits two feet wide and deep, and fill with well-prepared fermenting manure, and cover about a foot deep with soil. The pits should not be less than ten feet apart, and should be prepared about a week before planting, so that the soil may be properly warmed by the heat from the manure. The tops of compost-heaps, and hills of decaying leaves, manure, &c., will, however, afford the best possible situation for their growth.

Sowing, and Preparation of the Plants.—Sow early in April, in a pot or pan, filled with light soil, covering the seeds about half an inch; place in gentle heat, and as soon as the plants are sufficiently strong to handle, pot them off into 7-inch pots, putting two plants in each, and replace them near the glass in the warmth. When well established, remove to a cold frame, and gradually prepare for planting out, by a freer exposure to air, &c.

Planting and After-management.—Towards the end of May, or as soon as the weather is warm and appears to be settled, and the plants ready, plant them out, and protect them for a time by hand-glasses, or other means, and attend to watering until the roots get hold of the soil. Train and regulate the shoots, so as to prevent them from growing too closely together, and stop them if necessary, to forward the growth of the fruit. Do not allow the plants to feel the want of water at the roots, but if planted in suitable situations, watering will seldom be necessary.

The most approved varieties of the vegetable marrow are the following; each variety *4d.* per packet, or the collection for *3s. 6d.*

Barrel-shaped,—2 ft. long.
Cluster,—habit compact and bush-like.
Cream-colour,—large, 1½ ft. long.
Custard—a small handsome variety, particularly delicate in flavour.
Clear yellow,—10 inches long.
Egg-shaped,—1½ ft. long.
Green and orange,—1½ ft. long.
Melon-shaped,—large and extra fine.
Oval,—10 inches long.
Pear-shaped,—10 inches.
,, beautifully striped.
Small,—white.
,, miniature, very pretty, 6 inches long.
Warted,—oblong, very handsome, 1 ft. long.
,, large, cream, 14 inches long.
Yellow,—speckled, 9 inches long.
,, striped green, very handsome.

VEGETABE MOULD.

Vegetable mould, the richest of all garden soils, contains from 5 to 12 per cent. of *humus;* that is, decomposed vegetable and animal matter.

VENTILATION.

Wherever, for gardening purposes, artificial heat is employed, artificial ventilation, as a matter of course, must be provided. To frames upon hot-beds, and to garden-pits, this ventilation may easily be given by lowering or lifting the lights. In glass houses some machinery is requisite on account of the height and the greater heaviness of the glass covering. The plan introduced by Mr. Messenger is that generally approved.

Upright or side-lights, two feet high, which run the entire length of the house, are made to open and shut by means of a rod of iron, which runs the whole length also. To this rod are attached shorter rods at intervals of four or five feet, with joints; the other end of the shorter rods being attached to the lights, both ends of the short rod working on a joint. To one end of the long rod is fixed a long screw, working in slings made to receive it. To this screw is attached a grooved wheel, which is made to revolve in an endless chain, acted upon by another grooved wheel, turned by a handle placed in some convenient part of the house. By the action of the screw, the long rod is drawn backwards or forwards, which acts upon the short rods, and opens or shuts the light to any required point. The same system of raising the lights may be applied to one or more of the lights, or to the whole, as may be necessary.

The system of ventilation adopted by Mr. Messenger will be better understood by reference to the diagram, in which B, B are short rods, connected with the sling A at one end, and the lights at the other. The dotted lines, D, represent the upright divisions which support the roof; E, the screw-slings, in which the screw F is to work; G is a grooved wheel in which the endless chain is to work and turn the screw; in fact, this is its axis. The handle H is fixed to some convenient place on the front wall, being the mover of the whole apparatus. As the rod is moved from right to left, the short rods push the lights up and admit fresh air as they are acted upon: by reversing the screw, the opposite result is obtained. The ridge-ventilation is obtained in precisely the same manner; the lights under the coping being pushed out or drawn down by turning a handle attached to a long endless chain on the end wall.

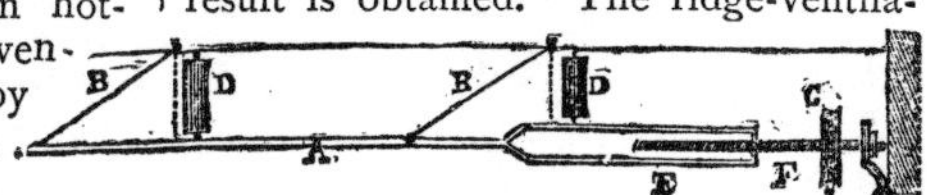

Fig. 1.

The results of this system, to use Mr. Messenger's words, are,

1. perfect ventilation; 2. non-interference with the plants; 3. no risk of broken glass by the lights falling down; 4. keeping out rain when the lights are open.

The roof of his houses Mr. Messenger makes of very light rafters, only three inches by two, strenghthening them by means of a tension-rod placed under each. These are firmly fixed at each end, and kept extended by means of two iron rods fixed in the rafters at equal distances from each other, and from the extremities. Between these rafters sash-bars are placed, which, when glazed and painted, are perfectly waterproof, and extremely light and elegant in appearance; the tension-rods being graceful, and the rafters light and airy, and yet strong enough for every purpose required. To his other patents, Mr. Messenger has added a new principle of glazing for greenhouse and other roofs, which is perfectly waterproof, and air-proof also, without putty. With this invention the roof may be nearly flat; thus effecting a great saving in material, no paint being required in connection with it.

The system of glazing patented by Mr. Messenger is simple and ingenious: the upper surface of the sash-bar, of which we give a section, is an open gutter, and the glazing is performed by bending the edge of the glass over the

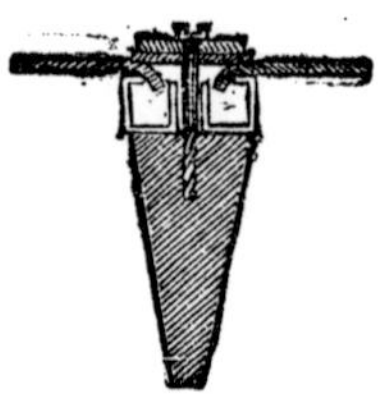

Fig. 2.

edge of the gutter. The accompanying engravings will make more clear the principle of this mode of glazing. The gutters are made of either lead, copper, zinc, or iron, or the sash-bar itself can be made with a gutter on its surface. The mode of securing the glass down to the gutter is shown by the section, fig. 2. It is done by a screw passing through a brass plate and India-rubber, into the wood or metal bar; the India-rubber pressing slightly upon both sides of the glass, keeps it in its place. If the glass is very heavy, zinc or copper clips are used

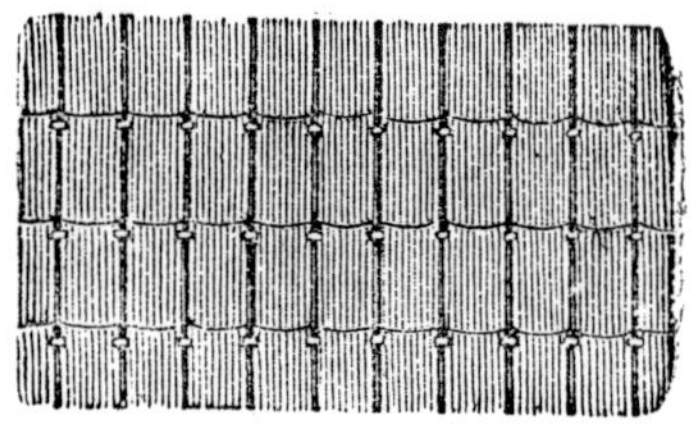

Fig. 3.

to prevent it slipping down. Fig. 3 is a plan of the roof, showing the brass plates and shape of glass, which is so arranged as to convey the condensed vapour as well as the external rain into the internal gutter, whence it escapes by a gutter attached to the wall-plate.

In the ventilation of the forcing-houses at Frogmore, an iron rod, which works on brass bearings or chains, runs the whole length of the house about a foot from the wall-plate. On this shaft, opposite each light, is a brass pinion working into a toothed quadrant attached to the bottom rail of each light. This shaft is turned by a handle, when the quadrants are either thrown out or drawn in, and the whole light thrown open or shut to the extent required. In the back wall of each intermediate light is a ventilating-frame, which is opened or shut by similar apparatus: above these frames over the glass is a corresponding number of open gratings. Flues or chambers in the wall open into the flues at the bottom, while the grating covers the opening at top. When it is desired to thoroughly ventilate the house, the fan-lights being open, it is only necessary to turn the screw or worm, which is connected by the rod attached to the lever; and the lever being attached to the end of an iron shaft running the whole length of the house, the whole are thrown open at once.

VERBE'NA (nat. ord. Verbena'ceæ).

One of the most useful of bedding plants, a native of South America. The named varieties are infinite; every year adds many novelties to the list. The plants seed freely, and are of easy cultivation by cuttings; they also root rapidly by being pegged down. The following management has been recommended by a very experienced gardener:—

"I have tried many different sizes of pots and pans for verbenas. I have found nothing so useful or successful as a score of cuttings in a 48-sized pot. The pots are filled one-third full of drainage, one inch of rough leaf-mould over it; then fill to within 1½ inch of the top with equal parts of loam, leaf-mould, or peat and sand, finishing with half an inch of sand; insert the cuttings in the usual manner, making sure that the *base* of the cutting is made firm. Water *level*—a point of great moment in excluding the air from the part where roots are to be emitted, as well as in the future watering of the cuttings,—and the work is finished. Verbenas are also best left in the store or cutting-pots until February; and, unlike calceolarias, if enough are kept over the winter for stock, spring-struck plants are best both for growth and flower. This last remark is equally applicable to petunias, ageratums, lobelias, &c. Verbenas and other soft-wooded plants may also be struck in water; but I see no benefit whatever in the practice. I may also state, for the very few who do not know how to make a cutting, that the usual practice is to cut part of a branch level across at the base of a single leaf or pair of leaves, to remove this leaf or leaves, and place this part, the bottom or thick end of the cutting, in the soil, water, or damp moss, until it is rooted."

The following list contains some of the best varieties:—

Admiral Dundas,—bright crimson.
Ariosto,—dark mulberry.
Ariosto improved,—rich mulberry; robust habit; large truss; continuous and fine bloomer; good bedder.
Blue Bonnet,—blue.
Cupid,—cerise pink; white eye.
Earl of Shaftesbury,—blush-crimson; white eye.
Fairest of the Fair,—white; violet eye.
Fire-fly,—rich scarlet; fine habit.
Foxhunter,—scarlet; white eye; fine.
Garibaldi,—rich indigo.
Géant des Batailles,—brilliant crimson.
General Simpson,—carmine.
Impératrice Elisabeth,—finely striped.
Invincible,—shaded slate-blue.
Julie,—pale peach; white eye.
King of Verbenas,—rosy purple.
Lord Raglan,—carmine-scarlet.
Moonlight,—nearly white.
Mrs. Elphinstone,—puce tints; fine.
Mrs. Woodroofe,—scarlet.
Ocean Pearl,—purple; white eye.
Odorata,—superb rosy purple.
Parfum de Madeline,—lilac.
Prince Arthur,—rose, shaded.
Pulchella alba,—white.
Purple King.
Reine des Amazons,—blush.
Rosea compacta,—pure lake.
Snow-flake,—good white.
Star,—deep rosy crimson; lemon eye.
Sultana,—rich crimson; good tinge.
Titian,—plum, shaded cerise.
Volunteer,—dark purple maroon; white eye.

VERO'NICA, the Speedwell (nat. ord. Scrophularia'ceæ).

The evergreen shrubs of this genus, when well grown, are amongst the most valuable of autumn-blooming plants. Their handsome spikes of flowers, which are produced in great profusion and in succession for months, make them invaluable for conservatory and sitting-room decoration, and for prominent positions out of doors, where with a dry sub-soil and somewhat sheltered situation, the plants will generally stand the winter uninjured. The miniature annual varieties *V. Syriaca* and *alba* make very pretty small beds and edgings during the summer and autumn, but in spring they are much more effective; we therefore recommend their being sown in autumn for the decoration of the spring garden.

VICTO'RIA REGI'NA.

A most splendid aquatic plant, requiring much space and a very warm house. Its native country is Guiana, where it was discovered by Sir R. Shomburgk, in 1837, who described it as a "vegetable wonder." The leaves are from six to seven feet in diameter, salver-shaped, with a broad rim of light green above and vivid crimson below. Its flower, which rests upon the water, is in character with the leaves; when it first opens it is white, with pink in the centre, which spreads over the whole flower as it advances in age. It is generally pink the second day after its expansion. The flower is very sweet-scented.

VIN'CA (nat. ord. Apocyna'ceæ).

This is the classical name of the common Periwinkle, and of its class there are many beautiful varieties. *V. major elegantissima*, *V. major reticulata*, *V. minor argentea*, and *V. minor aurea*, are all variegated and very showy. They grow in any soil, and look well on rock-work. Under the name Vinca also are included many choice greenhouse evergreens, as remarkable for their shining green foliage as for their handsome circular flowers. Plants raised from seed which has been sown early in spring will be found useful for the ornamentation of flower-beds and borders in warm situations.

Vinca rosea,—rose, 2 ft., from East Indies.
 ,, alba,—white, with crimson eye, 2 ft., from East Indies.
Vinca alba pura nova,—pure white, 2 ft.
 ,, lutea nova,—pure white with yellow eye, 2 ft.

VINES.

It is certain that our moist and cloudy climate is not favourable to the ripening of the grape; its cultivation in the open air, therefore, requires great care; and in many seasons the most skilful management will fail to bring it to perfection. Nevertheless, the graceful trailing habit and beautiful foliage of the vine render it highly ornamental on the walls of a house; and for this it is worth cultivating, with the prospect of some fruit in favourable summers. It is also certain that in former days vineyards of considerable extent were cultivated, some remains of which are still found in Gloucestershire.

The vine is propagated by cuttings and by layering. Cuttings, made early in March or the latter end of February may be planted about the middle of March. The cuttings must be shoots of last year, shortened to about 12 inches, or three joints each; and if they have an inch or so of last year's wood at the bottom, it will be an advantage. They may be planted either in nursery rows until rooted, or planted at once where they are to remain, observing in the latter case to plant them in a slanting direction, and so deep that only one eye or joint is above-ground, and that close to the surface.

Vines are propagated by layering of the shoot of last year, or of a part of the branch, laying them about four or five inches deep and covering them with soil, leaving about three eyes above the ground; they are also layered in large pots, either by drawing the branch through the drainage-hole and filling the pot with soil, or by bending the branch and sinking it four or five inches in the soil and pegging it down there; it may then either be grown as a potted vine or, when fully rooted, transferred to its permanent place on the wall or vine border; in the latter case the soil of the border should be dug out for three or four feet, as directed for other wall trees, a solid concrete bottom formed, with thorough drainage to carry off the water, and the border filled in again, first with bones and other animal remains, then with lime rubbish where that is available, and the surface with good loamy soil. In this soil the vine should be planted, the roots being previously trimmed and spread out horizontally, so as to radiate in a half-circle from the crown of the stem. Under such an arrangement as this the vine comes rapidly into bearing.

When the vine is approaching a bearing state, and the leaves have fallen, a general regulation of the shoots becomes necessary. In every part of the tree, a proper supply of last year's shoots, both lateral and terminal, should be encouraged, these being the principal bearers to produce next year's fruit. All irregular and superabundant shoots should be cut out, and with them all of the former year's bearers, which are either too close to each other or which are too long for their respective places. Where it is not desirable to cut out the branch entirely, prune it back to some eligible lateral shoot, to form a terminal or leading branch. Cut out also all naked old wood. The last summer's shoots thus left will in spring project from every eye or bud young shoots, which produce the grapes the same summer. The general rule is to shorten the shoots to three, four, five, or six eyes or joints in length, according to their strength, and cutting them back from half an inch to about a quarter of an inch at every eye, the strongest branches being limited to five or six joints, except where it is required to cover a vacant space on the wall. When left longer, the vines become crowded, in the following summer, with useless shoots, and the fruit is smaller in consequence. This pruning should be performed early in spring, even as early as February: in pruning at a later period, when the sap has begun to ascend, the wound is apt to bleed when the thick branches have been cut off. A second pruning should be performed about the middle of May, when the grapes are formed and the shoot has attained a length of two or three feet: at this time pinch off the shoot about six inches above the fruit and nail it to the wall in such a way that the fruit may be in contact with it. About midsummer a third pruning should take place, when all the branches should be gone over and the fruitless ones, not required for next year's wood, removed. A vigorous vine will require a fourth and final pruning in August, when the long shoots from the previous stoppings must be shortened back again, and all leaves lying too much over the bunches of fruit removed; taking care to prune, however, in such a manner that there is always a succession of young branches advancing from the lower part of the stem properly furnished with bearers, as well as a sufficient supply of young wood to replace the old as it becomes unserviceable. The pruning finished, let the branches be nailed or tied neatly to the wall or trellis, laying them regularly six, eight, or ten inches apart. Vine-pruning may be performed any time during the winter months, when the weather permits; but the sooner the work is done the better. The young shoots of last year produce shoots themselves the ensuing summer; and these are the fruit-bearers, which are to be trained horizontally or upright, according to the design of the tree.

In May the vines will shoot vigorously, producing, besides bearing and succession shoots, others which must be cut away, and bearing and other useful branches nailed or tied up close to the wall before they get entangled with each other; and all weak and straggling shoots, especially those rising from the old wood, should be cleared away. Much of this summer pruning may be effected by pinching off the young shoots with the finger and thumb while they are young and tender. This should be continued during June and July. Many small shoots rise, one mostly from every eye of the same summer's main shoots laid in a month or two ago: these must be displaced, in order to admit all the air possible to the advancing fruit. All new shoots whatever should now be rubbed off as they appear, except where they are required to cover the wall. In August, even these must be rubbed off, being utterly valueless even for that purpose. During this month, the fruit itself requires attention. Where the branches are entangled, or in confusion, let them be regulated so that every branch may hang in its proper position. All the shoots that have fruit hanging on them, or which are ranging out of bounds, may be stopped, and where the grapes are too much shaded during August and September, remove a few of the leaves which intercept the light and heat. They should now have all possible aid of the sun to enrich their flavour. It will be necessary now to protect them from birds, wasps, &c., by bagging the best bunches in gauze or paper bags. In October the bunches are ripe to bursting, and ready to gather, preparatory to a new year of growth and decay. Bear in mind that success depends on well-ripened wood — a short-jointed branch, ripened under an August sun, being a fruitful bearer of highly-flavoured fruit, and for this purpose a light porous earth is preferable to more tenacious clay soils. When the bunches of grapes are formed, pinch off the leading point of the growing shoot one joint above that from which the bunch proceeds. This is done to check the tendency of shoots to overlap one another. After the young points have been stopped, each joint below the stopping will put forth a side-shoot. These are termed lateral shoots. While this close stopping limits the extension of the tree, the size of the berry is much increased. This stopping is continued till the stoning period commences. This process occupies six or eight weeks, during which the growth of the fruit remains stationary, and the leading shoots may be suffered to push wherever they may.

During the swelling of the berry, the fruit begins to acquire flavour, and the buds plumpness and firmness. Henceforth they must have all the sunlight possible. To obtain this, all the lateral spray and others which shade the larger leaves must be stript away, leaving the larger leaves exposed to the sun; for the fruit receives its flavour through the agency of the leaves.

Pruning varies with the fancies of the operator. *Spur-pruning* consists of carrying up one leading shoot to the whole extent of the house or wall, either at one year's growth, or two or three, leaving spurs or lateral shoots to develop themselves at regular intervals on the stem. This is usually the result of three years' growth, the cane being allowed to make a third of the length the first year, a second third the second year, and the remaining third during the third year. There will thus be five branches the first year, ten the second year, and fifteen the third year. The subsequent pruning is confined to pruning each of the laterals back to the last eye at the base of the shoot.

Long-rod pruning consists in establishing a stump with three strong branches or collars, from each of which, in its turn, a shoot springs, which, by a regular system of pruning, is worked in successive lengths, the one running the whole length of the rafter, the second half the length, and the third, recently pruned back, is to produce the renewal-shoot.

Where the object is to cover a wall or house, the leading shoots are carried almost at random, the pruner selecting those which suit him, without heeding much, so long as they are short-jointed and strong, shortening back the renewal-shoots, according to the space they are to occupy, from three to six or eight eyes.

Sorts.—Early Black ripens in July, in situations where the Black Hamburgs fail. Miller's Burgundy, known by its white downy leaf, is very early and hardy. White Sweetwater is an early sort, with a fine large berry, but sets badly. White Muscadine, excellent for all purposes.

Black Hamburg ripens out of doors in fine seasons, but is very capricious in colour. White Frontignan is a fine early grape, sweet but insipid. Muscat of Alexandria requires artificial heat to ripen, but is one of the richest grapes in cultivation. West's St. Peter and the Cannon Mill grape are both favourites for house-culture.

Many expedients have been tried to expedite the ripening of the grape on open walls. The bunches have been put in empty flasks, run on tiles of the house roof, and trained on sloping walls: they ripen earlier in the flask, but acquire an insipid flavour; and sloping walls, while they catch more of the sun's rays, catch also all heavy rains. Nettings of muslin, sufficiently fine to keep out wasps and other insects in the ripening season, without intercepting the sun's rays, are, perhaps, the safest protection, unless a few movable sashes can be spared to cover the walls in cold and damp weather, and increase the radiation of heat.

We extract from *The Field* some most excellent observations on the subject, which cannot fail to prove interesting and useful to any who wish to see what can be done with vines out of doors in our climate. "Recently all the gardening papers have had articles advocating the culture of the vine against walls; most of the writers having seen it doing so well in the open air, with no care, as to justify the conclusion that with careful culture valuable results would be obtained. Some of those who warmly advocate this course are among the most skilful of our practical horticulturists; and we quite agree with them as to the practicability of growing good grapes in the open air, provided they are grown against white walls with a southern exposure, and properly cultivated and protected. Grapes are already grown finely in the open air in a few places,—by Mr. Darkin, at Bury St. Edmunds, for example, and by Mr. Fenn, in the rectory garden at Woodstock; so that there can be no doubt about the possibility of ripening good grapes over a considerable portion of the southern parts of England. All the best grapes for the Paris market are grown on walls near that city, where their culture becomes a speciality. The culture of the Chasselas de Fontainebleau, at Thomery, and other places in the vicinity of Paris, is the best example of open-air culture anywhere to be found; and this variety, more generally known in England as the Royal Muscadine, is also far the best for culture in the open air in this country. Therefore, we are confident that an account of the Thomery system from the pen of the best grower there will meet the wants of those who wish to try grape-growing out of doors. . . We may, nevertheless, add that we have never yet tasted the Chasselas de Fontainebleau or Royal Muscadine nearly so well flavoured as when grown in the open air, and that all who admire that grape would do well to attempt its culture on warm walls. The late Baron James Rothschild, with his magnificent gardens and numerous vineries at Longchamps and Ferrières, preferred this grape to any grown in England or in France, indoors or out. At Thomery, the soil is of a sandy and clayey nature, and mixed with pebbles in those parts which are near the river. The soil is at all times easy to work. Near the Seine it lacks depth,—so much so, indeed, that before cultivation it has to be dug and trenched, so as to remove some of the stony subsoil. Everywhere else the layer of vegetable mould measures from 4 feet 6 inches to 6 feet in thickness. This layer lies on a reddish clay of about the same thickness, and beneath the clay a broken-up stratum of building stone filled with fissures. This building stone is easily extracted. The grapes ripen a fortnight earlier in the flinty districts than in those parts in which the soil is deeper and richer. The gardens at Thomery, taken altogether, present much the appearance of those of Montreuil-sur-Bois. There is nothing but walls in all directions, distant from each other about 40 feet, and 10 feet high. This height has only obtained during the last fifteen years, before which period they were rarely higher than six or seven feet. This change has been advantageous for two reasons,—first, the grape-growers have been able to increase the space required for their purpose by taking possession of a larger portion of air, instead of having to bring fresh ground; and, secondly, the high walls are found to improve the appearance and quality of the grape. The walls are built of hard stone quarried in the neighbourhood, the stones being laid with mud only. The face of the wall is then covered with a mortar made of lime and sand, and is finally covered with the same material thinned to a cream. Every wall is topped with a roof of pantiles, surmounted by a row of gutter tiles. These roofs project about 10 inches, and below them are fixed at every yard iron rods, inclined slightly downwards. These supports project about 20 inches beyond the edge of the tiles, affording altogether a support of at least 2 feet 6 inches wide. Upon this is fixed, when occasion requires it, a strip of bituminized felt, or, where economy is necessary, a piece of thin plank. The bituminized felt is stretched on frames of wood, about 10 feet in length by 18 inches in width. The felt is stretched upon these frames by means of small nails. These frames are only used when the grapes are perfectly ripe, which is generally about September 15th, or when there is danger of the fruit being spoilt by heavy rains. Formerly, before these methods of shelter were employed, large quantities of grapes were continually lost through becoming rotten with the wet; since their adoption, however, there is no fear of such a result. The size of the frames to be used is always dependent on the aspect and height of the walls. With walls facing the south, and 10 feet high, frames containing felt at least 30 inches in width ought to be used. With a western aspect, they ought to be even wider, in order to avoid all danger from the heavy rains. With the old low walls, frames 24 inches wide for the south, 28 inches for the west, and 16 inches for the east were found to be quite sufficient. It is almost needless to give the preparation of the soil, pruning, &c., these are so simple. Nobody should plant in soil over rich, cold, or wet. The pruning may be performed in the ordinary spur fashion,— the shoots being trained erect on the walls, much as they are up the roof of a vinery. The really important points to bear in mind are—first, the warmer the exposure is, the better for the grape; second, that the walls are white, or nearly so—the vines get more heat on such walls than they do on dark ones, and are maintained in better health; third, that wide and efficient copings are used to permit the fruit to thoroughly ripen in autumn, and prevent its being spoiled by heavy rains. In addition, it is worthy of note that the higher walls are found to possess an advantage over the lower ones. After selecting a proper position and soil, the most important point is the sulphuring, to prevent the oidium. Sulphur is the effective cure for this pest, and it should be applied directly after the first pinching of the shoots, at a temperature below 96° Fahr. in the open air. If the heat is too great, the young skin of the grape is liable to become decomposed. In full sunshine at noon the fruit would be burnt up in an hour's time. Sulphuring may be carried on while the dew is falling. There is no fear, in this case, of soiling the grapes. The operation should not be deferred until the oidium has made its appearance. The second sulphuring should be performed when the grapes are about as large as a pea, or even earlier if the oidium has appeared at all. It would be preferable to sulphur while the vines are in flower. The operation is performed with sublimated sulphur, blown upon the vine with a pair of bellows specially contrived for the purpose. It may be effectively done without the operator standing an instant in one spot, but passing quickly along the line. In these latitudes heavy rains destroy in part the effect of the sulphur, and it is nearly always necessary to repeat the operation three or four times. If the grapes themselves are attacked, it is on them that the flower of sulphur should be spread. It has been remarked that under sunshine the oidium may be totally destroyed in one hour,—a result that may be attributed to the speedier disengagement of sulphuric acid gas by the heat of the sun. It is even possible to save the produce of a negleted vine, provided that the ends of the grape have not been blackened by the disease."

VIOLETS.

The common violet, *V. odorata*, is a native of our own island. It is found wild, both purple and white. "White violets," says Mrs. Loudon, "are generally found in calcareous soils, and the sweetest I ever smelt, were, I think, those I have gathered growing among the limestone rocks in the woods of Dudley Castle."

Violets may also be grown in pots, by placing two or three runners or offsets in a pot in May, and keeping them in the frame slightly shaded from the hot sun in summer. Loam and leaf-mould suit them admirably. Russian violets, and sometimes the Neapolitan, will flower all the winter. True violets flower in March and April.

Neapolitan Violets are so much and so deservedly valued that we will enter somewhat in detail upon the most successful cultivation of them. When the plants have flowered for the season, remove them from the soil in which they have been grown, divide them into single crowns, cutting off all runners and selecting the finest only; then plant them out with the trowel nine inches apart each way, pressing the ground firmly round the roots, selecting for the purpose a rich and well-prepared piece of ground with an east aspect, where they can receive the beams of the morning sun. In such a situation they are said to escape the ravages of the red spider and other pests, and to produce larger and brighter flowers. When the plants show signs of growth, stir the soil about their roots with a small hoe, and syringe them in the evenings of dry hot days with pure water, pinching off all runners as they appear, and keeping the bed free from weeds: nothing more is required for their culture during the summer months.

When the time arrives for forcing them, prepare the material for a hot-bed in the manner already described for making a cucumber-bed, either by building it up or by sinking it in the ground two feet, and treading down the dung to prevent an over-violent heat at first. Over this place the frame, and cover the bed a foot thick with prepared soil, consisting of the remains of an old cucumber-bed with a little leaf-mould added. The plants are then carefully removed, with as large a ball of earth round the roots as possible, and planted in rows close together, but not touching each other, and so arranged that the foliage may be close to the glass without touching it, as it will settle an inch or two after the lights are put on. When planted, give them a copious watering, even to saturation, and in warm showery weather take the lights off and give them the benefit of it: this will give them a clean, healthy appearance. The lights may be kept off all night with advantage when there is no appearance of frost, and all dead, decayed, or turning leaves should be removed as soon as they appear. Plants thus treated will yield a supply of violets from November to April.

It is immaterial, provided a succession is maintained by separating the crowns as soon as they have done blooming, whether the after-culture is on the bed or in pots plunged in the soil. For pot-culture, the best compost is formed of half-turfy loam that has been turned over two or three times during summer, and half-rotten dung and leaf-mould, well mixed together: this should be ready for use by the end of September. At that time the violet plants must be raised from the bed in which they have been growing during the summer with as much earth to their roots as possible. They should then be divested of all their side-shoots or runners. The proper sized pots are 7-inch ones. One strong plant should be put in each pot; but when they are weak, two or three. The pots should be well drained with broken bones instead of potsherds, for the roots of the violets will lay hold of the bones, which give vigour to the plants and make them bloom more profusely. The pots have the advantage of being available for the window garden, or for removal into the drawing-room or hall, as well as for cut flowers.

Having potted as many as are necessary for the season, a good supply of water should be given to settle the soil well about the roots. A sufficient number of old melon-boxes with the lights belonging to them should be arranged in a southern aspect, placing the boxes in such a manner that the lights will throw off rain quickly, and thereby prevent drip, which in winter not only rots the plants, but causes the flowers to be produced sparingly. The boxes being placed in position, a layer of old tan should be put into them four inches thick: in this the pots should be plunged up to their rims in rows till the boxes are filled. It will be necessary to leave three inches' space between the pots, where the plants are large, that air may be allowed to pass freely between and keep off damp, which is apt to destroy the plant. If they are so small as not to cover the top of the pots, they may be placed close together.

When the temperature is above 50°, the lights may be removed during the day, and at night they should be tilted up at the back for the admission of air. When the temperature is below 50°, the lights should be left on; but even then air should be admitted from behind during the daytime. When the temperature is below 40°, the admission of air should be very partial, if it be admitted at all. At no time after the plants begin to bloom should the lights be entirely removed, except for the purpose of watering or cleaning the plants, or gathering the flowers. When the weather is cold, coverings of mats should be applied at night. In hard frosts, two mats should be put on, as well as litter. The earth in the pots must never be allowed to freeze if it is possible to prevent it. The coverings must be removed in fine days. In March and April as much air as possible should be given if the weather is fine.

The pots should be examined at all times when the weather will permit. Weeds and decayed leaves must be removed, and a little water given when the soil is dry. Care must be taken to wet the leaves as little as possible. In March and April, if the plants have been properly managed, they will produce abundance of flowers, and consequently will require more moisture than during winter.

For summer and autumn flowering, runners should be laid in pots in February, and kept moist, and planted out separately in April.

VIRGINIAN CREEPER (nat. ord. Vita'ceæ).

A favourite plant for covering an ugly wall or shed. Its flowers are very insignificant; but this defect is amply compensated for by its beautiful leaves, which assume a most brilliant scarlet colour in autumn. Its growth also is very rapid: by some persons it is known as the Five-leaved Ivy.

VIRGINIA STOCK, the Malco'mia.

A pretty little annual, the seeds of which may be sown at almost any season. It is sure to grow and bloom abundantly.

Malcomia maritima,—½ ft., red and white; beautiful for margins. By constantly picking off the seed, and liberal waterings, it may be kept in flower the whole summer.

VISCA'RIA.

There are several varieties of pretty little annuals so named, suitable for borders, small beds, and single lines.

Viscaria oculata,—¾ ft., pink, dark eye.
" nana coccinea,—¾ ft, scarlet, dark eye.
Viscaria Damietta,—1 ft., white, dark eye.

VIS'CUM, the Mistletoe (nat. ord. Lorantha'ceæ).

A curious and beautiful parasite, which, in our own country, is generally found on old cankered apple-trees, and certainly not upon the oak, with which it is traditionally associated. It grows also on the white thorn, the lime, and the sycamore; indeed on several forest trees.

To many persons the cultivation of the mistletoe is looked upon with as much doubt as we are told the ancient Romans looked upon the cultivation of mushrooms. It may, however, be very readily cultivated by attending to the following directions:—Make an incision in the bark of an apple-tree (many other trees, as the pear, oak, white thorn, and even laurels, will answer equally well), and into this incision, in the spring of the year, insert some well-ripened berries of the mistletoe, carefully tying the bark over with a piece of bass, mat, or woollen yarn. This experiment often fails, from the birds running away with the berries from the place where they have been inserted, for they are very fond of them. To prevent this, the incision in the bark should be made on the underside of a hanging branch, where birds are not likely to rest. We must remember, however, that as the male and female blossoms of the mistletoe grow upon separate plants, the berries are not always fertile; so that in our efforts to cultivate, it will be well to select berries from several different plants.

VITTADIN'IA, the Australian Daisy (nat. ord. Compos'itæ).

A remarkably neat profusely-blooming miniature hardy perennial plant, admirably adapted for permanent edgings to small beds, &c.: grows freely in any good soil.

Vittadinia trilobata,—purple and lilac, ¼ ft., from Australia.

WALKS.

It is of the utmost importance that clean, dry walks be provided both for gardens and pleasure-grounds.

A good walk may be formed of concrete, consisting of six parts of coarse gravel and one of lime, four inches deep, with an inch of fine-sifted gravel sprinkled over and well rolled into the top; and six or seven inches deep, including gravel, will be a good average for walks formed of stones, &c., in the ordinary way. Perfect dryness is even of more importance upon walks than roads, as they should be clean and comparatively impenetrable in all weathers and at all seasons. Although some recommend walks to be sunk below, and others raised above, the general level, as here shown, yet they

generally look best on a level with the surface: they must be sunk half an inch at the edge, to leave this height of verge, which ought never to be exceeded in pleasure-ground walks. Half an inch is a sufficient convexity for a 10-feet walk. The wider the walk the smaller is the permissible rise in the centre, as nothing detracts more from the appearance of a gravel walk, say 15 or 20 feet wide, than variations in the level of its surface. A 6-feet walk, with two and a half or three inches rise in the centre, would not be so

offensive to the eye as the same amount of convexity in a walk 15 feet wide; all broad terraces and promenades should, therefore, be perfectly level; and if the removal of water renders a fall necessary, it should be so slight as to be imperceptible. For similar reasons, gratings are hardly ever admissible on such walks; rough stones, or rubble connected with underground drains, cropping out to within a few inches of the surface, being used instead for the removal of surface-water. The longer and wider a walk of this description is, the more offensive to good taste is the appearance of a grating and other irregularities of level. These views apply with double force to straight walks, and there are few gardens of any pretensions where either are now to be found. However beautiful curved walks may be elsewhere,—and they are exceedingly beautiful,—they can never be made to harmonize with the straight lines of architecture, and therefore should not be introduced near the mansion. Generally, there will be found plenty of scope for the introduction of both straight and curved walks; but where there is not, the former should have precedence, and the curved lines be introduced beyond the pleasure-grounds. Notwithstanding the dictum of Shenstone, who was, perhaps, a greater landscape-gardener than poet, and who tells us "that when a building or other object has been once viewed from its proper point, the foot should never travel to it by the same path which the eye has travelled over before," there are few persons who do not think a handsome seat or temple, a beautiful fountain, or a statue, a pleasing termination to a walk of 100 to 500 yards long. Certainly the rest the seat affords, and the pleasure imparted by the other objects, will not be the less refreshing or satisfactory because we are made aware of their proximity by walking right up to them. The size and importance of the terminal objects must, however, always correspond in magnitude and importance with the length and width of the walk, and architectural objects only are suitable termini for straight paths. Curved walks may have rustic buildings, moss, root, or heath-houses, of every variety of pattern and design, simple seats, secluded grottos with suitable inscriptions, ornamental bridges of antique shape, and rustic fountains, either as embellishments or as termini to them; for there is great truth in Shenstone's remark, that a rural scene is never perfect without the additon of some kind of building. Generally a walk should not terminate at any particular object: it is unsatisfactory to be compelled to return by the same route as we advance. Other walks should diverge from it, to give a choice of routes. The proper line of diverg-

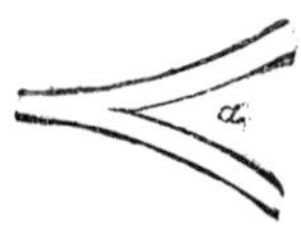

ence is of consequence; Repton says, where two walks separate from each other, it is always desirable to have them diverge in different directions, as at *a*, rather than give the idea of recurvity, as at *b*. When two walks join

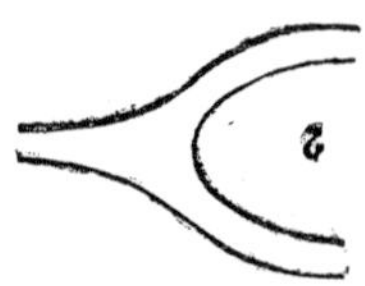

each other, it is generally better that they should meet at right angles, rather than leave the sharp point, as in the acute angle at *d*. The great thing is to avoid a stiff uniformity, and give

meaning to the curves on a walk by

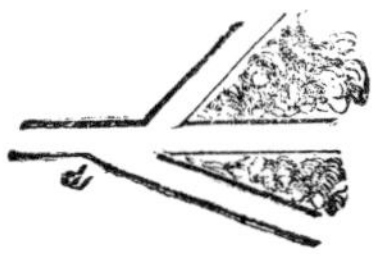

judiciously planting firs, limes, &c., as

here shown, so as to escape the force of such severe lines as these :—

> " Prim gravel walks, through which we winding go
> In endless serpentines, that nothing show ;
> Till, tired, I ask, 'Why this eternal round?'
> And the pert gardener says, ''Tis pleasure-ground.' "

Walks should always avoid skirting the boundary of pleasure-grounds, although they may occasionally approach it ; and, as a general rule, one should never be *vis-à-vis*, for any great distance, to another ; and then these walks should

be of different widths, according to their relative importance ; each walk should also maintain the same width throughout, unless it passes through rock-work, when it should be distinguished by irregularity of width,

abrupt bends, and capricious undulations ; the trim walk should then be lost in rugged attempts at the mountain

path, although the idea of safety must still be preserved. Grass walks are not so common as they were. On well-drained lawns the whole surface becomes a walk at pleasure, and grass walks ought never to be depended upon as necessary routes to or from any given place. When of great length, and 12 or 18 feet wide, however, they have a noble effect. The late Mr. Loudon recommends, where there is much traffic on grass walks, that their bottom should be formed with stone, as if for gravel; but it will be more satisfactory to make good gravel walks for the general traffic, and reserve the grass walks for delightful promenades in fine weather.

WALLFLOWER, Cheiranthus (nat. ord. Crucif'eræ).

For spring gardening these hardy perennials are as indispensable as the Crocus or the Tulip, and from the delicious fragrance of their beautiful flowers they are especial favourites, producing a splendid effect in beds or mixed borders. On account of their variety, much interest is excited in raising them from seed. Packets of the following are from 2*d.* to 1*s.* each.

Wallflower,—German, double, splendid mixed varieties, 2 ft.
Wallflower,—finest mixed, double, 1½ ft.
,, chameleon, single, 1½ ft.
,, dark, fine, single, 1½ ft., from Europe.
Wallflower,—dark, extra fine, single 1½ ft., from Europe.
Wallflower,—purple, single, very handsome, 1½ ft.
Wallflower, — yellow, single, 1½ ft., from Europe.
Wallflower,—mixed, fine, single, 1½ ft., from Europe.

WALLS.

The garden wall is as the setting to the gem ; without its inclosing fence the garden would be undistinguishable from the neighbouring fields, and its contents exposed to the depredations of man and beast, as well as to the "pitiless pelting" of every storm. But besides the protection it affords, the properly-constructed garden wall has other important conservative duties. Dr. Wells, in his interesting experiments on the origin of dew, found that a thermometer protected by a handkerchief sustained horizontally over it, marked a temperature from four to six degrees higher than the corresponding instrument placed in the open ground. The wall and its coping exercise a conservative power in preventing the radiation of heat in the one case which the handkerchief exercises in the other.

The wall performs another equally important office; during the heat of the day it absorbs the sun's rays in a ratio proportioned to its aspect and inclination to the sun; and, in common with all heated bodies, it radiates its heat in a ratio proportioned to the square of its distance; so that if an object placed a foot from the wall receives 1° of heat from it, at one inch it will receive heat equal to 144°. The reflection, also, of all unabsorbed rays impinging on the surface of the wall, greatly increases the temperature of the air in immediate contact with it. Besides this power of absorbing heat, moisture is also absorbed, both from rain and from the atmosphere, and, with the heat, is given out by radiation, tempering the atmosphere during the night: a wall is thus, in every sense, a source of protection; and it is of considerable importance that its height and form, as well as its workmanship and materials, should be well considered.

The countries of southern Europe, and Italy especially, can dispense with some of the conservative properties of the wall, and render architecturally ornamental that which we must make strictly utilitarian. The walls of Italian gardens are, therefore, frequently decorated with alcoves and balustrades, with a full complement of statuary and vases.

It has been already mentioned that the ha-ha fence, invented by Kent, has been considered the best form of external fence; it affords protection from without, and does not obstruct the view, but carries the eye uninterruptedly into the neighbouring domain. A light wire fence offers the best possible protection from game and other *feræ naturæ*. A holly or privet hedge may with advantage surmount the ha-ha on the east and west, especially if it is intended to have outside borders; where circumstances permit, a belt of trees on the north or north-east side of the ha-ha will also afford a desirable shelter.

Within this external fence the kitchen and fruit gardens usually form a separate inclosure, more or less extensive, according to the means of the proprietor; and the wall surrounding this inclosure we have now to consider. Garden walls have long been a subject for discussion, and will probably always remain so: like everything else connected with gardening, they depend on local circumstances. The walls which would be suitable for a moderate-sized kitchen-garden, in a flat or thickly-wooded country, would be very unsuitable for a loftier site, on the side of a hill, or in an open undulating country; while a plot of small extent, inclosed by walls 14 or 16 feet high, would be inadmissible both on artistic and physiological principles: on the first, it would seem as the walls of a prison; on the second, it would literally be so, excluding air, which is essential to the growth of plants.

The best practitioners consider that for small gardens, 8-feet walls are most suitable, provided the trees on them are planted so far apart as to admit of their horizontal extension. For gardens of larger size, 10-feet walls, and for an extensive garden, 12, and even 14 feet, will not be too great. Nicol thinks 10 or 12 feet a height convenient for pruning, watering, and gathering the fruit, giving also ample space for the expansion of the branches of most trees; but he adds, this should be influenced by the extent, or apparent extent, of the ground, the latter depending upon its cast: if it is a lengthened parallelogram, for instance, the ground will seem larger than it really is; if an exact square, it will seem smaller. So, if it is flat, it will seem smaller than if it is either undulating or sloping; while, on an elevation, loftier walls will admit a larger amount of atmospheric air than if placed in a hollow, or even in a flat country. Where an acre of ground, in the form of a parallelogram is inclosed, on a gentle elevation, he recommends a north wall 14 feet high, and the east, west, and south walls only 10 feet: if the slope of the ground is considerable, the difference may be less. In gardens of greater extent,—inclosures of four acres for instance, the walls may be higher, but in no instances more than 18 feet high for the north wall, 15 feet for the east and west walls, and 12 feet for the south wall.

In a parallelogram of 400 feet by 300, which is about two acres, and a well-proportioned piece of ground if the inclination of the land is an easy slope, Mr. McIntosh recommends a wall 16 feet high for the north wall, 14 feet for the east and west walls, and 12 feet for the south wall; but on level ground, while the north wall is still 16 feet, he would make the east and west walls 13 fest, and the south wall 10 feet. Rogers considers low walls much more convenient in management, more easily protected; and, seeing that the fruit-trees are most productive under horizontal training, he recommends two walls of six feet high, with the trees planted at good distances from each other, and asserts that such walls will produce more fruit in any given number of years than one 12-feet wall. "Low walls give free ventilation," he adds, "which is necessary at all times: even high winds do less damage than foul stagnant air, pent up within four high walls. Mr. P. Walker thinks walls should not be under eight feet from the ground-level to the coping, but 10 feet he considers the most useful height for general purposes; but where the garden area is flat, the appearance would be improved by raising the north wall a foot or two higher, carrying the rise round the north-east and north-west angles, and finishing with an appropriate canatto, or turret.

In reference to the really practical question of walls, the Caledonian Horticultural Society instituted, some years ago, a very interesting series of experiments on the comparative merits of a wall coloured black, an inclined wall at an angle of 50°, and a vertical wall of freestone. The results were very varied. At six p.m. in April, the average temperature of the sloping, the black, and the freestone wall was the same,—the brick wall was one degree lower. During May the temperature of the brick wall was considerably higher. At one o'clock in the day the average temperature of the sloping wall was seven degrees higher than the brick wall,—the black wall was three degrees, and the free stone five degrees, lower than the sloping wall; and at six o'clock the sloping wall was two degrees higher than the freestone and brick wall, and five degrees above the black stone; but in frosty weather the sloping wall was three degrees colder, in the night, than any of the others. It may therefore be assumed that, for all practical purposes, the brick and black walls are nearly equal, and only a shade in advance of the freestone wall.

The position of the walls being determined, as well as the material, the foundations should be excavated. Their depth must depend upon the subsoil, and the workmen should dig until they reach a solid bed. The trench completed, it should be filled up to within six inches of the surface, with concrete, consisting of six or seven parts of coarse gravel, stones, or brick rubbish, to one part of freshly-slaked lime, reduced to a thin paste, which may be thrown over a thin layer of the gravel; but the better foundation is formed by mixing the material thoroughly in a heap, and turning it out of the wheelbarrow into the trench, from a raised bank, raking each layer level as it is thrown in.

The thickness of the wall must depend on its height, and the foundation should be thicker by three or four inches than the wall itself, this thickness rising five or six inches above the surface-level. For a wall six or seven feet high, a single brick, or 9-inch wall, will suffice; for higher walls, it will require a brick in length and another in breadth, or 14 inches; beyond 12 feet and up to 18, two bricks in length, or 18 inches. Walls of these proportions are capable of supporting a lean-to greenhouse of corresponding height, if they are properly bonded, and hot lime or good cement is used. There is this practical difficulty in the more weak wall, that the bricks shrink unequally in drying. This inequality might be remedied by using the shorter ones as "stretchers," as bricks laid longitudinally on the wall are called, using the regular-sized bricks for "headers." But the bonding or tying, which is the object of laying headers and stretchers, would not be attained. It is, therefore, to be provided for by using half-bricks, and throwing out the short ones. The brick in length and breadth, and that in two lengths, are more easily laid and bonded; but the chief aim of the gardener, if he is charged with the superintendence of the work, is to see that the workmen use the proper bricks, and that they are bedded in a moderate quantity of mortar made of fresh-slaked lime or cement.

We have been so long accustomed to grow peaches and nectarines on walls, that many will still insist upon doing so; and therefore the best descriptions of walls, most approved methods of protection, &c., continue to be subjects of the first importance. No material for kitchen-garden walls can equal good red brick of medium hardness of texture. The joints should be formed as narrow as possible, of the best lime and sharp sand, and can either be left white, or the lime can be coloured a few shades lighter than the bricks. The bricks are better without any colouring whatever. This is not only the best-looking wall, but the plants are easier trained to it, and are probably subject to fewer alterations of temperature upon its surface than they would be upon a wall of any other substance or colour. Walls should never be less than eight or more than 14 feet high, and may vary from nine to 22 inches in thickness. From 10 to 12 feet is a good average height, and 14 inches in thickness will impart strength enough for that height. Sometimes walls 6 feet high are built only $4\frac{1}{2}$ inches thick, and in this form, to impart strength. A $4\frac{1}{2}$-inch curved

wall of this form will resist as much pressure as a straight wall nine inches thick without piers. As a rule, however, all kitchen-garden walls should be straight; and they are not safe without piers, unless formed of brick-and-a-half, or 14 inches thick. All walls for fruit-trees should also be furnished with a coping of stone, slate, or some other hard, durable material, of sufficient width to project four inches on each side of the wall. The top of the coping should be slightly convex, and the under surface as much concave, to facilitate the removal of water. A groove should also be formed half an inch deep, and three-quarters from the outside edge of the lower side, to intercept and throw off all drip. The coping should also be made in as long lengths as possible, to reduce the num-

ber of joinings. If stone is used, the joints should be formed of the best Portland cement; if slate, a mixture of white and red lead must be used. It would also be advisable to have the copings overlap, as they are comparatively useless unless waterproof. As in fine weather, frost falls in nearly perpendicular or vertical lines, a coping projecting over a wall will often protect the trees on its surface; and it will do this the more effectually if it has previously preserved them in a dry state. Permanent and temporary copings of much greater width than four inches are frequently used.

WALTONIAN CASE.

The flower-case so called is a portable pit intended for the propagation of different plants. It is constructed in such a manner that it may be placed in a drawing-room, or elsewhere in a dwelling-house. The general appearance is that of a 2-light box with glass sides, standing upon wooden legs; the bottom of the box being a zinc tray or boiler containing water, which is warmed by a lamp burning Colza oil, placed underneath it. This tray or boiler is strewed evenly with silver sand about an inch thick, kept moderately damp; and upon this sand the pots with their different cuttings are placed. "Those who possess the facilities for propagating on the orthodox plan," says Mr. Shirley Hibberd, "have no need for Waltonian cases. To such they would be mere toys; but to people who want only a few hundred plants for bedding, and some scores of annuals for the borders, it is the most useful invention of this more than half-gone century, because it will do whatever is done by dung-pits, hot-water tanks, &c., on a large scale; and do it, too, in precisely the same manner; and the only difference between a Waltonian case and a propagating-house is as to extent only." These cases may be bought of the maker, Mr. West, Victoria-road, Kingston; price 42*s*.

WARDIAN CASES.

These cases are greenhouses in miniature; they may be made of any shape and size, and to suit any situation, either outside or inside windows. At first they were entirely inclosed in glass, as if hermetically sealed; but experience has proved that they are far more generally useful when proper ventilation is provided. It is obvious to remark that in smoky cities such appliances are invaluable to those who love flowers.

WARMING.

In no department of industrial art has more ingenuity been exercised than in applying heat, whether it be to houses or horticultural buildings. Stoves, furnaces, and boilers, endless in form and principle,—hot air, hot water, and steam, have, in turn, been adopted, approved, and superseded; tubular furnaces, tubular boilers, in an endless variety of forms, have been invented, sometimes with most satisfactory, at other times with doubtful results; and we shall probably be approximating to the truth in stating that while all have had, and have, their advocates in the gardening world, no mode of heating is so universally approved as hot water circulating in iron pipes, with bottom-heat supplied from tanks heated by the same means. Even to this cleanly and convenient form of heating, however, there are objections: something is wanted that shall simulate the ammonial gaseous qualities of the vapour arising from hot dung, in which plants seem so to revel; and various expedients are adopted, by which this is partly attained. Mr. Fleming has introduced into the hot-water tanks at Trentham a mixture of pigeon-dung, in the proportion of an ounce to a gallon of water, to supply this desideratum to vegetation: others attain their object by watering the pots and beds with manured water, in varying proportions, according to individual judgment. Mr. Beaton suggests the application of vapour impregnated with tobacco or sulphur for the destruction of insects; while McIntosh recommends guano, pigeon-dung, and urine, used in the same manner by means of evaporating-pans attached to the pipes, in order to attain the fumes of the old-fashioned dung-bed, "so pre-eminently valuable for the restoration of sickly plants, and for promoting the vigorous growth of healthy ones."

We are indebted to the Dutch for the earliest edifices warmed with artificial heat, as for initiation into many other gardening secrets. Their trade with the East developed a taste for flowers as early as the fifteenth century; and they soon found that their cold moist atmosphere was unfitted for the successful culture of the delicate plants even of the Levant. They therefore erected houses for their reception, which they heated with the common earthenware stove of the country, equalizing the heat by earthenware pipes carried round the room. In course of time other countries adopted the idea, —in our own country by means of open fires outside the building, with connecting flues going round the house inside the walls; and there are not wanting, even now, gardeners who assert that as good crops of grapes were, and are, grown by these flued walls as can be produced by the modern innovations of hot-water pipes. The invention and application was, however, a great discovery for horticulture, and, accordingly, the names which are identified with it are both numerous and eminent in their art. Our space will only permit of our describing the principles on which the system acts, and naming a few of the leading inventions in general use.

The principle upon which hot water circulating in pipes is applied to warming houses is, that the hot water has a tendency to ascend, and to fall as it cools; the denser cold fluid displacing the more rarefied. This principle has been extensively applied to warming public and other large buildings; distance from the furnace, and height above the boiler, being no obstacle to the circulation of the fluid, the boiler being placed at the basement, while a water-box is placed at the top of the building, both being hermetically sealed. A flow-pipe connects and carries the hot water from the boiler to the water-box. After passing through it, the water descends again by the return-pipe, and by its greater density displaces a like amount of hotter fluid on the surface. A supply-pipe, regulated by the ordinary ball-cock, admits cold water into the water-box to replace that withdrawn by evaporation, while safety-valves, placed on the boiler, guard against too great a pressure from the expansion of the water. This principle is precisely that applied in heating horticultural buildings by hot water; but as it is seldom necessary to raise the water for this purpose, the amount of heat required is lower. Each hundred feet of 4-inch pipe contains 544 lb. of water, and will require 14 lb. of coal to raise its temperature to 180°. In a well-constructed boiler the water will lose 60° of heat hourly, and 200 cubic feet of air are heated 1° per minute by every foot of 4-inch pipe: it is easy, by cubing the contents of the building to be heated, and dividing it by 200, to calculate the quantity of pipe requisite to heat the building to the required temperature. When the temperature to be attained is 60°, the divisor should be 30; where it is to be 75° or 80°, 20 will be nearer; making allowanee always for loss by ventilation and the radiating power of glass, which is about one degree for every square foot and a half, and bearing in mind also that where smaller pipes are used, the body of water is smaller, and, consequently, the friction greater; for instance, in 2-inch pipes, the difference of temperature between the flow- and return-pipe will be four times greater than in a 4-inch pipe. In order to increase the rapidity of circulation, and equalize the temperature, Mr. Rogers proposes, when 2- or 3-inch pipes are used, that they should have a uniform rise of an inch in 20 feet, while in 4-inch pipes they should fall from the boiler in exactly the same proportion; for the velocity of circulation depends upon the difference in weight between the ascending and descending columns. Now the greater the height of these columns, the greater is the difference in their weight and in the velocity of circulation, and the higher the mean temperature of the pipes.

The inventor, or rather discoverer of the theory of the circulation of hot water, M. Bonneman, of Paris, had a calorifère so regulated that he could maintain a temperature scarcely varying half a degree of Réaumur, being regulated by the unequal dilation of metals. A rod of iron, screwed to another of brass, was inclosed in a lead tube terminating at its upper end in a ring of brass; the leaden tube was passed through the water in the boiler, by the side of one of the circulating pipes, and the dilation of the lead being greater than that of the iron, and the rod being inclosed within the lead, it was less heated; and the consequent lengthening of the leaden tube brought the brass ring into contact with a claw at the short end of a bent lever; the slightest increase of heat lengthened the tube, and pressed down the long end of the lever, and a wire connected with it opened or closed a valve, regulating the air admitted to the furnace. This, however, is a refinement on heating which is rarely practised or required.

Warming by steam is more expensive than by any other process, and rarely practised except in manufactories where it is used as a motive power.

The first successful attempt to introduce warming by means of hot water in this country seems to have been made by Atkinson. His idea is founded on the theory of fluids finding their level; for his first apparatus was merely a boiler, from which the water was made to flow and return by means of two pipes on a perfect level. At the extremity of the pipes a reservoir was considered necessary, exactly on a level with the top of the boiler, the reservoir being covered with an iron top, fitting into it with a flange; the boiler with a wooden one. Mr. Atkinson afterwards constructed boilers with closed tops; by which means he carried hot water 30 feet above the level of the boiler. An improvement upon this system of heating was attempted upon what was called the siphon principle. In an open boiler, the flow-pipe being placed a few inches below the surface of the water, where it is hottest, the lower, or return-pipe, descending nearly to the bottom of the boiler, a small tube or air-hole being placed in the upper pipe near to the bend at its highest elevation; the surface-water being the hottest, the heated particles are forced into the upper pipe, after dispelling the air, get cooled, and descend again into the lower pipe by the force of gravitation.

Numberless modifications of these principles have been proposed at various times, the chief of them being in the form of the boiler. After many experiments, Mr. Rogers was led to adopt a conical form of boiler, in place of a cylindrical one, the interior or furnace resembling in shape the sugar-loaf cone, supplied with coal from below. The boiler is also slightly conical. Cottam & Halen, and Burbidge & Healey, have each of them produced boilers extensively in use among gardeners; the object in both instances being to present the largest surface of the boiler to the flames; and both, though by different arrangements, carry the flame up the centre of the boiler. Mr. Thompson, of the Whitton Nursery, Hounslow, has invented a boiler which presents an immense surface to the action of the fire, and, from the mode of setting, admits the flame to play all round it, having projecting shoulders to extend the surface so exposed.

Where great heat is required from moderate space, the tubular boiler seems to have considerable advantages. Messrs. Weeks, Fowler, & Kewley seem to have been the earliest adapters of this system, now extensively used in horticultural buildings. Weeks seems to have adopted, and even patented, the well-known principle of the displacement of rarefied water by the pressure of the denser cold water, already explained; but his heating principle was a system of pipes placed round the fire, and communicating with the cistern, and with the warming-pipes. This he did at first in connection with a boiler; but the tubes were soon found to be perfectly efficient when ranged round the fire without any boiler. This apparatus is now constructed of upright tubes placed over the fire, and united together at top and bottom, the furnace bars being hollow tubes, through which the return-water passes before entering the upper part of the boiler; thus producing very rapid circulation, with great economy of fuel.

The last, and, as we are informed, not the least effective of the tubular boilers, is that patented by Mr. Messenger. The principal feature of this boiler, of which we give an elevation in the above engraving, is an arrangement of triangular tubes, round which the flames play in passing to the flue *b*. The tubes are horizontal, and placed over and round the fire, so that the heat in its upward course rebounds, as it were, from tube to tube; so that before it reaches the flue all the latent heat is expended. The furnace-bars are also tubes, through which the return-water passes; thus preventing them from burning, and increasing the rapidity of the circulation, and re-entering the tubes which form the boiler at a high temperature. It is obvious that the surface exposed to the action of the fire in this boiler is immensely increased by the form of the tubes. The boiler-surface entirely surrounds the flames, while, from its horizontal position, sufficient space is allowed for between the fire and the tubes for the introduction of atmospheric air, and the proper commingling of the gases; *a* being the brick setting round the boiler, *b* the flue through which the smoke escapes after passing round the tubes. The large surface of triangular bars exposed to the action of the fire, which in fact form the boiler, and through which water circulates, renders it, according to Mr. Messenger's statement, at once economical in its consumption of fuel, as well as highly

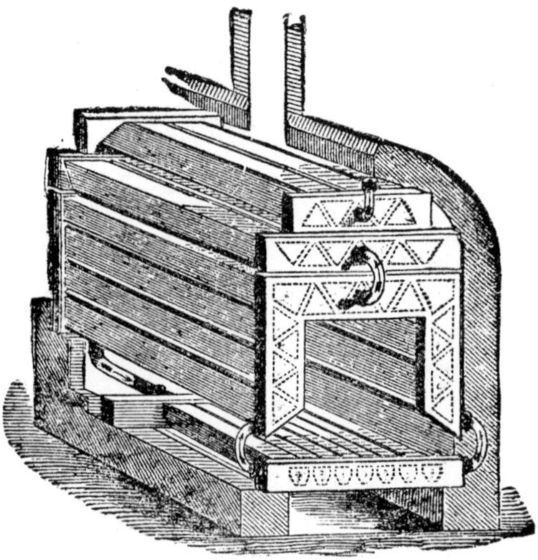

Elevation of Messenger's Boilers.

Warming.

efficient in its heating qualities ; while the facilities for cleaning it are such that it can be done at any time without interfering with its working. Besides its economical properties, neither the tubes at the sides and over the fire, nor

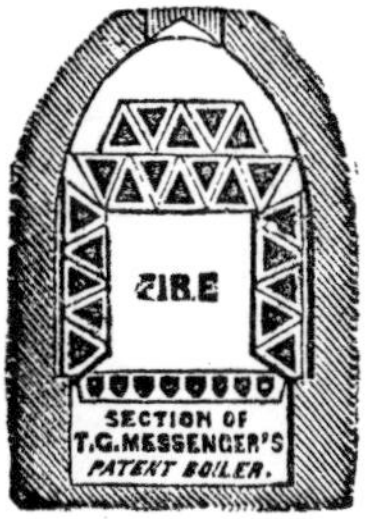

the furnace-bars under it, can be injured by the heat, as the water inside keeps them cool, and consequently protects them from its action.

The hot-water pipes are, of course, applied to the boiler by means of flanges, and the pipes themselves are of the usual circular shape, and of sizes calculated according to the superficial contents of the house to be heated, and temperature required. The tanks are to be heated by a flow- and return-pipe passing along their surface, at the level of the water, while a current of fresh air from below keeps the house pure and wholesome ; at the same time the air is heated in its progress to the temperature of the tanks. The only novelty introduced here consists in an exceedingly simple shutting-off valve which Mr. Messenger has patented, by which the circulation of the water can be cut off or introduced into any house or pit it is desired to keep at a higher or lower temperature than the others. These valves are said to be very simple, thoroughly effective, never get foul, and very durable; the prices being, for 2-inch pipes, 16*s*. 6*d*. ; for 3-inch pipes, £1. 1*s*.; and for 4-inch pipes, £1. 5*s*.

The system of heating houses by hot-water pipes was long objected to, as most improvements are. Probably the inefficiency of heating power, at first, was at the bottom of most of these objections; but the same objections have never been raised to the various modifications of it applied to heating tanks and gutters. These inventions supplied the gardener with many of the fertilizing results he had been in the habit of obtaining from the old dung-beds: he could obtain moisture, and, by mixing manure in his tank, he could obtain much of the old ammoniacal essence along with it. He was also enabled to obtain greater uniformity of temperature, for the mass of water contained in the tank was more easily retained at a regulated temperature than could be done in the pipes alone. Mr. Rendle, of Plymouth, has perhaps done more to introduce this system of heating than any other person.

Mr. Rendle recommends tanks of yellow deal, and eight or nine inches deep, for the purpose. They should be made thoroughly well-jointed, as the brewers' backs are made with 2-inch deal, and made water-tight by red lead, or lining with lead, and placed upon piers, at the required height; over the tank placing closely-fitted covering of slate. Through the tank, either by means of elbow-joints or by perforations in the tank, to be sealed up again by cement, the flow and return-pipe should pass with a sufficient coil of pipes to secure the degree of heat to the water which is required. The supply of water, of course, must be regulated by a ball-cock, and the usual measures taken to prevent damage by over-flow, by the use of a waste-pipe. Such a tank, coated with lead, would, of course, be more enduring, but not more efficient for the time. It will be obvious that the tank would only perform half the duty we have assigned it, if it did not, by some contrivance, give out some of its heat and moisture to heat the atmosphere of the house, and dispense the necessary vapour and moisture; but it may also be necessary to have a coil of pipes available for this purpose, independent of the tank, with a stop-cock attached, to turn the hot water on or off at pleasure. Perhaps the most efficient range of tanks are those fitted up by Mr. Rendle for Messrs. Veitch & Son, of Exeter, the description of which we quote from the *Gardener's Chronicle*, as supplied by Mr. Veitch, jun.:—"This tank," he says, "is formed of brick arches, worked in cement, with brick sides; the whole well coated with cement. The top is of slate, cemented down; the sides of the beds are of brick-work. The material used for plunging is a clear charp sand, which we find retains the heat for a considerable time. In one part of the bed we have put soil, in which the cuttings planted out have rooted most rapidly. The heated water is regulated by means of a division at the end of each house, through apertures in which communication is preserved by a short piece of 4-inch pipe, having plugs fitted into them. By this simple means one end, or the half of one end only, may be heated, or each bed may be regulated to a different degree of heat." This house is 51 feet 9 inches in length, 11½ feet wide, and 6 feet 9 inches high under the ridge.

Much as it has been approved by the best practical horticulturists, the tank system has its objections, which we find stated in the *Gardener's Chronicle.* "It is well known," the writer remarks, "that by means of a flow- and return-tank, the degree of bottom-heat in the pits can be very steadily maintained. Once the mass of soil on the beds is heated to the required pitch, very little is required to keep it up, and sudden changes of temperature do not much affect it: even such extremes of external temperature at 55° one night and 25° the next will only occasion a few degrees lower temperature in the beds. But the case is different as regards the air of the house itself; for under the above conditions, it would certainly be affected to a much greater extent,—perhaps as much as 20°. Presuming that the temperature of the beds is just what it ought to be, any attempt to counteract the coldness of the air in the pit on a cold night would cause an excess of bottom-heat, which, by repetition, must prove highly injurious to the plants. If the communication of heat from the tanks to the surface is only through the soil, the conduction of heat will be very slow, whilst its escape through the glass is rapid." The remedy for this, the writer goes on to say, is a separate command of heat for heating the house, which he proposes to supply by a 2-inch steam-pipe, running from the top of the boiler and ranging along the front of the house, immediately under the glass, terminating at the further end of the return-tank. Why steam, he does not say: perhaps a water-pipe would be sufficient for the purpose; but such is certainly an objection to which the system is open; and this is met in the range of houses proposed by Mr. Messenger, by hot-air chambers under the tanks, the air being carried up into the body of the house.

WASPS.

No class of insects give more annoyance in the garden than wasps: the sweetest and ripest of the wall-fruit become their prey, unless precautions are taken to prevent it. Towards the end of autumn, that is in September and October, every specimen of the common wasp should be sought for and destroyed; those individuals still left being females in search of a quiet corner in which to deposit their eggs and pass the winter. Each of these, if left undisturbed, is destined to become the foundress of a fresh nest. One of the best traps for catching wasps is formed by placing a couple of hand-lights on the top of each other, making a small hole at the apex of the lower one, attracting them into it by placing ripe half-eaten fruit beneath the under one. Another mode of dealing with wasps is as follows:—Having found the nest, rinse well with spirits of turpentine a common wine-bottle, and while the inside of the bottle is wet, thrust the neck of it into the chief hole of the nest, carefully stopping up all other holes with clods of moist earth, to prevent the egress of the wasps. This, of course, is best and most effectually done in the evening. The fumes of the turpentine will first stupefy, and then

Wasp and Nest.

destroy the wasps: in a few days the nest may be dug up. All persons interested in gardens should be careful, as we have just observed, to destroy the large female wasps which may be seen about singly late in autumn, and on fine days in the early spring; these, as we have already stated, are looking out for a wintering-place for their eggs.

WATER.

A good deal of our success in growing plants depends on the water we use for irrigation. The springs about Norwood defeated a friend of ours for years in his attempt to grow plants and flowers for show: it appeared to be charged with iron, and nothing did well with him until he sent for all the water he used to a pond a mile or two away from his house. Some pump-water, apparently clear, is too hard to do well for watering plants, but this hardness may be removed by keeping it in shallow tanks a considerable time before using. It is, however, far the best plan to contrive that every drop of rain-water be saved for the use of the gardener. Every roof that offers the opportunity should supply its contribution to tubs or tanks so placed as to receive it, and nothing but rain or river-water should on any account be used if it can be avoided. Plants under glass should always be watered from tubs or tanks kept at the same temperature as the plants are growing in; therefore some vessel must always be kept in the house. Nothing does much greater mischief to plants than chilling them with water of much lower temperature than the atmosphere they are in. On this account, even soft-water wells will not supply it so warm as it ought to be; and if it must be used direct from the well, it is desirable the chill should be taken off by a little heated water. This attention to the water used is most important in forwarding the cultivation of those occupants of the garden called, because they have been improved by seedling varieties, "florists' flowers and plants."

WATERING.

In watering fresh-potted plants, it is important that the whole of the soil be effectually moistened, which can only be accomplished by filling up two or three times with water. No fear need be entertained of over-watering: if the plants have been rightly potted, all surplus water, beyond what the soil can conveniently retain, will drain away. Irregular watering is frequently the cause of failure in plant-culture, even with experienced growers. A certain amount of tact is necessary in giving plants, which have been so neglected, just as much water as they should have, and no more. In watering, much depends on the weather, and also on the season: plants require less in winter than in summer. The proper time to water them in winter is when they are in bloom, or growing rapidly,—in summer, as soon as the least dryness appears; but a little practice will be more useful than a lengthy description. In giving air, it may be observed that all plants which are not tender, that is, all plants which are natives of temperate climes, may be exposed to the air at all times when the thermometer indicates a temperature above 40°, except in case of rough winds or heavy rains. Hardy plants may be exposed at any temperature above 32°; for, although frost will not kill them, it may spoil their appearance for a time. Plants in bloom should never be kept close, or exposed to wet or wind: the flowers last longest in a soft, mild atmosphere, free from draught. Plants should never be wetted overhead in cold weather, or, rather, while they are in a cold atmosphere; and never, except to wash off dust, should those having a soft or woolly foliage be so treated; but some plants, as the Camellia, Myrtles, Heaths, and others with hard leaves, may be plentifully syringed, or watered overhead from a fine rose, in warm weather, especially when in full growth.

WATER-POT.

These articles, so indispensable in gardens, are made of different shapes and sizes. They vary in price from 1*s.* to 5*s.* The patent "Alexandra Lady's Watering-can" is the last new invention. It is so constructed that ladies, when using it, can at pleasure shower the water upon the plants, or let it fall with the gentleness of a Scotch mist. Price from 1*s.* 6*d.* to 18*s.*

WEEPING ROSES.

Weeping Roses are roses of vigorous growth, and should be worked on stems four feet and upwards in height. In the first pruning they are cut close in; and to have one bud only is an advantage: the shoots are thinned out as with standards, shortening back the others to give vigorous growth. The habit of the roses being pendulous and the shoots long, they soon sweep the ground, and present a pyramid of flowers.

The nature of the stocks, whether the dog-rose or the Manetti be selected, limits the height to which weeping roses may be grown; but there seems to be no reason why either of them should not attain the height of 10 or 12 feet, with a proportionate thickness. In this case the chief support must be provided by a strong stake of wood or iron to which the stock may be fastened, while the head is extended outwards and directed downwards. For this purpose light iron rods and wire hoops, of sufficient circumference, will be found very useful. If grown simply as an object of decoration on the lawn, a standard seven feet high, with a head five feet in diameter, formed of some of the climbing roses, as the Evergreen rose, decorated with some of the perpetual hybrids, as La Reine, Colonel de Rougemont, or General Simpson, drooping to the ground in a curving line, or on a larger scale, making an arbour, will form a beautiful tree when in bloom.

Mr. Rivers gives a very instructive piece of gossip in his "Rose-Amateur's Guide." A friend of his, near Guildford, had his ground traversed by a railway, which was crossed by an unsightly brick bridge, and he was consulted how the bridge might be concealed. Ivy was too heavy, and he suggested evergreen roses. "They were planted with difficulty, the gravel being loosened with a pick, and some manure mixed with it. The roses grew with great rapidity, and soon covered every brick; but when they bloomed in large beautiful masses, some disappointment was expressed at the monotony of colour. I was prepared for this, and told my friend that they must be decorated. An incredulous smile met me with 'How?' This was in July, the budding season. I proceeded with the gardener to the rose-garden, and we took thence buds of the most beautiful hybrid perpetuals, not forgetting some of the bright rose-coloured tints, such as La Reine, Colonel de Rougemont, General Simpson, our great horse being General Jacqueminot. My budding hand had not forgot its cunning; so I and the gardener proceeded to place buds in every shoot favourable to our purpose. Nearly all the buds 'took,' to use the gardener's phrase; that is to say, lived, and many of them put forth fine clusters of bloom the following August and September. I paid my annual visit to my friend in June the next year. As I approached the bridge, what a glorious sight met my eye. Amid the masses of flowers of the pale climbing roses, shone forth large clusters of the Géant, Jacqueminot, Triomphe des Beaux Arts, Prince Noir, Comte Bobinsky, Louise Peyronny, Rougemont, Jules Margettin, and others. The bridge was a fairy avenue, so charming was the effect."

WELLINGTO'NIA (nat. ord. Conif'eræ).

The most gigantic and ornamental of cone-bearing plants; thrives in any good soil, and is uninjured by the most severe winters. Visitors to the Crystal Palace will find in the palm-house a specimen of this gigantic tree, consisting of bark brought from California. We are informed that in California specimens of this tree with trunks 300 feet high and of great diameter may be met with. It is known as *Wellingtonia gigantea.*

WESTRIN'GIA (nat. ord. Lobia'tæ).

A handsome greenhouse evergreen shrub from New Holland, about two feet high, bearing white flowers. It requires a light soil.

WINDOW GARDENING.

Our neighbours across the Channel are greatly in advance of us in the cultivation of house plants. "In Brussels," says M. Victor Paquet, "the balconies are turned into greenhouses and miniature stoves, gay with the brightest and greenest foliage; and in Paris there are many contrivances in use by means of which the rarest and most beautiful plants are produced. Passifloras cling to columns in the upper floors; water-plants start into blossom, in tiny basins, curiously contrived in solid brickwork; and limpid water flows down a miniature rockery, from whose crevices start up ferns and lycopodiums." It is not our intention to recommend any such fairy-like adjuncts as those belonging to the bedroom *au quatrième* of Paris; but there are many appliances, of a very simple character, by means of which our rooms may be made gay by flowers of home cultivation.

The most efficient contrivance for window gardeners is the Wardian case, which has already been described. (*See* Wardian Case.) It is obvious that those miniature greenhouses may be applied with great ease to any window: a pair of brackets on a level with the sill will form a stage, which may either support a case such as we have described, or a permanent greenhouse may be erected thereon. All that is required is a glazed frame, from 12 to 18 inches high in front, with glazed sides, rising to the window-sash at an angle of 30°, with a framework to receive a sash at the same angle, which may be hinged to the window-frame. If this frame only extends to three-fourths of the height of the window, it will not interfere very materially with the light of the room. Of course, the plants are watered and arranged from the room within. All manner of elegant projections may be thus formed, and large ornamental bell-glasses may be easily adjusted to vases for the hall and drawing-room. But whoever would have healthy plants in a sitting-room, of any kind whatever, should provide either a case or vase: the dry atmosphere which is agreeable to human beings is unsuitable for most plants.

A simple apparatus has been employed for the preservation of cut flowers for the decoration of our dwelling-houses, not dissimilar in principle to the Wardian case. A flat porcelain dish is filled with water, and a vase with cut flowers is placed on the dish; over the whole a bell-glass is placed, fitting to the edges of the porcelain dish. The air surrounding the flowers is thus kept in a moist state, supplying to the flowers the moisture yielded by the roots and leaves in their natural state, and maintaining them fresh and brilliant for a considerable time. But to return to our subject, which is window gardening.

Where a window happens to be in a recess, a wooden trough, lined with lead or zinc, may be used for holding earth, in which climbing plants may be planted and trained about the recess. For this purpose the Passion-flower is very suitable; if allowed, after crossing the top, to hang down before the window in festoons, displaying its naturally graceful pendulous habit, it will form a pleasant screen for a sunny window. A grape-vine may be grown in the same way, and it is always a graceful plant, while its fruit is excelled by no vegetable product when ripening in glowing clusters. But it is advisable to attempt nothing in this way which cannot be carried out perfectly; a single plant properly grown is to be preferred to the most elaborate attempts the working out of which has not been thoroughly considered; for instance, climbing plants must be very closely watched and carefully trained, or they become so entangled as to be anything but ornamental; they are apt, also, to harbour spiders and other insects, to drop their dead leaves and flowers, and, in common with other plants, they must be watered, which is always inconvenient in a room, for the pots must be well drained of superfluous moisture, otherwise the earth soddens in them. These are drawbacks to window-gardening; but the true lovers of Flora will find in them no obstacle; to such the sight of a window festooned with trailing plants, and gay with flowers, will be sufficient inducement to overcome every difficulty in the way of its production. If the plants are in ordinary pots, which are certainly best, let them be plunged in ornamental pots or vases, and fill up the vacancy between with moss or sand: they will not only look better, but the roots, being kept cool, will retain the moisture longer, and less watering will be necessary. This is of some consequence in a room; for although watering will be sometimes necessary, means should be taken to reduce the quantity required, by shading, plunging, and keeping the pots in feeders,—that is, pans or saucers, which are made to match with the pots or vases. This requires a little judgment: it will never do to let the roots of the plants stand in stagnant water. When the pots are placed in the pans or saucers, fill the vacancy with a mixture of silver-sand and finely-broken — not powdered — charcoal: this will absorb the water that runs through the pot, and yield it back again to the plant, besides preventing stagnation. The time to water a plant is just when the soil begins to present an appearance of dryness, which is best seen when the surface is pretty firm, although it is advisable to stir it sometimes; but if, after stirring, the plant wants water, give it from a fine rose. This will settle the soil again, so that it is easily ascertained when the plants want water afterwards. If any plants are infested with aphis or green-fly, brush it off with a small brush, without injuring the plant. A few plants may be kept free from this pest by this means, without having recourse to fumigating with tobacco. Various sorts of herbaceous plants may be cultivated outside, on the window-ledges: being hardy, they will stand all weathers, but are best protected from severe frost and a scorching sun.

Among these we may mention sedums or stonecrop, houseleeks, London Pride, with other saxifrages, campanulas, and a few phloxes.

Fast-growing plants, as fuchsias, geraniums, genistas, &c., grown under glass cases or in windows, should not be frequently turned, since they always make a face towards the light, and the process might weaken them: it would be better to train them out fanlike, by means of thin painted sticks. Fern-cases may be turned occasionally. The plants in these have a like tendency; consequently they show best from the light. By turning the case, the faces of the plants are brought facing the room. If they can receive light directly overhead, it will be so much the better. These fern-cases in windows may be planted with most of the British ferns, and a vast number of exotics are also suitable. Lycopodiums may be allowed to trail over the surface of the soil. *Pteris arguta* makes a good centre plant for a tall case; also *Adiantum pedatum*, one of the most graceful of ferns, but it dies down every winter. The Aspleniums offer an extensive and numerous family to choose from, particularly *A. viviparum, bulbiferum, paniculatum*, and others, producing young ferns on the old leaves, and roots in the air. The Scolopendriums are also suitable, and show well their broad shining leaves or fronds. Both the planting and management of these cases must depend a great deal on the situation or locality. In a dry warm room many ferns that are considered very tender may be grown successfully; but they will require more water, which should be warm when given, and less ventilation; for the dry air of a warm room, ill suited to most plants, is very injurious to ferns; and some of them naturally come from warm, humid climates; they must therefore be carefully treated in this respect. If an opening at each end of the case were made, and covered with fine wire gauze, it would admit air without any of its ill consequences. Plant-cases for winter-gardening have been greatly improved of late. One—the invention of an invalid lady—is ingeniously contrived so as to hold hot water. A cistern beneath this, being replenished once in twenty-four hours, maintains a soft genial heat, so that many stove-plants can be thus grown and displayed to advantage. The zinc trough at bottom is filled with sand and charcoal, in which the pots are plunged. This being kept moist, diffuses a soft dewy atmosphere in the body of the case, which is in form a double cube. These cases are made by Pickard & Co., King's Cross, London.

An admirable effect may be produced with plants, the beauty of which is in the foliage. Caladiums are almost too tender for window-culture, but several kinds of begonias will not only stand the air of a room, but thrive in it. There are also plants hardier still,—*Farfugium grande*, for instance, which produces a grand effect: it is closely allied to the Tussilago, or Coltsfoot family, and is very easily cultivated. Then, again, there is *Cineraria maritima*, with its white silvery foliage; also *Centaurea zymnocarpa* and *ragusina*, of similar habit; *Acacia lapantha, Fuchsia spectabilis*, and other plants of ornamental foliage, all of which have peculiar characteristics, and many of them admirably adapted to window decoration. I have known a plant of *Ficus elastica* kept for a dozen years in a window, maintaining a lively foliage and vigorous habit the whole time. This, and similar plants with shiny leaves, have this recommendation, that when the leaves get dusty they are easily cleansed with a damp sponge.

The various species of Cacti are also very suitable as permanent window-plants: the varieties of creeping Cereus may be grown in suspended baskets, and last for many years without requiring any change in the soil,—they naturally droop and hang down, which gives them an interesting appearance. The globular cacti are curious and interesting, and are very numerous, as every one must know who has seen the collection at Kew: a collection of these would be worth a case to themselves. There are some interesting selections grown in small pots, and arranged on shelves fixed in a miniature greenhouse, 4 feet by 2 feet 6 inches, being all labelled. The smaller kinds of aloes may be grown in the same way : many of these are curiously and prettily marked, and those who fancy this sort of plant consider them quite as ornamental as flowers. They are all succulent, and may be treated in the same way as the fig marigold, giving plenty of water in hot weather, and little or none in winter, taking care that the soil is well drained.

Beginners are very apt to make a mistake in supposing their first efforts in window plant-culture must, of necessity, be successful : the contrary is in general the case. First attempts, in ninety-nine cases out of every hundred, are merely so much profit and loss,—loss in plants, and knowledge gained of the necessary treatment. Gardening, like every other art, requires not only practice, but observation ; and those who have most failures, provided they observe the causes of failure, are likely to become the most skilful in the end.

The most necessary condition to successful window-culture is to have proper appliances,—that is, for instance, provided only one single window is available, then it should be fitted with a ledge or shelf, both inside and out, so that the plants can be close to the glass when inside, where they can have the full light; and also that they can be exposed to the open air on every occasion when the weather will permit. If a window is fitted in this way, half a dozen plants can be grown creditably, with very little trouble. They can be placed outside for the purpose of watering them, even in winter; and in wet weather they can be inside, with the window closed.

Again, supposing the window is fitted with double sashes,—in other words, a window-recess is fitted so as to form a sort of plant-case, giving the full height of it,—thereby sufficient head-room is obtained to grow tall plants or climbers : a trough lined with lead or zinc, or other non-corrosive material, will be necessary beneath. This should be sufficiently large to hold a proper quantity of soil,—say a foot in depth, and of length and breadth adapted to its position,—providing means for the exit of surplus water, and for ventilation, which should be perfectly under control. The size of such a plant-case must of necessity be a matter of taste or convenience ; but the larger it is the better for the plants.

Heat, light, moisture, air, and soil or earth, are essential matters to be brought into requisition in plant-culture : both the quantity and quality of these must be considered. Heat, probably the prime mover, must be supplied within certain limits, and regulated by the natural habitat of the plant : tropical plants must have tropical heat, unless they are natives of the temperate climates also, or of high mountains and table-land. Nothing will grow in a temperature under 32°, or over boiling-point. A happy medium of from 40° to 80° is best for most plants.

Light is most essential to the well-doing of plants of any kind ; the want of it is sure to be indicated by a weak, pale, and spindling growth, the result of placing the plants in a room far away from the glass : the more directly overhead plants receive light the better; but the ordinary variations of light and darkness are of no less consequence, since it is said that plants inhale under the influence of light, and respire in the dark.

Moisture, again, so necessary for the support of plants, must be supplied in proper quantities. When shall I water my plants? is a vexed question, yet one that will admit of no definite answer, as some plants want more than others ; some more or less at certain times, or under particular circcumstances. Observation and tact must be exercised,—useful qualities under any circumstances, and particularly necessary in the cultivation of plants.

Another question equally important, but far more difficult, is, how shall I manage my plants so that they will bloom again? This generally refers to plants purchased of hawkers or at the nursery, while in bloom, and which begin to decline in health simultaneously with the fading of the flowers. Many have attempted to answer the question, and rules have been laid down which have only had the effect of making the querist as wise as before. There are certain conditions necessary, not easy to define. The culture of a plant differs from a mechanical operation, inasmuch as the latter is under control; but in growing a plant, nature must do the work, while we supply the material. If left in a state of nature, a plant is usually placed where it can supply itself with material for supporting life and health; but if it is to grow where we choose to place it, it becomes necessary to ascertain the processes by which that object may be gained,—processes more easily learnt by observation than from any description.

WINTER CHERRY (nat. ord. Solana'ceæ).

This is a hardy perennial, which will grow under shade anywhere. The fruit is very pretty and much used for winter decoration: it is largely grown for the bouquet-makers in Covent Garden.

WINTER FLOWER-GARDEN.

Spring flower-gardens and flower-gardens for summer and autumn are everywhere to be found; but a winter flower-garden is a luxury enjoyed by comparatively few, and yet, to a greater or less extent, it is within reach of every possessor of a greenhouse, vinery, or orchard-house, and that without interfering with the legitimate occupants of either.

Boxes varying in depth from six to nine inches, and in width corresponding with the floor-space at command, should be provided, and in these hyacinths, early tulips, polyanthus, narcissus, ixias, &c., may be planted, with snowdrops, crocus, *Scilla siberica*, sparaxis, spring snowflakes, &c., in their front, all arranged in waving lines, or in whatever quaint and elegant device the fancy and taste of the cultivator may dictate. A portion of amalgamated cocoa-fibre and charcoal may with great advantage be incorporated into the soil with which these boxes are filled: it will greatly increase the beauty and vigour of the plants.

As, however, the plants named do not all flower at the same time, but yield a succession of bloom for upwards of two months, it is necessary, in order to secure an effective display, that they should be carefully grouped and classifiedf both as to colours, height, and time of flowering.

When the plants have done blooming, the boxes should be placed out of doors, that the roots may ripen. In orchard-houses also, bulbs should be planted in the borders, where a display combining effectiveness and beauty can be produced which will not readily be forgotten.

WIRE-TRAINING.

This mode of training is practised in many places with considerable success; at Trentham, for instance, there are five lines set out for the culture of choice apples and pears on the wire-training system: they are alternately cup or vase-shaped, and the reverse, or umbrella-fashion, which has an excellent effect, and appears to be very fruitful.

In the gardens of the Luxembourg, the quarters in the fruit-garden are surrounded with borders planted with cherry, plum, and apricot trees as standards, while others are trained in the vase-shape, on 4-foot stems. The head is formed hollow, the shoots being annually tied down to hoops of wood of the circumference required; and all shoots which spring up in the centre of the vase pinched off. Supposing a tree to have six shoots, they are tied to a hoop at equal distances all round, and shortened to a few inches above the hoop, so as to leave them about a foot in length. From each of these two other shoots are trained towards a wider hoop, parallel with the first, in the following season; and this is continued annually, until the desired form is attained, and the head of the tree completely balanced in its cup-like form. At Trentham and elsewhere this form is attained by means of a light iron wire frame, the umbrella form being produced in the same manner, the wires radiating from the centre corresponding with the number of shoots issuing from the stem, with hoops of thin wire on which the lateral shoots are trained.

Another arrangement of the cup-trained tree is recommended by M. Du Breuil. Starting with four primary lateral shoots, these are suffered to extend themselves horizontally for the first year. When they are tied to the hoop and stopped, each of these will throw out two shoots the second year, being kept at an equal degree of vigour by pinching. At the end of the second season, these eight shoots are cut back to a foot from their base, with two buds on each; those issuing on the left side of the shoot being trained on a hoop towards the left, at an angle of about 30°; those on the right, at the same angle, in the contrary direction; each thus crossing another at the same angle, and consequently at the same distance from each other. During the third year sixteen shoots are suffered to grow, the circle widening with each year, or rising at the same circumference, according to the taste of the trainer; and this special training is continued until it is seen fit to stop its further growth, each of the branches being grafted by approach to that which crosses.

The advantage presented by this mode of training is said to be a more equal distribution of the sap in the whole extent of its branches, and consequently a more equal distribution of fruit; the fruit on spurs being obtained in the same manner as in the pyramid trees.

WIREWORMS.

If any bed or favourite plant suffers much from wireworm, a good trap may be made by placing small potatoes with a hole in them just under the surface of the ground, at different intervals. The wireworms will, in general, prefer this to any other food, and a daily examination will serve to entrap a great many of them.

WOODEN FLOWER-STICKS.

Sticks should never be used, unless absolutely necessary, for they are not ornamental. When necessary, they should be concealed as much as possible and firmly fixed. Those painted green are least conspicuous. Price:—

	Plain. Per 100. s. d.	Painted. Per 100. s. d.
1 foot in length ..	1 6	2 6
1½ ,, ..	2 0	3 0
2 ,, ..	3 0	4 0
2½ ,, ..	3 6	4 6
3 ,, ..	4 0	5 6
3½ ,, ..	5 6	7 6
4 ,, ..	6 6	8 0
4½ ,, ..	7 6	9 6
5 ,, ..	8 6	10 6

WOODEN TALLIES.

These are useful for borders, pots, and for suspending to trees of different sorts. They are very cheap if bought in quantities. In Messrs. Barr & Sugden's list we find them priced:—

	Per 100. s. d.
4 inches in length	0 8
5 ,, ...	0 10
6 ,, ...	1 0
7 ,, ...	1 6
8 ,, ...	2 0
9 ,, ...	2 6
12 ,, ...	4 0
18 ,, ...	5 0
With holes for suspending:—	
3½ inches long	1 0
5 ,, ...	1 6

WOODLICE.

These insects are very destructive, especially to tender seedlings in a frame. They are so numerous in general that they clear a pot in a single night as soon as the seed-leaves appear. Indeed where woodlice abound many persons are often under the impression that the seed has never come up at all, for it requires a magnifying-glass to enable us to detect the minute stalks when deprived of their leaves. Woodlice congregate at the bottoms of pots in a hotbed and round the sides of the frame. They should be searched for every morning and destroyed by having boiling-hot water poured upon them.

WORMS IN LAWNS, TO DESTROY.

Take newly-slaked lime, in the proportion of 10 lb. of lime to about 30 gallons of water. Stir it often, and then let it stand to settle. Draw off this water clear from the sediment, and with a rose watering-pot spread it freely over the lawn. The worms will come to the surface, and may be swept up with a broom. This operation is most effectual if performed in damp weather, as the worms then lie nearer the surface. It may be repeated till the worms disappear.

XANTHORHI'ZA (nat. ord. Ranuncula'ceæ).

An American shrub, so called from its yellow root. It is perfectly hardy, and will grow in any common garden soil. The flower is dark purple.

XERAN'THEMUM (nat. ord. Compos'itæ). Hardy Annuals.

A showy class of Everlastings; the flowers, gathered when young, are valuable for winter bouquets: require a rich soil. They are best sown mixed, the sorts being,—

Xeranthemum album, 2 ft., from South Europe.
Xeranthemum atropurpureum, fl. pl.,—purple, very fine double variety, 2 ft.
Xeranthemum luteum, 2 ft.
,, purpureum, 2 ft.

XYTAPHYL'LA (nat. ord. Euphorbia'ceæ).

Stove plants, natives of the West Indies. They are remarkable for producing their flowers in the margins of their leaves.

YUC'CA (nat. ord. Lilia'ceæ).

These are popularly known as Adam's Needle. They are perfectly hardy plants, of quaint appearance, forming striking objects in garden scenery. *Y. recurva* has graceful drooping leaves, forming a most desirable plant for vases, or for planting as a specimen on lawns or in the parterre. They grow best in a dry sandy loam, and will succeed well if planted on rockwork, to which they impart quite a tropical aspect. The following are the varieties, price 2*s*. 6*d*. each:—

Yucca filamentosa,—white.
,, flaccida,—white.
,, gloriosa,—white.
,, recurva,—white.

ZAUSCHNE'RIA (nat. ord. Onagra'ceæ).

A very handsome Californian perennial plant, in bloom from June to October, with a profusion of beautiful tube-shaped flowers: succeeds best in dry gravelly soil.

ZE'A (nat. ord. Gramin'eæ).

This is the Indian corn, an annual plant, very ornamental. It should be raised in a hotbed early in spring and in May.

ZIE'RIA (nat. ord. Ruta'ceæ).

A remarkably pretty greenhouse

evergreen shrub: succeeds best in a mixture of sandy loam and peat.

Zieria macrophylla, — white, flowering in bunches, 3 ft., from North Holland.

ZIN'GIBER (nat. ord. Scitamin'eæ).

The Ginger plants, of which there are several species. All are with us stove plants. It is the root which is made use of for ginger. The flowers are not remarkable.

ZIN'NIA (nat. ord. Compos'itæ). Half-hardy Annuals.

A grand genus of autumn-flowering plants, combining the greatest richness and diversity of colour with unequalled profusion and duration of bloom. Amongst the novelties of recent introduction, the "New Double Zinnia" has proved to be one of the most important, its splendid double flowers rivalling in beauty, size, and form moderate-sized dahlias. In England the double zinnia has frequently greatly disappointed the expectations of most persons; that it can, however, be grown successfully in this country is proved by the large stand of handsome blooms exhibited at the Dahlia and Fruit Show of the Royal Horticultural Society. They are much admired by all, and very greatly praised by Mr. D. Beaton as an important acquisition. The universal success which has attended the cultivation of these plants on the continent abundantly establishes the high character awarded to them. Messrs. Barr & Sugden write :—"Our Sardinian correspondent, in the autumn, forwarded to us a photographed group of double zinnia flowers, the smallest of which, he informs us, was 3¾ inches deep, and 11 inches in circumference; another had 586 petals; one of the flowers is beautifully reflexed. In all respects the group proves our engraving to be faithful, and we may add this is the class of flowers from which the seed we offer has been saved. The photograph may be seen at our establishment. We recommend the seed being sown early in March, so as to have strong stocky plants to put out in June; they should be planted in the richest soil and the warmest situation possible. For flower-beds, borders, and conservatory decoration, the double zinnia is alike valuable."

Zinnia elegans, fl. pl., mixed, saved from splendid double flowers, 1½ ft.
Zinnia elegans, fl. pl.,—carmine, bronze, lilac, magenta, purple, violet, red, scarlet and violet.
Zinnia elegans coccinea,—single, scarlet, 1½ ft.
" " purpurea,—single, purple, 1½ ft.
" " choice mixed, from twenty splendid single varieties, 1½ ft.
Zinnia elegans,—fine mixed, 1½ ft.
" gigantea,—rose; a strong-growing free-flowering bushy variety, said to grow 8 ft. high.
Zinnia mexicana,—yellow, flushed with orange up to the centre of each petal; habit dwarf, bushy, and free-flowering; an exceedingly valuable plant for flower-beds, edgings, and borders, 1 ft., from Mexico.

ZIZ'YPHUS (nat. ord. Rhamna'ceæ).

Pretty fruit-bearing greenhouse evergreen shrubs, with extremely graceful foliage; succeed best in sandy peat and loam.

Zizyphus Jujuba,—purple and green, 6 ft., from East Indies.
Zizyphus sativus,—large berries and graceful drooping foliage, 5 ft.

ZONALE GERANIUMS.

During the last few years great attention has been paid to the cultivation of Zonale Geraniums, so called from the zone or zones with which their foliage is marked; and certainly few plants have better deserved the care and attention bestowed upon them. Each year is marked by great improvements. When this class of geraniums was first brought into notice, the foliage was looked upon as everything; now, however, the blossoms are receiving their fair share of attention, and many of the more recent varieties can boast of both foliage and blossoms which are

Zonale Geraniums.

deserving of the highest commendation. Mr. Shirley Hibberd, with his usual good judgment, makes the following selection as suitable for conservatories, though many of the varieties will be found equally good as bedders. They have the advantage of being very moderate in price, as they have now been before the public for some little time.

Six Scarlet and Crimson.—Adonis: fine form, pure white eye. Attraction: brilliant scarlet. Faust: large trusses, rich scarlet. Dr. Lindley: super form, trusses not large, not suited for bedding. Lord of the Isles: very large flower, light scarlet. Monsieur Gallard: rich scarlet flower, rather capped, finely formed.

Four Red and Red Shades.—Rubens: form excellent. Herald of Spring: blooms abundantly, and fine flower. Triomphe de Gergoviat: the best of the double-flowering kinds; colour crimson and red. Excellent: fine light red.

Four White.—White Perfection: surpasses Madame Voucher. Virgo Marie: pure white, a refined flower. Madame Werle: white ground, the petals delicately margined with pale rose. Galanthi-flora: dwarf grower, fine snow-white, abundant flowerer.

Four Rose-Pink.—Beauté du Suresne: broad petals, top petals white at base. Rose Rendatler: rose-pink, shaded lilac, a nosegay with peculiar long petals and huge showy trusses. Lady Cullum: a small-growing nosegay, the contour lilac-pink, peculiar and beautiful. Mrs. William Paul: flowers large and the form fine, petals rather flimsy, colour pale rose-pink.

Four Salmon. St. Fiacre: good form, deep rich salmon-red, most beautiful. Eugénie Mezard (also known as Madame Rudersdorf): when in the full sun in a bed, is a beautiful salmon-colour, but when grown in a pot and shaded from intense sunshine, the flowers are white, with salmon centre, delicate and beautiful, like wax. Amelina Grisau: white, with salmon centre, superb. Madame Chardine: shaded salmon and white. Rosamond: salmon flesh.

Six Variegated.—Mrs. Pollock: superb leaf and fine scarlet flower; when grown as a pot plant, cool treatment suits it best. Flower of Spring: very white margin and fine flowers. Queen of Queens: very white margin and fine scarlet flowers. The Countess: small growth, neat creamy-edged leaves, flowers rosy-scarlet. United Italy: a fine tricolor, with small leaves, white margins, and lively rosy zones.

All the above are good, but the newest varieties are—

Amelia,—flowers bright rosy crimson, large and compact truss, free-growing, leaves slightly zonate.

Fire-King,—most intense vivid scarlet.

Princess Dagmar; a cross between Madame Voucher and Beauté du Suresne, having the habit of the former and eclipsing the good qualities of the latter.

Star of the North,—a cross for Indian yellow, fine horse-shoe leaf, rosy crimson, shaded on yellow ground.

Bronze Model,—velvet-like golden leaf, with fine dark chocolate zone, flowers brilliant orange-scarlet, with white centre.

Golden Eclipse,—habit dwarf and compact, with circular-lobed leaves; the rich dark chocolate zones are finely effective upon a golden leaf-ground; flowers bright scarlet.

Soprano,—neat circular-lobed leaves, chocolate zone on golden ground, with outer margin.

The Queen,—unique and distinct in its section, with remarkably dwarf growth, golden leaf-ground, with narrower dark zone, the flowers being pure blush-white.

Of double-flowered Zonale Geraniums, the newest and best varieties are—

Madame Lemoine,—flower truss remarkably large, very double, in colour equal to a Provence rose.

Andrew Henderson,—a clear scarlet-like flower, very double, and imbricated like a ranunculus.

Emile Lemoine,—bright carnation-red, very free flowerer.

These, with the following new Tricolour Geraniums, may be seen in great beauty at Mr. Williams's Holloway Nursery.

Countess of Craven,—the leaf is perfectly flat and circular in outline: has an even and well-defined broad margin of clear golden yellow, with a rich crimson and bronze zone, encircling a deep green centre; habit compact and vigorous.

Crown Jewel,—centre of leaf green, with a broad well-defined zone, the greater portion of which is of a bright carmine approaching to scarlet, surrounded by a deep margin of clear yellow, into which the green portion never intrudes; habit remarkably robust and vigorous.

Miss Watson, Tricolor,—of fine robust growth, compact habit, and easy of cultivation; flower a lively salmon-colour, fine large truss, shape of old Compactum; leaves superbly coloured with deep red, and chestnut zone, and sulphur edge; as a bedding plant, or for pot-cultivation, it stands unrivalled.

Mrs. Dix,—of the Lady Cullum class, but far superior; the colours are decided and beautiful. The *Gardener's Magazine* for March 30th, page 133, says: "Mrs. Dix.—Yellow edge, olive and bronze, breaking into bold bars of clear brick-red (the red of wet bricks), the disc dull green, superb in every respect; the leaves round and flat, the plant compact and dense, covering a large extent of surface."

Sunrise,—centre green, with bright red and claret zone of medium size, the margin being remarkably broad and of a clear canary-yellow, changing to sulphur. The habit of the plant is very compact and close-jointed, resembling that of the Tom Thumb section.

Ivy-leaved Pelargonium, Duke of Edinburgh,—this variety possesses more pure white than any other kind, and is most remarkable; its growth is as free as that of the green varieties, and it is certainly the most effective of its class.

Golden Tricolour Geraniums.

Artemus Ward,—which is undoubtedly the finest in the gold and bronze section that has yet been offered, and from its bright and distinct markings, assuredly will remain a favourite among edging plants for a long time to come.

Fairy Spell,—a beautiful and effective dwarf branching variety, with well-expanded leaves of circular outline, the green disc belted with a bronze zone, finely belted and barred with carmine-scarlet upon a broad rich canary-yellow leaf-margin.

Howarth Ashton,—an exceedingly rich and beautifully-marked variety. Leaves of circular outline and great substance, with a well-proportioned and rich golden margin, the disc surrounded with a broad bronze zone, brilliantly suffused with flamed scarlet; growth vigorous and free, retaining its rich leaf-tints throughout the year—an improvement in the style of Beautiful Lucy Grieve.

Humming-Bird,—in the style of Lady Cullum, with sub-erect robust growth, and evenly-expanded leaves of good substance, marked by a broad metallic bronze zone, margined with rich flamed crimson in summer, and retaining a picturesque character by its violet-rose tints in winter.

Lady Sheffield,—a fine improvement on Sunset in its more brilliant and enduring zone-tints. Leaves even, of good substance and circular outlines, their rich golden leaf-margins finely contrasted with brilliant zones of flamed scarlet. By its free growth it will form a beautiful group or bed; and by retaining its decorative leaf-tints through the winter months, it is specially adapted for conservatory culture in pots or artistic vases.

Nellie Ray,—an elegant miniature variety, of dwarf and compact growth; leaves evenly expanded and circular in outline, showing a beautiful medium bronze-scarlet zone upon a rich sulphur-yellow border. A very effective and distinct summer variety for parterres or fancy vases.

Rustic Beauty,—a novel variety by its distinct coloured flowers; habit dwarf and compact; leaves roundly lobed, with a light flame-coloured zone, and bright lemon-yellow leaf-border, flowers clear white—a unique feature in its section.

Star of India,—this has been pronounced to be one of the most useful and attractive Tricolours ever offered. In general appearance it resembles Sunset; but the most cursory glance is sufficient to show its vast superiority over that variety, in the general freeness of its habit, and the brilliancy and distinctness of its markings.

Silver Tricolour Geraniums.

Charming Bride,—habit robust, free; leaves concave, with rich bronze zone barred with bright rose-carmine; flowers brilliant scarlet, fine truss.

Silver Cloud,—a compact and free-growing variety, with well-expanded mature foliage; bronze zone finely belted and barred with flamed rose-colour; flowers rich scarlet.

In a very useful article in a late number of the *Floral World*, Mr. Hibberd calls attention to the good effect produced by a quantity of seedling Zonale Geraniums used in what he terms the plunging system. Not only for its scenic effects, but as affording an excellent opportunity for selecting superior varieties, we think the plan well worth the notice of those who have the means of carrying it out. Premising that the seed only of good sorts should be selected, "If you have plenty of glass," says Mr. Hibberd, "and can keep a few hundred small plants through the winter, sow the seed as soon as ripe, and in due time pot the plants in the smallest pots, and winter them in a warm house near the glass. If not well off in respect of glass, sow in February or March, place the seed-pans in a gentle heat and grow the plants all the summer in a green-house or frame, and get them into 60-sized pots before the end of August. In March following shift them into 48-size, and as they fill these pots with roots, shift again to 32-size, and in this size let them flower: they are all to be allowed to grow as they please, no stopping, no pruning. In the course of the second summer—that is to say, fifteen months from the time the seed was sown—they will flower. We flower a great many in less than five months from the time of sowing the seed ; but we say nothing about these things now, because it is desirable to adapt these notes to the circumstances of the majority of private cultivators. All the seedlings should remain one full year in 32-sized pots, and after that time should be shifted into 24-size, or otherwise disposed of as may be considered most expedient. The system of cultivation proposed will produce robust plants, varying from two to five feet high, with fine heads and abundance of flowers of all colours. When packed closely together to form a group, the colours being mixed indiscriminately, their appearance will so far surpass all other geraniums, that a revolution in the district is pretty sure to follow. The seedlings are our stronghold from plunging effects, and it is so easy to raise geraniums from seed that I recommend all who take to plunging to accompany it with this great aid to success."

ZOSTE'RA (nat. ord. Fluvia'les).

A marine grass, very useful in aquaria.